ROME IN ETRURIA AND UMBRIA

ROME IN ETRURIA AND UMBRIA

BY

W. V. HARRIS

CLARENDON PRESS · OXFORD

1971

Oxford University Press, Ely House, London W.1

GLASGOW NEW YORK TORONTO MELBOURNE WELLINGTON
CAPE TOWN SALISBURY IBADAN NAIROBI DAR ES SALAAM LUSAKA ADDIS ABABA
BOMBAY CALCUTTA MADRAS KARACHI LAHORE DACCA
KUALA LUMPUR SINGAPORE HONG KONG TOKYO

PRINTED IN GREAT BRITAIN
BY WILLIAM CLOWES & SONS, LIMITED
LONDON, BECCLES AND COLCHESTER

PREFACE

THIS book was in an earlier version a thesis entitled *Roman Policies in Etruria and Umbria from the Conquest to the Early Empire*, which was submitted for the degree of Doctor of Philosophy at Oxford in January 1968. My greatest debt of gratitude is owed to my supervisor, Mr. M. W. Frederiksen, who guided me with unfailing skill and patience during the preparation of my thesis. Such a debt cannot be measured or repaid. I further wish to thank my examiners, Dr. P. J. Cuff and Dr. A. H. McDonald, and my colleague Professor Morton Smith, for their help with the whole text; and, for their expert advice on various topics, Mr. J. B. Ward-Perkins, Professor F. E. Brown, Dr. Mario Torelli, and Mr. M. H. Crawford. Finally for financial help I wish to thank the Craven Committee, which awarded me a Thomas Whitcombe Greene Scholarship for 1962–4, and the Council for Research in the Social Sciences of Columbia University, which gave me a summer grant to visit Italy in 1969.

Columbia University,
March 1970

W. V. HARRIS

CONTENTS

ABBREVIATIONS

Most of the abbreviations are those of *L'Année Philologique* or are otherwise well known. The following should be noted:

CIE	*Corpus Inscriptionum Etruscarum*, ed. C. Pauli, etc., vol. i and vol. ii 1.1–3, 2.1 (Leipzig, 1893–1935)
CII	*Corpus Inscriptionum Italicarum antiquioris aevi et Glossarium Italicum*, ed. A. Fabretti (Turin, 1867)
ILLRP	*Inscriptiones Latinae Liberae Rei Publicae*, ed. A. Degrassi, vol. i (2nd ed., Florence, 1965), vol. ii (Florence, 1963)
MRR	T. R. S. Broughton, *The Magistrates of the Roman Republic*, 2 vols. (New York, 1951–2) and *Supplement* (1960)
SE	*Studi Etruschi*
TLE	*Testimonia Linguae Etruscae*, ed. M. Pallottino (2nd ed., Florence, 1968)

E. Badian, *FC*=*Foreign Clientelae* (*264–70* B.C.) (Oxford, 1958)

[K.] J. Beloch, *It. Bund*=*Der italische Bund unter Roms Hegemonie* (Leipzig, 1880)

K. J. Beloch, *RG*=*Römische Geschichte bis zum Beginn der punischen Kriege* (Berlin-Leipzig, 1926)

R. S. Conway, *ID*=*The Italic Dialects*, 2 vols. (Cambridge, 1897)

W. Schulze, *ZGLE*='Zur Geschichte lateinischer Eigennamen', *Abhandlungen der Kgl. Gesellschaft der Wissenschaften zu Göttingen*, v, no. 5 (1904)

A. N. Sherwin-White, *RC*=*The Roman Citizenship* (Oxford, 1939)

R. Syme, *RR*=*The Roman Revolution* (Oxford, 1939)

L. R. Taylor, *VDRR*=*The Voting Districts of the Roman Republic* (Rome, 1960)

E. Vetter, *HID*=*Handbuch der italischen Dialekte*, vol. i (Heidelberg, 1953)

INTRODUCTION

THE Roman conquest of Italy and subsequent Roman policies in Italy constitute an important chapter in the history of Roman imperialism. Most existing accounts, however, even when they do not neglect the period after the military victory, deal summarily with Italy in general, neglecting the local conditions to which Roman policy had to respond. It is the purpose of this study to describe and explain Roman policies in two adjacent areas, Etruria and Umbria, in the period of the conquest and throughout the period when the Etruscans and Umbrians remained politically and culturally distinct from other Italians. In Etruria there is a particularly rich mine of local evidence, archaeological, epigraphical, and even literary, greater in quantity and much better known as a result of the work of recent years; combined with the Roman evidence, it enables us to infer certain facts about the political and social conditions of Etruria and, in consequence, to understand the methods by which Rome chose to exercise control there in the period between the military victory and the enfranchisement of the Etruscans after the Social War. Likewise the non-Roman as well as the Roman evidence is capable of throwing light on the gradual Romanization of Etruria, and on Roman policies and their effects in the century after the Social War, when Etruria underwent two periods of upheaval, brought about by Sulla and Augustus, and lost the last of its significantly Etruscan characteristics.

The best existing account of this subject is still that of R. A. L. Fell, whose book *Etruria and Rome*[1] attempted to combine the available Etruscan evidence with the Roman evidence on many points. However he dealt only cursorily with many of the main problems, especially the central one of Roman control and those concerning the period after the enfranchisement. His account is also in many respects necessarily out of date.

Less is known about Umbria than about Etruria, and a continuous narrative can hardly be written about Roman policies

[1] Cambridge, 1924, 108–74.

in Umbria alone. There are several strong reasons for dealing with the two areas together. There are close connections between Roman policies in the two regions: the conquest took place at almost the same time; afterwards, unlike the Sabines who divided them from the rest of Italy, most of the states of Etruria and Umbria remained formally independent; later, at the time of the Social War, the Etruscans and Umbrians apparently shared a similar attitude towards Rome. The differences between the two regions, particularly in the methods of Roman control and in the pace of Romanization, are also very instructive, and are analysed and explained whenever possible.

As for the chronological limits of this study, I do not attempt to deal with Rome's relations with the Etruscan states before the fourth century, or indeed in great detail before 311. It is with Roman expansion in the historical period that I am concerned. The last chapter of the work deals with the last major acts of colonization in these regions, the work of Augustus; that was also the period when the Romanization of Etruria was virtually completed. These are the natural limits of a study of Roman policies in Etruria and Umbria.

A note may be added about the northern boundaries of the areas occupied by the two peoples. Pisae, according to Polybius, is the first city of Etruria towards the west;[1] yet the third-century pseudo-Aristotelian work *περὶ θαυμασίων ἀκουσμάτων* places it by implication in Liguria,[2] and the archaeological evidence is against calling it an Etruscan town during our period.[3] Polybius' statement results from the fact that Pisae was in Roman hands for a long time before the rest of Liguria,[4] probably from the early third century—or (perhaps a more likely explanation) he was following writers who were referring to an earlier period of Etruscan domination at Pisae.[5] As far as

[1] II 16.2.

[2] Sect. 92. The phenomenon that is said to take place *ἐν τοῖς Λίγυσι* must be at the confluence of the Serchio (Ausar) and the Arno, where in fact it is said to have taken place by Strabo (V 2.5 222C).

[3] L. Banti, *SE* v (1931), esp. 171–6, and in *RE* s.v. Pisae (1950), col. 1769. Pisae was eventually put into the tribe Galeria, which later at least was particularly Ligurian (cf. E. Bormann, *CIL* xi. p. 273).

[4] Cf. F. W. Walbank ad loc.

[5] Cf. Ps.-Scylax (*GGM* i) 5, 17, Lyc. *Alex.* 1356–9, Cato fr.45P.

Umbria is concerned, some of the towns on the Adriatic coast (Ravenna, Ariminum) or near it (Butrium) could be described as Umbrian,[1] but it is clear that the coastal strip of what was later region VI was already occupied by Gauls by the time of the Roman conquest of Umbria,[2] and particular towns there are referred to as Umbrian because of some real or supposed earlier stage of their history.[3] Polybius says that the Umbrians inhabit both slopes of the Apennines, but he does not regard the coastal plain, which he says goes as far south as Sena, as being inhabited by Umbrians.[4] The Augustan regions VI and VII were larger than this, spreading respectively as far as the Adriatic coast from Pisaurum to Sena Gallica and as far as Luna, but it is with the area actually inhabited by the Etruscans and Umbrians that we shall here be dealing.

[1] Strabo V 1.7 214C, V 1.11 217C, V 2.1 219C, Plin. *NH* III 115.

[2] Cf. Polyb. II 17.7, Liv. V 35.3 (and R. M. Ogilvie ad loc.), Plin. *NH* III 112.

[3] Cf. G. De Sanctis, *Storia dei romani*, i (Turin, 1907), 102–3.

[4] II 16.3, II 16.5.

I

SOURCES

1. *The Historiography of Etruria*

THE emperor Claudius wrote twenty books of *Tyrrhenica*, complete recitals of which were to be given each year in the Museum at Alexandria. It is a cause for surprise that there was sufficient material for such a long work about the Etruscans, and we should ask what had been written about them before. How detailed and how accurate was the knowledge that Greek and Roman writers had about the Etruscans? How much did non-Etruscan writers gain from Etruscan or Etrusco-Roman literature? These questions are important for the present work because we need to assess the evidence of Greek and Roman writers about the political and social conditions in Etruria in the last period of its history, from the fourth century onwards. The whole view that is taken in this work of Roman policies in Etruria down to the Social War depends on the political and social structure of the Etruscan states, and as will be argued here and in Chapter IV it is possible to discover some fundamental facts about that structure from the existing literary evidence. In this chapter, while the limitations of the known writings about Etruria are emphasized (as against some recent views), an attempt is made to show that it was possible for some Greek and Roman writers to acquire authentic information about Etruscan society. Detailed consideration of the evidence about the class-division in Etruria is, however, reserved until Chapter IV.

A few thousand epitaphs and a small number of other inscriptions, largely unintelligible, are the only written sources that the Etruscans have left to us directly. Yet from a large miscellany of references something can be discovered about their literature, including works that referred to their history. Most of the references to Etruscan literature in Roman writers are to works dealing with the *disciplina*, the religious learning of the Etruscans; indeed Etruscan literature was very largely concerned with the *disciplina*, more so than has sometimes been realized. Here, however, questions about Etruscan literature that are of interest only for the religious history of the Etruscans will be avoided. The intention is to discover what Etruscan writing there was that dealt with Etruscan history and how far it was known outside Etruria.

Those Etruscan writings concerned with divination that became known in the outside world must have preserved some facts about Etruscan history and society. The terms in which the *libri haruspicini*, the *libri fulgurales*, the *libri fatales*, and the *ostentaria* referred to the future must have been revealing about the past and the present. The *disciplina* knew, for example, of *fulmina regalia* and *exta regalia*, technical terms that probably attest to the period of the kingship in the Etruscan cities.[1] There may be some references to Etruscan society in the ἐφήμερος βροντοσκοπία (a calendar of predictions from thunder) of Nigidius Figulus preserved in Ioannes Lydus' *De Ostentis*.[2] Pliny, in his discussion of divination by lightning, seems to be taking some references to historical events indirectly from an Etruscan source. The events are admittedly bizarre: Volsinii, the wealthiest city of the Etruscans, was completely burnt up by lightning;[3] on another occasion, when the territory of Volsinii had been devastated by a monster which they called Olta, and it was threatening the city, a flash of lightning was called down by Porsina, the king.[4] Surviving fragments of this kind are few, brief, and problematical; nor should we too readily assume that the books of divination ever preserved very much of the Etruscan past. It is evident that those who provided and interpreted them at Rome, generically known as *haruspices*, were professionals who regarded it as their business to meet contemporary conditions. They needed to be impressive—that is, to stick to the accepted style—and relevant, rather than simply to reproduce old documents. The *haruspices* had political importance because they dealt with contemporary affairs. We can identify a number of those who in the late

[1] C. O. Thulin, 'Die etruskische Disciplin', i, *Göteborgs Högskolas Årsskrift*, xi (1905), 70–1.

[2] Chs. 27–38 = fr. 83S.

[3] *NH* II 139.

[4] II 140—the source is *annalium memoria*.

Republic published works concerning divination, in some cases at least probably translating material from Etruscan. Some of them were of demonstrably Etruscan origin, such as A. Caecina,[1] Tarquitius Priscus,[2] and Nigidius Figulus;[3] such works are also known to have been written by Fonteius Capito and by more shadowy figures such as Julius Aquila, Umbricius Melior, and Caesius.[4] However, in spite of the Etruscan origins of at least some of them, these men were Romans, Nigidius a praetor and Fonteius a suffect consul, and in the first four cases something definite is known of their sympathies in Roman politics. It is difficult to believe that they published works about the *disciplina* without regard for present conditions, although the appearance of authenticity naturally had to be maintained. The great majority of the surviving 'Etruscan' texts about divination have been adapted to a Roman audience and the cases cited are usually Roman ones; that was probably already the case in the late Republic.

The most extensive of the surviving texts attributed to one of the writers about the *disciplina* is Nigidius' ἐφήμερος βροντοσκοπία. The full title given to it is ἐφήμερος βροντοσκοπία τοπικὴ πρὸς τὴν σελήνην κατὰ τὸν Ῥωμαῖον Φίγουλον ἐκ τῶν Τάγητος καθ' ἑρμηνείαν πρὸς λέξιν; and at the end there is added the note ταύτην τὴν ἐφήμερον βροντοσκοπίαν ὁ Νιγίδιος οὐ καθολικήν, ἀλλὰ μόνης εἶναι τῆς Ῥώμης ἔκρινεν. Although the general opinion has been against Wachsmuth's theory that Nigidius Figulus had nothing at all to do with the existing work,[5] it remains

[1] On the writings of Caecina see Sen. *NQ* II 39, 49, 56, Plin. *NH* II, index; A. H. G. Zimmermann, *De A. Caecina Scriptore* (Berlin, 1852), F. Münzer, *Beiträge zur Quellenkritik der Naturgeschichte des Plinius* (Berlin, 1897), 244–5, and in *RE* s.v. Caecina no. 7 (1899), M. Schanz–C. Hosius, *Geschichte der römischen Literatur* i⁴ (Munich, 1927), 602.

[2] On the writings of Tarquitius see *CIL* xi.3370 (and p. 1337), 7566, E. Bormann, *Archäologisch-epigraphische Mitteilungen aus Oesterreich-Ungarn*, xi (1887), 94–103, and *Jahresh. Oest. Arch. Inst.*, ii (1899), 129–36, W. Kroll in *RE* s.v. Tarquitius no. 7 (1932), Schanz-Hosius, l.c., J. Heurgon, *Latomus*, xii (1953), 402–17.

[3] On the writings of Nigidius see the works cited below, p. 5, and Schanz-Hosius, op. cit., 552–4.

[4] On Fonteius Capito, properly identified by S. Weinstock, *PBSR* xviii (1950), 44–9, and the less known writers on the *disciplina* see Schanz-Hosius, op. cit., 602–3.

[5] C. Wachsmuth, *Ioannis Laurentii Lydi Liber de Ostentis* . . .² (Leipzig, 1897), pp. xxxvii–xxxviii, followed by G. Schmeisser, *Quaestiones de etrusca disciplina particula* (Breslau, 1872), 23. Previous editors of Lydus, from C. B. Hase onwards, accepted

quite uncertain what his contribution to it was. For the present purpose it will suffice to point out that there are many elements in it that are not likely to be Etruscan, or at least are not likely to have been in the Etruscan version that Nigidius supposedly translated into Latin (or Greek?), itself probably the latest of a number of versions. At the most superficial level, the names of the months used in the calendar are those of the imperial Roman calendar; and the Rome to which the work was supposed to be relevant was ruled by a monarch (see the prophecies for 19 October, 16 November, 27 and 30 December, etc.).[1] Some have claimed to detect a number of references in the calendar to the personalities of Nigidius' own lifetime, particularly to Caesar and Pompey; and the same has been done with the *liber fulguralis* also preserved in Ioannes Lydus and perhaps the work of Nigidius;[2] these references remain hypothetical. As far as genuinely Etruscan allusions are concerned,[3] civil strife is continually mentioned in the calendar, and sometimes it is strife between classes (see the prophecy for 9 November);[4] but we cannot select entries of this kind and apply them to the Etruscans, when they may equally well belong to other strata of the calendar's formation, Babylonian, Roman, or Byzantine. The entry that seems to refer most definitely to a characteristically Etruscan social system is that of 11 September: *ἐὰν βροντήσῃ, οἱ ὑπεξούσιοι τῶν εὐγενῶν σκέψονταί τι καινὸν ἐν τοῖς κοινοῖς*. This has been translated as 'principes nobilitatis res novas molientur',[5] but in fact it must

that there was at least a Nigidian element; cf. T. Bergk, *Kleine Philologische Schriften*, i, (Halle, 1884), 653 and n. For criticism of Wachsmuth see A. Swoboda, *P. Nigidii Figuli operum reliquiae* (Vienna, 1889), 31–5; more recently W. Kroll in *RE* s.v. Nigidius no. 3 (1936), cols. 207–9, S. Weinstock, *PBSR* xix (1951), 140, A. Piganiol in *Studies in Roman Economic and Social History in Honor of A. C. Johnson* (Princeton, 1951), 79–87, and A. Della Casa, *Nigidio Figulo* (Rome, 1962), 128, have argued that the text was adapted by Nigidius.

[1] 19 October: *εἰ βροντήσῃ, δυνάστου πτῶσιν ἢ βασιλέως ἐκβολὴν ἀπειλεῖ . . .*; 16 November: *τῷ δὲ βασιλεῖ κίνδυνος*; 27 December: *ὁ βασιλεὺς πολλοὺς ὠφελήσει*; 30 December: *ἀνταρσίαν κατὰ τῆς βασιλείας*.

[2] See especially Weinstock, art cit., 139–40.

[3] That there was a genuinely Etruscan element was denied by Wachsmuth, l.c.; also now by W. and H. G. Gundel, 'Astrologumena, Die astrologische Literatur in der Antike und ihre Geschichte', *Sudhoffs Archiv, Vierteljahrsschrift für Geschichte der Medizin usw.*, Beiheft vi (1966), 138. Cf. also Kroll, art. cit., col. 208.

[4] *εἰ βροντήσῃ, δημοτῶν ἀνασκολοπισμοὶ ἔσονται, ἀλλὰ μὴν καὶ ἀφθονία τῶν ἐπιτηδείων.*

[5] Kroll, art. cit., cols. 208–9, followed by Weinstock, l.c.

refer to the *dependents* of the nobles,[1] dependents, however, who were capable of rebellion.

Also partly concerned with divination were the *libri rituales.* Their contents are described by Festus in terms that probably derive from Verrius Flaccus, the Augustan writer on *res Etruscae*: 'rituales nominantur Etruscorum libri, in quibus perscriptum est, quo ritu condantur urbes, arae, aedes sacrentur, qua sanctitate muri, quo iure portae, quomodo tribus, curiae, centuriae distribuantur, exercitus constituantur, ordinentur, ceteraque eiusmodi ad bellum ac pacem pertinentia'.[2] Among the *libri rituales* there should probably also be counted the *libri fatales,* and the Etruscan teaching on *saecula* and on the limitation of land.[3] The terms in which Festus describes the *libri rituales* create the suspicion that they had been thoroughly adapted to Roman conditions—'quomodo tribus, curiae, centuriae distribuantur' is particularly suspect;[4] yet tribes subdivided into *curiae* do seem to have existed in at least one Etruscan town.[5] However, authentically Etruscan books of this description were of almost exclusively antiquarian interest by the end of the Republic, and it is doubtful whether there are many traces of them in surviving texts. A reference in Servius Danielis to a book 'qui inscribitur terrae iuris Etruriae scriptum vocibus Tagae' may be one.[6] A fragment of Caecina concerning the foundation of Mantua may conceivably be another,[7] but the *origines* of Italian towns had been well studied by non-Etruscans. As far as teaching on the

[1] So C. B. Hase (*clientelae*), L. Legrand, *Publius Nigidius Figulus* (Paris, 1931), 154 (*clients*), A. Piganiol, art. cit., 80 (*clients*).

[2] Festus 358L.

[3] Thulin, 'Die etruskische Disciplin', i.2, extended the term *libri rituales* to cover all Etruscan works on divination except the *libri haruspicini* and *fulgurales.* The basis for this is Cicero's division of the Etruscan works on divination into 'haruspicini et fulgurales et rituales libri' (*Div.* I 72), where the MS. authority for the reading *rituales* is stronger than that for *tonitruales* (see A. S. Pease ad loc.).

[4] Cf. Thulin, 'Die etruskische Disciplin', iii, *Göteborgs Högskolas Årsskrift,* xv (1909), 47–51. S. Mazzarino, *Iura,* xii (1961), 32, takes this passage as proof of the existence of Etruscan *centuriae* (he also thinks that the terms included in it were translated from Etruscan by Verrius himself), but there is no supporting evidence.

[5] Serv. *Aen.* X 202 (on Mantua), pointed out by A. Momigliano, *JRS* liii (1963), 109 n. 60.

[6] Serv. Dan. *Aen.* I 2: 'terrae iuris Etruriae' is the MS. reading, where Bergk and Thilo wished to read 'litterae iuris Etruriae' and Thulin, op. cit., i.9, 'terrae ritus Etruriae'.

[7] Σ Veron. *Aen.* X 200.

saecula is concerned, some brief fragments on the subject survived; they are discussed later in this chapter. On the limitation of land, Etruscan knowledge was regarded by Varro as the origin of Roman practices,[1] and there survives in the gromatic corpus, besides the Prophecy of Vegoia, a fragment about limitation attributed to Mago and Vegoia;[2] but there is no other evidence that any authentically Etruscan writing on the subject survived into the Roman world.

It has recently been argued by Heurgon that there was a considerable amount of other Etruscan literature not concerned with divination.[3] He puts much weight on Diodorus' statement that the Etruscans γράμματα . . . καὶ φυσιολογίαν καὶ θεολογίαν ἐξεπόνησαν ἐπὶ πλέον, a statement probably taken from Posidonius.[4] Yet if Posidonius was thinking of Etruscan γράμματα as consisting of φυσιολογία and θεολογία, the passage is of little use in demonstrating the existence of an Etruscan literature beyond what has already been described, for φυσιολογία probably refers to Etruscan lore concerning lightning and natural *ostenta* in general.[5] As a proof of the existence of a wide range of literature, Livy's reference to the supposed ancient Roman custom of having their children educated in *litterae Etruscae*[6] carries even less weight. The story looks like a less accurate version of Cicero's statement that some of the sons of Roman *principes* used to be sent to learn the Etruscan *disciplina*;[7] it is certainly not evidence for a substantial body of Etruscan literature outside the *disciplina*.

[1] Varro *apud* Front. p. 27 Lachmann: 'limitum prima origo, sicut Varro descripsit, a disciplina Etrusca . . .'. Cf. Thulin, op. cit., iii.26–30.

[2] Pp. 348–50L: 'Ex libris Magonis et Vegoiae auctorum'.

[3] *La vie quotidienne chez les étrusques* (Paris, 1961), here referred to by its English translation, *Daily Life of the Etruscans* (London, 1964), 237–68; cf. B. Nogara, *Gli etruschi e la loro civiltà* (Milan, 1933), 405–36, M. Pallottino, *Etruscologia*[6] (Milan, 1968), 269–74. For a cautious estimate see also F. Altheim, *Epochen der römischen Geschichte*, i (Frankfurt-a.-M., 1934), 216–19.

[4] Diod. V 40.2. See below, p. 20.

[5] Cf. Serv. *Aen.* VIII 427: 'nam dicunt physici de sedecim partibus caeli iaci fulmina'. A Stoic like Posidonius regarded divination of this kind as dependent on φυσιολογία; cf. in particular Cic. *Div.* I 90.

[6] IX 36.3: 'Habeo auctores vulgo tum Romanos, sicut nunc Graecis, ita Etruscis litteris erudiri solitos'. This passage is heavily emphasized by Heurgon, op. cit., 238–9; cf. M. Sordi, *I rapporti romano-ceriti e l'origine della civitas sine suffragio* (Rome, 1960), 87 (she speculates that it may have derived from Fabius Pictor—it occurs in a story about Fabius Rullianus).

[7] *Div.* I 92: 'Quocirca bene apud maiores nostros senatus tum cum florebat

It is obvious that there was some other Etruscan literature of various genres. Leaving historical works aside for the moment, we happen to know from Varro that there was a certain Volnius 'qui tragoedias Tuscas scripsit', whose evidence Varro referred to on an etymological point.[1] There is some problematical supporting evidence for the existence of organized drama in Etruria;[2] but apart perhaps from a single reference to *fabulae Etruscae*, Volnius' Etruscan tragedies are an isolated phenomenon in the literary tradition. The information that Varro took from him looks as if it came from a *fabula praetexta*; in any case Volnius probably wrote in the second or first century (hardly before Naevius' *Clastidium*), and he cannot be used to prove the existence of a substantial body of literature.

Did the Etruscans have a historical literature?[3] Given their general cultural level and their knowledge of the Greek world, it is to be expected that there was something of the sort. Indeed many who were not Greeks, but were in touch with the Greek world, are known to have written histories of their own peoples in Greek, particularly after the time of Alexander the Great.[4] There is no corroboration of the view that there were histories by Etruscans written in Greek, but there is evidence for some Etruscan historiography. The scenes depicted in the François Tomb at Vulci surely show that the Etruscans maintained in some way historical traditions of their own.[5] The paintings show representative warriors of several Etruscan states and of Rome in combat with each other,[6] and among them

imperium decrevit ut de principum filiis sex [MSS.: X ex Christ, Pease, etc.] singulis Etruriae populis in disciplinam traderentur, ne ars tanta propter tenuitatem hominum a religionis auctoritate abduceretur ad mercedem atque quaestum'. Cf. Val. Max. I 1.1. Opinion is divided as to whether Cicero was referring to the sons of Etruscans or Romans; the latter is what the text seems to say. Pease (ad loc.) rejected the connection with Livy's story on the grounds that '*litteris* is hardly an appropriate term for the Etruscan discipline'; it is true that this interpretation makes Livy guilty of a certain misunderstanding.

[1] *LL* V 55.

[2] Cf. Heurgon, op. cit., 241–7 (over-optimistic).

[3] A strongly affirmative answer is given by Heurgon, op. cit., 247; cf. Sordi, op. cit., 178–9.

[4] Cf. A. Momigliano, *Rend. Acc. Linc.*, ser. 8, xv (1960), 314–15= *Terzo contributo alla storia degli studi classici e del mondo antico* (Rome, 1966), 61; he thinks that the Etruscans probably did so.

[5] Pointed out by W. Deecke in K. O. Müller–W. Deecke, *Die Etrusker*[2] (Stuttgart, 1877), i.111 n. 128.

[6] For description see especially F. Messerschmidt–A. Von Gerkan, *Nekropolen*

'Macstrna',[1] clearly identical with the Mastarna who, according to Claudius, was said by Etruscan sources to have been a king of Rome.[2] Various dates have been assigned to the paintings, but a date in the period 340–310 B.C. has now been very strongly argued and cannot be far wrong.[3] Although it has recently been suggested that it was Fabius Pictor who was responsible for introducing Mastarna to the Roman world,[4] there is no evidence that he was known to any non-Etruscan before Dionysius of Halicarnassus.[5] It follows that there must have been a tradition of some sort in Etruria that continued to carry Mastarna down to the first century B.C.[6]—and although the possibilities of an oral tradition cannot be excluded, presumably it was a literary tradition. The survival of Mastarna suggests that there may have been many other historical or pseudo-historical stories about the same period still current in the late Republic. Yet the scenes depicted in the François tomb are from a story that was probably well known in Etruria—so one may judge from the several appearances elsewhere of one or both of the brothers Vibenna.[7] There are no comparable cases, and the scenes in the tomb are more probably a version of the most famous indigenous Etruscan legend than excerpts from a historical narrative covering a long period.

Varro claimed knowledge of some *Tuscae historiae*: according

von Vulci (Berlin, 1930), 62–163, A. Alföldi, *Early Rome and the Latins* (Ann Arbor, 1965), 220–8, M. Cristofani, *Dialoghi di Archeologia*, i (1967), 186–219.

[1] *CIE* 5267.

[2] *ILS* 212, lines 22–3.

[3] Cristofani, art. cit. For a date *c.* 300, Messerschmidt–Von Gerkan, Alföldi, ll. cc.; cf. J. Gagé, *MEFR* lxxiv (1962), 82. The arguments for a later date (after *c.* 125) were put by Von Gerkan himself, *MDAI–R* lvii (1942), 146–50, and by M. Pallottino, *La peinture étrusque* (Geneva, 1952), 153–4. There is a large bibliography of the subject, cf. Alföldi, op. cit., 225–6, Cristofani, art. cit., 186–7 (add L. Banti, *Il mondo degli etruschi* (Rome, 1960), 70–1, S. Mazzarino, *Il pensiero storico classico* (Bari, 1966), i.192). G. A. Mansuelli, *SE* xxxvi (1968), 7, still favours a late date, but does not deal with Cristofani's arguments.

[4] Alföldi, op. cit., 215.

[5] See below, p. 26.

[6] Cf. Mazzarino, op. cit., ii.1 86.

[7] On a mirror from Bolsena, E. Gerhard–G. Körte, *Etruskische Spiegel*, v (Berlin, 1897), pl. 127, pp. 166–72; on a *bucchero* cup from Veii, M. Pallottino, *SE* xiii (1939), 455–7, *TLE* 35; on a red-figure *kylix* perhaps from Vulci, *CVA* (France), fasc. 16, pls. 28–30, pp. 39–41, J. D. Beazley, *Etruscan Vase-Painting* (Oxford, 1947), 256–7, J. Heurgon, *Mélanges d'archéologie, d'épigraphie, et d'histoire offerts à J. Carcopino* (Paris, 1966), 516–28, *TLE* 942. Cf. also G. Radke, *RE* s.v. Vibenna (1958), cols. 2456–7, Alföldi, op. cit., 229–30.

to Censorinus,[1] the Etruscans, with their skill in *haruspicium* and in their *disciplina*, carefully observed and recorded in books the portents that marked the end of an Etruscan *saeculum*. Consequently in the *Tuscae historiae*, which were written in the eighth Etruscan *saeculum*, as Varro testifies, it is stated how many *saecula* were awarded to the Etruscans, how long each of the past ones has been, or by what signs their ends have been designated. Thus it is written that each of the first four *saecula* was a hundred years long, the fifth 123, the sixth 119, the seventh the same, that the eighth was then in progress, and the ninth and tenth remained, after which the *nomen Etruscum* would come to an end. Clearly some important events in Etruscan history may have been recorded in such *historiae*, but we are not justified by Varro's description in assuming that they amounted to continuous works of history; they may have contained only portents and other matter concerning the *disciplina*. Nor can we assume that Varro had any first-hand acquaintance with them. Varro gives the date of the *Tuscae historiae* as during the eighth Etruscan *saeculum*, approximately 208–88 B.C. according to the usual calculation, but possibly somewhat earlier.[2] It has been suggested that they may have been influenced by the redaction of the *Annales Maximi* in about 123,[3] but that is improbable—there is not even any evidence or likelihood that the *Tuscae historiae* had an annalistic character.[4] With this fragment from Varro a cryptic notice in the *Suda* (s.v. Τυρρηνία) should probably be associated: ἱστορίαν δὲ παρ' αὐτοῖς ἔμπειρος ἀνὴρ συνεγράψατο.[5] The citation that follows is not from any ordinary history, but from a cosmology allocating twelve thousand years to creation and six thousand years as the life of the human race, a topic obviously related closely to the known passage from the *Tuscae historiae*. We still do not have any strong evidence that there was an actual history of the Etruscans that became known to non-Etruscan writers.

Varro knew something not only about the *Tuscae historiae*, but also about certain *fabulae Etruscae*: Pliny recounts a descrip-

[1] *De die natali* XVII 6.

[2] See below, pp. 35–7.

[3] Heurgon, *JRS* xlix (1959), 42 n. 14.

[4] As tends to be thought, cf. Nogara, op. cit., 423, Pallottino, *Etruscologia*[6], 273.

[5] iv, p. 609 Adler.

tion of the tomb of Porsenna at Clusium,[1] which was surmounted by gigantic pyramids—Varro was embarrassed to mention their height, which the *fabulae Etruscae* said was equal to the height of the whole edifice below them. *Fabulae Etruscae* with such subject matter are difficult to fit into any otherwise-attested category of Etruscan writing: but the alternative, which is to suppose that the story derived from a Hellenistic work like the περὶ θαυμασίων ἀκουσμάτων, is not attractive, for stories about inland Etruscans, even fanciful stories, were probably not numerous in Hellenistic writers. *Fabulae Etruscae* should probably be given their most obvious meaning, namely 'Etruscan plays'; like some at least of the works of Volnius, also known to Varro, they may have been *fabulae praetextae*; Porsenna's tomb may easily have been described in such a work.

Some recent writers have claimed to detect Etruscan sources in some parts of Livy's description of the siege of Veii in Book V.[2] Such views are without foundation. Far from being well informed about the political situation in Veii, Livy makes it conform to the needs of the dramatic situation; so too with the discussions in the Etruscan league. There is no reason whatsoever why the story of the prodigy of the Alban Lake should not have had Roman sources,[3] and Livy does not display any close knowledge of the *libri fatales*.[4] There is no single element in the whole account that shows any esoteric knowledge of Etruscan affairs of a kind that suggests that there was an Etruscan version of the siege of Veii behind it. More generally it may be said that when the literary sources for the political structure of the Etruscan states and the 'League of the Twelve Peoples' are collected,[5] there is little that looks securely authentic. Meetings of the *concilium* of the Twelve Peoples, for example, were surely products of literary embroidery.

[1] *NH* XXXVI 91–3. On this see J. L. Myres, *ABSA* xlvi (1951), 117–21.

[2] J. Bayet, *Tite-Live, Histoire Romaine*, v (Paris, 1954), 125–40, Sordi, op. cit. 10–16; the theory has been quite widely accepted, e.g. by A. H. McDonald, *CR* n.s. xi (1961), 269 (with some reservations), G. Vitucci in *Problemi di storia e archeologia dell'Umbria, Atti del I Convegno di Studi Umbri* (1963, publ. Gubbio–Perugia, 1964), 296, R. M. Ogilvie, *A Commentary on Livy Books 1–5* (Oxford, 1965), 628; for some criticism cf. J. Bleicken, *ZSS* lxxviii (1961), 450–1.

[3] V 15.

[4] As Bayet, op. cit., 128, appears to think.

[5] Cf. R. Lambrechts, *Essai sur les magistratures des républiques étrusques* (Brussels–Rome, 1959), 21–31.

At the beginning of the Empire, however, we begin to hear of treatises about the Etruscans that were apparently so detailed that their authors must have had some sort of access to Etruscan sources. Dionysius of Halicarnassus stated that he was going to write the political history of the Etruscans,[1] and it is reasonable to suppose that he already had some definite knowledge of the sources that were available. In the same passage[2] he mentions the Etruscan name for Etruria (Ῥασέννα), about which he was evidently correct;[3] and there are additional reasons to suppose that Dionysius had some rather esoteric knowledge about the Etruscans.[4] There were two writers who did succeed in producing works about the Etruscans, namely the Augustan and Tiberian writer Verrius Flaccus, who wrote on *res Etruscae*,[5] and Claudius, who wrote twenty books of *Tyrrhenica*,[6] and claimed to be able to follow the *auctores Tusci* over the story of Caelius Vibenna and Mastarna.[7] Whether or not any of these three writers had direct access to Etruscan sources, and whether or not Verrius Flaccus and Claudius wrote continuous histories of the Etruscans, these cases strongly suggest that in the Julio–Claudian period there was believed to be much good information available about Etruscan history and society.

Greek writers had of course possessed fragments of information and misinformation about the Etruscans (and most of the other peoples of Italy) before the fourth century; but it was then that the ethnographical writers formed a general view of the Etruscans, and it was one that influenced most later writing about them.[8] What we know of fourth-century writing about the Etruscans is very fragmentary and much of it depends on Athenaeus' interest in τρυφή. The τρυφὴ of the Etruscans was in fact a *topos*:[9] it occurs in Alcimus,[10] in a work

[1] I 30.4. [2] I 30.3. [3] Cf. *CIE* 439, 5360, etc.
[4] See below, pp. 25–6. [5] Σ Veron. *Aen.* X 183. [6] Suet. *Claud.* 42.
[7] *ILS* 212, lines 16–24.
[8] On the fourth-century ethnographers' writing on Etruria see K. Trüdinger, *Studien zur Geschichte der griechisch-römischen Ethnographie* (Basel, 1918), 48, E. Wikén, *Die Kunde der Hellenen von dem Lande und den Völkern der Apenninenhalbinsel bis 300 v. Chr.* (Lund, 1937), 182–8. T. S. Brown, *Timaeus of Tauromenium* (Berkeley–Los Angeles, 1955), 122 n. 71, mentions the possibility that there was an account of Etruria in an earlier logographer, but there is no sign of it.
[9] Cf. A. Passerini, *SIFC* n.s. xi (1934), 51, F. Jacoby on Alcimus *FGrH* 560 F 3.
[10] *FGrH* 560 F 3.

called *Τυρρηνῶν Νόμιμα* attributed to Aristotle,[1] in Theopompus' *Ἱστορίαι*,[2] in Heraclides of Pontus' work on *πολιτεῖαι*,[3] and in Timaeus' *Histories*.[4] The view recurs outside historical writing—Theophrastus, who wrote something about the Etruscans,[5] had a pupil nicknamed *Τυρρηνός, ὅτι τῶν αὐλητρίδων τὰ ἱμάτια περιέδυεν*, according to Athenaeus.[6] The fullest surviving account of Etruscan *τρυφή* is that of Theopompus, who attributed it to a number of other peoples;[7] Timaeus and Alcimus are cited by Athenaeus in the same section, and it can be assumed that their full descriptions largely overlapped that of Theopompus. According to Theopompus, the Etruscans hold their women in common; the women pay great attention to their bodies and exercise often in the company of men, for it is not a disgrace for them to be seen naked; they dine with any men they please and toast anyone they please; they are formidable drinkers and very beautiful; the Etruscans bring up all their children, not knowing who the fathers are; they make love in public, and indulge in homosexuality and the shaving of their bodies. Some at least of these stories are fanciful,[8] and there are various possible explanations of them. Some of them may have been genuine misunderstandings;[9] but the bitterness aroused by the activities of the Etruscan pirates probably encouraged them,[10] and also the reputation of the Lydians for effeminacy; later, Roman propaganda about the Etruscans may have helped to maintain this view of them. On the other hand, Theopompus' description was not totally unconnected with the real Etruscan world, for it does seem likely that women were somewhat less repressed there than they were in Greece.

There may have been other *topoi* about the Etruscans. A story about them that was often repeated later derived from

[1] Fr. 607 Rose.

[2] *FGrH* 115 F 204.

[3] *FHG* ii.217 fr. 16.

[4] *FGrH* 566 F 1, F 50.

[5] Σ Pind. *Pyth.* II 2: *Θεόφραστος ἐν τῷ περὶ Τυρρηνῶν*. Cf. O. Regenbogen in *RE* s.v. Theophrastos no. 3, Supplementband vii (1940), col. 1521.

[6] XIII 607f.

[7] Listed by Trüdinger, op. cit., 62.

[8] For some remarks on their inaccuracy cf. A. J. Pfiffig, *Gymnasium*, lxxi (1964), 17–36.

[9] G. Körte in *RE* s.v. Etrusker (1907), cols. 754–5.

[10] Heurgon, *Daily Life of the Etruscans*, 32. The explanation offered by H. J. Rose, *JRS* xii (1922), 113, is to be rejected.

Aristotle:[1] the Etruscan pirates had a singularly cruel way of treating their prisoners, which was to bind them to decaying corpses (the condition of the prisoners was, according to Aristotle, similar to that of the soul bound to the human body). The attribution of cruelty to the Etruscans was no new thing, however, in the fourth century: Herodotus had already done it.[2]

Fourth-century and Hellenistic writers about Etruria did concern themselves with some other aspects of Etruscan life. Presumably an Aristotelian work with the title *Τυρρηνῶν Νόμιμα* dealt with other things as well as *τρυφή*, and Theophrastus wrote a whole work, or at least a whole section of a work, *περὶ Τυρρηνῶν*, in which it was recorded that after the battle of Himera Gelo forbad the practice of human sacrifice among the defeated.[3] It is also very likely that some more general account of the Etruscans was to be found in some of the other ethnographies. Heraclides' knowledge of them was not restricted to their *τρυφή*: they had *πλεῖσται τέχναι*, they treated their guests well, and defaulting Etruscan debtors were followed everywhere by children with empty purses *εἰς δυσωπίαν*. We do not know how extensive these works were, but it seems unlikely that any of their authors had the inclination or time to dig deeply into Etruscan affairs; their information presumably had its ultimate origin in brief reports made by Greek travellers. Nothing in the meagre surviving fragments suggests that they had any knowledge of the Etruscans that was at all esoteric.

There were other brief references to Etruscan affairs in third- and second-century Greek writers. In the third-century work *περὶ θαυμασίων ἀκουσμάτων* attributed to Aristotle,[4] there

[1] Fr. 60 Rose=*Fragmenta Selecta*, ed. Ross, *Protrepticus* 10b=Cicero, *Hortensius* fr. 95 Müller=fr. 112 Grilli; cf. Val. Max. IX 2 ext. 10, Serv. *Aen.* VIII 479, Serv. Dan. *Aen.* VIII 485. Cf. J. Carcopino, *Bulletin de la Société Nat. des Antiquaires de France* (1927), 211–12, J. Gagé, *MEFR* xlvi (1929), 127–8.

[2] I 167; Gagé, l.c., J. Brunschwig, *Revue philosophique*, cliii (1963), 173.

[3] Σ Pind. *Pyth.* II 2.

[4] For discussion of its date see A. Westermann, *Παραδοξογράφοι, Scriptores Rerum Mirabilium Graeci* (Braunschweig, 1839), pp. xxv–xxviii, H. Schrader, *Fleckeisens Jahrbücher für classische Philologie*, xcvii (1868), 217–19. The case for putting it much later (A. Gercke, *RE* s.v. Aristoteles no. 18 (1896), col. 1048, W. Christ–W. Schmid–O. Stählin, *Geschichte der griechischen Literatur*, i[5] (Munich, 1908), 686) is without substance as far as sects. 1–151 are concerned. In particular there is no reason why sects. 87 and 91 should be later than Posidonius, and no reason to identify the Pantheon of sect. 51 with the Hadrianic Pantheon at Athens

is a story about a river situated ἐν τοῖς Λίγυσι where the waters rose so high that one could not see across the river;[1] Strabo describes the phenomenon as being at the river confluence at Pisa.[2] This evidently came from no very well-informed source. On the other hand two further sections of the περὶ θαυμασίων ἀκουσμάτων do suggest a rather closer acquaintance with Etruria: one contains some information about copper and iron mining on Elba,[3] the other a strange description of the town of Οἰναρέα, which was ruled by slaves.[4] Other writers also seem to have gone beyond the stereotype of τρυφή. The brief description of the Etruscan empire given by Polybius shows that he knew of more than the ethnographical commonplaces.[5] There is a tantalizing fragment of the philosopher, orator, and propagandist Metrodorus of Scepsis;[6] he is reported by Pliny to have claimed that the Romans attacked Volsinii (sc. in 265) on account of the two thousand statues there,[7] not, as the Roman annalistic tradition claimed, to honour an obligation to their allies. Metrodorus probably wrote a work περὶ ἱστορίας,[8] and it probably contained some ethnographical material.[9] It is more likely, however, that Metrodorus made this accusation in a list of instances of the *avaritia* of the Roman imperialists.[10]

In Plutarch's life of Romulus a version of the birth of Romulus is attributed to one Promathion, who wrote a ἱστορία Ἰταλική;[11] it has been suggested that the story that he recounted was taken from an Etruscan source.[12] 'Promathion' may perhaps be a

(see J. Geffcken, *Timaios' Geographie des Westens* (Berlin, 1892), 86, K. Ziegler in *RE* s.v. Pantheion (1949), cols. 718, 721–2).

1 Sect. 92. 2 V 2.5 222C 3 Sect. 93. 4 Sect. 94.

5 II 17: τοὺς ἱστοροῦντας τὰς Τυρρηνῶν δυναστείας οὐ χρὴ ποιεῖσθαι τὴν ἀναφορὰν ἐπι τὴν νῦν κατεχομένην ὑπ' αὐτῶν χώραν, ἀλλ' . . . .

6 On whom see W. Kroll in *RE* s.v. Metrodorus no. 23 (1932), H. Fuchs, *Der geistige Widerstand gegen Rom in der antiken Welt* (Basel, 1938), 43–4, S. Mazzarino, *Il pensiero storico classico*, ii.1 208–9.

7 *NH* XXXIV 34.

8 Σ Ap. Rhod. IV 834=*FGrH* 184 F 2.

9 Cf. Steph. Byz. s.v. Ὕπανις=F 18.

10 Cf. Fuchs, l.c., for the possibility of a special work of Metrodorus attacking the Romans.

11 *Rom.* 2. S. Mazzarino, *Studi Romani*, viii (1960), 390–1, *Il pensiero storico classico*, i.584–5, misguidedly rejects the title in an attempt to give Promathion a fifth-century date; against this see E. Gabba, *Entretiens Fond. Hardt*, xiii (1966), 148.

12 F. Altheim, *Griechischer Götter im alten Rom* (Giessen, 1930), 51–2, Heurgon, op. cit., 254–6; cf. W. Schultz, *Memnon*, iii (1909), 157–8, F. Marbach in *RE* s.v. Tarchetios (1932), col. 2295.

mistake for 'Promathidas',[1] but if not Promathion is undatable except by reference to the Plutarch passage. A Hellenistic date is most likely.[2] Tarchetius, king of Alba, and perhaps Teratius, his herdsman, who are leading characters in the story, have Etruscan names;[3] but the theory that Promathion had an Etruscan source does not inspire much confidence, for surely a Greek who had been ingenious enough to discover a story of the Etruscans about the birth of Romulus would have attributed it to them.

Members of the Fabian family were especially active in the Roman conquest of Etruria, and it is probable that they subsequently had some clients there. It is tempting to suppose that Fabius Pictor had access to some Etruscan historical traditions and made use of them.[4] Yet the Fabian connections with Etruria after the conquest are poorly documented,[5] and there is among the fragments of Fabius Pictor nothing that looks Etruscan.[6] Nothing that we know about him suggests that he will have been eager to discover non-Roman versions of the events that he was describing, and if he had done so at all assiduously there would surely have been more sign of it in later writers.

From the time of Cato we can distinguish some specifically Roman writing about Etruria. In Books II and III of his *Origines*, in which he described 'unde quaeque civitas orta sit Italica',[7] much information must have been gathered. The *Origines* acquired a great reputation for *diligentia*,[8] and it is possible that Cato read ἱστορίαι ἐπιχώριοι of the Sabines[9]—but he had lived among the Sabines,[10] and so nothing can be inferred from that about his use of Etruscan sources. It is in fact

[1] Suggested by C. Müller, *FHG* iii.202–3.

[2] W. Christ–W. Schmid–O. Stählin, op. cit., ii[6] (Munich, 1920), 400 n. 1 (late Hellenistic), F. Jacoby, *FGrH* iii. C p. 893 (? third century).

[3] Heurgon, l.c.

[4] Heurgon, op. cit., 252–3; cf. Mazzarino, *Il pensiero storico classico*, ii.1 86.

[5] Much has to be made of the Fabii who appear in inscriptions, *TLE* 471 (bilingual and admittedly important), *CIL* xi.2202, 2202a.

[6] Fabius Rullianus' Etruscan education has been derived from him (see above) as has the Roman discovery of king Mastarna (but see below, p. 26).

[7] Nepos, *Cat.* 3, cf. Dion. Hal. I 11.1.

[8] H. Peter, *HRR* i[2]. cxlii–cxliii.

[9] Cf. Dion. Hal. II 49.2–5. The question is discussed by Peter, op. cit., cxxxiv.

[10] Nepos, *Cat.* 1.

unlikely that he had the advantage of much Etruscan information about Etruria.[1] He is the first writer who is known to have recorded a period of Etruscan dominance in Italy[2]—although there had long been a tradition of a period of Etruscan sea-power.[3] Yet it is hardly likely that Cato obtained his idea of Etruscan land-power from Etruscan writers or from works like the *Tuscae historiae*;[4] it is more probable that he made an inference from the appearance of Etruscans in many local legends. We happen to know that there appeared in the *Origines* a version of a story known to us in most detail from Dionysius of Halicarnassus,[5] according to which one Arruns of Clusium secured the alliance of the Gauls by enticing them with wine and olive-oil so that they would support him against the son of Lucumo, who had seduced his wife. This story, Heurgon alleges, is of Etruscan origin—Cato, or perhaps an earlier annalist, found it in the local records of Clusium.[6] This hypothesis is most unconvincing: the story reflected badly on all the citizens of Clusium involved, it provided a conveniently anti-Etruscan explanation for a Roman writer wishing to explain the arrival of the Gauls in central Italy,[7] it has a close similarity to the story of the sons of Demaratus,[8] its Etruscan names are feeble and unconvincing, and it even seems to repeat the *topos* of Etruscan τρυφή.[9] Cato did know about Mezentius, king of Caere,[10] perhaps from a local source, and about foundation legends and early history of some other towns near to Rome.[11] But there is no evidence that he was acquainted with local sources from any of the main, not yet Romanized, towns of Etruria. The remaining fragments that concern Etruria deal

[1] *Pace* L. Banti, *Il mondo degli etruschi* (Rome, 1960), 8.

[2] Serv. *Aen.* XI 567=fr. 62P: 'quia in Tuscorum iure paene omnis Italia fuerat'.

[3] *Hymn to Dionysus* [VII] 6–8; cf. Palaephatus, περὶ ἀπίστων, 20 (Mythographi Graeci, ed. N. Festa, vol. iii, fasc. ii).

[4] *Pace* Ogilvie on Liv. V 33.7.

[5] Dion. Hal. XIII 14–19, cf. Polyb. II 17.3, Liv. V 33.3. It appears in fr. 36P, recognized as a reference to this story by A. Wagener, *M. Porcii Catonis Originum Fragmenta* . . . (Bonn, 1849), 49.

[6] *Daily Life of the Etruscans*, 252.

[7] Ogilvie on Liv. V 33.3; cf. J. Wolski, *Historia*, v (1956), 38.

[8] Ogilvie, l.c.

[9] Dion. Hal. XIII 15: καὶ οὐκέτι κρύβδα ἀλλ' ἀναφανδὸν ἐζήτει αὐτῇ διαλεγεσθαι; Cato, fr. 36P.

[10] Frr. 9–12.

[11] Falerii, fr. 47; Capena and Veii, fr. 48.

with the history of the Etruscans at Pisa,[1] but his source for that may well have been Greek, and with the Latin etymology of the colony of Graviscae, founded in 181.[2] Nor do the meagre known fragments concerning *origines* written by the annalist Cn. Gellius suggest that he will have made use of local Etruscan sources.[3]

Heir both to the Greek and to the Roman traditions of historiography about the regions of Italy was Posidonius. It is not safe to assume his influence in accounts of Etruria other than that of Diodorus, for example in that of Strabo;[4] but the description given by Diodorus,[5] although it was at one time attributed by Jacoby to Timaeus,[6] is undoubtedly from Posidonius.[7] The parallel between the quotation from Book II of Posidonius attributed to him by Athenaeus in which the dining arrangements of the Etruscans are discussed[8] and the discussion of the same topic in Diodorus[9] is very close indeed. Eating and drinking habits are admittedly a commonplace subject in ethnographies;[10] but since Diodorus elsewhere often mentions Posidonius, and Posidonius dealt with the subject of dining arrangements, it is unreasonable to doubt that this passage is Posidonian. Its tone is reminiscent of the relative fairness of Posidonius' other descriptions of barbarian peoples.[11] The context, presumably in the second book of the history after

[1] Fr. 45. [2] Fr. 46.

[3] Frr. 8–10P. Dion. Hal. I 11.1, incidentally, does not say, in spite of P. A. Brunt, *JRS* lv (1965), 100, that others besides Cato traced the origins of the peoples of Italy.

[4] On Strabo see below, pp. 24–5. S. Mazzarino also attributes to Posidonius Plutarch's knowledge of the Etruscan *saecula* (*Sull.* 7), *Il pensiero storico classico*, ii.1 172.

[5] V 40=*FGrH* 87 F 119. [6] On Timaeus *FGrH* 566 F 1.

[7] K. Müllenhoff, *Deutsche Altertumskunde*, ii² (Berlin, 1906), 177–89; J. Heurgon, *Hommages à A. Grenier* (Brussels, 1962), ii. 799, traced this view back to Heyne (1784), reprinted in Dindorf's Diodorus, ii. p. xviii.

[8] IV 153cd=*FGrH* 87 F 1: *παρὰ δὲ Τυρρηνοῖς δὶς τῆς ἡμέρας τράπεζαι πολυτελεῖς παρασκευάζονται ἄνθιναί τε στρωμναὶ καὶ ἐκπώματα ἀργυρᾶ παντοδαπά, καὶ δούλων πλῆθος εὐπρεπῶν παρέστηκεν ἐσθήσεσι πολυτελέσι κεκοσμημένων.*

[9] V 40.3=*FGrH* 87 F 119: *παρατίθενται γὰρ δὶς τῆς ἡμέρας τραπέζας πολυτελεῖς καὶ τἄλλα τὰ πρὸς τὴν ὑπερβάλλουσαν τρυφὴν οἰκεῖα, στρωμνὰς μὲν ἀνθεινὰς κατασκευάζοντες, ἐκπωμάτων δ' ἀργυρῶν παντοδαπῶν πλῆθος καὶ τῶν διακονούντων οἰκετῶν οὐκ ὀλίγον ἀριθμὸν ἡτοιμακότες· καὶ τούτων οἱ μὲν εὐπρεπείᾳ διαφέροντές εἰσιν, οἱ δ' ἐσθῆσι πολυτελεστέραις ἢ κατὰ δουλικὴν ἀξίαν κεκόσμηνται.*

[10] Cf. Trüdinger, op. cit.

[11] Cf. H. Strasburger, *JRS* lv (1965), 47.

Polybius,[1] must have been an ethnography of the whole empire.

The descriptions of the Etruscans in Diodorus runs together a number of elements already known from previous literature about the Etruscans and some that cannot be traced.[2] It falls roughly into four sections, concerning the power of the Etruscans in an early period of their history, some of their inventions, their *disciplina*, and their decadence. It is not to be hoped that we can work out in detail what Posidonius' sources were for this description, but it is worthwhile to isolate the elements which are not known from earlier sources. The wide territorial power of the Etruscans[3] was already known to Cato and Polybius, and their sea-power was well known much earlier. From their territorial power their outstanding ἀνδρεία at that time was an obvious inference, even if it had not been commented on before; and the same applies to the naming of the Tyrrhenian Sea (already so called in classical Greece) as a result of their naval power. In the aetiological section, the Etruscan σάλπιγξ was well known to fifth-century and Hellenistic writers.[4] On the other hand, neither the Etruscan origin of the Roman *insignia imperii* nor the Etruscan peristyle (περίστῳα) is known from earlier sources. The statement about the *insignia imperii* suggests that he had an unusually good source about Etruscan affairs. The view is first known elsewhere in Sallust,[5] who may indeed have known it from Posidonius, though it may well have appeared in the Sullan annalists.[6] The statement about the peristyle is mysterious, since the peristyle seems to have been of Greek origin.[7] As far as the *disciplina* was concerned, Posidonius presumably had some special knowledge, for he considered the Etruscans in his

[1] See Jacoby on F 1.

[2] On this description see Trüdinger, op. cit., 102, Heurgon, *Daily Life of the Etruscans*, 35–7.

[3] V 40.1.

[4] Cf. Maux in *RE* s.v. *Salpinx* (1920), Wikén, op. cit., 131.

[5] *Cat.* 51.38, *Hist.* I in Ioannes Lydus, *de mensibus* I 37.

[6] It is common later: Strabo V 2.2 220C, Dion. Hal. III 61–2, Plin. *NH* VIII 195, App. *Pun.* 6. On the truth of the tradition see R. Lambrechts, op. cit., 29–31, against P. De Francisci, *SE* xxiv (1955–6), 33–7; cf. Ogilvie on Liv. I 8.

[7] One may suspect that there is some confusion with the *cavum aedium Tuscanicum* mentioned by Varro, *LL* V 161—which had no columns.

περὶ μαντικῆς;[1] but his remarks here[2] hardly go beyond what was already known in Rome (and it is surprising that he refers to divination by thunder, when divination by lightning had a more important place in the tradition);[3] the *haruspices* were already well established in Rome in the second century.[4] The last section of the description,[5] concerning the fertility of the land of the Etruscans and their τρυφή, reverts to a standard theme, and although Posidonius' theory that the former was the cause of the latter is not known to us from any earlier writer, it conforms to a fairly common Hellenistic view about the relationship between national character and national environment.[6] The theme of Etruscan luxury is commonplace, but here again Posidonius has some previously unknown information—not only did the rulers have private houses, but most of the free men (thus the emended text). The statement has produced considerable dispute, but, as will be argued in detail in Chapter IV, it is likely to correspond to reality. Posidonius accepted much of the standard literary view about Etruscan decadence, and when he moderates the versions of Theopompus and others it may be partly from general distrust of them; but his reservations were at least partly based on better information about Etruria. It is unlikely that the good pieces of information that Posidonius had went back to Greek sources earlier than the second century; Posidonius, or some other Greek writer or writers of not much earlier date, managed to acquire pieces of authentic information about Etruria, some of it probably in Rome (the *insignia imperii*), but some of it probably more directly. It will be argued later that Posidonius may have been responsible for discovering a Caeritan view of some parts of the history of Caere that is preserved by Strabo.

After Posidonius some of the commonplaces about the

[1] K. Reinhardt in *RE* s.v. Posidonius (1953), cols. 792–805, cf. Weinstock, *PBSR* xix (1951), 124.

[2] Diod. V 40.2.

[3] On Etruscan divination by thunder see Thulin, *Die etruskische Disciplin*, i.53–6.

[4] Weinstock, art. cit., 152 (cf. Mazzarino, op. cit., ii.1 172), holds that Posidonius was responsible for arousing Roman interest in Etruscan divination, but that is in my opinion unlikely.

[5] V 40.3.

[6] Cf. particularly Timaeus *FGrH* 566 F 50, Onesicritus *FGrH* 134 F 17, Posidonius *FGrH* 87 F 10 (the cities of Syria), F 102; Trüdinger, op. cit., 37–43, 51–9, 104, F. W. Walbank on Polybius IV 20–1.

τρυφὴ of the Etruscans continued to circulate. The theme reappears in Catullus ('pinguis Umber aut obesus Etruscus'),[1] in Diodorus, in Dionysius of Halicarnassus (who was quite well informed about the Etruscans),[2] and it probably affected the reputation of Maecenas.

There were also some other attempts at serious study of the Etruscans. The date and quality of the *Τυρρηνικὰ* of Sostratus, attested by Stobaeus,[3] are most uncertain, but a date in the first half of the first century B.C. seems most likely.[4] Since Stobaeus' citation is from the second book, the *Τυρρηνικὰ* was presumably an independent work of some dimensions. It seems to have made no impression on later students of the subject.

Some of the late republican writers of Etruscan origin who dealt with the *disciplina* are known to have concerned themselves with matters other than divination. It might be hoped that they would show signs of acquaintance with Etruscan historical literature, but the point cannot be established from the surviving fragments. Nigidius Figulus in particular seems to have written on matters unrelated to the *disciplina* or Pythagoreanism. According to Servius, while Varro excelled in *theologia*, Nigidius excelled in *communes litterae*.[5] Servius quotes a passage in which he characterized the Ligurians as *latrones, insidiosi, fallaces, mendaces*;[6] the title of the work in which Nigidius wrote this is given as *de terras*, and it is much better to infer the title *de terra* or *de terris* than to take this as a reference to his work *de sphaera*.[7] If then Nigidius wrote some kind of ethnographical work, and had an acquaintance with Etruscan literature, he may have been responsible for passing on some historical information that was to be found in it.[8]

[1] XXXIX 11. [2] II 38.3. [3] *Flor.* IV 20.72=*FGrH* 23 F 3.

[4] E. Bux in *RE* s.v. Sostratus no. 7 (1927). [5] *Aen.* X 175.

[6] *Aen.* XI 715=fr. 101S. This had been the reputation of the Ligurians at least since the time of Cato (cited in Servius, l.c.).

[7] *De sphaera*, Masvicius; *de terris*, J. Klein, *Quaestiones Nigidianae* (Bonn, 1861), 26, W. Kroll in *RE* s.v. Nigidius no. 3 (1936), col. 206; *de terra*, F. Boll, *Sphaera* (Leipzig, 1903), 351–2.

[8] Tarquitius Priscus also seems to have written on a subject other than the *disciplina*: 'Tarquitius de illustribus viris disserens' is mentioned by Lactantius, *Inst.* I 10.2. Etruscan origins have also been attributed to some other Latin writers of the same period, the Sasernae, father and son, agricultural writers before the time of Varro, whose name has an Etruscan termination (on them see F. Münzer in *RE* s.v. Hostilius nos. 22–4 (1913), Heurgon, op. cit., 115–17)—but there is no sign that they were not thoroughly Roman. And to Santra, a writer *de antiquitate*

Varro knew of the *Tuscae historiae* and of some of their contents and their supposed date, of *fabulae Etruscae* describing Porsenna's tomb, and of Volnius who wrote Etruscan tragedies and could be cited on a point of etymology. Yet the fragments of the *Antiquitates*,[1] which are fairly numerous, do not have much to offer about Etruria: Mezentius, king of Caere, already known to Cato,[2] and the supposed derivation of the name of Caere from Greek χαῖρε,[3] obviously not a very esoteric piece of information.[4]

Information about monuments in Etruria was collected in the late Republic by one Cincius, probably to be distinguished from the annalist L. Cincius Alimentus.[5] What he said about the temple of Nortia at Volsinii is cited by Livy,[6] who regarded him as 'comparere diligens talium monumentorum auctor'. He may have been of ultimately Etruscan origin.[7]

Strabo made a journey to Populonium on the Etruscan coast and made some observations of his own on the way.[8] Since he also acquired some esoteric information from literary sources, it would be useful to trace them. Posidonius is clearly a possibility. On the one hand, Strabo's explicit references to Posidonius in Book V stop after one that concerns the Ligurians,[9] and none of them concerns the Etruscans. On the other hand, there are some specific indications that Posidonius was used. Neither the early strength of the Etruscans, which Strabo attributed to their obedience to a single ruler (while their decline was caused by the violence of their neighbours),[10] nor the Tarquinian origin of the Roman *insignia imperii*,[11] are

verborum and *de viris illustribus* under the very late Republic or Augustus (Schanz–Hosius, op. cit., i⁴.584), whom Schulze (*ZGLE* 143, 342, 369) thought to be of Etruscan origin. Such a termination is only found in Etruscan names when they are adapted from Gk. -andra, -andros, which Santra evidently was not.

[1] Collected by P. Mirsch, *Leipziger Studien*, v (1882); on the work see Schanz–Hosius, op. cit., i⁴.564–9, H. Dahlmann in *RE* Supplementband vi (1935), cols. 1229–37.

[2] Plin. *NH* XIV 88=Bk. II.fr. 17 Mirsch; cf. Cato, frr. 9–12P.

[3] Serv. *Aen.* X 183=Bk. III.fr. 7 Mirsch.

[4] Also known to Hyginus (Serv. *Aen.* VIII 597=fr. 12P) and Strabo (V 2.3 220C); see Sordi, op. cit., 44 and n. 2, for the various forms of the story. For the more esoteric view of Verrius Flaccus on the subject, see below.

[5] Cf. Peter, *HRR* i².cix, Schanz–Hosius, op. cit., i⁴.175.

[6] VII 3.7; cf. XXIII 20.3.

[7] R. Syme, *Historia*, xiii (1964), 114, J. Heurgon, *Athenaeum*, xlii (1964), 432–7.

[8] V 2.6 223C.

[9] V 2.1 219C.

[10] V 2.2 219C.

[11] V 2.2 220C.

really distinctive elements; but when Strabo turns to Caere, he is more revealing. He refers to a defeat of the Gauls by the Caeritans after the former had captured Rome, a story first known in Diodorus.[1] There follows an account of Caere that emphasizes the φαυλότης of the Roman rulers who were ungrateful to the Caeritans after they had helped Rome during the Gallic invasion, and the good repute of the Caeritans in Greece, partly a result of the fact that they, unlike the rest of the Etruscans, abstained from piracy. It certainly looks as if Strabo was for some of his account using, however indirectly, a source that gave a Caeritan view of some parts of Caeritan history;[2] when this source became known to non-Caeritans cannot be ascertained, but since Diodorus, who knew of the Caeritan victory over the Gauls, made much use of Posidonius, and Posidonius is known to have had an interest in piracy,[3] the latter may well have been Strabo's source. Two further passages in Strabo are connected with ones in the περὶ θαυμασίων ἀκουσμάτων—one concerns the confluence of the Arno and the Ausar at Pisa,[4] the other mining on Elba.[5] Ultimately there must have been a common source in one of the fourth- or third-century ethnographies. Strabo's description of Volaterrae has also been referred to the περὶ θαυμασίων ἀκουσμάτων,[6] without any justification.[7] A quite detailed description of the site of the town is followed by a brief account of the two-year siege conducted by the forces of Sulla; it is tempting to see Posidonius here as well, although according to most scholars his history did not run down to such a late date.[8]

Dionysius said that he would write about the Etruscans: πόλεις δ᾽ ἅστινας ᾤκισαν οἱ Τυρρηνοί, καὶ πολιτευμάτων οὕστινας

[1] Strabo V 2.3 220C, Diod. XIV 117.7. Beloch, *RG* 141–2, and Sordi, op. cit., 32–6, take this story back to Philistus via Timaeus, a speculation.

[2] Sordi, op. cit., 42–9.

[3] H. Strasburger, art. cit., 42–3, 49–51.

[4] V 2.5 222C.

[5] V 2.6 223C.

[6] W. Aly, *Strabon von Amaseia* (Bonn, 1957), 242, following J. Geffcken, *Timaios' Geographie des Westens* (Berlin, 1892), 95–6.

[7] The town mentioned in περὶ θαυμασίων ἀκουσμάτων, 94, has a different name (Οἰναρέα) and different physical characteristics (it was on a hill thirty stades high, not fifteen); the fact that made it worthy of note (it was ruled by slaves) is not mentioned by Strabo.

[8] The view that Posidonius covered events long after 86 has been revived by Strasburger, art. cit., 44.

κατεστήσαντο κόσμους, δύναμίν τε ὁπόσην ἐκτήσαντο καὶ ἔργα εἴ τινα μνήμης ἄξια διεπράξαντο, τύχαις τε ὁποίαις ἐχρήσαντο, ἐν ἑτέρῳ δηλωθήσεται λόγῳ.[1] He may mean merely that he intended to discuss these things later in the *Roman Antiquities*; but there is no other evidence that he did so, and since it is difficult to see how, for example, a list of cities founded by the Etruscans would be introduced later in the work, it is much better to suppose that he is promising to write a separate work. His programme for this work is strikingly detailed, and, to judge from what we know of them, not one that could easily have been fulfilled by means of the existing Greek and Roman sources. It does not entail an over-estimation of Dionysius as a historian if we point out that he knew the Etruscan name for Etruria and that he was unusually well-informed about the Etruscan social system (argued in Chapter IV). Further, it seems to me likely that it was Dionysius, not Claudius, who first discovered that there was an Etruscan tradition that Mastarna was a king of Rome.[2] At the beginning of Book IV he gives the Roman versions of the origins of Servius Tullius, but at the end of the previous book, as has recently been pointed out,[3] he alludes to a different tradition when he describes Servius as a foreign exile.[4] It is possible that some non-Etruscan writer before Dionysius knew of Mastarna's existence, but, given Dionysius' interest in the Etruscans, there is no need to go beyond him.

Verrius Flaccus was the first writer to produce a treatise on the Etruscans about the contents of which we know something substantial. It contained at least two books.[5] The surviving fragments give the Etruscan name of Caere, Cisra,[6] otherwise unknown but not very esoteric, and information about the foundation of Mantua,[7] with which A. Caecina and probably others had dealt. If, as seems likely, Verrius was the source of

[1] I 30.4.

[2] The discovery is generally attributed to Claudius; cf. A. Momigliano, *JRS* xlvii (1957), 113=*Secondo contributo alla storia degli studi classici* (Rome, 1960), 86.

[3] A. Alföldi, *Early Rome and the Latins* (Ann Arbor, 1965), 215.

[4] III 65.6: (Servius Tullius) *ἄνδρα γενναῖον μὲν τὰ πολέμια καὶ φρονεῖν τὰ δέοντα ἱκανώτατον, ξένον δὲ καὶ ἄπολιν.* This diverges from the Roman account of Servius, but corresponds to Claudius' 'postquam varia fortuna exactus cum omnibus reliquiis Caeliani exercitus Etruria excessit', *ILS* 212.

[5] Σ Veron. *Aen.* X 183: 'Flaccus primo Etruscarum . . .'.

[6] Ibid.

[7] Σ Veron. *Aen.* X 200.

Festus' *De verborum significatu*,[1] Verrius cited Tarquitius Priscus,[2] and described the contents of the *libri rituales*;[3] it is indeed possible that most of Verrius' work on the Etruscans was taken up with the *disciplina*. He may have been the first Roman writer to mention Mastarna by name,[4] but that remains hypothetical, and nothing else that we know about the *Res Etruscae* suggests that he used sources other than easily accessible Roman ones.

There is very little direct evidence about the contents of Claudius' *Tyrrhenica*.[5] Perhaps the best evidence comes from the version of Claudius' famous speech to the Senate recorded in the Lugdunum inscription;[6] there the story of Mastarna is told according to *auctores Tusci*, and presumably the same information was to be found in the *Tyrrhenica*. It has been suggested that the story was known to Dionysius, and the name Mastarna may already have appeared in a Roman source. How close then did Claudius come to Etruscan sources? His researches were not very highly thought of by most scholars[7] until Heurgon pointed out the full number of persons of Etruscan descent who were in his family circle.[8] This was thought to mean that Claudius had the 'best sources' for his inquiries. Yet the persons of Etruscan descent were his first wife Plautia Urgulanilla and some of her relatives—her

[1] R. Reitzenstein, 'Verrianische Forschungen', *Breslauer Philologische Abhandlungen*, i. no. 4 (Berlin, 1887); cf. L. Strzelecki, *Quaestiones Verrianae* (Warsaw, 1932), 1–2; Schanz–Hosius, op. cit., ii[4].366–7, A. Dihle in *RE* s.v. Verrius no. 2 (1958), col. 1645.

[2] Festus 340L (s.v. *Ratitum quadrantem*): '[. . .] Tarqui [. . .]'. The supplement 'Tarqui[tius]' originated with Fulvio Orsini.

[3] Festus 358L.

[4] Festus 486L (s.v. *Tuscum vicum*): '[. . .]entes fratres Caeles et Vibenn⟨a⟩ [. . .] Tarquinium Romam secum max[. . .]'. V. Gardthausen, *Mastarna oder Servius Tullius* (Leipzig, 1882), 40 n. 2, suggested that Max[tarna. . .] should be read; accepted by G. De Sanctis, *Klio*, ii (1902), 98, etc.; cf. A. Momigliano, *JRS* liii (1963), 97. Verrius is not, however, likely to have been the first to allude to Mastarna, since he probably wrote after Dionysius.

[5] For the bibliography of Claudius' Etruscan studies see Schanz–Hosius, op. cit., ii[4].426, Momigliano, *Claudius, the Emperor and his Achievement*[2] (Cambridge, 1961), 84–6, 128–9, Alföldi, op. cit., 213 n. 2.

[6] *ILS* 212.

[7] Alföldi, l.c.

[8] *CRAI* 1953, 92–7; cf. *Daily Life of the Etruscans*, 248. Scribonius Largus, the famous doctor who accompanied Claudius to Britain in 43, may also have been of Etruscan origin; cf. Heurgon, *Mélanges d'archéologie et d'histoire offerts à A. Piganiol* (Paris, 1966), 657, and below, p. 199.

imperious grandmother Urgulania (the friend of Livia), and Urgulanilla's mother Lartia and sister-in-law Vibia, and Claudius was married to Urgulanilla only rather briefly and in his youth.[1] Furthermore it is very doubtful whether such people would have been much help to an Etruscologist in Claudius' time. They almost certainly did not know the Etruscan language well, if at all; and the recollection of Etruscan nomenclature by the wife of Claudius' brother-in-law was surely mere affectation.[2] Snobbery rather than scholarship made Claudius' relatives look to their Etruscan ancestry. The suspicion must nonetheless be strong that Claudius did in fact discover a great deal about the Etruscans. His interest was certainly lively, being attested by the twenty books of the *Tyrrhenica* and the story of Mastarna; it also seems likely that the Twelve Peoples of Etruria set up a statue of Claudius at Caere,[3] and it is tempting to suppose that the flowering of interest in local Etruscan history that is represented by the *Elogia Tarquiniensia* was partly stimulated by the emperor. As to what stories, besides that of Mastarna, Claudius may have exhumed from Etruscan sources, it is only possible to speculate.[4]

At some date during the first century of the Empire a number of *elogia* were put up at Tarquinii.[5] *Elogia* of the same period from Arretium and Pompeii all have Romans as their subjects,[6] but the suggestion of Heurgon that the subjects of the Tar-

[1] Suet. *Claud.* 26.2: 'uxores deinde duxit Plautiam Urgulanillam triumphali et mox Aeliam Paetinam consulari patre'. He divorced Urgulanilla during her second pregnancy, ibid. 27.1.

[2] *ILS* 964: 'Vibia Marsi f. *Laelia nata* Pulchri'.

[3] L. Canina, *Bull. Inst.*, 1840, 92–4, etc.; cf. A. Momigliano, op. cit., 83–4, W. Helbig, *Führer durch die öffentlichen Sammlungen klassischer Altertümer in Rom*, i[4] (Tübingen, 1963), pp. 756–7.

[4] An interesting question arises, for example, about how Tacitus came to be the first Roman writer to say that Porsenna succeeded in capturing Rome (*Hist.* III 72.1, cf. Plin. *NH* XXXIV 139); cf. R. Syme, *Tacitus* (Oxford, 1958), 398. This was hardly to be found in Ennius, *pace* O. Skutsch, *JRS* xliii (1953), 77–8.

[5] On these *elogia* see P. Romanelli, *NSA* 1948, 258–66 (with suggestions of A. Degrassi), Heurgon, *CRAI* 1950, 212–15, *MEFR* lxiii (1951), 119–37, *Daily Life of the Etruscans*, 256–8, M. Pallottino, *SE* xxi (1950–1), 147–71, U. Kahrstedt, *Symbolae Osloenses*, xxx (1953), 68–76, E. Vetter, *Glotta*, xxxiv (1955), 59–62, F. Della Corte, *SE* xxiv (1955–6), 73–8, S. Mazzarino in G. Giannelli–S. Mazzarino, *Trattato di storia romana*, ii (Rome, 1956), 52 n. 1, J. Reynolds, *JRS* l (1960), 206, M. Torelli, *SE* xxxvi (1968), 467–70. They are dated to the first century of the Empire by Pallottino, art. cit., 151, to the middle of the first century A.D. by Della Corte, art. cit., 74, to 40 A.D. by Heurgon, *Daily Life of the Etruscans*, 257.

[6] They are collected by Degrassi in *Inscriptiones Italiae*, xiii.3.

quinii *elogia* were characters of local Tarquinian history has been universally accepted,[1] and it is confirmed by some newly published fragments.[2] Only one possibly comparable case of an *elogium* of a local figure is known in Italy, at Brundisium,[3] and the similarity is not very great, for the events recorded in it were events of Roman history (the Hannibalic War), and there was an obvious continuity in a Latin colony which may well have been lacking in an Etruscan town that had been thoroughly Romanized by a date in the early Empire. Yet it is clear that the subject of the best preserved *elogium* was a character of local and not of Roman history—Velthur Spurinna, son of Lars, who led an expedition to Sicily.[4] Who was responsible for putting up these texts? Since the two families that are known to have been commemorated in the *elogia* are the Spurinnae and the Caesennii,[5] and since there were prominent Roman families with these names in the early Empire, families that in all probability came from Tarquinii,[6] it seems likely that it was these prominent families with local connections that erected the *elogia* to commemorate their own ancestors.[7] But where did they find the material for the historical claims that are made in the *elogia*? Perhaps in old local traditions, as is widely supposed.[8] Certainly no absurd claims are made for the subjects of the *elogia* in the few surviving fragments, and it is quite likely that both families did play a prominent part in Tarquinian history. However, amid the prevailing optimism about the authenticity of the historical statements made in the *elogia*, some contrary points need to be made. Tarquinii was by the time of Claudius a thoroughly Romanized place, and ex-

[1] Heurgon, *CRAI* 1950, 212–13.

[2] M. Torelli, art. cit.

[3] E. Gabba, *Athenaeum*, xxxvi (1958), 90–105 (on *AE* 1954, no. 216), Reynolds l.c., *MRR Suppl.* 2–3, A. Guarino, *Labeo*, ix (1963), 89–95; but the subject was a Roman in the view of G. Vitucci, *RFIC* xxxi (1953), 43–61, *Annali della Facoltà di Lettere e Filosofia, Università degli Studi di Perugia*, i (1963–4), 3–14, followed by F. Cassola, *Labeo*, viii (1962), 307–16, and Mazzarino, *Il pensiero storico classico*, ii.1 322–4.

[4] Torelli, art. cit., 467.

[5] Spurinna: Romanelli fragments, nos. 18b, 45–8, 77. Caesennius: Romanelli fragments, nos. 5, 43. See Torelli, art. cit., 467–8.

[6] Torelli, art. cit., 468–9; on the Caesennii cf. H.-G. Pflaum, *Historia*, ii (1953–4), 444, R. Syme, *Historia*, xiii (1964), 113, and below, p. 284.

[7] Torelli, l.c.

[8] Heurgon, ll.cc., Pallottino, art. cit., 152, etc.

cept perhaps among a very few people it is most unlikely that the Etruscan language survived there.[1] It is possible that local Etruscan traditions had already been translated into Latin in an earlier period, but if they had not been they would have become very inaccessible by this date. The Caesennii and the Vestricii Spurinnae were thoroughly Roman families, and their better-educated members must have been aware of some of what Greek and Roman writers had to say about events that had taken place in Etruria, but it must be doubtful whether they were capable of using sources in the local language. Furthermore Etruscan ancestry had a well-attested snob value in the early Empire, and Etruscan genealogies could be elaborated to a ridiculous degree.[2] Was it not singularly fortunate that the two most aristocratic families of the period that came from Tarquinii could find in some local sources information about the exploits of their ancestors of at least 300 years, and perhaps much longer, before? There is indeed no explicit evidence that there ever existed Etruscan writings of the right kind, detailed records of the military achievements of magistrates. All this strains belief in the antiquity and authenticity of the statements made in the *elogia*. There was probably some basis for the *elogia* in local traditions, which were perhaps conveyed orally or by monuments rather than by written histories. On the other hand, the suspicion must be strong that the authors of the *elogia* elaborated these traditions out of their own imaginations. The problem may be affected by the discovery of further fragments of *elogia* on the same site.

There were then some Etruscan writings that could be revealing about the history and society of the Etruscans, works on the *disciplina*, including the *libri rituales*, and also perhaps works similar to the *fabulae praetextae*. More important, there seem to have been some Etruscan historical sources from which some non-Etruscan writers benefited: this we may conclude in particular from Varro's reference to the *Tuscae historiae*, from the good information apparently acquired by Posidonius, from

[1] See below, p. 182. As far as we can tell from the existing evidence, Kahrstedt, art. cit., 68–9, was quite wrong to think that Tarquinii was much less Romanized than Arretium.

[2] The ancestry of Maecenas may be an instance. Note Persius III 27–8: 'an deceat pulmonem rumpere ventis / stemmate quod Tusco ramum millesime ducis / . . . ?'.

remarks made by Dionysius of Halicarnassus, from the known facts about Claudius' Etruscology, and from the *elogia* of Tarquinii. Of course there continued to be much poor information and misinformation in circulation about the Etruscans: Diodorus and Strabo derived many of their assertions from ill-informed Hellenistic sources, Dionysius and Livy wrote much about the Etruscans that was no better than romance, and Virgil was capable of making a Latin colony of the third century into an important Etruscan town.[1] But there was some knowledge of the historical Etruscans, and it will be argued in Chapter IV that the basic facts of the Etruscan social system can be known through the existing sources.

2. *Vegoia's Prophecy*

Two short texts in the gromatic corpus are attributed to Vegoia, one with the heading 'Ex libris Magonis et Vegoiae auctorum',[2] the other with the heading 'Idem Vegoiae Arrunti Veltymno'.[3] The first concerns the technique of limitation and is not important for the present purpose, but the authenticity of the second, Vegoia's Prophecy, which is quite different in tone and content, needs detailed discussion. The text is as follows:

IDEM VEGOIAE ARRUNTI VELTYMNO

Scias mare ex aethera remotum. Cum autem Iuppiter terram Aetruriae sibi vindicavit, constituit iussitque metiri campos signarique agros. Sciens hominum avaritiam vel terrenum cupidinem, terminis omnia scita esse voluit. Quos quandoque quis ob avaritiam prope novissimi octavi saeculi data sibi ⟨. . .⟩ homines malo dolo violabunt contingentque atque movebunt. Sed qui contigerit moveritque, possessionem promovendo suam, alterius minuendo, ob hoc scelus damnabitur a diis. Si servi faciant, dominio mutabuntur in deterius. Sed si conscientia dominica fiet, caelerius domus extirpabitur, gensque eius omnis interiet. Motores autem pessimis morbis et vulneribus afficientur membrisque suis debilitabuntur. Tum etiam terra a tempestatibus vel turbinibus plerumque labe movebitur. Fructus saepe ledentur decutienturque imbribus atque grandine, caniculis

[1] Cosa, *Aen.* X 168. If it existed, it was insignificant. For speculation that much in Virgil derived from Etruscan sources see Sordi, op. cit., 177–82.

[2] *Die Schriften der Römischen Feldmesser*, ed. K. Lachmann, i (Berlin, 1848), 348–50.

[3] Ibid. pp. 350–1.

interient, robigine occidentur. Multae dissensiones in populo. Fieri haec scitote, cum talia scelera committuntur. Propterea neque fallax neque bilinguis sis. Disciplinam pone in corde tuo.

Apparatus: 1: *ex aethera remotum*:*ex aere et terra natum* Lachmann; *e terra remotum* Latte; but see A. Piganiol, *CHM* i (1953), 345. 4: *scita*:*saepta* or *sancita* suggested by Lachmann. 5–6: *quis . . . homines*:*quis* removed by Turnebus; for *data sibi* Lachmann suggested *lascivi:* J. Heurgon, *JRS* xlix (1959), 44–5, pointed out the lacuna after *sibi* and suggested the supplement *bona pro nihilo ducens aliena appetiverit*, for which see below. 15: *occidentur. Multae*: *occident*:*erunt multae* suggested by Lachmann.

It is generally believed that the prophecy contains at least a kernel of authentic Etruscan material,[1] although Mommsen on some occasions expressed disbelief.[2] There are a number of difficulties that arise from the text, and although some of them remain insoluble, it is to be accepted as probable that the prophecy derived from an authentic Etruscan text.

There is, not surprisingly, no reference to this text in any ancient source; however, it is worth pointing out at the beginning that the general tone of the prophecy is strikingly similar to that of late republican prophecies made by the *haruspices*, as they are reported by Cicero.[3] That at least suggests that the text does not belong primarily to any late imperial date. Yet of Vegoia herself we have explicit testimony from only two sources, Ammianus Marcellinus, who refers to the *libri Vegoici* or *Vegonici* together with the *libri Tagetici* as a source for a particular piece of Etruscan teaching about lightning;[4] and Servius, who states that the Sibylline books were kept in the temple of Apollo on the Palatine, as were also those of the Marcii and of the nymph Begoe, 'quae artem scripserat fulguritarum apud Tuscos'.[5] It is not legitimate to infer from Servius' statement that the books of Begoe (Vegoia) were pre-

[1] K. O. Müller–W. Deecke, *Die Etrusker*, ii^{2} (Stuttgart, 1877), 30–1, 298–9, 312, W. M. Von Goethe, *De Fragmento Vegoiae* (Heidelberg, 1845), T. Mommsen, *Römische Chronologie*^{2} (Berlin, 1859), 189 n. 372, C. O. Thulin, *Die etruskische Disciplin*, i.3–8, etc. (also in *RE* s.vv. *Etrusca disciplina* (1909), *haruspices* (1912)), L. Piotrowicz, *Klio*, xxiii (1930), 336, K. Latte, *Philologus*, lxxxvii (1932), 268–70, L. Zancan, *A & R* ser. 3. vii (1939), 203–19, S. Weinstock in *RE* s.v. Vegoia (1955), S. Mazzarino, *Historia*, vi (1957), 111–12, *Iura*, xii (1961), 24–39, *Il pensiero storico classico*, ii.1 171–2, 525–6, Heurgon, *JRS* xlix (1959), 41–5; cf. also A. J. Pfiffig, *Gymnasium*, lxviii (1961), 55–64.

[2] In *Die Schriften der Römischen Feldmesser*, ii (Berlin, 1852), 181, and *GS* vii.474–5 (=*Jahrbücher des Vereins von Altertumsfreunden im Rheinlande*, xcvi–xcvii (1895), 283–4).

[3] Cf. Müller–Deecke, op. cit., ii.22 n. 11. [4] XVII 10.2. [5] *Aen.* VI 72.

viously in the temple of Jupiter Capitolinus;[1] but it is an argument in favour of their age and therefore of their authenticity. In fact there is no definite evidence at all that Vegoia was known as a prophetess at a date when the Etruscan language and people survived. The personal name Vegoe is attested once in an inscription,[2] and there is a possible Etruscan root in the name Vecu(i).[3] Veltymnus too was definitely an Etruscan name, as the etruscanizing name of the third-century emperor C. Vibius Afinius Gallus Veldumnianus Volusianus and the Etruscan name Ultimne make clear.[4] The other document attributed to Vegoia in the gromatic corpus is of imperial date, for it refers to the town of Florentia,[5] which may have been a Sullan but was probably a triumviral colony. Thulin supplemented *CIL* xi.3370, one of the inscriptions that refers to the *disciplina* expert Tarquitius Priscus, with a reference to Vegoia ('Arus a m⟨agistra edoctus⟩'), but given the limitations of our knowledge of Vegoia, it is only a guess.[6] The antiquity and authenticity of the *libri Vegoici* are not then beyond question, but it can reasonably be argued that Vegoia cannot have been *invented* under the Empire and that a document attributed to her rather than to, say, the better known Tages is likely to be genuine.

What Etruscan features does Vegoia's Prophecy present? Some are in general conformity with Etruscan ideas without having exact parallels. Thus the reference to a cosmogony[7] and to Jupiter as the author of the prevailing land-divisions[8] may be taken as Etruscan, but their authenticity cannot be proved.

[1] As do Müller in Müller–Deecke, op. cit., ii.31, Weinstock, art. cit., col. 577; *contra* Deecke, ii.31 n. 46. See Suet. *Aug.* 31: 'solos retinuit Sibyllinos'.

[2] *CIL* xiv. 1738 (Ostia); cf. Thulin, *MDAI–R* xxii (1907), 262–3.

[3] *CIE* 1494–1503 (Clusium); cf. Thulin, art. cit., 263. An Etruscan mirror, E. Gerhard–G. Körte, *Etruskische Spiegel*, i (Berlin, 1840), pl. xxxvii, apparently gives the name of a companion of Minerva as *lasa vecu* or *lasr vecu*; cf. Thulin, *Die etruskische Disciplin*, iii.147 n. 2.

[4] Schulze, *ZGLE* 251–2. On Veldumnianus cf. Heurgon, *SE* xxiv (1955–6), 102–3. Heurgon goes beyond the evidence when he says that 'Arruns Veltymnus' was 'a seer or prince from Clusium', *JRS* xlix (1959), 41.

[5] 349.15L.

[6] Thulin, op. cit., iii.148, Heurgon, *Latomus*, xii (1953), 404, *JRS* xlix (1959), 41. The inscription is *CIL* xi. 3370.

[7] Lines 1–2. The unclear question of the Pahlavi or Chaldaean origin of the concept expressed in the first sentence of the Prophecy need not be decided here.

[8] Lines 1–4. See R. Pettazzoni, *SMSR* iv (1928), 218–20, Zancan, art. cit., 212; cf. Virg. *Georg.* I 126–7.

The reference to the doctrine of the *saecula*[1] may be a sign of Etruscan authorship, but it was fairly widely known that the Etruscans had a system of *saecula*, and it is conceivable that such a reference as 'ob avaritiam prope novissimi octavi saeculi'[2] could be devised by someone who knew the theory that eight (not ten) *saecula* was the allotted life-span of the Etruscans, which is mentioned by Plutarch in his life of Sulla.[3] Two other concepts in the text of the Prophecy deserve attention. One of these is the class-division between *domini* and *servi*. Now it is the main purpose of this discussion to establish that Vegoia's Prophecy is sufficiently authentic for us to be able to use it as evidence for the reality of this class-division; but it can be said here that it fits well into the other evidence on that subject and that it is very difficult to fit it into the land-holding system of any period of Roman history. The essential part of the text is: 'Si servi faciant, dominio mutabuntur in deterius. Sed si conscientia dominica fiet, caelerius domus extirpabitur, gensque eius omnis interiet.' There is more obscurity in this than has generally been recognized. The situation that is being envisaged may be that the slaves will move the boundary-markers, either with or without the *conscientia* of their own masters, at the expense of neighbouring landowners.[4] But there is no mention of the possibility that the masters may move the the boundary-markers on their own. The Prophecy is directed against the *servi* and also against any *domini* who may consent to the actions of the *servi*; it looks as if the conflict that is envisaged is a conflict of classes, *servi* against *domini*. In that case, since the *servi* have some *termini*, they must already have some claim of rights to land. This is evidently a quite un-Roman situation. In addition there is one other idea in the Prophecy that seems to be particularly Etruscan, the emphasis on the sin of deceitfulness;[5] one may compare the sentence of exile on the

[1] Lines 4–6.

[2] Following G. Schmeisser, *Die etruskische Disciplin vom Bundesgenossenkriege bis zum Untergang des Heidentums* (Liegnitz, 1881), 6 n. 10, and Heurgon, art. cit., 42, I translate this as 'on account of the greed of the eighth *saeculum* now almost at its end'. Mazzarino, *Il pensiero storico classico*, ii.1 525, retains his view that it means 'of the eighth and final *saeculum*, which is coming near'; but that is simply not what the Latin means.

[3] *Sull.* 7.

[4] That this is a possible interpretation was suggested to me by Prof. Morton Smith.

[5] Lines 16–17.

descendants of *periuri*, said by Servius Danielis to be prescribed by the *ius terrae Etruriae*.[1]

One concept that does have Roman parallels is the central one of *termini moti*.[2] The most obvious purpose of the Prophecy is to forbid the moving of boundary-stones, which we happen to know was dealt with in laws of the late Republic,[3] but it is reasonable to suppose that the Etruscans too had rules on this subject. Other signs of later revision, if not authorship, have been held to be Christian:[4] Proverbs 24:32 is quoted: 'posui in corde meo et exemplo didici disciplinam'. If there was any such rewording it was very superficial indeed.

The Prophecy claims to date itself by the words 'ob avaritiam prope novissimi octavi saeculi', and this has led to the attempts of various scholars, most recently Heurgon, to give the Prophecy a precise context. It has generally been held that the eighth *saeculum* here referred to is the eighth *saeculum* mentioned by Plutarch in his life of Sulla,[5] the *saeculum* during which, according to Varro, the *Tuscae historiae* were written.[6] Dealing with the portents of 88, Plutarch says that after the greatest of them, a terrifying trumpet-blast from a clear sky, *Τυρρηνῶν . . . οἱ λόγιοι μεταβολὴν ἑτέρου γένους ἀπεφαίνοντο καὶ μετακόσμησιν ἀποσημαίνειν τὸ τέρας*. He goes on to give their supposed explanation of the *γένη*: there were eight of them, differing in their customs, and to each one god had allotted a certain number of years making up a great year. When such a period comes to an end and another begins an amazing sign is sent from earth or heaven so that it is immediately clear to those who have pondered and understood such things that a different

[1] Serv. Dan. *Aen.* I 2: 'Est enim in libro qui inscribitur terrae iuris Etruriae scriptum vocibus Tagae, eum qui genus a periuris duceret, fato extorrem et profugum esse debere . . .'. The comparison with Vegoia's Prophecy was made by Thulin, op. cit., iii.53. Compare also Nigidius Figulus' description of the Ligurians, above, p. 23.

[2] See R. Taubenschlag in *RE* s.v. *terminus motus* (1934).

[3] In the Lex Mamilia Roscia Peducaea Alliena Fabia, *FIRA*[2] (ed. Riccobono) i. no. 12 (ch. 55); and in a Caesarian law referred to in *Dig.* XLVII 21.3; cf. Hor. *Od.* II 18.23.

[4] Zancan, art. cit., 217, Heurgon, *JRS* xlix (1959), 41 nn. 5–6.

[5] Mommsen, *Römische Chronologie*, Piotrowicz, Latte, ll.cc., etc.

[6] Mazzarino's argument that the eighth *saeculum* must still have been in progress when Varro wrote, op. cit., ii.1 526, for otherwise he would have stated its actual length, is without foundation.

kind of human race has come into being. When one age succeeds another, everything changes—at some times divination is more respected than at others. All this is attributed to *οἱ λογιώτατοι Τυρρηνῶν*.[1] There is some further evidence that the eighth Etruscan *saeculum* ended at about this time: Dio tells us that in 19 A.D., 106 years later, there was a portent at Rome in the form of a trumpet-blast, and a prophecy followed that a nine-hundred-year period was ending—although, as Dio says, this was obviously not true of Rome.[2] Thus it was shortly before 88 that Vegoia's Prophecy claimed to have been written. It is plain enough that it may refer to a situation created by one of the agrarian laws of the period, and Heurgon[3] has recently elaborated the case for dating it to 91.

It was, however, apparently a matter of dispute when the eighth Etruscan *saeculum* did come to an end. Some held that it did so in 88, but there was another occasion when a *haruspex*, beyond doubt an Etruscan, proclaimed the end of a *saeculum*: one Vulcanius or Vulcatius said in a *contio* that the comet that appeared after Caesar's death signalled the end of the ninth *saeculum*.[4] There are a number of puzzling matters about this story, as about Plutarch's story, but it is clear that on both occasions it was claimed that an Etruscan *saeculum* was coming to an end.[5] However if all *haruspices* agreed that the eighth *saeculum* came to an end in 88, Vulcanius could hardly have declared the end of the ninth *saeculum* in 44—a forty-four year *saeculum* was an impossibility. The system of *saecula* expounded by the *haruspices* in the first century was disputed among them.[6]

[1] Apparently Plutarch derived this material from Livy or Diodorus, *Suda* s.v. *Σύλλας*, iv.455 Adler (Diodorus XXXVIII/XXXIX 5).

[2] Dio LVII 18.3–5. The portent occurred when the consul Norbanus, who was a keen trumpeter, blew a loud blast early one morning. Cf. R. Syme, *Tacitus* (Oxford, 1958), 772.

[3] *JRS*, art. cit.

[4] Serv. Dan. *Ecl.* IX 46: 'Baebius Macer . . . Sed Vulcanius [MSS: Vulcatius Masvicius] aruspex in contione dixit cometen esse, qui significaret exitum noni saeculi et ingressum decimi; sed quod invitis diis secreta rerum pronuntiaret, statim se esse moriturum; et nondum finita oratione, in ipsa contione concidit. Hoc etiam Augustus in libro secundo de memoria vitae suae complexus est'.

[5] Thulin, op. cit., ii.73, followed by Zancan, art. cit., 205–6, suggested that the *saeculum* that ended in 44 was a Roman one; it would have been possible for a Roman *saeculum* to end at that date, but as M. P. Nilsson pointed out, *RE* s.v. *Saeculares ludi* (1920), col. 1707, the stated number of the *saeculum*, the ninth, means that it must have been Etruscan.

[6] Cf. Mazzarino, op. cit., ii.1 526.

It had also been adapted to its Roman audience. According to the *Tuscae historiae* cited by Varro, the Etruscan *saecula* concerned the Etruscan people—presumably their endings would be declared by portents in Etruria. There is no reason to think that in seeking to meet the needs of their Roman clientele, the *haruspices* will all have been consistent with each other in such matters; they certainly seem to have disagreed with each other about whether there were to be eight or ten *saecula* in the history of the Etruscans.[1] Knowledge of the system of *saecula* was an arcane business, as Vulcanius' statement shows, and it could, within limits, be manipulated. There is no reason to think that the *haruspices* will have been prevented from doing that by religious principles.[2] As Weinstock says, they 'always aimed to be up-to-date'.[3] In both 88 and 44 there was a considerable incentive to make such spectacular announcements.

In spite of all this, however, we can say some definite things about the end of the eighth *saeculum*; in a sense the incidents of 88 and 44 support each other—since there were two different versions of the *saecula* doctrine that both put the end of the eighth *saeculum* in the period *c.* 150–88 it is virtually certain that that was the period to which Vegoia's Prophecy claimed to belong.

The other arguments that are used to date the Prophecy precisely to 91 are that the Etruscans were in particular danger from Livius Drusus' agrarian law and are known to have reacted strongly against him,[4] and that the 'most significant' of the *prodigia* of that year came from Etruria. Opposition to the confiscation of land is not precisely what the Prophecy expresses, but even if it is so interpreted, there were other occasions for such opposition, particularly 133, and also 99, when an agrarian bill proposed by one Titius, an ally of Saturninus, was opposed by the *haruspices*.[5] There does indeed seem to be a

[1] On the confusion about the Etruscan *saecula* in extant texts see Weinstock, *Glotta*, xxi (1932), 50–2. Thulin, op. cit., iii.63, suggested that the scheme of eight *saecula* described by Plutarch may have been a mistaken notion arising from the fact that it was the eighth *saeculum* that was ending on that occasion; but Plutarch's original source did at least have detailed information on the subject.

[2] As does Zancan, art. cit., 208.

[3] *PBSR* xix (1951), 123.

[4] App. *BC* I 36.163.

[5] Obsequens 46.

lacuna in the text of the Prophecy,[1] but it is not permissible to introduce into the lacuna a reference to Drusus. As for the *prodigia*, 91 was indeed a year when an exceptional number were registered[2]—as was 63, according to Cicero's testimony.[3] From about 108 B.C. onwards there appear in Obsequens' lists of *prodigia* some from the allied towns of Etruria, though there are few other entries in his catalogue concerning allied states. In addition to the *prodigia* recorded by Obsequens and Orosius, there was an earthquake at Mutina in 91 which Pliny found 'in Etruscae disciplinae voluminibus' and described in detail.[4] However there is no reason to associate the Prophecy with these or any other particular *prodigia*, for they were the normal accompaniment of any important event in Etruria.

The language of the Prophecy presents a considerable problem,[5] which no scholar has answered in such a way as to determine its date or authenticity. It is not the language of a literate Roman of the late Republic or early Empire—the suggestion that it was translated by Tarquitius Priscus[6] is impossible. The effects of a close translation from Etruscan have sometimes been detected, as have those of Christianity and the idioms of everyday speech. The first of these explanations might clear away all the linguistic difficulties, but it necessarily remains guess-work; not surprisingly no one has been able to point out any strictly linguistic feature of the Prophecy that is Etruscan.[7] *Caelerius* is quite unknown elsewhere, even in post-classical Latin; *terrenus cupido* for 'desire for land' is quite unparalleled, but is the sort of difficulty that is covered by the translation hypothesis. *Dominium* (in this sense of *domini*

[1] Heurgon, *JRS* xlix (1959), 44–5. Mazzarino, op. cit., ii.1 525, rejects this suggestion, but offers no real alternative.

[2] Cf. Cic. *Div.* II 54.

[3] *Div.* I 17–22.

[4] *NH* II 199; Heurgon, art. cit., 43–4.

[5] See in particular Zancan, art. cit., 217, Mazzarino, *Historia*, vi (1957), 112, and *Il pensiero storico classico*, ii.1 525, Heurgon, art. cit., 41 n. 5, K. Latte, *Römische Religionsgeschichte* (Munich, 1960), 288 n. 3.

[6] Heurgon, *Daily Life of the Etruscans*, 233; Mazzarino, op. cit., ii.1 526.

[7] Mazzarino's argument on this point, *Historia*, vi (1957), 112 n. 2, is that there are two Graecisms in the Prophecy, 'prope novissimi octavi saeculi' (which should in fact be interpreted otherwise), and 'ex aethera' (which may merely be a mistake); that 'grecismi e volgarismi si accoppiano sempre', and that vulgarisms and 'Italian' language and Etruscanisms are all the same thing. The weakness of these arguments needs no comment.

potestas) and *dominicus* occur once each in comedy under the late Republic,[1] and occasionally in later writers until they become common in the third century. In fact a complete study of all the verbal oddities produces no firm conclusion about the date. Mazzarino was perhaps right to emphasize the 'vulgarisms' in the language of the Prophecy, but it is difficult to resist the idea that the peculiarities of its language result from a translation (and not from Greek) by a person with imperfect Latin. They are in any case strong evidence against any suggestion that the Prophecy was a forgery.

Once the probability is accepted that the Prophecy derives from an Etruscan text we can come back to the question of historical context. The text may have been used in a campaign against a Roman agrarian law, as has often been suggested. That can hardly have been the purpose of the original Etruscan text, for in 91 there was no question of slaves contending with masters for the possession of land in Etruria—those who were to benefit from Drusus' agrarian law were Roman citizens. Such disputes were apparently of the past, but the propaganda survived. It was the propaganda of the *domini*, determined to maintain the existing land-holdings; there is enough evidence of conflict between *domini* and *servi* in Etruria in the third and second century to make its background clear. Some scholars have attributed the Prophecy to the side of the *servi*,[2] but the phrase *conscientia dominica* makes that quite impossible; the *termini* may be moved by the slaves on their own, or a result of the connivance with them of some of the *domini*, and the writer does not envisage such a thing being done by the *domini* in general in the interests of their class. *Termini* might on other occasions be regarded as a defence of the small land-holder against the large; but there is no reason to think that that was the situation to which Vegoia's Prophecy applied. It seems likely that the dispute between *domini* and *servi* that originally produced the Prophecy was well before any possible end of the eighth Etruscan *saeculum*, and the reference to the end of the *saeculum*, which is not essential to the prophecy, was added to it when it was applied to a Roman situation; that is to say, the

[1] Laevius fr. 22, Afranius *Com.* 282.

[2] Zancan, art. cit., 214 n. 20, Mazzarino, art. cit., 112; *contra* H. M. R. Leopold, *SMSR* v (1929), 47 n. 4, Piotrowicz, l.c., Heurgon, art. cit., 44.

reference was added by a *haruspex* who was adapting the text to a Roman situation and chose to make use of one of the versions of the *saecula* doctrine.

It is disappointing not to be able to specify 91 or some other particular occasion as the date of the Prophecy. But the important conclusion of this discussion is that in spite of the difficulties there is no doubt that it was in origin an Etruscan document and that most of the existing text derives from that document. Since the division between *domini* and *servi* is quite essential to the Prophecy, it is safe to use it as evidence on that subject.

II

THE WARS OF CONQUEST

1. *Roman Expansion in Etruria before 311*

THE preliminary stages of Roman expansion in Etruria will be described briefly. In the early fourth century the Romans in effect established a frontier within southern Etruria, running through the Tolfa and Ciminus hills from the sea to the Tiber. The first important step was the subjugation of Fidenae on the east bank of the Tiber, a strategic site long contested between Rome and Veii. It came permanently under Roman control in the later part of the fifth century, its final defeat being recorded by Livy both under 435 and under 416.[1] The conquest must have strengthened Rome enormously in her rivalry with Veii, since Fidenae was in a position to exercise power over trade along the river, trade that was evidently important both to Rome and to Veii.[2] Further wars between Rome and Veii followed, culminating in the siege and capture of Veii itself, in (Varronian) 396 according to Livy,[3] in 388 according to Diodorus.[4] After the capture, although the town itself continued to exist,[5] the Veientane survivors were probably enslaved,[6] and their territory was divided among Roman settlers in lots of uncertain size.[7] Not long after the fall of Veii, in 389 according to Livy's chronology, those who had deserted to Rome from Capena, Falerii, and Veii were rewarded with

[1] IV 22 (cf. 25.8), 31–4.

[2] There is, however, a lack of trustworthy evidence about this trade, J. Le Gall, *Le Tibre, fleuve de Rome dans l'antiquité* (Paris, 1952), 56.

[3] See esp. V 22.8.

[4] XIV 93.4–5.

[5] J. B. Ward-Perkins, *PBSR* xxix (1961), 52–7, xxxvi (1968), 145–6.

[6] Liv. V 22.1: 'postero die libera corpora dictator sub corona vendidit.' This is entirely plausible, but it is not possible to tell when such notices in Livy became authentic (cf. R. M. Ogilvie ad loc.).

[7] Liv. V 30.8. Diodorus (XIV 102.4) says that the allotments were of four πλέθρα, or according to another version of twenty-eight πλέθρα. Whether Diodorus intends to refer to real πλέθρα or to *iugera*, we have three different figures, and it is unlikely that any of them was annalistic (*pace* Ogilvie ad loc.).

Roman citizenship and grants of land;[1] and it was then thought necessary to create four new rural tribes, the Stellatina, Tromentina, Sabatina, and Arnensis.[2]

The fall of Veii exposed the smaller Etruscan towns beyond, Capena, Sutrium, and Nepet, to Roman attacks, and prepared the way for Roman conflict with the more powerful towns of Falerii and Caere. Capena, which had apparently fought on the side of Veii in the final struggle with Rome,[3] was in a very exposed position after 396. Rome defeated Capena in the following year and the defeat seems to have been final: 'ea clades Capenatem populum subegit; pax petentibus data'.[4] From imperial inscriptions it appears that Capena was a *municipium foederatum*,[5] and there was a praetorship there,[6] facts which strongly suggest that the town became a *municipium* before the Social War.[7] From these facts it is not possible to reconstruct a definite political history of Capena. Presumably the *foedus* was made in 395 or shortly afterwards. The deserters who were enfranchised are not likely to have been more than a small proportion of the surviving inhabitants, and since Livy specifies that it was to deserters that the citizenship was given, it is to be presumed that the other local inhabitants did not receive the citizenship at that time.[8] It is very likely that some Romans were awarded plots of land in the territory of Capena, and that they, with the deserters, became members of the tribe Stellatina, afterwards the tribe of all members of the community of Capena.[9] It must have been later that the rest of the population of Capena was enfranchised and the town became a *municipium*: a date between 338 and the 270s is perhaps most likely.[10] Capena was then, in the period immediately after the

[1] Liv. VI 4.4: 'Eo anno in civitatem accepti qui Veientium Capenatiumque ac Faliscorum per ea bella transfugerant ad Romanos, agerque his novis civibus adsignatus.' Some modern writers make Roman policy too generous by interpreting this to refer to a wider class of Veientane well-wishers of Rome, e.g. J. Bayet, *Tite-Live, Histoire Romaine*, vol. v (Paris, 1954), 116.

[2] Liv. VI 5.8; cf. Festus 464L.

[3] Liv. V 8.4, 13.9, 17.6, etc.

[4] Liv. V 24.3, cf. 27.10.

[5] *CIL* xi.3932 (=*ILS* 5770), cf. 3873 (=*ILS* 409), 3876a (if genuine), 3878, 3935, 3936 (=*ILS* 6588). I reject the supposed local federation—see below, p. 87.

[6] *CIL* xi.3873, 3876a (if genuine).

[7] Beloch, *It. Bund* 119, *RG* 446.

[8] Cf. Beloch, *RG* 446.

[9] See below, p. 331.

[10] Beloch, *RG* 446, pointing out that it is unlikely that Capena was the oldest *municipium*, suggests that it became one *c.* 293.

conquest, something of a constitutional oddity, but that is not surprising, for the early fourth century was a period when Rome was having to adapt her institutions to relatively large extensions of her power.

The histories of Sutrium, Nepet, and Falerii are closely connected and, although it is sometimes supposed that Sutrium and Nepet were before the Roman conquest dependencies of Veii,[1] it is obvious from the topography that they are far more likely to have been within the Faliscan sphere of influence.[2] Falerii was allied with Veii in that city's last war with Rome, and, after Veii fell, Falerii was in considerable danger. The sources agree that Falerii fell to Rome not long after Veii,[3] and according to Livy the Faliscans agreed to pay the cost of the Roman army for the year as an indemnity;[4] but it is to be doubted whether the surrender of Falerii ever took place,[5] for the Faliscans are said to have surrendered voluntarily because they were favourably impressed by an example of *fides Romana* and by the *iustitia* of Camillus.[6] There must have been some conflict between Rome and Falerii at this time, leading to the foundation of the Latin colonies at Sutrium and Nepet, but it is unlikely that Falerii itself fell to Rome. Supposed conflict before the Gallic invasion between Rome and Volsinii and its allies the Salpinates[7] is also open to doubt.[8]

About the Latin colonies of Sutrium and Nepet there is conflicting evidence: in Velleius' list of colonies Sutrium is said to have been founded seven years after the Gallic sack of Rome,

[1] G. De Sanctis, *Storia dei romani*, ii (Turin, 1907), 149 ('probably'), A. Alföldi, *Early Rome and the Latins* (Ann Arbor, 1965), 396.

[2] Beloch, *RG* 306, etc.

[3] Liv. V 27.11–15, Diod. XIV 96.5, 98.5, Dion. Hal. XIII 1–2, Plu. *Cam.* 10, Zonar. VII 22.

[4] V 27.15, cf. Plu. *Cam.* 10.7.

[5] See De Sanctis, op. cit., ii.150, R. A. L. Fell, *Etruria and Rome* (Cambridge, 1924), 94; otherwise R. M. Ogilvie (on Liv. V 26–7).

[6] Except in the brief notices of Diodorus.

[7] Liv. V 31–2, Diod. XIV 109.7. The site of Etruscan Volsinii was in my opinion probably Orvieto (cf. W. V. Harris, *PBSR* xxxiii (1965), 113; for some further discussion see A. Andrén, *SE* xxxv (1967), 77–9). Where the Salpinates dwelt is not known; in spite of R. M. Ogilvie, who prefers the form 'Sapienates' (n. on Liv. V 31.5), and G. Baffioni (*SE* xxxv (1967), 125–57), who wishes to replace them by the Capenates, 'Salpinates' seems best; cf. Lyc. *Alex.* 1361.

[8] De Sanctis, op. cit., ii.149, etc.

and Nepet ten years after that,[1] but Livy, who does not mention the foundation of the Sutrium colony, says that the Senate appointed triumvirs to found a colony at Nepet in 383.[2] Furthermore, when Sutrium appears in Livy's account of 311 B.C., it is described as an *urbs socia*;[3] but Diodorus refers to Sutrium as being a colony at a date shortly after the Gauls retired from Rome and before Camillus supposedly defeated them at Veascium[4]—he seems to assume that Sutrium was already a colony before the Gallic invasion. There is no obviously correct solution to this puzzle, but an explicit statement that a colony was founded at a certain time is much more important evidence than a passing, possibly careless, allusion to the status of a town. The main problem is then to reconcile Velleius' statements with Livy's date for the foundation of Nepet. It is most likely that one of them reversed the true order of the foundation dates; there is little to choose between the two, but Sutrium encroached less severely on the territory of Falerii and may well have been the earlier of the two foundations.

Livy twice refers to the Sutrini as *socii* of Rome in the period before 383.[5] Since there presumably continued to be some pro-Roman Sutrini, they probably became full members of the colony. In any case, all that the sources have to say about the foundation of the colonies puts them in this period,[6] and so at least from 373 Latin territory extended very close to Falerii: the *claustra Etruriae*[7] were in Roman hands.

[1] I.14.2: 'Post septem annos quam Galli urbem ceperant, Sutrium deducta colonia est et post annum Setia novemque interiectis annis Nepe, deinde interpositis duobus et triginta Aricini in civitatem recepti.'

[2] VI 21.4.

[3] IX 32.1; M. Sordi, *I rapporti romano-ceriti e l'origine della civitas sine suffragio* (Rome, 1960), 137–8, suggested that Rome lost these colonies to Falerii in the war of 357–351, but quite apart from other difficulties it is unlikely that in such circumstances Rome would have agreed to a *foedus* with Falerii in 343, or that Sutrium could have been said to be allied with Rome in 311, or that Rome and Falerii would have remained at peace until 293.

[4] XIV 117.4. It is arbitrary to emend *Σούτριον μὲν ὥρμησαν* in XIV 98.5 to *Σούτριον μὲν ᾤκισαν*, as do many scholars (e.g. De Sanctis, op. cit., ii.149 n. 3, Ed. Meyer, *Kleine Schriften*, ii (Halle, 1924), 311 n. 1, Sordi, op. cit., 135, following J. F. Wurm's suggestion); cf. Beloch, *RG* 305.

[5] VI 3.2, 9.12; this is probably a doublet (cf. Beloch, *RG* 319).

[6] Beloch, *RG* 306–7, and some others, refuse to believe that Rome can have controlled an area as far north as Sutrium and Nepet until the war of 357–351, but that means discarding all the evidence.

[7] The phrase is used of Sutrium and Nepet by Livy VI 9.4, cf. IX 32.1.

The Romans also extended their influence in the coastal area of southern Etruria in the early fourth century. Rome's relations with Caere have been much discussed, and the general opinion of scholars has been that the Caerites became *cives sine suffragio* in 353 or between 353 and 338.[1] There is much to be said against this.[2] According to a strong tradition, apparently known to Aristotle,[3] the *sacra* and priests of the Roman people were received and protected by the Caeritans at the time of the Gallic attack.[4] In Livy's version the Caeritans were subsequently rewarded when Camillus proposed that 'cum Caeritibus hospitium publice fieret',[5] and he never mentions the *civitas sine suffragio* of Caere, holding that in 353 the town concluded *indutiae* of a hundred years' duration with Rome.[6] According to others, when the Gauls withdrew, Rome bestowed the *civitas sine suffragio* on the Caeritans,[7] though there was disagreement about whether this showed sufficient gratitude.[8] Other events in the history of relations between Rome and Caere were a war in 353, followed by the *indutiae* of a hundred years (Livy); and a rebellion or suspected rebellion in 274 or 273, followed by the confiscation of half of the Caeritan land (Dio).[9] When we set out to solve this problem, it is no use assuming either that the *civitas sine suffragio* was a privilege for the Caeritans or that it was ignominious;[10] that can be decided,

[1] See the list, beginning with Mommsen, *Römisches Staatsrecht*, iii.572, given by Sordi, op. cit., 38 n. 3; add R. Werner, *Der Beginn der römischen Republik* (Munich–Vienna, 1963), 359 n. 1, W. Dahlheim, *Deditio und Societas: Untersuchungen zur Entwicklung der römischen Aussenpolitik in der Blütezeit der Republik* (Munich, 1965), 101, *Struktur und Entwicklung des römischen Völkerrechts im dritten und zweiten Jahrhundert v. Chr.* (Munich, 1968), 115. For the view of Pais and others that *civitas sine suffragio* was given to Caere in 274 or 273, see below, p. 46 n. 1. T. Frank, *Klio*, xi (1911), 377 n. 2, argued against both of these dates.

[2] Sordi, op. cit., esp. 36–49, has argued forcefully for a date shortly after the Gallic invasion. My arguments differ in some respects from hers.

[3] Fr. 568 Rose=Plu. *Cam.* 22.4; cf. Sordi, op. cit., 49–52.

[4] Liv. V 40.7–10, 50.3, VII 20.3–8, Strabo V 2.3 220C, Val. Max. I 1.10, Plu. *Cam.* 21, Gellius, *Noct. Att.* XVI 13.7, Festus 38L, *CIL* i². 1 p. 191, VI=*Inscriptiones Italiae*, xiii.3 no. 11, Σ Acro and Ps.-Acro on Hor. *Epist.* I 6.62.

[5] V 50.3.

[6] VII 20.8.

[7] Strabo (πολιτείαν γὰρ δόντες οὐκ ἀνέγραψαν εἰς τοὺς πολίτας, ἀλλὰ καὶ τοὺς ἄλλους τοὺς μὴ μετέχοντας τῆς ἰσονομίας εἰς τὰς δέλτους ἐξώριζον τὰς Καιρετανῶν), Gellius ('Primos autem municipes sine suffragii iure Caerites esse factos accepimus . . . pro sacris bello Gallico receptis custoditisque'), the scholiasts on Horace.

[8] Strabo thought not.

[9] Fr. 33.

[10] A. N. Sherwin-White, *RC* 53.

if at all, only when the context in which it was given has been discovered. The most serious objection to the usual interpretation (that the Caerites received the *civitas sine suffragio* in the period 353–338) is that it conflicts with *both* the main ancient accounts: Strabo, Gellius, and the scholiasts on Horace were supposedly wrong to think that they received it in the aftermath of the Gallic war, Livy was supposedly wrong to think that the *indutiae* were the only arrangement that Rome made with Caere in a long period from 353. It is surely better to cleave to one account or the other,[1] and several points can be made against Livy's. Strabo seems to have had a remarkably detailed knowledge of this period of Caeritan history,[2] and his evidence on this topic is stronger evidence against Livy than his evidence on other topics would be. Gellius furthermore had made some attempt to discover the precise facts of the case. Lastly, there was some similarity between *hospitium publicum* and *civitas sine suffragio*,[3] and confusion between the two was possible,[4] so that it is easier to alter Livy's account of 390 than his account of 353.

It seems unlikely that the Romans gave Caere any ignominious status in the period 390–353. In 353 Caere made war against Rome, and there is no reason to doubt that the war ended with *indutiae* of a hundred years.[5] Rome will naturally have regarded that as an unsatisfactory conclusion, but it re-

[1] E. Pais, *Storia di Roma*, i.2 (Turin, 1899), 308–12, *Storia di Roma dalle origini all'inizio delle guerre puniche*, iv (Rome, 1928), 212–14, 434–40, Beloch, *RG* 363–5, and now A. J. Toynbee, *Hannibal's Legacy* (Oxford, 1965), i. 410–24, put the award of *civitas sine suffragio* in 274–273. That date is more plausible than 353–338, since it makes necessary the rejection of only one of the two ancient accounts, and it may even have been Livy's date; but it does make it necessary to reject one account altogether, whereas the view defended in the text supposes only one mild error (Livy refers to *hospitium publicum* instead of *civitas sine suffragio*). Furthermore, when Gellius said that the Caerites were the first *municipes sine suffragii iure*, and when the scholiast on Horace said that the Caerites rebelled after they had received the citizenship, they may have had solid reasons—and both statements exclude 274–273.

[2] See above, p. 25.

[3] Cf. Sordi, op. cit., 110–13.

[4] It is conceivable that Livy assimilated their reward to the *hospitium publicum* given to Timasitheus of Liparae, V 28.4.

[5] According to A. J. Pfiffig, *Die Ausbreitung des römischen Städtewesens in Etrurien und die Frage der Unterwerfung der Etrusker* (Florence, 1966), 34, Livy had no right to refer to *indutiae* of a hundred years' duration as *pax* (no doubt he should not have done it if he had wanted to speak with technical accuracy, cf. Gellius, *Noct. Att.* I 25.1–4), and therefore the *indutiae* were fictitious. Pfiffig rejects by far the most solid part of Livy's narrative in VII 20, namely the *indutiae* of a hundred years, and substitutes a fiction of his own.

flected the limits of her military power. In the final series of Etruscan wars that began in 311, Caere seems to have taken no part; when they were finished, or very nearly so, Rome threatened to bring to an end the anomaly of Caere's *indutiae*-governed status, and Caere obtained a final settlement only on the harsh condition that she surrendered half her territory—a consequence, no doubt, not only of Caere's military weakness in the face of Rome, but also of a Roman wish to punish a state that had 'rebelled' (in 353) after it had been well treated. Nonetheless the Caeritans regained their citizenship at some date before the Social War, as the survival of the office of dictator at Caere under the Empire shows.[1] The *tabulae Caerites*, 'in quas censores referri iubebant, quos notae causa suffragiis privabant',[2] were undoubtedly ignominious, but there is no great difficulty in supposing that they acquired that character long after the Caerites received their *civitas sine suffragio*.[3] Citizens whom the censors deprived of their *suffragium* were added to the list, and after a certain date (we do not know when) the original *cives sine suffragio* had received the full citizenship; the former were the only names left on the list of *cives sine suffragio*, but the list retained its old title.

Apart from the colonization of Sutrium and Nepet, and an excursion into Tarquinian territory,[4] there was no attempt to extend Roman power in Etruria between the Gallic invasion and the 350s; the effects of the invasion had been too severe[5] and Rome was preoccupied with the Latins until the reconstitution of the confederacy in 358–354. In the 350s, there was inconclusive conflict with Falerii, Caere, and Tarquinii. In the Roman version at least, the initial attack was made in 358 by Tarquinii,[6] and the Faliscans sided with them,[7] as did the

[1] Cf. Beloch, *RG* 498, G. De Sanctis, *Scritti in onore di B. Nogara* (Rome, 1937), 151.

[2] Gellius, *Noct. Att.* XVI 13.7.

[3] Sordi, op. cit., 40.

[4] Liv. VI 4.8–11.

[5] Cf. Polyb. II 18.5, Liv. VII 12.7. This explanation is surely sufficient and it is unnecessary to have recourse to the unattested Roman accord with Etruscan states north of Caere or the allegedly pro-Etruscan government of the Fabii and Licinii hypothesized by Sordi, op. cit., 73–7, followed by Ogilvie, op. cit., 627–8 (on the Licinii cf. L. R. Taylor, *AJPh* lxxxii (1961), 450).

[6] Liv. VII 12.5–6.

[7] Liv. VII 16.2.

Caeritans in 353.[1] Not much trust is to be put in the statement that the whole Etruscan *nomen* took part in the fighting against Rome.[2] Some engagements were fought in Roman territory,[3] others in the territory of the Etruscan states—at least the Romans devastated some territory of the Faliscans and of the Tarquinians,[4] but they fought no battles with the armies of these states nor did they attack the towns. The Caeritans, according to Livy, were so frightened of war with Rome that they begged for peace in the most pathetic way;[5] but the only reliable element in this narrative is the result, the *indutiae* of a hundred years. Similarly, the *indutiae* of forty years that Rome made with Tarquinii and with Falerii in 351 are by far the most solid elements in the account of these wars with the two towns. Thus the new series of wars achieved nothing for Rome. The conflict was broken off still undecided, perhaps because of the new Gallic invasion of Latium.[6]

Only one change is known to have taken place in Roman–Etruscan political relations between 351 and 311. The Faliscans in 343 requested a *foedus* to replace their *indutiae*,[7] and it was presumably granted to them; in 293 they were considered to have been for many years in the friendship of Rome.[8] The *foedus* of 343 must have been on equal or nearly equal terms, since the Faliscans had not been forced into submission;[9] on her side Rome probably wished to make a more lasting agreement in order to protect Nepet and Sutrium, which were exposed to attack from Falerii.

Whatever immediate reasons Rome had for making war against Etruscan states in 311–308, her activities were not merely defensive, and we must attempt to explain what restrained Roman aggressiveness in the preceding forty years. To explain why the Etruscans did not attack Roman territory is not so difficult, though we do not have the evidence with which to weigh up the various possibilities.[10] The obvious answer to the

[1] Liv. VII 19.6. [2] Liv. VII 17.6. [3] Liv. VII 12.5–6, 17.6, 19.8.
[4] Liv. VII 20.9, 22.4–5. [5] Liv. VII 20.1–8.
[6] Liv. VII 23–6; there was renewed restiveness among the Latins in 349, VII 25.5–6.
[7] Liv. VII 38.1. [8] Liv. X 45.6.
[9] Livy explains their request by the Roman defeat of the Samnites at Suessula.
[10] For possible explanations see De Sanctis, *Storia dei romani*, ii. 328–9, R. A. L. Fell, op. cit., 108–9.

problem of Roman restraint in the period 351–311 is that they were preoccupied elsewhere, in Latium, with the Volsci, and with the Samnites; since the Samnites were a continuous threat to Campania, it was more important to defeat them than to attack the central Etruscan states. It is not very plausible to argue that there was a group at Rome that would have preferred a war of expansion in the north, and that war was made against the Etruscans in 311–308 because this group had become dominant.[1] It is possible—but in 312–311, the crucial period, Ap. Claudius Caecus, the proponent of the supposed 'southern' policy, had hardly fallen from power, and Q. Fabius Maximus Rullianus, cos. I in 322, dictator in 315, cos. II in 310, was hardly a new influence in Roman politics. That is not to deny that Fabius was more aggressive during the Etruscan war than others wished him to be;[2] but the Samnite war obviously had priority until the defeats at the Caudine Forks (321) and at Lautulae (315) had been counteracted. After 315 the war was evidently progressing well enough[3] for the Romans to consider an additional war acceptable, and in the event they did manage to pursue both the Samnite and the Etruscan wars successfully at the same time.[4]

2. *The War of 311–308*

The evidence for the final series of wars between Rome and the Etruscans, and for the closely connected wars between Rome and the Umbrians, like the evidence for the other contemporary wars, is problematical. The evidence has been exposed to much scepticism: since Niebuhr[5] historians have whittled away from the Livian account of the conquest of Italy those elements that have seemed incredible. The most advanced degree of scepticism shown in a comprehensive discussion was

[1] E. T. Salmon, *Samnium and the Samnites* (Cambridge, 1967), 240.

[2] See below, p. 58.

[3] Salmon, op. cit., 236–40.

[4] It is tempting to suppose that the forty-year *indutiae* with Tarquinii made in 351 were a restraining influence, since the Etruscan war began in 311 (cf. De Sanctis, op. cit., ii.328); in Livy the peace lasted for only thirty-seven years, since he rejected the three intervening dictator-years, but it is possible that the Etruscan war ended in Varronian 354; cf. Pais, *Storia di Roma*, i.2 130–1.

[5] His account is in *Römische Geschichte*, iii[3] (Berlin, 1853), 320–506 *passim*.

reached by E. Pais[1] and similar views were later expressed by K. J. Beloch;[2] subsequently many of their conclusions have been accepted in less detailed works[3] and there has been no full examination of the issues raised.[4] Here the Livian tradition will be dealt with in two sections, one for the war of 311–308, another for the wars of 302–293; in a third section the wars of 292–264 will be reconstructed.

Livy's narrative of the first of these wars covers the years 311, 310, and 308, 309 being a dictator-year which he ignores.[5] The war begins at Sutrium, but in Livy it extends far northwards into Etruria in 310 and again in 308. Beloch's conclusion is: 'so bleibt von den Kriegsereignissen in diesem Jahre nur der etruskische Angriff auf Sutrium'.[6] This is an excess of disbelief.

After rumours of war in 312,[7] fighting breaks out in 311, the war being assigned to the consul, Q. Aemilius Barbula.[8] All the peoples of Etruria except the Arretines besiege Sutrium, and the consul, trying to relieve the town, fights a battle that is reported by Livy as a Roman victory; afterwards the Etruscan forces are still encamped at Sutrium.[9] In 310 the campaign was taken over by the consul Q. Fabius Maximus Rullianus,[10] who

[1] *Storia di Roma*, i.2 (Turin, 1899), substantially repeated later, for example in *Storia critica di Roma durante i primi cinque secoli*, iv (Rome, 1920). In the former he gives a valuable bibliography of nineteenth-century criticism, 375 n. 1. De Sanctis' account in *Storia dei romani*, ii (Turin, 1907) is more moderate.

[2] *RG*, esp. 412–59.

[3] E.g. by R. A. L. Fell, *Etruria and Rome* (Cambridge, 1924), 108–34, F. E. Adcock in *CAH* vii, 581–616, L. Pareti, *A & R* ser. 2. xii (1931), 211–30=*Studi minori di storia antica*, i (Rome, 1958), 345–63; cf. also E. T. Salmon, op. cit., 240–69. M. Sordi, *Roma e i sanniti nel IV secolo a.C.* (Rocca San Casciano, 1969), 93–104, follows in this tradition and offers an imaginative and somewhat arbitrary reconstruction of Rome's external relations in the period 311–295.

[4] Salmon, l.c., has dealt with the Samnite wars in detail. The account of the Etruscan wars given by A. J. Pfiffig, *Historia*, xvii (1968), 307–50, consists mainly of a not very accurate paraphrase of Livy, with some arbitrary corrections.

[5] The whole of the tradition seems to be against the dictator-years with the exception of the *Fasti Capitolini*, and this seems to have continued to be the case after their redaction (cf. for example the figure of forty-six years given in Tac. *Ann.* I 9, where the number in the *Fasti Cap.* was forty-nine (on this point see *MRR* i.170 n. 2)). For discussion see Beloch, *RG* 44–5, A. Degrassi, *Inscriptiones Italiae*, xiii.1 (Rome, 1947), 110, R. Werner, *Der Beginn der Römischen Republik* (Munich–Vienna, 1963), 200–1.

[6] *RG* 414; Sordi, op. cit., 95–6, rejects all fighting between Rome and the Etruscans in 311–308.

[7] IX 29.1–5.

[8] IX 31.1.

[9] IX 32–3.

[10] IX 33.1.

fought another battle near Sutrium that was evidently successful in lifting the siege.[1] There follows the story of how a Roman who knew the Etruscan language—his identity variously reported—penetrated the Ciminus with a single slave companion and made an alliance with Camerinum;[2] then there was a plundering expedition north of the Ciminus that was carried out by Q. Fabius' army and a victory over the Etruscans who opposed it; when Fabius returned to his camp he found that the Senate had sent instructions that he was not to cross the Ciminus.[3] The plundering expedition provoked another Etruscan expedition to the territory of Sutrium, which was defeated there by the consul with Etruscan losses of 60,000 killed or captured; but 'quidam auctores' said that the victory was won near Perusia; then ambassadors from Perusia, Cortona, and Arretium arranged *indutiae* of thirty years' duration.[4] Later in 310 an Umbrian army was defeated, and at the Lake of Vadimon another Etruscan army was defeated; 'ille primum dies fortuna vetere abundantes Etruscorum fregit opes'.[5] Still in the same year Q. Fabius defeated the remnants of the Etruscans near Perusia when the Perusines and others broke the *indutiae*; the town surrendered and he celebrated a triumph.[6] Consequently Fabius was re-elected as consul for the next year (308, that is), but the war with the Etruscans was assigned to his colleague P. Decius Mus. Decius frightened Tarquinii into seeking *indutiae* of forty years' duration and captured some *castella* belonging to Volsinii. His devastations led the whole *nomen Etruscum* to ask Rome for a *foedus*; instead, *indutiae* for one year were made. There follows a war with the Umbrians, who had only been involved in war with Rome before when an army had passed through their territory; they persuaded most of the Etruscans to rebel; this made Decius retreat towards Rome and Fabius arrive from Samnium. The latter defeated some Umbrians in a battle at Mevania, with the result that all the peoples of Umbria surrendered to Rome; Ocriculum was accepted into *amicitia*.[7]

[1] IX 35. [2] IX 36.1–8. [3] IX 36.9–14.

[4] IX 37. Livy makes it clear that in his opinion this was agreed by all the authorities: 'Sed ubicumque pugnatum est, res Romana superior fuit. Itaque a Perusia et Cortona et Arretio . . .'

[5] IX 39. [6] IX 40. [7] IX 41.

Diodorus has two short notices dealing with the war,[1] in length a small fraction of Livy's account. The first, dealing with 310, refers to a battle fought at Sutrium with both consuls present, evidently the battle described by Livy in IX 35; a plundering expedition and a victory for Fabius in Etruria; another battle of his near Perusia; truces (ἀνοχαί) with Perusia, Cortona, and Arretium; and lastly the lifting of the siege of Sutrium by means of the capture of the town of *Καστόλα*. In 308, according to the second notice, both consuls crossed the territory of the Umbrians, invaded Etruria, and captured *Κάπριον*;[2] then they made truces of forty years' duration with Tarquinii and of one year's duration with the rest of the Etruscans.[3] Not surprisingly there are various elements in the Livian narrative that are simply omitted by Diodorus' summary: for example, the campaign of Q. Aemilius in 311; the Sutrium battle of IX 37.1–10; the defeat of the Umbrians in IX 39.4; the battle at the Lake of Vadimon; the victory over the Etruscans near Perusia after the breaking of the *indutiae*, the surrender of Perusia, and the triumph of Fabius; and from the notice of 308 there is omitted in particular the war with the Umbrians.

In the *Fasti Triumphales* two triumphs are recorded for the war of 311–308: in 311 Q. Aemilius triumphed *de Etrusceis*, then Q. Fabius as proconsul, i.e. in the dictator-year 309, also *de Etrusceis*;[4] there is no literary reference to the former, but the latter presumably corresponds to the triumph of 310 attributed to Fabius by Livy.[5]

Which elements in these accounts are to be rejected? Two preliminary observations should be made. In his account of the wars described in Books IX and X, Livy frequently tells us of the discrepancies that he found between his sources. We have no reason to doubt that when he claims to have consulted a number of authors on a particular point he had in fact generally done so,[6] and no reason to doubt that the discrepancies com-

[1] XX 35.1–5, 44.8–9. [2] For the reading see below, p. 60.

[3] Not 100 years, as stated by Sordi, *I rapporti romano-ceriti*, 126.

[4] Degrassi, op. cit., 70–1.

[5] IX 40.15.

[6] This is not to deny that Livy sometimes exaggerated the number of writers that he had consulted: claims to have consulted *all* writers on any topic are obviously suspect, e.g. IV 20.5 (on Cossus and the *spolia opima*), where 'omnes ante

pelled him to be more careful than usual. The record of discrepancies actually increases the value of Livy's account, and makes it more difficult to reject whole sections of his narrative. Diodorus' method of working also needs careful attention; in particular it should be noticed that for almost all topics in the Roman history of this period nothing whatsoever can be demonstrated by Diodorus' silence, since he excerpted and abbreviated in an erratic manner.[1]

The whole campaign of 311 has been rejected as a doublet of part of the campaign of 310.[2] A question of principle arises from this: the war with the Etruscans was a protracted one in which there must have been repeated fighting over the territory of the same towns, and it is therefore not reasonable to reject one battle outright as a doublet of another unless there is some specific resemblance other than that they were fought somewhere on the territory of the same Etruscan state. In this case the only points of resemblance between the campaign ascribed by Livy to 311 and the first campaigns ascribed by Livy and Diodorus to 310 are that they were Roman victories in the neighbourhood of Sutrium.

There are other difficulties in Livy's narrative of 311. According to him the war with the Etruscans was under the command of the consul Q. Aemilius Barbula, but according to Diodorus[3] both consuls were engaged in the war with the Samnites. It is perfectly possible that Aemilius fought in both areas, all the more so as the Etruscan war was a new affair, probably at first a piece of Etruscan initiative, and the scene of fighting in Etruria was easily accessible from Rome. It is also quite possible that Diodorus' phrase *οἱ τῶν Ῥωμαίων ὕπατοι*, without the names, is merely a slovenly version of a source that referred simply to the actions of the Romans in general.[4] The *Fasti Triumphales* attribute a triumph to Aemilius that is not

me auctores' is demonstrably exaggerated (see R. M. Ogilvie ad loc.)—yet this is certainly a special case. Such definite claims of comprehensiveness are in fact not common, cf. F. Hellmann, *Livius-Interpretationen* (Berlin, 1939), 13–14. P. G. Walsh, *Livy, his Historical Aims and Methods* (Cambridge, 1963), 142, seems to me to be too sceptical about this.

[1] Cf. A. Klotz, *RhM* lxxxvi (1937), 210–16, a judicious assessment, often unheeded by subsequent writers.

[2] De Sanctis, op. cit., ii.329 n. 2, Adcock, op. cit., 604–5.

[3] XX 26.3.

[4] Cf. Klotz., art. cit., 214.

mentioned by Livy, and it has been disbelieved.[1] By the Augustan period there was, to say the least, some confusion about the triumphs won during these wars; but for all the faults in the *Fasti* it has not really been shown that Livy's silence is a fatal point against a triumph that they list—Aemilius' may be right—and at any rate there was probably another annalist besides the one followed by Livy who held that Aemilius fought in Etruria. In fact the description of Aemilius' military success arouses the strong suspicion that he was in reality defeated;[2] and when the campaign was over, the Etruscans remained encamped near Sutrium.[3] Furthermore, it is unlikely that the Etruscan forces comprised 'omnes Etruriae populi praeter Arretinos', for the league of Etruscan states does not seem to have cohered sufficiently at this period to have produced such an effect.

Livy's account of the campaigns in Etruria and Umbria in 310 is, apart from other difficulties, impossibly crowded.[4] If the general opinion is right that there was no such year as 309, some events must be removed from the account as having taken place either at other dates or never. Two fundamental events of the year that come at different points in the narratives of Livy and Diodorus, but (unlike the battles) are not likely to have been repeated during the year, are the raising of the siege of Sutrium and the making of the truces between Rome and Perusia, Arretium, and Cortona. The tradition was, as far as we know, unanimous that both events took place in 310 (or 309). In Livy the siege of Sutrium was raised as a result of the first battle in Etruria in 310;[5] in Diodorus it comes at the end of the campaigns of the year, after the truces with the three towns.[6] This account makes Diodorus' own narrative unintelligible, for the expedition to Perusia[7] would have been militarily

[1] Klebs in *RE* s.v. Aemilius no. 34 (1894). According to Beloch's theory, *RG* 86–95, the *Fasti Triumphales* are authentic from 306 at the earliest; but it is necessary to judge each one on its merits in this period.

[2] C. P. Burger, *De bello cum Samnitibus secundo* (Haarlem, 1884), 89, Pais, *Storia di Roma*, i.2 405–6, C. Delplace, *Latomus*, xxvi (1967), 455. What Livy says is (IX 32.9–10): 'Nullo unquam proelio fugae minus nec plus caedis fuisset, ni obstinatos mori Tuscos nox texisset, ita ut victores prius quam victi pugnandi finem facerent. Post occasum solis signum receptui datum est; nocte utroque in castra reditum.'

[3] IX 32.11, cf. 33.1.

[4] Cf. Pais, op. cit., 520.

[5] IX 35.8.

[6] XX 35.5.

[7] XX 35.4.

impossible while Sutrium was still besieged. In his account the penultimate event is the making of the truces, which is preceded by the expedition to Perusia (this *may* have been the version of the 'quidam auctores' referred to by Livy),[1] whereas in Livy's main account the expedition to Perusia comes after the truces (and is followed by various other military events). Thus there were at least two radically different outlines of the Etruscan wars of 310 that agreed that there was fighting well to the north of the territory of Sutrium. The truces themselves have been called into question: Beloch rejected them as a doublet of the truces made with Perusia, Arretium, and Volsinii in 294,[2] the latter erroneously attributed by him to Q. Fabius who made the truces of 310[3]—but since the list of towns and the duration of the truces are different in the two cases and there are no other significant resemblances, the earlier as well as the later ones should be accepted as historical, provided that they fit into a coherent narrative of the war.

Another doublet has been detected in Diodorus XX 35.3, where Q. Fabius passes through Umbria on the way to Etruria διὰ τῆς τῶν ὁμόρων χώρας, and XX 44.9, where the consuls pass through Umbria on their way to Etruria in the following year διὰ τῆς τῶν Ὀμβρικῶν χώρας.[4] Whatever the correct text in the former passage,[5] the sense is the same. There does seem to have been an annalistic version that made no mention of an expedition across Umbria in 310, Livy's version—though he seems to refer to it when he discusses the Umbrian war of 308.[6] Yet there are no other resemblances between the two Diodoran notices. The question needs to be examined from the point of view of military possibility.

Some other parts of the accounts of 310 given by Livy and Diodorus are clearly suspect. The reconnaissance to the north of the Ciminus (a version of which is also told in Frontinus)[7] has some romantic elements, for example the description of the

[1] IX 37.11. So Münzer in *RE* s.v. Fabius no. 124 (1909), col. 1804, Beloch, *RG* 444, C. Delplace, art. cit., 460.

[2] Liv. X 37.4–5.

[3] *RG* 413.

[4] Discussed by Beloch, *RG* 413.

[5] Ὀμβρικῶν was suggested by Niebuhr, followed by De Sanctis, op. cit., ii.334 n. 1, etc.; cf. R. A. L. Fell, op. cit., 112 n. 1.

[6] IX 41.8: 'defectio Umbrorum, gentis integrae a cladibus belli, nisi quod transitum exercitus ager senserat.'

[7] *Strat.* I 2.2.

Ciminus itself,[1] and Livy himself expresses reserve about some parts of the story.[2] The only geographical reference in the story, apart from the Ciminus, is Camerinum, with which the famous *foedus* was supposed to have been made on this occasion. Camerinum comes into the narrative again in 295 when a battle was probably lost there by an army of Q. Fabius; that mention of the town, and the exceptional Camerinum treaty, which required an explanation, render the story of its making in 310 suspect.[3] Yet there must at one time have been official records of the treaty, and a plausible explanation of its being made in 310 can be found: Camerinum was threatened by the Senonian Gauls.

The battle of the Lake of Vadimon[4] is generally regarded as a doublet of the Roman victory over the combined Boii (or Senones)[5] and Etruscans at the same site in 283 that is described by Polybius.[6] The site of the battle is so specific[7] that it is necessary to reject one or the other, and in spite of the difficulties about the campaign of 283, the battle clearly belongs to that year.[8]

Again in 308 there are considerable differences between

[1] 'Silva erat Ciminia magis tum invia atque horrenda quam nuper fuere Germanici saltus, nulli ad eam diem ne mercatorum quidem adita. Eam intrare haud fere quisquam praeter ducem ipsum audebat . . .'; yet presumably the Etruscans had crossed it to besiege Sutrium. It was simply hostile territory, favourable to defenders. Cf. A. Schwegler–O. Clason, *Römische Geschichte*, iv (Berlin, 1873), 301, Pais, op. cit., 519, etc.

[2] The single slave companion, IX 36.4 (*dicitur*), penetration as far as Camerinum, 36.7 (*dicuntur*).

[3] It is transferred to 295 by Beloch, *RG* 443. According to Sordi, *Roma e i sanniti*, 96–7, the treaty was made not with Camerinum, but with Clusium, which according to Livy (X 25.11) was once called Camars (cf. below, p. 70).

[4] Liv. IX 39.4–5. The lake is the Laghetto di Bassano on the Tiber four miles upstream from Orte; it is described by Plin. *Ep.* VIII 20.3–10, with no mention of the battle.

[5] It is argued below that the Boii, not the Senones, were on the side of the Etruscans in the 283 battle.

[6] Polyb. II 20.2–3. The doublet: Pais, op. cit., 529, De Sanctis, op. cit., ii.331 n. 3; denied with no good reasons by J. Gröseling, *Rom und Etrurien von der Eroberung Veiis bis zur Mitte des 3. Jahrhunderts v. Chr.* (Leipzig, 1913), 38. W. B. Anderson wished to strike the reference to Vadimon from the text of Liv. IX 39.4–5 (see his edn., pp. 249–50, and Walters–Conway ad loc.).

[7] Pais, op. cit., 530 n. 1, and others, also point to a similarity between Liv. IX 39.11 ('Caesum in acie, quod Etruscorum roboris fuit') and Polyb. II 20.3 (ἐν δὲ τῇ μάχῃ ταύτῃ Τυρρηνῶν μὲν οἱ πλεῖστοι κατεκόπησαν . . .).

[8] Note that Livy fails to name the Roman commander in the battle of 310.

Livy's account of the Etruscan and Umbrian wars and the notice given in Diodorus. Partly it is a matter of omission: Diodorus does not mention the Umbrians except to say that the consuls crossed their territory,[1] while in Livy they are the opponents in an important war, and their actions impel the Etruscans to rebel after the making of the *indutiae*.[2] The absence of the war from Diodorus and also from the *Fasti Triumphales* does not seriously affect the credibility of Livy's version, nor is it of much importance to the historicity of his account that the Romans already had troubles in Etruria (as a matter of fact they may have expected a year's respite as a result of the *indutiae*), or that Umbria remained independent after the campaign of 308.[3] The formal *amicitia* with Ocriculum, established according to Livy in 308,[4] *may* have been the reason why Ὀκρίκολα was mentioned in Book XVIII of Dionysius,[5] a book that dealt with the Third Samnite War which began in 298, but Livy's notice about Ocriculum is supported by the colonization of Narnia in 299, which would otherwise have been separated from Rome by hostile territory. It has been suggested that the whole Umbrian war of 308 is a *Vorausnahme* of the Sentinum campaign of 295, when Fabius and Decius were again the consuls in command.[6] Yet in spite of the fact that Livy's narrative is relatively detailed about both campaigns, there are no other real resemblances between them.

The other major difference between the two accounts of 308 is that in Diodorus the whole campaign is jointly commanded by the two consuls, whereas in Livy it is assigned to P. Decius Mus, and Q. Fabius only joins in after the *indutiae* with the Etruscans have been made and broken.[7] As in 310, Diodorus can probably be disregarded on this point. Again in this year there were partially divergent traditions which agreed that there was fighting well to the north of the Ciminus.

[1] XX 44.9.

[2] IX 41.9: 'magna parte Etruscorum . . .'.

[3] The reasons for scepticism that are rejected here are given by De Sanctis, op. cit., ii.334. Delplace, art. cit., 464–5, gives some weak reasons for rejecting the Umbrian war.

[4] IX 41.20.

[5] Steph. Byz. s.v. Ὀκρίκολα. That this was why Ocriculum was mentioned is suggested by Beloch, *RG* 424–5.

[6] This is argued by Beloch, l.c.; cf. De Sanctis, op. cit., ii.334 n. 1.

[7] Fabius is also supposed to have fought in Campania (Liv. IX 41.3–4) and among the Marsi (Diod. XX 44.8).

So much for the source-criticism that can be applied to the war of 311–308. Since considerable emphasis has sometimes been placed on arguments from military and geographical reasonableness by those who have examined the evidence for this war, such considerations are now treated as far as possible separately.

How much can we tell about the likely course of the war from the circumstances in which it broke out? The war seems to have begun as an Etruscan attack on Roman territory, the real contest at the beginning concerning continued Roman possession of Sutrium. This is perhaps an acceptable description of the war of the year 311, all the more so if Aemilius was defeated, the Romans having been caught somewhat unawares. Yet we are obliged to be sceptical about any train of events that tends to suggest that a Roman war was a *iustum bellum*, and no altogether satisfying explanation is available of why the Etruscans should suddenly in 311 have begun to try to recover what they had lost before. Livy's description of the Ciminus has tended to count too much against possible Roman wars to the north of the hills, in spite of the fact that it is obviously exaggerated and that there was some record of earlier Roman conflict with Tarquinii and Volsinii in the fourth century. If an Etruscan army could cross the Ciminus from the north, it might be desirable or necessary for a Roman army to cross it (not that it was necessary to enter central Etruria by this route, rather than for example up the Tiber valley). Again, there is a fairly clear tradition of disputes at Rome in this period about the type of external policy to be followed, with Q. Fabius as a proponent of aggression;[1] it may be believed that the Senate gave Fabius instructions 'ne saltum Ciminium transiret'[2] (though the incident has some similarity to some later events),[3] either after his expedition (Livy) or even before it.[4] Another factor in favour of the Roman expeditions north of the Ciminus during these wars is the tradition that the Etruscan response to Roman invasion was to withdraw into

[1] Cf. E. Staveley, *Historia*, viii (1959), 432.

[2] Liv. IX 36.14.

[3] The order given to Flaminius in 223 concerning the Insubres and the debate about the African expedition in 205—but in these cases it is Fabius Maximus who is trying to impose restraint.

[4] Cf. Florus I 12.3.

their fortified towns, which the Romans were for some time incapable of capturing by assault.

In 311 Livy says that 'omnes Etruriae populi praeter Arretinos'[1] were involved in the war against Rome, an obvious type of exaggeration. This sort of combination would not necessarily have been the result of the operation of the league, but there is no evidence that the league of Etruscan states,[2] or anything else, was at this time capable of inspiring such co-operation.

It is clear that in 310 the Romans were not on the point of reducing Perusia, Arretium, and Cortona to permanent subjection, but that is no reason why *indutiae* should not have been made, at least in 308 if not in 310; the Etruscan states in the north were probably more ready to make temporary agreements with Rome because they were more immediately threatened by the Gauls than by the Romans. Similar considerations make the Camerinum agreement quite plausible, for the enemy from whom they had most to fear were the Senones.[3]

Obviously there is plenty of exaggeration and invention in the accounts of 310 for the benefit of national glory and that of Q. Fabius in particular. Sixty thousand Etruscans were killed or captured in a battle at Sutrium;[4] Perusia surrendered easily and a garrison was stationed there.[5]

Roman attention in 310 seems to have been concentrated partly on the defence of Sutrium—hence the capture of the unidentified town of *Καστόλα*, which according to Diodorus relieved the siege;[6] and attention was also concentrated in 310 and in 308 on the area of Perusia, and on the Topino valley, the most obvious way of getting to Perusia.[7] The *amicitia* of Ocriculum was clearly a part of the same policy of securing a route up the Tiber and Nera valleys, a policy the next stage of

[1] IX 32.1.

[2] De Sanctis, op.cit., ii.329, thought that the league was becoming more political, a belief for which there is no evidence. The league existed, but there is no evidence that it was an effective unit in these wars. See below, p. 96 n. 4.

[3] Cf. De Sanctis, op. cit., ii.334. [4] IX 37.10. [5] 40.19–20.

[6] XX 35.5. Emendation of *Καστόλα* is pointless, since there is no obvious substitute and so many towns are unidentified. It was probably some *castellum*, perhaps one of those Volsinian *castella* that were captured early in 308, Liv. IX 41.6; cf. Salmon, op. cit., 243 n. 1. There is no point in transferring the capture of *Καστόλα* to 308, as Pfiffig does, art. cit., 315.

[7] Cf. the mention of Mevania, Liv. IX 41.13.

which was the colonization of Narnia in 299; attacks on the *castella* of Volsinii are also related to this policy. Meanwhile the frontier with Tarquinii was kept peaceful; when *indutiae* for one year were made with the whole *nomen Etruscum* in 308, i.e. with a number of Etruscan states, *indutiae* were made with Tarquinii for forty years, precisely forty years having passed, as has been pointed out,[1] since the last forty-year *indutiae* were made. Some other geographical indications that appear in the sources should be mentioned, although their meaning is unknown. In 308, according to Diodorus, the consuls, coming from the territory of the Marsi, crossed Umbria and took by siege *τὸ καλούμενον Κάπριον φρούριον*,[2] which is unidentified (but it is to be preferred to *Καίριον* = Caere, for *Κάπριον* is read by all MSS. in the contents list of Book XX and by one MS. in the text, and Caere is a quite impossible place for a Roman army to capture by siege in this war).[3] At the battle of Mevania the Umbrians were impelled to fight by 'plaga una—Materinam ipsi appellant', another place completely unknown (although identification with Matilica has been suggested).[4] In fact these pieces of mysterious geography may serve as a further ground for confidence in the factual basis of the annalists' accounts, in that they were clearly quite as mysterious to the Augustan writers as they are to us; they are hardly likely to be recent decoration added to the narrative.

It can be seen then that we do not have as much reason to suspect the annalistic basis of Livy's account as many have supposed. Victories were exaggerated and sometimes invented; enemies were multiplied; the order of events was often confused; all manner of literary decoration was added; and a few bad mistakes, like the double battle of Vadimon, entered the tradition. Yet the record of agreements with other states and of military conflicts with other states seems in outline to be quite strong.

The peace of 308 was of the most temporary possible kind, with the exception of the *indutiae* for forty years made with

[1] Beloch, *RG* 414.
[2] XX 44.9.
[3] '*Κάπριον*' is also the *difficilior lectio*; Sordi, *I rapporti romano-ceriti*, 126, reads '*Καίριον*' without discussion.
[4] Pais, op. cit., 537.

Tarquinii.[1] No new permanent political arrangements with any other state were made as a result of the war, apart from those made in Umbria with Camerinum and Ocriculum. The one-year *indutiae* showed that Rome intended to make war on states well outside her previous area of influence when the occasion arose; when it arose would be determined by the more pressing needs of the Samnite war.

3. *The War of 302, down to 293*

The notices in Livy's tenth book concerning the Etruscan and Umbrian wars may be listed first without discussion. The Samnite war effectively came to an end in 304 and did not begin again until 298. In 303 Livy recounts a small expedition to Umbria, with bizarre details.[2] In 302 there was a rebellion of Etruscans, beginning at Arretium,[3] a defeat of the *magister equitum*,[4] a successful campaign of the dictator in the territory of Rusellae,[5] *indutiae biennii* with the Etruscans;[6] then various alternative versions known to Livy.[7] In the next year, 300 (301 was a dictator-year), there was peace in Etruria;[8] but in Umbria the siege of Nequinum was begun by one of the consuls,[9] being finished by one of the consuls of 299; a colony, Narnia, was founded there against the Umbrians.[10] In 299 the Etruscans planned to make war against Rome in spite of the *indutiae*, but they were delayed by the difficulties of making an agreement with the Gauls who were pressing them from the north;[11] war eventually broke out.[12] In the next year there was a war with Etruscans that involved Volaterrae and the Faliscans,[13] and later in the same year there were fears of another Etruscan war.[14] In 297 there was news at Rome that the Etruscans were discussing the seeking of peace terms.[15] In 296 the Samnites are first heard of in Etruria preparing war against Rome in conjunction with the Etruscans;[16] an alliance is formed also with

[1] De Sanctis, op. cit., ii.333–4, followed by Pfiffig, art. cit., 315, thought that there must have been 'qualche cessione territoriale' in this case, but that is never known to have happened with *indutiae*.

[2] X 1.4–6. Subsequent references in this section are to Livy X unless otherwise specified.

[3] 3.1–2. [4] 3.6–8. [5] 4.1–5.12. [6] 5.12, cf. 6.2. [7] 5.13–14. [8] 6.1–2. [9] 9.8–9. [10] 10.1–5. [11] 10.6–12. [12] 11.1–6, 11.8. [13] 12.3–8. [14] 13.2–4. [15] 14.1–3. [16] 16.3–17.1.

Gauls and Umbrians,[1] and these four peoples make war against Rome in Etruria.[2] In 295, after a dispute about which consul shall have charge of the war against these peoples,[3] there follows the Sentinum campaign,[4] another campaign at the same time against Etruria including Clusium and Perusia,[5] an account of exaggerated versions of the Sentinum campaign,[6] and some concluding details;[7] later in the same year another war was provoked by the Perusini, who were defeated.[8] In 294, although the Samnites were expected to reappear in Etruria,[9] when war broke out there, it was against the Etruscans; there was fighting in the territory of Volsinii and Rusellae, and at the end of the campaign the forty-year *indutiae* were made with Volsinii, Perusia, and Arretium;[10] finally variant versions of the wars of the year are discussed.[11] In 293 further warfare with Etruscans, including Faliscans, is described,[12] then the capture of the unidentified town of Troilum and the *indutiae annuae* made with the Faliscans.[13] References to later incidents in the war that are given in the Periochae of the second decade are described in the next section.

The following are the relevant triumphs mentioned in the *Fasti Triumphales*:[14] in 301 M. Valerius Maximus [*de*] *Etrusceis*; in 299 M. Fulvius Paetinus *de Samnitibus Nequinatibusque*; in 298 Cn. Fulvius Maximus *de Samnitibus Etrusceisque*; in 295 Q. Fabius Maximus *de Samnitibus et Etrusceis*; in 294 L. Postumius Megellus *de Samnitibus et Etrusceis* and M. Atilius Regulus *de Volsonibus et Samnitibus*.

'Et huius anni parum constans memoria est', says Livy of the year 294,[15] having dealt earlier in Book X with various problems that he found in the annals of the Third Samnite War. Some have taken the existence of these problems to show that it is even harder to discover any facts about this war than about the Etruscan and Umbrian war of 311–308,[16] but it also shows that on certain points Livy had consulted a greater number of accounts than he had for the Second Samnite War. When Livy can be compared directly with Polybius on the subject of the

[1] 18.1–2.
[2] 18.3–7, 18.9–20.1, 21.1–4, 21.11–15.
[3] 24.1–18. [4] 25.1–29.20. [5] 30.1–2. [6] 30.4–7.
[7] 30.8–10. [8] 31.1, 31.3–4. [9] 32.2. [10] 37.1–12.
[11] 37.13–14. [12] 45.2–8, 45.11. [13] 46.10–16. [14] Pp. 72–3.
[15] 37.13. [16] Pais, op. cit., 531.

war of 302–293, he does not come out of it well, and a number of other defects can be found in his account; yet again a basic annalistic record seems to survive the process of criticism. Particular difficulties will now be examined, as far as possible in chronological order.

The small expedition that the consuls made to Umbria in 303, 'quod nuntiabatur ex spelunca quadam excursiones armatorum in agros fieri',[1] may have been based on an authentic annalistic notice, for it is difficult to see why it should otherwise have been inserted at this point in the narrative—although there was a shortage of military events for the year; the attack on Nequinum, an obvious beginning for any strategy aimed at the conquest of Umbria,[2] looks like the first move in a Roman campaign in Umbria. The details of the story of 303 are strange and incredible.

Livy knew two versions of the Etruscan war of 302, one of which he gives at much greater length than the other. They had in common only the *seditiones Arretinorum* and the fact that those were eventually ended by the dictator M. Valerius Maximus Corvus;[3] from the secondary version all the memorable battles were absent. There are various arguments for and against Livy's main version. He gave Valerius a triumph,[4] while the *Fasti Triumphales* gave him one over the Etruscans in the next year, a dictator-year, which can be associated with this campaign—that is to say that there was another version besides that of Livy that agreed that there was serious fighting in this period between a Roman army under Valerius and the Etruscans. There was another disagreement among those who accepted this war about the identity of Valerius' *magister equitum*[5] (see below). The story of the campaign naturally contains elements of romantic anecdote[6] and commonplace description (Valerius restraining his troops with difficulty when they wanted to make up for their earlier defeat),[7] but these

[1] 1.4. [2] Cf. Adcock, *CAH* vii.609, on the strategic importance of the site.

[3] Whether this was the father or the son need not be discussed here; cf. *MRR* i.170 n. 2, F. Cassola, *I gruppi politici romani nel III sec. a.C.* (Trieste, 1962), 200–2, etc. Livy (X 3.4) implies that in his view the dictator of 302 was the son.

[4] 5.13. [5] 3.4–8. [6] 4.8–10.

[7] 5.2–3. For the analysis of Livy's narrative technique in describing this defeat and the subsequent victory, see H. Bruckmann, *Die römischen Niederlagen im Geschichtswerk des T. Livius* (Münster, 1931), 34–6.

things do not show that no major campaign took place. The mention of Rusellae[1] is surprising—a campaign there seems too far from Arretium to be plausible in these circumstances, and it is rather a long way to the north for a new Roman war against the Etruscans; yet arbitrary limits should not be set on possible Roman movements, especially as, according to Livy at least, the Romans fought the war in the countryside while the Etruscans withdrew into their walled towns, the first of which is not known to have fallen until 294 (Rusellae).[2] Beloch somewhat arbitrarily transferred the campaign of 302 to 299,[3] when Valerius as suffect consul again held command in Etruria. Pais pointed to the similarities between Livy's account of 302 and his account of 294;[4] he concluded from this and other arguments that the 294 account is to be rejected; but it is hard to see how the 294 account of Rusellae can have been the origin of the (quite different) one of 302, or vice versa. Pais also criticized Livy's account of the part played by Valerius in the internal struggle at Arretium.[5] There can easily have been some exaggeration of the importance of Roman intervention in settling the *seditiones*. Pais suggests that the part played by Valerius in this process ('pacatam ab dictatore Etruriam esse seditionibus tantum Arretinorum compositis et Cilnio genere cum plebe in gratiam reducto')[6] was suspiciously similar to the parts played by this and other members of the *gens* on a number of occasions in Rome.[7] The case is rather insubstantial, however, since Valerius Antias transferred so many events to members of the Valerian *gens*,[8] while the tradition seems to have been unanimous that Valerius was active at Arretium in 302, or at least that he fought in Etruria (*Fasti Triumphales*)—that story at least was not the invention of a Sullan annalist. The mention of the Cilnii, the supposed ancestors of Maecenas and

[1] 4.5. [2] 37.3.

[3] *RG* 423; Sordi, *Roma e i sanniti*, 101, regards the Etruscan wars of 302 and 299 as duplicate versions of a single war.

[4] Pais, op. cit., 527–8; Salmon, op. cit., 256 n. 5, takes the incursion into the territory of Rusellae to be an anticipation of 294.

[5] Op. cit., 529.

[6] 5.13. In the main version it is not explicitly stated that the Cilnii were restored to favour; but it is implied—cf. 'tantum'.

[7] See Pais, op. cit., 528.

[8] Cf. most recently R. M. Ogilvie, *A Commentary on Livy, Books 1–5* (Oxford, 1965), 12–16.

the only Etruscans named by a Roman annalist after King Tolumnius of Veii, also arouses suspicion, but there is no strong reason to suspect more than the name. Whatever is to be made of some of the fighting in Livy's main version, most of his secondary version at least should be retained.

In the *Fasti Capitolini*[1] Valerius' dictatorship is given in the dictator-year and two other names are given for the year, those of Q. Fabius Maximus Rullianus and M. Aemilius Paullus, the other consul of 302. Livy explains why he prefers to think that Aemilius rather than Fabius was Valerius' *magister equitum*:[2] Fabius had too many honours to be subordinate to Valerius—he might have considered that most writers believed that the Valerius concerned was consul for the first time as early as 348; Fabius, he says, would not have lost the battle; and Fabius would not have fought it *dictatoris iniussu* in the first place—but he has just said that the *magister equitum* found himself in battle involuntarily.[3] Quite apart from the fact that Livy does not seem to know the implied version of the *Fasti*, that there were two *magistri equitum* at different times, the feebleness of his reasoning is apparent; yet at least he has taken the trouble to record divergent views.

In 300 the consul Q. Appuleius Pansa began the campaign against the Umbrian town of Nequinum that was finished in 299 by the consul M. Fulvius Paetinus,[4] and in 299 the colony of Narnia was established there. There is no reason why any part of this account, apart from the embroidery on the story of the treachery by which the town was won, should be rejected. That the campaign and colonization were not finished in one season receives some support from the fact that *Νηκουία, πόλις Ὀμβρικῶν* (=Nequinum) was mentioned in Book XVII of Dionysius and *Ναρνία* in Book XVIII.[5] There was one minor divergence in the tradition, for the *Fasti Triumphales* give Paetinus a triumph *de Nequinatibus*, of which there is no mention in Livy.

[1] Pp. 38–9.

[2] 3.6–8.

[3] Livy also refers to the suggestion that confusion had arisen from the *cognomen* Maximus, 3.4.

[4] That the consul concerned was Fulvius is implied by 11.1.

[5] Steph. Byz. s.vv. The latter is erroneously said to be a Samnite town (for theories about this cf. Beloch, *RG* 426, Adcock, *CAH* vii.609 n. 1).

For the Etruscan war of 299 we have a notice of Polybius[1] as well as Livy. According to the latter the Etruscans planned to make war against Rome and made preparations but were distracted from this by a Gallic invasion of Etruria. There was an Etruscan alliance with the Gauls but they failed to agree on terms on which to attack Rome and the Gauls were bribed by the Etruscans not to cause destruction in Etruria; then later in the year there was an Etruscan war in which the Gauls took no part. Livy states specifically that there was no Gallic attack on Rome, but only *fama Gallici tumultus*.[2] Polybius on the other hand says that the Gauls attacked Roman territory via Etruria, ὁμοῦ συστρατευσαμένων σφίσι Τυρρηνῶν, καὶ περιβαλόμενοι λείας πλῆθος, ἐκ μὲν τῆς Ῥωμαίων ἐπαρχίας ἀσφαλῶς ἐπανῆλθον . . . This seems to be a case where some annalists tried to conceal a Roman defeat,[3] part of which was perhaps the allegedly accidental death of the consul T. Manlius Torquatus, who died before the Etruscan war could really get going.[4] Then there follows the election of Valerius as suffect consul and unopposed plundering by him in Etruria, which may be accurate or may be an annalistic way of filling up a period of office for Valerius when no information was available.[5]

In itself Livy's account of the war of 298 raises only minor difficulties. The consul L. Cornelius Scipio Barbatus fought a battle near Volaterrae which was claimed as a victory.[6] That he should have fought so far north is surprising,[7] particularly as he then withdrew to the territory of Falerii[8]—but again it is possible if it really was Etruscan policy to retire into the towns. Livy was, however, apparently unaware that there was in one respect at least a different version of the war, one that gave a different commander. He gave Etruria to Scipio and the

[1] II 19.1–4. [2] 10.8–12. [3] Pais, op. cit., 531.

[4] For the view that he is likely to have been killed in battle see Beloch, *RG* 440.

[5] 299/8 is incidentally the last date at which we hear of Etruscan mercenaries, Diod. XXI 3.1 (under Agathocles). 298 is also the last definite date at which we hear of Etruscan piracy (*IG* xi.148, line 73 (Delos); cf. W. W. Tarn, *Antigonos Gonatas* (Oxford, 1913), 85–6), though a reference in *SIG*³ 1225 seems to be somewhat later (cf. H. H. Schmitt, *Rom und Rhodos* (Munich, 1957), 43–5).

[6] 12.4.

[7] The Volaterrae battle is rejected by Münzer in *RE* s.v. Cornelius no. 343 (1901), col. 1440, Beloch, *RG* 438. Salmon, op. cit., 260 n. 3, suggests that Livy mistakenly substituted Volaterrae for Volsinii.

[8] 12.7.

Samnites to the other consul, Cn. Fulvius Maximus Centumalus, who triumphed over them.[1] The *Fasti Triumphales* give Fulvius a triumph over both Samnites and Etruscans. Scipio's *elogium* says that he captured Taurasia and Cisauna, two towns in Samnium, and subdued Lucania,[2] but it says nothing about fighting in Etruria (Livy's account has in consequence often been rejected).[3] There are no other clear testimonia about the consuls' provinces, though Frontinus tells of a Fulvius Nobilior in Samnium and more especially in Lucania,[4] and of a Cn. Fulvius in the territory of the Faliscans,[5] and both have been held to be references to Cn. Fulvius Maximus Centumalus, the consul of 298.[6] There is no answer to this problem; it was not, as the *Fasti* show, simply a matter of transposing the two names. The important conclusion is that Livy's acquaintance with the annalists was at this point poor.

In 297 there is only the notice of news that the peoples of Etruria were discussing the seeking of peace terms, news that was supposed to have come from *legati* of Sutrium, Nepet, and Falerii.[7] Such a notice may have been an attempt to fill a gap in a year when Etruria was known not to have been assigned to either of the consuls, and the *legati*, who if authentic will have been recorded in the *annales*, may be a subsidiary fiction.

From 296 there is an additional cause for confusion in that the Samnite and Etruscan wars begin to combine, a Samnite army having retreated into Etruria.[8] Livy pretends to describe the Samnites' plea for Etruscan co-operation with what he regarded as suitable commonplaces.[9] An agreement seems to have been made that included Umbrians and Gauls: 'Tusci fere omnes consciverant bellum; traxerat contagio proximos Umbriae populos, et Gallica auxilia mercede sollicitabantur; omnis ea multitudo ad castra Samnitium conveniebat'.[10] This Samnite camp was clearly in Etruria. There follows an extended account of the military failure of the consul Ap.

[1] 12.3, 13.2.

[2] *CIL* i².7=*ILS* 1.

[3] Mommsen ad loc., etc.

[4] *Strat.* I 6.1–2, 11.2.

[5] *Strat.* II 5.9.

[6] For the former view, *MRR* i.174; for the latter, Beloch, *RG* 438. For another view of II 5.9 see below, p. 74.

[7] 14.3.

[8] 16.3.

[9] Cf. P. G. Walsh, *Livy, his Historical Aims and Methods* (Cambridge, 1963), 84.

[10] 18.2.

Claudius Caecus, to whom Etruria had been assigned, and the eventual success of Caecus and the other consul, L. Volumnius Flamma Violens, when the latter arrived in Etruria from Samnium. There was a dispute between the two consuls (which received more attention from the annalists than the war), known in a variety of versions and further complicated by the accounts of the behaviour of the same individuals in the following year. There were some themes in the tradition that could be elaborated at length, that Claudius was an incompetent general,[1] and that he was the representative of the Senate while Volumnius was the representative of the plebs. The only point in the narrative that Livy discussed was one that could hardly be decided, namely whether there was a letter from Claudius to Volumnius summoning him to Etruria; this version he found *in trinis annalibus*,[2] but apparently elsewhere he found the statement that Claudius claimed that he had sent no such letter. The dispute between the consuls that was imagined to have taken place when Volumnius arrived in Etruria is recounted at length and very much in favour of Volumnius.[3] When the battle with the Samnites and Etruscans began, Claudius vowed a temple to Bellona,[4] the dedication of which is referred to in his *elogium* and by Ovid.[5] It was possible to believe another story about the foundation of the temple—Pliny[6] attributes it to the Ap. Claudius who was consul in 495—yet the more widely known and much more credible foundation legend supports the tradition concerning the war (even though it was obviously the cause of the invention of some of the details of the story).[7] We are not told where this great battle took place,[8] but we are told the enemy casualties, 7,800 killed and 2,120 taken prisoner.[9] Such figures are given for a number of

[1] On the large subject of the denigration of the Claudii, cf. Walsh, op. cit., 89–90.

[2] 18.7.

[3] 18.9–19.13.

[4] 19.17–18, cf. 19.21.

[5] *CIL* i².1 p. 192, X, Ovid, *Fasti* VI 199–208 ('Tusco . . . duello', 201).

[6] *NH* XXXV 12.

[7] On the temple see S. B. Platner—T. Ashby, *Topographical Dictionary of Ancient Rome* (Oxford, 1929), 82–3.

[8] According to De Sanctis, op. cit., ii.354 n. 3, a precise site is always given for a battle of which we have an authentic tradition; but that is too sweeping, cf. H.-G. Plathner, *Die Schlachtschilderungen bei Livius* (Breslau, 1934), 24.

[9] 19.22.

subsequent battles, and in all the cases in the Etruscan and Umbrian wars they are theoretically possible figures, but they are to be rejected, not so much because no attempt is usually made to give Roman casualties,[1] as because even in later times Roman commanders did not apparently make great efforts to record the number of the enemy dead.[2] Yet in general there seems to be a solid tradition concerning the main events of this campaign, much elaborated as it is with other material.

There were fears of another war in Etruria later in the year:[3] after Volumnius had withdrawn again, there was information that the four peoples that had fought against Rome in the previous campaign were taking up arms. All this is conventional enough. The reports were taken so seriously at Rome that the Senate ordered a *iustitium* and a special levy. 'Nec ingenui modo aut iuniores sacramento adacti sunt sed seniorum etiam cohortes factae libertinique centuriati; et defendendae urbis consilia agitabantur summaeque rerum praetor P. Sempronius praeerat.'[4] Details about the *iustitium*[5] and the levy are likely to have been preserved in the annals and are likely to have formed the basis for this account. There follows some rhetorical elaboration of the anxiety at Rome about war with the four peoples.

The annalists built up the war of 295 into an elaborate set-piece. First of all in Livy there was a stylized dispute between the consuls P. Decius Mus and Q. Fabius Maximus Rullianus about who should have command in Etruria, that is of the war against the *quattuor gentes*, the one representing the plebeians, the other the patricians, the one youth, the other age.[6] The account is thoroughly pro-Fabian, Fabius winning the command by a unanimous vote of the people as well as of the Senate. Ap. Claudius Caecus had been in command in Etruria as praetor, and Fabius marched to Aharna, Arna in Umbria,[7]

[1] That seems to have been an established Roman tradition, cf. Oros. VII 10.4.

[2] Even in the *De Bello Gallico* such figures are few and approximate.

[3] 21.1–4, 21.11–15.

[4] 21.4.

[5] On *iustitia* in the annals see Ogilvie on Liv. III 3.6.

[6] A good analysis of the use of these motifs is provided by O. Schönberger, *Hermes*, lxxxviii (1960), 217–30.

[7] Livy does not distinguish at all carefully between places in Etruria and places in Umbria, apparently placing Aharna and Sentinum in Etruria.

to the camp of Claudius. Then there follows the story of how Fabius was so confident that he ordered the destruction of the stockade round the Roman camp (this is also recounted by Zonaras),[1] a story which is heavily biased against Claudius, like the story of his dispute with Volumnius in the previous year.[2]

In Livy the first battle of 295 takes place at Clusium, 'quod Camars olim appellabant', when Fabius had gone back to Rome 'ad consultandum de bello',[3] leaving the propraetor L. Scipio in charge of one legion. This force was besieged by the Senones Galli and eventually defeated.[4] This is clearly the first of the two battles that Polybius mentions in his account of the year,[5] saying that the Gauls and Samnites defeated the Romans *ἐν τῇ Καμερτίων χώρᾳ*. Various problems arise from this battle: on the topographical point, Livy is clearly misapplying his learning when he puts the battle at Clusium, and Camerinum was its real site.[6] There was some disagreement, as in the case of the battle of Sentinum, about who the peoples were who fought against Rome; Polybius says that they were Gauls and Samnites, Livy Gauls, but Livy knew some other versions of the battle besides his main one: 'Sunt qui Umbros fuisse non Gallos tradant, nec tantum cladis acceptum. . . . Similius vero est a Gallo hoste quam Umbro eam cladem acceptam, quod cum saepe alias tum eo anno Gallici tumultus praecipuus terror civitatem tenuit.'[7] Polybius must be right about the presence of the Gauls, in spite of the feebleness[8] of Livy's arguments for this view; but although their presence may merely have been inferred from the fact that the battle took place in Umbria, Umbrians may have been present on the anti-Roman side. Different versions of the battle gave different amounts of discredit to L. Scipio, and the version accepted by Livy (Polybius does not tell us who the Roman commander was) tried to exonerate Fabius by implausibly sending him off

[1] VIII 1.5. [2] 24.18–25.10. [3] 25.11.
[4] 26.7–13. [5] II 19.5–6.
[6] Niebuhr, *Römische Geschichte*, iii³.441 n. 637, De Sanctis, op. cit., ii.355 n. 2, and most scholars; otherwise R. Werner, *Der Beginn der Römischen Republik* (Munich–Vienna, 1963), 88–9, on the inadequate ground that Polybius should have written *Καμερίνων* instead of *Καμερτίων χώρα*.
[7] 26.12–13.
[8] Pais, op. cit., 531 n. 4.

to Rome for consultation at a time when his army was obviously likely to be attacked.[1] This question of blame is related to another matter about which Livy found controversy in his sources—did Fabius return to Rome for consultation *sponte sua* or at the summons of the Senate ('nam in utrumque auctores sunt'),[2] or was he compelled to return by Ap. Claudius, who in Rome exaggerated the dangers of the war? This last version is elaborated.[3] Fabius then graciously accepts the additional appointment of Decius to a command in Etruria.[4] 'Invenio apud quosdam extemplo consulatu inito profectos in Etruriam Fabium Deciumque sine ulla mentione sortis provinciarum certaminumque inter collegas quae exposui.'[5] Others gave more details of a quarrel between Claudius and the consuls and a quarrel between the consuls themselves. From the beginning of the war itself, Livy erroneously believes, 'constare res incipit'.[6] This extensive confusion was what happened when a personage whose career was glorified in the account of at least one important annalist was responsible for a major defeat of a Roman army. Livy's limitations in dealing with the variant versions are clear enough; his preference seems to be for the mean between extreme accounts, and he is naturally unable to resist the story of the conflict between Fabius and Decius. Yet at least he seems to regard this as one of the most disputed passages in these wars, on which point he was surely right.

The victory at Sentinum seems to have come to be regarded as a victory over the Gauls more than anyone else—as a nearby temple frieze of the second century suggests.[7] Others specified

[1] On the attempt to create an alibi for Fabius cf. Beloch, *RG* 440. He rejects altogether L. Scipio's propraetorship, because the praetorship is not among the offices mentioned in his *elogium*; so too S. Mazzarino, *Il pensiero storico classico* (Bari, 1966), i.2 288.

[2] 25.12.

[3] 25.13–18.

[4] 26.1–4.

[5] 26.5. This version presumably admitted Fabius' responsibility for the defeat.

[6] 26.7.

[7] The frieze of Cività Alba, fewer than five miles from Sentinum, described by A. Andrén, *Architectural Terracottas from Etrusco-Italic Temples* (Lund–Leipzig, 1940), 297–308, portrays the Gallic sack of Delphi and the repulse of the Gauls: surely the subject will have had a local reference in such a place. For this view cf. now S. Mazzarino, op. cit., i.2 284. The frieze is dated by Andrén to *c.* 180 B.C. (cf. P. J. Riis, *An Introduction to Etruscan Art* (Copenhagen, 1953), 108); by M. Zuffa, *Studi in onore di A. Calderini e R. Paribeni* (Milan, 1956), iii.288, to shortly after 150.

that Etruscans and Umbrians took part in one or both of the battles mentioned by Polybius, and the state of the annalistic tradition on that point needs discussion. As far as Polybius is concerned, his account is so brief that some marginal participation by the Etruscans and Umbrians could have gone unmentioned. Livy, however, preferred a version in which they were not present at the battle of Sentinum: in the main account the Etruscans and Umbrians were encamped separately from the Samnites and Gauls[1] and 'inter ipsum certamen Etrusci Umbrique iussi castra Romana oppugnare'.[2] This plan having been revealed to the consuls by spies from Clusium, an attack on the territory of Clusium was ordered that succeeded in diverting the Etruscans to defending it.[3] During the main course of the battle neither the Etruscans nor the Umbrians were present.[4] Livy rejects the account of those who wrote that the enemy forces consisted of 600,000 infantry (if this is the right reading), 46,000 cavalry, and 1,000 chariots, and that they included the Etruscans and Umbrians.[5] He himself, however, proceeds to mention the triumph of Fabius over the Gauls, Etruscans, and Samnites.[6] Some of our other sources state or suggest that the Etruscans were present: thus the *Fasti Triumphales* give Fabius a triumph over the Samnites, Gauls, and Etruscans, and (less important) *de viris illustribus* says that he triumphed over the Gauls, Umbrians, Marsi, and Etruscans.[7] Other sources follow Livy's main version, i.e. that the Etruscans were compelled to retire to the defence of their own territory,[8] and they added that the Umbrians did likewise. Information about the battle was distorted at an early date: the contemporary Duris said that there were 100,000 enemy casualties,[9] a figure that Livy cut down to 25,000.[10] There was also a natural

[1] 27.2. [2] 27.3.

[3] Adcock, *CAH* vii.612, comments sceptically on this plan; even if it is fictional that does not invalidate the view that the Etruscans and Umbrians were separate from the rest of the enemy. It is not clear where Frontinus (*Strat.* I 8.3) thought that the diversionary attack was made: 'adsicium' and 'adsitium' in the MSS. have been interpreted as 'ad Clusium' (Modius, to correspond with Livy) or 'ad Asisium' (Tennulius, followed now by Pfiffig, art. cit., 329); 'ad Clusium' in Livy X 27.5 should not be emended in any case, *pace* Pfiffig.

[4] 27.11. [5] 30.5.

[6] 30.8. [7] 32.1.

[8] Frontin. *Strat.* I 8.3, Oros. III 21.1–6.

[9] Diod. XXI 6.1 = *FGrH* 76 F 56.

[10] 29.17.

tendency to exaggerate the number of enemy peoples defeated (the theme being 'quattuor gentes conferre arma'),[1] and so Livy was probably right to reject any substantial presence of Etruscans or Umbrians.

Much of the account of the battle of Sentinum itself is inevitably a literary confection, redounding to the credit of Fabius. When the opposing armies were drawn up for battle, an omen was offered by the behaviour of a wolf and a hind.[2] When the battle begins, Fabius attempts to tire the enemy like Fabius Cunctator,[3] while Decius fights in a characteristically youthful way and eventually repeats the *devotio* that his father was supposed to have made at the battle of Veseris in 340,[4] anticipating the one that his son was supposed to have attempted at the battle of Ausculum in 279.[5] Whether the *devotio* of 295 was historical remains an open question.[6] There were, however, probably some authentic details of the battle in Livy's account, the death of the consul and also Fabius' vowing of a temple and the spoils to Jupiter Victor.[7]

As well as giving the casualty figures of the Gauls and Samnites, more moderate than some, but still surely imaginary, Livy claims to know the number of the Roman dead, 7,000 killed in the army of Decius and 1,700 in the army of Fabius; it must be suspected that these figures are also imaginary ones.[8]

Livy comes back later to Sentinum itself to discuss the exaggerated versions that he knew.[9] With the exaggerated estimates of the size of the enemy forces went the alleged additional presence on the Roman side of L. Volumnius as

[1] 21.12.

[2] The story is also told in Zonaras VIII 1.6. There may have been an annalistic notice. J. Bayet, *Hommages à A. Grenier* (Brussels, 1962), i.244–56, put forward an absurd theory that 'pro-Celtic, if not Celtic' versions lay behind parts of Livy's account of the battle; he seems unaware of the role of an initial Roman setback in a Livian battle-narrative.

[3] For a view of the influence of Cunctator on Rullianus, see Pais, op. cit., 570–1.

[4] 28.12–18, cf. VIII 9.12.

[5] Dio. fr. 40.43, Zonar. VIII 5.

[6] For, Münzer in *RE* s.v. Decius no. 16 (1901), col. 2283, De Sanctis, op. cit., ii.357 n. 2, Salmon, op. cit., 208 n. 1; against, B. Niese, *De annalibus Romanis observationes* (Marburg, 1886), p. iv, Beloch, *RG* 440–2, Pfiffig, art. cit., 329–30.

[7] 29.14, 29.18. On the temple see Platner-Ashby, op. cit., 306–7; and cf. S. Weinstock, *HTR* l (1957), 215–21, 246–7, on the historical context of the foundation.

[8] Roman casualty figures are also given in 31.7.

[9] 30.4.

proconsul with his army; but 'in pluribus annalibus' Livy found that the consuls alone won the victory while Volumnius was in Samnium, and of the minority version nothing more is known.[1] Then there was Fabius' triumph and the spoils received by each soldier: 'aeris octogeni bini sagaque et tunicae, praemia illa tempestate militiae haudquaquam spernenda'.[2] The number of eighty-two *asses* may suggest an accurate record, or, as with the casualty figures, an attempt to supply it.

There was some further fighting in 295 against the Clusini and Perusini, presumably as a result of the attempt to distract the Etruscans from Sentinum. Cn. Fulvius Maximus Centumalus, a propraetor, commanded an army that caused more than 3,000 casualties to these states and captured some twenty *signa militaria*.[3] There is nothing to show that this campaign was a duplicate of that of Fulvius in 298,[4] and there was probably an authentic annalistic notice behind it. Earlier in the year Cn. Fulvius had been stationed in the territory of the Faliscans,[5] and so this is probably the occasion of the story told by Frontinus according to which a Cn. Fulvius fought against a Faliscan army that had taken up a position 'in finibus nostris'.[6] There was in Livy's account still further fighting in Etruria in 295, for after Fabius withdrew war broke out again 'Perusinis auctoribus'.[7] This was dealt with by Fabius, and Livy gives some terse details; 4,500 Perusini were killed and 1,740 were taken prisoner and ransomed at 310 *asses* each, while all the rest of the booty was given to the soldiers.[8] These casualty figures have the same status as those of 296, and the size of the ransom is exposed to the same doubts as the one paid after Sentinum; in fact the whole incident may be a doublet of Fulvius' campaign against Clusium and Perusia.[9]

In Livy's main account of 294 a campaign was fought in Etruria by the consul L. Postumius Megellus.[10] He devastated

[1] 30.6–7. [2] 30.8–10. [3] 30.1–2.

[4] As Münzer, *RE* s.v. Fabius no. 114 (1909), col. 1810, and Beloch, *RG* 444, thought.

[5] 26.15, 27.5.

[6] *Strat.* II 5.9. Cf. Münzer in *RE* s.v. Fulvius no. 88 (1912), col. 264.

[7] 31.1.

[8] 31.3–4.

[9] So Münzer in *RE* s.v. Fabius no. 114 (1909), col. 1810.

[10] The campaigns of this year are discussed by Münzer in *RE* s.v. Postumius no. 55 (1953), cols. 936–8; cf. Cassola, op. cit., 194–5.

the territory of Volsinii, and defeated the inhabitants in a battle in which they suffered 2,800 casualties.[1] He then went to Rusellae, and having devastated its territory captured the town, the first major Etruscan town to fall to Rome in Livy. Here again casualty figures are given, prisoners 'amplius duo milia', killed 'minus duo milia'.[2] There follow the *indutiae* with Volsinii, Perusia, and Arretium, and a fine of 500,000 *asses* on each of the three states. All of this is acceptable, with the exception of the numbers of Etruscans killed. Postumius' successes were followed by a claim for a triumph, which was refused by the Senate and opposed by some tribunes—'posteroque die auxilio tribunorum plebis trium adversus intercessionem septem tribunorum et consensum senatus celebrante populo diem triumphavit.'[3] This triumph and the precedents cited[4] look like an attempt to claim popular authority over the granting of triumphs, an argument appropriate to the first century. The triumph appears in the *Fasti Triumphales*, but the circumstances in which it was granted, if not the fact itself, will have been invented.

Livy's main version of the commands of 294, according to which Postumius fought first against the Samnites and later in Etruria, and the other consul M. Atilius Regulus in Samnium and Apulia, is given also by Zonaras.[5] Livy goes on to discuss the divergent accounts of the wars of 294: according to Claudius Quadrigarius, Postumius campaigned unsuccessfully in the south, while Atilius campaigned in Etruria and earned a triumph. According to Fabius Pictor both consuls fought in Samnium and at Luceria (this was Atilius' battle in Livy's main version) and then an army was transferred to Etruria, by which consul he did not say; Fabius also told a version of the story of the vowing of the temple of Jupiter Stator at the battle of Luceria,[6] as did Livy in his main version.[7] Finally there are the *Fasti Triumphales*, in which Postumius triumphed over the Samnites and Etruscans and Atilius over the Volsones, i.e. Volsinienses, and the Samnites (in Livy's main version it was Postumius who fought against the Volsinienses). An exhaustive discussion of the development of the tradition is not possible here. The Jupiter Stator story is a solid element, though it may have

[1] 37.1–2. [2] 37.3. [3] 37.12. [4] 37.10. [5] VIII 1.8–9.
[6] 37.15. Cf. Platner-Ashby, op. cit., 303–4.
[7] 36.11.

been omitted from Claudius Quadrigarius' account. Presumably the *Fasti Triumphales* were trying to have the best of all possible versions by putting both consuls in both areas.[1] Since Livy reports Claudius' version in a single sentence, it is impossible to know how much he differed from Livy's main version—his reversal of the roles of the consuls may have been only part of the divergence. 'Et huius anni parum constans memoria est'[2]—yet even in this year there was some discernible agreement among differing accounts about which Etruscan towns (Volsinii and Falerii) were the targets of military operations.

In 293, 'legationes sociorum, a M. Atilio praetore in senatum introductae, querebantur uri ac vastari agros a finitimis Etruscis quod desciscere a populo Romano nollent . . .'[3] The *finitimi Etrusci* probably included the Faliscans, since they were largely involved in the subsequent war. The Faliscans were reported 'arma Etruscis iunxisse',[4] and after the *fetiales* had been sent *ad res repetendas*,[5] a fact that was surely mentioned in the *annales*, war was declared against them. This war was assigned to the consul Sp. Carvilius Maximus,[6] who attacked the town of Troilum, site uncertain,[7] and having agreed with 470 of the richest inhabitants to let them go for a consideration, took it by assault. 2,400 of the inhabitants were killed, fewer than 2,000 taken prisoner.[8] He also granted *annuae indutiae* to the Faliscans in exchange for 100,000 *asses* and a year's pay for his army.[9] He then celebrated a triumph, and with these and his Samnite spoils he paid *inter alia* for the building of the temple of Fors Fortuna. Most of this account can be accepted as based on annalistic notices, the number of Etruscans killed again being very suspect. Only the triumph that Carvilius celebrated over the Samnites is mentioned in the *Fasti Triumphales*, but that need not cause doubt about his activity in Etruria, since by any account his main fighting was in Samnium. The foundation

[1] Cf. Beloch, *RG* 444. [2] 37.13. [3] 45.4.
[4] 45.6. [5] 45.7. [6] 45.11.
[7] But Cluver's identification of Troilum with Trossulum, a town nine Roman miles to the south of Volsinii (Plin. *NH* XXXIII 9), is attractive, in spite of the objections of De Sanctis, op. cit., ii.362 n. 2.
[8] 46.10–12.
[9] This is rejected by Pfiffig, art. cit., 333–4, but the sources he cites do not say that the expedition of 292 was the first one undertaken in the new war against Falerii.

story of the temple of Fors Fortuna,[1] though not told elsewhere, is a strong element in the account.

It is not intended to defend Livy's use of his material as much as the quality of information available to him about this series of wars. Livy's vices as a historian have been exhaustively catalogued by many scholars. Not to mention the characteristics which his literary purposes give to the work, in this short section alone we can see that he did not read widely (298 B.C.), that when he did choose to discuss variant versions he sometimes chose problems that were inherently unanswerable (299, 295), and that the reasoning in his discussions is often puerile (302, 295). There were of course many things wrong with the annalistic tradition of the wars of 311 to 293: there were some confusions even in the lists of the highest magistrates and their provincial assignments (Livy at least attempted to discuss these problems); there was at least one doublet (Vadimon); the order of events was sometimes confused (310); defeats were concealed (311, 299); the number of the enemy was exaggerated (310); and it is clear that at the end of the second pentad of Livy the tradition was still very much affected by the standard view of several of the major *gentes*, the Valerii who reconciled the plebs, the Fabii (so often engaged in the Etruscan wars) with their selflessness and other virtues, the Claudii with their *superbia* and other vices. What has been established in this discussion of Livy is that there is seldom good reason to doubt the record when it concerns lists of those against whom war was made, embassies and public agreements, and the foundation stories of temples. Thus in existing modern accounts the influence of Pais and Beloch has led to an excessive degree of scepticism.

The wars with the Etruscans and Umbrians were not of course finished in 293,[2] but since our detailed knowledge of the

[1] Cf. Platner-Ashby, op. cit., 212–13.

[2] Some modern writers overstate the finality of the peace agreements that were made in 294. There is no reason to think that the *indutiae* made with Volsinii, Perusia, and Arretium were really *foedera*, or that the other Etruscan towns also made such agreements, as De Sanctis asserted, op. cit., ii.359 n. 3. Our knowledge of the years after 293 is slight, not only because of the loss of Livy, but because there is a lacuna in the *Fasti Triumphales* that extends in effect from 291 to 282. In spite of this it is clear that, even if they survived the campaign of 293, the *indutiae* with Volsinii were fairly soon broken (see below).

annalists' account of them ends then, it is convenient to summarize the military state of affairs. The danger to Rome in this war came from combinations of other powers, but on the north side of Rome the battle of Sentinum seems to change the balance of the situation, at least in the eyes of the annalists. Before that, Roman territory could still be entered by a combined army of Gauls and Etruscans; it was threatened by *finitimi Etrusci* in 293, but the Faliscan war of 293–292 must have been a desperate last, or rather penultimate,[1] measure—they were in danger of losing their independence, as the colonization of Nequinum must have shown them. For the first time in 294 a major town in central Etruria, Rusellae, fell to Rome, and though some of the towns were virtually impregnable, they were dependent at least for their military strength on the territory outside the towns themselves; that territory had now suffered from ten years of Roman depredation, and also from a major incursion by the Gauls in 299 (and no doubt from other minor ones). Of the Umbrians we hear relatively little during this decade; unlike the Etruscans they had scarcely been a threat to Roman territory even before Sentinum. When the Camerinum and Ocriculum alliances were supplemented by the colony of Narnia in 299 it was merely a question of when the Romans would choose to push their control further and what methods they would use.

4. *The Wars of 292–264*

The Faliscan war was carried on in 292, with some wider repercussions in Etruria; this we happen to know from Zonaras.[2] Then we have no specific information about the Etruscans or Umbrians for any particular year until 284. At the end of the *Periocha* of Livy XI there is the statement that the book 'res praeterea contra Vulsinienses gestas continet', which has a *terminus ante quem* of 284 because of the murder of the Roman *legati* at the beginning of Book XII; but the war does not necessarily belong to the end of the period 292–284. The *indutiae* of 294 were certainly broken, but it looks as if there was relatively little fighting between Romans and Etruscans in the span of Livy XI.

[1] There was a rebellion in 241.

[2] VIII 1.10. This is rejected by De Sanctis, op. cit., ii.362 n. 2, as a repetition of 293, without sufficient reason.

The campaigns in Etruria and the *ager Gallicus* in 284–282 have been the subject of extensive debates.[1] A brief attempt will be made to clarify the sequence of events, and also (something that has not been so often discussed) the effects on the Etruscans and Umbrians.

Polybius describes the war in his list of Gallic invasions:[2] ten years after the invasion of 295, i.e. in 284,[3] a large expedition of Gauls appeared and besieged Arretium; the Romans attacked them there and were defeated, ἐν . . . τῇ μάχῃ ταύτῃ Λευκίου τοῦ στρατηγοῦ τελευτήσαντος. M'. Curius was selected in his place. He sent *legati* to the Gauls to negotiate about prisoners, but they were killed. In their indignation the Romans immediately (ἐκ χειρός) invaded Gaul, and meeting the Senones in battle they killed most of them and expelled the rest, occupying the country and founding the colony of Sena. The Boii[4] were frightened by the expulsion of the Senones, and asked for and obtained the help of the Etruscans against Rome. The combined forces were defeated at Vadimon, ἐν δὲ τῇ μάχῃ ταύτῃ Τυρρηνῶν μὲν οἱ πλεῖστοι κατεκόπησαν, τῶν δὲ Βοίων τελέως ὀλίγοι διέφυγον. In spite of this the two peoples combined again in the next year to fight against Rome, but again they were defeated, καὶ διαπρεσβευσάμενοι περὶ σπονδῶν καὶ διαλύσεων, συνθήκας ἔθεντο πρὸς Ῥωμαίους. This happened in the third year before Pyrrhus' crossing into Italy[5] and the fifth year before the sack of Delphi. The other surviving notices of the war[6] are often referred to as if they were a single tradition, although they disagree considerably among themselves,[7] and none of them really purports to be a narrative as full as that of

[1] Apart from the works already mentioned, note Mommsen, *Römische Forschungen*, ii (Berlin, 1879), 365–75, E. T. Salmon, *CPh* xxx (1935), 23–31, G. Forni, *Athenaeum*, xxxi (1953), 204–14; cf. also B. Bruno, *La terza guerra sannitica* (Rome, 1906), 116–20, *MRR* i.188 n. 2, R. Werner, op. cit., 89–96.

[2] II 19.7–20.6.

[3] διαγενομένων δὲ πάλιν ἐτῶν δέκα.

[4] Here, it is generally held, the narrative passes into the next year, 283, although Polybius does not say so (cf. Walbank ad loc.); the assumption is not strictly necessary that that was what Polybius meant, cf. Forni, art. cit., 210–11.

[5] On chronological reckoning from this event, cf. G. Nenci, *Historia*, vii (1958), 277.

[6] Liv. *Per.* 12, Florus I 8.21, Eutrop. II 10, Oros. III 22.12–13, Dion. Hal. XIX 13.1, App. *Gall.* 11, *Sam.* 6, Dio fr. 38, Augustine *CD* III 17.2 and probably Frontin. *Strat.* I 2.7.

[7] Cf. Forni, art. cit., 209–10.

Polybius. In spite of this these notices have been used since Beloch to correct the Polybian account. In fact Mommsen's and De Sanctis'[1] faith in the Polybian version of these events can be shown to be substantially justified.

The supposed weaknesses in Polybius' account have been greatly overemphasized.[2] The most serious one is the disappearance from most, but not all,[3] of the non-Polybian tradition of the victory won by M'. Curius Dentatus,[4] and this can best be answered by supposing that Polybius' account of the victory was exaggerated[5] (and it may very well have been the case in 284 that the Senones had no intention in 284 of coming much further south than Arretium, so an immense victory was in fact not necessary); although in any case it is only in Appian that the silence on the subject is significant. Appian and Dionysius attributed the victory to P. Cornelius Dolabella, which was simply a confusion with the battle of Vadimon. Again, it is asked, if the Boii were almost wiped out in the battle of Vadimon in 283, how did they fight once more in 282? Some allowance can be made for rhetorical exaggeration of the slaughter at Vadimon, and in any case it is evident that the whole Boian nation was not involved in that battle. Again, if the colony of Sena (Gallica) was founded in 284, how did the Boii manage to get to the battle of Vadimon? This question misconceives the nature of a new citizen colony with 300 members.

There are some specific points on which other accounts contradict Polybius: as has been said, some sources give Dolabella as the successful commander in the battle against the Senones, but that was as a result of what happened at Vadimon. Polybius says that it was the Boii who lost the Vadimon battle,

[1] Op. cit., ii.376–9.

[2] The objections dealt with in this paragraph are those of Beloch, *RG* 453, largely followed by Salmon, art. cit., 24–5.

[3] As Forni points out, art. cit., 208 n. 2, though Cicero, Plutarch, and others give Curius three triumphs, in the *Fasti Triumphales* his triumph over the Samnites and Pyrrhus in 275 is given as his fourth (pp. 74–5); the third one must have come between 290, the date of his first two, and 282, when the lacuna in the *Fasti* ends.

[4] This has generally been explained by the theory that the Roman tradition wanted to date the Roman victory over the Gauls as soon as possible after the defeat, cf. Beloch, *RG* 452–3, Salmon, art. cit., 29; for a different solution, Forni, art. cit., 211–13.

[5] Cf. Salmon, l.c.

while Florus and Appian make it clear that they thought that it was the Senones. They simply failed to make the relatively subtle distinction between different varieties of Gauls that was familiar to Polybius. In the version of Livy's *Periocha* and Orosius, the Roman *legati* were murdered before, not after, the defeat of Lucius (Caecilius); Polybius' order is supported by Appian. There is not much to choose between these alternatives;[1] the whole story is in any case rather suspect,[2] all the more so since its chronological place in the narrative is uncertain. Another difficulty concerns the dating of the colony of Sena—again rather an open question, but not one where it can be shown that Polybius is likely to have been wrong. Lastly there is the praetorship of L. Caecilius: Polybius says that Caecilius was *στρατηγός*, i.e. probably consul,[3] when he lost the battle and his life, i.e. that these events took place in 284, which fits Polybius' statement that there had been ten years since 295. However, according to Livy's *Periocha*, Orosius, and Augustine, Caecilius was praetor at this time, which must be in 283; this is also by implication the view taken in the *Fasti Capitolini*.[4] That the war should have been put in the charge of a *praetor suffectus* (so to speak) after such a disaster seems most unlikely and the suspicion arises that the whole tradition of the involvement of a praetor depends upon a mistaken translation of *στρατηγὸς* in (say) Polybius or Fabius Pictor as 'praetor'.

Some information is added to the Polybian account by the other sources, but it is not of such a type that its omission is surprising. The full name of 'Lucius' and the Roman casualties in the battle near Arretium (seven tribunes of the soldiers and 13,000 men) are given, and after the battle there is said to have been a general rebellion of the Etruscans (Liv. *Per.*, Oros., Augustine). As stated above, the battle of Vadimon was won by P. Cornelius Dolabella in his consulship (283). Then lastly there is some information about the campaign of 282, if Beloch

[1] I fail to understand Pfiffig's reason (art. cit., 340) for rejecting Polybius' order.

[2] Beloch, *RG* 454 (but the absence of their statues from the *rostra* is not important—statues were sometimes taken down because of crowding); Salmon, art. cit., 31 n. 39, Walbank on Polyb. II 19.9, S. Mazzarino, *Il pensiero storico classico* (Bari, 1966), ii.1 286–7.

[3] On this cf. Mommsen, op. cit., 367; Walbank on Polyb. II 19.7; for other discussions cf. Werner, op. cit., 91 n. 1.

[4] In favour of Polybius cf. R. Syme, *CPh* l (1955), 129, against *MRR* i.188 n. 2.

was right to attribute a story of Frontinus to that year.[1] From Dionysius we know that the consul Q. Aemilius Papus was in command of the Etruscan war;[2] what Frontinus says is that a consul called 'Aemilius Paulus', fighting in an Etruscan war, 'apud oppidum coloniam [*sic*] demissurus exercitum in planitiem', detected an ambush of 10,000 Boii, whom he then defeated. Since both Frontinus and Dionysius say that Aemilius was fighting an Etruscan war, it creates unnecessary difficulties to refer *coloniam* (or whatever the correct text is) to Sena Gallica;[3] it is not possible to choose decisively between the Etruscan towns that may be meant.[4]

To what extent did the Etruscans participate in these campaigns? Here it is probably legitimate to make an addition to Polybius' account of the campaign of 284: when the Gauls besiege Arretium he makes no mention of Etruscans fighting on the anti-Roman side, but his account is brief, and Appian describes the anti-Roman force as consisting of Etruscans and Senones, the latter serving for pay.[5] Orosius also says that Caecilius was defeated by Etruscans as well as Gauls. There is no great difficulty in supposing that the Etruscans were divided, the Arretines on the Roman side, others against them. Polybius is clear that the Etruscans co-operated with the Boii in the following year,[6] and both peoples fought at Vadimon.

The only further information that we have about this war with the Etruscans comes from the *Fasti Triumphales*, which give a triumph [*d*]*e Etrusceis* to Q. Marcius Philippus, cos. 281, and one [*de V*]*ulsiniensibus et Vulcientib.*, i.e. over Volsinii and Vulci, to Ti. Coruncanius, cos. 280,[7] and from the *Periocha* of Livy XIII, where the notice 'res praeterea contra . . . Etruscos prospere gestas continet' refers to events between about the

[1] *Strat.* I 2.7; see *RG* 454–5. Some wish to refer this to 225, Forni, art. cit., 207 n. 4. The argument hinges on whether the latter could be called a *bellum Etruscum* as easily as the former, which I doubt. Cf. now Pfiffig, art. cit., 342 n. 117.

[2] XIX 13.1.

[3] So Salmon, art. cit., 26; the supposed manuscript reading 'apud oppidum coloniam' looks quite impossible.

[4] Populonium and Vetulonia have been most favoured.

[5] *Sam.* 6.1, cf. *Gall.* 11 (in the latter passage Pfiffig, art. cit., 340 n. 103, erroneously reads κατὰ Ῥωμαίους, which he takes to mean 'on the side of the Romans', for κατὰ Ῥωμαίων).

[6] II 20.1.

[7] Pp. 72–3.

middle of 280 and the middle of 278. Pyrrhus' arrival in Italy (May 280) was included in Livy XII, and since it quickly led to Coruncanius' withdrawal from Etruria for service in the Pyrrhic war,[1] Livy XIII probably dealt with fighting in Etruria later than Coruncanius' victory over Volsinii and Vulci. There is no further sign of the Etruscans in the *Fasti Triumphales*, although there are gaps in 275 and 272 where they could theoretically be restored. Evidently the συνθῆκαι of 282[2] were broken in the cases of some of the Etruscan towns.

In addition to the conflict with Caere in 274 or 273,[3] there was in fact one further outbreak of fighting in Etruria, a rebellion at Volsinii in 265. The implications of the incident for the type of settlement that had been made in Etruria and for the social system in the town are to be discussed later. There are some basic difficulties in our short notices: according to Florus[4] and Zonaras[5] the consul Q. Fabius Maximus Gurges was sent to deal with the situation. According to Zonaras he was killed in battle, and the silence of Florus can be explained by the brevity of his notice; in the *Fasti Capitolini* there seems not to be room for a suffect consul,[6] but Fabius' death need not have taken place early enough for the election of one. Zonaras refers to another consul, unnamed, who finished off the war.[7] Two other individuals are mentioned in the sources, M. Fulvius Flaccus, cos. 264, who was given a triumph *de Vulsiniensibus* by the *Fasti Triumphales*,[8] and Decius Mus, who according to *de viris illustribus* was the man who put down the revolt;[9] no office is specified for the latter. There is not room for all three of these men—Decius Mus either began or finished the war, or took *no* part in it. Decius is clearly the intruder, and

[1] Cf. App. *Sam* 10.3, Zonar. VIII 4.

[2] Polyb. II 20.5.

[3] See above p. 45. Sordi, *I rapporti romano-ceriti*, 128–33, suggested that 293 provided a better context than 273 for the notice about this in Dio. fr. 33—it was displaced to 273–272 because the coss. of 293 were also those of 272; but the text of Zonaras seems to indicate that the incident was supposed to have taken place in 274 or 273, not 272 (Sordi's note on this, p. 129 n. 3, is special pleading); cf. A. J. Toynbee, *Hannibal's Legacy* (Oxford, 1965), i.414 n. 1.

[4] I 16.

[5] VIII 7.

[6] Degrassi, p. 112, confirmed by his photograph.

[7] VIII 7.8.

[8] Fulvius' presence at the capture of Volsinii is confirmed by Festus 228L.

[9] 36.2.

his presence in the tradition can be explained by reference to one of his father's joint consulships with Fabius Rullianus and in particular by reference to 308 when his father made war against Volsinii.[1]

Our knowledge of Roman warfare against the Umbrians in the last stage of the conquest is even more scanty. In 266 the *Fasti Triumphales* give the consuls D. Iunius Pera and N. Fabius Pictor triumphs *de Sassinatibus*,[2] the Sassinates being the most northerly of the Umbrians. 'Umbri et Sallentini victi in deditionem accepti sunt' in Livy's *Periocha* must refer to the period 268–265 inclusively:[3] presumably the Sassinates surrendered in 266 and were the last Umbrians to do so.

For a time it might have been possible for the Etruscans to look forward to maintaining their political independence if they could obtain the co-operation of some at least of the Gallic tribes that were near enough to fight in Etruria; but the weakening or at least discouragement of those tribes in the Sentinum and Vadimon wars left the Etruscans without even those uncomfortable allies. The defeats suffered by the combined armies of Etruscans and Boii in 283 and 282 showed that even that co-operation was no longer effective, at least as far as central Etruria was concerned. After the final defeat of the Etruscans, the Umbrians were surrounded by those who were either allies or direct subjects of Rome, and it was a matter of small effort on Rome's part to reduce them to surrender; and after the final settlement in Samnium it was duly done.

[1] Liv. IX 41.6. [2] Pp. 74–5. [3] XV.

III

THE ROMAN *FOEDERA*

1. *The* Foedera *in Etruria*[1]

WHAT constitutional form did Rome's relations with the Etruscan states north of the Ciminus assume after the conquest?[2] In the absence of Livy's account of the crucial years we have to rely on miscellaneous indications from later periods and arguments about what the Romans are likely to have done. In fact a good case can be made for believing that Rome contracted *foedera* with the Etruscan states, and that case is argued in this section. The fact that there is no explicit reference to such a *foedus* except in the case of Falerii[3] is, in the absence of Livy's account, of no significance—their existence can be inferred from other evidence. To argue that the *foedera* were the constitutional form of Rome's relations with Etruria

[1] An earlier version of this section, making substantially the same points, appeared in *Historia*, xiv (1965), 282–92.

[2] Previous discussions by K. J. Beloch, *It. Bund* 119–21, 160–4, *RG* 451–9, 607–12, A. N. Sherwin-White, *RC* 115–17; cf. G. De Sanctis, *Storia dei romani*, ii (Turin, 1907), 397–8, T. Frank, *Klio*, xi (1911), 376–81, J. Göhler, *Rom und Italien* (Breslau, 1939), 19–20, E. T. Salmon, *Phoenix*, xvi (1962), 116–17. A. J. Pfiffig, *Die Ausbreitung des römischen Städtewesens in Etrurien und die Frage der Unterwerfung der Etrusker* (Florence, 1966) (cf. *Historia*, xv (1966), 193–6), is wayward, and not all of his opinions are discussed here. On *foedera* in general see Mommsen, *Römisches Staatsrecht* (Leipzig, 1887), i³.246–57, iii.590–606, E. Täubler, *Imperium Romanum*, i (Leipzig, 1913), H. Horn, *Foederati* (Frankfurt-a.-M., 1930), A. Heuss, *Die völkerrechtlichen Grundlagen der römischen Aussenpolitik in republikanischer Zeit* (*Klio, Beiheft* xxxi, Leipzig, 1933), U. von Lübtow, *Das römische Volk* (Frankfurt-a.-M., 1955), 641–4, E. Badian, *FC*, esp. 25–8, Ernst Meyer, *Römischer Staat und Staatsgedanke*² (Zürich–Stuttgart, 1961), 229–30, F. De Martino, *Storia della costituzione romana*, ii (Naples, 1954), 30–43, 93–6, W. Dahlheim, *Deditio und Societas, Untersuchungen zur Entwicklung der römischen Aussenpolitik in der Republik* (Munich, 1965), substantially reproduced in *Struktur und Entwicklung des römischen Völkerrechts im dritten und zweiten Jahrhundert v. Chr.* (Munich, 1968).

[3] 'The fact remains that there is only one example of a *foedus* between Rome and an Etruscan state' (Falerii), Sherwin-White, *RC* 117; cf. Salmon, art. cit., 116. Cf. also Beloch, *RG* 609: 'Der Abschluss eines *foedus* mit Rom wird überhaupt . . . nur von Volsinii ausdrücklich berichtet' (for the evidence for this see below).

is not of course to neglect the fact that the political realities of Rome's relations with Etruria after the conquest had many other aspects: they are dealt with in Chapters IV and V. Here the fact of the *foedera* is established, and in Section 3 their terms are discussed.

In an inscription of the third century A.D.[1] the inhabitants of Tarquinii refer to themselves as *Tarquinienses foederati*, an allusion to a supposed *foedus* of republican date between Tarquinii and Rome.[2] To this allusion there are two parallels. The first is provided by the Umbrian Camertes, who in a well-known inscription[3] thank Septimius Severus for the confirmation of their *foedus*, a *foedus* in this case which is attested by Cicero and Livy.[4] The second parallel, which has been debated, is that of Capena, and although Roman arrangements with the town, which was conquered well before the towns under discussion, are not directly relevant to those which she made with the main body of Etruscan towns, it is to the point to discover whether Capena was in fact referring to a supposed republican *foedus* with Rome, and if so, whether that *foedus* was authentic. The *Capenates foederati* appear in nine inscriptions.[5] In two of these the town is called the *municipium Capenae foederatum*,[6] in one it is called the *municipium Capenatium foederatorum*[7] and in another it is called a *municipium*.[8] The earliest of these inscriptions belongs to the second half of the first century A.D. Since Beloch, it has generally been admitted that there was a small category of Italian *municipia* that had *foedera* with Rome (though there have been various explanations of this phenomenon),[9] and

[1] P. Romanelli, *NSA* 1948, 267; =*AE* 1951, no. 191.

[2] Cf. P. Veyne, *Latomus*, xix (1960), 429–31. Pfiffig, op. cit., 43–4, implausibly supposes that the *foedus* was a local synoecism like the one that he and others have imagined at Capena (see below).

[3] *CIL* xi.5631=*ILS* 432.

[4] Cic. *Balb.* 46, Liv. XXVIII 45.20.

[5] *CIL* xi.3873 (=*ILS* 409), 3876a (Bormann expressed doubt about the genuineness of this inscription), 3932 (=*ILS* 5770), 3936 (=*ILS* 6588); and five further inscriptions published by G. Mancini in *NSA* 1953, 18–28 (nos. 1–3, 5–6). Of these 3932, dedicated by T. Flavius Aug. Lib. Mythus and his wife, is probably the earliest; cf. Veyne, art. cit., 429 n. 4.

[6] *CIL* xi.3932, Mancini no. 6. 'MCF' in Mancini no. 5 may be an abbreviation for this or for *municipium Capenatium foederatorum*.

[7] Mancini no. 3.

[8] *CIL* xi.3936.

[9] *It. Bund.* 117–23, *RG* 376–81; for further references see A. J. Toynbee, *Hannibal's Legacy* (Oxford, 1965), i. 397–403, Dahlheim, *Deditio und Societas*, 99 n. 1, *Struktur und Entwicklung*, 113 n. 7 (Dahlheim is himself doubtful).

Capena surely was one of them. It has sometimes been suggested[1] as an alternative explanation that the federation concerned was not with Rome at all but was a sort of synoecism of three towns of the *ager Capenas* itself. This is improbable.[2] Comparisons which are cited are with Cirta (Numidia), the Vocontii (Narbonensis), and Aricia. At Cirta the relevant inscriptions do not employ the term *foederatus.*[3] In the case of Aricia (a town that received *civitas sine suffragio* in 338), when Cicero refers to it as a 'municipium ... vetustate antiquissimum, iure foederatum, propinquitate paene finitimum, splendore municipium honestissimum',[4] he is emphasizing the strength of its ties with Rome, and the *foedus* that he mentions is clearly with Rome and not with the other members of the old religious league that had its centre at Aricia.[5] Indeed in order to provide a parallel Cicero would have to be referring to a *foedus* that existed among the Aricini themselves, and of that there is no trace. As for the Vocontii, Pliny lists 'Vocontiorum civitatis foederatae duo capita Vasio et Lucus Augusti'.[6] This case is theoretically more open,[7] but it is worth noticing that he lists one other state in this section as *foederata*, namely Massilia, whose *foedus* was with Rome.[8] Thus there is no real evidence that *Capenates foederati* could have meant Capenatans federated

[1] First by G. B. De Rossi in *Bulletino di Archeologia Cristiana*, ser. 4.ii (1883), 115; followed by Sherwin-White, *RC* 52–3, A. Bernardi, *Athenaeum*, xx (1942), 93–4, by the archaeologists who have discussed the enlarged corpus of Capenatan inscriptions, Mancini, art. cit., 27, G. D. B. Jones, *PBSR* xxx (1962), 124–5, xxxi (1963), 107–10, and now by Pfiffig, op. cit., 19–21 (cf. also De Sanctis, op. cit., ii.433). For an early critique see Bormann, *CIL* xi. p. 571. The question was also examined, without a decision, by E. Manni, *Per la storia dei municipii fino alla guerra sociale* (Rome, 1947), 43–4.

[2] As Veyne points out, art. cit., 431, there is no known instance in which *foederati* means *foederati inter se.*

[3] *CIL* viii.8318, 8319 (=*ILS* 5533); on the Cirta federation cf. J. Heurgon, *Libyca*, v (1957), 7–24, P. Veyne, *Latomus*, xviii (1959), 571–5.

[4] *Phil.* III 15.

[5] Dahlheim, ll.cc., attempting to detract from the accuracy of Cicero's remarks, says that Aricia was not the oldest *municipium*—but Cicero does not say that it was.

[6] *NH* III 37, cf. VII 78.

[7] *TLL* (s.v. *foederatus*, col. 994.77 (Vollmer)) takes the Vocontii to have been federated with Rome. So H. Rolland in *RE* s.v. Vocontii (1961), col. 705.

[8] III 34. This is the only explicit reference to the Massiliot *foedus*, other than a vague one in Justin XLIII 5.3, but in view of the town's well-known friendship with Rome (cf. H. Philipp, *RE* s.v. Massalia (1930), cols. 2132–5, Dahlheim, *Deditio und Societas*, 130–3, *Struktur und Entwicklung*, 138–41) it must have been with Rome that Massilia was federated.

among themselves, and the natural interpretation is a *foedus* with Rome. Nor is the positive evidence for the alleged synoecism of Capena at all strong. To enjoy all the honours of three towns, as did a man who appears in *CIL* xi.3939 (from Capena),[1] was not extraordinary,[2] and it was a mistake to associate the three *decuriae* which occur in *CIL* xi.3888 and 7764 with the supposed three towns of the *ager Capenas*.[3] The existence of a Roman settlement at Nazzano, so-called *Civitas Sepernatium*,[4] the supposed site of the third town of the federation, may be admitted; but its administrative identity (which is argued from the *decuriones* and *seviri* of *CIL* xi.3871) is perhaps open to question. The *Capenates foederati inter se* are then probably chimerical, and the town was in fact claiming to recall an ancient *foedus* with Rome.[5] Though the making of this *foedus* is nowhere explicitly recorded, it was presumably made when *pax* was given to the Capenates in 395:[6] Livy implies that the peace was to be permanent (and so could not have had *indutiae* as its instrument). The cases of both Camerinum and Capena thus provide some support for the view that Tarquinii had an

[1] 'trium cibitatium o m onoribus fuctum'.

[2] Cf. De Ruggiero, *Diz. Ep.* s.v. *honos*, 948.

[3] Jones, *PBSR* xxx.124–5. The *decuriae* concerned are a well-attested part of the organization of the *apparitores* of the capital. For *scribae librarii quaestorii trium decuriarum*, etc., see *CIL* vi.1802–35, 1869–70, 32294–6, 32312 (=xi.3888), ii.3596; cf. *ILS* ch. vii; E. Kornemann in *RE* s.v. *scriba* (1923), cols. 850–6; A. H. M. Jones, *JRS* xxxix (1949), 38–55=*Studies in Roman Government and Law* (Oxford, 1960), 151–75.

[4] First devised by De Rossi, art. cit., 125–6. For details of the evidence, see Jones, *PBSR* xxxi.107–10. The name of the site is of little importance for the present purpose: but the three fragmentary inscriptions *CIL* xi.3868–70 do not settle the issue, for they give no indication that a place name is being used.

[5] The view was first stated by P. L. Galletti, *Capena municipio de' Romani* (Rome, 1756), 3; so Beloch, *It. Bund* 119–20, etc.

[6] See above, p. 42. I agree with Dahlheim, *Deditio und Societas*, 99 n. 1, *Struktur und Entwicklung*, 113 n. 7, that the purpose of referring to the *foedus* under the Empire was 'die Verleihung einer gewissen Ehrenstellung', but that is not adequate evidence that there had never really been one (and Capena is not, *pace* Dahlheim, known to have been a Caesarian colony—cf. below, p. 308. Veyne, *Latomus*, xix (1960), 434, also suggests that the claim of the Capenates to an ancient *foedus* may have been false, adducing as another example of such pseudo-antiquarianism an inscription from Thuburnica in Proconsular Africa (P. Quoniam, *CRAI* 1950, 332–6=*AE* 1951, no. 81) in which an allegedly false claim was made that Marius founded the colony; but the fact that Pliny listed T. as an *oppidum civium Romanorum* (*NH* V 29) does not show that the claim was false—cf. *MRR* ii.645, L. Teutsch, *Das Städtewesen in Nordafrika in der Zeit von C. Gracchus bis zum Tode des Kaisers Augustus* (Berlin, 1962), 17–18.

ancient *foedus* with Rome, for they too commemorated under the Empire *foedera* that were of solely antiquarian interest.

In 216 B.C. a 'Perusina cohors' is said to have fought with the Roman army,[1] and that in Campania and not in defence of the (probably already devastated) *ager Perusinus*. At their first appearance the Perusini are said to have been 'eodem nuntio quo Praenestini paucos ante dies Casilinum compulsi'. 'Compulsi' is an inappropriately strong word to use in this context unless the Perusini were providing their cohort *ex foedere*;[2] and the Praenestini had probably been given a *foedus*.[3] In 208 a force of 180 Etruscan cavalry is said to have fought with M. Claudius Marcellus in Apulia.[4] Etruria thus made a contribution to the war in manpower as well as in supplies, and there is no reason whatsoever to believe that these occasions were the only ones on which contributions of manpower were made. Several times during this war the Etruscans are referred to by Livy as 'socii', whose sufferings at the hands of Hannibal are supposed to have provoked C. Flaminius in 217.[5] In XXVIII 45.13–20 Livy gives a detailed account of the contributions of material made by allies to Scipio Africanus' forces in 205.[6] He passes directly from his description of the contributors as *socii* to the statement that the first contributors were the

[1] Liv. XXIII 17.11, 20.3.

[2] Cf. L. E. Matthaei, *CQ* i (1907), 195–200, on the differences in Roman behaviour towards those who provided military assistance *ex foedere* and those who provided it more voluntarily.

[3] Beloch, *RG* 380.

[4] Liv. XXVII 26.11.

[5] XXII 3.7, 4.1.

[6] 'Scipio cum ut dilectum haberet neque impetrasset neque magnopere tetendisset, ut voluntarios ducere sibi milites liceret tenuit et, quia impensae negaverat rei publicae futuram classem, ut quae ab sociis darentur ad novas fabricandas naves acciperet. Etruriae primum populi pro suis quisque facultatibus consulem adiuturos polliciti: Caerites frumentum sociis navalibus commeatumque omnis generis, Populonenses ferrum, Tarquinienses lintea in vela, Volaterrani interamenta navium et frumentum, Arretini tria milia scutorum, galeas totidem, pila gaesa hastas longas, milium quinquaginta summam pari cuiusque generis numero expleturos, secures rutra falces alveolos molas quantum in quadraginta longas naves opus esset, tritici centum viginti milia modium et in viaticum decurionibus remigibusque conlaturos; Perusini Clusini Rusellani abietem in fabricandas naves et frumenti magnum numerum; abiete et ex publicis silvis est usus. Umbriae populi et praeter hos Nursini et Reatini et Amiternini Sabinusque omnis ager milites polliciti. Marsi Paeligni Marrucinique multi voluntarii nomina in classem dederunt. Camertes cum aequo foedere cum Romanis essent cohortem armatam sescentorum hominum miserunt'.

Etruscans, the people of Caere, Populonium, Tarquinii, Volaterrae, Arretium, Perusia, Clusium, and Rusellae. Among the contributors listed, Caere and most of the Sabines probably possessed *civitas sine suffragio* (some at least of the latter were already full citizens);[1] but the Marsi, Paeligni, and Marrucini all had *foedera* with Rome,[2] as did the Camertes. So most of those whom Livy describes as *socii* may well have been regarded by him as federated with Rome. Matthaei, who first analysed the usage of the term *socius* in a systematic way, asserted that it had a strict sense—'it may be taken for granted without discussion that all *socii* were *foederati*'.[3] However Horn, who analysed the Ciceronian evidence, defined a *socius* simply as 'alles, was nicht civis und nicht hostis ist, d.h. was der grossen Interessengemeinschaft des römischen Reichs angehört'.[4] This may be rather too sweeping, but it is much nearer to the truth than Matthaei's view.[5] Of course *foedera* produced *societas*, and so there is a natural connection between the two terms,[6] but by itself Livy's description of the Etruscans as *socii* does not show that they were *foederati*. Similarly Polybius' description of the Sabines and Etruscans as σύμμαχοι is not very helpful:[7] elsewhere he uses the word about states that did not have *foedera* with Rome.[8]

Some have thought that the material contributions of 205

[1] For the case for thinking that most of the Sabines were still *cives sine suffragio*, see L. R. Taylor, *VDRR* 59–66, and (for the view that the Sabines enfranchised in 268 were the people of Cures) A. Afzelius, *Die römische Eroberung Italiens 340–264 v. Chr.* (Copenhagen, 1942), 21–3. P. A. Brunt now argues (*Hommages à M. Renard* (Brussels, 1969), ii.121–9) that the Sabines had all received the full citizenship.

[2] Liv. IX 45.18.

[3] Art. cit., 188. This view of hers is misunderstood by S. I. Oost, *CPh* lxii (1967), 150.

[4] Op. cit., 11. The passages of Cicero which he cites are *II Verr.* I 85, II 166, III 9, V 133, V 139, *Manil.* 48, *Dom.* 85, *Balb.* 27, *Prov. Cons.* 12, *Lig.* 2, *Leg.* III 18.

[5] Dahlheim's objections, *Deditio und Societas*, 161 n. 1, *Struktur und Entwicklung*, 163 n. 1, are without force; cf. Oost, l.c. The breadth of meaning that the word has in Livy can readily be seen in D. W. Packard, *A Concordance to Livy* (Cambridge, Mass., 1968). For example, when Rhodes did not have a *foedus* with Rome (Polyb. XXX 5.6, Liv. XLV 25.9), *socius* and cognate words could be applied to it (XLII 19.8, 45.4, etc., cf. H. H. Schmitt, *Rom und Rhodos* (Munich, 1957), 68).

[6] Cf. for example, Liv. XXXI 29.2–3, XXXVI 42.1.

[7] II 24.4–5; Pfiffig, *Historia*, xvii (1968), 336, is in error.

[8] For example at I 40.1—Panormus, which was a *civitas libera*, Cic. *II Verr.* III 13. For this usage cf. Horn, l.c., E. Bikerman, *RPh* lxv (1939), 346–7.

were (nominally at least) voluntary,[1] as the soldiers in Scipio's army were volunteers. Livy does not say so, and they may have been made *ex foedere*. To one critic the material character of the contributions 'recalls the war indemnities which were earlier the regular accompaniment of the *indutiae*'.[2] More will be said of the unconvincing suggestion that Rome's relations with Etruria continued after the final conquest to be governed by *indutiae*; in any case there is no reason to suppose that federated states did not make material contributions but only contributions of manpower. Examples of such contributions on the part of some undeniably federated states are not hard to find: grain was provided by Naples in 215[3] and by the Marrucini in 207.[4]

Zonaras says that it was because they were ἔνσπονδοι with Volsinii that the Romans intervened there on behalf of the local *domini* in 265.[5] *Indutiae* for forty years had been made in 294,[6] but quite apart from the fact that these *indutiae* could hardly have formed the legal basis for the action of 265, they must have been annulled, for fighting had taken place on at least two occasions between the two dates.[7] The word ἔνσπονδος must normally imply a formal agreement of some kind,[8] and if the σπονδαὶ really were the legal basis on which Rome intervened, they can hardly have been other than a *foedus*. Florus tantalizingly says that the Volsinienses were the last of the Italians to *venire in fidem*, 'implorantes opem adversus servos quondam suos ...',[9] which leaves unclear the position of Volsinii before 265. There was, admittedly, a temptation for the Romans to bestow legal propriety on their actions after the event even if there had been no real legal basis for intervention,

[1] Mommsen, *History of Rome* (Eng. trans.), ii.354, and recently E. T. Salmon, *Phoenix*, xvi (1962), 117 n. 25, A. J. Pfiffig, *Historia*, xv (1966), 205–6. For assistance offered by *foederati* beyond what was required *ex foedere* cf. Liv. XXXVI 4.5–10, Matthaei, art. cit., 196.

[2] Sherwin-White, *RC* 117. [3] Liv. XXIII 46.9. [4] XXVII 43.10.

[5] VIII 7.4: πρὸς Οὐλσινίους ἐστράτευσαν ἐπ' ἐλευθερίᾳ αὐτῶν· ἔνσπονδοι γὰρ ἦσαν αὐτοῖς.

[6] Liv. X 37.4.

[7] Liv. *Per.* 11; *Fasti Triumphales* for 280, Degrassi, pp. 72–3, 545.

[8] Mommsen, *Römisches Staatsr.*, iii.654 n. 3, held that the term ἔνσπονδοι could be applied to those who were *sine foedere liberi et immunes*; certainly τὸ ἔνσπονδον is sometimes contrasted with τὸ ὑπήκοον in Dio (e.g. XXXVIII 10.1, LIV 9.1), and Britain in 57 B.C. is ἔνσπονδος (XXXIX 1.2).

[9] I.16.

and a cynical view of Roman motives in this case was expressed by Metrodorus of Scepsis. The intervention was made in order to reinstate the *domini*, an action that was fully in accord with general Roman policy in Etruria, as will be argued in detail in the next chapter. It is indeed even possible that the *foedus* made some specific provision for Roman assistance to the *domini*, for their security from the *servi* was already threatened by the time that the war with Rome ended. In any case, though Zonaras' statement is obscure, it adds some support to the view that there was a *foedus* between Rome and Volsinii by 265.

In 211 Cn. Fulvius Flaccus, who as a praetor in the previous year had been badly defeated by Hannibal in Apulia and was now facing a charge of *perduellio*, went into exile at Tarquinii.[1] 'Id ei iustum exilium esse scivit plebs', Livy reports. This *plebiscitum* has been thought anachronistic,[2] but it seems a natural course to take to impede the return of an exile. On balance, however, it is better to take this *plebiscitum*, for which we know no precise parallel, not as a regular formality but as a measure specially required for some reason by Fulvius' case. The special circumstance which made the *plebiscitum* necessary has sometimes been found in Fulvius' choice of Tarquinii as his place of exile,[3] but more probably the *plebiscitum* represented some form of *damnatio*, similar to that passed in the case of M. Postumius Pyrgensis in the previous year,[4] declaring that Fulvius deserved to be in exile. If Livy had intended to describe a declaration that *exilium* at that place was *iustum*, he could easily have done so; and in any case such a decision would very probably have been the prerogative of the Senate. Fulvius had not yet been tried of course—the case was to have been heard on the day when he in fact left Rome.[5] If this interpretation is

[1] Liv. XXVI 3.12.

[2] M. I. Henderson, *JRS* xli (1951), 72 n. 11, cf. Sherwin-White, *RC* 119. Mrs. Henderson thought that Livy's statement that the plebs passed acts of recognition of this *exilium* and that of 212 sounded 'illogical and suspicious'. No reason for such an act existed, she argued, before the existence of *aquae et ignis interdictio*; but see the text.

[3] Mommsen, *Römisches Staatsr.*, iii.49 n. 3; Sherwin-White, *RC* 118–19.

[4] Liv. XXV 4.9–11.

[5] On the legal problems raised by Livy's phrase see, for the most recent detailed discussion, G. Crifò, *Ricerche sull' 'exilium' nel periodo repubblicano*, pt. i (Milan, 1961), 167–91. Crifò holds (183–4) that the *plebiscitum* declaring *iustum exilium* is

correct, there was already *ius exilii* at Tarquinii. Of the places where it was permitted to spend exile, Polybius says: ἔστι δ' ἀσφάλεια τοῖς φεύγουσιν ἔν τε τῇ Νεαπολιτῶν καὶ Πραινεστίνων, ἔτι δὲ Τιβουρίνων πόλει καὶ ταῖς ἄλλαις πρὸς ἃς ἔχουσιν ὅρκια.[1] Places in Italy which are known to have received exiles between this period and the Social War are Tibur and Praeneste,[2] Naples[3] and Nuceria.[4] All these towns had *foedera*.[5] Some have supposed that it would have been pointless for Polybius to specify Naples, Praeneste, and Tibur if there was *ius exilii* at all *civitates foederatae*,[6] but they could easily have been picked out as the most usual though not the sole legally permissible recipients of exiles.[7] Tarquinii, like the other towns to which exiles went, probably had a *foedus* with Rome. Even if the *plebiscitum* of 211 referred to the legality of Fulvius' place of exile, Tarquinii is not thereby shown to have lacked a *foedus*, but only a *foedus* containing this *ius*.

Taken separately each of the positive arguments that have been set out in favour of *foedera* between Rome and most of the

simply an indication that the exile had taken advantage of a legally permissible means of avoiding the judgement of the plebs on a specific crime 'che l'assemblea della plebe aveva competenza o interesse a conoscere'; its function, he claims, was to inform the plebs that the right of judging the crime continued to exist (presumably even if the exile claimed to have exchanged his Roman citizenship for that of another state). This is possible. But the view of H. Legras, *Nouvelle Revue hist. de droit fr. et étr.*, xxxii (1908), 598–601, that the *plebiscitum* contained an attribution of guilt to the exile (cf. J. Bleicken, *Das Volkstribunat der klassischen Republik* (Munich, 1955), 111 n. 7) is more attractive. Ordinary judgement presented serious difficulties if the accused was absent. This is not the context in which to debate these issues: the point is that good sense can be made out of Livy XXVI 3.12 without supposing that he refers to the establishment of a Tarquinian *ius exilii*, which, if the town had a *foedus*, should probably have existed already.

[1] VI 14.7.

[2] Liv. XLIII 2.10.

[3] XXIX 21.1.

[4] Cic. *Balb.* 28.

[5] For Tibur and Praeneste, cf. Liv. VIII 14.9; for Naples, VIII 26.8; for Nuceria, IX 41.3.

[6] F. W. Walbank ad loc., following Schweighäuser's translation of ταῖς ἄλλαις πρὸς ἃς ἔχουσιν ὅρκια as 'aliis urbibus quibus hoc iure foedus intercedit cum Romanis'; also followed by Sherwin-White, *RC* 118 n. 5.

[7] Crifò, op. cit., 127 n. 6, denies that a *foedus* was a prerequisite of *iustum exilium* on the grounds that Cicero says that the treaty of Gades contained nothing about citizenship (*Balb.* 35); but 'nihil est enim aliud in foedere nisi ut pia et aeterna pax sit' is obviously not true in a literal sense, and in any case the *foedus* was quite abnormal. The view that a *foedus* was a prerequisite of *iustum exilium* goes back to L. M. Hartmann, *De exilio apud Romanos inde ab initio bellorum civilium usque ad Severi Alexandri principatum* (Berlin, 1887), 3–6.

Etruscan states could possibly be discounted: together they are very strong indeed. Furthermore we know of no alternative mechanism of Roman policy which could have seemed appropriate for this case. Our knowledge of the legal framework on which Rome built her external policies at this period is admittedly very imperfect—no ancient source attempts to give a systematic and comprehensive account of its development[1]—but it seems highly improbable that a whole category of relationships has disappeared from the sources. What instruments other than *foedera* do we know of? No relationship based merely on *sponsio* is ever said to have been established in any case remotely similar to that of the Etruscans.[2] In Sicily during the First Punic War, a very few years after the end of the Etruscan wars, the policy of awarding freedom without a treaty was already being applied (as Badian has convincingly argued).[3] The case was quite different, however, from the one which we are discussing: it is inconceivable that Rome relied on a 'strong moral claim' for the security of Etruria.[4] *Amicitia* without a *foedus* was inappropriate too: it was only an indication that diplomatic relations existed,[5] and it could have no place in a vulnerable frontier area close to the city, especially when that area was one about which Rome was (according to Livy at least) habitually over-anxious.[6] It is most unlikely that *indutiae* were made the permanent basis of Roman relations with Etruria, for while much about *indutiae* is obscure, at least it is

[1] Some remarks are made by Polybius of course (VI 13.4–5, 14.11, 15.9–10); cf. the description given by Antiochus' envoy Menippus of the three types of *foedus*, Liv. XXXIV 57.7–9 (a Polybian passage, cf. H. Nissen, *Kritische Untersuchungen über die Quellen der vierten und fünften Dekade des Livius* (Berlin, 1868), 162–4).

[2] Cf. 'Ocriculani sponsione in amicitiam accepti' (Liv. IX 41.20) (probably in 308, in spite of Beloch, *RG* 424–5); 'pax per sponsionem facta' (IX 5.2) after the Caudine Forks—although in this case most held that a *foedus* was made.

[3] *FC* 37–43, against the view of Sherwin-White, *RC* 150, that it dated from Flamininus' declaration of Greek freedom at the Isthmian Games of 196.

[4] Badian's phrase, *FC* 44, for Rome's relations with Sicily. Hiero's anti-Roman record was scarcely comparable with that of the Etruscans.

[5] Cf. Badian, *FC* 68, etc.

[6] For this over-anxiety, see VI 22.1, VII 21.9, IX 29.2 ('nec erat ea tempestate gens alia cuius secundum Gallicos tumultus arma terribiliora essent . . .'), X 4.1, XXVII 24.6. But since it may have been theorized that *metus Etruscus*, like *metus Punicus*, had once kept the Romans united (cf. M. Gelzer, *Philologus*, lxxxvi (1931), 275 = *Vom Römischen Staat* (Leipzig, 1943), i.94 = *Kleine Schriften*, ii (Wiesbaden, 1963), 51, A. La Penna, *Athenaeum*, xli (1963), 262), it may never have existed.

clear that they were only made when Rome regarded the resulting peace merely as an interval in unfinished hostilities—and this applied to *indutiae* of long duration as well as to the shortest. There is no evidence that they did anything more than stop the fighting and (generally but probably not in every case) establish a penalty which the weaker party had to pay.[1] While an enemy seemed likely to continue significant resistance, a *foedus* was a privilege which was not permitted to him, for a *foedus* had the function of making a permanent settlement of the constitutional relations of the two states and frequently of defining what part of the territory of the defeated was to be Roman *ager publicus*, and it sanctioned the terms of the settlement with fetial ritual, which called down destruction on the party 'per quem . . . fiat quominus legibus dictis stetur'.[2] On several occasions before their final defeat Etruscans made requests for *foedera* and received instead only *indutiae*,[3] but when in 343 the Faliscans asked for a *foedus* (presumably accepting that the terms would be seriously disadvantageous to themselves) this was taken to be a token of the end of their resistance.[4] Finally, it used to be maintained by some that a few at least of the towns north of the Ciminus received a grant of *civitas sine suffragio*—Tarquinii and Vulci were the cases suggested.[5] This too is improbable: we should have expected perhaps to have heard of these grants of citizenship in accounts of the events of 91 and 90 (for example at Appian, *BC* I 49.213), and known uses of the device are decidedly different.[6]

[1] On *indutiae* see especially F. De Martino, *Storia della costituzione romana*, ii (Naples, 1954), 34–40.

[2] Liv. IX 5.3 (cf. XXXIV 57.7). Mommsen (*Römisches Staatsr.* i³.251 and n. 1) doubted whether the fetial ritual was always enacted (cf. Täubler, op. cit., 147, Beloch *RG* 128), but the cases which he cites do not prove his point.

[3] E.g. Liv. IX 37.12, 41.7.

[4] Liv. VII 38.1: 'Huius certaminis fortuna et Faliscos, cum in indutiis essent, foedus petere ab senatu coegit'; translated by Sherwin-White, op. cit., 116, as 'the result of this battle forced even the Faliscans, although they enjoyed a truce, to ask the Senate for a treaty.' This, he claims, 'stresses the rarity' of Rome's contracting *foedera* in Etruria. But the sentence continues, 'et Latinos iam exercitibus comparatis ab Romano in Paelignum vertit bellum'; it is better to translate, 'the result of this battle both forced the Faliscans . . . and turned the Latins . . .'

[5] Beloch, *It. Bund* 58–61; accepted by Bormann, *CIL* xi. p. 510, for Tarquinii. Dahlheim, *Struktur und Entwicklung*, 33, thinks that Falerii probably received the *civitas sine suffragio* after the rebellion of 241, but there is no evidence.

[6] Anagnia, Arpinum, and Trebula, and some at least of the Aequi and Sabini

It could scarcely have fulfilled its function if it had been extended to states as alien from Rome as Tarquinii and Vulci were at this time. Some *praefecturae* were established in Etruria after the conquest, Saturnia, Statonia, and Praefectura Claudia Foroclodii,[1] but they were not on the sites of the leading towns with whose rulers Rome made peace.

Need we suppose that all the Etruscan towns north of the Ciminus had the same or closely similar relations with their Roman conquerors? The final series of major campaigns against Etruria which began in 311 is known to have involved most of the chief towns: Arretium, Clusium, Cortona, Perusia, Rusellae, Tarquinii, Volaterrae, and Volsinii are mentioned by Livy, and Vulci appears in the *Fasti Triumphales.* All resisted Rome: it is difficult to find in the sources any reason why Rome should have treated them differently after their defeat. All the contributors of 205 listed by Livy, except Populonium, are thus specifically known to have taken part in these wars. Of the towns that are known to have fought, only Volsinii[2] and Cortona[3] are absent from the 205 list. There is little evidence that the famous League of the Twelve Peoples was a coherent political force in the century before the conquest,[4] and it cannot

were the most recent cases (cf. Liv. IX 43.24 for Anagnia; X 1.3 for Arpinum and Trebula; for the evidence on the Aequi see Taylor, *VDRR* 56 n. 35, 81 n. 7; on the Sabines, see above p. 90). All were more susceptible to assimilation, although some of them were further from the city, than Vulci and Tarquinii. Cf. P. Fraccaro, *Atti del Congr. internaz. di diritto romano* (Rome, 1933), i.200–3= *Opuscula* i (Pavia, 1956), 107–10. All the recipients of *civitas sine suffragio* mentioned here had offered only brief resistance to Rome (cf. IX 43.2—the Anagnini were *novi hostes*) or, in the cases of the Sabini and Aequi, had been submissive for a considerable period before their final subjugation; and the sites were of obvious importance in still unfinished wars.

[1] See below, pp. 149–52.

[2] The town may have been given more generous terms after the collaboration of the ruling class with Rome in 265 and the transference of the surviving loyalists from Orvieto to Bolsena.

[3] Cortona had suffered particularly severely at the hands of Hannibal in 217, Liv. XXII 4.1: 'quod agri est inter Cortonam urbem Trasumennumque lacum omni clade belli pervastat . . .' Pfiffig, art. cit., 197 n. 18, is perverse on this point.

[4] L. Pareti, *RPAA* vii (1929–31), 89–100=*Studi minori di storia antica*, i (Rome, 1958), 283–94, and G. Camporeale, *PP* xiii (1958), 5–25, have argued against the political character of the League. P. Lambrechts, *Essai sur les magistratures des républiques étrusques* (Brussels–Rome, 1959), 25–8, and V. Bellini, *RIDA* ser. 3.vii (1960), 273–305, are insufficiently critical towards the sources. The only specific reference to the Twelve Peoples in the last century of independent Etruria is Liv. VII 21.9 ('terror inde vanus belli Etrusci, cum coniurasse duodecim populos

be cited as an argument for the probability of a unified Roman policy in Etruria; but the decision to withstand Rome was common to all the towns of the region.

The problem of deciding what ultimate sources there were concerning the *foedera* contracted by Rome and what documentary evidence there was on Rome's relations with other states in unsolved. For practical reasons there must surely have been at Rome in the third century B.C. documentary evidence of some kind on this subject, at least a record of *ex foedere* obligations to Rome. Polybius' list of the Roman and Italian forces of 225 probably derives in the end from documentary evidence,[1] and Livy believed that the names of the *sponsores* of the *pax Caudina*, which must also have derived from a document, were still known.[2] A *formula sociorum* is a document particularly likely to have been preserved,[3] and it is difficult to believe that the *annales* failed to preserve an accurate record of *foedera* for this period. Locally, there must also have been records of the *foedera*, and the *Tarquinienses foederati* inscription may have had such backing.[4]

The Etruscan *foedera* were the instrument of an intelligible Roman policy. Colonization was limited—in the area of the federated states only Cosa,[5] in the territory of the Vulci, followed closely after the peace, and even after the foundation of the citizen-colony of Saturnia in 183, a strikingly small proportion of Etruria was occupied by Roman colonists, by comparison with, for example, Umbria. Various explanations have been offered of this state of affairs in Etruria, for example that the Etruscans had not fought hard enough against Rome to deserve the harshness of colonization[6]—which is hardly true; or that

fama esset . . .'), which is uninformative. The only clear reference to a *concilium* of the *principes Etruriae* is Liv. X 16.3; almost all the Etruscans were brought to agreement—but the meeting looks suspiciously dramatic.

[1] II 24.

[2] IX 5.4: 'nominaque omnium qui spoponderunt extant'; hence problems, however, cf. Beloch, *RG* 397–8.

[3] Referred to by Liv. XLIII 6.10, XLIV 16.7, cf. XXII 57.10. Whether it was identical with the *formula amicorum* is unclear; cf. most recently A. J. Marshall, *AJPh* lxxxix (1968), 54 n. 35 (who thinks that they were more probably not separate documents).

[4] Cf. M. W. Frederiksen, *JRS* lv (1965), 187.

[5] For the evidence concerning colonization in Etruria between the conquest and the Social War see the first section of Chapter V.

[6] T. Frank, *Klio*, xi (1911), 378–9.

Rome wished to win the co-operation of the Etruscans in resisting the Gauls[1]—but the Etruscans could obviously not be relied upon to fight with the Romans and against the Gauls unless some active form of control was exercised in Etruria; or that the Apennines were at this point good protection against the Gauls and the Etruscans 'could bear the brunt of the invasion'[2]—which again assumes too much loyalty to Rome on the part of the Etruscans. It has been suggested that colonization was limited by the supposed Roman belief that the Etruscans were unusually unsusceptible to assimilation[3]—but assimilation was not in any case among the conscious purposes of Roman colonization in the third century.[4] Etruscan society in fact offered to the conquerors a more economical method of ensuring security than colonization. It was so sharply divided between the class of the *principes* and the serf class that Rome was able to enlist the help of the former against the latter. In some at least of the towns concerned the position of the *principes* was insecure; Rome gave them her invaluable support—on condition that they maintained the loyalty of their towns to the Roman state. The evidence for this class-division, and Roman policy concerning it, are discussed in the next chapter.

2. *The* Foedera *in Umbria*

About the arrangements made in Umbria after the conquest there are only scraps of information.[5] According to Livy,[6] 'Umbri et Sallentini victi in deditionem accepti sunt', probably in 266: this, however, probably concerned only the most northern of the Umbrians, since there is no sign of any other warfare in Umbria after 295, and the enemy of 266 appear in the *Fasti* as the Sassinates; whatever the arrangements were with the majority of the Umbrians, they were probably made at some time before 266. Apart from the colonization of Narnia in 299, we have evidence of Roman agreements with two Umbrian states well before the conquest of the greater part of Umbria, namely the agreements with Camerinum and Ocriculum in 310 and 308.[7]

[1] Ibid., 379.
[2] Fell, op. cit., 150.
[3] Frank, *CAH* vii.661.
[4] See below, pp. 158–9.
[5] See Beloch, *It. Bund* 164–5, *RG* 559–61, 605–7, Salmon, art. cit., 116–17.
[6] *Per.* 15.
[7] Liv. IX 36.7–8, 41.20.

Except for the colony at Narnia, probably all the Umbrian states had *foedera* with Rome after their defeat. Spoletium became a Latin colony in 241, and there were a number of citizen-communities (Fulginiae and probably Interamna Nahara, Plestia and Tadinum) of unknown date—the evidence for these is discussed in Chapter V. The Umbrians in general appear later as allies of Rome: among those who provided troops for Rome in 225 were *οἱ . . . τὸν ᾿Απεννῖνον κατοικοῦντες Ὄμβροι καὶ Σαρσινάτοι*,[1] and *Umbriae populi* were among the contributors to the African expedition of 205.[2]

There is some evidence concerning the *foedera* of particular towns. There was a strong tradition of the *aequum* or *aequissimum foedus* of Camerinum, mentioned by Cicero ('Camertinum ⟨foedus omnium⟩ foederum sanctissimum atque aequissimum'),[3] and by Livy,[4] and 'renewed' by Septimius Severus.[5] There are difficulties in Livy's story of the making of this *foedus* in 310,[6] and the terms described are inappropriate to the *foedus omnium aequissimum*—the Roman envoy was told to inform the Romans that 'commeatum exercitui dierum triginta praesto fore, si ea loca intrasset, iuventutemque Camertium Umbrorum in armis paratam imperio futuram'. In spite of these difficulties, Livy's notice probably corresponds to an authentic record of a *foedus* with Camerinum, and the *aequissimum foedus* resulted from exceptional circumstances. The *foedus* clearly continued to exist until the Social War, Marius having on a famous occasion enfranchised two cohorts of Camertes. A recent attempt to revive an old view that the Camertes were already Roman citizens in the time of the elder Cato was entirely misguided.[7]

[1] Polyb. II 24.7.

[2] Liv. XXVIII 45.19.

[3] *Balb.* 46. The supplement is Madvig's: the meaning of the text is in any case clear. The *foedus* is also mentioned in s. 47.

[4] XXVIII 45.20. The *foedus* is also mentioned by Val. Max. V 2.8.

[5] *CIL* xi.5631=*ILS* 432: 'Imp. Caesari L. Septimio Severo . . . caelesti eius indulgentia in aeternam securitatem adque gloriam iure aequo foederis sibi confirmato Camertes p.p.' (A.D. 210).

[6] See above, p. 56.

[7] G. Radke, *Gymnasium*, lxxi (1964), 216; cf. H. Nissen, *Italische Landeskunde*, ii (Berlin, 1902), 388. The view is based on Cato's statement (Festus 268.9–14L=*ORF*[2] fr. 56) 'Camerini cives nostri oppidum pulchrum habuere, . . . Cum Romam veniebant, prorsus devertebantur pro hospitibus ad amicos suos.' The reference is obviously to the old Latian town of Cameria or Camerium (Liv. I 38.4, Tac. *Ann.*

Iguvium had an explicitly attested *foedus*,[1] which like that of Camerinum is known still to have been in existence at the time of Marius. That the people of Ameria were *peregrini* shortly before the Social War can be inferred, as has been pointed out,[2] from Cicero's statement that the elder Sex. Roscius was 'gratia atque hospitiis florens hominum nobilissimorum',[3] if he was using the word *hospitium*, as he regularly did, in its strict sense, to refer to a relationship between a Roman and a *peregrinus*; that contributes to the view that Ameria had a *foedus* with Rome, for it eliminates the only other real possibility—that the Amerini were Roman citizens. The people of Ocriculum were in 308 'sponsione in amicitiam accepti',[4] and that presumably led to a *foedus*. Tuder is also a case where we have evidence that the town did not have Roman citizenship before the Social War: it was in Book IV of his history that Sisenna stated that they received it.[5]

There is good evidence then for Roman *foedera* with Camerinum and Iguvium and some evidence for Roman *foedera* with Ameria, Ocriculum, and Tuder. It cannot be established that any other particular town in Umbria was a *civitas foederata*, but the evidence cited indicates that most of them were. Furthermore, while we know that a considerable number of towns had a separate administrative existence at a later period of their history, there are few for which this was demonstrably the case in the third century; yet the physical character of the territory makes it easy to believe that it was politically very much fragmented. The towns concerned are Arna,[6] Asisium, Attidium, Fulginiae, Hispellum, Matilica, Mevania, Mevaniola, Pitinum Mergens and Pisaurense, Sarsina, Sentinum, Sestinum,

XI 24, etc.); Cato's past tenses as well as the other evidence about the *foedus* of Camerinum make that clear. Weissenborn anticipated Nissen in associating this passage with Camerinum (on Liv. IX 36.7, 4th edn., 1870); since Nissen does not even mention Cameria in this passage, one may suspect that it was an oversight, not a considered view. Radke has also argued that friendly relations between Rome and Camerinum went back to the early fourth century, but see G. Vitucci in *Problemi di storia e archeologia dell'Umbria, Atti del I convegno di Studi Umbri* (1963) (publ. Gubbio–Perugia, 1964), 292–7.

[1] Cic. *Balb.* 46–7.

[2] L. R. Taylor, *VDRR* 85 n. 18.

[3] *Rosc. Am.* 15.

[4] Liv. IX 41.20.

[5] Fr. 119P: 'Tamen Tudertibus senati consulto et populi iusso dat civitatem.'

[6] On the status of Arna, Fulginiae, and Matilica cf. below, pp. 153–4.

Tifernum Mataurense and Tiberinum, Trebiae, Tuficum, Urvinum Hortense and Mataurense, and Vettona. Although Umbrian peoples naturally allied themselves with each other for military purposes, there is no evidence worthy of the name that there was an Umbrian League of any importance above the individual states.[1]

There were thus many *civitates foederatae* in Umbria as in Etruria, but Roman control was exercised in different ways in the two regions. At least after the Roman citizen-communities had been established in Umbria, probably in the third century, the area was in a sense dominated by the colonies in Umbria itself and in the *ager Gallicus* and by the other Roman territory in Umbria and immediately to the south and east among the Sabines.

3. *The Character of the* Foedera

Were the *foedera* that Rome made with the Etruscan and Umbrian states *foedera aequa*? There is one excellent case of a *foedus* in this region that was *aequum* and indeed *omnium aequissimum*, namely that of Camerinum; thereafter argument begins. Recently it has been maintained that *foedera aequa* were widely used in Italy,[2] and also that the Etruscans and Umbrians were privileged in this respect.[3] It is my contention that there were few if any *foedera aequa* in Etruria or Umbria other than that of Camerinum.

One misconception about the Umbrian *foedera* needs to be eliminated at once, that the character of the Camerinum *foedus* provides any evidence for that of the others.[4] The date of the *foedus* was probably based on reliable evidence, and it is difficult to believe that Cicero and Livy were in error when they insisted on its exceptionally favourable terms. The Umbrians did not fight as hard to defend their independence from Rome,

[1] *Contra* U. Coli, *Problemi di storia e archeologia dell'Umbria, Atti del I Convegno di Studi Umbri*, 154–7.

[2] Badian, *FC* 25–8, Dahlheim, *Deditio und Societas*, 106 n. 2, 109, *Struktur und Entwicklung*, 119 n. 21, 121.

[3] E. T. Salmon, *Phoenix*, xvi (1962), 116–17, hesitant about the exact nature of these privileges, but seeming to favour *foedera aequa* in both areas; on Umbria cf. G. Vitucci in *Problemi di storia e archeologia dell'Umbria*, etc., 291, who takes the Camerinum *foedus* as typical.

[4] Salmon, Vitucci, ll.cc.

at least in the period described in Books IX and X of Livy, as the Etruscans did, but there is no reason to doubt that most if not all of the other Umbrian states (with the exception of Ocriculum, for which see below) had helped to make war against Rome. That being the case, the circumstances in which they made *foedera* with Rome were quite different from Camerinum's circumstances in 310.

No third-century treaty between Rome and an Italian state was made between equal powers, yet Rome made concessions in the form of *foedera aequa* when circumstances suggested or required them. What is difficult to decide is whether, in the cases of states that had been defeated by Rome and had come *in dicionem p.R.* or *in fidem*, the inequality of the states was always made explicit in the subsequent *foedera*. Badian compares the situation in Italy with the Delian League, and suggests that when many of the Italian states came into alliance with Rome they were unequal *de facto* but not *de iure*.[1] Yet it was patent that the majority of the *foedera* were the consequences of military defeats, and there is no real reason to suppose that the Romans attempted to conceal behind a mask of diplomatic language the real obligations (for which see below) that the *foedera* imposed on most of the allies. For practical reasons these obligations must have been made clear and they were surely embodied in the *foedera*; and if the *iustum bellum* was already a Roman preoccupation[2] there was all the more reason to make explicit the obligations of allies who might one day rebel.

The description of the *tria genera foederum* that Livy puts into the mouth of Antiochus' envoy Menippus,[3] speaking before the Senate, is not without its value in this respect: 'unum cum bello victis dicerentur leges; ubi enim omnia ei qui armis plus posset dedita essent, quae ex iis habere victos, quibus multari eos velit, ipsius ius atque arbitrium esse; alterum, cum pares bello aequo foedere in pacem atque amicitiam venirent...' Juridical precision is not to be expected in these words, but their implication that an *aequum foedus* was made only when the parties were *pares bello* or (the third type of *foedus*) when they had not

[1] *FC* 26–7.
[2] On this issue see M. Gelzer, *Hermes*, lxviii (1933), 165=*KS* iii (Wiesbaden, 1964), 91, and *KS* ii (1963), 319 n. 34.
[3] XXXIV 57.7–9. Cf. above, p. 94 n.1.

been at war at all is not without force. It is somewhat difficult to suppose that Polybius or Livy can have produced a seriously erroneous account of the *tria genera*. Sherwin-White complained that Livy omitted from between the first and second types precisely the situation that the Romans experienced most often in Italy—'cum impares bello iniquo foedere in pacem atque amicitiam venirent'[1]—but the actual circumstances in which a so-called *foedus iniquum* was made could perfectly well be described by the words 'cum bello victis dicerentur leges'. The weaker party to the *foedus* retained its independence, but the terms of the *foedus* were imposed. Menippus' description does not establish that no state that made a *foedus* with Rome after suffering any military defeat *ever* had a *foedus aequum*, but it supports the view that those who were not *pares bello* were not generally given *foedera aequa*.

Of what *foedera aequa* other than the Camerinum *foedus* do we know between 338 and the end of the conquest of Italy?[2] Heraclea had a *foedus* that was *aequissimum*,[3] but it was also said by Cicero to have been 'prope singulare',[4] that is to say almost uniquely favourable, and it is obvious why it should have been so favourable, since it was made 'Pyrrhi temporibus C. Fabricio consule' (278 B.C.).[5] Naples and Heraclea hesitated to accept the Lex Julia of 90 'cum magna pars in iis civitatibus foederis sui libertatem civitati anteferret',[6] and it can therefore be assumed that the *foedus* of Naples was quite a favourable one.[7] Livy's statement that in 326 the Neapolitans came back voluntarily into the friendship of Rome ('ipsos in amicitiam redisse')[8] suggests that it was a *foedus aequum*, yet the proconsul Q. Publilius Philo was given a triumph 'quod satis credebatur obsidione domitos hostes in fidem venisse'.[9] It is certainly of interest that Livy can say of the same occasion that the Neapolitans came *in fidem* and that they came *in amicitiam*; but we

[1] *RC* 113.

[2] This paragraph and the succeeding one are directed against the arguments of Badian, l.c.

[3] Cic. *Arch.* 6.

[4] *Balb.* 50.

[5] Ibid.

[6] Ibid. 21.

[7] Horn, op. cit., 85.

[8] VIII 26.6.

[9] 26.7. The triumph was over the Palaeopolitans according to the *Fasti Triumphales*. On this incident see especially De Sanctis, op. cit., ii.301–2, Dahlheim, *Deditio und Societas*, 34–6, *Struktur und Entwicklung*, 63–4.

do not know for certain that the Neapolitan *foedus* was technically *aequum*,[1] or that it reached its final form in 326—may not Naples too have profited from the presence of Pyrrhus? Furthermore Livy does recognize that it was rather illogical to award a triumph in such circumstances. The case scarcely establishes that states that came *in fidem* after military defeat were regularly given *foedera aequa*. Again, it may have been in the war with Pyrrhus that Velia, which seems to have had some ostensibly independent foreign relations after it has been conquered by Rome in 293,[2] received its favourable *foedus*. Badian further suggests that the *foedus* made with the Picentines in 298[3] was *aequum*,[4] which is reasonable, and that the ones made in 304 with the Marrucini, Marsi, Paeligni, and Frentani also were—however the Marsi and Paeligni at least were *not* 'quite undefeated'.[5]

Two other cases mentioned by Livy are supposed to show the ready availability of *foedera aequa*. The Teates Apuli had a *foedus* with Rome, broke it, were defeated, and received another *foedus*. The way in which Livy describes the making of this second *foedus*[6] is taken to show that a rebellious *civitas foederata* would ordinarily, when it was reconquered, receive a *foedus aequum*. The passage is to be understood quite differently: the reason that Livy gives as the (only) one for the Teates' being able to aspire to a *foedus aequum*—and this reason turned out not to be strong enough for them to get one—is given in the first part of the crucial sentence ('id audacter spondendo . . .'). They boldly promised that they would ensure that the Romans enjoyed peace throughout Apulia, but even that was not enough in the circumstances to get them a *foedus aequum*. All this tells us in fact is that in Livy's view a state could in theory receive a *foedus aequum* even after it had been defeated and had made a *deditio* to Rome, if it could provide Rome with some really important benefit. Another passage that has been somewhat

[1] See Dahlheim, *Deditio und Societas*, 106 n. 2, *Struktur und Entwicklung*, 119 n. 21.

[2] H. Bengtson, *Historia*, iii (1954–5), 457–8, Badian, *FC* 27 n. 5.

[3] Liv. X 10.12.

[4] *FC* 27, cf. Sherwin-White, *RC* 114 n. 5.

[5] Badian, ibid.; see Liv. IX 41.4, E. T. Salmon, *Phoenix*, xiv (1960), 53.

[6] IX 20.7–8: 'Inclinatis semel in Apulia rebus Teates quoque Apuli ad novos consules . . . foedus petitum venerunt, pacis per omnem Apuliam praestandae populo Romano auctores. Id audacter spondendo impetravere ut foedus daretur neque ut aequo tamen foedere sed ut in dicione populi Romani essent.'

misused is Terentius Varro's statement to the Campanians after Cannae: speaking of the Capuan *deditio* of 343, he says 'foedus aequum deditis . . . dedimus'.[1] The *deditio* referred to here was, at least in Livy's view, not of the kind made by states that surrendered in war, but it was a voluntary submission, made with a request for Roman protection against a third party (the Samnites).[2] This was not the kind of act of *deditio* that most Italian states made in the late fourth and third centuries. The specific evidence concerning the *foedera aequa* in Italy is thus far from showing that they were commonly given. They were only available to states much stronger in relation to Rome than most *dediticii* were, and much stronger than most of the Etruscan and Umbrian states were.

It is not to be assumed then that any state in Etruria or Umbria had a *foedus aequum* with Rome unless some specific evidence can be cited. Apart from Camerinum, Ocriculum is the state most likely to have had one,[3] since when the *sponsio* was made in 308 there had evidently been no military conflict. There is no real reason to add Iguvium,[4] for although its *foedus* is mentioned by Cicero in conjunction with that of Camerinum,[5] that was merely because Marius had enfranchised an Iguvine as well as some Camertines;[6] in fact Cicero's silence about Iguvium when it was worthwhile to mention the equality of the Camertine *foedus* suggests that the Iguvine *foedus* was not *aequum*.

It is obviously very unlikely that any of the states that had land taken away from them to become Roman *ager publicus* (see below) had *foedera aequa*; Tarquinii and Vulci at least are thus excluded.

Certain conclusions can be reached about the detailed terms of the *foedera* other than *foedera aequa* that were made with the Etruscan and Umbrian states. The clause 'maiestatem populi

[1] Liv. XXIII 5.9.

[2] On this type of *deditio*, which was also in Livy's mind when he wrote about Naples, see Heuss, op. cit., 80–3, Badian, *FC* 35, Dahlheim, *Deditio und Societas*, 22–40, *Struktur und Entwicklung*, 52–67.

[3] Thus Sherwin-White, *RC* 114.

[4] As does De Sanctis, op. cit., ii.349.

[5] *Balb.* 47.

[6] Given the context nothing definite can be inferred from the words 'dicat (Marius) . . . a se ex coniunctissima atque amicissima civitate fortissimum quemque esse delectum; neque Iguvinatium neque Camertium foedere esse exceptum', etc.

Romani comiter conservanto' that Cicero regarded as a mark of the inequality of the *foedus* with Gades,[1] may or may not have been part of unequal third-century Italian *foedera*;[2] there must in any case have been more detailed provisions. There must, first of all, have been detailed provisions concerning the obligations of the allies to provide troops for Rome.[3] In a number of cases there must have been clauses about the confiscation of allied land. The allied Etruscan states that are known to have lost part of their land to Roman settlements of various kinds, Vulci, Tarquinii, and perhaps others,[4] probably lost it by the *foedera*, although, as has been said, there was only one colony that was set up in the immediate aftermath, namely Cosa. Graviscae was sent out in 181 'in agrum Etruscum, de Tarquiniensibus *quondam* captum',[5] which suggests that the land was confiscated at the time of the conquest. How much *ager publicus* was created in the territory of the other Etruscan and Umbrian states? There is no clear evidence on this point from the period just before the Social War, and Plutarch's famous story about Tiberius Gracchus' observations in Etruria can be understood without supposing that there was other *ager publicus* besides that already mentioned.[6] In 274 or 273 Rome confiscated no less than half its territory from Caere, apparently on the mere pretext that the Caeritans wanted to make war against Rome.[7] It looks as if Rome was being inordinately voracious of territory at this time; on the other hand coastal territory near Rome was obviously particularly useful to Rome, and nothing definite can

[1] *Balb.* 35–7: 'Nihil est enim aliud in foedere [with Gades] nisi ut PIA ET AETERNA PAX sit. Quid id ad civitatem? Adiunctum illud etiam est, quod non est in omnibus foederibus: MAIESTATEM POPULI ROMANI COMITER CONSERVANTO. Id habet hanc vim, ut sit ille in foedere inferior. Primum verbi genus hoc 'conservanto', quo magis in legibus quam in foederibus uti solemus, imperantis est, non precantis. Deinde cum alterius populi maiestas conservari iubetur, de altero siletur, certe ille populus in superiore condicione causaque ponitur cuius maiestas foederis sanctione defenditur.' Cf. Proculus in *Dig.* XLIX 15.7.1 on the significance of such a clause. For a similar clause in the Aetolian treaty, cf. Polyb. XXI 32.2, Liv. XXXVIII 11.2.

[2] For, Sherwin-White, *RC* 114–15; against, Badian, *FC* 26; no definite conclusion is possible. Cf. H. G. Gundel, *Historia*, xii (1963), 293–4.

[3] There is no reason to think that the military obligation 'restava nell' ombra', as De Martino holds, op. cit., ii.94.

[4] See Chapter V, Section 1.

[5] Liv. XL 29.1.

[6] See below, pp. 203–4.

[7] Dio fr. 33.

be inferred from this about the treatment of, say, Clusium and Perusia. The confiscation of land was a fairly regular procedure when unequal *foedera* were made: witness the treatment of the Marsi when they were given their second *foedus*[1] and the Frusinates, who lost one-third of their territory,[2] again, however, when a particular punishment was thought necessary.[3] Appian implies[4] that the confiscation of land to become *ager publicus* was general, but it is not safe to apply this to every area and period without further evidence. Unequal *foedera* could surely be made *without* the confiscation of land, and the question must remain open whether most of those that were made with the Etruscan and Umbrian states involved confiscation. There are, however, no grounds for supposing that Etruria and Umbria were particularly well-treated in this respect, and the balance of probabilities is in my opinion rather in favour of there having been *ager publicus* in many of the states where it is not explicitly attested.

The relationship that developed between Rome and the Italian allies in general in the time between the making of the alliances and the Social War has been the subject of detailed study,[5] and it is not my intention to traverse all of the same territory. However, on one fundamental question existing accounts are unsatisfactory, the question of how often the Romans trespassed on the constitutional independence of the Italian allies that had been left to them by the *foedera*. The answer to this question is of direct importance for our understanding of the relations between Rome and the allied states of Etruria and Umbria.

The independence of the *civitates foederatae* was of course

[1] Liv. X 3.6.

[2] Liv. X 1.3, cf. Diod. XX 80.4.

[3] Cf. the case of Privernum, which lost two-thirds of its territory after its *defectio* (Liv. VIII 1.1–3).

[4] *BC* I 7.26–7: *Ῥωμαῖοι τὴν Ἰταλίαν πολέμῳ κατὰ μέρη χειρούμενοι, γῆς μέρος ἐλάμβανον καὶ πόλεις ἐνῴκιζον ἢ ἐς τὰς πρότερον οὔσας κληρούχους ἀπὸ σφῶν κατέλεγον. καὶ τάδε μὲν ἀντὶ φρουρίων ἐπενόουν, τῆς δὲ γῆς τῆς δορικτήτου σφίσιν ἑκάστοτε γιγνομένης τὴν μὲν ἐξειργασμένην αὐτίκα τοῖς οἰκιζομένοις ἐπιδιῄρουν ἢ ἐπίπρασκον ἢ ἐξεμίσθουν, τὴν δ' ἀργὸν ἐκ τοῦ πολέμου τότε οὖσαν, ἣ δὴ καὶ μάλιστα ἐπλήθυεν, οὐκ ἄγοντές πω σχολὴν διαλαχεῖν ἐπεκήρυττον ἐν τοσῷδε τοῖς ἐθέλουσιν ἐκπονεῖν ἐπὶ τέλει* . . . Cf. Plu. *TG* 8.1.

[5] See in particular De Sanctis, op. cit., iv.1 (1923), 563–71, T. Frank, *CAH* viii.350–4, Sherwin-White, *RC* 112–25, Göhler, op. cit., 39–69, A. H. McDonald, *CHJ* vi (1939), 124–46, *JRS* xxxiv (1944), 11–33, Badian, *FC* 141–53.

always limited, and the obligation that made the allies feel their subjection to Rome most of all, the supplying of troops, existed from the first. As far as political and administrative interference are concerned, the evidence is very uneven; it is often said that the Second Punic War sharply increased the readiness of the Romans to interfere and of the Italian allies to tolerate interference—but without the second decade of Livy we hardly know how Rome behaved towards the allies before the war. When Roman security was really threatened, as it was during the war, the allies could be treated as subjects; the experience could not be forgotten, but after about 196 political normality had apparently returned to most of Italy, and the evidence for the subsequent period has to be examined on its own. It is worth making a careful distinction too between Roman behaviour towards the Latins and towards the Italian allies.

Badian's analysis of the extent of Roman interference in the period down to 133, the most recent detailed one, is one-sided. Emphasizing the effects of the Second Punic War in forming habits of Roman intervention and allied acquiescence, he argues that after the war 'it had become natural for the Senate to send instructions on matters of importance; we can be certain . . . that no excuse was given and that neither side felt the need for one'.[1] He further maintains that what prevented even more extensive Roman intervention in allied affairs was not the legal restraint of the *foedera* but the Senate's 'ingrained unwillingness to assume avoidable administrative responsibilities'.[2] That, I agree, had an important effect in limiting the amount of Roman interference. But both this and the constant difficulty in finding enough troops in the second century surely also meant that the Senate needed to avoid antagonizing the allies unduly; therefore it could not ignore the remaining autonomy of the allies as it was defined in the *foedera*. When we examine the known acts of Roman intervention in the period after the last disturbances directly attributable to the war, they turn out to be too few to justify Badian's interpretation. (I omit here events arising from the establishment of new colonies, and also actions that concerned the Latins but not the Italian

[1] *FC* 145–6. [2] *FC* 144.

allies.) Polybius describes the Senate's powers in Italy in a well-known passage: ὁμοίως ὅσα τῶν ἀδικημάτων τῶν κατ' Ἰταλίαν προσδεῖται δημοσίας ἐπισκέψεως, λέγω δ' οἷον προδοσίας, συνωμοσίας, φαρμακείας, δολοφονίας, τῇ συγκλήτῳ μέλει περὶ τούτων. πρὸς δὲ τούτοις, εἴ τις ἰδιώτης ἢ πόλις τῶν κατὰ τὴν Ἰταλίαν διαλύσεως ἢ (καὶ νὴ Δι') ἐπιτιμήσεως ἢ βοηθείας ἢ φυλακῆς προσδεῖται, τούτων πάντων ἐπιμελές ἐστι τῇ συγκλήτῳ.[1] The question of how much these powers were actually used in Polybius' time is complicated by the fact that Roman intervention may well have been invited by local magistrates on various occasions when there is no evidence to that effect, and also by the fact that there were Roman citizens to be found all over Italy.[2] The activities of L. Postumius, pr. 185 with the *provincia* Tarentum, in breaking up *pastorum coniurationes* and preventing *latrocinia* in Apulia in 185–184[3] were presumably welcomed by law-abiding local allies even if they did take place on allied territory[4]—although of course Postumius was engaged in an act of brutal repression, 7,000 men being condemned. In 174 it was representatives, *legati*, from Patavium itself who reported to the Senate the *seditio* there and the internal war brought about by the rivalry of the *factiones*.[5] Arbitration between states was only provided, Polybius implies, on request[6]—but there may have been cases where only one side in a dispute wanted the Senate to give judgement. The allies of Rome collaborated with her in such matters. That was probably also true to some extent in the most famous case of Roman intervention, the crisis of the Bacchanalia.[7] Although the *ager Teuranus*, where the surviving copy of the consuls' letter on the subject was put up,[8] was probably Roman territory,[9] although

[1] VI 13.4–5. On this passage see McDonald, *JRS* art. cit., 13–17, as well as Walbank's commentary.

[2] The affair of the murders in the *silva Sila* in Bruttium in 138 (Cic. *Brut.* 85) may very well have concerned Roman citizens; the *silva Sila* may very well have been in Roman territory, McDonald, art. cit., 15 n. 31. Badian, *FC* 145 n. 2, assumes that the affair concerned the allies.

[3] Liv. XXXIX 29.8–9, 41.6.

[4] McDonald, l.c., tends to the view that this too took place in Roman territory.

[5] Liv. XLI 27.3–4.

[6] For the cases see McDonald, art. cit., 14 n. 20.

[7] On this case in particular see McDonald, art. cit., 26–33 (with bibliography, 26 n. 116).

[8] *FIRA*[2] (ed. Riccobono) i. no. 30, pp. 240–1 = *ILLRP* 511.

[9] M. Gelzer, *Hermes*, lxxi (1936), 278 n. 15 = *KS* iii.259 n. 15, U. Kahrstedt, *Historia*, viii (1959), 176, 191, P. A. Brunt, *JRS* lv (1965), 100 n. 67.

there are difficulties in the interpretation of the word 'foideratei' in the inscription,[1] and although the consuls seem to have felt some embarrassment at issuing their instructions,[2] it remains the case that the Senate did issue orders to allies on this occasion—'Bacas vir nequis adiese velet ceivis Romanus neve nominus Latini neve socium quisquam'.[3] However the crisis was thought to be one of the greatest importance to Roman security, and what we know about Roman actions on this occasion does not justify the belief that there was other direct intervention in allied affairs on less vital occasions. It is a mistake to think of the Roman response to the crisis as a typical Roman action towards the allies. There are, it is true, some other instances of Roman interference in this period. We happen to know of a *senatus consultum*, generally but rather insecurely dated *c.* 159, in which the Senate censured the Tiburtes;[4] the reason for doing this is quite unknown, and it is in fact possible that it was because of some action, concerning the levy for example, that was a legitimate concern of Rome by the most legalistic definition. There are also minor instances of apparent interference: a *supplicatio* of three days throughout Italy,[5] king Gentius and family entrusted to the custody of the Iguvines (after Spoletium had refused),[6] more than a thousand leading Achaeans similarly entrusted to the cities of Etruria.[7] In 133

[1] Line 3. See Degrassi's references, *ILLRP* ii. p. 18.

[2] For this view see McDonald, art. cit., 30.

[3] Lines 7–8. Cf. Liv. XXXIX 14.6–8: 'iubent (patres) . . . sacerdotes eorum sacrorum . . . non Romae modo sed per omnia fora et conciliabula conquiri, ut in consulum potestate essent; edici praeterea in urbe Roma et per totam Italiam edicta mitti, ne quis qui Bacchis initiatus esset coisse aut convenisse sacrorum causa velit, neu quid talis rei divinae fecisse. Ante omnia ut quaestio de iis habeatur, qui coierint coniuraverintve, quo stuprum flagitiumve inferretur. Haec senatus decrevit'. Copies of the letter will certainly have been sent to Etruria, since it was thought to have been the immediate source of the cult.

[4] *FIRA*² (ed. Riccobono) i. no. 33, pp. 247–8=*ILLRP* 512. This dating goes back to F. Ritschl, *RhM* ix (1854), 160. The identification of the praetor L. Cornelius Cn. f. with the cos. of 156 is to some extent supported by the names of the other three senators mentioned. E. H. Warmington, *Remains of Old Latin*, iv (London, 1940), 261, dates it to the late second or early first century.

[5] Liv. XL 19.5.

[6] Liv. XLV 43.9.

[7] Paus. VII 10.11. According to Plin. *NH* III 138, XXXIII 78, an old *senatus consultum* forbad the working of *metalla* in Italy. We do not know the date of this *s.c.* (? second century), whether it applied to allied states, whether it ever really went into effect, or (if it did) for how long. Ore was mined on Elba in the time of Strabo (V 2.6 223C).

there was a significant change in the treatment of the allies: whether or not the optimate charge reproduced by Cicero,[1] that the *lex agraria* violated the *foedera* of the allies, was strictly accurate, those of the allies who had long occupied *ager publicus* suffered from a very radical change in Roman policy. Previous known incidents do not, however, justify even a cautious judgement like Walbank's about the extent of Roman interference:[2] we do not know that Rome 'often' explicitly told the allies what to do in their own affairs.

There is the further question, not without importance, of the application of Roman laws in allied states.[3] Recent writers have said that at least some Roman laws were made to apply in the allied states, as Mommsen thought.[4] Alleged instances of this are the Lex Sempronia *de pecunia credita* of 193, the Lex Appuleia and the Lex Furia, laws of uncertain date but probably of this period which are usually referred to as laws *de sponsu*, and two sumptuary laws, the Lex Fannia (161) and the Lex Didia (143). In reality, however, the Lex Sempronia probably applied to Latins and Italians only in cases in which Roman citizens were also involved, and the other laws did not apply to non-citizens at all.[5] The purpose of Lex Sempronia was 'ut cum sociis ac nomine Latino creditae pecuniae ius idem quod cum civibus Romanis esset';[6] the law was intended to protect Roman debtors, and there is no hint that it was thought necessary to take the drastic further step of extending Roman law to debts

[1] *Rep.* I 31, III 41.

[2] On Polyb. l.c.: 'In general, public safety was a local responsibility: but when offences seemed likely to have extensive repercussions, and especially when extraordinary measures proved necessary within districts under Roman jurisdiction, the Romans often required the *socii* to take similar action through their own magistrates.'

[3] My view will appear in detail in *Historia*, xxi (1972).

[4] *Römisches Staatsr.*, iii.696, G. Niccolini, *Rend. Acc. Linc.*, ser. 8.i (1946), 112, J. Carcopino in G. Bloch–J. Carcopino, *Histoire romaine*, ii³ (Paris, 1952), 147–8, Badian, *FC* 146 n. 3 ('the question whether laws passed in Rome could normally apply to allied states is entirely theoretical. When it suited Rome, they did . . .'), Dahlheim, *Deditio und Societas*, 109 n. 1, *Struktur und Entwicklung*, 121 n. 25, cf. E. T. Salmon, *Samnium and the Samnites* (Cambridge, 1967), 324 (referring to the sumptuary laws discussed below).

[5] M. Wlassak, *Römische Processgesetze*, ii (Leipzig, 1891), 152–4, De Sanctis, op. cit., iv.1 564–6, J. Göhler, op. cit., 53–5, 58–9, A. H. McDonald, *CHJ* art. cit., 126–7, H. H. Scullard, *Roman Politics, 220–150* B.C. (Oxford, 1951), 146.

[6] Liv. XXXV 7.5.

between allies.[1] The view that the Lex Appuleia and the Lex Furia were imposed on the allies derives from Gaius' statement 'nam Lex quidem Furia tantum in Italia valet, Appuleia vero etiam in ceteris provinciis';[2] the jurist makes no mention of *peregrini*, and it is much better to suppose that it was Roman citizens in Italy and in the provinces who were the subjects of these laws.[3] Similarly with the Lex Fannia and the Lex Didia. According to Macrobius,[4] the Lex Didia followed the Lex Fannia by eighteen years—'Eius ferundae duplex fuit causa, prima et potissima ut universa Italia, non sola urbs, lege sumptuaria teneretur, Italicis existimantibus Fanniam legem non in se sed in solos urbanos cives esse conscriptam; deinde. . . '. The best interpretation of this is that the law was intended to refer to Roman citizens in Italy and not only to the *urbani cives*.[5] The imposition of Roman law in Italy in the second century would have presented very serious practical problems, and there is no evidence that Rome was prepared to extend her administration in this way. No doubt the laws of the allied states in Italy came to resemble the laws of Rome more and more during the second century, but of the actual imposition of Roman laws there is little evidence—in fact there is no definite case in which the *foederis libertas* of an Italian state was thus infringed.

Quite apart from the rights that Rome possessed by treaty, the fact that she chose to rule in a rather indirect way did not prevent her from ruling; and no doubt the growing tendency of individual Roman magistrates to misbehave in their relations with the Italian allies,[6] beginning with the incident of the consul L. Postumius at Praeneste in 173,[7] was accompanied by a decrease in the respect that the Senate showed for the interests of the allies. On the other hand a striking degree of trust was sometimes shown towards the allies: when Perusia and Tuder,

[1] This is the interpretation of M. Voigt, *Das ius naturale, aequum et bonum und ius gentium der Römer*, iv.1 (Leipzig, 1875), 179–80, etc., against Mommsen, *Geschichte des römischen Münzwesens* (Berlin, 1860), 327, etc. (cf. above, p. 111 n. 4).

[2] *Inst.* III 122.

[3] Voigt, op. cit., ii (Leipzig, 1858), 688 n. 791, etc., against Mommsen, *Römisches Staatsr.*, l.c., etc.

[4] *Sat.* III 17.6.

[5] Cf. M. Wlassak, op. cit., ii.154–6, L. Mitteis, *Römisches Privatrecht*, i (Leipzig, 1908), 69 n. 19, etc., against Mommsen, l.c., etc.

[6] On this see for example De Sanctis, op. cit., iv.1 566–7, Badian, *FC* 148–9.

[7] Liv. XLII 1.7–12.

to name only two examples, were permitted to build substantial city walls in the second century,[1] it was not expected that they would ever rebel. The administration of the Italian states remained in the hands of the local magistrates; such trust of course presupposed the loyalty of the ruling classes everywhere in Italy, but in Etruria, where colonies were relatively few, that loyalty was especially important.

[1] On the walls of Perusia and Tuder see M. E. Blake, *Ancient Roman Construction in Italy from the Prehistoric Period to Augustus* (Washington, 1947), 199–201, G. Lugli, *La tecnica edilizia romana* (Rome, 1957), 280–1.

IV

THE ALLIANCE WITH THE ETRUSCAN *PRINCIPES*

1. *The Structure of Etruscan Society*

THERE can be no doubt that there were at various times and in various places in Etruria class-conflicts between the ruling classes and slaves or people of slave-like status. A conception of Etruscan society in general as one deeply divided between two such conflicting classes has been elaborated by means of epigraphical and archaeological evidence, as well as literary evidence.[1] Some of the difficulties of understanding the situation have recently been emphasized,[2] and since the complete body of evidence has never been properly discussed, a full defence will be made of the proposition that in the Roman period such a deep division did exist. No attempt will be made in this section to describe the changes that took place in Etruria in the period immediately before the Social War.[3]

The Literary Evidence

Livy speaks of Etruscan *principes* and Dionysius of the δυνατώτατοι and the πενέσται of Etruria in a fifth-century context, but it will clearly be better to consider first the relevant incidents from the period when the annalistic sources have a

[1] An early expression of such a view is to be found in Niebuhr, *Römische Geschichte*, i (Berlin, 1811), 79–83, (1873 ed.), 100–104; the first detailed discussion is that of K. O. Müller (1828), for which see K. O. Müller–W. Deecke, *Die Etrusker*, i² (Stuttgart, 1877), 350–5. The main modern discussions are the following: J. Heurgon, *Historia*, vi (1957), 63–97, esp. 69–71, S. Mazzarino, ibid., 98–122, T. Frankfort, *Latomus*, xviii (1959), 3–22, J. Heurgon, ibid., 713–23, R. Lambrechts, *Essai sur les magistratures des républiques étrusques* (Brussels–Rome, 1959), 22–5, H. Rix, *Das etruskische Cognomen* (Wiesbaden, 1963), esp. 356–78; the supposed division is dismissed without discussion by A. J. Pfiffig, *Historia*, xv (1966), 193.

[2] Rix, op. cit., 370, 373–4.

[3] See Chapter VI, Section 1.

greater claim to reliability, and in particular the incidents in which a class-conflict of some kind is an essential part of the narrative, not a merely decorative element; later the references that seem more incidental will be considered.

It has been argued that the Livian account of the Etruscan wars that began in 311 is within limits trustworthy, so discussion can begin with the *Arretinorum seditiones* of 302.[1] A general Etruscan 'rebellion' began as a result of these *seditiones* and subsequent fighting took place in the *ager Rusellanus*.[2] The target of the disturbance at Arretium was the *Cilnium genus*, evidently a family group of some kind, said by Livy to have been 'praepotens divitiarum'. He also implies that the Cilnii were friendly to Rome,[3] and that the attempt to expel them was an attack on Roman interests. The story could possibly have been invented or distorted to justify Roman intervention, but since the *Cilnium genus* is described unfavourably that it is not a very likely hypothesis. About the opposition to the Cilnii we learn nothing from Livy's main account except that it was armed and strong enough to rebel. In the brief alternative account of the campaign[4] Etruria was pacified 'seditionibu tantum Arretinorum compositis et Cilnio genere cum plebe in gratiam reducto'. In both versions Livy apparently found the same or similar accounts of the events at Arretium—they differed only about the rest of the war. It is to be noticed that Livy regarded the opposition as the plebs of Arretium, that is not as slaves. In the incident of Sp. Carvilius and the town of Troilum (293 B.C.),[5] the distinction that Livy makes between two categories of Etruscans is again one of wealth. The consul agreed for a large price to let 470 *ditissimi* leave the town before he captured it. Those who stayed behind and resisted were the 'cetera multitudo'—again nothing about servile status.

The rebellion at Volsinii in 265–264 is described in six surviving accounts, that of Zonaras being quite detailed.[6] The account in the *περὶ θαυμασίων ἀκουσμάτων* of a revolution at *Οἰναρέα*[7] will be considered separately. Between the other

[1] Liv. X 3–5.
[2] X 4.5.
[3] Cf. IX 32.1: 'omnes Etruriae populi praeter Arretinos ad arma ierant' (311 B.C.)—but perhaps that was because of their remoteness from Rome. Thirty-year *indutiae* were established in 310, IX 37.12.
[4] X 5.13.
[5] Liv. X 46.10–12.
[6] VIII 7.4–8.
[7] Ps.-Aristot. *περὶ θαυμασίων ἀκουσμάτων* 94.

accounts, those of Zonaras, Valerius Maximus,[1] Florus,[2] Orosius,[3] *De viris illustribus*,[4] and John of Antioch,[5] there are very few discrepancies, none of them sufficiently considerable to suggest that there was any serious disagreement about the incident in the annalistic tradition.[6] Yet there is some variation in the terms used to describe the two contending groups at Volsinii. According to Zonaras, the *Οὐλσίνιοι* had previously had a stable political system, *πολιτείᾳ τε εὐνομουμένῃ ἐκέχρηντο*, but after their conquest by the Romans they drifted into luxuriousness and turned the administration of the town over to their *οἰκέται*, and they generally carried on their campaigns by means of these slaves. Finally they encouraged them to the point where the *οἰκέται* had both power and spirit and felt that they were worthy of freedom. As time went on they actually obtained it *δι' ἑαυτῶν*. The former slaves gained more and more power, until their former masters prevailed on the Romans to intervene; after the capture of the town, the latter put to death *τοὺς . . . ἀφελομένους τὰς τῶν κυρίων τιμάς*, resettled their masters elsewhere, and with them *εἴ τινες τῶν οἰκετῶν χρηστοὶ περὶ τοὺς δεσπότας ἐγένοντο*, presumably returning the latter to the condition of slavery if they too had previously been manumitted. The slaves are referred to three times as *οἰκέται*, never by any other term. Their masters are twice called *δεσπόται* (and their masters' wives are called *δεσποίναι*), but several other terms are used. After the manumission it is the *ἀρχαῖοι πολῖται* who can no longer endure the slaves, that is the slaves are assumed to have acquired citizenship on manumission, like Roman slaves. The slaves had seized the honours of the *κύριοι*. The latter are also called the *αὐθιγενεῖς*, Dio apparently assuming that slaves were of foreign origin, although that was probably not true of the great majority of slaves in Etruria in the early third century. If there was a *βουλὴ* at Volsinii, as is stated, there may have been some gradations among the free men, but even so Zonaras sees the conflict as one between the

[1] IX 1 ext. 2.
[2] I 16.
[3] IV 5.3.
[4] Ch. 36.
[5] *FHG* iv.557 fr. 50.
[6] Other sources: the *Fasti Triumphales* for 264, *Inscr. Ital.* xiii.1, pp. 74–5, 547; on the removal of the Volsinian god Vertumnus to Rome by M. Fulvius Flaccus, cos. 264, Varro *LL* V 46, Propert. IV 2.3–4, Festus 228L; cf. also Plin. *NH* XXXIV 34, W. Eisenhut in *RE* s.v. Vertumnus (1958), cols. 1669–77.

masters in general and the slaves in general, with the exception of those who were χρηστοί.

The other sources all speak of the *domini*[1] or the δεσπόται[2] on the one side, and the *servi* or οἰκέται on the other. Other terms used in descriptions of the ruling class are οἱ ταύτην οἰκοῦντες τὴν χώραν[3] and *ingenui*;[4] there are also references to a senate in writers other than Zonaras.[5] Concerning the status of the slaves, we are explicitly told by Florus, Orosius, and *De viris illustribus*, as by Zonaras, that they had been manumitted. Zonaras also tells us that the citizens had already handed over the administration of the town before the manumission, and already carried on their military campaigns through the slaves. There is a certain chronological difficulty in this account, because these innovations are attributed to the ἁβρότης of the citizens that followed their defeat by Rome—are we to suppose that some defeat by Rome before the final one was a cause of this ἁβρότης? Since τρυφὴ was a standard charge with which to malign the Etruscans[6] this difficulty can be ignored. The important point is that Zonaras is unlikely to have said that the slaves did anything as unusual as administering the state and serving in the army unless he thought that he had good reason to do so.

There are certain suspect elements in the story of the Volsinian revolt, besides the decadence of the citizens, which is referred to by all the sources. It was claimed that the former masters had themselves been enslaved and that the purpose of the Romans was to free them.[7] Roman actions certainly needed justification, and the resettlement of the survivors in a different place shows that in reality other motives were at work besides a wish to restore the *domini*[8] (and Metrodorus of Scepsis asserted that Volsinii was conquered—though not necessarily on this occasion—for the sake of 2,000 statues).[9] These, however, are very far from being sufficient grounds to make us doubt

[1] Val. Max., Flor., Oros., *De vir. ill.*, ll.cc.
[2] John of Antioch, l.c.
[3] John of Antioch.
[4] Val. Max.
[5] Val. Max., *De vir ill.*
[6] See above, p. 14.
[7] ἐπ' ἐλευθερίᾳ (Zonaras); ἠλευθέρωσαν (John of Antioch); cf. the words *dominatio* (Val. Max., Oros.), *dominari* (Florus), *oppressi* (*De vir. ill.*).
[8] Cf. the transfer of Falerii after the rebellion of 241, Polyb. I 65.2, etc., part of an obviously harsh Roman response. The removal of Vertumnus must also be indicative of Roman policy.
[9] Plin. *NH* XXXIV 34.

the general accuracy of the surviving accounts of the events at Volsinii or in particular the accuracy of the descriptions that they give of the social system of Volsinii.

In the *περὶ θαυμασίων ἀκουσμάτων* we are told of the Etruscan town of *Οἰναρέα* or *Οἴνα*,[1] where the inhabitants, in fear of a tyranny, were said to have set over themselves some of their slaves, *οἰκέται*, whom they had manumitted, the freedmen ruling by annual magistracies.[2] Apart from the motive of fear of tyranny, the description bears some resemblance to conditions at Volsinii before 265, where slaves had been manumitted and held office. Attempts to identify *Οἰναρέα* (the better form of the name)[3] have failed,[4] for Venaria[5] was an insignificant island off the Etruscan coast, the Etruscan name of Volsinii was probably Velzna,[6] and the *λόφος* thirty stades high could be found at several other sites besides Orvieto. Wherever *Οἰναρέα* was, the story is useful as non-Roman confirmation of the fact that some Etruscan slaves rose far above their servile status. Note that here as at Volsinii the slaves are still regarded as a separate class even after their manumission.

In the Hannibalic War it was the senators at Arretium[7] and the *nobiles*[8] and *principes*[9] in Etruria who were held responsible for the behaviour of their states;[10] the rest of the population is

[1] It appears in this form in Steph. Byz.

[2] *Ἔστι δέ τις ἐν τῇ Τυρρηνίᾳ πόλις Οἰναρέα καλουμένη, ἣν ὑπερβολῇ φασὶν ὀχυρὰν εἶναι· ἐν γὰρ μέσῃ αὐτῇ λόφος ἐστὶν ὑψηλός, τριάκοντα σταδίους ἀνέχων ἄνω, καὶ κάτω ὕλην παντοδαπὴν καὶ ὕδατα. φοβουμένους οὖν τοὺς ἐνοικοῦντας λέγουσι μή τις τύραννος γένηται, προΐστασθαι αὐτῶν τοὺς ἐκ τῶν οἰκετῶν ἠλευθερωμένους· καὶ οὗτοι ἄρχουσιν αὐτῶν, κατ' ἐνιαυτὸν δ' ἄλλους ἀντικαθιστάναι τοιούτους.* Such things might be exaggerated in the Greek world (cf. *SIG*^{3} 543).

[3] Cf. Mazzarino, art. cit., 122.

[4] Volsinii has been favoured by many of those who have expressed a preference, cf. Heurgon, *Historia*, art. cit., 70 n. 5; Volaterrae also has often been suggested. A third-century Greek writer is more likely to have known about a coastal or nearly coastal town than an inland one; the previous section refers to Aithalia (Elba) and Populonium.

[5] Plin. *NH* III 81.

[6] According to the accepted interpretation of the François tomb at Vulci, where this form appears in *CIE* 5269= *TLE* 297.

[7] Liv. XXVII 24.2.

[8] XXIX 36.11.

[9] XXX 25.12. For definition of this term see L. Wickert, *RE* s.v. *princeps* (*civitatis*) (1954), esp. cols. 2029–41.

[10] Livy mentions 'septem principes senatus' at Arretium who escaped with their children, and gives as 120 the number of children of other senators thereafter taken as hostages. For discussion of this incident, see below, p. 139.

described only once in this context, as *populi sui*.[1] Then in 196 there was a *coniuratio servorum* in Etruria, which, it is implied, affected a large part of the area: the Romans suppressed it, crucifying some, returning others to their *domini*.[2]

It has been argued that the surviving Prophecy of Vegoia has authentic Etruscan origins.[3] It predicts what will happen if the *servi* move the boundary-stones and what will happen if it is done with *conscientia dominica*. Among the results of the latter event will be 'multae dissensiones in populo'. It is certainly implied that the *servi* and *domini* are the two main elements in society. But the *servi* are not ordinary *servi* in the Roman sense, for they seem to have some property-rights—it is presumably their own property (in some sense) that they may hope to increase by moving boundary-stones, and their status is not the lowest that is imaginable—'si servi facient, dominio mutabuntur in deterius'. Yet 'servi' was the nearest Roman term available to describe them.

On his famous journey through Etruria in 135 Tiberius Gracchus saw οἰκέτας ἐπεισάκτους καὶ βαρβάρους working the land, so his brother said;[4] of that it only need be said here that it is not good evidence that the indigenous serf class had disappeared. It has been suggested that Tiberius' journey lay largely through *ager Romanus* on the Via Aurelia,[5] and that is likely enough, but slaves in general would be assumed to be ἐπείσακτοι, and no importance should be attached to the term.[6]

There are a number of more incidental references to the social structure of Etruria. In the description of Etruria that he based on Posidonius, Diodorus elaborated two common themes, the Etruscan sources of various inventions and the τρυφή of the Etruscans.[7] Among the inventions was the peristyle—ἔν τε ταῖς οἰκίαις τὰ περίστῳα πρὸς τὰς τῶν θεραπευόντων ὄχλων ταραχὰς ἐξεῦρον εὐχρηστίαν—but it is not clear that he had any real evidence that there were such noisy crowds of

[1] XXIX 36.11.

[2] XXXIII 36.1–2: 'Etruriam infestam prope coniuratio servorum fecit. Ad quaerendam opprimendamque eam M'. Acilius Glabrio praetor . . . cum una ex duabus legione urbana est missus.'

[3] See above, pp. 31–40.

[4] Plu. *TG* 8.

[5] Heurgon, *Daily Life of the Etruscans* (London, 1964), 56.

[6] For this interpretation see below, pp. 203–4.

[7] V 40.

slaves (clients?) in Etruria. Naturally the luxurious banquets of the Etruscans were served by large numbers of expensive *οἰκέται*, dressed more richly ἢ *κατὰ δουλικὴν ἀξίαν*.[1] A paradoxical statement follows: *οἰκήσεις τε παντοδαπὰς ἰδιαζούσας ἔχουσι παρ' αὐτοῖς οὐ μόνον οἱ θεράποντες ἀλλὰ καὶ τῶν ἐλευθέρων οἱ πλείους*. Some have accepted this text as it stands,[2] supposing it to refer to 'clients' who all had private houses and were better off than the free-born, but it is a quite impossible remark for Diodorus to have made. He could have believed it, but he would have had to express it differently—'not only the slaves . . . but also the majority of the free . . .' would have seemed nonsensical to his readers. The emendation *ἄρχοντες* for *θεράποντες* (Vogel), though not very attractive, is the best that has been proposed, and the passage remains useful evidence of the wealth of the *ἐλεύθεροι*.

Other references to the *principes* of Etruria in the first decade of Livy,[3] and to their *concilia*,[4] are probably only pieces of colouring. Livy believed that they were a part of the Etruscan system and had no difficulty in inserting them into such incidents; the same will apply to the *intestina discordia* at Veii,[5] the band of performers, *artifices*, of the king of Veii, 'quorum magna pars ipsius servi erant',[6] and the *principes* and *multitudo* of Nepet.[7] However, imaginatively conceived as these passages were, there is nothing to show that Livy was wrong to regard the Etruscan states of this period as having been dominated by *principes*.[8]

In Veii's war against Rome set in 480 'undique ex Etruria

[1] V 40.3.

[2] Mazzarino, art. cit., 114–15, J. Heurgon, *Hommages à A. Grenier* (Brussels, 1962), ii.803–8. The former imagines that the *θεράποντες* were *lautni* (=*clientes* in his opinion), who were 'sostenuti dal patrocinio dei signori' and therefore better off than the free. Heurgon, also believing that the *θεράποντες* were 'clients', suggests that Diodorus' *οὐ μόνον* and *ἀλλὰ καὶ* were his own clumsy addition to a remark of Posidonius to the effect that 'chez eux les *θεράποντες* ont des demeures particulières; d'ailleurs c'est le cas aussi de la plupart des hommes libres', not only of a minority of them; the statement remains impossibly inept. He also criticizes the emendation *ἄρχοντες* for *θεράποντες* on the pedantic grounds that *ἄρχοντες* means 'magistrates' not 'the ruling class'.

[3] II 44.8, IX 36.5, X 13.3, X 16.3.

[4] II 44.8, X 16.3.

[5] IV 58.2.

[6] V 1.5.

[7] VI 10.2, 5.

[8] Dion. Hal. V 3.2–3 refers to the *ἐκκλησία* and *δῆμος* at Tarquinii to which Tarquinius Superbus is supposed to have appealed; they are mere decoration.

auxilia convenerant'.[1] The 'auxilia' are described in more detail by Dionysius:[2] συνεληλύθεσαν γὰρ ἐξ ἁπάσης Τυρρηνίας οἱ δυνατώτατοι τοὺς ἑαυτῶν πενέστας ἐπαγόμενοι. Again the description of the orders is anachronistic, and is based on Dionysius' knowledge of the Etruscan system in the third century or later. It is important to decide how much significance can be attached to Dionysius' use of the precise term πενέσται, the name of the Thessalian serf class.[3] The use of such an unusual term suggests that it may have had some particular appropriateness for the dependents of the Etruscan δυνατώτατοι that, say, ὑπήκοοι or πελάται[4] or helots did not have. Dionysius' interest in writing a work about the Etruscans is of course attested[5] and he may well have acquired some detailed knowledge by the time that he wrote this passage. He also claimed to know something about the Thessalian system[6] and about the πενέσται in particular.[7] Heurgon has suggested[8] that Dionysius regarded the Etruscan class concerned as 'clients' but avoided using πελάται, his usual word for clients,[9] because he wanted to avoid making them equivalent to the πελάται who followed the Fabii;[10] he matched the outlandishness of the Etruscans[11] with an outlandish description of their client-class. As for the first part of this explanation, πενέσται did not in fact mean 'clients', and it has to be established that Dionysius erroneously thought that it did; he does indeed say that the Thessalians called their πελάται πενέσται,[12] but he is showing how the Romans improved on various Greek institutions, and he knew that in fact the Thessalians treated their πελάται very differently from the way in which the Romans treated their clients—ἐκεῖνοι [the

[1] II 44.7.
[2] IX 5.4.
[3] On the Thessalian πενέσται see esp. F. Miltner, *RE* s.v. *Penesten* (1937), J. Heurgon, *Latomus*, art. cit., D. Lotze, *ΜΕΤΑΞΥ 'ΕΛΕΥΘΕΡΩΝ ΚΑΙ ΔΟΥΛΩΝ, Studien zur Rechtsstellung unfreier Landbevölkerungen in Griechenland bis zum 4. Jahrhundert v. Chr.* (Berlin, 1959), 48–53.
[4] This was Dionysius' considered translation of Lat. *clientes*, as II 9 shows; cf. Heurgon, *Latomus*, art. cit., 720.
[5] I 30.4.
[6] He claimed to know the title of the Thessalian rulers, V 74.3, but MSS. merely give the title as ἀρχούς; Bücheler took that to be a gloss for ταγούς.
[7] Cf. his description in II 9.2.
[8] *Latomus*, art. cit., 720–2.
[9] See above, n. 4.
[10] IX 15.12.
[11] Cf. I 30.2.
[12] II 9.2: ἐκάλουν δὲ Ἀθηναῖοι μὲν θῆτας τοὺς πελάτας ἐπὶ τῆς λατρείας, Θετταλοὶ δὲ πενέστας ὀνειδίζοντες αὐτοῖς εὐθὺς ἐν τῇ κλήσει τὴν τύχην.

Thessalians] *μὲν γὰρ ὑπεροπτικῶς ἐχρῶντο τοῖς πελάταις ἔργα τε ἐπιτάττοντες οὐ προσήκοντα ἐλευθέροις, καὶ ὁπότε μὴ πράξειάν τι τῶν κελευομένων, πληγὰς ἐντείνοντες καὶ τἆλλα ὥσπερ ἀργυρωνήτοις παραχρώμενοι.*[1] Dionysius did not then think of the *πενέσται* as being simply clients, and he does not seem to strive to insert outlandish terminology into his descriptions of the Etruscans. Of course a number of Dionysius' Greek terms for Roman institutions involve him in inaccuracy,[2] but that results from the use of a commonplace Greek term (*γερουσία, προβούλευμα*)—*πενέσται*, by contrast, does not look like a facile Greek equivalent for anything.

Did Dionysius mean by his use of this term for the Etruscan lower class only that they were the victims of a particularly primitive and inhuman form of *clientela*?[3] He accepts the crude etymological connection with *πένομαι, πένης*,[4] but it is not the basis of the description that he gives of *πενεστεία*. *πενεστεία* was not only a primitive and inhuman condition, it was actually slave-like: they had tasks imposed upon them that were *οὐ προσήκοντα ἐλευθέροις*, presumably forced agricultural labour, and the Thessalians, i.e. the ruling class among the Thessalians, imposed orders on them (of any kind?), and punished disobedience as if the *πενέσται* had been the lowest type of slave, *ἀργυρώνητοι*. So much for Dionysius' knowledge. In fact the *πενέσται* were, like the helots, one of the categories that Pollux refers to as *μεταξὺ ἐλευθέρων καὶ δούλων*, between free men and slaves.[5] The allusions of ancient writers to these statuses naturally tend to be imprecise (there was a shortage of suitable terminology in Greek and even more in Latin)—the *πενέσται* were bundled together with the helots, the Cretan *κλαρῶται*, and the *Μαριανδυνοὶ* of Heraclea Pontica.[6] They were often regarded as slaves,[7] yet they could also be wage-labourers,[8] and

[1] II 9.2.

[2] Cf. Heurgon, art. cit., 718, and references there.

[3] As Heurgon suggests, art. cit., 723.

[4] Also referred to by Σ Aristoph. *Vesp.* 1271.

[5] *Onomast.* III 83. He had here what should have been an excellent source, Aristophanes of Byzantium, the Alexandrian librarian.

[6] For example they are compared with the helots and *κλαρῶται*, Aristot. *Pol.* II 6.2, with the helots, Theopomp. 115 F 122, with the helots and *Μαριανδυνοί*, Plato *Lg.* VI 776cd (on this passage see the next paragraph).

[7] E.g. Theopomp. 115 F 81.

[8] Theocrit. XVI 34–5: *πολλοὶ ἐν Ἀντιόχοιο δόμοις καὶ ἄνακτος Ἀλεύα / ἁρμαλιὴν ἔμμηνον ἐμετρήσαντο πενέσται.*

even grow richer than their masters.[1] Of the disabilities mentioned by Dionysius we also have evidence from other sources: it is clear that, like others who were 'between free men and slaves', they were tied to the land in some way,[2] and that they were subject to punishments exacted by their 'masters'—who were (merely) forbidden to exile or to kill them.[3]

We have seen that there is some specific evidence that the slaves of various states in Etruria had rights greater than those of Roman slaves—at Volsinii before the manumission (Zonaras), in the case of the *servi* in Vegoia's Prophecy and—a very strange situation—at *Οἰναρέα*. The Thessalian *πενέσται* could perform military service,[4] like the 'slaves' at Volsinii, and had some property rights,[5] like the *servi* in the Prophecy—conditions were of course probably not identical in either case. The wealth of the *πενέσται*[6] is also reminiscent of Etruria. (The *πενέσται* were also supposedly an indigenous population enslaved by outsiders.[7]) The Etruscan serf class from time to time came into active conflict with its masters; that is some indication that their status was higher than that of Roman slaves, for rebellions of chattel-slaves were decidedly unusual in the Roman world except during the period 139–71, as indeed they were in the Greek world.[8] The Thessalian *πενέσται* on the other hand, like the helots, were frequently in conflict with their 'masters'[9] (of this Dionysius may have been aware)—their greater freedom and resources gave them greater opportunities than those of ordinary slaves.

There exist some other literary references to the Etruscan social system which by themselves would not amount to much, but which fit quite well with the evidence reviewed here. A

[1] Archemachus 424 F 1: *καὶ πολλοὶ* [!] *τῶν κυρίων ἑαυτῶν εἰσὶν εὐπορώτεροι.*

[2] Archemachus, l.c.: *παρέδωκαν ἑαυτοὺς τοῖς Θεσσαλοῖς δουλεύειν καθ' ὁμολογίας, ἐφ' ᾧ . . . αὐτοὶ . . . τὴν χώραν αὐτοῖς ἐργαζόμενοι τὰς συντάξεις ἀποδώσουσιν.*

[3] Archemachus, l.c.: *οὔτε ἐξάξουσιν αὐτοὺς ἐκ τῆς χώρας οὔτε ἀποκτενοῦσιν.*

[4] But how regularly they did so is unknown; cf. Lotze, op. cit., 52.

[5] Archemachus, l.c. (*οὔτε ἐξάξουσιν κτλ.*), probably implies that.

[6] Archemachus; cf. Plato's statement that the *Μαριανδυνοὶ* and the *πενέσται* had an easier lot than the helots, *Lg.* VI 776cd.

[7] In that respect the ruling class differed from the ruling class of Etruria, believed by Dionysius to be indigenous; cf. Heurgon, *Historia*, art. cit., 71 n. 4; but not much can be made of the point.

[8] M. I. Finley, *Comparative Studies in Society and History*, vi (1963–4), 235–6.

[9] Aristot. *Pol.* II 9.2, cf. Xen. *Hell.* II 3.36, and also Lotze, op. cit., 52–3.

reference to *οἱ ὑπεξούσιοι τῶν εὐγενῶν* in Nigidius Figulus' *βροντοσκοπία* has already been mentioned.[1] In the *libri fulgurales*, *haruspicini*, and *rituales* there were evidently references to the Etruscan social system,[2] but it has been argued that the known fragments are not to be relied on as uncontaminated evidence about the Etruscans.[3] The value of these and other allusions is in any case entirely subordinate to that of the more solid evidence already discussed.

Are we entitled to believe that the social structure of all or most of the Etruscan states was similar or the same? Most of the confusions that arise in the sources can be explained if the lower class was 'between free men and slaves'. Specific literary evidence deals with only one or two towns—yet the slave revolt of 196 was not confined to them, and Dionysius regarded the *πενέσται* as a general Etruscan phenomenon. Again, there is no reason to think that Vegoia's Prophecy referred to the conditions of only one or two towns. In the territory of some towns there is a complete lack of Etruscan inscriptions containing the crucial term *lautni*, an equivalent of *libertus* (for these inscriptions see the next section), but that certainly does not show that the status was unknown there, and in fact a large number of different areas do have some such inscriptions. The fairly widespread distribution of some Etruscan magistrates' titles,[4] and the single *ius* that seems to have concerned Etruscan land,[5] also suggest that the social structure was everywhere broadly similar. On the other hand the Etruscan states were independent of each other, and exactly identical development did not take place in all of them. That there must have been a number of rather different systems at any given time no one will deny, but the combined weight of the literary evidence establishes that the deep social division did exist.

The Epigraphical Evidence

Inscriptions from Etruscan tomb-groups are sometimes said to show that Etruscan society had an aristocratic structure of

[1] Above, p. 7.

[2] E.g. Servius on *Aen.* II 649, and Macrobius, *Sat.* III 7.2; Heurgon, art. cit., 69–71, builds too much on these references.

[3] See above, p. 5.

[4] See R. Lambrechts, op. cit.

[5] See Mazzarino, art. cit., esp. 111; some of his arguments are speculative, to say the least.

some kind.[1] At Volaterrae the literary evidence for the power of the *gens Caecina*[2] is strongly supported by the inscriptions,[3] although there were certainly other well-to-do families. There is some epigraphical support for at least the existence of the Cilnii at Arretium.[4] An aristocratic system is indicated by the relative youth of some of those who held the senior office of *zilath*—it was possible to have obtained the office by the age of twenty-nine, if not younger.[5] But more is needed than this—we need to know what the relationship was between the well-to-do families and the rest of the population. A thorough survey of the late Etruscan sites in the territory of one of the allied states, on the pattern of the surveys carried out by the British School at Rome in the most southerly parts of Etruria, might produce some illuminating results. More than forty years ago an attempt was made by R. Bianchi Bandinelli to produce a demographic map of the territory of Clusium;[6] he based his demographic conclusions on the epigraphical evidence from the tombs of the region—evidence that was in a chaotic state, since there had been a total lack of intelligent excavation. The possible conclusions of such an investigation can be regarded as at best tentative—yet his knowledge of the region was clearly quite good. In the Roman-Etruscan period (not precisely defined, but apparently beginning with the final wars) he believed that a considerable area around Clusium was in the hands of some twenty families. 'Questa espansione topografica di un numero ristretto di famiglie, potrebbe testimoniare l'esistenza di quei latifondi, coltivati da schiavi, che furono uno dei principali germi di decadenza...'[7] Similar conclusions might be drawn from the surprising scarcity of late Etruscan sites in some of the territory around Bolsena and Orvieto.[8] None of this

[1] Discussions of some of the evidence are to be found in the works of Heurgon, Mazzarino, Frankfort, Lambrechts, and Rix cited above, p. 114 n. 1.

[2] Cic. *Caec.* 104: 'amplissimo totius Etruriae nomine'; *Fam.* VI 6.9: 'te, hominem in parte Italiae minime contemnenda facile omnium nobilissimum'.

[3] See *CIE* 18–42, etc., some of which must go back at least to the early second century.

[4] *CIE* 408 = *TLE* 674, *CIE* 409.

[5] *TLE* 169, from Musarna, near Viterbo. Lambrechts, op. cit., 97.

[6] *MAAL* xxx (1925), cols. 209–552; for the area covered see col. 499.

[7] Col. 500.

[8] This appeared from an investigation of the course of the Via Cassia in the area, W. V. Harris, *PBSR* xxxiii (1965), 113–33.

evidence can be used with any confidence for the present purpose, however; to mention only one additional difficulty, the literary evidence strongly suggests that, in the period of the final wars at least, there were outside the main town-sites numbers of concentrations of population in *vici* and *castella*.[1]

Two bilingual inscriptions give us an Etruscan word equivalent to *libertus*, namely *CIE* 3692 (Perusia), 'L. Scarpus Scarpiae l. Popa / larnth scarpe lautni',[2] and *CIE* 1288 (Clusium), 'l. eucle phisis lautni / L. Phisius L.l. Eucl[es]'; material doubts about the correct reading arise in the latter case, but the one given (H. Rix) seems the most likely.[3] The equation *lautni*=*libertus* has been generally accepted,[4] and the bilinguals are supported by the structure of the names in many of the *lautni* inscriptions, which shows that the *lautni* were in some way dependents.[5] There are in all about 150 inscriptions in which *lautni* appears in some form (see below on their distribution).[6] A further examination of the condition of the *lautni* is relevant here only if it can be shown to support, or weaken, the literary evidence about the division in Etruscan society. The dangers of identifying the *lautni* with any particular group mentioned in the sources are easy to see,[7] but if there was a substantial class whose status was 'between free men and slaves', there is some confirmation of the literary evidence. In the first century the subjects of *CIE* 1288 and 3692 must have been *liberti* in the sense of the *liberti* of Roman law;

[1] Liv. X 12.8 (*castella, vici*), 46.11 (*castella*), 11.6 (*vici*, but also *villae*).

[2] = *TLE* 606. On the text, H. Rix, *SE* xxv (1957), 532.

[3] = *TLE* 470. On the text, H. Rix, *Das etruskische Cognomen*, 366 n. 159.

[4] Denied only by L. Deroy, *Glotta*, xxxvi (1958), 286–300, who entirely failed to deal with the evidence in favour of the identification, and on several strange hypotheses translated *lautni* as Lat. *laudatus*; for criticism see Frankfort, art. cit., 8, Rix, op. cit., 356 n. 85. The equation *lautni*=*libertus* was first made by G. F. Gamurrini, *Bull. Inst.*, 1874, 13–17; the known *lautni* material was then discussed by W. Deecke (*Bezzenbergers*) *Beiträge zur Kunde der indogermanischen Sprachen*, iii (1879), 26–53; the most important subsequent discussions (giving references to the other literature) are those of S. P. Cortsen, 'Die etruskischen Standes- und Beamtentitel, durch die Inschriften beleuchtet', in *Kgl. Danske Videnskabernes Selskab, Historisk-filologiske Meddelelser*, xi.1 (Copenhagen, 1925), 3–76, F. Leifer, 'Studien zum antiken Aemterwesen', *Klio Beiträge*, xxiii (Leipzig, 1931), 145–6, E. Vetter, *Jahresh. Oest. Arch. Inst.*, xxxvii (1948), Beiblatt, cols. 74–112, H. Rix, op. cit.; some other recent remarks by A. J. Pfiffig, *Beiträge zur Namenforschung*, xi (1960), 256–9, U. Coli, *Nuovo saggio di lingua etrusca* (Florence, 1966), 11–13.

[5] Rix, op. cit., 360–2.

[6] Rix, op. cit., 357.

[7] Cf. Rix, op. cit., 373 n. 176.

it does not follow that the earlier *lautni* had had an exactly equivalent status. What was the earlier status of the *lautni*?

Scholars have been reluctant to believe that the Etruscan *lautni* were exactly like the Roman freedmen. The interpretation 'cliens', or something similar, has been put forward.[1] 'L'équivalence [*lautni*=*libertus*] ait porté plutôt sur la dépendance du *lautni* par rapport au *pater familias* que sur la notion d'émancipation de l'esclave'[2]—but an essential part of that idea is the widely accepted translation of *lautn* as *familia*,[3] which is in fact quite unproven. The name-formulae of the *lautni* fall into two obvious categories, in the smaller of which the *lautni* have both citizen *praenomina* and *gentilicia*, while in the larger they have merely a single personal name, with the *gentilicium* (and sometimes some other name) of the *patronus* in the genitive. The two bilinguals fall into the former category, which suggests that the *lautni* in the latter category did not necessarily have the precise status of Roman freedmen[4]—indeed it is most unlikely that they did, since there is no doubt that a great number of them belong to the time before the Social War. On the other hand the Etruscans must have had a word for a man who had been manumitted, i.e. who once having had a certain servile status had risen to a more free but still restricted status.

The geographical distribution of the *lautni* inscriptions is uneven: they are relatively numerous in the territories of Clusium and Perusia, and they are also to be found in the territories of Arretium,[5] Populonium,[6] Volaterrae,[7] and elsewhere[8] in northern Etruria. This shows that there was a similar

[1] A. Torp, 'Etruscan Notes' in *Skrifter udgivne af Videnskabs-Selskabet i Christiana, Hist.-filos. Kl.*, i (1905), 48; the interpretation has been favoured in varying degrees by Cortsen, Mazzarino, Heurgon, and Frankfort.

[2] Heurgon, *Historia*, art. cit., 95.

[3] C. Pauli, *Etruskische Studien*, iii (Göttingen, 1880), 98–9.

[4] Rix, op. cit., 356–66.

[5] *CIE* 372=*TLE* 659 ('la⟨u⟩tni').

[6] *CIE* 5211=*TLE* 380 ('lautnita', line 10).

[7] *CIE* 49=*TLE* 387 ('lautuniś'), *CIE* 129=*TLE* 393 ('lauṭni'—Rix, op. cit., 116 n. 41, supplies the correct reading, but I cannot accept his interpretation of the word as a name), *CIE* 159 ('lautnei'—surely genuine, but again not to be interpreted as a name, in spite of Rix, l.c.), *CIE* 4613 ('lautni'); *CII* 359 ('laṿtni'—the reading is not certain), *CII* 1031 ('lavtnei'—on the provenance of the inscription see Rix, l.c.) are questionable cases—Rix again interprets the word as a name, l.c.

[8] *CIE* 316=*TLE* 443 ('latni', S. Quirico d'Orcia, perhaps within the territory of Clusium), *CIE* 4622 ('lautn', Rapolano—taken to be a name by Rix, op. cit., 361 n. 121).

or identical status in each of these places, but the absence of *lautni* from the surviving inscriptions of Tarquinii (this is an open case),[1] Vulci, Volsinii,[2] Rusellae, Vetulonia, Cortona,[3] and Faesulae (less numerous than those of Clusium and Perusia) does not establish that a status similar or identical to that of the *lautni* was lacking in those states.

There is also epigraphical evidence for others in Etruria whose status was probably below that of the full citizens, but who are not specifically called *lautni*; these people have recently been the subject of a suggestive discussion by H. Rix.[4] Some of the points that he raises will be discussed later when the condition of Etruscan society immediately before the Social War comes under consideration.[5] Here it is only necessary to say that there is further evidence for the existence of a (quasi-) servile class in Etruria quite apart from the *lautni*, and that no case has been made out either by the literary evidence or by the inscriptions that the old Etruscan serf class had disappeared by the mid-second century B.C.[6]

In this discussion it is assumed that *lautni* is the only title referring to a servile status of any kind that is known to us. *Etera* has continued to be translated as *servus* (Mazzarino),[7] πενέστης (S. P. Cortsen),[8] client (Heurgon);[9] any of which would be very surprising in view of the style of the burial of the *etera*.[10] However, the only piece of evidence that should ever have carried any weight in favour of such a translation was the type of name-formula that supposedly indicated the depen-

[1] It seems doubtful whether 'lavtn' *et sim.* in *CIE* 5407 = *TLE* 100, *CIE* 5470 = *TLE* 135 and *SE* xxxii (1964), 107–29 = *TLE* 880, are the same as 'lautn', though Pallottino, *SE* xxxii (1964), 118–19, and Coli, op. cit., 11–13, believe so. For a doubtful case at Caere see *NSA* 1915, 384 (R. Mengarelli), M. Cristofani, *Mem. Acc. Linc.*, ser. 8. xiv (1969), 217.

[2] A very doubtful case in an inscription published by M. Cristofani, *SE* xxxiv (1966), 343–5 ('lavthṇ . . .').

[3] *CIE* 469 = *TLE* 637 is misreported in both collections and does not contain the word, see Rix, op. cit., 361 n. 121.

[4] Op. cit., 349–56, 374–6.

[5] Chapter VI, Section 1.

[6] For Plu. *TG* 8, on which Rix places far too much weight (374), see below, pp. 203–4.

[7] Art. cit., 113; similarly Pallottino, but he now gives *cliente, servo* with a question mark, *Etruscologia*[6] (Milan, 1968), 419.

[8] Op. cit., 77–91; both these suggestions were made by W. Deecke.

[9] *Historia*, art. cit., 95–6, followed by Frankfort, art. cit., 9–11, and by M. Capozza, *Movimenti servili nel mondo romano in età repubblicana*, i (Rome, 1966), 126.

[10] For which see Frankfort, art. cit., 10.

dence of the *etera*; the evidence was never very strong, and Rix, following Leifer, has demolished it.[1] In such Perusine inscriptions as 'au. semthni etera helvereal'[2] and 'la. venete la. lethial etera',[3] *helvereal* and *la. lethial* merely represent filiation; and names ending in -ś, found in conjunction with *etera* at Perusia, are merely gentilicial names of a quite common kind.

None of this epigraphical evidence would be sufficient in itself to justify the belief that there was a deep social division in Etruscan society that produced active conflict, but it is useful in varying degrees in confirming that parts at least of the literary evidence refer to real elements of Etruscan society.

Marginally useful for the same purpose are various representations of servile figures in Etruscan art; they are most useful in establishing that there were such persons in Etruria by the late sixth century (the Tomba della Caccia e Pesca at Tarquinii).[4] Some further archaeological evidence has been cited by Boëthius as relevant to the social system in allied Etruria;[5] in particular he believes that the existence of free lower and middle classes is attested 'by the dwellings along the streets of San Giovenale and Vetulonia', which are on a fairly small scale.[6] However there is no reason why most of these houses could not have been occupied by members of a serf class of the type that I have described.

Such is the sum of the evidence for the deep division in Etruscan society; at Arretium, at Troilum, at Volsinii, at Οἰναρέα, in Etruria in general, such a division makes its appearance, and the serf class 'between free men and slaves' that I have described can be recognized in the inscriptions. In Chapter VI, Section 1, it will be argued that the system survived in its essentials until the period of the Social War.

2. *The Alliance at Work*

This being the social structure of Etruria, as far as it can be known, what reasons have we for holding that Rome made an

[1] Op. cit., 371 n. 165, cf. Leifer, op. cit., 159–69 (but it is not necessary to accept his interpretation, 'nobilis').

[2] *CIE* 3965.

[3] *CIE* 4144.

[4] For a survey of the iconographical evidence see Frankfort, art. cit., 11–13.

[5] A. Boëthius, *Etruscan Culture, Land and People* (New York, 1962) (Eng. version of *San Giovenale, Etruskerna Landet och Folket*, Malmö, 1962), 75.

[6] For the San Giovenale evidence see K. Hanell in Boëthius, op. cit., 299–310.

arrangement with the local *principes* whereby their local power was supported in return for co-operation with the Roman government? The annalistic tradition offers us some particular incidents, and some general considerations strengthen the theory.[1]

The incidents at Arretium in 302, at Troilum in 293, and at Volsinii in 265–264 have already been examined. At Arretium the relatively pro-Roman Cilnii were probably restored to power by Roman intervention; that is specified in Livy's secondary version,[2] and it is implied that it was the case in the main version also. The Troilum incident, such as it is, shows that a Roman commander was willing to favour the richest section of the community, and that they were willing to co-operate with him; by itself it does not carry us very far, but it is some confirmation of the rest of the case. These incidents of course preceded the *foedera*, but that does not make them irrelevant to what happened later. The rebellion at Volsinii gives the clearest evidence of the policy: the masters or rather ex-masters sent representatives to Rome[3] asking for help (most clearly in the accounts of Florus and *De vir. ill.*).[4] Roman intervention followed because of the *foedus* with Volsinii (Zonaras), and the restoration of the masters was carried out,[5] although the transportation of the population is obviously not something that will have been desired by the masters.

Any Etruscans who in the two generations after the conquest had any hope of re-establishing their independence from Rome must have looked upon the Gallic tribes as the most likely if not the most desirable source of the necessary outside support. Yet the Gallic invasion of 225 was not the signal for an Etruscan

[1] The support of the allied ruling classes in general for the Roman government has often been commented on (see for example M. Gelzer, *Neue Jahrb.*, xxiii (1920), 17=*Von Römischen Staat* (Leipzig, 1943), ii.35=*KS* i (Wiesbaden, 1962), 172–3; E. T. Salmon, *Samnium and the Samnites* (Cambridge, 1967), 293). On Etruria cf. some remarks by O. W. Von Vacano, *The Etruscans in the Ancient World* (Eng. version, London, 1960), 165, 168, and D. W. L. Van Son, *Mnemosyne*, ser. 4.xv (1963), 268–9.

[2] X 5.13.

[3] Zonaras VIII 7.

[4] Florus I 16, *De vir ill.* 36, cf. Zonaras VIII 7, Oros. IV 5.3 *ad fin.*

[5] As the majority of accounts make clear; Zonaras VIII 7, Oros. IV 5.3, *De vir ill.* 36, cf. John of Antioch (*FHG* iv), p. 557 fr. 50, but not Val. Max. IX 1 ext. 2, Florus I 16.

rebellion. Far from it: Etruscans (and Umbrians) contributed on a large scale to the Roman forces.[1] The Gauls do not seem to have made any attempt to win over possibly dissident Etruscan opinion: *καταράραντες εἰς τὴν Τυρρηνίαν ἐπεπορεύοντο τὴν χώραν, πορθοῦντες ἀδεῶς.*[2] According to Polybius the inhabitants of Italy thought that they were fighting against the Gauls not for the sake of Roman supremacy but because their own cities and territories were endangered.[3] This statement, which probably goes back to Fabius Pictor, with the failure of the Etruscans to defect to the side of their former allies, surely indicates that Rome had established a stable understanding with the ruling classes of the Etruscan towns.

The great test of the Roman settlement in Italy came in the Hannibalic War;[4] the submissiveness of the Etruscans to Rome was tested by the sudden weakening of Roman military power in 217–216, which gave the Etruscans the best opportunity for rebellion that they had had since the conquest, by the gradual exhaustion of Rome during the rest of the war, and also by the heavy demands that the Romans made on Etruscan resources. There was indeed some disaffection in Etruria and in Umbria as well. Hannibal's propaganda repeatedly claimed that he intended to free the Italian allies of Rome from Roman domination (the most detailed statement is in Polyb. III 77.4–7),[5] and he took some practical measures to support this claim. Deserters from the Roman side before the battle of the Trebia were turned to good use[6] and captives were let off leniently.[7] He

[1] Polyb. II 24.5–7. The figures—4,000 cavalry and 50,000 infantry from the Sabines and the Etruscans, 20,000 Umbrians—have been thought to represent the number available by the *formula togatorum* (De Sanctis, *Storia dei romani*, iii.1 (Turin, 1916), 307 n. 2) rather than those who actually took up arms on this occasion. The fact that the Sabines and Etruscans were put under the command of a mere praetor is not a sufficient ground for this view; cf. Walbank on II 24.

[2] Polyb. II 25.1. Walbank (on II 23.4) suggests that they hoped to find Etruscan allies once more, but since the consul Aemilius Papus was at Ariminum, this supposition is not necessary to explain why the Gauls entered Etruria.

[3] II 23.13, cf. 21.7.

[4] An attempt to disprove the existence of the Roman policy described here was made by A. J. Pfiffig, *Historia*, xv (1966), 193–210, concentrating on the Hannibalic War.

[5] B. L. Hallward, *CAH* viii.33–5, gives a sensible account of Hannibal's strategy.

[6] Liv. XXI 48.2: 'Ad duo milia peditum et ducenti equites . . . ad Hannibalem transfugiunt; quos Poenus benigne adlocutus et spe ingentium donorum accensos in civitates quemque suas ad sollicitandos popularium animos dimisit.'

[7] 48.10.

released the Italian allies whom he captured at the Trebia, at Trasimene and at Cannae without requiring any ransom;[1] this he did in spite of his probable financial troubles.[2] The policy was an obvious enough one for him to follow,[3] but it did not dictate all his actions in Italy.

According to Livy Hannibal entered Etruria 'eam quoque gentem, sicut Gallos Liguresque aut vi aut voluntate adiuncturus',[4] and he devastated territory in north-eastern Etruria before the battle of Trasimene[5] and in Etruria and Umbria after the battle.[6] This was of course a policy likely to alienate the Etruscans and Umbrians. It might be argued that these alleged actions of Hannibal fit too neatly into a pro-Roman description of the war;[7] furthermore the motive attributed to Hannibal by Polybius and Livy,[8] namely that he wanted to entice the reckless Flaminius into battle, was probably elaborated to excess.[9] Yet the fact of the devastation is hardly to be doubted, especially if we consider the size of Hannibal's army, how far removed it was from its base, the presence of the Gallic allies, and the ripening crops. The region devastated before Trasimene will not have been the whole of Etruria and it will not have reached almost to Rome.[10] Livy speaks vaguely of the middle of Etruria (and there is an uncertainty in the text);[11]

[1] 'sine pretio', Liv. XXII 58.1–2 (there is some obscurity about what happened after Cannae, for a ransom was set in XXII 52.3); after the Trebia, Polyb. III 77.4, Zonaras VIII 24; after Trasimene, App. *Hann.* 10, cf. Liv. XXII 7.5.

[2] For which see Liv. XXII 61.2.

[3] But see below, p. 137 and n. 5, for the irrelevance of earlier Carthaginian connections with Etruria.

[4] XXI 58.2.

[5] Polyb. III 80.4–5, 82.1–3, Liv. XXII 3.6–4.1, Plu. *Fab.* 2.2, App. *Hann.* 9, Zonaras VIII 25.

[6] Polyb. III 86.8–9, Liv. XXII 9.1–2, Zonaras, l.c.

[7] Cf. App. *Pun.* 134 (Hannibal destroyed 400 towns in Italy), etc.

[8] Polyb. III 80–2, Liv. XXII 3.5.

[9] De Sanctis, op. cit., iii.2 (Turin, 1917), 37–8; but cf. Walbank on Polyb. III 82.

[10] As Appian, *Hann.* 9, and Polyb. III 82.6 respectively assert.

[11] XXII 3.6. The MSS. have 'et laeva relicto hoste Faesulas petens medio Etruriae agro praedatum profectus . . .'. Flaminius being at Arretium, Hannibal cannot have been making for Faesulae, and indeed any mention of Faesulae is out of place (so Conway's *praeteriens* for *petens* will not do). The error may have arisen from Polyb. III 82.1 (Walbank, etc.), but I do not think that a geographical confusion on Livy's part is a likely answer (*aliter* T. A. Dorey, *Euphrosyne*, iii (1961), 213–14, attributing the error to a Carthaginian source). R. L. Dunbabin restored the obvious sense with 'Cortonam petens', *CR* xlv (1931), 125–6, but it is not an

more precisely the area was that south of Arretium, but not very far from it,[1] especially 'inter Cortonam urbem Trasumenumque lacum'[2]—but he may also have been further south before the battle.[3] The detail of the paths taken by Hannibal's troops after the battle are as uncertain as those of earlier ones: he marched to the Adriatic somewhere in Picenum,[4] that is, he passed through Umbria. Various topographical indications are given in various sources, and one chronological one,[5] which is usually taken to be crucial, namely that he reached the Adriatic δεκαταῖος. Since, however, it is unclear when the period of time thus referred to began,[6] and since Hannibal had a substantial cavalry force, each indication of place has to be taken on its merits. Appian's statement that he went as far north as one day's march from Ariminum[7] is not very likely, and Narnia[8] was unnecessarily far out of his way, but that he reached as far south as the territory of Spoletium is plausible.[9] There is a further problem about the battle at the *Πλειστίνη λίμνη*,[10] which I take to be an indication that at least part of Hannibal's army moved eastwards from the area of Fulginiae into the valley of the eastward-flowing river Chienti.[11] The

easy change even though Faesulae has been named shortly before. Omission of the two words (Jordan) produces a clumsy sentence. *Non liquet.*

[1] Polyb. III 80.4, 82.1–3.

[2] Liv. XXII 4.1.

[3] Something is needed to explain Polyb. III 82.6; perhaps a cavalry expedition.

[4] Polyb. III 86.9, cf. Liv. XXII 9.3.

[5] Polyb. l.c.

[6] This is crucial in particular to the views that have been taken of the attack on Spoletium, rejected by L. Pareti, *RFIC* xl (1912), 544=*Studi minori di storia antica*, iii (Rome, 1965), 217, U. Kahrstedt in O. Meltzer, *Geschichte der Karthager*, iii (Berlin, 1913), 192, 413 n. 4, Walbank on Polyb. III 86.9, accepted by De Sanctis, op. cit., 121, and A. Klotz, *RhM* lxxxv (1936), 101–2 (and elsewhere). It would have been extremely easy for some of Hannibal's force to reach the territory of Spoletium along the Topino valley.

[7] *Hann.* 12.

[8] Zonaras VIII 25.

[9] Liv. XXII 9.1, cf. Zonaras, l.c.

[10] App. *Hann.* 9, 11.

[11] Again there has been much dispute and the topography cannot be discussed at length here. The version given by Appian of this stage of the Carthaginian advance is unique, and a doublet has been suspected of events elsewhere in 212; cf. Walbank on Polyb. III 86.1–7. But Hannibal is in any case likely to have passed very close to Plestia near the river Chienti; the *Πλειστίνη λίμνη* will have been the 'Padule di Colfiorito' (J. Kromayer, *Antike Schlachtfelder*, iii.1 (Berlin, 1912), 194, referring to earlier works).

sources agree that Hannibal's path was one of devastation; the communities affected will have been Perusia and all those in the long valley to the south-east of Perusia as far as Spoletium (the Val di Topino).

As far as we know from Polybius and Livy, there was no disaffection worth mentioning in Etruria and Umbria before the battle of Cannae, but one source, namely Zonaras,[1] though less detailed, refers to an important rebellion in Etruria; he says that after the Trebia Hannibal released allied prisoners to gain favour: *ἀμέλει καὶ τῶν λοιπῶν Γαλατῶν πολλοὶ καὶ Λιγύων καὶ Τυρσηνῶν τοὺς Ῥωμαίους τοὺς παρ' αὑτοῖς ὄντας οἱ μὲν φονεύσαντες, οἱ δὲ ἐκδόντες μετέστησαν*. This is most unlikely as far as the Etruscans of 218 are concerned,[2] and indeed it is rather an exaggeration for any stage of the war. Zonaras' account, though it may go back through Coelius Antipater to Silenus, has its inaccuracies and confusions;[3] and it is a crude form of source-criticism to explain the silence of Polybius and Livy about the supposed widespread revolt in Etruria as the 'official version of Fabius Pictor'[4]—upon whom Polybius was certainly not exclusively dependent. There are other points which help to make it unlikely that there was a general revolt in Etruria—or Umbria—while Hannibal was in the region. He went to the south because that was where he could expect support, and his short stay in Etruria and Umbria (he was in Picenum by early July in 217) shows that there were not easy gains to be made there. There is no reason to think that he was welcomed in the towns of north-eastern Etruria, and at no time did he have access to the Etruscan coast[5] in spite of the activities of a Carthaginian fleet in that area.[6] Polybius and Livy make Cannae the beginning of Rome's really serious difficulties with the allied states,[7] but there is no mention of the Etruscans or Umbrians in Livy's list of those who rebelled after the battle. It is unlikely that there were any widespread acts of rebellion,

[1] VIII 24.

[2] As is recognized even by A. J. Pfiffig, art. cit., 198, who prefers the account that Zonaras gives of Etruria to the implications of Polybius and Livy.

[3] On Dio's account of 218–216 see De Sanctis, op. cit., 195–202.

[4] Pfiffig, art. cit., 198 n. 21.

[5] Polyb. III 87.4.

[6] Polyb. III 96.8–10, Liv. XXII 11.6.

[7] Polyb. III 118.1–5, Liv. XXII 61.10–12.

especially since without the close presence of a Carthaginian army they would probably not have got very far. What Zonaras should have written was that many rebelled, (many) Gauls and (many) Ligurians and (some) Etruscans.

From 212 until 200 there was a Roman army, generally of two legions, continually stationed in Etruria (see table below, pp. 145–6). Its obvious purpose was to restrain rebellions, although that danger is only specified for 209–207 and 204–203, and there is also said to have been danger of invasion by Hasdrubal in 216[1] and more seriously from 210,[2] and later of invasion by Mago.[3] Etruscan discontent may well have been increased by special purchases of grain that were made, no doubt on Roman terms, in 212[4] and in 210,[5] as well as by the more regular exactions caused by the war. In 211, when Hannibal marched on Rome, he probably made a brief appearance in south Etruria,[6] but in 210 it was thought to be safe to settle Campanian prisoners in the territory of Veii, Sutrium, and Nepet,[7] an action quite inconsistent with great anxiety about the loyalty of Etruria as a whole. In the following year, according to Livy,[8] the discontent of the Latins and allies, occasioned by the transfer of their troops to Sicily, began to reach serious proportions. There was anxiety about a *defectio* in Etruria, beginning at Arretium, but because of the fear of Roman reinforcements the Etruscans kept quiet;[9] precautions

[1] Liv. XXIII 27–8. [2] Liv. XXVII 7.3.

[3] Cf. e.g. Zonaras IX 11 *ad fin.* for Mago as the target of M. Cornelius Cethegus, the consul to whom Etruria had been assigned in 204. From about 213 Rome was able to conduct a more forward policy in Gaul; see Liv. XXX 19.6–8 for the activities in Gaul of C. Servilius Geminus, the consul of 203 whose province was Etruria and Liguria.

[4] Liv. XXV 15.4, 20.3 (bought by the praetor who held Etruria as a province), cf. 22.5.

[5] Liv. XXVII 3.9.

[6] Liv. XXVI 11.8–13, the sack of Lucus Feroniae. This is doubted by De Sanctis, op. cit., 341, but cf. the inscriptions published by R. Bloch and G. Foti, *RPh* ser. 3.xxvii (1953), 65–77=*AE* 1953, nos. 195–6=*ILLRP* 93a–b.

[7] Liv. XXVI 34.7, 10. [8] XXVII 9.1–6.

[9] Liv. XXVII 21.6–7. '... sollicita civitas de Etruriae defectione fuit. Principium eius rei ab Arretinis fieri C. Calpurnius scripserat, qui eam provinciam pro praetore obtinebat. Itaque confestim eo missus Marcellus consul designatus, qui rem inspiceret ac, si digna videretur, exercitu accito bellum ex Apulia in Etruriam transferret. Eo metu compressi Etrusci quieverunt.' Cf. Plu. *Marc.* 28.1: παραλαβὼν δὲ τὴν ἀρχὴν πρῶτον μὲν ἐν Τυρρηνίᾳ μέγα κίνημα πρὸς ἀπόστασιν ἔπαυσε καὶ κατεπράϋνεν ἐπελθὼν τὰς πόλεις.

were also taken at Arretium in 208, one Roman commander being forbidden to leave the town before the arrival of his successor, who was told to guard against sedition.[1] There follows the exaction of hostages from the senators of Arretium and the patrolling of the whole of Etruria by C. Hostilius Tubulus to prevent possible rebellions.[2] Zonaras refers to an actual rebellion in Etruria, apparently in 208: οἱ δ' ἐν τῇ Ἰταλίᾳ καὶ ἐκ νόσου ἐπόνησαν καὶ μάχαις ἐταλαιπώρησαν, Τυρσηνῶν νεωτερισάντων τινῶν, which again seems to be overstated.[3] There were more alarms in 207: Hasdrubal had to be prevented from arousing the Cisalpine Gauls, or Etruria, 'erectam in spem rerum novarum',[4] and some Etruscans and also Umbrians were suspected to have discussed plans to rebel when he arrived, and to have helped him with supplies, *auxilia*, or other things; the consul M. Livius Salinator was sent to make an investigation.[5] (This incidentally is the only reference during the war to disloyalty in Umbria.) We know of no town in Etruria or Umbria that declared openly for Hasdrubal—not surprisingly, since he did not enter the territory of either people[6]—but clearly he received some covert support. It seems that in 209–207, in spite of Hasdrubal's invasion, the Romans kept Etruria and Umbria quiet with two legions, the regular garrison since 212, temporarily increased by one legion in 208.[7] Mago's invasion of Liguria was the occasion of similar troubles in Etruria. In 204 the consul M. Cornelius Cethegus 'non tam armis quam iudiciorum terrore Etruriam continuit, totam ferme ad Magonem ac per eum ad spem novandi res versam. Eas quaestiones ex senatus consulto minime ambitiose habuit . . .',

[1] Liv. XXVII 22.13: 'C. Calpurnius vetitus ab Arretio movere exercitum, nisi cum successor venisset; idem et Tubulo imperatum ut inde praecipue caveret ne qua nova consilia orerentur.'

[2] Liv. XXVII 24.7: 'C. Hostilium cum cetero exercitu placet totam provinciam peragrare et cavere ne qua occasio novare cupientibus res daretur.'

[3] IX 9.1. Cf. De Sanctis, op. cit., 474 n. 47.

[4] XXVII 38.6.

[5] Liv. XXVIII 10.4–5: '. . . in Etruriam provinciam ex senatus consulto est profectus ad quaestiones habendas qui Etruscorum Umbrorumve populi defectionis ab Romanis ad Hasdrubalem sub adventum eius consilia agitassent quique eum auxiliis aut commeatu aut ope aliqua iuvissent.' *Populi* implies that whole communities were involved, but the implication cannot be pressed.

[6] Hasdrubal's intention of meeting Hannibal in Umbria (Liv. XXVII 43.8) evidently referred to the *ager Gallicus* east of the Apennines.

[7] Liv. XXVII 24.6.

and many Etruscan nobles who had either gone to Mago themselves or had sent messages to him about the defection of their communities were condemned.[1] A last specific reference to disaffection in Etruria is made in 203—the consul C. Servilius Geminus held 'quaestiones ex senatus consulto de coniurationibus principum'.[2] Similar activities presumably continued until 200 (when there was nothing for the commander to do),[3] the last year when Etruria was assigned as a province and had a garrison. Again, it is clear that the co-operation with the Carthaginians was serious, but still covert.

Before all this evidence about the behaviour of the Etruscans during the war can be analysed in more detail, some recent misconceptions must be cleared out of the way.[4] It is most unlikely that the memory of Etruscan alliances with Carthage in the fourth century will have had any practical effect in the Hannibalic War.[5] It is pure fantasy to suppose that Livy's inability to find any record of the ultimate fate of the *Perusina cohors* of 216 shows that it deserted.[6] Too much has also been made of the behaviour of the Etruscan cavalry in the reconnaissance expedition near Petelia that was fatal to the consuls of 208. Marcellus selected for the task cavalrymen whom he had particular reason to trust[7]—as well he might—a force of 180 Etruscans and forty Fregellani;[8] when the Carthaginians sprang their ambush, the Etruscans were the first to take to flight. In spite of the circumstances, Livy says, 'extrahi tamen diutius certamen potuisset, ni coepta ab Etruscis fuga pavorem ceteris iniecisset' (that seems rather wishful thinking). 'Non tamen

[1] Liv. XXIX 36.10–12.

[2] Liv. XXX 26.12. The conflict in Livy's sources about whether the elections of 203 were held by the consul, or by the dictator 'quia eum res in Etruria tenuerint quaestiones ex senatus consulto . . .' is probably not relevant, but note that the consul was active in Gaul as well as in Etruria.

[3] Liv. XXXI 47.5.

[4] These are the creations of Pfiffig, art. cit.

[5] Implied by Pfiffig, art. cit., 197. He refers to the recently found gold sheets of Pyrgi, written in Punic and Etruscan; they are dated by most scholars to the early fifth century, by Pfiffig to the late fifth century; cf. J. Heurgon, *JRS* lvi (1966), 1–15. Etruscans fought with Agathocles (cf. Diod. XX 61.6–7) as well as with Carthage.

[6] Liv. XXIII 20.3. Pfiffig, art. cit., 202–3.

[7] Plu. *Marc.* 29.

[8] Plu., Liv. XXVII 26.11.

omisere pugnam deserti ab Etruscis Fregellani.'[1] This is supposed to be an example of the 'passive resistance' of the Etruscans to Rome,[2] although Marcellus, who clearly knew what the feelings of the Etruscans were at this time from his activities in Etruria in the previous year,[3] was using particularly trustworthy troops; it is not a likely interpretation. Nor is there any real basis for the implied view[4] that the alleged 'passive resistance' of the Etruscans was led by two Etruscan officers in command of the detachment of 180 cavalrymen. There were two *praefecti socium* in the reconnaissance expedition, L. Arrenius and M'. Aulius (we are not told explicitly that they were in command of the Etruscans or that they fled with the Etruscans), but whatever the regional origins of these *nomina* were, and they are far from certain,[5] and whether or not Livy was right in thinking that *praefecti socium* were at this time normally Roman citizens,[6] L. Arrenius was obviously the L. Arrenius who was tribune of the people in 210,[7] while Aulius was already a

[1] Liv. XXVII 27.5. Polyb. X 32 is the other main source for this incident, but he does not give the relevant details. For a sceptical discussion cf. De Sanctis, op. cit., 474 n. 49.

[2] Pfiffig, art. cit., 201.

[3] Liv. XXVII 21.7, cf. Plu. *Marc.* 28 *ad init.*

[4] Pfiffig, l.c.

[5] According to Pfiffig the name Arrenius 'entspricht dem etr. Gentilis *arni/arntni*', for which he refers to the (bilingual) tomb-group of the *arni/arntni* at Clusium, *CIE* 1468–9, *TLE* 502–3, where the Latin form used is Arrius; and to Schulze, *ZGLE* 125, 430, who incorrectly reports (125) that Arrenius is common in *CIL* xi as well as in *CIL* vi. There are some interesting cases of similar names, e.g. of Arinius in *CIE* 4767–8 (Clusium) and Etr. *arinei* in *CIE* 1159 (Clusium); there is nothing in *CIL* i². The case is better than that of Aulius, which appears in *CIL* i² 92–5, 2450 (all *vetustissimae* from Praeneste), 1508 (Cora), as well as in *CIE* 899=*CIL* xi.2294 (Clusium); see below for its early appearance in Rome.

[6] Livy's opinion is inferred from XXIII 7.3: 'Praefectos socium civisque Romanos alios . . .'. Some were well-known citizens, cf. XXXIII 36.5. For this view see J. Marquardt, *Römische Staatsverwaltung*, ii² (Leipzig, 1884), 396, J. Kromayer–G. Veith, *Heerwesen und Kriegführung der Griechen und Römer* (Munich, 1928), 276, followed by Walbank on Polyb. VI 26.5. As R. Syme pointed out in his review of *MRR* (*CPh* l (1955), 136), 'some of the prefects commanding allied troops in the third and second centuries B.C. are foreigners themselves', e.g. Marius Statilius, Vibius Accaus, and Salvius the Paelignian; there were of course separate native officers as well as the Roman *praefecti socium* (cf. Marquardt, l.c.); with the former Livy seems to withhold the actual title *praefectus socium* and to make a point of mentioning their nationality. It is always possible that Livy was mistaken in thinking Arrenius and Aulius Roman citizens, or rather it would be possible were it not for our other information about the names.

[7] Liv. XXVII 6.3.

consular name.[1] Some misconceptions that have arisen from Livy's list of the Etruscan states that contributed to Africanus' forces in 205 have already been discussed;[2] it is most improbable that the list of contributing towns is a list of the ones that had rebelled against Rome, or bears any relation to rebellions.

The following then were the dimensions of the Etruscan revolt: when, after several years of war, the Etruscans, like the other allies who remained officially loyal to Rome, began strongly to resent the burdens of the war, and when there was some prospect of Carthaginian forces arriving in Etruria itself, there was some Etruscan co-operation with Carthage.[3] The incident recounted by Livy in more detail than any other action of the Etruscans during the war was the exaction of hostages at Arretium in 208:[4] the town (which for simple geographical reasons was more likely than almost any other to see Hasdrubal) was considered to need a garrison of a legion even after the taking of hostages. Yet there was no armed rebellion, and the incident is surely given in relative detail because it was the most serious resistance to Rome that was encountered in Etruria. Even on this occasion Livy seems to regard the Roman reaction as rather exaggerated—'Is [C. Terentius Varro, the pro-magistrate] omnia suspectiora quam ante fuerant in senatu fecit. Itaque *tamquam imminente Etrusco tumultu*, legionem unam . . . ducere iussus . . .'[5] The garrison that was stationed in Etruria from 212 to 200 was obviously intended to maintain the loyalty of the allies there, but it must have had other purposes too, guarding what was in effect the

[1] Cos. 323, 319, *mag. eq.* 315; there are some difficulties about the correct name in the first case at least, cf. *MRR* i.149 n. 1, 154 n. 1, but they are not important here.

[2] Above, pp. 90–1.

[3] D. W. L. Van Son, *Mnemosyne*, ser. 4.xvi (1963), 267–74, argues that the rebellious movement of 209 was ill-timed, since Hasdrubal was not in fact on the point of arriving and that the 'turbulent mood' of the *principes* can only be explained by their belief that the end of a *saeculum* was approaching. It is reasonable to suppose that a *saeculum* did end at about this time (cf. above, p. 12), but any connection between this and the political decisions of Etruscans in 209 remains entirely speculative.

[4] XXVII 24.

[5] Liv. XXVII 24.6. For other occasions when Livy held that there was undue alarm about the Etruscans in Rome, see above, p. 94 n. 6.

Roman frontier with the Gauls and resisting the forces of Hasdrubal and Mago.

Besides the literary evidence concerning the actions of the Etruscans during the war, there is some numismatic and epigraphical evidence that may be relevant. A bronze coin issue that seems to have been minted in or near the Chiana valley in north-eastern Etruria depicts an elephant and a negro head.[1] Many scholars have been inclined to associate these coins with Hannibal,[2] but an earlier date also seems quite possible.[3] If the coins were minted during the war, they were 'an isolated pair of seditious types',[4] probably connected with the disaffection at Arretium in 208–207. There must certainly have been individual Etruscans who favoured Hannibal. A fascinating piece of epigraphical confirmation of this has recently come to light, in the form of a funerary inscription from Tarquinii.[5] On the most likely interpretation of the text the subject fought with Hannibal at Capua in 212–211.

The fact that there was some disloyalty to Rome in Etruria during the war does not disprove the existence of the understanding between Rome and the local *principes*;[6] indeed the relatively modest scale of the opposition shows that Rome had

[1] E. Babelon, *Rev. num.*, ser. 3.xiv (1896), 1–13=*Mélanges numismatiques*, iii (Paris, 1900), 153–65 (with references to earlier publications, n. 1), A. Sambon, *Les monnaies antiques de l'Italie* (Paris, 1903), 81 (type no. 145), R. Pedani, *SE* ii (1928), 645, H. H. Scullard, *Num. Chron.*, ser. 6.viii (1948), 162–3, W. Gowers and H. H. Scullard, *Num. Chron.*, ser. 6.x (1950), 278–80, E. S. G. Robinson, *Num. Chron.*, ser. 7.iv (1964), 46–8, F. P. Rosati in *Studi Annibalici* (Cortona, 1964), 176–80. The geographical origin is generally agreed (but cf. Rosati, l.c., for doubts).

[2] Babelon, Pedani, Scullard, Robinson.

[3] Thus Rosati, l.c., referring them to the First Punic War. The old suggestion of R. Garrucci, *Monete dell' Italia antica* (Rome, 1885), 58, that associated them with Pyrrhus' invasion is a possibility, especially as it seems to be agreed that the elephant is Indian (Gowers and Scullard, l.c.); for the first known representation of an elephant in Etruria (Capena—but the painter was not Etruscan) see J. D. Beazley, *Etruscan Vase-Painting* (Oxford, 1947), 211–15 (shortly after Pyrrhus).

[4] Robinson, art. cit., 48.

[5] M. Torelli, *SE* xxxiii (1965), 472–3=*TLE* 890. The text as now read by Pallottino (*TLE*) is 'felsnas la. lethes / svalce avil CVỊ / murce cạpuẹ / tleche ḥanipaluscle'. Torelli read the last word as 'ạanipaluscle', but his very detailed drawing makes the correct reading clear. He gave the inscription a second-century date. On the reading see further Pallottino, *SE* xxxiv (1966), 355–6, Pfiffig, *SE* xxxv (1967), 659–63 (independently detecting Hannibal), *Historia*, xvii (1968), 118.

[6] As apparently assumed by Pfiffig, *Historia*, xv (1966).

some hold in addition to the military one—two legions after all were not enough to prevent a general rebellion. Clearly the Romans knew that it was of the very greatest importance to maintain peace and, as far as possible, support in Etruria. A general Etruscan rebellion would have been disastrous, and indeed the loss of Etruscan resources, the extent of which is vividly illustrated by the contributions made in 205,[1] would in itself have been a very serious blow. The *principes* were held responsible for the behaviour of their states, and if they decided to be disloyal to Rome in the hope of receiving benefits from the Carthaginians, that was a reasonable calculation based on the view that the Carthaginians would bring about a permanent decrease in Roman power over the Italian states. Afterwards the loyalty of the *principes* was carefully examined by the Romans, and of course in many cases it was found wanting—but at the end of the Hannibalic War those who could establish that they had remained loyal had a strong claim to Rome's favour; and there was no easily available alternative to the previous system, for manpower was extremely scarce.

There are only three references that tell us anything directly about the behaviour of the *principes* during the war. The first concerns the Arretine incident mentioned above,[2] in which hostages were demanded of the local senators, and 120 of their children were taken to Rome after 'septem principes senatus', presumably implicated with Carthage, had managed to escape; the property of these seven was then sold off. We are told of investigations in Etruria in 204 and 203 (no towns are specified), as a result of which many Etruscan nobles were condemned or went into exile.[3] The consul of 204 conducted these cases in accordance with a decree of the senate 'minime ambitiose', and since the reference to the condemnation of many nobles immediately follows this, it is reasonable to suppose that the consul was forbidden not only to favour individuals but also to favour the *nobiles* in general—there may then be an implication that Rome normally looked favourably upon the *nobiles*.

[1] Liv. XXVIII 45.15–18, quoted above, p. 89 n. 6.

[2] Liv. XXVII 24.

[3] Liv. XXIX 36.10–12, XXX 26.12. The punishments of those who remained and were condemned were physical ones ('corporibus subtractis', XXXIX 36.12), cf. Pfiffig, art. cit., 208.

It is obvious that Roman arrangements in Etruria were severely shaken by all these events—how unstable the situation was immediately after the war we can learn from the brief notice concerning the slave-rising of 196.[1] Livy makes it clear that this rising was not brought about by Carthaginian prisoners like the one in Latium in 198[2]—it was too widespread,[3] and the slaves whose lives were spared were afterwards returned to their *domini*.[4] The rebels were clearly members of the local serf class, their position relatively strengthened by the Roman punishment of members of the class of *principes*. The Romans showed that the pre-war policy was being maintained—they could hardly do anything else—by suppressing the revolt, crucifying some of their prisoners, and returning others to their masters.

Livy believed that there was a uniform social pattern for all the disputes between pro- and anti-Romans in Italian towns during the Hannibalic War. Thus at Nola in 216: 'senatus ac maxime primores eius in societate Romana cum fide perstare; plebs novarum, ut solet, rerum atque Hannibalis tota esse.'[5] Discussing the Bruttian attack on Croton in 215, he generalizes the conditions: 'Crotone nec consilium unum inter populares nec voluntas erat. Unus velut morbus invaserat omnes Italiae civitates ut plebes ab optimatibus dissentirent, senatus Romanis faveret, plebs ad Poenos rem traheret.'[6] Even at Croton, however, the ambiguous behaviour of the popular leader Aristomachus[7] suggests that the situation was more complicated than that. Badian[8] points to several states where Livy's generalization seems to be at odds with his own facts, namely Locri, Arpi, and Tarentum,[9] and he suggests that 'Livy's account of class

[1] Liv. XXXIII 36.1–3.

[2] Liv. XXXII 26.

[3] 'Etruriam infestam prope coniuratio servorum fecit'; but the praetor suppressed the revolt with one urban legion.

[4] The hypothesis of Capozza, op. cit., 140, that the rebellion had Carthaginian inspiration, fails to convince.

[5] Liv. XXIII 14.7; cf. XXIII 6 for Capua.

[6] XXIV 2.8; cf. XXI 48.2.

[7] XXIV 2.9–11, 3.11–13.

[8] *FC* 147–8; my opinion expressed in *Historia*, xiv (1965), 292 n. 68, has changed somewhat. For a too sweeping attack on Livy's rule cf. J. S. Reid, *JRS* v (1915), 112–24.

[9] On which see respectively Liv. XXIII 30.8 (contrast XXIV 1–2), XXIV 47.6, XXIV 13.3.

divisions in Italy during the War . . . is a second-century myth, invented to uphold oligarchy in Italy'. It is clear at least that special factors were at work in some cases that ran contrary to Livy's rule, for example the general conflict between Greeks on the one hand and Lucanians and Bruttians on the other,[1] the calculations of the powerful *princeps* of Arpi Dasius Altinius,[2] and at Tarentum the division between *iuniores* and *seniores*,[3] the slaughter of hostages by the Romans,[4] and Hannibal's tactful restraint.[5] In fact Livy does not try to force his rather excessively schematic view of the social pattern of defections to Hannibal on to the events in Etruria—where in any case, as he was at least partially aware, the social system was quite different from that of the Greek and Campanian states to which his generalizations mainly refer.

The Roman system of supporting the local *principes* against their own local subjects was particularly well adapted to the social structure of Etruria, where the *principes* from time to time certainly needed support (Arretium in 302, Volsinii in 265, many areas in 196) and where there was no alternative to supporting them which would not involve radical social change. Unless the *principes* could be relied upon, an elaborate programme of colonization and settlement was necessary; indeed after the Hannibalic War the system was strengthened by some additional colonization and settlement, both in Etruria proper and to the north where the colonies were primarily relevant to other areas. During the second century there is evidence that Rome 'upheld oligarchy' in others parts of Italy,[6] as she often did outside Italy,[7] but it may also have happened earlier in areas with social systems different from the Etruscan one. There is, however, only one piece of evidence for this, namely Livy's

[1] Liv. XXIV 1–3, etc.

[2] Liv. XXIV 45.

[3] Cf. Polyb. VIII 30.1, Liv. XXV 8.3, etc.; P. Wuilleumier, *Tarente des origines à la conquête romaine* (Paris, 1939), 105.

[4] Liv. XXV 7.11–8.2.

[5] There was no devastation of Tarentine territory, Liv. XXIV 20.10, 15.

[6] Cf. the restriction of the *ius migrandi*, the intervention at Patavium in 174, the *civitas per magistratum*.

[7] For a balanced appraisal of this element in Roman policy towards the Greek world see J. Briscoe, *Past and Present*, xxxvi (1967), 3–20 (with bibliography, to which add A. H. M. Jones, *The Greek City from Alexander to Justinian* (Oxford, 1940), 170–1).

account of the action of L. Volumnius in Lucania in 296—'Lucanorum seditiones a plebeiis et egentibus ducibus ortas summa optimatium voluntate per Q. Fabium . . . compresserat',[1] and it is possible that the relevant details are apocryphal.

The Romans did not make their decision not to colonize extensively in Etruria primarily, if at all, because the Etruscans seemed alien to them and unlikely to become Romanized,[2] but because there was an excellent method of maintaining security in Etruria that made colonization largely unnecessary. Yet the choice of this method of control, together with the continuing willingness of the Roman government to leave to the allied states in Etruria, as elsewhere in Italy, a high degree of autonomy in their internal affairs (Chapter III, Section 3), necessarily affected the speed of Romanization in Etruria. How colonization affected this process in both Etruria and Umbria, how other factors did, and the chronology of Romanization in the two regions are questions that are dealt with in the next chapter.

[1] Liv. X 18.8.

[2] See above, pp. 97–8, for this and other supposed reasons for the Roman decision.

APPENDIX TO CHAPTER IV

A List of Roman Officials and Armies in Etruria between 212 and 200[1]

DATE	OFFICIAL	RANK	ARMY	REFERENCES
212	M. Iunius Silanus	pr.	2 urban legions of 213	Liv. XXV 3.2, 3.4 (cf. XXIV 44.3), 20.3
	C. Servilius	legate		XXV 15.4
211	M. Iunius Silanus	propr.	the same two legions	XXVI 1.5
210	C. Calpurnius Piso	propr.	2 urban legions of 211	XXVI 28.6, XXVII 6.1, 7.10, 21.6, 28.4, 28.6
	temporarily replaced by C. Sempronius Blaesus	legate of the dict.		XXVII 6.1
	P. Aquilius M. Ogulnius	legates		XXVII 3.9
209	C. Calpurnius Piso	propr.	2 urban legions of 210	XXVII 7.10, 21.6
	for taking the new legions to Etr. and old ones back to R. C. Fulvius Flaccus	legate of cos.		XXVII 8.12
	M. Claudius Marcellus	cos. des.		XXVII 21.7, cf. Plu. *Marc.* 28.1
208	C. Calpurnius Piso	propr.		XXVII 22.13
	replaced by C. Hostilius Tubulus	propr.	2 legions	XXVII 22.4, 22.13, 24.1, 24.7, 35.2
	C. Terentius Varro	propr.	1 legion	XXVII 24, 35.2
207	M. Livius Salinator	cos.		XXVIII 10.4–5
	C. Terentius Varro	propr.	2 legions of *volones*	XXVII 36.13, XXVIII 10.11
206	M. Livius Salinator	procos.	the same 2 legions	XXVIII 10.11
205	M. Livius Salinator (ordered to Ariminum with his army because of Mago)	procos.	the same 2 legions	XXVIII 45.10, 46.13
	M. Valerius Laevinus	? [2]	2 urban legions	XXVIII 46.13

[1] B. L. Hallward gives a 'Table of Legions and Commanders in the Second Punic War', *CAH* vii, facing p. 104; for Etruria it is not complete.

[2] He must have received *imperium* from the urban praetor to transport the two legions; see *MRR* i.303 and n.

DATE	OFFICIAL	RANK	ARMY	REFERENCES
204	M. Cornelius Cethegus	cos.	the same 2 legions	XXIX 13.1, 36.10, Zon. IX 11 *ad fin.*
203	C. Servilius Geminus (also assigned Liguria)	cos.	the same 2 legions	XXX 1, 19.6
202	C. Servilius Geminus	procos.		XXX 27.6, 38.6, 39.4
	M. Servilius Pulex Geminus	cos.	2 legions	XXX 27, 39.4, 41.3, cf. Zon. IX 14
201	M. Servilius Pulex Geminus	procos.	2 legions	XXX 41.3
200	L. Furius Purpurio (assigned Gaul, but later sent by cos. to Etr.).	pr.	5,000 allied troops	XXXI 6.2, 10.5, 11.3, 21.1, 47.4–6

V

THE ROMANIZATION OF ETRURIA AND UMBRIA

THE Romanization of Etruria and Umbria, the process by which the inhabitants came to be and to think of themselves as Romans, has never received the attention that it deserves. It is of course closely bound up with Roman policies in the two regions during most of the period covered by the present work: Roman policies affected the manner and the pace of Romanization, and if we are to understand the Roman policies of the period of the Social War a careful analysis of Romanization is essential. The process itself was, needless to say, one of the greatest complexity, and only certain parts of it can be revealed by the existing evidence. By concentrating on those parts I do not mean to diminish the possible importance of factors that cannot be examined in detail, for example the service of Etruscan and Umbrian soldiers with the Roman army; indeed it will be possible to make more accurate surmises about such matters when the available facts have been examined. First the framework of colonies and other Roman settlements and of Roman roads that developed during the third and second centuries will be discussed; then the best type of evidence that we have for the progress of Romanization, that which concerns the changes from the use of the Etruscan and Umbrian languages to Latin; then the possibility of Roman influence upon certain institutions of the allied states, with particular reference to the *kvestur* of the Iguvine Tables; and finally there will be examined the question of the enfranchisement of individuals from the allied states of Etruria and Umbria before the Social War.

1. *Colonization*[1]

In Etruria only one colony was certainly founded in the period from 311 to 264, namely the Latin colony of Cosa in

[1] Lists of colonies with references were made by De Ruggiero, *Diz. Ep.*, s.v.

273[1] on the territory of Vulci.[2] An early third-century date for this colony is supported by the archaeological evidence.[3] Before the Second Punic War there were probably four citizen-colonies on the south coast of Etruria in territory taken from Caere. Of these *coloniae maritimae*[4] Alsium and Fregenae were probably founded in 247 and 245 respectively.[5] Two colonies called Castrum Novum,[6] one in Etruria, the other in Picenum, are known much later from inscriptions, while Livy's *Periocha* gives the foundation of a colony at 'Castrum' in the period 290–286[7] and Velleius says that 'Castrum' became a colony in 264.[8] It is very possible that there was only one colony called Castrum Novum at any early date.[9] However, while the *Periocha* refers rather more easily to the Picene site (Castrum is mentioned with Sena, i.e. Sena Gallica, and Hadria, in the same area),[10] Livy's reference to 'Castrum Novum' in 191 is shown by the context

colonia, 452–4, E. Kornemann, *RE* s.v. *coloniae* (1901), cols. 514–22, E. Pais, *Mem. Acc. Linc.*, ser. 5.xvii (1924), 323–55. A full doxography of the dating of each colony is unnecessary here, especially as there is so little evidence.

[1] Vell. I 14.7, cf. Liv. *Per.* 14.

[2] Cosa Volcientium, Plin. *NH* III 51.

[3] See esp. F. E. Brown, *MAAR* xxvi (1960), 9 n. 5 (referring to 'the earliest dateable deposit in the Forum area, in which the only coins are issues of the early third century'). M. Lopes Pegna attempted to revive the theory that the Livy and Velleius passages did not refer to Cosa in Etruria, *SE* xxii (1952–3), 411–20 (the view goes back through Pais, art. cit., 331, and Mommsen, *Geschichte des römischen Münzwesens* (Berlin, 1860), 315 n. 75, to Madvig and Ruhnken). Following Pais, he imagined a town of Cosa in the valley of the Silarus (= Sele) near Paestum as the colony of 273; to explain its disappearance he devised a strange theory of its transference to the Etruscan site in 199. The whole view is obviously mistaken, and an exhaustive refutation is not necessary here. There is no need whatsoever to suppose that Cosa was situated in the vicinity of Paestum.

[4] On *coloniae maritimae* see E. T. Salmon, *Athenaeum*, xli (1963), 3–38.

[5] Vell. I 14.8, cf. Liv. *Per.* 19. The foundation of Fregenae is mentioned before the censorship of 247 by Liv. *Per.*, with the foundation of the colony at Brundisium, which Velleius (I 14.8) puts in 244 with a consular date. Velleius' date for Fregenae is slightly preferable to one in the period 249–7.

[6] See Salmon, art. cit., 20–3, M. Torelli, *SE* xxxv (1968), 342–7, on the foundation-dates of these two colonies.

[7] *Per.* 11. How many years after 290 this could be is uncertain, since there is a lack of firm dates in *Per.* 11, cf. *MRR* i.184 n. 2, 186 n. 2 (under 287 B.C.), 187 n. 1 (under 285 B.C.). *MRR* (i.189 n. 2) suggested that Livy may have gathered together notices of foundations with which Curius Dentatus was connected (he died in 270).

[8] I 14.8: 'initio primi belli Punici'.

[9] As L. R. Taylor, *VDRR* 91 n. 36, points out.

[10] This argument should not be discounted altogether, as by Salmon, art. cit., 20.

to refer to the site in Etruria,[1] and the context also makes it probable that the colony was founded before the Second Punic War.[2] There is now some archaeological confirmation that there was a colony at Castrum Novum in Etruria in the third century.[3] Dio says[4] that the Agyllaeans (i.e. Caeritans) surrendered half their territory to Rome, and that is generally referred to 274 or 273,[5] in which case the 264 date for Castrum Novum must be the right one.[6] It seems likely that this was the foundation-date of Castrum Novum in Etruria. Pyrgi was also a *colonia maritima* in the same district in 191,[7] and it too was probably founded before the Second Punic War and indeed before 241.[8]

After the war it continued to be Roman policy to leave most of allied Etruria free of colonies. Apart from Luca (a Latin colony about 178) and Luna (a citizen colony of 177), both in districts that were not really Etruscan, there was only one area where this did not apply. Saturnia was established as a citizen-colony in 183 in the *ager Caletranus*.[9] Saturnia is also one of the towns listed by Festus as a *praefectura*,[10] and some have thought that the colony was the *praefectura*,[11] which is conceivable. But

[1] Liv. XXXVI 3.6: 'Ostia et Fregenae et Castrum Novum et Pyrgi et Antium et Tarracina et Minturnae et Sinuessa fuerunt, quae cum praetore de vacatione certarunt.' Cf. E. Bormann, *CIL* xi. p. 530—all the other colonies listed are on the west coast and they are given almost in order; *contra* Weissenborn.

[2] The case is parallel to that of Pyrgi, for which see below.

[3] M. Torelli, l.c.

[4] Fr. 33.

[5] See above, p. 83.

[6] Recently it has been argued in favour of *c.* 289 that 264 was an obvious date for Velleius to have supplied for this colony (Salmon, art. cit., 22–3—but he now favours 264 as the foundation-date of Castrum Novum in Etruria, *Roman Colonization under the Republic* (London, 1969), 79, 180 n. 119)—which does not carry us very far—and that Cosa must have been supported by other colonies on the south coast of Etruria, an argument that has some force but can be discounted by the fact that unlike *coloniae maritimae* Cosa was large enough to look after itself except in extreme emergencies.

[7] Liv. XXXVI 3.6.

[8] Cf. G. Tibiletti, *Athenaeum*, xxviii (1950), 196 n. 1, E. T. Salmon, *Phoenix*, ix (1959), 70 n. 31, *Athenaeum*, art. cit., 23–4: the fact that the *coloni maritimi* could claim *vacatio militiae* in 191 suggests the pre-war date, since the colonies of 194 (among which Salmon had counted Pyrgi, *JRS* xxvi (1936), 48) had probably never had it. The omission of Pyrgi from the list in Liv. XXVII 38.4 does not prevent this, cf. Tibiletti, art. cit., 187 n. 2.

[9] Liv. XXXIX 55.9.

[10] 262.15L.

[11] Mommsen, *Römisches Staatsr.*, iii.581 n. 4, 814, H. Rudolph, *Stadt und Staat im römischen Italien* (Leipzig, 1935), 145–7.

in default of any good example of a colony which was at the same time a *praefectura*,[1] it is better to follow Beloch[2] in supposing that the *praefectura* of Saturnia was an earlier stage of its development than the colony of 183. When the *praefectura* came into being necessarily remains unknown. Graviscae was set up as a citizen-colony in the territory of Tarquinii in 181.[3] The other known colony in Etruria that is probably of pre-Sullan date is Heba, evidently the *oppidum Herbanum* in Pliny's town-list;[4] it was a colony under the Empire,[5] and the silence of ancient writers about its foundation suggests a date before 133 B.C., and the period 167–157 is perhaps most likely.[6] Such a date remains speculative.

Also attested as a settlement of Roman citizens before the Social War is Statonia,[7] described as a *praefectura* by Vitru-

[1] The possible cases are Capua, Puteoli, Liternum, and Volturnum, besides Saturnia; but see M. W. Frederiksen in *RE* s.v. Puteoli (1959), col. 2040 (and references there). The most important text is in Festus himself (262L): 'Praefecturae eae appellabantur in Italia in quibus et ius dicebatur et nundinae agebantur; et erat quaedam earum r.p., *neque tamen magistratus suos habebant*.' On *praefecturae* cf. U. Kahrstedt, *Historia*, viii (1959), 174–5.

[2] *It. Bund* 115, *RG* 455.

[3] Liv. XL 29.1, cf. Vell. I 15.2. Velleius gives 182, but one of the founding commissioners of Graviscae, C. Terentius Istra, was then praetor in Sardinia. Velleius' dates for Graviscae and Pisaurum (and others) can easily be made to correspond with Livy's; see Salmon, *JRS* xxvi (1936), 49–50.

[4] *NH* III 52.

[5] As was shown by an inscription published by A. Minto, *NSA* 1919, 199–206= *AE* 1920, no. 97 ('Genio Coloniae Hebae . . .'); dated to the second century A.D. by E. Pais, *Mem. Acc. Linc.*, ser. 6.i (1925), 394 n. 1.

[6] Beloch, *RG* 608, suggested a date after the break in Livy, perhaps in the second half of the second century; but between the 150s (I continue to assign Auximum to the 150s, in spite of E. T. Salmon, *Athenaeum*, xli (1963), 4–13, who attempts to move it to 128), if not the 170s, and the 120s there was a period without colonization, and from the 120s onwards we are relatively well-informed. Tibiletti, art. cit., 185–8, has pointed out the incompleteness of the sources on colonization even for the period before 167, but no omissions are known as serious as the total omission of a new colony. Salmon, *Roman Colonization under the Republic*, 114–15, now argues for a foundation-date in 128.

[7] The exact site is uncertain. The problem of identifying it is complicated by the difficulty of identifying the *lacus Statoniensis* (the Lake of Bolsena or of Mezzano?—the latter is about 4½ miles west of Lake Bolsena and very small). Poggio Buco and Castro, both in the Fiora valley, are the most favoured sites (G. Pellegrini, *NSA* 1898, 429–50, *A & R* ii (1899), cols. 2–13, G. Matteucig, *Poggio Buco, the Necropolis of Statonia* (Berkeley—Los Angeles, 1951), 1, *Hommages à M. Renard* (Brussels, 1969), iii.437–40, and M. Pallottino, *Etruscologia*[6] (Milan, 1968), 188, favour Poggio Buco, but cf. E. H. Richardson, *The Etruscans* (Chicago, 1964), 23, who points out the smallness of the town-site attached to the cemetery of Poggio Buco. J. B. Ward-

vius,[1] a status that it must have received before the Social War.[2] If Statonia was like most other *praefecturae*, its inhabitants were locals with Roman citizenship, and this view has been taken of Statonia.[3] But the local people of this area must have been relatively poor candidates for the citizenship, remote from the main lines of communication and all means of Romanization. There is no evidence to suggest that Statonia could or would be treated separately from Vulci, the federated town in the territory of which Statonia probably lay. It is better to suppose that Statonia was populated at least in part with Roman settlers who had assignments of *ager viritanus*;[4] the literary records of such grants are obviously very far from complete. The date of the settlement cannot be determined. Visentium[5] was governed by *duoviri* under the Empire, and has therefore been regarded as a citizen-community from before the Social War. It would be plausible to associate it with the settlement of Statonia,[6] but there is no evidence. Thus a large band of territory from the lower Albegna valley (if we include Heba) eastwards almost as far as Lake Bolsena (and perhaps as far as Visentium on the lake) seems to have been settled by the first half of the second century.[7]

The four *fora* known to have been established in Etruria should also be mentioned.[8] If Forum Subertanum in Livy[9] is

Perkins is definite in his preference for Castro (oral communication)—a view put forward by T. Lotti and F. Rittatore, *SE* xv (1941), 299–305). Poggio Buco is favoured somewhat by the Etruscan inscription *statnes* (this seems to be the best reading) on some sling-bullets found there (the number and provenance of these has now been clarified by Matteucig, art. cit.; previous descriptions of them, including *TLE* 347 and *ILLRP* 1119, should be forgotten); and it is possible that Statonia was a very small town.

1 II 7.3.

2 Cf. Beloch, *RG* 576–7, Sherwin-White, *RC* 138.

3 G. De Sanctis, *Storia dei Romani*, ii.398.

4 A. Afzelius, *Die römische Eroberung Italiens* (*340–264 v. Chr.*) (Copenhagen, 1942), 117. Note that some of the people of Poggio Buco spoke Etruscan in its Roman period, Pellegrini, *NSA* 1898, 440–1.

5 The name is reconstructed from adjectival forms, cf. E. Bormann, *CIL* xi. pp. 444–445.

6 Beloch, *RG* 510, 566, Taylor, *VDRR* 86 n. 21.

7 Suana (=Sovana) in the Fiora valley was probably in Roman territory (Beloch, *RG* 608), but there is no reason to think that it was a separate *praefectura* (as E. Manni supposed, *Per la storia dei municipii fino alla guerra sociale* (Rome, 1947), 74).

8 On the status of *fora* cf. Beloch, *RG* 581, Sherwin-White, *RC* 70–2.

9 XXVI 23.5, 211 B.C.

represented by the Subertani in Pliny's list,[1] then it was in Etruria, but the site is uncertain.[2] The other three *fora* were situated on the main roads, the Via Aurelia, the Via Clodia, and the Via Cassia. All three roads were probably organized within the period 200–144 (see the following section). Forum Clodii was in any case established early enough to be counted as a *praefectura*.[3] Forum Aurelii was situated on territory that had belonged to Vulci, Forum Clodii on that of Caere, and Forum Cassii on that of Tarquinii.[4]

I do not believe that there were any Gracchan colonies in Etruria, and if there was much Gracchan settlement there it was probably short-lived; the Sullan settlement had more effect as far as Romanization was concerned. Both the Gracchan and the Sullan settlements are discussed in detail below.[5]

In Umbria the Latin colony Narnia was planted in 299.[6] Spoletium was made a Latin colony, probably in 241.[7] East of the Apennines, in the part of region VI that was outside Umbria proper, a number of colonies and other settlements were made in the territory taken from the Senones after their defeat: there was possibly a citizen-colony at Aesis in 247[8] and certainly one at Pisaurum in 184.[9]

[1] *NH* III 52.

[2] Possibly it is Suvureto, north-east of Populonia, off the Via Aurelia (H. Kiepert, *Formae Orbis Antiqui*, xx (Berlin, 1902), p. 6), but it is not a typical *forum* site; and (against) cf. Dennis, *Cities and Cemeteries of Etruria*, i² (London, 1878), 479 n. 3, G. Alessio, *Atti Acc. Pontaniana*, n.s. ix (1959–60), 293–321.

[3] Plin. *NH* III 52, cf. *CIL* xi.3310a=*ILS* 904.

[4] See Weiss in *RE* s.vv.

[5] Pp. 204–6, 259–67.

[6] Liv. X 10.5.

[7] Vell. I 14.8, cf. Liv. *Per.* 20, Cic. *Balb.* 48. But Velleius also says that the *Floralia* began in the same year, an event that Pliny (*NH* XVIII 286) dated to 238 (after Varro). Cf. E. Pais, *Mem. Acc. Linc.*, ser. 5.xvii (1924), 336, *MRR* i.219–20. It is hardly possible that Tuder was a Latin colony, *pace* A. Alföldi *Early Rome and the Latins* (Ann Arbor, 1965), 272.

[8] 'Aefulum [or Aesulum] et Alsium', Vell. I 14.8; 'Aesis' was produced by Mommsen, *Geschichte des römischen Münzwesens*, 332 n. 113; accepted by Beloch, L. R. Taylor, *VDRR* 86 n. 20, etc.; rejected by Salmon, *Phoenix*, ix (1955) 66 n. 15, etc. Aefulum may perhaps have been Aefula near Tibur (for which see L. Cozza, *Rend. Acc. Linc.*, ser. 8.xiii (1958), 248–50), in spite of the fact that it is not coastal.

[9] Liv. XXXIX 44.10, cf. Vell. I 15.2. On the date cf. p. 150 n. 3. Further references (arising from the fact that Ennius was among the colonists): Cic. *Brut.* 79, *Arch.* 22, Jerome on Ol. 160.2 (on this passage see F. Marx, *RE* s.v. Accius no. 1 (1894), Salmon, *JRS* xxvi (1936), 50). Cf. Tibiletti, art. cit., 201.

Some other places in Umbria probably received Roman settlers. Fulginiae eventually became a *praefectura*,[1] and it probably received some settlers, although the Umbrian *maronatus* and the Umbrian language seem to have survived there until quite late.[2] Various other Umbrian towns have been held to be citizen-communities in which grants of *ager viritanus* were made to Romans. The possible cases are, from south to north, Interamna Nahars, Carsulae, Plestia, and Tadinum. For Interamna its Latin name is the best evidence, and the total case is strong.[3] Carsulae's Roman status is very hypothetical, depending primarily on one Augustan 'IIvir iure dicundo' of the town[4] as against a number of *quattuorviri*.[5] The citizen-community of Plestia is argued from the appearance there of the octovirate;[6] that is convincing, but it also suggests that Plestia should be considered more Sabine than Umbrian (although it was later in region VI).[7] The possibility that Tadinum was a citizen-community before the Social War depends on whether the *duovir* in *CIL* xi.5802 held office there; it is an open case.[8] Of these four towns only Interamna is more likely than not to have been a citizen-community in Umbria. Since it can be shown that several of the main Umbrian towns became *civitates foederatae*, we should not assume that any particular place within the region was a Roman citizen-community without specific

[1] Cic. *pro Vareno* fr. 6 Puccioni.

[2] See below, p. 185.

[3] L. R. Taylor, *VDRR* 83–5, argues that I.N. was a community of Roman citizens before the war; her other reasons are (i) that Interamna was in the tribe Clustumina, and (ii) that it had strong connections with Sabine territory. Neither argument is in itself strong. It was an allied town until the war in Beloch's view, *RG* 606.

[4] *CIL* xi.4575.

[5] It 'may well have been a foundation of Roman citizens' according to Taylor, *VDRR* 85. On the *IIvir* at Carsulae, cf. A. Degrassi, *Mem. Acc. Linc.*, ser. 8.ii (1950), 335–6. Also allied until the war according to Beloch, l.c.

[6] *CIL* xi.5621.

[7] Plestia as a citizen community before the war: Beloch, *RG* 500, Taylor, *VDRR* 92 n. 37. It is surely easier to believe that Plestia was not originally Umbrian (cf. T. Frank, *Klio*, xi (1911), 368 n. 2) than that the Sabine octovirate made this one appearance in Umbria, in spite of almost all who have written on the octovirate (see most recently P. A. Brunt, *JRS* lv (1965), 103 n. 97).

[8] E. Bormann argues for this, *CIL* xi. pp. 823, 853 (pointing out that neither Sentinum nor Iguvium, the neighbouring states, had *duoviri*, and that Sentinum, unlike the subject of the inscription, was not in the tribe Clustumina). Cf. Beloch, *RG* 561, Taylor, *VDRR* 85 n. 19. But the inscription was found rather far from Tadinum, and on the Via Flaminia.

evidence.[1] In Umbria there was also Forum Flaminii,[2] presumably established in 220 with the Via Flaminia.[3] The location of two other Umbrian *fora* mentioned by Pliny, those of the *Foroiulienses cognomine Concupienses* and the *Forobrentani*, is unknown.[4] Thus all the Roman settlement in Umbria was probably in the south of the region, on or to the east of the Via Flaminia. Unless Carsulae was an isolated pocket (which is unlikely), or Tadinum was, these settlements formed a number of extensions of the Roman territory taken from the Sabines.

In order to find out why particular colonies were sent out and why viritane settlements were made in particular places, we need to look both at the historical contexts of the foundations and also at their sites and physical character. It is widely agreed that the main reasons for sending out colonies in Italy were, before the Gracchi, military ones, although this explanation is scarcely exhaustive and leaves unidentified the forces that produced Roman expansion. It has been applied to the Latin colonies and to the large citizen-colonies of 183 and later, as well as to the earlier type of citizen-colony.[5] This was an interpretation of the colonization of this period given by later Roman writers: the *maiores* 'colonias sic idoneis in locis contra suspicionem periculi conlocarunt ut esse non oppida Italiae sed propugnacula imperi viderentur', Cicero claimed.[6] Compare Appian's phrase ἀντὶ φρουρίων[7] and Siculus Flaccus' explanation of colonies:[8] 'Coloniae autem inde dictae sunt quod Romani in ea municipia miserint colonos, vel ad ipsos priores municipiorum populos coercendos, vel ad hostium incursus repellendos.' This explanation, as Flaccus knew, covers a

[1] Beloch, *RG* 561, mentions the possibility of Nuceria Camellaria as a Roman community; E. Manni, op. cit., 149–50, suggests Matilica as a *praefectura*, Arna as a *conciliabulum*. None of these is supported by any substantial testimony.

[2] Plin. *NH* III 113.

[3] Cf. Festus 74L. The site is discussed by G. Radke, *RE* s.v. Vicus Forum Flaminii (1958), cols. 2563–7.

[4] Plin. *NH* III 113. Forum Sempronii was outside Umbria proper.

[5] Salmon, *JRS* xxvi (1936), 51–55, dealing with the period from the Second Punic War to the Gracchi; cf. now *Roman Colonization under the Republic*, 14–17, 95–109.

[6] Cic. *Agr.* II 73—*propugnaculum* was evidently a common description, cf. Cic. *Font.* 13 (Narbo Martius), Tac. *Hist.* III 34 (Cremona).

[7] *BC* I 7.27.

[8] Siculus Flaccus, *de cond. agr.* 135. 20–23L.

variety of different circumstances. It seems obvious that Narnia was founded in 299 to hold down the local population in a new area,[1] like the colonies in Samnium, but it could also serve the purpose of resisting intrusions by Gauls.[2] The military purpose of the foundation of Cosa in 273 is more complicated. It may have been intended to provide some control over the coastal Etruscan states—the active resistance of Vulci had lasted at least until 280—yet by 273 Etruscan naval power was at an end and the coastal site suggests that there was also already an intention of establishing a naval base that could be used against the other naval power of the western Mediterranean, the Carthaginians, who controlled Sardinia.

Saturnia (183) is the most difficult colony to explain. According to the 'military' explanation it controlled 'an easy road to and from the littoral along the valley of the Albinia and was admirably placed to prevent raids on central Etruria from the sea'.[3] Saturnia is certainly a highly defensible site, which suggests that it was meant to deal with some military threat or other. But the Ligurian pirates cannot have been a serious danger to central Etruria. Never at their most successful are they known to have appeared south of the *ager Pisanus*. Massilia complained of their activities in 181,[4] but they must have been regarded by Rome as a temporary nuisance, and in the same year thirty-two ships were taken from them.[5] The colony of Graviscae (181) was an obvious step if the naval strength of Rome on this coast needed increasing, but it does not show that there was a military need for Saturnia.[6] The usefulness of Saturnia in dealing with pirate raids would in any case have been extremely limited, since it was some twenty miles from Telamon and even further from Cosa. Cosa itself, supported by

[1] Cf. 'adversus Umbros', Liv. X 10.5.

[2] Cf. P. Fraccaro, *Atti del Congr. internaz. di diritto romano* (Rome, 1933), i.114= *Opuscula*, i (Pavia, 1956), 207.

[3] Salmon, art. cit., 53; A. H. McDonald, *CHJ* vi (1939), 128 (prevention of piracy and customs control); followed with less confidence by Tibiletti, art. cit., 202 n. 2.

[4] Liv. XL 18.4.

[5] Liv. XL 28.7.

[6] Saturnia as a strategic position: E. Martinori, *Via Cassia e sue deviazioni* (Rome, 1930), 197 n. 1, detects roads running in many directions from Saturnia; preliminary investigations of the area by J. B. Ward-Perkins, G. C. Duncan (notes in the possession of J. B. Ward-Perkins), and by myself tend to support this, but the dates of these roads are quite uncertain.

the coastal colonies to the south, was much better placed and would have been able to deal with anything less than a great invasion. As for the possibility that Saturnia was intended to hold down the local population, there had been, it is true, some need for Roman troops in Etruria as recently as 190;[1] the praetor P. Iunius Brutus had been given Etruria as his province with one Roman legion and 10,000 infantry and 4,000 cavalry of allies and Latins,[2] in 189 his command had been continued,[3] and later in the year when he was sent to Spain he had been told to leave his army in Etruria under *legati*.[4] Where in Etruria troops were thought to be necessary is not known. It is difficult to think that the security of Etruria was so uncertain in 183 that further colonization was thought necessary to maintain it, or that Saturnia, already a *praefectura*, was in or near a disaffected area, or that it was at all well placed for dealing with disaffection in other parts of Etruria.[5]

Some other explanation is needed, and two not mutually exclusive ones may be offered. Saturnia, with Parma and Mutina (also of 183), was the first inland colony (except perhaps for Aesis) to have Roman rather than Latin status. It also probably had far more colonists than the old *coloniae maritimae*, perhaps 2,000 like Parma, Mutina, and Luna.[6] These new colonies were of course the successors of the old Latin colonies, and they were Roman partly because the citizenship was now valued more highly.[7] An important effect of the colonization of Saturnia was to raise the financial standing of the Roman citizens who settled there; thus many of the colonists must have become liable for military service for which their census had previously been too low, and they will have been more likely to

[1] That Etruria was actively disaffected in 191 is hardly shown by Liv. XXXVI 7.16, as M. Capozza, *Movimenti servili nel mondo romano in età repubblicana* (Rome, 1966), 140, seems to suggest.

[2] Liv. XXXVII 2.1, 2.9.

[3] Liv. XXXVII 50.13.

[4] Liv. XXXVII 57.3.

[5] An elaborate road-system can hardly have been built very quickly around its otherwise rather inaccessible site.

[6] For Saturnia Livy does not specify the number, as he does for Parma, Mutina, and Luna. The number is often assumed for Saturnia (e.g. Sherwin-White, *RC* 74), but Livy's silence could imply that there was the hitherto normal number of colonists, i.e. 300.

[7] Cf. Sherwin-White, *RC* 73–5. It was now necessary to give 50 *iugera* to a Latin colonist.

bring up families. In view of the fairly frequent references to the shortage of men for the *dilectus* during this period,[1] it seems likely that this was one reason, if not the only reason, for sending out the colony of Saturnia.[2] It is also possible that the citizen-colonies of 183–177 were a method of continuing to admit Latins to the Roman citizenship and making use of their man-power.[3] This explanation can also be applied to the viritane assignments made in the same period; since there was not a great demand for land away from Rome on the part of Roman citizens, it is to be supposed that the Roman government held that it was necessary to encourage settlement to maintain military manpower.

Another variety of explanation helps to account for Saturnia and for other colonies. The personal advantages for the individual colonists are clear enough, and although some colonies were unpopular because of the dangers that threatened the settlers,[4] there must have been many who were quite eager to accept land at Saturnia. It has been shown that after the Second Punic War there was a shortage of people who could be sent out as settlers,[5] and even in 186 Sipontum and Buxentum, recently founded colonies, were found to be deserted;[6] but there apparently continued to be sufficient volunteers in 183 for a heavy programme of colonization. It was of course a small number of senators that played the major part in deciding to establish colonies, sometimes without the support of the potential colonists.[7] The commissioners who founded a colony apparently became its *patroni*,[8] and such *clientelae* had obvious uses. A successful colony furthermore generated much construction and much new wealth for the colonists, and we cannot suppose

[1] E.g. Liv. XL 26.6–7 (181 B.C.), XLIII 14.2–10 (169)—though the situation differed if large spoils were expected. Cf. D. C. Earl, *Tiberius Gracchus, a Study in Politics* (Brussels, 1963), 30–4, etc. Unfortunately the lowering of the required census of the fifth class from 11,000 to 4,000 *asses* cannot be dated.

[2] That such was one of the purposes of Latin colonies even earlier was argued by Salmon, *Phoenix*, ix (1955), 65 (cf. Liv. XXVII 9.11, XXXIV 58.13). Since the manpower of Roman citizens was needed, the colonists of 183 had to be settled in citizen-colonies, cf. Salmon, *JRS*, art. cit., 65.

[3] As suggested by R. E. Smith, *JRS* xliv (1954), 20.

[4] Liv. XXXVII 46.10 (Placentia and Cremona).

[5] Tibiletti, art. cit., 193–210, Salmon, *Phoenix*, art. cit., 71.

[6] Liv. XXXIX 23.3–4.

[7] Liv. XXXVII 46.10, XLIII 17.1 (Aquileia).

[8] Cf. Badian, *FC* 162–3.

that all leading senators were indifferent to the possible profits of colonization.[1]

The view has sometimes been put forward that some Roman colonies of this period were founded with the conscious intention of bringing about Romanization.[2] There was no widely ranging policy of systematic Romanization in allied Italy,[3] and it is most doubtful whether the Romans would have made any clear distinction between holding down the subject populations and bringing about Romanization. However Romanization was, and this must have been realized, an inherent part of the colonizing system. In the second century Latin colonies contained Italians in large numbers, although Fregellae, where there were 4,000 families of Samnites and Paelignians by 177,[4] was probably an extreme case. When in 197 Cosa eventually obtained 1,000 extra colonists,[5] it is clear that some at least were expected to be Italians.[6] On the one hand the Latin colonies did retain some genuine independence from Rome in the second century,[7] and they preserved some local traditions, as can be seen in Etruria and Umbria from evidence at Cosa[8]

[1] Little is known about direct Roman economic exploitation of Etruria or Umbria before the first century, but known incidents such as the exaction of supplies in 205, Liv. XXVIII 45.15–18 (quoted above, p. 89 n. 6), do not suggest moderation.

[2] W. Ihne, *History of Rome*, i (London, 1871), 543–5. De Ruggiero, *Diz. Ep.* s.v. *colonia*, 427 (Latin colonies were intended for defence and 'la propagazione del romanesimo'), cf. Tibiletti, *Athenaeum*, xxvi (1948), 181.

[3] See in particular J. Göhler, *Rom und Italien* (Breslau, 1939), 2, 21–2.

[4] Liv. XLI 8.8; on this figure cf. Tibiletti, *Athenaeum*, xxviii (1950), 204 n. 3, E. Malcovati, *Athenaeum*, xxxiii (1955), 138 n. 4. At Narnia in 199 there were apparently Italians passing themselves off as colonists, Liv. XXXII 2.6.

[5] Liv. XXXIII 24.8–9, cf. XXXII 2.7.

[6] Liv. XXXIII 24.8–9: 'Cosanis eo tempore postulantibus ut sibi colonorum numerus augeretur mille adscribi iussi, dum ne quis in eo numero esset qui post P. Cornelium et Ti. Sempronium consules [218] hostis fuisset.' Cf. Göhler, op. cit., 37 n. 187, A. Bernardi, *NRS* xxx (1946), 284, Tibiletti, *Athenaeum*, xxviii (1950), 194. According to P. A. Brunt, *JRS* lv (1965), 91, 'the Latin colonists were mainly of Roman descent', but the passages that he cites do not sustain his view.

[7] Sherwin-White, *RC* 99–103.

[8] The Etruscan affinities of some of the archaeological material from Cosa (at least in architecture) do not necessarily show either that the Etruscan element in its population was strong or that the non-Etruscan colonists were affected by local influences in a more than superficial way—but they suggest the former. Cf. tombs S1 and N1, F. E. Brown, *MAAR* xx (1951), 96–102; and the terracottas of the temple of Jupiter (*c.* 240–220 B.C.?), L. Richardson, *MAAR* xxvi (1960), 151–70, and of Temple D (*c.* 170–160), ibid., 184. Professor Brown has told me that in his opinion the colonists made use of Etruscan workmen in the first phase of construction.

and Spoletium[1]—and in other regions. On the other hand, as can now be seen very well at Cosa, they were decidedly Roman towns[2]—the discovery of the *curia* and *comitium* brings home what was meant by *quasi effigies parvae simulacraque*.[3] The appearance of the town and its public life fostered the feeling that Rome was the central power. Non-Romans in Latin colonies such as this must have come to feel that they owed their loyalty to Rome, as the behaviour of all the Latin colonies except Venusia in the Social War tends to show, and those members of the colonies who were not Latin speakers probably became such very soon.[4]

Among the 300 colonists of a *colonia maritima* the non-Romans are not likely to have been numerous, although Latins were legally able to join them,[5] and provisions were sometimes made for Italian allies to do so.[6] For the much larger citizen-colonies

[1] *CIL* i².366=xi.4766=*ILLRP* 505=R. S. Conway, *ID* note xlii (i.397), a public inscription from Spoletium dated shortly after 241 by Conway and Degrassi, contains in Conway's judgement five words 'showing marks of Umbrian influence' in a total of about sixty. Some six other inscriptions of republican Spoletium are known.

[2] On the topography of Cosa see F. E. Brown, art. cit., and (with E. H. Richardson and L. Richardson), *MAAR* xxvi (1960) (whole vol.); also L. Richardson, *Archaeology*, x (1957), 49–55.

[3] A phrase of Gellius, XVI 13.9; cf. *specula populi Romani*, Cic. *Font.* 13.

[4] Too much has sometimes been made (e.g. by T. Frank, *CAH* vii.659) of the supposed occasional failures of Latin colonies to use Latin. As far as can be seen from published evidence, Oscan can be supposed to have been used on the coins of three Latin colonies only, Aesernia (founded in 263), Vetter, *HID* no. 200 (B) (6) (a)=Conway, *ID* no. 185, Luceria (founded in 314), Vetter no. 200 (E) (3), and Paestum (founded in 273), Vetter no. 200 (F) (2)=Conway no. 24. In the first case (assuming that the coin-type is later than 263 B.C.) we are asked to believe that the legend 'aisernio' (in Latin script)=Oscan **aiserniú*, in spite of the several versions of Lat. *aisernino* that appear on other types. The Paestan type is perhaps better dated before 273 (see Conway i.14). Even if the Luceria type belongs to the colony it must have given way fairly quickly to the Latin types. Some of the inscriptions showing Oscan influence in Latin colonies cited by E. T. Salmon, *Samnium and the Samnites* (Cambridge, 1967), 316 n. 3, probably antedate the colonies.

[5] Latins could and did become members of citizen-colonies, as Liv. XXXIV 42.5–6 (195 B.C.) shows—see the interpretation of R. E. Smith, art. cit., 18–20 (against Mommsen, Salmon, Sherwin-White); at least that was the case until the *ius migrationis* was restricted.

[6] De Ruggiero, *Diz. Ep.* s.v. *colonia*, 433 (followed by Tibiletti, art. cit., 213, Smith, art. cit., 20) is surely right as far as the older citizen-colonies are concerned in thinking that there were few Italians who were admitted to them, but not much significance can be given to the fact that we only know specifically of the case of

of 183–177, including Saturnia, the net may have been cast more widely. There is no specific literary or archaeological evidence that the colony of Saturnia contained Etruscans or other Italians,[1] but it is likely that some Italians became members of it.

What was the effect of the colonies on the neighbouring non-Roman states? Some indication of the answer comes from the epigraphical evidence for the Latinization of the two regions, which is examined in Section 3 of this chapter. Here some other points need to be made clear. A colony took land away from the local population, and initially the planting of colonies must have increased hostility towards Rome.[2] On the other hand it emphasized the permanence of the Roman settlement of Italy, the unalterable fact of Roman domination, and in a wide variety of obvious ways it brought the surrounding Italians into continuous contact with Romans, Roman institutions, and the Latin language. Admittedly there were some barriers between those who did and those who did not have the *ius commercii* and the *ius conubii*; but in default of evidence on the point it would be unwise to assume that this distinction meant that there was not very much actual trade and intermarriage between Roman and Latin settlers and Italians. Diodorus perhaps had some evidence that there had been extensive intermarriage between Romans and Marsi before the Social War,[3] and it is likely to have been most common where there were colonies. The Romanization eventually took place of areas in Etruria that were remote from any such settlers, but before the Social War the colonies were the most important of the Roman policies that led to Romanization.

Ennius (at Pisaurum or Potentia). The procedure in that case is surely likely to have been a regular one. C. Gracchus seems to have enrolled Italian allies for Iunonia, App. *BC* I 24.104.

[1] I know of no Etruscan material from the period of the Roman colony at Saturnia—but A. Minto's survey, *MAAL* xxx (1925), is not a good basis for discussion. Pliny's entry 'Saturnini qui antea Aurini vocabantur' (*NH* III 52) is not evidence that the colony contained locals (*pace* E. Pais, *Mem. Acc. Linc.*, ser. 5.xvii (1924), 348 n. 2).

[2] Cf. Salmon, *Athenaeum*, art. cit., 12.

[3] Diod. XXXVII 15.2. So taken by P. Brunt, *JRS* lv (1965), 99; but there is some error in Diodorus, for the extensive intermarriage can hardly have been the result of the νόμος τῆς ἐπιγαμίας.

2. *The Roman Road-System*

The general statement that the Roman road-system that came into being in Etruria and Umbria in the third and second centuries was an important means of Romanization is obvious enough. A full description of the effects of the system is not possible, and will not be at least until a full examination has been made of the archaeological evidence not only for the roads themselves but also for the pattern of settlement in the whole region.[1] The system consisted eventually of four main roads, the Via Aurelia parallel to the coast, the Via Clodia going through central Etruria, west of Lake Bracciano, at least as far as Saturnia, the Via Cassia through central Etruria as far (originally) as Arretium, the Via Flaminia through south Etruria across Umbria and the Apennines to the Adriatic coast, and a considerable variety of lesser roads. In southern Etruria, the area covered by the published parts of the survey of the British School at Rome, namely the territories of Veii, Sutrium, and Capena,[2] is now known in great detail, and the roads of the *ager Faliscus*, and a section of the Via Cassia between Bolsena and Clusium, have been studied with attention to their effects on the surrounding areas;[3] elsewhere the remains of the Via Flaminia itself, if not of the whole area through which it passed, are well known.[4]

[1] A full bibliography of modern references to the road-system would be excessive. H. Nissen, *Italische Landeskunde*, ii (Berlin, 1902), 282–410, and R. A. L. Fell, *Etruria and Rome* (Cambridge, 1924), 151–8, are still useful. The most recent general works are those of G. Radke, *Gymnasium*, lxxi (1964), 204–35, *Mus. Helv.* xxiv (1967), 221–35, F. T. Hinrichs, *Historia*, xvi (1967), 162–76, T. Pekáry, *Untersuchungen zu den römischen Reichsstrassen* (Bonn, 1968). All of these leave much to be desired; see T. P. Wiseman's forthcoming article 'Roman Republican Road-Building', *PBSR* xxxviii (1970), which the author has kindly shown me in MS. Some of his chronological conclusions differ from mine, but my objections will have to appear elsewhere.

[2] See especially J. B. Ward-Perkins, *PBSR* xxiii (1955), 44–72, *JRS* xlvii (1957), 139–43, G. Duncan, *PBSR* xxvi (1958), 77–91, G. D. B. Jones, *PBSR* xxx (1962), 116–207, xxxi (1963), 100–58 *passim*; the important earlier discussions of the roads of southern Etruria were D. Anziani, *MEFR* xxxiii (1913), 169–244, T. Ashby, *Mem. Pont. Acc. Rom. Arch.*, i.2 (1924), 129–75, *SE* iii (1929), 171–85, *Klio*, xxv (1932), 114–17. Cf. also the references below to particular roads.

[3] M. W. Frederiksen and J. B. Ward-Perkins, *PBSR* xxv (1957), 67–208, W. V. Harris, *PBSR* xxxiii (1965), 113–33.

[4] The most important works are T. Ashby and R. A. L. Fell, *JRS* xi (1921), 125–90, E. Martinori, *Via Flaminia* (Rome, 1929), M. H. Ballance, *PBSR* xix (1951), 78–117 (on the bridges).

It has been well established since Anziani that there already existed in Etruria a road-system constructed by the Etruscans themselves. It was not as elaborate as the Roman system later became, and it was constructed for purposes different from those of the Roman trunk-roads, consisting mainly of roads that merely linked centres of population to other neighbouring ones. It is quite certain, though still often overlooked, that the Romans for a considerable time contented themselves with this system, making changes no doubt, but without establishing any great new trunk-roads. In some areas the developed Roman system performed the same function as the Etruscan one, and simply by making movement between the main centres easier, it exposed them to a faster process of Romanization. On the other hand the great trunk-roads were built with military purposes in mind, and it can easily be seen that the Aurelia and Flaminia in particular took the lines that would lead them most quickly towards Liguria and the *ager Gallicus* respectively,[1] even if that meant that they missed by some distance towns that had previously flourished; new communities were established on these roads, and some of the population and resources that they gained they gained at the expense of the older communities away from the roads. A *forum* on one of the main roads, even if most of its population was of local origin, was obviously likely to be an effective instrument of Romanization in spite of its meagre institutions. It is the aim of this section to discuss briefly two questions that arise from this Roman system, namely its chronology and the extent to which the roads drove the population into new and more Roman communities.

There is a general tendency to suppose that the main roads must have been organized in the third century rather than the second,[2] but it should be resisted. The one main road for the date of which we have explicit literary evidence is the Via Flaminia, built by C. Flaminius in his censorship in 220,[3] but it is likely that the roads across the Apennines were those most in need of creation or re-creation—hence the Flaminia will have

[1] On this aspect of the Flaminia cf. R. A. L. Fell, op. cit., 152.

[2] Cf. A. J. Pfiffig, *Historia*, xv (1966), 196, for continuing belief in this.

[3] Liv. *Per.* 20 has a lacuna, but the sense is fairly clear and is supported by Plu. *Quaest. Rom.* 66 (279f–280a). Festus 79.16–17L dates the road to Flaminius' consulship in 223, Strabo V 1.11 217C to his son's consulship in 187.

had precedence over other projects,[1] and from the time when Roman power spread into the Po valley the road that the younger Flaminius built in 187 from Arretium to Bononia[2] will have been a pressing need. With the help of archaeological evidence one road can be dated to the third century, namely the Via Amerina, running northwards from a junction with the later Cassia through Nepet and Falerii Novi to southern Umbria; it was organized in 240,[3] but its range was obviously more restricted than that of the main trunk-roads. The date of the Cassia must be 171 or a later year, for that was the date of the first consulship held by a member of the *gens*, yet obviously a road was needed earlier. This should make us cautious about third-century dates for the organization of the Clodia and Aurelia, and in fact second-century dates seem more likely for both of them. It is also instructive to see that the road from Arretium to Bononia was built *before* the organization of the Cassia between Rome and Arretium.

The date that has been most favoured for the Via Aurelia is 241,[4] the date of the only known censorship held by a member of the *gens*, but it is not necessary to suppose that the road was the work of a censor. A *terminus ante quem* is provided by a reference in Cicero,[5] and an earlier one has been suggested on the grounds that in 109 Aemilius Scaurus built a road through Liguria to Dertona[6]—it could, however, have fitted on to a still unreorganized Etruscan road.[7] Yet the Aurelia is most unlikely to have dated from after 100, for at least three bridges on the road seem to date at the latest from the second half of the second century.[8] That leaves nine consulships (252, 248, 200,

[1] The road led to Flaminius' settlements in the *ager Gallicus*.

[2] Liv. XXXIX 2.6.

[3] See below, p. 168.

[4] E.g. Nissen, op. cit., ii.299, De Sanctis, *Storia dei romani*, iii.1 310 n.110, Hinrichs, art. cit., 164. The occasion was quite a suitable one. 200 has recently come into favour, A. J. Toynbee, *Hannibal's Legacy* (Oxford, 1965), ii.660–1, Radke, *Mus. Helv.*, art. cit., 224—but not all the evidence was considered.

[5] *Cat.* II 6.

[6] Hülsen, *RE* s.v. Aurelia via (1896); for the sources on Scaurus' road, cf. *MRR* i.545.

[7] The same will apply to the road of T. Quinctius T.f. Flaminius, cos. 150 or 123, which led to Pisa from the upper Arno (*CIL* i^2.657=*ILS* 5808=*ILLRP* 458, cf. *MRR* i.512).

[8] These are the two Santa Marinella bridges, dated by G. Lugli (*La tecnica edilizia romana* (Rome, 1957), 356) to the second half of the second century; cf. M. E. Blake, *Ancient Roman Construction in Italy* (Washington, 1947), 210 (though one of her photographs shows a bridge from Civitavecchia, not Santa Marinella),

157, 144, 126, 119, 108 (a suffect consulship), and 103) as well as the censorship as possible dates; of these 252, 248, and 126 can be excluded, for the consuls concerned were occupied elsewhere. A milestone found on Bartoccini's excavation at Vulci can be brought into the argument. The text reads: '. . .]AUṚ [. . . / C]OTTA · CO[S. . . / M(ilia) A RUMA · ↓ XX[. . .'.[1] It was found at the edge of the *decumanus* within the town, and although in the absence of the complete numeral it is not possible to be certain, this was probably its original site. It is usually assumed that from the first the Aurelia avoided the town of Vulci and passed straight along the coast, a supposition for which the only positive evidence is provided by late imperial sources, the *Peutinger Table* and the *Antonine Itinerary*.[2] Whether the original Aurelia went to Vulci or not, the Aurelius Cotta named on the milestone was probably responsible for important road-works, and is surely likely to have been the man after whom the road was named.[3] If this is the case the censor and those Aurelii who were not Cottae can be eliminated from the list, and there remain the consuls of 200, 144, and 119. Bartoccini wished to exclude any date for the inscription after

S. Bastianelli, *Centumcellae (Civitavecchia), Castrum Novum (Torre Chiaruccia)* (Rome, 1954), 58 (these are sites 100 and 101 in *La Via Aurelia da Roma a Forum Aureli, Quaderni dell'Istituto di Topografia Antica della Università di Roma*, iv (1968)). The third bridge is the so-called Cloaca di Porto San Clementino, Blake, op. cit., 197 (though it 'may possibly have been built by Etruscan engineers, it was almost certainly erected under Roman supervision to carry the Via Aurelia over the Marta'), cf. W. J. Anderson, R. P. Spiers, and T. Ashby, *Architecture of Ancient Rome* (London, 1927), 5 n. 1, and other references given by Blake; it is site 147 in *La Via Aurelia da Roma a Forum Aureli*. The bridge may seem small to have carried the Via Aurelia over the Marta, but air photographs show conclusively that it was on the line of the road (F. Melis and F. R. Serra in *La Via Aurelia da Roma a Forum Aureli*, 98, and figs. 247, 351).

[1] *ILLRP* 1288. Cf. R. Bartoccini, *Vulci, Storia–Rinvenimenti–Scavi* (Rome, 1960), 12–17; the same account is given in *Atti del VII Congr. internaz. di archeologia classica* (Rome, 1958, publ. 1961), ii. 266–71. The inscription is also discussed by A. Degrassi, *Hommages à A. Grenier* (Brussels, 1962), i. 508–10.

[2] Diodorus' statement (IV 56) that Telamon was 800 stades from Rome need not be precise (*pace* Radke, *Gymnasium*, art. cit., 224), and cannot be used to calculate the course of the Aurelia.

[3] Bartoccini, op. cit., 15–16, prefers to associate the milestone with another road, known from *Itin. Anton.* (p. 300) to have passed from Rome to Cosa via Careiae, Aquae Apollinares, and Tarquinii (the distances known suggest that it then joined the Aurelia); he is forced to suppose that the name 'Aurelia' may have passed from this road to the main road 'per analogia'. Degrassi (op. cit., 509–10) assumes that the inscription belonged to the builder of the Aurelia and that the main road went to Vulci.

the middle of the second century,[1] but the consul of 144 remains possible.[2] The consul of 200 was assigned Italy[3] and seems to have been somehow involved in the war with the Ligurians,[4] although it was not his formal responsibility, whereas the Ligurian wars had substantially finished before 144.[5] On the other hand the consul of 144, about whose activities little is known,[6] is rather favoured by the silence about the road in the extant portion of Livy.[7] 144 seems to be the better of the two dates.[8]

In its developed form, known to us from the Itineraries, the Via Aurelia certainly missed all the old Etruscan towns of any importance on or near the coast—Caere, Tarquinii, Vulci, Telamon, Vetulonia, and probably Populonium—and it is unlikely that the last three at least were ever served by anything better than *diverticula* of the Roman road.[9] Some sites that were more accessible than these three were probably avoided from the beginning—even in the second century the Aurelia preferred Graviscae to Tarquinii, as is shown by the arch of the so-called Cloaca di Porto San Clementino, which was probably a bridge carrying the Aurelia.[10] Perhaps it went to Vulci, but what Forum Aurelii (in the territory of Vulci) and Graviscae gained, they gained in part at the expense of Vulci and Tarquinii—and the new towns were Roman from the beginning.[11]

[1] Op. cit., 15 (he preferred the cos. of 200). Neither the letter-form ↓ (on which see Bartoccini, l.c.) nor the form RUMA really helps us to decide between the available dates. The latter incidentally is an Etruscan form, for elsewhere it is found only in the François tomb at Vulci in an Etruscan inscription (*CIE* 5275= *TLE* 300), for which the most likely date is the late fourth century.

[2] The double t in Cotta would be striking in an inscription as early as 200. An allegedly mid-third-century milestone from Sicily (A. Di Vita, *ΚΩΚΑΛΟΣ*, i (1955), 10–21=*AE* 1957, no. 172=*ILLRP* 1277) refers to Aurelius Cottas, but cf. Degrassi ad loc. and in *Hommages à A. Grenier* (Brussels, 1962), i. 499–508, on the chronological problem. On coins of 135–26 (Sydenham, *Roman Republican Coinage* (London, 1952), nos. 429–30) 'Cota' is still used.

[3] Liv. XXXI 6.1.

[4] Liv. XXXI 10–11.

[5] Cf. De Sanctis, op. cit., iv.1 423.

[6] At least he was *not* in Spain, Val. Max. VI 4.2.

[7] For this reason Degrassi, art. cit., 510, prefers 144 or 119.

[8] If the argument from the Vulci milestone is wrong, then 241, 157, 108, and 103 are also possible dates.

[9] Cf. F. Castagnoli, *La Via Aurelia da Roma a Forum Aureli*, 6.

[10] See above, p. 163 n. 8.

[11] Degrassi, l.c., assumes that the Aurelia continued to pass through the old Etruscan centres until they declined for other reasons. He refers to the changes

In the cases of the Via Cassia and the Via Clodia there were Etruscan roads already in existence, and no definite dates are known for the Roman reorganization, but the possibilities can be narrowed down. The two roads shared the same course for a stretch north of Rome, and since Ovid, the earliest writer who mentions the Via Clodia, indicates that this section was known as the Clodia,[1] it was probably the earlier of the two.[2] For the Clodia a *terminus ante quem* earlier than Ovid is set by the *praefectura Claudia Foroclodi*,[3] which must have been created before the Social War and presupposes the existence of the Via Clodia. The Ponte della Rocca at Blera, which can hardly be later than the Gracchi,[4] suggests a still earlier *terminus ante quem*. Of the consulships and censorships held by the various Claudii between 312 and 136[5] at least eighteen appear to be possible occasions for the organization of the Clodia.[6] The dedication to their *patronus* C. Clodius C.f. Vestalis, proconsul, by the 'Claudienses ex Praefectura Claudia Urbani' of Forum Clodi[7] strongly suggests that he was of the family that founded the town and built the road.[8] But who was Vestalis? The cognomen might suggest a connection with the Claudii Pulchri,[9]

that had been made in the Aurelia by A.D. 147, by which date there was a Via Aurelia Nova and a Via Aurelia Vetus (*CIL* xiv.3610=*ILS* 1071), but that does not show that the old Aurelia went to Vulci, and we know from the Cloaca di Porto San Clementino that the Aurelia missed Tarquinii.

[1] *Ex Ponto* I 8.44: 'Flaminiae Clodia iuncta viae'.

[2] Ward-Perkins, *JRS* xlvii (1957), 140–1, argues that the Clodia 'is patently the earlier of the two roads', partly (it seems) because the Clodia had the more limited aim of consolidating Rome's authority in the immediate area of the road, partly because (for some of its course) it conformed to the old Etruscan road-system rather than the pattern of a Roman trunk-road; but presumably a road of the former type could always be built if the occasion arose.

[3] Plin. *NH* III 52, cf. *CIL* xi.3310a=*ILS* 904.

[4] G. Säflund, *Le mura di Roma repubblicana* (Uppsala, 1932), 259, dates it to the period of the Gracchi or even later, others somewhat earlier; but cf. Blake, op. cit., 209, and references.

[5] No Clodii held appropriate offices until after the Social War; it may be that the Clodia is more likely to be the work of a plebeian than of a patrician Claudius. Radke, *Gymnasium*, art. cit., 220, does not succeed in establishing that the correct name of the road was the Claudia.

[6] 225 has been the date most favoured, e.g. by Nissen, op. cit., ii.353–4, Hinrichs, art. cit., 164.

[7] *CIL* xi.3310a, cf. 3311.

[8] As Mommsen suggested when the inscription was discovered, *Zeitschrift für Numismatik*, xv (1887), 204.

[9] The daughter (*RE* no. 384) of Ap. Claudius Pulcher, cos. 143, was clearly the illustrious Vestal among the Claudii.

but since the tribe of Forum Clodi was Arnensis or Quirina[1] the founder was probably a Claudius Marcellus (or possibly a Claudius Nero).[2] 287, 196, 189, 183, 155, and possibly 222 are the available dates. The question arises whether the organization of the road had anything to do with the foundation of Saturnia, which was probably its destination;[3] this seems at least very plausible, and 183 is thus the best date. The conclusion is, however, obviously speculative.

The Clodia is in some ways the most interesting of the main Roman roads of the region, since its military function, like that of the colony of Saturnia, is less obvious, and although part of its course is direct and 'typically Roman'[4] further north it did not avoid the old Etruscan centres such as Blera and Norchia.[5] The Clodia was never under the Republic a main route to northern Etruria or beyond.[6] All this being the case, a relatively large amount of traffic on the Clodia must have been local, between Etruscan centres, and its Romanizing effect must have been smaller than that of the other main roads.

The date of the Cassia has been discussed elsewhere.[7] Various dates from 171 to 107 are possible, the most likely being 171 and 154.[8] The road has the characteristic appearance of a Roman trunk-road, at least in its southern section as far as Bolsena, and Vicus Matrini, Forum Cassi and Aquae Passeris were accompaniments of this development. Further north the preceding road-system continued to have its influence at one point at least long after the Cassia was established, for even

[1] See below, p. 332.

[2] No Claudius Nero really seems to be available. The Claudii Pulchri were in the Palatina.

[3] The *Peutinger Table* continues the road northwards beyond Saturnia to Succosa, which is in fact south of Saturnia; the *Ravenna Geography* (iv.36) takes the road to Saturnia, but the *Antonine Itinerary* (p. 286) only as far as Forum Clodi.

[4] Ward-Perkins, art. cit., 140.

[5] Ward-Perkins, l.c.; cf. E. Wetter in A. Boethius, *Etruscan People, Land, and Culture* (New York, 1962) (Eng. version of *San Giovenale, Etruskerna Landet och Folket* (Malmö, 1962)), Map i opposite p. 198.

[6] Cf. Cic. *Phil.* XII 22.

[7] Harris, art. cit., 114, cf. C. Hardie, *JRS* lv (1965), 129–30. 125 is widely favoured, e.g. by Nissen, op. cit., ii.313, Hinrichs, art. cit., 165.

[8] I gave 171, 164, 154, 127, 125, 124, 107, 96, and 73 as possible dates, but the Ponte Cammillari, just outside Viterbo, 'is certainly not later than the second century before Christ' and is 'to be associated with the Via Cassia' (Blake, op. cit., 209).

after the Etruscan town of Orvieto (Volsinii in my view) declined in importance in the third century, the Cassia made a considerable detour towards the site instead of taking a more direct route northwards from Bolsena, as is shown most clearly by the Colonnacce bridge near Orvieto;[1] the great physical difficulties of the alternative were considered to be excessive, until the time of Trajan. Further north the Cassia could scarcely avoid the old towns of Clusium and Arretium, but it is an open question whether the Via Flaminia went to Faesulae,[2] and it seems likely that the Cassia missed some smaller Etruscan settlements that had been served by the previous road-system.

In the case of the Via Amerina, which must have been laid out at least in part in or soon after 240,[3] when the inhabitants of defeated Falerii were forced to resettle in the new town, the road obviously improved Roman access to the area further north, and also helped to make the new town more prosperous than it would otherwise have been. Furthermore, in the period after the suppression of Falerii Veteres there was 'an unmistakable concentration of settlement along the Via Amerina.'[4] Yet the history of the road-system and its effects in this area are not likely to be typical of the whole of Etruria, since the forced transfer of population is only known to have taken place elsewhere at Volsinii.

The Via Flaminia, as has often been said, was an extremely direct road, strikingly so for example in its most southerly stretch, on the west side of the Tiber.[5] The Roman communities in Umbria that were on or near the road have already been discussed,[6] and it is easy to see in a general way how the communities on the road gained from it. Listing the towns on the Flaminia north of Mevania, Strabo says that there are other settlements that are filled with people because of the road rather than διὰ πολιτικὸν σύστημα, Forum Flaminium, Nuceria, and Forum Sempronium.[7] Such places surely contributed in

[1] On the Colonnacce bridge and its significance, Harris, art. cit., 126–7.

[2] Hardie, art. cit., 129.

[3] M. W. Frederiksen and J. B. Ward-Perkins, art. cit., 107, 182.

[4] Ibid., 189.

[5] T. Ashby, *SE* iii (1929), 175.

[6] I cannot incidentally follow Radke's argument (*Gymnasium*, art. cit., 211–12, *RE* s.v. Umbri, *Supplementband* ix (1962), col. 1795) for supposing that the original Flaminia went to Camerinum, Sentinum, and Sena Gallica.

[7] V 2.10 227C.

only the most marginal way to the military purposes of the road—they were not garrison towns, but market-places used by the local population.

Thus the Romans did make some attempt, beyond the simple construction of the roads, to make the trunk-roads effective in the regions through which they passed. The new settlements along the main roads were—in some cases—fundamentally lacking in πολιτικὸν σύστημα, but that did not prevent them from bringing about some Romanization. The most important factor in the changing balance of population between different centres was of course the Roman peace itself, which meant that considerations of defence became less important and considerations of trade more important.[1] As a result of the peace the Roman communities on the roads, both colonies and lesser ones, had a good basis on which to build.

3. *The Spread of the Latin Language*

The displacement of the Etruscan and Umbrian languages by Latin is the only part of the process of Romanization about which we have a considerable body of evidence. The inscriptions have their limitations as evidence for this change; they probably do not reflect the practices of the poorest part of the population—though they get quite close to doing so—and on the other hand funerary inscriptions may conserve an otherwise dead language. But from the inscriptions and from the meagre literary references some important facts about Romanization and its chronology can be established.

The general causes of the change are not difficult to see.[2] It was not brought about by any systematic *Sprachenpolitik*,[3] but

[1] Emphasized by Ward-Perkins, *JRS*, art. cit.; but it is worth noting the imposing town-walls that were built in a number of places after the conquest (above, p. 112).

[2] The best discussions are by J. Safarewicz, *Meander*, ix (1954), 163–7, *Eos*, li (1961), 317–25 (both in Polish; I am grateful to Prof. H. B. Segel of Columbia University for translating them for me), E. T. Salmon, *Report of the Annual Meeting of the Canadian Historical Association*, 1960, 33–43, and P. Brunt, *JRS* lv (1965), 97–101. Some useful points are also made by G. Devoto, *Storia della lingua di Roma* (Rome, 1940), *passim*, and *CHM* iii (1956), 443–62=*Scritti Minori* (Florence, 1958), 287–304. There have been some useful descriptions of the spread of Latin in other areas, e.g. K. Jackson, *Language and History in Early Britain* (Edinburgh, 1953), 96–112.

[3] M. Gelzer, *HZ* cxxvi (1923), 189–92=*KS* i.270–2, J. Göhler, *Rom und Italien* (Breslau, 1939), 2, 23–4.

by a variety of inter-related circumstances, most of them the products of Roman political domination. Colonization and the road-system have already been discussed, and also the progress of Roman political interference in the affairs of the allied states. Etruscans and Umbrians served in the Roman army, and although that did not necessarily make all soldiers learn Latin (they served in local units),[1] some must have done so. Some Etruscans and Umbrians will have left their regions to carry on business elsewhere, although this was much less common than in some other areas of Italy,[2] and they will have used Latin, or Greek, to do so. Rome itself and other Latin-speaking areas must have become steadily more important in the commercial activities of Etruria and Umbria. As Rome became more powerful and Italy became more Romanized, relations of *clientela* between powerful Roman citizens and citizens of the allied states in Etruria and Umbria must have increased.[3] A few men from these states gained the Roman citizenship, and they retained their local connections thereafter. As in other parts of Italy, some Romans and other Latin speakers probably took up residence in the allied states.[4] There was probably some intermarriage between local families and Latin-speaking ones—how much there was we have no way of telling.[5] Finally it is reasonable to suppose that, by the late second century at least, local *nobiles* sent their sons to Rome to advance their education, and to suppose that in spite of the local culture of Etruria and its surviving contacts with the Hellenistic world some Etruscan interest was aroused in the Latin-speaking culture of the second century. The political and economic facts made it inevitable that in almost all departments of life Etruria and Umbria became more and more provincial, Rome more and more central.

How did the Romans regard the use of the local Italian languages? A story of Valerius Maximus, unusually lacking in

[1] Salmon, art. cit., 38–9.

[2] J. Hatzfeld, *Les trafiquants italiens dans l'orient hellénique* (Paris, 1919), 240. This negative point is confirmed, though not with exhaustive arguments, by A. J. N. Wilson, *Emigration from Italy in the Republican Age of Rome* (Manchester, 1966), 105–11, 152–5.

[3] See below, pp. 225–8, for the evidence concerning such *clientelae* in 91.

[4] There were 2,000 Romans at Nola in 90, App. *BC* I 42.185, a number at Asculum, 38.174, and in other rebellious towns, 42.190.

[5] See above, p. 160.

specific reference, is often quoted.[1] Magistrates of the old days, in order to establish respect for Latin, for themselves, and for the Roman state, obstinately refused to give answers to Greeks except in Latin and compelled them to make their representations in Latin.[2] The story is very 'Catonian' and rather overstates the case.[3] No doubt Roman magistrates were reluctant to speak or listen to Greek in the second century, and although the story has no necessary connection with their attitude to the Italian languages it seems unlikely that Rome was at all willing to conduct any official business except in Latin. There must have been Etruscan and Umbrian equivalents of the Oscan law of Bantia; if the translation was made on Roman initiative, and particularly if the translation was made at Rome—an unproven hypothesis[4]—some concession was made to the desire to communicate with non-Latin speakers,[5] but it would not follow that other concessions of this kind were made.[6] Such second-century references as there are, by Titinius and Lucilius, suggest that Romans looked down on the Italian languages,[7] as indeed

[1] Val. Max. II 2.2. Cf. Göhler, op. cit., 28, Brunt, art. cit., 99.

[2] 'Magistratus vero prisci quantopere suam populique Romani maiestatem retinentes se gesserint hinc cognosci potest, quod inter cetera obtinendae gravitatis indicia illud quoque magna cum perseverantia custodiebant, ne Graecis umquam nisi Latine responsa darent. Quin etiam ipsos linguae volubilitate, qua plurima valent, excussa per interpretem loqui cogebant non in urbe tantum nostra, sed etiam in Graecia et Asia, quo scilicet Latinae vocis honos per omnes gentes venerabilior diffunderetur . . . nulla non in re pallium togae subici debere.'

[3] For Cato's views cf. esp. Plu. *Cat. Ma.* 12.4–5, and H. H. Scullard, *Roman Politics, 220–150* B.C. (Oxford, 1951), 112; but others felt similarly, cf. Plu. *Mar.* 2. Livy finds it noteworthy that Aemilius Paullus should have addressed Perseus in Greek after Pydna (XLV 8.6) and that Cn. Octavius should have translated the peace-terms into Greek after they had been read out in Latin; these incidents show that some compromises were made.

[4] Put forward by E. Schönbauer, *RIDA* ser. 3.ii (1955), 356–7, on the grounds that the engraver did not know Oscan (on which the fullest commentary is that of E. Vetter, *HID* pp. 13–28); the text is so bad that it is surely unlikely to have been prepared at Rome, as is pointed out by M. W. Frederiksen, *JRS* lv (1965), 187 n. 21. It is surely more plausible to suppose that publication clauses like that in the Tarentine *lex de repetundis* (lines 12–19—see the text of G. Tibiletti, *Athenaeum*, xxxi (1953), 47–52) left translation as a local responsibility rather than that there were official translations made into numerous languages at Rome.

[5] The inscription was, however, written in the Latin alphabet.

[6] See below, pp. 173–4, for Latin laws at Clusium in the second century.

[7] Titinius: 'Qui Obsce et Volsce fabulantur, nam Latine nesciunt', *CRF* 104 Ribbeck. Quintil. I 5.56: 'Taceo de Tuscis et Sabinis et Praenestinis quoque; namut eorum sermone utentem Vettium Lucilius insectatur' (which does not refer just to the Praenestine language, as Devoto, *Storia della lingua di Roma*, 126, thought).

they tended to look down on the Italians themselves.[1] That does not mean that they took active steps to eliminate the official, still less the private, use of other languages. The only explicit evidence of Roman language-policy concerns the permission granted in 180 to the *praefectura* Cumae 'ut publice Latine loquerentur et praeconibus Latine vendendi ius esset'.[2] That suggests that there was little likelihood of a federated state's using Latin for its own official purposes—yet eventually some of them came to do so, and we know of a probable Umbrian instance at Asisium.

Among the inscriptions of allied Etruria[3] the earliest Latin ones (which antedate the earliest bilinguals) are inscribed on articles that were or may well have been imported into Etruria. Such were the various Cales cups, probably of the third century;[4] and the series of *pocula* of various deities, which were probably made in Latium but apparently intended in part for an Etruscan market, also of the third century.[5] There is a Praenestine mirror, probably of the third century, found on the same site as Etruscan inscriptions and near but not definitely within the territory of Cosa (founded in 273), showing 'Venos', 'Iovem', and 'Prosepnai', the last probably an Etruscan form.[6]

[1] As the outrages committed by Roman magistrates in various Italian towns in the second century indicate (cf. E. T. Salmon, *Samnium and the Samnites* (Cambridge, 1967), 323–7, for the evidence but not for the interpretation). For the Roman attitude to the Etruscans cf. below, pp. 187, 194.

[2] Liv. XL 42.13.

[3] Some of this evidence is discussed briefly by R. A. L. Fell, *Etruria and Rome* (Cambridge, 1924), 147–9. Caere and Falerii, special cases requiring lengthy treatment, are generally excluded from my discussion.

[4] *CIL* i².406 d–f (Tarquinii), h (Caere), 407–8, 411a=*ILLRP* 1213 (Caere), 412 a–c=*ILLRP* 1214–15 (Tarquinii); for *CIL* i².406 see *ILLRP* 1209. The production of Cales cups is generally set in the period 250–180, cf. A. Rocco in *EAA* s.v. Caleni (1959), *ILLRP* pp. 345–6.

[5] i².439=*ILLRP* 32; 444–5=*ILLRP* 173, 68 (Vulci); 440=*ILLRP* 40 (Clusium); 441=*ILLRP* 55 (Florentia); 442=*ILLRP* 72, 446=*ILLRP* 202, 450=*ILLRP* 254 (Horta); 447=*ILLRP* 239, 451=*ILLRP* 274 (Tarquinii); 453=*ILLRP* 288 (Tarquinii or Vulci); 2495 (Caere). Cf. J. D. Beazley, *Etruscan Vase-Painting* (Oxford, 1947), 209–16, who adds two uninscribed ones from Etruria, from Tarquinii (his no. 6) and Capena (no. 11). According to Beazley they were 'probably made in Latium' (210—'certainly', 215), 'quite likely by Tarentine settlers' (215). The majority of the nineteen are known to have come from Etruria, and none of those with a known origin comes from anywhere else, except Rome. On the date, Beazley accepts Ryberg's 'a little earlier than the middle of the third century'. Cf. P. Moreno in *EAA* s.v. *pocola* (1965).

[6] i².558=*ILLRP* 1203=Vetter no. 366 (l). Fourth-century, Degrassi in *ILLRP* ('ut videtur'), C. Koch, *Hermes*, lxxxiii (1955), 3; third-century, Degrassi,

More importantly a third-century date has also been ascribed to a dedication recently discovered at San Giuliano,[1] although a second-century date also seems possible; the site of its discovery was probably within the territory of Blera but not far from the territory of the Latin colony of Sutrium. This evidence, such as it is, suggests that it was the areas best situated to trade with other parts of Italy, especially the southern half of the Etruscan coast, that felt the first impact of Latin.

Our dating of the second-century Latin inscriptions from allied Etruria is largely dependent on their spelling, which provides very inexact indications (it is clear that some of the main changes to classical spelling took a long time, and even official texts often have inconsistencies), and on the even less exact criterion of letter-forms. On these grounds it is safe to put *CIL* i².595–6, two fragments of laws on the two sides of a bronze tablet first known at Montepulciano (*ager Clusinus*), in the second century.[2] It seems by these criteria to belong to much the same period as the Lex Repetundarum,[3] but in theory any

Auctarium (Berlin, 1965), p. 262, R. Bloch, *RPh* ser. 3.xxvi (1952), 179–86. Vetter counts the ending -epnai as Etruscan, cf. *CIE* 5091 'Phersepnai'; this seems a more likely explanation than Greek influence, but cf. Bloch, art. cit., who also suggests that -ai represents the genitive. i².580=*ILLRP* 6=*ILS* 9233 may have come from Cortona (cf. *CIL*): it is either of the fourth century (Degrassi, *ILLRP* and *Auctarium*, p. 66) or of the third (H. L. Wilson, *AJPh* xxviii (1907), 452–3). i².475, a name inscribed on a vessel found near Bomarzo, may be correctly classified among the *vetustissimae* (i.e. pre-202 B.C.) in *CIL*.

[1] P. Villa D'Amelio, *NSA* 1963, 65, 68–9: 'A(ulus) S(e)mo(nius) Ti(beri filius) / Apolo(ni) d(edit)'. The text and date are those of Degrassi.

[2] i².595–6, discussed by A. Rudorff, *Abh. Ak. Wiss. Berlin*, 1861, 485–8 (i².596), Mommsen and Lommatzsch in *CIL*, G. Bruns, *FIRA*⁷ pp. 117–20, G. Rotondi, *Leges Publicae Populi Romani* (Milan, 1912), 483–4, E. H. Warmington, *Remains of Old Latin*, iv (London, 1940), 310–15 (i².596), G. Tibiletti, *Athenaeum*, xxxi (1953), 78 n. 3. Facsimiles are given in Ritschl, *Priscae Lat. Mon. Ep.* (Berlin, 1862) plates iii A and iii B. 'Aetati Gracchanae vel non multo posteriori et hanc legem [595] et in postica perscriptam [596] vindicant scripturae *literai* ant. v.6 cum t non geminata et ai pro ae; *pronontiare* ant. v.1, post. v.7; *sorticolis singolis* post. v. 7; *tolerint* post. v.11; *tabolam* post. v.12', Mommsen, Lommatzsch. The doubling of the t in *literae* would have been quite possible even in the early second century; by the time of the Lex Repetundarum the choice seems to be completely open; by the time of the Lex Agraria the doubling is more common. With *literai* cf. *li*]*terae*, post. 13; nom. pl. in -ai probably begins to go in the first half of the second century and is definitely uncommon by the last twenty years of the century. The Lex Repetundarum is mixed in its use of -o- and -u-, the pre-classical practice being uncommon by the end of the century; on the other hand it sometimes has *ioudicium*, whereas i². 596 has *iurare* and *iubeto* (lines 1, 10).

[3] i².583.

date between *c.* 175 and *c.* 100 is possible. The script of the two sides, and indeed the spelling, are not identical,[1] but they are probably very close in time, even if not parts of the same law. Both apparently concern a *quaestio perpetua*; possibilities are the Lex Calpurnia of 149, the Lex Iunia that preceded the Lex Repetundarum,[2] and the Lex Cassia tabellaria of 137.[3] *CIL* i².597 comprises four inscribed fragments of a bronze tablet found at Clusium, with Latin on one side and Etruscan on the other.[4] The spelling on the Latin side favours a date in the latter half of the second century.[5] The Latin text concerns the paying of a reward to the successful accuser in a *quaestio perpetua*; the surviving Etruscan text is a list of names, perhaps officials of some kind, which does not help us to determine its date. This document, with the other official Latin inscriptions in allied states,[6] has been taken as evidence that the upper classes at least were bilingual.[7] No doubt Latin was understood at Clusium to some extent, but there is no need to suppose that the text of the laws was put up in Latin alone, and furthermore a Latin version may surely have been put up even if it was little understood at Clusium—it may have been necessary to do so to satisfy a clause concerning publication, and the Latin text was the authentic text, difficult to translate with precision. It can unfortunately only be a supposition that this was the source of the conjunction of the Etruscan and Latin texts; it remains possible that it merely results from the re-using of a bronze tablet that contained an out-of-date Etruscan text. Also probably of the second century is a bronze statuette from Orvieto inscribed with the words 'C. Pomponio(s) Virio(s) pos(uit)', which has hitherto been wrongly transcribed; the spelling is again the most re-

[1] Pointed out by Warmington, op. cit., 310.

[2] i².583, line 74.

[3] It does not seem to be possible to fit the fragments into the Lex Repetundarum itself.

[4] i².597=*CIE* 3230; W. Deecke, *Die etruskischen Bilinguen* (Stuttgart, 1883, vol. v in the series W. Deecke–C. Pauli (ed.), *Etruskische Forschungen und Studien*), 121–33; Bruns, op. cit., 121; Rotondi, op. cit., 484 (fr.a); Tibiletti, art. cit., 78.

[5] Cf. *quei, utei, boneis, uxorei, pequnia* (a), *quai* (b), -ereito (c), among which *quai* is the best evidence of early date; but cf. *quae* in (a), which also has *praedibus, quaestio*; and *-nae* in (c).

[6] Some are to be found in places more remote than Clusium, as at Genua in 117 (i².584=*ILLRP* 517) and among the Veneti in the same period (i².633–4, 2501, which all=*ILLRP* 476, i².636=*ILLRP* 477).

[7] Brunt, art. cit., 100.

liable indication of the date.[1] Other second-century Latin inscriptions are hard to identify: *CIL* i².1993 with the dative 'Iunone Regina' must be one, but Cellere where it was found was perhaps in the territory of the *praefectura* Statonia.[2] In fact the other epigraphical evidence suggests that Latin was not the primary language of Clusium, or of most parts of allied Etruria, until the first century, and indeed that they did not become truly bilingual until then (*some* of the local upper classes had obviously acquired Latin much earlier).

The chronological problem of the change is important for the whole process of Romanization and in particular for the history of the Social War. The inscriptions of the period of transition can be divided into three main categories, the bilinguals, the last Etruscan inscriptions, and the remaining Latin inscriptions of the Republic.

1. *The Bilinguals*[3]

Of some thirty-one bilingual inscriptions,[4] almost all of them funerary,[5] only the Clusium law[6] has any pre-classical spelling and several have spelling that probably belongs to the first

[1] The correct reading has been pointed out to me by Dr. M. Torelli. It has previously been read as 'C. Pomponi Quiri(na) opos', i².546=*ILLRP* 1249; cf. F. Ritschl, op. cit., plate i B b. It is generally assigned to the third century, as in *CIL*, though G. Q. Giglioli, *SE* xxii (1952–3), 58, suggested the first century, without discussion.

[2] i².1993=*ILLRP* 172. Another Latin inscription from nr. Orvieto, consisting of a single name, probably also belongs to the second century, P. Mingazzini, *NSA* 1932, 482–3.

[3] The most important discussions are W. Deecke, op. cit., O. Skutsch in *RE* s.v. Etrusker (1909), cols. 790–1, U. Coli, *SE* xix (1946–7), 277–83, H. Rix, *Beiträge zur Namenforschung*, vii (1956), 147–72.

[4] There are some marginal cases where what is written in the Latin alphabet may or may not be in the Latin language. Where possible I give the *CIE* number only; those marked with an asterisk also appear in *TLE*. The list is: *CIE* 272* (Saena), 378*, 428*, *TLE* 930 (Arretium), *CIE* 739*, 808 (here the Latin as well as the Etruscan is written *sinistrorsum*), 890*, 1048*, 1060*, 1288*, 1290*, 1416*, 1437*, 1468–9*, 1487*, 1671*, 1729*, 2106*, 2647*, 2965*, 3023*, *TLE* 462 (Clusium), *CIE* 3500, 3692*, 3763*, 4190* (Perusia), *TLE* 697 (Pisaurum—the arguments of I. Zicari, *Studia Oliveriana*, xi (1963), 30, against the truly bilingual character of this inscription are to be rejected). *CIE* 3230=i².597 (discussed above), i².2382 (Orvieto), and *CIE* 4844=xi.7179 (Perusia) might be added, though the surviving Etruscan and Latin texts do not correspond.

[5] The last two may be excluded from this category, as well as the Clusium law.

[6] i².597.

century.[1] Four of the bilinguals contain the name of a Roman tribe, and so probably date from after the Social War.[2] Three of these and some thirteen other bilinguals contain in the Latin version filiation with the father's initial;[3] that has been held to be evidence that the fathers were Roman citizens,[4] and in an official Roman context it would be, but since the Etruscans made fairly extensive use of patronymics as well as metronymics,[5] they may have continued to do so in Latin even before their enfranchisement. It has also been suggested[6] that only a non-citizen could use a non-Roman *praenomen* such as Ar. (=Aruns, Arnth), found in the Latin form of *CIE* 2965,[7] but this was not a firm rule.[8] It is not possible to establish any definite dates before the Social War for bilingual inscriptions by reference to the ossuaries themselves or to their tomb-groups. Some late dates can be established in this way. In particular *CIE* 3763, inscribed on the marble ossuary that ends the series in the Volumnius tomb at Perusia, is generally thought to be Augustan—but it is so detached in style from the other ossuaries in the tomb (or anywhere else) that the inscription may be nothing more than a piece of archaizing.[9] Some Arretine pottery was found with the ossuary bearing *TLE* 930 and the period 40–30 B.C. may be taken as a *terminus post quem*.[10]

[1] Thus the double consonants in *CIE* 378, 1468–9, 1729, *TLE* 462, and ae in *CIE* 808, 890, 3692, and *fulguriator* in *TLE* 697.

[2] *CIE* 428 and *TLE* 930 (Arretium), *CIE* 1469 (Clusium) and *TLE* 697 (Pisaurum, with the tribe Stellatina, whereas Pisaurum itself was in the Camilia; various Etruscan towns, enfranchised before as well as after the Social War, were in the Stellatina; the theory that the subject came from Ferentium, S. Ferri, *Rend. Acc. Linc.*, ser. 8.xiii (1958), 323–6, G. Forni, *Studia Oliveriana*, vii (1959), 25–31, remains a theory).

[3] Of the last four all except *CIE* 1469; and also 378, 890, 1048, 1060, 1416, 1437, 1468, 1671, 1729, 2647, *TLE* 462, *CIE* 3763, 4190.

[4] Rix, art. cit., 154–6.

[5] Cf. Rix, art. cit., 154, S. Mazzarino, *Historia*, vi (1957), 117 n. 3, etc.

[6] Rix. art. cit., 156.

[7] 'ath trepi thanasa [in Etr. script] Ar. Trebi Histro [in Lat. script].'

[8] 'Vel. Vibius Ar Pansa Tro(mentina)', *CIE* 3615, is a counter-instance, and this is a small category of inscriptions.

[9] On this tomb see A. Von Gerkan–F. Messerschmidt, *MDAI-R* lvii (1942), 122–235, J. Thimme, *SE* xxiii (1954), 132–47, Rix, art. cit., 164–5, J. Heurgon, *Archeologia Classica*, x (1958), 151. See below, p. 211 n.3.

[10] Material published by G. Maetzke, *SE* xxiii (1954), 353–6, M. Pallottino, ibid. 399–402; and see Rix, art. cit., 147–8. The exact date at which Arretine pottery was first produced is still disputed, cf. A. Stenico, *EAA* s.v. Aretini (1958), pp. 612–13, C. Goudineau, *La céramique arétine lisse* (*MEFR*, Suppl. vi, 1968).

The bilingual from Pisaurum, *TLE* 697, the epitaph of a *haruspex*, can hardly be pre-Augustan to judge by the style of the Latin lettering, but it need not be later.[1] There is no reason then to put any of the bilinguals, apart from the Clusium Law, outside the first century B.C.[2]

2. *The Last Etruscan Inscriptions*

There is ample evidence that Etruscan was in use in funerary inscriptions down to the end of the second century.[3] What evidence is there, besides that of the bilinguals, that it continued in use after the Social War? There are a number of Etruscan inscriptions that in the present state of knowledge it is impossible to assign definitely either to a date before 100 or to a date after 100. These include tombs with Etruscan inscriptions, the Tomba del Cardinale at Tarquinii, and the tomb of the Volumnii at Perusia.[4] In the last generation art-historians have tended to give later dates to certain monuments, and in some cases at least that tendency has gone too far.[5] I list the cases relevant to this study by site, as far as possible in order of increasing remoteness from Roman influences.

One at least of the paintings in the Tomba del Tifone at Tarquinii, which contains *CIE* 5407–14, has been dated to the first century and even to the second half of it,[6] and the inscriptions must have the same date. The painting, representing a funeral procession, has stylistic connections with the Ara Pacis as well as with the Pergamum frieze, but the former are probably not sufficient to exclude a second-century date, to which

[1] Cf. M. Lejeune, *REL* xl (1962), 161.

[2] So Rix, art. cit., 150.

[3] Cf. in particular the evidence of the tomb-groups cited below, pp. 181–2.

[4] The Tomba del Cardinale: *CIE* 5376, 5378; the Volumnii: *CIE* 3754–67.

[5] Cf. R. Bianchi Bandinelli, *SE* xxi (1950–1951), 485–9 (dealing with an extreme manifestation of this tendency); and A. Rumpf, cited in the next n. The dating of the François tomb, which has now returned to a relatively early period (cf. above, pp. 10–11), is a case in point.

[6] *CIE* 5407–8 = *TLE* 100–1, 5410 = *TLE* 102, 5413–14 = *CIL* i².1997, 1996. M. Pallottino, *La peinture étrusque* (Geneva, 1952), 125–6, 128, dates the tomb to the first century, and thinks even the second half possible; first century accepted by R. Lambrechts, *Essai sur les magistratures des républiques étrusques* (Brussels–Rome, 1959), 62; some reviewers of Pallottino retain earlier dates, as A. Rumpf, *AJA* lx (1956), 76 ('the very short *toga exigua* points here undoubtedly to the second century B.C.'); cf. also C. C. Van Essen, *Bibliotheca Orientalis*, xii (1955), 216–17. The new discussion of the tomb by M. Cristofani, *Mem. Acc. Linc.*, ser. 8.xiv (1969), 213–56, came to me only during proof-reading.

some art-historians adhere. Some more reliable indications can be drawn from the inscriptions themselves: 5410 refers to a *zilath*, a magistrate, who is not likely to be merely a translated *quattuorvir*;[1] 5413–14 are in Latin and the subject of 5413 was a *quattuorvir*, but the spelling 'anos' for 'annos' (5413) and 'optuma' (5414) tends to support a date early in the post-90 period for these two inscriptions, and in any case the relationship of the persons mentioned to those mentioned in the Etruscan inscriptions cannot be established.[2] Thus we scarcely have here a definite case of the use of Etruscan after 90.

The author of the best recent study of tomb-groups of the period from the third to the first centuries[3] has argued strongly that some of them continue beyond the Social War and continue to use Etruscan, including in particular the Larthia Seianti tomb at Clusium, and he gives such a date to *CIE* 1211; he compares this sarcophagus with one from the Tomba delle Tassinaie at Clusium[4] which he also dates to the first century.[5] It certainly seems to be established that such dates are stylistically possible; but that emphasizes sharply how dependent these post-war dates are on suppositions about the effects of the war itself.

The statue of the 'Arringatore', bearing *CIE* 4196, was found either at Pila in the territory of Perusia or (less probably) at Sanguineto in the territory of Cortona.[6] Its largely Roman character is apparent,[7] but although recent scholars have tended to move it from the second century to the first quarter of the first century, unanimity has not been reached.[8] Two works

[1] A point not mentioned by any of those who favour the first-century date.

[2] The names Tercenna (obviously Etruscan) and Aurelia have no connection with the other names in the tomb.

[3] J. Thimme, *SE* xxiii (1954), 25–147, xxv (1957), 87–160, for which R. Herbig, *Die jüngeretruskischen Steinsarkophage* (Berlin, 1952), was an important foundation.

[4] *SE* xxv.112.

[5] *SE* xxiii.31; cf. 'l'époque vers 100 av.J.C.', Van Essen, op. cit., 215.

[6] *CIE* 4196= *TLE* 651. T. Dohrn has tried to reassert the case for Pila, *Problemi di storia e archeologia dell'Umbria, Atti del I Convegno di Studi Umbri* (1963, publ. Gubbio–Perugia, 1964), 197–9, *Bollettino d'Arte* xlix (1964), 97–114, though according to G. Susini, *Archeologia Classica*, xvii (1965), 141–6, the question is still open; the balance seems to be in favour of Pila.

[7] P. J. Riis, *Introduction to Etruscan Art* (Copenhagen, 1953), 110, E. H. Richardson, *MAAR* xxi (1953), 113, *The Etruscans* (Chicago, 1964), 167–8, etc.

[8] P. Ducati, *Storia dell'arte etrusca* (Florence, 1927), 546 ('forse anche posteriore al 100 a.C.'); O. Vessberg, *Studien zur Kunstgeschichte der römischen Republik* (Lund–Leipzig, 1941), 172, arguing for 150–100; B. Schweitzer, *Die Bildniskunst der*

of statuary from San Martino alla Palma in the territory of Faesulae or Florentia bear *CIE* 15 and 16; the material is marble, but may not be Luna marble,[1] so there is no reason to assume a date in the second half of the first century.[2] Another statue from Volaterrae bearing an Etruscan inscription also seems to have been of non-Luna marble,[3] and has now been dated back to the third century.[4]

The most important epigraphical evidence for the late use of the Etruscan language is, however, the tomb of the Hepenii at Asciano, probably in the territory of Saena,[5] which contained urns inscribed in both languages, and in three of those inscribed in Etruscan, coins of Augustus.[6] This is the first incontrovertible evidence that Etruscan was still in use at that time, and the Latin inscriptions show that even there it came to an end shortly afterwards.[7]

Such is the evidence, although there are numbers of other late Etruscan inscriptions that could belong to the post-war

römischen Republik (Leipzig–Weimar, 1948), 144, for 80–70; Riis, l.c., for 100–75, cf. Dohrn, *Problemi*, etc. 207–11, *Bollettino d'Arte*, art. cit., 108–10, *Der Arringatore* (Berlin, 1968), 16–17; R. Brilliant, *Gesture and Rank in Roman Art* (New Haven, 1963), 30, for the late second century; Richardson in her later work, l.c., argues for a first-century date.

[1] Cf. A. Andrén, *Antike Plastik*, vii (1967), 34, 36.

[2] *CIE* 15–16=*TLE* 682, 681. G. Buonamici, *SE* iv (1930), 267–86, discussed the latter and argued for a late first-century date (279); this is accepted by M. Pallottino in *TLE*, who also assigns the other to the first century with a question mark. On the first use of Luna marble at Rome, see Plin. *NH* XXXVI 49–50 (Mamurra), but at Luna itself there was a marble *abacus* of a column set up in 155 to honour the consul M. Claudius Marcellus (i².623=*ILLRP* 325). On the whole question of the first use of Luna marble see L. Banti, *Luni* (Florence, 1937), 114–15.

[3] *CIE* 76=*TLE* 397; cf. Andrén, art. cit., 36.

[4] R. Bianchi Bandinelli, *Dialoghi di Archeologia*, ii (1968), 234–5; G. Radke, *RE* s.v. Volaterrae (1961), cols. 733, 736, had dated it to the first century.

[5] Published by A. De Agostino, *SE* xxvii (1959), 277–300 (Tomb ii). On the genealogy of the family cf. A. J. Pfiffig, *Beiträge zur Namenforschung*, xiii (1962), 28–39, *SE* xxxi (1963), 239–40.

[6] Urns 21, 57, 65 (on the texts of the first two cf. H. Rix, *Das etruskische Cognomen* (Wiesbaden, 1963), 113, 118, respectively). The coins in 21 and 65 have the legend CAESAR AUGUSTUS TRIBUNIC POTEST / L. SURDINUS III VIR A.A.A.F.F. S.C.; cf. H. Mattingly–E. A. Sydenham, *Roman Imperial Coinage*, i (London, 1923), p. 66 no. 75 (23 B.C.), E. Babelon, *Monnaies de la république romaine*, ii p. 250 no. 12 (*c.* 15 B.C.), M. H. Crawford, *Roman Republican Coin Hoards* (London, 1969), Table xviii (17 B.C.). Urn 57 has a similar type, but the moneyer's name is illegible.

[7] Urn 1, which has a Latin inscription, 'L. Hepenius L.f. ocisus ab comilitone' [*sic*], has an Augustan coin issued by a member of the same college, P. Plotius Rufus, Mattingly–Sydenham i.65 no. 69, Babelon ii. p. 93 no. 306=p. 328 no. 22.

period. Two useful distinctions can be made. The first-century bilinguals and the Clusium and Asciano inscriptions are little more than name-formulae, and the same could be said of *CIE* 15 and 16. The 'Arringatore' inscription, which consists of twelve words, is the most likely instance of a longer Etruscan inscription of such a date. These formulaic inscriptions could represent conservative burial-practices on the part of people who in fact had lost most of the use of Etruscan, an interpretation that receives some support from the Etruscan funerary inscriptions of those whose everyday names were Roman.[1] Again, ossuaries surely did not start to have Latin inscribed on them, even in bilingual inscriptions, until Latin was the dominant spoken language. The other distinction is geographical. Etruscan retreated northwards and away from Roman centres; the Asciano tomb is the most striking evidence, inaccessible from any of the main roads and even from the Augustan colony of Saena.

3. *Latin Inscriptions in the Period of Transition*

The very large number of urns of Etruscan type from Clusium and Perusia that bear inscriptions in Latin makes it likely that Latin was the dominant language there in the first century B.C. Spelling is a poor guide to the date of a modest funerary inscription, but it is significant that among the Latin inscriptions from Etruscan burials, those Latin inscriptions that have metronymics and those that come from bilingual tomb-groups (for which see the next paragraph), there are very few pre-classical spellings indeed.[2] Many metronymics use the genitive form -ae, only some three the form -ai.[3] The form -ae

[1] 'Auleśi Meteliś', the Arringatore's name, is authentically Etruscan, but *cuinte* (Quintus) and *pupli* (Publius) used as *praenomina* in Etruscan are evidently translations from Latin, cf. Rix, *Beiträge zur Namenforschung*, vii (1956), 158.

[2] Cf. 'Septumia' as a metronymic (*CIE* 711), and the cases given in p. 181 n.3. In some cases primitive (or illiterate) forms were used at demonstrably late dates, as in the Augustan inscription from Asciano quoted in p. 179 n. 7, and in the Salvius tomb at Ferentium, where i².2511=*ILLRP* 589 (with the spelling 'omneis') belongs to 67 B.C. and i².2634=*ILLRP* 588 ('anorum', 'Ferentei', 'oena' (? =*una*)) is also later than the Social War. Note that *ILLRP* 589 apparently gave the date by the Etruscan as well as by the Latin month (A. Degrassi, *RPAA* xxxiv (1961–2), 73–5).

[3] Pointed out by Fell, op. cit., 148. There are at least twenty-two of the former; the latter in *CIE* 724, 2860, 4774 and cf. 1151 (all from Clusium).

began to be used in the early second century, but it did not achieve this degree of prevalence until the first century.[1] Consequently it is not possible that more than a small minority of the Latin inscriptions from Clusium and Perusia are earlier than the Social War.

Tomb-groups in which inscriptions in both languages are found are very important in this respect, especially as they are numerous (more than forty).[2] In some cases early spelling occurs, notably in the Rufius tomb at Perusia,[3] but it is easily outweighed by classical spelling. Clear evidence of the date of the change of language in particular tomb-names is generally lacking, but *CIE* 2721–2 (Clusium) may be representative of the usual situation; 2721 is in Etruscan, 2722 probably belonging to a son of the owner of 2721 is in Latin and gives the tribe Arnensis, so that the change probably did not take place until the Social War or at the earliest shortly before. The Tomba delle Iscrizioni at Vulci[4] had perhaps begun to use Latin by *c.* 100 B.C., for Caia Postumia's *praenomen* would be anachronistic later.[5] Yet much closer to Rome, at Caere, the change of language in the family that owned the Tomba delle Iscrizioni cannot have taken place much before the Social War; the author of a recent detailed and acute study of the tomb set the first use of Latin in the period

[1] The use of ai in some positions certainly continued in the 80s, e.g. in *ILS* 8888=*ILLRP* 515, *ILS* 873=*ILLRP* 356 (the latter a dedication to Sulla at Clusium—'Sullai').

[2] Far more of the cases are from Clusium and Perusia than from anywhere else, but there are also cases from Caere, Tarquinii, Tuscana, Vulci, Saena, and Volaterrae.

[3] The Rufius tomb (*CIE* 3469–3506) has 'Ar*os* Ruf*is* Atin*ea* natus' (3498) and 'L. Ruf*is* Cotonia natus' (3501), cf. 'Ar. Rufi V[...] natus Cepa' (3469). It is interesting to note that the first word of the first of these inscriptions was originally written 'Arus' and then altered, cf. A. J. Pfiffig, *SE* xxxii (1964), 187. Add 3453, 3514, 3722 (Perusia), 4774 (Clusium), 5413–14 (Tarquinii, Tomba del Tifone).

[4] Discovered in 1958 and published by M. T. Falconi Amorelli and M. Pallottino, *SE* xxxi (1963), 185–98.

[5] Pointed out by M. Cristofani, *La Tomba delle Iscrizioni a Cerveteri* (Rome, 1965), 64. For female *praenomina* see H. Thylander, *Etude sur l'épigraphie latine* (Lund, 1952), 73–7; the chronological point is, however, far from certain—*ILLRP* 632 (Nursia), a probable instance, seems to belong to the first century B.C. Following F. Messerschmidt–A. von Gerkan, *Nekropolen von Vulci* (Berlin, 1930), 16, Cristofani, op. cit., 63, also dates the earliest Latin inscription of the Tarna tomb at Vulci (*CIE* 5293) to the end of the second century.

115–80 and the final disappearance of Etruscan in the period 80–45.[1]

The epigraphical evidence that Latin was the dominant language in Etruria after the 80s is clear, but such evidence as there is suggests that at least in the central and northern part the change had *not* taken place in the second century. As far as the non-official use of the language was concerned, the Social War was certainly not at the end of the process of change; it was the Romanizing influences of the subsequent period, including notably the colonization of Sulla and of Augustus, that finally killed the language. Knowledge of name-formulae at least survived in some relatively remote places until the time of Augustus, and in some of them the language may still have been spoken. Thereafter it disappeared.

Some Etruscan texts survived until well into the first century at least. Ioannes Lydus[2] refers to the fact that Nigidius Figulus had translated (καθ' ἑρμηνείαν πρὸς λέξιν) his prophetic calendar from the Tagetic books.[3] That can be believed, without any necessity of accepting all of the existing text as Etruscan in origin. Nigidius can hardly have done this much before the 80s or 70s at the earliest.[4] A puzzling passage in Lucretius has sometimes been referred to contemporary texts about *fulmina* written in Etruscan, but probability is against this interpretation.[5] There was clearly some interest, however, in preserving such texts for those who wished to maintain that it was 'Tusci bene praedicere',[6] and the language may have lasted longest among the *haruspices*; thus in A.D. 14 it was apparently possible to interpret an omen concerning Augustus by reference to the

[1] Cristofani, op. cit., 61–2. His calculations are based partly on the family tree (but note the criticisms of E. H. Richardson, *AJA* lxxii (1968), 191); cf. also the classical Latin spelling 'Murria', xi.3629.

[2] *De ostentis* c.27.

[3] Cf. above, pp. 6–8.

[4] The only evidence concerning his date of birth is his praetorship in 58.

[5] 'Hoc est igniferi naturam fulminis ipsam / perspicere . . . , / non Tyrrhena retro volventem carmina frustra / indicia occultae divum perquirere mentis', VI 379–83, first referred to Etruscan script by Niebuhr, also by Deecke, Heurgon, et al.; that is 'exceedingly improbable' according to C. Bailey ad loc., but, in the absence of an exact parallel for 'retro volvere'='unroll', still possible. Other texts cited by A. Budinszky, *Die Ausbreitung der lateinischen Sprache über Italien und die Provinzen des römischen Reiches* (Berlin, 1881), 52, namely Dion. Hal. I 30 and Liv. V 33.11, do not show that the language continued to be spoken.

[6] Cf. Lucilius fr. 611 Marx.

fact that 'aesar' was the Etruscan for 'gods',[1] and the *haruspex* L. Cafatius was probably responsible for one of the very latest of all the Etruscan inscriptions.[2] That is not, of course, evidence that the language was still in use among ordinary Etruscans.

It has, however, been maintained that Etruscan survived for a long time as a spoken language even under the Empire, and that idea can most easily be discussed here. In Aulus Gellius a pretentious advocate is described who used some incomprehensible old terms for bread and wine—'post deinde, quasi nescio quid Tusce aut Gallice dixisset, universi riserunt'.[3] Gallic was still spoken in the second century. Did Etruscan also survive as an *agrestis sermo*?[4] All that is necessary to the sense of the Gellius passage is that some obscure individual words should have been believed to survive, and antiquarians had indeed recorded a number of Etruscan words.[5] Surviving Tuscan words of possibly Etruscan origin[6] do not help the case very much, for it would hardly be surprising if the local Latin-speakers preserved some Etruscan words for such things as plant names. None of these arguments tells at all strongly against the complete absence of Etruscan inscriptions. Admittedly, if notices could be painted in Oscan on the walls of Pompeii not long before the eruption of 79,[7] similar notices could have been painted on the walls of some Etruscan towns at the same period. On the other hand inscriptions from

[1] Suet. *Aug.* 97.2, Dio LVI 29.4 (the interpretation was made by the μάντεις); for the word cf. Hesych. s.v. αἰσοί (= *TLE* 804).

[2] *TLE* 697.

[3] *Noct. Att.* XI 7.4.

[4] The case is made by S. Mazzarino, *Historia*, vi (1957), 98–9, 120–1. Liv. X 4.9 refers to a distinction between *agrestis* and *urbanus sermo* in Etruria, no doubt a real one at some time.

[5] Cf. the *glossae* collected by Pallottino, *TLE* 801–58.

[6] The best case is Tuscan 'gíghero'=Lat. *arum*; according to Dioscorides II 167 (= *TLE* 834) the Etruscan word γιγάρουμ referred to the plant known as ἄρον in Greek (but cf. Pallottino ad loc.). Mazzarino, art. cit., 98, refers to 'sondro', 'illatro', 'ramarro', all north Tuscan words of obscure etymology, on which cf. C. Battisti, etc., *Dizionario Etimologico Italiano*, s.vv. ('ilatro'), G. Alessio, *SE* xx (1948–9), 113, 140. The view that Etruscan aspiration was the origin of the famous Tuscan *gorgia* (see, e.g., C. Battisti, *SE* iv (1930), 249–54) is a pleasing fantasy. For some sceptical remarks on such survivals see now G. Rohlfs, *Studi linguistici in onore di V. Pisani* (Brescia, 1969), ii. 857–61.

[7] R. S. Conway, *Indog. Forsch.*, iii (1894), 85, *ID* i. pp. 55, 70—he infers from the condition of the inscriptions nos. 60–76 that 'Oscan was spoken there till well within the 1st century A.D.' Cf. R. von Planta, *Grammatik der oskisch-umbrischen Dialekte*, i (Strassburg, 1892), 33.

Etruria are plentiful under the Empire, some of them of quite low social origins, some of them from very remote places, but there is not a whisper of the Etruscan language.

The evidence about the change from Umbrian to Latin, a much smaller quantity, seems to indicate that it was completed sooner than the change in Etruria.[1] As early as the time of Plautus, a man from remote Umbrian Sarsina could become Romanized,[2] although the other evidence shows that Latin is unlikely to have made much progress there by the late third century.

Two inscriptions set up by the magistrates of Asisium, one in Umbrian, the other in Latin, give some indication of the date of the change.[3] The Latin inscription refers to the *marones*, and so is more likely than not to be earlier than the Social War, for the constitution was surely changed very soon afterwards.[4] Members of two of the same families also appear in the Umbrian inscription: in one of these two cases the same man seems to appear in both inscriptions, in the other the father seems to appear in the Umbrian inscription, his son in the Latin one.[5] It is likely that the magistrates of the town used Latin for their own official purposes before the war, but that they had only begun to do so within a period of (say) twenty years before the Latin inscription; that inscription itself cannot be dated with great precision, but it is rather unlikely to have been earlier than 125.[6]

[1] For discussions of the change in Umbria see J. Safarewicz, *Eos*, xlix (1957–8), 65–71 (in Polish, kindly translated for me by Prof. H. B. Segel), J. Heurgon, *Problemi di storia e archeologia dell'Umbria, Atti del I convegno di Studi Umbri* (1963, publ. Gubbio–Perugia, 1964), 113–31.

[2] The origin of Plautus is inferred from *Mostellaria* 770, cf. Festus 274–5L ('Umber Sarsinas'), Jerome p. 135H ('Sarsinas'). Doubt is possible.

[3] Vetter no. 236=*CIL* xi.5389; i^{2}.2112=*ILLRP* 550=*ILS* 5346. The script of the Umbrian inscription 'appears to be of the Sullan period', Conway, *ID* i. p. 398 no. 355 (repeated by subsequent writers), but it can be earlier.

[4] Now, however, we have better evidence that there were some *marones* in Umbria after the enfranchisement of the allied towns—see the Latin inscription published by S. Nessi, *Bollettino della Deputazione di storia patria per l'Umbria*, lx (1963), 61–2, and, with G. Giacomelli, *SE* xxxiii (1965), 553–7. It was found in a church at Montefalco, i.e. probably in the territory of Mevania, but it may have originated elsewhere.

[5] Ner. Babrius T.f. in the Latin inscription probably corresponds to Ner. T. Babr(ie) in the Umbrian; T. V. Voisiener is probably the father of V. Volsienus T.f.

[6] Spelling only offers weak indications in this case.

This Umbrian inscription from Asisium was written in the Latin alphabet, not the Etruscan one that the Umbrians had used earlier, and so it was part of an intermediate stage to which two Umbrian inscriptions from Fulginiae, both referring to *marones*, also belong. To judge by the poor criterion of the lettering, these two inscriptions date from soon after 150, if not earlier.[1] To this stage belong the later parts of the most important monument of the Umbrian language, the *Iguvine Tables*;[2] the whole document is in Umbrian, but from *Table* v.b, line 8, onwards it is in the Latin alphabet (v.b.8–18 and vii.b.1–4 representing new regulations, vi.a–b and vii.a representing a new draft of i.a–b). At this point only the dating is important. Devoto's limits of 240–150 B.C. for the tables in Etruscan script and 150–70 for those in Latin script have been widely accepted,[3] and for the script itself these dates are probably the closest that can be given. Two contrary arguments have been used to settle the question of whether the tables in Latin script were written later than the Social War. According to some the figure of six *asses* that seems to be given as the equivalent of a dinner for two men[4] is excessively large unless it was already the semi-uncial *as*, probably introduced in 88, that was in question.[5] But this argument is without value, since it is substantially based on prices in the Po valley that Polybius knew to be extraordinarily low,[6] and the price of three *asses*

[1] Vetter no. 233=Conway p. 398 no. 354: 'Gracchan period', Conway, second half of the second century, Vetter; no. 234, of the same period, 'doch etwas älter', Vetter. Conway also dated Vetter no. 235 (=his no. 354 *bis*=*ILLRP* 260) to the Gracchan period, but whether the two words are in Umbrian or Latin is not clear. Heurgon, art. cit., 115–18, claims to see a *terminus post quem* for Vetter no. 233 in the use of *n.*=Lat. *nummus* for *nummus sestertius*, a usage which, he thinks, does not occur at Rome until Lucilius (440M).

[2] Editions and commentaries are numerous; note C. D. Buck, *A Grammar of Oscan and Umbrian*[2] (Boston, 1928), G. Devoto, *Tabulae Iguvinae*[3] (Rome, 1962), *Le Tavole di Gubbio* (Florence, 1948), E. Vetter, *HID*, V. Pisani, *Le lingue dell'Italia antica oltre il latino* (Turin, 1953), G. Bottiglioni, *Manuale dei dialetti italici* (Bologna, 1954), J. W. Poultney, *The Bronze Tables of Iguvium* (Baltimore, 1959), A. Ernout, *Le dialecte ombrien* (Paris, 1961); cf. also U. Coli, *Il diritto pubblico degli Umbri e le Tavole Eugubine* (Milan, 1958), J. Untermann, *Kratylos*, v (1960), 113–25, K. Olzscha, *Glotta*, xli (1963), 70–138 (these last two are *Forschungsberichte*).

[3] Devoto, *Tabulae Iguvinae*[3], 51–5

[4] v. b. 10, 15.

[5] Devoto, *Tabulae Iguvinae*[3], 405–6, 415, *Le tavole di Gubbio*, 4–5, Vetter, *HID* p. 228, Poultney, op. cit., 225–6.

[6] II 15.4.

accords perfectly well with such other evidence as we have about prices.[1] On the other hand there is frequent mention in these tables in Latin script of the 'tota iiouina' (in various forms),[2] which definitely means something like 'civitas Iguvina' or 'populus Iguvinus', from which it has been inferred that the tables must be earlier than the extinction of the independent state of Iguvium after the Social War.[3] The argument too is of questionable value, for if the people of Iguvium continued to use Umbrian after the Social War, they may have been compelled by lack of a more suitable Umbrian term to refer to the *municipium* at the *tota*.[4] In fact, however, there is no reason to think that any of the *Iguvine Tables* dates from after the war.[5]

The only inscription with a strong claim to be bilingual in Umbrian and Latin, names inscribed on a bronze strainer from an unknown part of the region, is probably of the second century.[6] There is no evidence that Umbrian was used in any inscription after the Social War, and its total disappearance is therefore likely to have been earlier than that of Etruscan.

Some other Latin inscriptions from Umbrian states other than colonies also date from before the Social War. Among the *vetustissimae* in *CIL* i² there is only a Latin name on a jar from Interamna[7] and two Cales cups; but a dedication to 'Iove Optumo Maxumo' from Ameria is not likely to be much later than 150,[8] and the spelling of i².2110 (Mevania), i².2116–17 (Hispellum), and i².2118 (Asisium) probably places them before

[1] See F. W. Walbank on Polyb. II 15.1; Martial IV 68 is irrelevant; perhaps the best comparison is between the price of grain in the Po valley and at Rome, the latter some seven times as high in the second century according to T. Frank, *Economic Survey of Ancient Rome*, i (Baltimore, 1933), 191–6 (cf. his price-list, 200).

[2] vi. a.5, 18, 23, 24, 25, etc.

[3] Coli, op. cit., 69–93, esp. 79–82, 93.

[4] Coli admits, l.c., that this term and the corresponding one in Oscan proper had a wider meaning than *civitas*.

[5] Heurgon, l.c., argues that the last section of the tables that is written in the Etruscan alphabet cannot be earlier than the period of Lucilius because of the appearance of *numer* in v. a.17, 19, 21. Cf. above, p. 185 n. 1.

[6] *ILLRP* 1206. On this cf. M. Lejeune, *REL* xxx (1952), 98–100. The Umbrian origin of the inscription depends in effect on the Umbrian character of the genitive 'Numesier'; cf. Coredier, *Tab. Ig.* vi. b.45, Voisenier, Vetter no. 236, Poultney, op. cit., 98–9. *ILLRP* 687 seems more likely to be in Gallic and Latin, cf. R. S. Conway–J. Whatmough–S. E. Johnson, *Prae-Italic Dialects* (Cambridge, Mass., 1933), ii. 175–8.

[7] i².428.

[8] *ILLRP* 183.

the war.[1] The 'Popillius' cups made at Mevania and Ocriculum inscribed with the makers' names in Latin and exported to Etruria may not have been produced until the first century, but a second-century date is also possible.[2] When it is set against the total body of Umbrian inscriptions, about ten, this evidence strengthens the view that the change of language was somewhat earlier in Umbria than in Etruria. However, the limitations of our knowledge of the process should constantly be remembered.

Several factors will have helped to bring about the differences between the regions. Of course speakers of Oscan and Umbrian must have found difficulty in making the change, but the speakers of a non-Indo-European language must have found it even more difficult. The partially Hellenized culture of Etruria was much more likely to continue to satisfy local needs in the third and second centuries than anything that was known in Umbria.[3] Most important of all, the places in Umbria where we know Latin to have been spoken at an early date are all relatively very close to Latin colonies and to the main road to the north, the Via Flaminia. Since Umbria and Etruria differed in these ways, it is perhaps not surprising that an Umbrian poet could amuse a Roman audience with a derogatory reference to the relatively alien Etruscans.[4]

4. *Roman Influence on Local Magistracies*

That some allied states in Italy gave Roman titles to some of their magistracies is generally accepted.[5] Did this happen in

[1] 'C. Laaro' (2110, 'lapis similis urnae Etruscae', Bormann); 'obeit' (2116); 'Deum Maanium' (*ILLRP* 215—this may be the earliest instance of this formula, cf. K. Latte, *Römische Religionsgeschichte* (Munich, 1960), 99); 'coiugi carisumae' (2118, but the inscription has an illiterate appearance, and may be later).

[2] See A. Gallina in *EAA* s.v. Popillius (1965); cf. *CIL* i^2.418–38, *ILLRP* 1222–7.

[3] For a description of Umbrian culture, as far as there was anything worthy of the name, cf. G. Devoto, *Gli antichi Italici* (Florence, 1931), 188–98. The weakness of the local culture probably contributed to the relatively swift Latinization of the Marsi, E. Peruzzi, *Maia*, xiv (1962), 118.

[4] Plaut. *Cist.* 561–3 (cf. Hdt. I 93!)—surely not just a reference to the *vicus Tuscus* at Rome, in spite of *Curculio* 482.

[5] F. De Martino, *Storia della costituzione romana*, ii (Naples, 1954), 94–5, P. Brunt, *JRS* lv (1965), 100–1; the most recent detailed study is that of G. Camporeale, *Atti e Memorie dell'Accademia Toscana di scienze e lettere 'La Colombaria'*, xxi (1956), 31–108. For some new evidence concerning the Vestini cf. E. Mattiocco, *Archeologia Classica*, xvi (1964), 296–7.

Etruria or Umbria? Everywhere in Italy the evidence for such practices is epigraphical and fragmentary, but it is possible to base some cautious generalizations on the available evidence.

For Etruria the answer must be essentially negative. In two highly speculative cases the influence of Latin terminology has been seen. One of the inscriptions in the Tomba Golini I at Orvieto contains the term *ailf* [...] in a context that allows it to be the name of a magistracy,[1] and W. Deecke and others have connected it with Lat. *aedilis*.[2] Furthermore on a sarcophagus from Tuscana,[3] again in a context that allows it to refer to a magistracy, there is the term *macstrevc*,[4] which Deecke and others have connected with Lat. *magister*.[5] Since the date of the Orvieto tomb is probably in the fourth century and is in any case not much later than 300,[6] imitation of a Latin title would be startling; we are not after all dealing with a primitive Italic state that had felt no need of a complicated political hierarchy until after it came into close contact with Rome. The etymology is in itself theoretically possible,[7] but the authentic titles of Etruscan magistrates occur relatively frequently, and it is not advisable to accept the view that *ailf* [...] is a magistrate's title on the strength of one inscription, especially as some

[1] *CIE* 5094 = *TLE* 234. On the text see R. Lambrechts, *Essai sur les magistratures des républiques étrusques* (Brussels–Rome, 1959), 52–4 (there are some uncertainties, and the painted inscription has been completely destroyed).

[2] W. Deecke, *Die etruskischen Beamten- und Priester-Titel* (Stuttgart, 1884, vol. vi in the series W. Deecke–C. Pauli (ed.), *Etruskische Forschungen und Studien*), 57, S. Mazzarino, *Dalla monarchia allo stato repubblicano* (Catania, [1945]), 136–40, M. Sordi, *I rapporti romano-ceriti e l'origine della civitas sine suffragio* (Rome, 1960), 80 n. 2 ('probabilmente prestito dal latino'), J. Heurgon, *Entretiens Fond. Hardt*, xiii (1966), 103.

[3] *CII* 2100 = *TLE* 195. On the text see Lambrechts, op. cit., 78–9.

[4] The final *c* is probably enclitic, = Lat. *-que*.

[5] Deecke, op. cit., 45, S. P. Cortsen, 'Die etruskischen Standes- und Beamtentitel, durch die Inschriften beleuchtet', in *Kgl. Danske Videnskabernes Selskab, Historisk-filologiske Meddelelser*, xi.1 (Copenhagen, 1925), 131, F. Leifer, 'Studien zum antiken Aemterwesen', *Klio Beiträge*, xxiii (Leipzig, 1931), 242–5, L. Pareti, *SE* v (1931), 160 = *Studi minori di storia antica*, i (Rome, 1958), 318, Mazzarino, op. cit., 188–9, G. Devoto, *Historia*, vi (1957), 31–2, J. Heurgon, *Historia*, vi (1957), 75, M. Pallottino, *Etruscologia*[6] (Milan, 1968), 423.

[6] See Lambrechts, op. cit., 52, for the bibliography of this question.

[7] *Aedilis* could fairly well appear in the form **aifilis* (cf. Faliscan *efile(s)* = ? *aediles*, Vetter nos. 264a–b); the metathesis that is then required is somewhat strange if the word is a conscious borrowing. For sceptical views see Camporeale, art. cit., 50, Lambrechts, op. cit., 110.

of the adjacent words in it are unintelligible.[1] The *macstrevc* inscription is probably of the third or second century,[2] and again the term is a unique one, occurring in a partly untranslatable inscription—it is surely not likely that Etruscans borrowed from Rome such a general term (for which there must have been some equivalent in Etruscan). Indeed it is a strong argument against any such borrowing of terminology by Etruscans that they had a complex system of their own titles for magistrates, a system quite independent of the Roman one and surely in no need of being supplemented by it. The titles of the old magistracies, *zilath*, *maru*, and *purth*, continued in use after the Roman conquest—indeed the majority of the instances of these titles are from after that date.

We should be prepared to find a different situation in Umbria, which was more receptive to Romanization in general and in some places had relatively rudimentary political institutions or at any rate relatively rudimentary terminology with which to describe its institutions. The evidence that we have to consider concerns the *kvestur* of the *Iguvine Tables*. The term itself occurs in v.a.23 and v.b.2, and *kvestretie*, evidently the name of the office, in i.b.45 and ii.a.44. Whether the *kvestur* was a public official of Iguvium or an official of the fraternity of the *frater atiersiur* has been disputed.[3] In the first two passages he plays a part in the ritual of the fraternity as an alternative to the *fratreks*, and it can scarcely be supposed that he is anything other than an official of the fraternity like the *fratreks*. The other two passages are more difficult to interpret: at the end of i.b and at the end of ii.a there appears the statement that '(? Vovicius or Lucius) son of Titus Tetteius' did something represented by the verb *usaie* or *usaçe* 'in his quaestorship'. Etymology alone does not offer any definite meaning for this verb, but it is possible to translate it in the sense 'saw to the

[1] Lambrechts, l.c.

[2] Cf. Lambrechts, op. cit., 78, 125, 127.

[3] With varying degrees of conviction the *kvestur* has been held to be a state official by, e.g., G. Devoto, *Gli antichi Italici* (Florence, 1931), 258, G. B. Pighi, *Studi in onore di G. Funaioli* (Rome, 1955), 374, Camporeale, art. cit., 54–5, C. Gioffredi, *Labeo*, iv (1958), 354, J. W. Poultney, *The Bronze Tables of Iguvium* (Baltimore, 1959), 23; but an official of the fraternity by, e.g., C. D. Buck, *A Grammar of Oscan and Umbrian*[2] (Boston, 1928), 301, F. Ribezzo, *RIGI* xviii (1934), 185, E. Vetter, *HID* p. 201, U. Coli, *Il diritto pubblico degli Umbri e le Tavole Eugubine* (Milan, 1958), 39–41, A. Momigliano, *JRS* liii (1963), 115.

transcription (of this)';[1] it is not necessary to introduce the idea of legislation by the *kvestur*—the *kvestur* alone is not likely to have been empowered to approve the prescription for the ritual. This interpretation to some extent favours the view that the *kvestur* was an official of the fraternity, not of the state, and in any case it would be awkward if the term *kvestur* had two different meanings within the *Tables*. We are here of course treading upon thin philological ice: some reputable scholars have doubted whether *usaie/usaçe* is a verb at all.[2] If we are correct to conclude that the *kvestur* was an official of the fraternity, it is still possible that there was also an office of *kvestur* in the Iguvine state organization as well,[3] but in any case it rather favours the view that the *kvestur*-ship was a very long-established Iguvine institution.

What in fact are the arguments for supposing that the title of *kvestur* arrived at Iguvium from Rome?[4] The alternative is to suppose that it was part of some sort of Italic *κοινή* of a period earlier than the spread of Roman power,[5] a view that necessarily takes us back into speculation about Italian pre-history. Among the many things that are completely unknowable about this supposed *κοινή* is whether it included any uniformity of political institutions, but without positive evidence it must be regarded as unlikely. It is not possible to settle the question of the origin of the Iguvine *kvestur*-ship chronologically, for the earliest tables cannot be shown to be too early for possible Roman influence (see below), and indeed we do not know of any quaestor in an Italian state who antedated the possibility of Roman influence. The diffusion of the Italic equivalents (Faliscan, Oscan, and Umbrian) of Lat. *quaestor* in the allied states is so much wider than that of any non-Roman magistrate's title that a survival from a notionally more uniform prehistoric period is improbable. Inscriptions record quaestors

[1] See Coli, op. cit., 40.

[2] Older scholars took it as an adjective (Bücheler, Pauli, Ribezzo, Blumenthal, Von Planta); cf. V. Pisani, *Le lingue dell'Italia antica oltre il latino* (Turin, 1953), 185; the suggestion that it was a verb was made by Devoto, *Mélanges linguistiques offerts à H. Pedersen* (Copenhagen, 1937), 223, *Tabulae Iguvinae*[3] (Rome, 1962), 302, 477.

[3] Coli, op. cit., 39–40.

[4] Cf. Camporeale, art. cit., 54–5.

[5] The notion of this *κοινή* reaches its extreme form in Mazzarino's 'comune travaglio costituzionale', op. cit., 175 and *passim*.

(variously spelt) from Abella,[1] Bantia,[2] Pompeii,[3] and Potentia,[4] among the Marsi[5] and from Falerii,[6] as well as at Iguvium and in territory directly controlled by Rome. It is probable that in some of these cases, and others where other Roman magistracies were borrowed, increasingly complicated administration required institutions that had not existed before.[7] In any case it is easily understandable that the titles of magistrates should have been borrowed if they had previously been extremely simple—at Capua there had been only *meddices* and in Umbria the only title certainly belonging to a public official that we encounter in our admittedly meagre epigraphical evidence is that of *maro*.[8] It is also possible that some cities borrowed titles from Rome because they wished to associate themselves with Roman dignity.[9]

The dates of the tables that are written in Etruscan script are quite uncertain, but such an early date has sometimes been proposed for them that Roman influence would be surprising. The ritual banishment and cursing of the peoples of some other states—'totar tarsinater, trifor tarsinater, tuscer naharcer iabuscer nomner', 'the people of Tadinum, the tribe of Tadinum, the Tuscan, Naharcan, and Iapudic name'[10]—is commonly held to presuppose the continuing political independence of the state of Iguvium and in particular its ability to conduct its own foreign relations,[11] which they no longer could after the early third century; evidently the text was composed before Gauls and Romans became the chief dangers to the Umbrian states. This argument is, I think, quite irrelevant to the date of the first appearance of the *kvestur*: no real state of war is envisaged between Iguvium and the other places mentioned,[12] and we know that a similar formula continued to play a part in the ritual long after it ceased to have any practical

[1] Vetter no. 1.

[2] Vetter no. 2.

[3] Vetter nos. 11–12, 16–19.

[4] *κϝαιστορ*, Vetter nos. 180, 181a.

[5] Vetter no. 228d=*ILLRP* 286.

[6] Vetter no. 322 i=*ILLRP* 582; cf. *ILLRP* 47.

[7] Cf. A. Rosenberg, *Der Staat der alten Italiker* (Berlin, 1913), 101, A. N. Sherwin-White, *RC* 122, Camporeale, art. cit., 44.

[8] I accept the main lines of Coli's argument (op. cit., 45–50) for the religious character of the office of *uhtur*.

[9] Cf. Camporeale, art. cit., 56.

[10] vi. b.53–54, cf. i. b.16–17, etc.

[11] R. S. Conway, *ID* p. 407, Coli, op. cit., 93.

[12] *Pace* Coli, l.c.

significance, for it appears in vi.b and vii.a, which were written in Latin script. Such elements may obviously have survived from the distant past, but that does not mean that the *kvestur*-ship, an element of more practical importance in the ritual, need have done so as well. It is then likely that the Iguvines borrowed the title of *kvestur* from Rome and that the borrowing took place in the third century, or even later.

There is no real justification for thinking that there was any Roman influence on the titles of magistracies in Etruria before the Social War. In Umbria on the other hand the *kvestur* of Iguvium provides a good case, and there were probably others —there is nothing to make Iguvium an exceptional place in this respect. This conclusion is consistent with other evidence that Romanization proceeded slowly in Etruria before the war, but somewhat more quickly in Umbria.

5. *Acquisition of Roman Citizenship Before the Social War*

Some Etruscans and Umbrians received individual grants of Roman citizenship between the conquest and the Social War.[1] There are a few definite and well-known cases, beneficiaries of Marius, namely the Camertine cohorts, M. Annius Appius of Iguvium, and also the Latin colonist T. Matrinius of Spoletium; but Marius probably enfranchised few if any others in this area (see below). There are other cases to be investigated, men of Etruscan or Umbrian origin who may have acquired the citizenship during this period.

It was not Roman policy to make the citizenship available to large numbers of individual members of Italian allied states at any time during this period. By what means could they acquire it? A few became members of citizen-colonies. Large numbers migrated to Latin colonies, and until the expulsions of 187 and 177, and the effective annulment of the *ius migrationis* in 177[2]

[1] There has not previously been a systematic discussion of this question. C. E. Goodfellow, *Roman Citizenship* (Bryn Mawr, 1935), 32–3, gives a list of *singillatim civitate donati*; E. Badian gives a list for 'the last few generations of the Republic', *FC* 302–8.

[2] XLI 8.6–12, 9.9–12. The law of 177: 'Legem dein de sociis C. Claudius tulit ex senatus consulto et edixit, qui socii [ac] nominis Latini, ipsi maioresve eorum, M. Claudio T. Quinctio censoribus postve ea apud socios nominis Latini censi essent, ut omnes in suam quisque civitatem ante Kal. Novembres redirent.' 'Ac' is usually removed from the text in 8.9 and 9.9, so that the restriction concerns only

there was a channel by which the Italians could reach the Roman citizenship (see below for illegal *migratio* after 177). There was no legal progress to the citizenship by regular channels, it is generally thought, between 189 (the date to which the Lex Claudia of 177 retroactively referred) and the 120s. Then it seems likely that the citizenship became available to Latins *per magistratum*,[1] and the Lex Repetundarum made it available to successful prosecutors in *repetundae* cases,[2] even to Italians (until the Lex Servilia Caepionis restricted the privilege to the Latins).[3] After the 170s there were virtually no more new colonies by which Italians could acquire a better status.

Citizenship could also be awarded to individuals by a special vote of the Roman people.[4] In the second century L. Mamilius, the dictator of Tusculum in 460 who was given the Roman citizenship for his prompt military help,[5] was a known precedent.[6] The known instances are almost all of persons who performed some important military service, such as Sosis of Syracuse, Moericus the Spaniard, and Muttunes the Liby-phoenician in the Second Punic War.[7] It was among the rewards that might be given to those who performed acts of treachery. At a critical stage of the war it was offered 'ob virtutem' to the soldiers of Praeneste,[8] who refused it;[9] and it

the Latins; surely that is at least what Livy should have written, for the other Italians did not come into the matter (Badian, however, wishes to keep 'ac', *FC* 150 n. 4).

[1] That this became possible after the revolt of Fregellae was argued by G. Tibiletti, *RIL* lxxxvi (1953), 45–63. D. W. Bradeen, *CJ* liv (1958–9), 221–8, argued that it was not possible until after 89 at the earliest; his arguments cannot be examined in detail here, but what seems to be his main argument against Tibiletti, namely that the rule concerning the incompatibility of citizenships would have prevented it, does not seem very strong; cf. P. Brunt, *JRS* lv (1965), 90 n. 4.

[2] *FIRA*² i (ed. Riccobono), no. 7, lines 76–8, 83–5.

[3] On the Lex Servilia see Cic. *Balb.* 54; in holding this to refer to Caepio's law, not Glaucia's, I follow E. Badian, *CR* n.s. iv (1954), 101–2.

[4] On this in general see Mommsen, *Römisches Staatsr.*, iii.132–4.

[5] Liv. III 18.2, 29.6.

[6] Cato fr. 25P. H. Peter's doubts about referring this to the story in Livy seem to have stemmed from a failure to consider III 29.6.

[7] Sosis and Moericus betrayed Syracuse to M. Claudius Marcellus in 212, Muttunes betrayed Agrigentum in 210. Cf. Cic. *Balb.* 41 *ad init.*

[8] Liv. XXIII 20.2.

[9] Tibiletti, art. cit., 49 n. 13, suggests that the Praenestines refused because their own law forbade *civitatis mutatio*.

was given to 300 faithful *equites Campani* who, Capua having defected from Rome, 'quorum hominum essent scire se ipsi negabant'.[1] As well as the Praenestines there was a cohort from Perusia fighting at Casilinum,[2] but, Livy tells us, their case was more obscure, 'quia nec ipsorum monumento ullo est illustratus nec decreto Romanorum'.[3] That is to say that some reward might have been expected in this case (but not necessarily the Roman citizenship—the Praenestines were also given *duplex stipendium* and five years' *vacatio militiae*). The *equites Campani* were restored to the condition that they had enjoyed before the defection of Capua, and the Praenestines were probably regarded as much better candidates for enfranchisement than any of the allied Etruscans or Umbrians. In fact it is quite possible that there were some cases of enfranchisement of Etruscans and Umbrians *virtutis causa* during the war; Livy's silence is not of great significance, for all the cases that he does mention are in some way more spectacular than the enfranchisement of a very small number of Italian allies would have been.

There was another small category of enfranchised individuals: the priestesses of Ceres, who generally came from Neapolis or Velia, were, according to Cicero,[4] given the citizenship because 'maiores nostri . . .' (no date is specified, but Cicero is clearly sure that the practice is older than the recent case of Calliphana of Velia) 'sacra pro civibus civem facere voluerunt, ut deos immortalis scientia peregrina et externa, mente domestica et civili precaretur'. Will not something similar have applied to some of the *haruspices* at Rome who are mentioned frequently from the Second Punic War onwards? They aroused the hostility of Ti. Sempronius Gracchus, cos. 177, and the derision of Cato,[5] but their importance was considerable: in 152, for example, they caused all the magistrates

[1] Liv. XXIII 31.10–11. Having been members of the *municipium* of Capua, they were now made members of the *municipium* of Cumae. For Campanian bonds of marriage with Romans see Liv. XXIII 4.7, XXVI 33.3.

[2] Liv. XXIII 17.11.

[3] Liv. XXIII 20.3.

[4] Cic. *Balb.* 55.

[5] Cic. *ND* II 11: 'An vos Tusci ac barbari auspiciorum populi Romani ius tenetis et interpretes esse comitiorum potestis?'; *Div.* II 51: 'Vetus autem illud Catonis admodum scitum est, qui mirari se aiebat quod non rideret haruspex haruspicem cum vidisset' (cf. Cato, *R.R.* V 4).

to resign,[1] and their power is implicit in the story of the elections of 163 that occasioned Gracchus' outburst.[2] That such power should have been possessed by *peregrini* seems almost inconceivable. But it is probable that *haruspices* were generally Etruscans; virtually all the early *haruspices* who are known by name, even outside Etruria itself, have at least partially Etruscan names,[3] and Gracchus was not addressing men of Roman blood. The case is not upset by the fact that there were thought to have been *haruspices* at Rome much earlier.[4] Nor is it difficult to see why Cicero should have preferred to mention the case of the priestesses of Ceres: there was the case of the priestess Calliphana that the urban praetor had referred to the people (*c.* 96).[5]

Wishing to cite authoritative cases in which citizenship had been granted to individuals in *civitates foederatae*, Cicero turned at once to Marius and produced two cases, the two cohorts of Camertes[6] and M. Annius Appius of Iguvium.[7] Marius' action in enfranchising the Camertine cohorts and Appius was technically illegal, for there was no act of the Roman people, and there were probably no other cases in 101, for otherwise they would surely have been cited. Yet it is hard to believe that Marius was in fact the first to promise the citizenship to individual *peregrini* in the field, *virtutis causa*. A way in which this may have been done is suggested by the case of T. Matrinius of Spoletium, 'unus ex iis quos C. Marius civitate donasset', who had his citizenship impugned, not on the grounds that the

[1] Obsequens 18. De Sanctis, *Storia dei romani*, iv.2.1 (Florence, 1953), 364 n. 1068, is unduly sceptical about this event.

[2] Cf. C. O. Thulin, *Die etruskische Disciplin*, iii.88, and in *RE* s.v. *haruspices* (1912), col. 2433.

[3] Thulin, art. cit., col. 2441—'tragen alle gut etruskische oder in Etrurien geläufige Namen.' Outside Etruria cf. *ILLRP* 791 = *TLE* 697 (Pisaurum), *ILLRP* 128 (Ostia—Salvi(u)s), *ILLRP* 186 (Rome—Volcacius, on which see Appendix I). However Thulin somewhat exaggerates—cf. Aemilius Potensis (Obsequens 44, 102 B.C.).

[4] Cf. Liv. VIII 6.12–340 B.C.

[5] The other known case of an individual enfranchisement before the 120s is that of the Peloponnesian doctor Archagathus, who came to Rome in 219 (Cassius Hemina fr. 26 Peter, *apud* Plin. *NH* XXIX 12).

[6] Cic. *Balb.* 46—the two cohorts are restored from s. 50. They are also mentioned in Val. Max. V 2.8; Plutarch, the other source for the story (*Mar.* 28, *Mor.* 202cd) gives *χίλιοι*.

[7] Cic. *Balb.* 46—with 'Iguvinatem' restored from s. 47.

populus Spoletinus had failed to agree to it, but because of the lapsing or the invalidation[1] of Saturninus' law whereby Marius was permitted 'in singulas colonias ternos cives Romanos facere'.[2] This was surely a regular thing in citizen-colonies: Fulvius Nobilior, as a *triumvir coloniae deducendae*, was instrumental in obtaining the Roman citizenship for Ennius by enrolling him in the colony of Pisaurum (or Potentia) in 184,[3] and Cicero did not think that there was anything extraordinary in enfranchising a man in that way. If, as seems quite likely, this was a nominal enrolment in the sense that Ennius did not go off and take up residence at Pisaurum, it fits well with evidence that we have about some later enfranchisements. Among the 5,000 whom Caesar settled at Novum Comum were 500 Greeks—*οὐ μέντοι ᾤκησαν αὐτόθι*;[4] and in Octavian's letter about Seleucus of Rhosus it can be seen that an individual *peregrinus* who was enfranchised was expected to enrol nominally in an Italian town.[5] Both these incidents look like relics of a system in which the normal way of obtaining the Roman citizenship for a *peregrinus* was to enrol him in a citizen-colony; that was probably what happened in the second century. The clause in Saturninus' law may well have been intended to allow Marius to enfranchise individuals to whom he had already promised it.[6] As far as the emendation of Cicero's *ternos* to *trecenos* is concerned there are good arguments on both sides,[7] but on balance it is probably better to retain *ternos*, for the privilege of enfranchising even three men in each colony was still a privilege worth having. Marius' grants of citizenship evidently seemed excessive to some, but there is no need to think that they were more extensive than our specific evidence leads us to believe.

Some important questions of law arise. Was the enfranchisement of the Camertes, as Valerius Maximus asserts, 'adversus

[1] On the dispute about what happened to Saturninus' laws of 100 see E. Badian, *Historia*, xi (1962), 219 n. 87.

[2] Cic. *Balb.* 48.

[3] Cic. *Brut.* 79.

[4] Strabo V 1.6 213C.

[5] *FIRA*[2] i (ed. Riccobono), no. 55=R. K. Sherk, *Roman Documents from the Greek East* (Baltimore, 1969), no. 58, lines 24–7. On this case cf. Taylor, *VDRR* 20.

[6] Cf. G. Samonati, *BMIR* viii (1937), 34, Badian, *FC* 206.

[7] *Ternos* has been rejected by many since W. Ihne, *History of Rome*, v (London, 1882), 163 n. 1; cf. Badian, *FC* 206 n. 1; it is defended by E. Gabba on App. *BC* I 29.132.

condicionem foederis'?[1] (There were other grounds than this for holding the act illegal, and they can explain Marius' remark that in the clash of arms he was unable to hear the voice of the law.[2]) If there was a clause forbidding *civitatis mutatio* in this and other Italian *foedera*, no doubt before Marius it had its effect. There were such clauses in some second-century *foedera*,[3] but Cicero asserts that neither in the Iguvium nor in the Camerinum *foedus* was there a clause 'quo minus eorum civibus a populo Romano praemia virtutis tribuerentur'.[4] To be precise, Cicero puts the view that there were no such clauses into the mouth of Marius, in a sort of προσωποποιία in indirect speech, the argument being that the most learned interpreters of *foedera* are those 'qui iam imperia ac bella gesserunt'.[5] Valerius Maximus' statement may merely be based on a misunderstanding of what was an emotional, not a legal, objection to Roman policy on the part of the allies[6]—the Romans were taking away allied manpower while continuing to demand allied troops. Yet doubt remains about whether Cicero was expressing the only possible view when he denied the existence of clauses forbidding *civitatis mutatio*.[7]

There were then a number of *singillatim civitate donati* even before the Lex Repetundarum, men who received legally respectable grants; but the number was evidently small.

The individuals listed in Appendix I as Roman citizens were domiciled at Rome. It is unlikely that there were any citizens of the *civitates foederatae* resident in their own towns who possessed the Roman citizenship, at least until the time of the Lex Repetundarum. Attempts have been made to show that, contrary to Cicero's view,[8] it was possible in some cases to have

[1] Apparently accepted by G. Niccolini, *Rend. Acc. Linc.*, ser. 8.i (1946), 117; rejected by Badian, *FC* 261 n. 1.

[2] Val. Max., Plu. ll.cc. Plutarch alone suggests that the enfranchisement of the Camertes was challenged in court: δοκοῦντος εἶναι τούτου παρανόμου καί τινων ἐγκαλούντων (*Mar.* 28.3).

[3] Cic. *Balb.* 32.

[4] Cic. *Balb.* 47.

[5] Cic. *Balb.* 45.

[6] Badian, l.c., suggests that he or an excerptor had merely misunderstood *Balb.* 46, but he must have had some other source.

[7] If the *foedera* contained some general provision that was held to exclude *civitatis mutatio*, the sort of *exceptio* clause referred to in *Balb.* 32 might not have been necessary.

[8] Cic. *Balb.* 28–9.

both the Roman citizenship and that of another state.[1] There is no evidence that that was possible before the Social War, although the situation was made rather anomalous by the *municipia*, separate *respublicae* inhabited by Roman citizens, and after 126 (if that is the correct date) by the *civitas per magistratum*.[2]

There was also illegal assumption of the Roman citizenship, although the best evidence concerning the allies all comes from the year 95; in discussing assumption of citizenship in 177 Livy seems to refer only to Latins.[3] In the period just before the Lex Licinia Mucia[4] large numbers were involved—*μυρίους . . . ἐκ τῶν τὰς εὐθύνας φοβουμένων* is Diodorus' phrase.[5] There is also the case of the father of M. Perperna, the consul of 130, who according to a story in Valerius Maximus was found after his son's consulship to have assumed the citizenship illegally (at a date before 168).[6] There are many difficulties in the story,[7] but even so it suggests that it was held to be possible to acquire the citizenship without any of the legal means. It is not difficult to see how the citizenship could be illegally assumed—a man could act as a citizen even if his name was not on the list, and no doubt there were technical difficulties and marginal cases in the census-taking itself,[8] especially if, as Velleius implies, the

[1] What was fundamentally the Ciceronian and also Mommsenian (*Römisches Staatsr.*, iii.47–8) view was well restated by V. Arangio-Ruiz, *Scritti giuridici in onore di F. Carnelutti* (Padua, 1950), iv. 53–77. For a formulation of an opposing view see F. De Visscher, *Bull. Ac. Roy. Belg.*, ser. 5.xl (1954), 49–67 (cf. *Studi in onore de P. De Francisci* (Milan, 1956), i. 37–62). De Visscher makes a distinction among *peregrini* who were given the Roman citizenship between those who came to Rome and those who stayed in their former homes; the latter, he thinks, were able to have double citizenship. There is no evidence that there was any legal sanction for such a privilege as early as the *Pro Balbo*. Some people are likely to have got away with infractions of the law; cf. the Roman citizens ('imperitos homines') who took the citizenship of Athens as well (*Balb.* 30), and Nepos, *Att.* 3.

[2] For the development of ideas on this subject see A. N. Sherwin-White, *RC* 54.

[3] Liv. XLI 8.11.

[4] On which see esp. Cic. *Off.* III 47: 'Male etiam qui peregrinos urbibus uti prohibent eosque exterminant . . . Nam esse pro cive qui civis non sit rectum est non licere; quam legem tulerunt sapientissimi consules Crassus et Scaevola; usu vero urbis prohibere peregrinos sane inhumanum est.' Cf. the Lucilius fragment (1088M): 'Accipiunt leges, populus quibus legibus exlex.'

[5] Diod. XXXVII 13. Cf. 'magna pars eorum pro civibus Romanis se gereret', Asc. 67C.

[6] III 4.5.

[7] See below, pp. 322–3.

[8] Cf. G. Tibiletti, *SDHI* xxv (1959), 115–17.

censors began to entrust some census-taking to local officials from 120 onwards.[1]

It was then possible for Etruscans and Umbrians to gain the Roman citizenship by a variety of paths. From other *civitates foederatae*, apart from Tibur and Praeneste, particular cases are difficult to find, but that should not prevent us from accepting cases of Etruscans and Umbrians, particularly since names of Etruscan origin are relatively distinctive. A list of the most likely is given in Appendix I.

The limitations of the evidence on which the list is based should be made clear. A number of historical Romans much earlier than the 270s had names as Etruscan in character as any that are known later, for example Ogulnii and Volumnii,[2] and there were no doubt other such families before the 270s whose names are not known until later. It is possible, too, that some Etruscans from Caere have intruded into the list. Again, a number of names appear in inscriptions that are bilingual in Etruscan and Latin or Umbrian and Latin, but that does not mean that all Caesii are derived from Etr. *ceinzna*[3] or all Scribonii from Etr. *zicu* or *zichu*.[4] This applies when the Latin name chosen is closely related to the translation of the Etruscan name (Etr. *zich*=Lat. *scribere*, it is generally agreed),[5] as well as when the Latin name is chosen merely because of some resemblance in form. Furthermore the Etruscans certainly did not have a completely exclusive stock of family names, at least in the period from the fourth century onwards when we can compare other areas. A number of names that have Etruscan forms and are common in Etruria, for example Etr. *an(n)e*, Lat. *Annius*,

[1] Vell. II 7.7–8. 'In legibus Gracchi inter perniciosissima numerarim, quod extra Italiam colonias posuit. Id maiores . . . diligenter vitaverant et cives Romanos ad censendum ex provinciis in Italiam revocaverant. Prima autem extra Italiam colonia Carthago condita est.' On decentralized census-taking after the Social War, see below, pp. 234–5.

[2] On the Ogulnii see Schulze, *ZGLE* 150–1, Münzer, *Römische Adelsparteien und Adelsfamilien* (Stuttgart, 1920), esp. 83–9; on the Volumnii, Schulze, *ZGLE* 258–9.

[3] *TLE* 521=*CIE* 890=i².2016: 'arth ceinzna [or 'canzna'?] varnalisla C. Caesius C.f. Varia nat'.

[4] *TLE* 472=*CIE* 1416=xi.2218: 'Q. Scribonius C.f. vl zicu'.

[5] This translation, proposed by W. Deecke, *Literarisches Centralblatt*, xxxiii (1881), 1186 (see H. Rix, *Beiträge zur Namenforschung*, vii (1956), 169, for argument and later references), is based on the use of the verb form *zichuche*, e.g. in *CIE* 4538, 8413, as well as on the bilingual inscription.

are common elsewhere it Italy;[1] and as has recently been pointed out,[2] names that have an excellent claim to Etruscan origin could be well established outside Etruria and could reach Rome from outside Etruria.

As far as the identification of those who became Roman citizens in this period is concerned, the difficulties are obvious. A crucial question concerns the length of time that must have elapsed between the arrival of a new citizen and the possibility of his descendants' holding office.[3] I have excluded from my list all families that are known to have reached senatorial rank before the end of the Second Punic War; of those who are known to have reached senatorial rank after the Social War I have included only those whose enfranchisement before the war is certain or nearly certain. Unfortunately none of those who appear on the list lack filiation in a context where that could provide evidence about the date when citizenship was acquired.

With all these provisos the Carrinas, Maecenas, Nigidius, Perperna, Saenius, Vibius Pansa, and Volcacius families emerge as Etruscans who were enfranchised before the Social War. Some other possible cases are also discussed in Appendix I. Since some of the most important evidence on which the list is based is extremely fortuitous, it is reasonable to assume that there must have been other cases.

We do not know through which channel any of these families were enfranchised. It would be possible to suppose that some of those who appeared in Rome at the end of the second century were the enfranchised magistrates of Latin towns, and that those who appeared earlier did so in virtue of the Latin *ius migrationis*, but the Volcacii Tulli at least probably derived directly from Perusia (a town that seems to have been particularly favoured by grants of citizenship).

What part did these families play in the process of Romanization after their enfranchisement? For them to have been acceptable as Roman citizens and even as Roman officials they must have been thoroughly Romanized. There was a real *civitatis mutatio*, confirmed by the fact that by comparison with

[1] *CIE* 1729: 'C. Annius L.f. Coelia gnat vel anne cupsnal'. For the diffusion of Annii, cf. Taylor, *VDRR* 190–1.

[2] R. Syme, *Historia*, xiii (1964), 164.

[3] Cf. Münzer, op. cit., 47–62.

some other Etruscan families most of those on the list have names that are rare in the Etruscan inscriptions, and none of the known political families, the Cilnii of Arretium, the Caecinae of Volaterrae, or various *zilath*s, are known to have been enfranchised before the Social War. However, the newly enfranchised will have retained their local interests, or at least property. Various connections with Etruria survived a number of generations: it cannot be accidental that so many Etruscan names are to be found in the entourage of Sertorius, or rather of his ally Perperna, and yet Perperna had at least three Roman generations behind him. The Nigidii and Saenii (to which cases some doubts are attached) also show evidence of different kinds of Etruscan connections some three generations after the name appears at Rome. Some of those who became Roman citizens will no doubt have had formal relations of *hospitium* with Etruscan towns, as Balbus had with the Gaditani.[1] By these continuing relations with Etruria they will have helped to spread the Latin language, Roman ideas, and loyalty to Rome.

[1] Cic. *Balb.* 41–2.

VI

THE SOCIAL WAR

1. *Etruscan Society in 91*

AFTER the conquest Roman policy aimed at the maintenance of security in Etruria by means of the local ruling class, and therefore at the maintenance of the existing social system, that is the dominance of the ruling class over the depressed but in some cases actively discontented serf class. Some have held that this system is in some way relevant to the actions of the Etruscans during the Social War, when they (and also the Umbrians, who are discussed separately) behaved differently from the majority of the Italian allies. First of all it is necessary to discuss the question whether the system had survived in its essentials; for some have simply assumed that this was the case[1] and others that it was not.[2] Writers about the Etruscans have tended to believe that the system did survive,[3] but recently an important attempt has been made to revise this view.[4]

There is of course little evidence. Vegoia's Prophecy and two other pieces of literary evidence, both well-worn, the story of Tiberius Gracchus' journey through Etruria[5] and the story of Marius' landing at Telamon in 87,[6] will be examined; then the arguments that H. Rix has drawn from his study of Etruscan nomenclature; then a body of epigraphical and archaeological evidence that has not previously been brought into the discussion.

It has been argued that Vegoia's Prophecy is in substance an authentically Etruscan document—so much is in fact generally accepted—and on that basis it can obviously be used to show

[1] E.g. E. Gabba, *Athenaeum*, xxxii (1954), 50.
[2] E.g. Badian, *FC*.
[3] Cf. J. Heurgon, *JRS* xlix (1959), 43–4.
[4] H. Rix, *Das etruskische Cognomen* (Wiesbaden, 1963), 325–78.
[5] Plu. *TG* 8.
[6] Plu. *Mar.* 41.

that the social structure of Etruria had remained stable. If its precise historical context is the Social War, so much the better, but whatever its exact origins and whatever the exact purposes were to which it was put in the late Republic, it is clear that it must have been held to be extremely relevant to the Etruscan situation at least as late as the time of the Gracchi.[1] In the Prophecy land-holding is discussed in terms of two classes, *domini* and *servi*,[2] and those two classes alone. The Prophecy asserts in the strongest terms the sacredness of the present boundaries of land-holdings: 'Cum autem Iuppiter terram Aetruriae sibi vindicavit, constituit iussitque metiri campos signarique agros. Sciens hominum avaritiam vel terrenum cupidinem, terminis omnia scita esse voluit.'[3] The implication is that land-holdings were regarded as having been stable for a long period, and the social order likewise (and it also seems to be the case that the danger to the existing order comes from the side of the *servi*, with connivance (*conscientia*) from some of the *domini*). This evidence for the survival of the Etruscan social system cannot be rejected without the relegation of Vegoia's Prophecy to the category of forgery.

Plutarch describes the condition of Italy at the time of Tiberius Gracchus' tribunate: throughout the country there was a dearth of free men and it was filled with barbarian slaves, with which the rich farmed their estates, having driven away the citizens. Then Plutarch offers various explanations of Tiberius' having taken action on the subject: as the majority say, it was the fault of Diophanes and Blossius; some joined Cornelia in the responsibility; others thought Tiberius' rival Sp. Postumius was responsible—*ὁ δ' ἀδελφὸς αὐτοῦ Γάϊος ἔν τινι βιβλίῳ γέγραφεν εἰς Νομαντίαν πορευόμενον διὰ τῆς Τυρρηνίας τὸν Τιβέριον, καὶ τὴν ἐρημίαν τῆς χώρας ὁρῶντα καὶ τοὺς γεωργοῦντας ἢ νέμοντας οἰκέτας ἐπεισάκτους καὶ βαρβάρους, τότε πρῶτον ἐπὶ νοῦν βαλέσθαι, κτλ.* But, says Plutarch, what most incited Tiberius were the demands of the *δῆμος* that he should recover the public land for the poor. Considerable weight has been put on this passage as evidence of the state of affairs in allied

[1] No one has ever suggested to my knowledge that the Prophecy could have reached its present form at an earlier date than that.

[2] *servi*, 351.1L; *conscientia dominica*, 351.2–3L.

[3] 350.18–22L.

Etruria,[1] and indeed even if the event itself was distorted by Gaius' propaganda,[2] the allusion to Etruscan conditions remains important. Yet it is not at all certain that the observations concerned were made in allied territory. Only a relatively small strip of Etruria just north of Rome was in the *ager Romanus*, it is said,[3] and so it would seem that Tiberius' observations must have been made in allied territory; but if Tiberius was on his way to Spain, he surely travelled by the Via Aurelia,[4] and much of the territory in Etruria through which the Aurelia passed (and much in particular of the *ager publicus* through which it passed) was no longer in the area of allied states, but in that of various colonies and other settlements, at least as far north as Cosa and possibly farther. The situation that Tiberius is said to have encountered will have been the result of the enormous influx of slaves into Rome in the second century; it is obvious that that must have had an effect in Etruria, as elsewhere, but there is no reason to suppose that the old system necessarily came to an end as a result—especially as the serf class seems to have had some property rights. Even if what Tiberius saw was in allied territory, there is a further point that weakens the story as evidence for a change in the social system: slaves were normally ἐπείσακτοι and βάρβαροι,[5] particularly in the mouth of Tiberius, one of whose main points it seems to have been that the slaves in Italy were intruders.[6] There are so many points of weakness in the story that it is impossible to use it to show that the social system in Etruria had completely changed.

At this point it is necessary to consider whether the activities of the Gracchan land commission brought about any long-lasting changes in Etruria. There was *ager publicus* in Etruria and it is virtually certain that there was some that was eligible for distribution by the commission. Of the twelve known Gracchan boundary-markers, not one comes from Etruria (or

[1] Rix evidently regards it as decisive evidence that the whole system had changed, op. cit., 374.

[2] Cf. Badian, *FC* 172.

[3] Ibid., followed by D. C. Earl, *Tiberius Gracchus, A Study in Politics* (Brussels, 1963), 21.

[4] Cf. above, p. 119.

[5] Cf. δεσμωτηρίων βαρβαρικῶν in this chapter.

[6] Cf. App. *BC* I 9.36, 11.44. References to Appian in Chapters VI–VIII are to *BC* I unless otherwise specified.

Umbria),[1] and there are enough from other places to suggest that there was, at most, relatively little distribution of land in Etruria. We know that there was some eligible land in Italy that was never recovered or distributed by the Gracchan commission.[2] In the *Libri Coloniarum* there are references to the activities of the commission and of Gaius Gracchus in Etruria: there were *Gracchani limites* at Arretium;[3] 'colonia Ferentinensis lege Sempronia est adsignata' (this seems to be a reference to Etruscan Ferentium rather than Volscian Ferentinum);[4] and 'colonia Tarquinios lege Sempronia est adsignata'.[5] A variety of otherwise unauthenticated Gracchan assignments and colonies are referred to,[6] yet while it is plausible that there was eligible *ager publicus* in the territory of Arretium, none of these statements can be accepted,[7] so bad are the *Libri Coloniarum* when they can be checked with other sources.[8] On the other hand Gaius is hardly likely to have advertised Etruria as an area where reform had been particularly needed if in fact the commission had not done something there.[9] Thus it is likely that some local *possessores* of large estates lost land and some of the serf class was displaced. Appian asserts that fifteen years after Gaius' legislation the work of the Gracchan commissioners had been completely undone:[10] οἱ πλούσιοι παρὰ τῶν πενήτων ἐωνοῦντο, ἢ ταῖσδε ταῖς προφάσεσιν ἐβιάζοντο . . . ὅθεν ἐσπάνιζον

[1] *ILLRP* 467–75; cf. *CIL* i².639–44, 696, 719, *ILS* 24–6, 28, L. R. Taylor, *VDRR* 93 n. 40. In Italy two come from Campania, six from Lucania, three from Apulia, and one from the *ager Gallicus* (Monte Giove, near and surely in the territory of Fanum Fortunae; not far away along the Via Flaminia was Forum Sempronii).

[2] Such may be inferred from τὴν μὲν γῆν μηκέτι διανέμειν, ἀλλ' εἶναι τῶν ἐχόντων (App. 27.122); cf. Gabba ad loc.

[3] 215.3L.

[4] 216.3L. It is in the section dealing with 'Tuscia', cf. 211.22L.

[5] 219.1L. That one of Gaius' colonies should have been sent out without leaving any trace except in the *Libri Coloniarum* is much harder to believe than that there were otherwise unattested *viritim* distributions.

[6] Abellinum, Caiatia, Corfinium, Suessa Aurunca, Velitrae, etc.

[7] As they are even by some careful scholars, e.g. Gabba, art. cit., 47. The notices are accepted uncritically by R. J. Rowland, *TAPhA* xcvi (1965), 367 and n. 31, A. J. Pfiffig, *Die Ausbreitung des römischen Städtewesens in Etrurien und die Frage der Unterwerfung der Etrusker* (Florence, 1966), 43, 58, 66.

[8] See below, pp. 305–6, for an assessment of their unreliability on the Augustan colonies.

[9] Cf. Gabba, l.c.

[10] 27.121–4. The question of when Appian's fifteen-year period was supposed to have begun need not be answered here; cf. E. Badian, *Historia*, xi (1962), 211.

ἔτι μᾶλλον ὁμοῦ πολιτῶν, κτλ. The *πλούσιοι* who acquired this land are more likely to have been Roman citizens than members of the allied states[1]—and so to a limited extent there was probably a change in the type of occupation of land in Etruria, with a consequent weakening of the *principes* and displacement of the serfs. In their place there will presumably have been proprietors who farmed largely by means of slaves. Yet it should be emphasized that this is likely to have happened only in restricted areas of Etruria.

The story of Marius' landing at Telamon in 87 also needs analysis.[2] Clearly Marius is likely to have landed at Telamon, when returning from Africa to Italy, for some particular reason. The proximity of his colony in Corsica has been suggested as an explanation,[3] but something more than that is needed. Marius was in fact in serious need of troops, for he landed with some 500[4] or 1,000 men,[5] many of them Africans according to Plutarch;[6] and more troops he did manage to collect, a total of 6,000 Etruscans.[7] Were these Etruscans in the proper sense of the word, or inhabitants of territory that had long been in Roman hands? Telamon itself had once been an independent community,[8] and although there is no sign that it ever became a *municipium* under the Romans, and some have thought that it must have been in the territory of Cosa or of Heba,[9] on balance

[1] There seems to be no specific evidence for land-holding by individual Romans in allied Etruria or Umbria in this period.

[2] Plu. *Mar.* 41: *ταῦτα τῷ Μαρίῳ πυνθανομένῳ πλεῦσαι τὴν ταχίστην ἐφαίνετο· καὶ παραλαβὼν ἐκ τῆς Λιβύης Μαυρουσίων τινὰς ἱππότας καὶ τῶν ἀπὸ τῆς Ἰταλίας τινὰς καταφερομένων, συναμφοτέρους οὐ πλείονας χιλίων γενομένους, ἀνήχθη. προσβαλὼν δὲ Τελαμῶνι τῆς Τυρρηνίας καὶ ἀποβὰς ἐκήρυττε δούλοις ἐλευθερίαν· καὶ τῶν αὐτόθι γεωργούντων καὶ νεμόντων ἐλευθέρων κατὰ δόξαν αὐτοῦ συντρεχόντων ἐπὶ τὴν θάλατταν ἀναπείθων τοὺς ἀκμαιοτάτους, ἐν ἡμέραις ὀλίγαις χεῖρα μεγάλην ἤθροισε καὶ τεσσαράκοντα ναῦς ἐπλήρωσεν.*

[3] E. Wiehn, *Die illegalen Heereskommanden in Rom bis auf Caesar* (Marburg, 1926), 59, favoured by Badian, *FC* 238 n. 4.

[4] App. 67.305.

[5] Gran. Licin. 16F, cf. Plu. l.c.

[6] On the contradictions between these three sources about the make-up of Marius' force, cf. A. Passerini, *Athenaeum*, xvii (1939), 68–9, who points to the Marian veterans in Africa.

[7] App. 67.306, cf. Gran. Licin. 16F, 'mox legionem voluntariorum conscripsit', Plu. l.c.

[8] As its coins (on which see W. Deecke, *Das etruskische Münzwesen* (Stuttgart, 1876, vol. ii of *Etruskische Forschungen*), esp. pp. 43–4, Beloch, *RG* 608) surely show.

[9] Cosa according to Bormann, *CIL* xi. p. 416, Heba according to Beloch, l.c.

it seems more likely that it was still inhabited by Etruscans.[1] On the other hand the total force collected by Marius in Etruria was too large to have come from Telamon alone, and much of the neighbouring territory was in Roman hands (at Saturnia, as well as Heba and Cosa). So Marius probably looked both to old citizens and to new. Marius' first action when he landed, according to Plutarch, was to offer freedom to slaves. Arming of slaves was a standard charge,[2] and we have other evidence that it was made against Marius in this war without explicit reference to Etruria.[3] So much in fact is said about the slaves whom Marius armed and the objections to the behaviour of some of them (the *Βαρδυαῖοι*) expressed after the victory by Sertorius and even by Cinna,[4] that it is probable that there were some armed slaves in Marius' army, and by far the most likely occasion on which Marius could have acquired this force was immediately after his landing at Telamon.[5] It is tempting to see in the rebellious slaves of Telamon members of the Etruscan serf class or slaves who saw an opportunity in the collapse of the old ruling class. But it appears from Plutarch that the majority of the supporters whom Marius collected in Etruria were free farmers (not from the same area, one would suppose, as the slaves to whom Marius offered their freedom), not necessarily or probably small landowners, but tenant farmers or even free labourers from large estates;[6] many of them may have been veterans of Marius' armies,[7] and many of them will have been old Roman citizens. The conclusion of

[1] On the destruction at Telamon in this period cf. *NSA* 1888, 682–91 (G. F. Gamurrini), R. A. L. Fell, *Etruria and Rome* (Cambridge, 1924), 164, H. Philipp in *RE* s.v. Telamon no. 4 (1934). A *terminus post quem* of *c.* 85 is given by a coin of L. Iulius Bursio (Sydenham no. 728c) (information of Mr. M. H. Crawford about the coins cursorily referred to by Gamurrini), but the destruction may have been a number of years later. Cf. below, p. 258.

[2] R. Syme, *Sallust* (Cambridge, 1964), 82.

[3] The Marians were accused of having incited slaves to rebellion in 88, App. 60.271. On 87, Florus II 9.11, Plu. *Sert.* 5, *Mar.* 44, Σ Gronov. p. 286.8–9St.

[4] Plu. ll.cc.

[5] App. 67.305 says that he brought with him from Africa the slaves of his followers, but naturally they are not likely to have been freed. Σ Gronov. is too brief and vague to tell us where Marius' slave forces came from. On the name *Βαρδυαῖοι* see H. Bennett, *Cinna and his Times* (Menasha, Wis., 1923), 23 n. 112.

[6] The 'small landowners' of Badian, *FC* 222, was corrected by E. Gabba, *RFIC* xxxvii (1959), 197 n. 2, cf. Badian, *Historia*, xi (1962), 227 n. 106.

[7] Badian, *FC* 238; *κατὰ δόξαν αὐτοῦ*, however, may represent another motive.

all this, as with the story concerning Tiberius Gracchus, is that we have no secure information at all that would lead us to think that the old social system in Etruria had changed, but some slight indication that it survived.[1]

Rix's study of the nomenclature of Etruria is a model of precision and caution, but the sociological conclusions that he draws are by their nature extremely speculative and in fact go far beyond the evidence. The best way to approach this evidence without getting involved in technical linguistic problems that have no place here is to emphasize the facts that in his opinion point to changes in the system since the third and early second centuries. Too much weight, first of all, is placed on the story of Tiberius Gracchus: as we have seen, there is no need to see in it accurate description of the predominant social system of allied Etruria in 135, still less to think that it points to a social *Neuordnung* there.[2] He is also compelled to be evasive about Vegoia's Prophecy.[3]

The problem that Rix is attempting to solve is that of the second gentilicial name that many Etruscans bear, or, as he puts it, the use of gentilicial names as *cognomina* (there are also other *cognomina*, which he calls the genuine ones).[4] Examples of gentilicial names used in this way are the name *cacni* in the name 'au. anei cacniś au.'[5] and the name *asate* in 'v. caeś asate'.[6] These gentilicial names used as *cognomina* are almost always found in conjunction with *nomina* of a particular kind, namely *Vornamengentilizia*, that is gentilicial names that are 'formally identical' with *praenomina* or individual names,[7] the commonest of these being *cae* (*cai*), *vipi*, and *tite*. As an explanation of this conjunction Rix puts forward the theory that the ancestors of the bearers of these *Vornamengentilizia* were 'non-citizens' (in fact he thinks that they were the πενέσται),[8] who

[1] Another piece of literary evidence has been brought into this question: R. M. Haywood, *AJPh* liv (1933), 145–6, supposed that the *coloni* enlisted by Domitius Ahenobarbus, cos. 54, in the *ager Cosanus* in 49 (Caes. *BC* I 34) were descendants of the Etruscan serf class and that they had as such an obligation to military service; this seems to be taken seriously by Gabba, *RFIC*, l.c.; but there cannot have been such people in a Latin colony.

[2] As Rix thinks, op. cit., 376.

[3] Ibid., 374.

[4] Earlier opinions on this matter are reviewed, ibid., 325–31.

[5] *CIE* 3905.

[6] *CIE* 401. A full list can be found in Rix, op. cit., 338–9.

[7] Ibid., 331.

[8] Ibid., 375.

when they became citizens acquired proper citizen-names by converting their former personal names into gentilicial names; when such persons took another gentilicial name and used it as a *cognomen*, the name that they used for this purpose was the gentilicial name of their former *patronus*. Thus it is argued that a class of non-citizens, equated with the πενέσται, began to acquire the status of full citizens; this process is said to have begun after *c*. 150 because the tombs of the bearers of the *Vornamengentilizia* at Clusium do not go back beyond that date,[1] and to have produced a social *Neuordnung* by the time of Tiberius' journey through Etruria in 135 (but see above).[2] Rix then proceeds to make some inferences about the relatively good relations between the social classes at Perusia from the fact that there the bearers of *Vornamengentilizia* tended to use gentilicial names as *cognomina*, i.e. the names of their own *patroni*, rather than genuine *cognomina*.[3]

Rix's array of facts is impressive, but his sociological conclusions rest upon too many hypotheses to weigh at all heavily against the other evidence. To begin with, we do not really know anything about the origin of the bearers of the *Vornamengentilizia*, whose names are in fact virtually unknown as individual names in Etruria;[4] certainly we have no direct evidence at all that their ancestors recently lacked citizen status (it can be accepted that at Clusium on the whole they tended to have rather poorer burials than others did).[5] The chronological point seems to be of fundamental importance to this scheme; yet there were some bearers of *Vornamengentilizia* much earlier than 150,[6] and it is simply guess-work to say that there was a great increase in the relative number of such people after 150. Further, it seems to be an error of method to put as much trust as Rix does in name-formulae as indications of legal status[7]—

[1] Ibid., 343, 376.

[2] This conclusion is accepted by M. Pallottino, *Etruscologia*[6] (Milan, 1968), 233.

[3] Op. cit., 377–8.

[4] As Rix says, op. cit., 348–9.

[5] Ibid., 342–4.

[6] Ibid., 343–4.

[7] I do not doubt that in ancient Italy 'Name und Rechtsstellung so eng miteinander verknüpft sind' (ibid., 372, though the article of V. Gardthausen, *RhM* lxxii (1917–18), 353–73, to which Rix refers, does not show that this was true in Etruria). The dangers of this idea become clear when Rix argues that a particular class of *lautni* had the same status as Roman *liberti*, because they each had 'ein etruskisches Bürgerpraenomen und ein Gentile, was auf eine grundsätzliche Gleichberechtigung mit dem Vollbürgern deutet' (op. cit., 366).

the chief difficulty here arising from the fact that it is very difficult, if not impossible, to discover a clear relationship between the bearers of the *Vornamengentilizia* and the *lautni*;[1] in such a situation it is surely preferable to assume that the known Etruscan term *lautni* had a precise meaning rather than to rely on the quite unevidenced legal implications of the name-formulae. A number of other difficulties arise, which have no bearing on the point at issue here—enough has been said to show that it is not possible by this means to show that the old social system was already dissolved by the time of the Social War.

Some useful archaeological evidence on this question has been neglected. The stability of Etruscan society can be inferred to a limited extent from the continuity of some of the more prosperous families as it appears from their tomb-groups. In particular the work of J. Thimme on various tomb-groups at Clusium and on the tomb of the Volumnii at Perusia has established fairly clearly both the number of generations for which certain tombs were in use, and as far as possible their absolute dates.[2] The latter point is one of considerable difficulty, for certain assumptions have to be made about the effects of known political events; in particular catastrophic effects tend to be attributed to the Social War,[3] which there is no need to believe that it actually brought about in Etruria, and which are in fact more likely to be due to Sulla. Yet Thimme's dates must generally be within a decade or two of the correct ones. He shows that at Clusium there were four generations of burials in the Granduca tomb, running from *c.* 190 to *c.* 100,[4] four in the Pellegrina tomb, continuing to *c.* 135,[5] four in the Tutna Fastntru tomb continuing to *c.* 130,[6] burials covering about

[1] The two classes partially overlap, ibid., 375.

[2] *SE* xxiii (1954), 25–147 ('Thimme i' hereafter) and xxv (1957), 87–160 ('Thimme ii').

[3] Cf. Thimme i.70, ii.113, e.g.; on the evidence for absolute dates see below, p. 211 n. 3.

[4] Thimme i.60–73, *CIE* 1158–65. The family stemma becomes rather uncertain in the last generation (Thimme 69–73), but if we accept his *terminus post quem* for the series it must go down at least very nearly to the last decade of the second century.

[5] Thimme i.98–132.

[6] Thimme ii.96–106, *CIE* 941–51 (cf. Rix, op. cit., 105).

eighty years in the second century in the Purni tomb,[1] and also some continuity in the second century in the Matausni, Ceicna, and Larthia Seianti tombs.[2] There was also a period of continuity in the tomb of the Volumnii at Perusia from *c.* 160 to *c.* 110.[3] In other cases not discussed by Thimme the chronological basis is less secure, but there are various tombs in the territory of Tarquinii where the continuity of a particular family seems to belong to this same period, one for example that belonged to a distinguished family at Tuscana,[4] and the Pulena and Curuna tombs, as well as the Tomba del Tifone, at Tarquinii itself.[5] It is obvious that important social and economic changes could take place without there being any evidence of them in such tomb-groups, but taken as a whole, the evidence from Clusium, and also from Perusia and Tarquinii, strongly suggests that the economic position of the ruling class was fairly stable throughout the second century—and since that position

[1] Thimme ii.119–34, *CIE* 1342–52. 1638, 1640, 4889, 4907, Rix, op. cit., 328–9.

[2] The Matausni tomb: Thimme i.73–98, *CIE* 1385–91. The Ceicna tomb: Thimme ii.87–95. The Larthia Seianti tomb: Thimme ii.106–18, *CIE* 1211–17 (cf. Rix, op. cit., 64 n. 107, E. H. Richardson, *The Etruscans* (Chicago, 1964), 169–70).

[3] i.132–47, *CIE* 3754–64, *TLE* 566–8, 605. The siege of Perusia (41–0 B.C.) has been used as a *terminus ante quem* for this tomb, for example by A. von Gerkan (in his article with F. Messerschmidt in *MDAI–R* lvii (1942), 122–50). Basing himself exclusively on the assumption that the inscriptions on the main group of urns were the immediate and direct predecessors of the famous bilingually-inscribed marble urn of P. Volumnius A.f. Violens Cafatia natus, he dated them to the period 75–60. But stylistically they resemble much more closely Thimme's *Entwicklungsstufe* iii, which, at Clusium at least, belongs to the second half of the second century (Thimme i.134). On absolute dates: for finds associated with the urns discussed by Thimme and comparable ones, cf. F. Messerschmidt, *MDAI–R* xlv (1930), 178, R. Herbig, *Die jüngeretruskischen Steinsarkophage* (Berlin, 1952), 122. The uncial *as* in the Larthia Seianti tomb (*NSA* 1877, 140, R. Bianchi Bandinelli, *MAAL* xxx (1925), col. 306) does not give any precise help in the present apparent state of uncertainty about the dating of such coins.

[4] F. N. Pryce, *Catalogue of Sculpture in the Department of Greek and Roman Antiquities of the British Museum*, vol. i part ii (London, 1931), 193–200, who refers to earlier descriptions; *CII* 2108=*TLE* 180, *CII* 2101=*TLE* 194. There are various difficulties in this case: there is no apparent connection between the two inscriptions, so that the tomb may not after all have been used by a single family—a known phenomenon of late Tarquinii, cf. M. Pallottino, *MAAL* xxxvi (1937), col. 385.

[5] A summary of information about the Pulena tomb is given by Pallottino, art. cit., cols. 520–1, 544; about the Curuna tomb, cols. 515, 525, 544; about the Tomba del Tifone, cols. 397, 408–9, 429–30, 516–17, 525; on the date of the last, see above, p. 177 n. 6. To these may now be added the Tomba Giglioli at Tarquinii, a second-century tomb used for perhaps three generations, *SE* xxx (1962), 285–91 (L. C. Vanoni), 301–2 (Pallottino).

was based on the labour of the serfs, that the social system in general was fairly stable.

On the existing evidence it is not possible to give a completely conclusive proof that the Etruscan social system had survived in its essentials until the Social War, but there is some evidence that it had and virtually none that there had been any change. That there had been some influx of new slave labour and that there had been some tendency towards *latifundia* does not have to be denied, but given that Roman and Etruscan intentions had been to preserve the system after the Hannibalic War, it is quite wrong to assume that it had disappeared a hundred years later. The problem remains of course of defining when and how the system did break up, and to that there is no simple answer. Its legal and political terms were radically changed by the settlement or rather settlements made after the war, a process that is examined in the next two chapters; yet the power of some of the old ruling families survived in some cases right through to the end of the Republic and beyond.

2. *Etruria and Umbria in 91 and 90: the Sources*

The problems raised by the explicit references in the sources to Etruria and Umbria in 91–90, some of them problems that have been repeatedly discussed,[1] need to be examined first. These are first the problems raised by Appian, *BC* I 36. 162–4, and secondly those raised by the fighting in 90 and the acceptance of the Lex Iulia.

The Ἰταλιῶται, Appian tells us, were frightened about Drusus' νόμος τῆς ἀποικίας, because under it they expected to lose the possession of Roman *ager publicus*. Etruscans and Umbrians, fearing the same things as the Ἰταλιῶται,[2] and apparently brought to Rome by the consuls to murder Drusus

[1] An exhaustive bibliography of the Social War in general need not be given here; much of it is to be found in R. Thomsen, *C & M* v (1942), 13–14, Badian, *FC* and *Historia*, xi (1962), esp. 223–8. Since then the causes of the war have been discussed by E. T. Salmon, *Phoenix*, xvi (1962), 107–19, P. A. Brunt, *JRS* lv (1965), 90–109.

[2] Evidently meaning 'the Italians in general' or perhaps 'the Italians who started the Social War'; I cannot agree with the view of P. J. Cuff, *Historia*, xvi (1967), 182, that we should, because of this passage, take Ἰταλιῶται to mean 'the Italians who started the Social War' throughout the early chapters of *BC* I.

but ostensibly to denounce him, openly protested against the law and awaited the day of the δοκιμασία. Drusus heard of these things and went out seldom, doing business in the *atrium* of his house, where he was murdered.[1] Obviously much is missing from Appian's account that is known from other sources, but it makes sense by itself—if the nullification of the agrarian and judiciary laws is not mentioned, neither is their passing in the first place described at all explicitly.[2] It is assumed by Appian that the allies in general wanted the Roman citizenship,[3] and as the text stands it is clearly stated that the law against which the Etruscans and Umbrians protested, with the agreement of the consuls, was the νόμος τῆς ἀποικίας. What then was the day of the vote for which they waited? The agrarian law had been passed long before the death of Drusus, probably at the beginning of the year, before the decline of Drusus' influence that the δοκιμασία, whatever it was, shows to have taken place. It has been suggested[4] that the vote was the vote taken in the Senate to settle whether the Leges Liviae had been passed *contra legem Caeciliam Didiam*, by which they were in fact invalidated.[5] That is what Appian may have meant; but he chose a very obscure way of saying it—no one would know from his account that there was ever any question of a senatorial vote on the validity of Drusus' laws.[6] Appian himself has in fact made

[1] (162) *οἱ Ἰταλιῶται δ', ὑπὲρ ὧν δὴ καὶ μάλιστα ὁ Δροῦσος ταῦτα ἐτέχναζε, καὶ οἵδε περὶ τῷ νόμῳ τῆς ἀποικίας ἐδεδοίκεσαν, ὡς τῆς δημοσίας Ῥωμαίων γῆς, ην ἀνέμητον οὖσαν ἔτι οἱ μὲν ἐκ βίας, οἱ δὲ λανθάνοντες ἐγεώργουν, αὐτίκα σφῶν ἀφαιρεθησομένης, καὶ πολλὰ καὶ περὶ τῆς ἰδίας ἐνοχλησόμενοι* (163). *Τυρρηνοί τε καὶ Ὀμβρικοὶ ταὐτὰ δειμαίνοντες τοῖς Ἰταλιώταις καί, ὡς ἐδόκει, πρὸς τῶν ὑπάτων ἐς τὴν πόλιν ἐπαχθέντες ἔργῳ μὲν ἐς ἀναίρεσιν Δρούσου, λόγῳ δ' ἐς κατηγορίαν, τοῦ νόμου φανερῶς κατεβόων καὶ τὴν τῆς δοκιμασίας ἡμέραν ἀνέμενον* (164). *ὧν ὁ Δροῦσος αἰσθανόμενός τε καὶ οὐ θαμινὰ προϊών . . .*

[2] Cf. 35.156–7.

[3] Cf. 35.155, 49.213.

[4] E. Marcks, *Die Ueberlieferung des Bundesgenossenkrieges 91–89 v. Chr.* (Marburg, 1884), 10, and independently Badian, *FC* 219, *Historia*, xi (1962), 226 n. 104, followed by Brunt, art. cit., 94.

[5] Cic. *Dom.* 41. The only specific fault in the laws that is mentioned in the sources is that they were 'contra auspicia . . . latas' (Ascon. 68C).

[6] Gabba, *RFIC* xxxvii (1959), 196, objected to Badian's interpretation on the grounds that δοκιμασία elsewhere in Appian (e.g. 10.42, 29.132) refers to assembly votes on laws, to which Badian replies, *Historia*, l.c., that there is no known Greek word for the procedure that took place in the Senate and that δοκιμασία could well be used for this purpose. But the word does in that case indicate a bad misunderstanding on Appian's part, as Badian recognizes—whereas in Gabba's interpretation Appian only has to be 'fortemente sunteggiato'.

no explicit remark about the previous passing of the colonial law and until section 164 starts and we find that we are on the eve of the murder of Drusus, that could be the δοκιμασία to which he is referring. Where exactly the defect comes in Appian's account is a difficult question; it is usually held to come between sections 163 and 164,[1] for it is only in section 164 that the reader realizes that something must be wrong. Yet the last sentence of 163 is closely connected with 164—the Etruscans and Umbrians were brought to Rome to kill Drusus (ὡς ἐδόκει), and then he is killed. If there is some sort of fault in Appian's narrative *before* the bringing of the Etruscans and Umbrians to Rome, then the δοκιμασία is cut off from the colonial law and it can (but does not have to) refer to the *rogatio de sociis*. This tortuous line of argument seems to be the only one by which the view[2] that the Etruscans and Umbrians were protesting against the *rogatio de sociis* can be saved, and it is not convincing—it goes too far in assuming that Appian could write nonsense. I conclude that it is much more likely that Appian meant to say that the Etruscans and Umbrians protested against the colonial law—yet his clarity on this point has sometimes been overrated. (Whether it is likely that the Etruscans and Umbrians were in fact opposed to the *rogatio de sociis* is discussed in the next section.)

A further inference from 163–4 has been put forward by Brunt,[3] namely that by the time of the protest of the Etruscans and Umbrians and the δοκιμασία (the Senate vote, as he thinks) the *rogatio de sociis* was already a lost cause, so that those who protested against the colonial law were not even showing that they preferred their lands to gaining the Roman citizenship, all hope of the latter having passed. Various arguments tell against this: it was not until very late that any of Drusus' schemes was a lost cause, for his position seems to have been strong, if hotly contended, until the Ides of September,[4] and something surely had been done by that time to organize the influx of Etruscans and Umbrians,[5] especially if the common assumption is correct

[1] Cf. Gabba, *Athenaeum*, xxxii (1954), 47, *Appiano e la storia delle guerre civili* (Florence, 1956), 22.

[2] L. Piotrowicz, *Klio*, xxiii (1930), 335–6; also Carcopino, Pareti, Gabba.

[3] Art. cit., 95.

[4] Cic. *de Or.* III 1 (Brunt recognizes this, art. cit., 107).

[5] Cf. below, p. 226 n. 5.

that the death of Drusus took place in October.[1] If, as Brunt believes, the Etruscans and Umbrians wanted the Roman citizenship in 91, and did not mind losing land in order to obtain it, it is very difficult to imagine their consenting to campaign for Philippus against Drusus, when Philippus had led the opposition to Drusus' scheme to bring that about.[2] There remains then, in my view, some evidence that the Etruscans and Umbrians concerned were less willing than the other allies to make the exchange of land for citizenship, at least on the precise terms on which the offer was made in 91.

It is clear that in 91 and in the first part of 90 neither Etruscans nor Umbrians took part in the fighting against Rome. About their actions in the latter part of 90 there is a conflict between Appian and the Livian tradition. According to the former,[3] as a result of defeats suffered by the forces of Italia, the Etruscans and Umbrians on the other side of Rome and some other nations that were neighbours of theirs, πάντες ἐς ἀπόστασιν ἠρεθίζοντο. Consequently the Senate feared that Rome would be encircled; they arranged a guard of freedmen for the coast of Campania, and voted that the Ἰταλιῶται who still remained in the alliance should be Roman citizens, the thing that they above all desired. They sent news of this to the Etruscans, who gladly accepted the citizenship. Later, not having heard of the μετάνοια of the Etruscans, the rebels on the Adriatic coast sent a force of 15,000 men over a difficult and long path into Etruria ἐπὶ συμμαχίᾳ. Thus the Etruscans, if not the Umbrians, are described as being among the beneficiaries of the enfranchising law, that is as having remained in the alliance up to that time. The Epitomator of Livy reports that both the Etruscans and Umbrians rebelled, and were conquered by A. Plotius, a *legatus*, and L. Porcius, 'praetor' (in fact propraetor), respectively;[4] this is in 90, though clearly late in the year, for Cato was consul in the following year, and had time to turn his attention to the Marsi during the winter.[5] Orosius says that the victories of Plotius and Cato were brought about

[1] Carcopino, *Histoire romaine*, ii (Paris, 1929), 360, etc.

[2] Further it may be the case that when Appian says (49.213) that in 90 the Etruscans ἄσμενοι τῆς πολιτείας μετελάμβανον he is implying a contrast with their attitude in 91.

[3] 49.211–50.216.

[4] *Per.* 74.

[5] App. 50.217.

'plurimo sanguine impenso et difficillimo labore',[1] a characteristic exaggeration, as has been pointed out.[2] Florus also exaggerates the extent of the war, to a ridiculous degree[3]—all of Latium and Campania were involved as well as *omnis Etruria*, and so on; the victory of Cato over the Etruscans is mentioned[4] and that of Plotius over the Umbrians.[5] Some further geographical details are offered in a rhetorical flight: 'ecce Ocriculum, ecce Grumentum, ecce Faesulae, ecce Carseoli, Aesernia, Nuceria, Picentia [*sic*] caedibus ferro et igne vastantur.' (There is no reason to emend Faesulae to Pausulae here.[6]) He simply seems to be listing one place from the territory of each of the main peoples of Italy, and although in several cases we know that fighting actually took place (at Grumentum, Aesernia, and Nuceria, also in Picenum), Ocriculum and Faesulae cannot be assumed to have taken part in the war. In fact it is possible to suppose that fighting took place at Ocriculum between the forces of Italia and Rome—Ocriculum itself, near to Rome and with a relatively favourable *foedus*, does not make a plausible centre of rebel activity; Faesulae is a more open case, and there may be some marginal confirmation of the activity of Cato there in the hoard of coins minted by a contemporary M. Cato, possibly the brother of the consul of 89, and found at Faesulae.[7] And it is one thing for Florus to exaggerate by saying that the whole of Etruria took part in the Social War, another to intrude Etruria into his account without any grounds at all. We do have some further

[1] V 18.17.

[2] Brunt, art. cit., 94, referring to *praef.* 9f.; otherwise Badian, *Historia*, xi (1962), 226 n. 103.

[3] II 6.5. Cf. E. T. Salmon, *TAPhA* lxxxix (1958), 160. I. Haug's view, *WJA* ii (1947), 211, that he was referring to the areas where fighting took place, hardly saves him.

[4] II 6.13.

[5] II 6.6—though Plotius appears in a list of rebel commanders.

[6] Suggested by G. Samonati, *GIF* xi (1958), 117–19; rejected by Gabba, *RFIC*, art. cit., 197 n. 1.

[7] For the hoard see E. Sydenham, *Roman Republican Coinage*, p. liv, M. H. Crawford, *Roman Republican Coin Hoards* (London, 1969), no. 227. The moneyer could be the son of the cos. of 118 (favoured by H. A. Grueber, *Coins of the Roman Republic in the British Museum*, ii.303–4) or of Salonianus (Mommsen, Babelon) who was also the father of the cos. of 89. Cf. F. Miltner in *RE* s.v. Porcius nos. 11 and 12 (1953). The legend ST on the reverse was taken by Borghesi to stand for *stipendium* (tentatively accepted by Grueber), which would fit in well. On the date of these coins cf. also Crawford, *Num. Chron.*, ser. 7.iv (1964), 141.

reasons to think that various towns in Etruria and Umbria took part in the war. The argument from tribal assignments made after the war was misused sometimes in the past for the purpose of identifying the rebels,[1] but a case can be made out for thinking that the Clustumina, to which at least nine communities in Umbria were assigned,[2] was a 'punitive' tribe.[3] Also there were in Book IV of Sisenna references to three towns in this area, Iguvium, Perusia, and Tuder;[4] the last of these at least may indicate a scene of rebellion.[5]

Velleius describes the beneficiaries of the Lex Iulia as 'qui arma aut non ceperant aut deposuerant maturius',[6] and though the enfranchisement of those who had rebelled but had already surrendered is not envisaged in Appian's description of the terms of the law, that was probably what happened in the case of a number of Etruscan and Umbrian communities. Some probably took no part in the war and were enfranchised at once; others needed special votes later on, as in the case of Tuder (and we do not know under which law the town was enfranchised). Appian is probably wrong to think that no town was enfranchised by the Lex Iulia that had ever left the alliance, though some special procedure, perhaps including a *senatus consultum*, was probably necessary in the cases of those who had, and he is certainly wrong to imply that there was no rebellion in Etruria or Umbria.

Appian's account is then one that plays down the efforts of the Etruscans and Umbrians on the side of Italia; one may compare the way in which the responsibility for the death of Drusus is attributed to them in 36. 163. It may be inferred that those who were favourable to the cause of Italia regarded the

[1] Piotrowicz, art. cit., 336. He held that Arretium and Volsinii (Pom.) and Clusium (Arn.) were put in tribes that were reserved for ex-rebels.

[2] Ameria, Arna, Iguvium, Pitinum Mergens, Sestinum, Tifernum Mataurense, Tifernum Tiberinum, Tuder, and Vettona, in addition to Carsulae, Interamna Nahars, and Tadinum.

[3] See below, pp. 238–40.

[4] Fr. 94P: 'itaque postero die legatos Iguvium redeuntis apiscitur'; 95; 'tum postquam apud Iguvinos ac Perusinos eius facti mentionem proiecit'; 119: '*tamen* Tudertibus senati consulto et populi iusso dat civitatem.'

[5] The fragment concerning Tuder is so interpreted by G. Niccolini, *Rend. Acc. Linc.*, ser. 8.i (1946), 113.

[6] II 16.4. The enfranchising laws are discussed in the next chapter.

Etruscans as having been definitely hostile to the cause and hostile to the settlement offered by Drusus in 91.

As far as the Umbrians are concerned, it is to be assumed that some of them at least were given the citizenship in 90 under the Lex Iulia, and that Appian does not omit them in 49. 213 and 50. 216 for any reason other than brevity.

3. *Explanations of the Behaviour of the Etruscans and Umbrians in the Social War*

Simply to explain the military inactivity of the Etruscans and Umbrians in 91 and the first part of 90 does not seem very difficult. Various suggestions have been advanced as parts of more general theories concerning the origins of the war. Sherwin-White,[1] holding that what the Italians in general fought for was 'equality of treatment and opportunity' and protection from 'the undivided and unchecked *imperium* of Roman magistrates', and that they did not fight for the right to take part in Roman politics, pointed to the supposed fact that the *foedera* that governed Rome's relations with the Etruscans and Umbrians were milder than those with the rebellious states as an explanation of the inactivity of the former in the Social War. However, as has already been argued, the *foedera* between Rome and the towns of Etruria were probably not in fact more mild than those made with the states of Italia,[2] and there is no reason to think that the levy for the Roman army had been particularly uncommon in Etruria. In Umbria, although Camerinum did have the *foedus omnium aequissimum*, it was clearly regarded in the first century as quite exceptional and there was probably only one other town in Umbria, namely Ocriculum, that may have had a *foedus aequum*.[3] It is further said that the recent *viritim* grants of citizenship in Umbria had been part of a generous Roman policy, tending to make the Umbrians less eager to fight against Rome, but, as has been argued, there were probably few cases of enfranchisement other than those mentioned by Cicero in the *Pro Balbo*,[4] and they

[1] *RC* 126–8.

[2] This has also been taken by Salmon to be the explanation of the behaviour of the Etruscans in 91, *Phoenix*, art. cit., 116–17; so too C. Nicolet, *L'ordre equestre à l'époque républicaine* (*312–43 av. J.-C.*) (Paris, 1966), 394 n. 20.

[3] Above, p. 105. [4] See above, p. 195.

hardly made a great impression except in the town of Camerinum, which was in any case untypical.

Seeking for a more convincing answer to the question of what the Italians who fought for Italia hoped to gain by becoming *κοινωνοὶ τῆς ἡγεμονίας*, Gabba[1] elaborated a theory that the main force behind the rebels in 91, a force that was not in existence in 125, was the desire of the successful new commercial classes of Italy, in particular of those *negotiatores* who operated wholly or in part in the East, to look after their own interests by exerting influence in Roman politics. In Hatzfeld's view only a very small proportion of the Italian *negotiatores* in the East derived from Etruria and Umbria,[2] and while some points of detail in the argument for this conclusion can be disputed, it is obvious even without exhaustive discussion that this is true for Etruria. The inference is made that the upper classes of Etruria and Umbria did not have the same motives as the upper classes of most of the rest of Italy for wanting the Roman citizenship—their commercial involvement in Roman foreign policy was relatively slight.[3] As the explanation of the Social War, the theory is clearly unsatisfactory: it is quite unproven that the eastern *negotiatores* exercised much influence in the states of Italia,[4] or that they felt a particular serious need for the Roman citizenship,[5] and most of all it is unproven that they wanted to make war on Rome in 91.[6] A number of critics have pointed out these and other defects in the theory.[7]

[1] *Athenaeum*, art. cit.

[2] J. Hatzfeld, *Les trafiquants italiens dans l'Orient hellénique* (Paris, 1919), 240; the evidence was collected by him in *BCH* xxxvi (1912), 5–218. There are virtually no names of definitely Etruscan form. Cf. above, p. 170 n. 2.

[3] Gabba, art. cit., 57–61.

[4] Cf. J. P. V. D. Balsdon, *Gnomon*, xxvi (1954), 344, etc. Even the geographical correspondence between Italia and the homes of the *negotiatores* lacks evidence; cf. T. R. S. Broughton, *Second International Conference of Economic History, Aix-en-Provence, 1962* (Paris, 1965), i. 155.

[5] As Hatzfeld and others have pointed out, Italians and Romans were known indifferently as Ῥωμαῖοι in the East.

[6] That the Italian *negotiatores* wanted to make war on Rome in 91 in order to get an aggressive Asian policy put into effect seems even more far-fetched if one considers what the actual situation was in Asia Minor in 91: Socrates Chrestos having been repulsed by the Senate 'early in 91' (D. Magie, *Roman Rule in Asia Minor* (Princeton, 1950), i. 207—the chronology of these events can be disputed, but Magie's is acceptable), Nicomedes IV was turned out of Bithynia, and at the same time Ariobarzanes I was turned out of Cappadocia (App. *Mithr.* 10).

[7] A. N. Sherwin-White, *JRS* xlv (1955), 168–70, Brunt, art. cit., 104.

Whether the fact that there were relatively few Etruscan and Umbrian *negotiatores* in the East—and it was not necessarily so in other provinces, for example in Spain—made any real difference to the situation in Italy remains a matter for conjecture: it probably was the case that rich men other than those who were mainly landowners were more influential in (say) Campanian towns than in Etruscan ones.

There are some obvious factors that tended to prevent military activity in Etruria and Umbria in 91 and 90. The Umbrians are unlikely to have felt that Roman policy about the citizenship had been particularly generous, but the influence of those who had been enfranchised, especially in Etruria, and had retained some interests there, would be against war;[1] on the other hand it is hard to believe that there were many such people whose origins were among the central Italian tribes. Naturally the pro-Roman *principes* will have been relatively unwilling to rebel, whatever the precise issues were in 91. There were also some practical military difficulties that impeded rebellion: between the rebellious tribes and Etruria and Umbria was a continuous stretch of Roman territory, and at least as important, some of the most impassable regions of the Apennines—when the 15,000 rebels did arrive in Etruria in late 90 they had covered a path ἀτριβῆ καὶ μακράν. How weak the contact was between Etruria and Italia is suggested by the fact that the 15,000 had not heard of the μετάνοια produced in Etruria by the Lex Iulia.[2] The rebellion required concerted preparation, and when it began it must have seemed to some extent to be a national cause of an Oscan-speaking nation quite alien to the Etruscans; it would in fact have been remarkable if in such circumstances rebellion had broken out in Etruria at exactly the same time as in central Italy. Yet the fact that there was no fighting in Etruria or Umbria until the war had been going on for so long also suggests the important conclusion that in Etruria and Umbria there was not the overwhelming desire that there was in central Italy to fight for the claimed rights of the allies, in particular the Roman citizenship—a desire that in the latter region had clearly been welling up for a number of years. There was then a difference between the attitude of the

[1] See below, pp. 226–7, for the behaviour of some individuals in this category.
[2] App. 50.216.

Etruscan and Umbrian states and those of central Italy towards the citizenship.

In 91 the Italians were in effect offered the citizenship in exchange for some of their land,[1] an exchange which according to Appian they had been offered by Fulvius Flaccus in 125, and which, he says, they then accepted *ἄσμενοι*.[2] The Etruscans and Umbrians were unwilling to accept these terms when they were offered in 91, it has here been argued—a point that was indeed made with clarity long ago by A. Kiene.[3] The two elements in the situation, the *rogatio de sociis* and the land distributions, need to be examined in more detail from the point of view of the Etruscans and Umbrians.

Brunt[4] has argued that the process of Romanization had gone so far in Italy, including Etruria and Umbria, that the acquisition of the Roman citizenship now seemed to the Italians obviously just and necessary.[5] That this was the case in many places will not be disputed, and it is not my intention here to assess the progress of Romanization in other parts of Italy. However a detailed examination of the existing evidence for the Romanization of Etruria shows that it had certainly not gone as far as Brunt suggested.[6] There were in southern Etruria, which is not in question here, and in Rome, various thoroughly Romanized Etruscans, but although we do not of course have any explicit evidence concerning the views about Rome held by Etruscans in the allied states there is every reason to think that they still felt themselves to be a separate and to some extent independent unit. This is not to say that the Etruscans did not want the Roman citizenship, but if they did want it it was not because of their advanced degree of Romanization. It has been argued that Umbria had advanced further in this direction; the Umbrians are discussed separately below. Following a theory put forward by L. Piotrowicz,[7] some have

[1] Badian, *FC* 217; *contra* Sherwin-White, *RC* 127.

[2] 21.86–7.

[3] *Der römische Bundesgenossenkrieg* (Leipzig, 1845), 185–6.

[4] Art. cit., 97–101.

[5] The assimilation of language and institutions does not of course show the strength of political loyalty; in Ireland in 1901 only 14 per cent of the population could speak Irish, more than 99 per cent English.

[6] Chapter V, esp. Section 3.

[7] Art. cit.

attempted to explain the attitude of the Etruscans and Umbrians towards the *rogatio de sociis* by supposing that it threatened the power of the upper classes of Etruria and Umbria in their own states.[1] These upper classes will have been among those people whom Fulvius Flaccus expected in 125 to be unwilling 'civitatem mutare'.[2] However it is not difficult to think of others who would have been expected to fall into that category at that date, Naples and Heraclea for example. According to Piotrowicz, the Drusan *rogatio* may not have offered the allies the option of refusing the citizenship—but that is an unlikely hypothesis.[3] The chief point of this type of theory is that the spread of the Roman citizenship would have given new political rights to the mass of the population in the Etruscan and Umbrian states; it is said for example that the upper classes of Etruria would have been 'sconvolti da un'eventuale situazione di parità' with the lower classes.[4] It has also been suggested that the upper classes resisted the Drusan settlement because they wished to retain possession of the *ager publicus* that the agrarian law intended to take away from them, while the 'have-nots' of both Etruria and Umbria supported Drusus.[5] Although the direct contacts of the consuls who brought Etruscans and Umbrians to Rome to oppose Drusus were obviously with the upper classes,[6] there is unfortunately no explicit evidence at all either that the demonstrators represented the possessing classes or that when fighting began in 90 it was the work of the dissident lower classes.[7]

Did the *rogatio de sociis* really offer to the lower classes in Etruria 'la possibilità di impadronirsi del potere in alcune città'?[8] What could the upper classes of Etruria expect the

[1] See especially Gabba, art. cit., 50.

[2] Val. Max. IX 5.1.

[3] We know of no case in which such a thing happened; it would surely have been contrary to the *foedera* of the allies. For evidence that refusal would be possible, cf. Liv. IX 43.23.

[4] Gabba, l.c.

[5] Badian, *FC* 221.

[6] For specific evidence, see below, pp. 226–7.

[7] Gabba once suggested (*Athenaeum*, art. cit., 50) that the latter view was supported by Liv. *Per.* 74 and Oros. V 18.17, but it would certainly be fanciful to see such an implication in the Epitomator's phrase 'cum uterque populus defecisset'. Gabba was more tentative about this in *RFIC*, art. cit., 197–8.

[8] Gabba, *Athenaeum*, l.c.

effects of the *rogatio* to be on the internal affairs of their own towns? In theory Roman instead of local law would surely be expected to prevail in all important respects; yet no one can have thought that if the whole of Italy was suddenly enfranchised local jurisdiction would be taken from the hands of the local magistrates and put into Roman hands, for that would have been a practical impossibility.[1] It is difficult to envisage the magistrates of the Italian towns, many of them no doubt quite ignorant of Roman law, suddenly beginning to administer Roman law in purely local cases;[2] it must have been expected that local practices would continue to operate. Rudolph[3] put forward the view that the local courts in fact lost all their powers after the enfranchisement, but it has generally and rightly been rejected;[4] there was some local jurisdiction over law-suits after the war, and that must have been expected by the allies; and it is likely that some local law survived as well. Thus the local magistrates and the curial class from which they came will have retained considerable discretion in dealing with their fellow-citizens. When the change to the Roman system came, recourse to a Roman court would remain a purely theoretical possibility for a poor Etruscan in conflict with a social and economic superior. What was there to expect in the political sphere? Again, it must have been expected that the local rulers would retain their actual power or much of it, for there was from the Roman point of view no practical alternative; but this depended of course on their retaining the economic basis of their power, in particular their land. While they kept this power, and while the Roman assemblies continued to be as undemocratic as the rulers of the Etruscan towns no doubt well knew them to be, there was little likelihood that the lower classes of the towns would be able to make their votes in Rome into useful political instruments for themselves, even if they managed to cast them at all. On the other hand it might very well be useful to the ruling classes of the towns to have their dependents endowed with the Roman franchise. Appian[5]

[1] Cf. Brunt, art. cit., 102, with whose assessment of what the Italians could expect in the way of independence if they became Roman citizens I am in general agreement.

[2] Cf. M. Radin, *Tulane Law Review*, xxii (1947), 155.

[3] *Stadt und Staat im römischen Italien* (Leipzig, 1935), esp. 238–9.

[4] Sherwin-White, *RC* 136–40, etc.

[5] 49.215 *ad fin.*

thought that some of those who were enfranchised by the Lex Iulia may have been content that their votes should be rendered useless by the arrangement of the new voters in the tribes (*ὅπερ ἢ λαθὸν αὐτίκα ἢ καὶ ὣς αὐτὸ ἀγαπησάντων τῶν Ἰταλιω-τῶν . . .*), and although that may merely have been guess-work on his part, it is reasonable to suppose that it applied to many members of the upper classes in Etruria.

These being the circumstances, it is easier to understand why the Etruscans should have put other things before the Roman citizenship in 91 and why they accepted it *ἄσμενοι* in 90. There might well be some hesitation on the part of the ruling classes of the Etruscan towns, for their political future would pass further out of their own control, and who was to know when Marius or some other politician might not seek to give to the rabble power greater than was fitting in order to effect his own purposes? Furthermore, as has been argued, it is most unlikely that the majority of Etruscans felt themselves to be Romans in everything but legal rights. Yet in 90 the risks in the situation were outweighed by the concrete and less concrete advantages that the Etruscans could see in the citizenship.

Whatever the precise feelings of the Etruscans about the proposed Drusan settlement, it is likely that Appian meant to say that the Etruscans were opposed to the agrarian law; it is in any case very reasonable to expect that they would have been opposed to it, since there were considerable areas of *ager publicus* in Etruria that were probably in Etruscan hands. All that we know about Drusus' agrarian or rather colonial activity is that he intended to send out many colonies in Italy and Sicily that had been voted a long time before but not founded,[1] presumably because it has been difficult to find land for them; that it was expected that *ager publicus* in Italy would be used for this purpose;[2] that Drusus actually held office as 'Xvir a.d.a. lege sua et eodem anno Vvir a.d.a. lege Saufe⟨i⟩a';[3] and perhaps that one of his colonies was at Vibo in Bruttium.[4] Neither in Sicily nor apparently at Vibo was there any danger of war

[1] App. 35.156.

[2] 36.162.

[3] *CIL* i².1, p. 199, *elogium* no. 30.

[4] *CIL* x.44 (with p. 1003). This is the interpretation of C. Cichorius, *Römische Studien* (Berlin–Leipzig, 1922), 116–25; cf. *MRR* ii.24 n. 10.

if land was used for Roman colonization. What evidence then is there that the theoretically available land in Etruria that was likely to be more hotly defended was an object of Drusus' attentions?

One important way in which *clientela* with a Roman politician could help an Italian in the late Republic was in protecting the latter's land-holdings from the ambitions and reforms of other politicians. When Drusus' colonial intentions became known all vulnerable Italians will have looked to their Roman connections for protection, as they had on past occasions, while no doubt those who were in good standing with Drusus himself or with leading members of the *factio* that supported him would be able to feel confident that they would not suffer; by contrast those who had connections primarily with the *inimici* of the Drusan group will have expected the worst. Now it is obviously impossible to delineate properly the Italian *clientela* of any of the important figures of 91, with the possible exception of Marius, but some facts are known and they are suggestive.

Drusus himself was a man of exceptional wealth,[1] and he is almost certain for that reason alone to have had important Italian connections. One connection is very well attested, namely his friendship with Poppaedius Silo,[2] leader of the Marsi and Italic consul.[3] Among Drusus' ancestors in the direct line was the Capuan aristocrat Pacuvius Calavius, father-in-law of M. Livius Salinator, censor in 204, and it can be believed that there were still connections with Campania.[4] A less secure indication of where Drusus' interests lay is given by the notice of the (undated) attack on the younger Caepio made by T. Betucius Barrus of Asculum[5]—it is hard to believe that it was without political implications.[6] Unfortunately the specific Italian connections of L. Crassus and Scaurus are unknown, although we know that the latter was influential among those

[1] Diod. XXXVII 10.1. Cf. Plin. *NH* XXXIII 141.

[2] Plu. *Cat. Mi.*2, cf. Val. Max III 1.2, *De vir. ill.* 80.

[3] On Poppaedius' status, cf. Diod. XXXVII 2, 13, E. T. Salmon, *TAPhA* lxxxix (1958), 171.

[4] So H. C. Boren, *CJ* lii (1956–7), 28.

[5] Cic. *Brut.* 169.

[6] Cf. Gabba, *Athenaeum*, xxxi (1953), 271; otherwise Badian, *Historia*, vi (1957), 327 n. 85=*Studies in Greek and Roman History* (Oxford, 1964), 66 n. 85 (further references to this article are given by the page number in *Studies*, etc.).

who were later referred to as the *rustici*,[1] and both must have had some connections in Cisalpine Gaul.[2] It is scarcely worth pursuing all the possible connections of those who were more or less committed to Drusus in 91,[3] but it can be stated that there are among them no definite connections with Etruria or Umbria.[4]

On the other side the summoning of the Etruscans and Umbrians by the consuls of 91, in which it is probable that Philippus was more active than his colleague,[5] is a strong indication that there were established connections between them and the areas concerned. For Philippus[6] this is confirmed by his connection with M. Perperna, his colleague as censor in 86, and consul in 92; it is reasonable to think that he helped Philippus to avoid another *repulsa* in the elections for 91,[7] and the two were probably also connected through the Claudii.[8] The Etruscan origin of the Perpernae is well established and it

[1] Cic. *Att.* IV 16.6.

[2] Scaurus was consul there in 115 and constructed the Via Aemilia there as censor in 109; Crassus had the province of Gaul in 95–94.

[3] On the Vibo commission (see above, p. 224 n. 4) were [C. D]ecidius C.f. Rufus and C. M[amilius –.f. Limetanus] according to Cichorius' suggestions. The name Decidius, not previously known at Rome, belongs to a Samnite of this period (Cic. *Clu.* 161, Tac. *Dial.* 21.6), and -idius is probably Oscan (cf. Syme, *RR* 80 n. 1). Mamilius Limetanus had connections at Caere, but his membership of the commission is very speculative (cf. Cichorius, op. cit., 124–5).

[4] The young C. Aurelius Cotta may well have derived some connections from the construction of the Via Aurelia by one of his ancestors, but much of it was in Roman territory.

[5] Sex. Caesar is mentioned little in 91. He was probably out of Italy after the *feriae Latinae* (*MRR* ii.31, nn. 11, 18; Badian, *Studies*, etc. 51–2), but he is not for that reason to be dissociated, as he is by Gabba (*ad* 163), from the summoning of the Etruscans and Umbrians. In default of other definite information Appian must be taken to mean what he says. Clearly, however, Philippus was the leader of all actions taken against Drusus.

[6] J. Van Ooteghem, *Lucius Marcius Philippus et sa famille* (Brussels, 1961), is uninformative on this topic.

[7] Philippus' *repulsa* in 94 is attested by Cic. *Mur.* 36, *Brut.* 166. Since he was connected with the Perpernae and with the Claudii Pulchri (next n.), and since C. Claudius Pulcher, a brother of Philippus' mother, was a candidate, it is unlikely that Philippus stood in 93 (otherwise E. S. Gruen, *Roman Politics and the Criminal Courts, 149–78* B.C. (Cambridge, Mass., 1968), 241). In 92 he will have been unbeatable.

[8] Apart from 92, there was the suffect consulship of Ap. Claudius Pulcher in 130, the consulship of a Perperna, and when the Perpernae are first heard of at Rome it is because of a legate of Ap. Claudius Centho in 168; cf. F. Münzer, *Römische Adelsparteien und Adelsfamilien* (Stuttgart, 1920), 95–7, Badian, *JRS* lii (1962), 56=*Studies*, etc. 223.

is virtually certain that they still had influence in Etruria.[1] It is tempting to think that Philippus' ancestor, Q. Marcius Philippus, the consul of 281, who triumphed over the Etruscans in that year at a late stage of the Etruscan wars, acquired *clientela* there[2] and passed it on. Another connection between Etruria and the opponents of Drusus can be seen in the opposition of the leading *eques* C. Maecenas, one of the three mentioned as opponents by Cicero[3]—admittedly it was over the *lex iudiciaria*. The family is first known in Rome in this generation and surely retained its influence in Etruria.[4]

Much has been written about the *clientelae* of Marius, some of it rather rash. Obviously they were substantial, but Marius had in his lower class veterans a body of support throughout Italy quite unlike that of any other Roman politician,[5] and on occasion (as in 87) he showed himself relatively unconcerned about the feelings of the substantial citizens of the Italian towns. Speaking of the Etruscans and Umbrians, Badian says: 'It is clear that, when Marius saw his programme stolen by his enemies, he roused his own clients to defeat the plan'.[6] But first of all, although Badian has insisted on the contrary, there is no evidence that Marius was openly aligned against Drusus, while the *adfinitas* with L. Crassus[7] and perhaps his behaviour during the war[8] make it decidedly unlikely that he opposed Drusus' programme. As for rousing his own clients to defeat Drusus, there is no evidence at all: the support that Marius is

[1] See above, p. 201.

[2] Cicero asserts (*Off.* I 35) that 'tantopere apud nostros iustitia culta est, ut ii qui civitates aut nationes devictas bello in fidem recepissent, earum patroni essent more maiorum'; but cf. Badian, *FC* 156–7.

[3] *Clu.* 153.

[4] See above, p. 201.

[5] For the class element in Marius' support (in 108), see Sall. *Jug.* 73.6: 'denique plebes sic accensa, uti opifices agrestesque omnes, quorum res fidesque in manibus sitae erant, relictis operibus frequentarent Marium . . .'; and cf. *Jug.* 84.2.

[6] *Historia*, xi (1962), 227.

[7] The date of the marriage of the younger Marius (b. about 109) with the daughter of Crassus has been disputed, cf. E. Frank, *CJ* l (1955), 151 (late 92), Badian, *Athenaeum*, xxxiv (1956), 112 (94 or 93), *Studies*, etc. 57 (95), *FC* 211 (95 or later), M. Gelzer, *KS* i (Wiesbaden, 1962), 214 (about 92), E. Gruen, *Historia*, xv (1966), 43 n. 67 (betrothal by 95). The evidence is simply that Marius and Crassus were *adfines* by the time of Matrinius' trial under the Lex Licinia Mucia (Cic. *Balb.* 49); the trial does not have to be in 95, but it is probably better to put it early in the period 95–92 rather than late.

[8] Brunt, art. cit., 106.

known to have had in Etruria he surely had in most other parts of Italy,[1] while his known clients in Umbria, who incidentally do not show that the area was his particular fief, were most of them in no danger in 91—the Camertes with their *foedus omnium aequissimum* did not have to worry about the requisitioning of *ager publicus*, nor did a Latin from Spoletium—there is left only M. Annius Appius of Iguvium.

Further investigation of the Italian *clientelae* of the relevant figures of 91 seems excessively speculative; in particular we cannot in my opinion really identify any of the Roman ἐπιτήδειοι of Italian peoples referred to by Appian.[2] However the evidence that has been mentioned makes it even more probable that Drusus' colonial programme discriminated against the Etruscans, or rather seemed to them to be unfair. It also makes it more plausible to suppose that the *rogatio de sociis* was a bill in which the *clientes* of the Drusan *factio* benefited more than the Etruscan connections of Drusus' enemies.[3] In 90 of course the offer made to the Etruscans will have had no such disadvantages.[4]

Umbrians, as well as Etruscans, participated in the opposition to Drusus in 91 (so Appian tells us), and in Umbria, as well as in Etruria, there was eventually in 90 some rebellion against Rome. The evidence is not such as to allow us to weigh up the possible explanations of these facts about Umbria at all precisely. It must be supposed that the terms of the Drusan settlement were un-

[1] Badian, *FC* 224, compares Marius' reception in Etruria with the treatment that he received in Campania when he was travelling in the other direction in 88, a part of his career about which some strange and not altogether consistent stories were told. That some Campanians acted against him in such circumstances does not upset my contention, nor does Badian's (mostly convincing) attack on the supposed upper-class Campanian *clientela* of Marius, *Studies*, etc. 59–61 (replying to Gabba, *Athenaeum*, xxix (1951), 256–61).

[2] 38.170. Salmon, *TAPhA*, art. cit., 168, is excessively optimistic about this.

[3] Gabba, *Athenaeum*, xxxi (1953), 263, argued that Scaurus never in fact wanted to give the citizenship to the allies, which is possible. But the contention of A. Bernardi, *NRS* xxviii–xxix (1944–5), 92–3, and E. Gruen, *JRS* lv (1965), 61, *Roman Politics and the Criminal Courts, 149–78* B.C., 211–12, that Crassus too was not a supporter of the *rogatio de sociis* lacks positive evidence and seems most unlikely in view of what we know of his behaviour on the Ides of September—there were some supporters whom Drusus could certainly not dispense with.

[4] For what it is worth we know of a probable Etruscan connection in the family of L. Iulius Caesar, cos. 90, namely Sextilius, the *hospes Etruscus* at Tarquinii of his brother C. Caesar Strabo: on the connection cf. below, p. 253.

attractive there as well as in Etruria, although it might be expected that in more Romanized Umbria desire for the citizenship would be strong. Here unfortunately the prosopographical evidence is too tenuous to be of any help: Marius' *clientela* has already been discussed, and the case of Ameria, in spite of the information in the *Pro Roscio*, is not very illuminating. There may be some reason to think that the 'good' Roscii would have been protected by the Drusus–Crassus–Scaurus faction in 91, but it is far from clear.[1] One factor that may have had some influence in Etruria in 91 was probably very important in Umbria, namely the sheer military difficulty of the situation for potential rebels. The area was dominated in this sense by the Roman settlements on and to the east of the Via Flaminia. In 90, when the military future for a time looked very perilous to the Romans, and the Etruscans were also prepared to fight, it became more reasonable to take up arms.

[1] Cicero dilates on the close relations of his client's father 'cum Metellis, Serviliis, Scipionibus' (15), but the person who seems to have been really important to him at one time was Caecilia (27, 147), Metellus Balearicus' daughter, who was married to Philippus' uncle, Ap. Claudius Pulcher (so I continue to think against E. Gruen, *Roman Politics and the Criminal Courts, 149–78* B.C., 266 n. 52, who thinks that she was Appius' sister-in-law).

VII

THE ENFRANCHISEMENT OF THE ETRUSCAN AND UMBRIAN COMMUNITIES

1. *The Acts of Enfranchisement and the Date of the Distribution of the Italians in the Thirty-One Tribes*

We know of three enfranchising laws passed during or after the Social War, the Lex Calpurnia, the Lex Iulia, and the Lex Plautia Papiria. The Lex Iulia, which was afterwards regarded as the main law by which the Italians had received the citizenship,[1] has already been discussed; whatever other provisions were necessary in order to enfranchise towns that were still in arms at the time that the law was passed, it is clear that the Lex Iulia was sufficient to offer the citizenship to most of the towns of Etruria and Umbria. Some other enactments were also used: since the Lex Iulia was passed late in 90[2] and provided for enfranchisements *virtutis causa*,[3] it is likely that the Lex Calpurnia, also of 90[4] and also providing for enfranchisements *virtutis causa*,[5] was passed earlier in the year;[6] although we do not have any specific evidence that any Etruscan or Umbrian allies fought on the Roman side in the Social War, it is reasonable to suppose that some did so and they may well have been rewarded in this way. In order to enfranchise a town that remained in arms at the time of the Lex Iulia, it is likely that a *senatus consultum* at least was passed; this view is supported by the fragment of Sisenna

[1] Cf. in particular Cic. *Balb.* 21, quoted below, p. 231 n. 4.

[2] Cf. most recently P. A. Brunt, *JRS* lv (1965), 105. E. Badian, *Historia*, xi (1962), 227, unfortunately accepted the erroneous view of G. Niccolini, *Rend. Acc. Linc.*, ser. 8.i (1946), 110–11, that it was early in the year.

[3] As *ILS* 8888 shows ('virtutis causa', line 1).

[4] R. Syme, *Historia*, iv (1955), 58, *MRR Suppl.* 13.

[5] Cf. Sisenna fr. 120P: 'Milites, ut lex Calpurnia concesserat, virtutis ergo civitate donari . . .'

[6] Brunt, l.c.

concerning the enfranchisement of Tuder.[1] Since the Lex Iulia was regarded as the main law by which the Italians, including those who were still in arms against Rome, were enfranchised, the law referred to in this case was probably the Lex Iulia itself. It is virtually certain that by the end of 89 all the Etruscan and Umbrian communities had received the citizenship—the Lex Plautia Papiria, which probably belongs to the tribunician year 89/88, seems to have had a very limited purpose incidental to the main enfranchisement.[2]

Provisions for a restrictive method of allocating the new citizens to the tribes were promptly devised, and are likely to have been contained in the Lex Iulia itself.[3] No law of 90 can have specified precisely which towns were to go into each tribe, since each town had to pass a *fundus factus* provision if it was to receive the *civitas*,[4] but a general clause concerning restrictive allocation is easy to envisage. The censors of 89, namely L. Iulius Caesar, the proposer of the law, and P. Licinius Crassus, founded the *lustrum*, but they did not complete the census.[5] That in itself did not prevent the new citizens from enjoying most of the *iura* of citizens, and any for whom a law *had* enacted tribal assignments, among these probably the Latins,[6] could vote in the tribal assembly.[7] The arrangements for tribal assignments that most of the Italians themselves desired were contained in the law that Sulpicius Rufus proposed and carried,[8] a law to divide τοὺς ἐκ τῆς Ἰταλίας νεοπολίτας, μειονεκ-

[1] Fr. 119P: 'Tamen Tudertibus senati consulto et populi iusso dat civitatem.'

[2] Sherwin-White, *RC* 132–3, gave the correct explanation of the only known clause of this law, which concerned *ascripti* of allied communities (Cic. *Arch.* 7). Badian wants to take this further, arguing that this clause was the main one (*Proc. Afr. Class. Assoc.*, i (1958), 3–5=*Studies in Greek and Roman History* (Oxford, 1964), 75–6), which may well be right. *MRR* (ii.34), Gabba (on App. *BC* I 53.23), Taylor (*VDRR* 101), and now G. Pieri (*L'histoire du cens jusqu'à la fin de la république romaine* (Paris, 1968), 163) are in error.

[3] Taylor, *VDRR* 102 n. 6, Brunt, art. cit., 108; cf. App. 49.214–15.

[4] Cic. *Balb.* 21: 'ipsa denique Iulia, qua lege civitas est sociis et Latinis data, qui fundi populi facti non essent, civitatem non haberent.' There were of course disputes at Heraclea and Neapolis about whether to accept the Roman citizenship, ibid.

[5] Cic. *Arch.* 11: 'nullam populi partem esse censam'.

[6] See below, pp. 237–8.

[7] A man's *domus* had to be established of course. On the right to vote in the tribal assembly, see Taylor, *VDRR* 106, 119; cf. Badian, *JRS* lii (1962), 206.

[8] App. 56.249.

τοῦτας ἐπὶ ταῖς χειροτονίαις . . . ἐς τὰς φυλὰς ἁπάσας.[1] The Lex Sulpicia was annulled by Sulla,[2] and in 87 Cinna agitated unsuccessfully for the distribution of the new citizens in all the tribes,[3] proposing a bill which was vetoed. As Octavius' régime collapsed (Marius had already captured Ostia) it passed a *senatus consultum* giving the citizenship 'Italicis populis',[4] but probably not accepting the principle of distributing the new citizens in all the tribes.[5]

When Marius and Cinna seized power, the laws passed under Sulla were overturned.[6] It is generally thought that the Leges Sulpiciae came back into force as an automatic consequence,[7] but there is no evidence that they did, and certainly none that the law on the distribution of the new citizens did.[8] There followed the census of 86–85, and then the *senatus consultum* of 84 by which, according to the Epitomator of Livy (our only evidence on this event), 'novis civibus . . . suffragium datum est'.[9] This took place after the death of Cinna, and there is no reason to suppose that it was his measure; the fact that it was passed soon after his death rather suggests the contrary. Nor

[1] 55.242. Cf. Liv. *Per.* 77: 'ut . . . novi cives libertinique in tribus distribuerentur', Ascon. 64C.

[2] App. 58.268: *διελύετο ὡς οὐκ ἔννομα*; Cic. *Phil.* VIII 7. Probably a *s.c.* was passed (Mommsen, *Hermes*, xxii (1887), 102=*GS* v.263, G. W. Botsford, *Roman Assemblies* (New York, 1909), 405), declaring that the laws had been passed *per vim* (cf. Gabba ad loc., A. Biscardi, *BIDR* n.s. xvi–xvii (1953), 231–2, and the references given there).

[3] App. 64.287–65.299, Vell. II 20.2.

[4] Liv. *Per.* 80: 'Italicis populis a senatu civitas data est'; Gran. Licin. 21F 'dediticiis omnibus civitas data qui polliciti multa milia militum vix XVI cohortes miserunt'. The *s.c.* is not mentioned in Appian; the chronological point in his narrative is 68.309.

[5] Cf. Taylor, *VDRR* 104: scarcely sixteen cohorts were sent, because the Marians offered better terms. Octavius' régime was also unwilling to go as far in pleasing the Samnites as the Marians were (App. 68.309–10, etc.).

[6] App. 73.339: *ἀνατροπαί*. Biscardi, art. cit., 255–9, argued that there was no formal abrogation, claiming that *ἀνατροπή* meant 'sconvolgimento' and that Appian here avoided the technical terms in his vocabulary. But *ἀνατροπαὶ* does not exclude the idea that the laws were annulled, it merely emphasizes that they were overthrown violently.

[7] Strachan-Davidson and Gabba on 73.339.

[8] Cf. T. F. Carney, *A Biography of C. Marius* (Assen, 1961), 69 n. 293. It is not known (*pace MRR* ii.46, Badian, *FC* 241, Carney) that Marius technically repossessed his Mithridatic command, which might imply the revival of all the Leges Sulpiciae; on this the evidence is App. 75.346, Plu. *Mar.* 41, 45.

[9] Liv. *Per.* 84.

can we say definitely that it was Carbo's measure, for he was not in control of the Senate.[1] The arrangements contained in the *senatus consultum* were probably accepted by Sulla, the old opponent of wide distribution, when in 82 he made the *foedus* with the Italians by which he agreed not to take away their *civitas* and *ius suffragii*.[2] A census was necessary if the new citizens were to be able to vote in the centuriate as well as the tribal assembly, and this Sulla is likely in effect to have conducted.[3] The alternative is to suppose that the proper registration did not take place until 70–69,[4] and it is surely impossible to think that this can have happened without producing any signs of discontent in the 70s.

Was it then the censors of 86 who distributed all the new citizens among the thirty-one rural tribes,[5] or were they only distributed by the *senatus consultum* of 84 and the next censors thereafter?[6] Attempts to combine both views do not carry conviction.[7] There are persuasive arguments on both sides, but it

[1] Cf. the incidents recorded in App. 78.358–9, Liv. *Per.* 84, Val. Max. VI 2.10. The Senate had tried to negotiate with Sulla even before Cinna's death (App. 79.360–2). Afterwards Carbo prevented it from accepting Sulla's terms (Liv. *Per.* 84: 'quae condicio, cum iusta senatui videretur, per Carbonem factionemque eius, cui bellum videbatur utilius, ne conveniret, effectum est') and his faction carried through a *s.c.* enacting general disarmament (ibid.). Between these two events (in Livy's account) the Senate prevents Carbo from exacting hostages from the Italians and passes the *s.c.* on the *suffragium*. Gabba on 79.362 holds that the *s.c.* was Carbo's; Biscardi, art. cit., 261, interprets it as an act of the 'partito aristocratico', which is unlikely.

[2] Liv. *Per.* 86: 'Sulla cum Italicis populis, ne timeretur ab his, velut empturus civitatem et suffragii ius nuper datum, foedus percussit.'

[3] There was not a proper census, as the list in Cic. *Arch.* 11 shows. The idea that Sulla's powers included those of a censor goes back to A. W. Zumpt, *RhM* xxv (1870), 469–80, xxvi (1871), 37. See G. Tibiletti, *SDHI* xxv (1959), 121–2, supporting the theory; 'while systematizing the state completely' with his 'unlimited powers' Sulla must have drawn up an actual list of citizens. The irregularity of Sulla's proceedings would have helped to keep this action out of *Arch.* 11.

[4] L. R. Taylor, *Party Politics in the Age of Caesar* (Berkeley–Los Angeles, 1949), 52, Brunt, art. cit., 107; cf. C. Nicolet, *L'ordre équestre à l'époque républicaine (312–43 av. J.-C.)* (Paris, 1966), 395–6.

[5] As Taylor, *VDRR* 105, C. Meier, *Res Publica Amissa* (Wiesbaden, 1966), 230, believe. I return in the next section to Taylor's idea (*VDRR* 310) that the tribes 'had been determined before the death of Marius' on 13 January 86.

[6] A. Biscardi, *PP* vi (1951), 252, Badian, *FC* 240–2, *Studies*, etc. 223, E. S. Gruen, *Roman Politics and the Criminal Courts, 149–78* B.C. (Cambridge, Mass., 1968), 246.

[7] Thus Tibiletti, art. cit., 121 n. 102; the mention of the *s.c.* in Liv. *Per.* 'gives us a precious information: namely that the census taking of 86 lasted until 84'. The census-taking began 'presumably at the end of the eventful year 86'. There is no

seems more likely that the distribution belongs to 84. The following reasons may be given:

(i) This interpretation coincides with the known census figures for the period. The last known total before 85 is that of 115, given as 394,336 by the Epitomator of Livy.[1] Jerome's figure for 85 is 463,000,[2] an increase of only 18 per cent (an error of transmission is of course always possible).[3] The next known figure, that of 69, is given by the Epitomator of Livy as 900,000,[4] an increase of 94 per cent since 85.[5] The most obvious explanation of these figures is that in 86–85 some Italians were recognized as citizens by the censors, but not the majority, who only obtained recognition by the censors at the next census. Miss Taylor discounts this argument against the 86–85 distribution, arguing that the numbers were kept down by the difficulties of making a journey to Rome for registration—it was the relatively rich, she thinks, who did come.[6] But for most parts of Italy the difficulties were not so much greater than they were in 70–69, and in any case it is most unlikely, in my opinion, that all citizens had to attend in person. Local officials were available and probably used—it is hard to think that such arrangements were an innovation in the Heraclea Table, which merely concerns itself with some mechanics of the situation, and it is clearly assumed in the *Pro Archia*[7] that if Archias had been registered as a citizen of Heraclea his Roman citizenship would have been unquestionable. The records of Heraclea, unfortunately destroyed by fire, would have been relied on in deciding the question of Roman citizenship. So there was no question of a mass movement of the Italian population being

other reason to think so. He also suggests the possibility of a term of office extended beyond the normal eighteen months. The belief that the *s.c.* of 84 was in some way part of the census of 86 is found in Beloch, *It. Bund.* 37. According to Mommsen, *History of Rome* (Eng. trans.), iv.70, the *s.c.* merely confirmed the work of the censors—but that was quite unnecessary.

[1] *Per.* 63.

[2] p. 151H.

[3] Beloch suggested the simple emendation to 963,000, *Bevölkerung des griechisch-römischen Welt* (Leipzig, 1886), 352, which seems too high for the conditions of 86–85, but is conceivable. J. Carcopino, in *Mélanges en hommage à la mémoire de Fr. Martroye* (Paris, 1940), 73–9, attempted, without success in my opinion, to show that there was no census completed in 86–85 and that Jerome's figure referred to the total number of inhabitants in the city of Rome.

[4] *Per.* 98.

[5] Phlegon of Tralles gives 910,000, *FGrH* 257 F 12.

[6] *VDRR* 105.

[7] Cic. *Arch.* 8–11.

necessary for their registration.[1] It might be thought that a low total was to be expected after the destruction of the records and the general dislocation of the preceding wars, but surely not such a low total as that actually achieved. The census figure tells us that the censors of 86–85 refused to carry out a full registration. The restrictive policy concerning the tribes was of course a separate matter, but a restrictive method of allocating the tribes was a natural concomitant of reluctance to register Italians at all.

(ii) The reference in the *Periocha* of Livy to the *senatus consultum* of 84 is even more difficult to explain if the full distribution had taken place before 84. Carelessness on the part of the Epitomator has been suggested[2]—but displacements of events in his account seem to be limited to the reversal of the order of two consecutive events. It has been suggested that Livy was referring only to a *senatus consultum* confirming assignments already made by the censors of 86, or that the *senatus consultum* of 84 made available to the Italians who had not been registered in 86–85 the vote in the tribal assembly[3]—but both procedures were quite unnecessary. It has to be admitted that the explanation of the passage here adopted is not completely satisfying—the Epitomator simply does not say that by the *senatus consultum* of 84 the new citizens were distributed in the

[1] Mommsen, *Römisches Staatsr.*, ii³.368, held that the census-taking of the *municipia* was decentralized from 86 onwards, according to rules like those in the *Heraclea Table* (*FIRA*² i (ed. Riccobono), no. 13), lines 142–56. This is not generally accepted, but cf. now Pieri, op. cit., 169–72. The case cannot be argued in full here. There had been appropriate magistrates in many allied towns before the war; for local censors in a *municipium* after the war see Cic. *Clu.* 41. For a precedent in Latin colonies see Liv. XXIX 15.9–11, 37.7 (pointed out by Sherwin-White, *RC* 146). Against my view are, e.g., E. G. Hardy, *Some Problems in Roman History* (Oxford, 1924), 264, T. Frank, *CPh* xix (1924), 334 (partially), L. R. Taylor, *Party Politics*, etc. 200 n. 11, *VDRR* 103 n. 7, G. Tibiletti, art. cit., 122, T. P. Wiseman, *JRS* lix (1969), 67–9. The reference in Cic. *I Verr.* 54 to 'haec frequentia totius Italiae', 'quae convenit uno tempore undique comitiorum ludorum censendique causa' is not strong evidence against the view taken here. Cf. above, pp. 198–9.

[2] Mommsen, op. cit., iii.180 nn. 1, 2.

[3] This is Taylor's explanation, *VDRR* 106; according to her view the Italians who had been registered in the census of 86–85 were the better-off men in the Italian towns, who had been able to get to Rome to register (this I reject—see above). As Badian pointed out, *JRS* lii (1962), 206, those who were not registered in 86–85 could in any case, on Taylor's own view, already vote in the tribal assembly; once they had been allocated to the tribes, which she thinks had happened by 13 January 86, no further measures were necessary.

thirty-one tribes. Yet such imprecision on the part of the Epitomator is easier to swallow than any of the other hitherto suggested explanations of the passage.

(iii) Of the censors of 86 Philippus had been a strong opponent of Italian enfranchisement in 91, and regretted it still in 77. That he was *not* in favour of a restrictive method of allocating the new citizens to the tribes in 86 is hard to believe, and Perperna will have co-operated with Philippus in carrying out a restrictive policy.[1] That Cinna made such a compromise with Philippus and his allies can be accepted, although he probably made it with some reluctance.[2] Whatever view should be taken of the relations between Cinna and the censors, it is most unlikely that the latter attempted to carry out anything like a full Marian–Sulpician policy about the enfranchisement.

The main argument that has been used in favour of distribution in 86–85 is that Cinna had made promises to Italians that he must have redeemed when he came to power. The policy of distributing the new citizens in all the tribes was more truly the policy of Marius than of Cinna, but Cinna certainly had some debts to pay,[3] and some of them were probably paid. The 18 per cent increase of citizens registered in 86–85, or an even greater proportion of the total,[4] may represent new Italian citizens.[5] However, most Italians were still not registered.

2. *Explanations of the Tribal Allocations in Etruria and Umbria*

The tribes allocated to the great majority of the towns of Etruria and Umbria are known, and the evidence is catalogued

[1] His connection with Philippus is discussed above, p. 226.

[2] Cf. Brunt, art. cit., 109.

[3] According to Vell. II 20 Cinna promised that he would distribute the new citizens in all the tribes. Appian's version is more detailed: the distribution was the *ἐνθύμημα τοῦ Μαρίου* when he was in exile in 87 (64.287); Cinna aligned himself with the new citizens perhaps for a bribe (288); Marius made promises to the Etruscans about the *χειροτονία* (67.306), and the Marians promised citizenship to the Samnites (68.310).

[4] The censors will have failed to register the old citizens who were serving with Sulla.

[5] If any particular area of Italy was favoured when Cinna was in control, it was presumably Campania; cf. App. 65.294, 65.298, Vell. II 20.3. The meaning of Exuperant. 7 (in late 83 'erat autem Etruria fidissima partibus Marianis, quia ab ipsis Romanam quam non habebant acceperant civitatem') is unclear; it may refer to the provisions of the *senatus consultum* of 84.

and discussed separately in Appendix II. Various explanations have been offered of these allocations, but no really satisfying account has been written.

First it is necessary to establish what the tribal allocations in Etruria and Umbria had been before the war. The Roman and Latin communities in the area have already been identified, and one preliminary remains—to decide whether the Latin colonies already had in effect had tribes allocated to them before the war when their magistrates were enfranchised. I agree with Taylor[1] that such allocations had taken place, but since the view has recently been challenged[2] the arguments in its favour may be given:

(i) The Latin magistrates who gained the citizenship before the war must have been put into tribes, and probably into the same tribes in the cases of magistrates of each town, as is suggested by Caesarian and later practice and perhaps by the treatment of the Transpadanes after 89.[3] Even in some allied towns the new citizens were put into tribes which already contained individuals who had been enfranchised (see below).

(ii) There is no reason why the Latins, who, with the exception of Venusia, had been loyal during the Social War, should have been treated restrictively in the tribal allocations.[4] No one says that they were or that the Latin colonies were dissatisfied with the arrangements made. Admittedly Tibur and Praeneste do seem to have been dissatisfied,[5] but they may well have been classed with the other allies rather than with the other Latins as far as *civitas per magistratum* was concerned, that is to say excluded from the privilege;[6] Cinna certainly seems to have singled them out for attention in 87.

(iii) Even if there were temporarily arrangements to which

[1] *VDRR* 107–9.

[2] Brunt, art. cit., 108.

[3] Thus Taylor, *VDRR* 109.

[4] Ibid. 107. According to Brunt, l.c., this contention 'can carry little weight'—I disagree, all the more so because I believe that the tribal allocations were connected with the behaviour of the Italians during the war.

[5] App. 65.294.

[6] Taylor, *VDRR* 107, argues that like the ordinary allies Tibur and Praeneste had not enjoyed *civitas per magistratum*, relying on Ascon. 3C, which does not help, as Brunt points out, art. cit., 108; and on the suggestive but not conclusive fact that two Tiburtes of the 'office-holding' class had to acquire citizenship through prosecutions (Cic. *Balb.* 53–4).

all the Latins objected in 87, the later ones may have been a restoration of the pre-war tribal allocations.

The following then were the tribes to be found in Etruria and Umbria before the war: the Arnensis, Sabatina, Stellatina, and Tromentina, which had originally been created for south Etruria in the fourth century, the Sabatina having subsequently gained Heba, Saturnia, and Visentium, the Stellatina Capena, Graviscae, and the Latin colony Nepet, and the Arnensis (perhaps) Forum Clodi; also the Lemonia (Pyrgi) and Voturia (Caere) although both cases are uncertain; the Papiria (the Latin colony at Sutrium); and in the north the Galeria (Luna)[1] and Fabia (the Latin colony Luca). The Sergia, Quirina, Voltinia, and even Pomptina are also possible. The tribe of the Latin colony Cosa is still unknown.

The Clustumina (Interamna Nahars and probably Carsulae and Tadinum), Cornelia (Fulginiae) and Oufentina (Forum Flaminii and Plestia) were to be found in Umbria proper, with the Horatia and Papiria respectively for the Latin colonies Spoletium and Narnia; and in the *ager Gallicus*, the Camilia (Pisaurum, Suasa), Pollia (Aesis, Fanum Fortunae, Forum Sempronii, Ostra), and Pupinia (Forum Brentanorum).

After the Social War fifteen allied towns in Etruria proper were allocated to seven tribes, and three other towns, Falerii,[2] Pisae, and Pistoriae[3] to three more tribes. In Umbria twenty-four (all in Umbria proper) were allocated to nine tribes, with nine new towns in a single tribe, the Clustumina. These figures are, of course, subject to slight revision.

First I shall examine the effects of the allocations on the towns themselves. The contrast has often been pointed out between on the one hand Etruria and the part of Umbria outside the Clustumina, and on the other hand the areas where whole peoples or large parts of them were put into single tribes—the

[1] I have included all the towns in the Augustan regions VI and VII in this chapter—see below, p. 330. Luna was in fact associated with Liguria in the allocation of the tribes—Genua and Pisae (also Veleia) were afterwards put into Gal.

[2] Taylor supposes, *VDRR* 94, following Beloch, *RG* 495, 515–16, that the *colonia Iunonia* at Falerii may have been of the Gracchan period and thus that the Horatia was already allocated there; but the argument from silence carries some weight against such a colony. The question is a difficult one; see below, p. 307.

[3] Since Pisae is listed among *municipia* that received the Roman citizenship after the Social War in Festus 155L it was probably enfranchised then. It is only an assumption that Pistoriae was as well.

Clustumina (which contained after the war Ameria, Arna, Iguvium, Pitinum Mergens, Sestinum, Tifernum Mataurense, Tifernum Tiberinum, Tuder, and Vettona, in addition to Carsulae, Interamna Nahars, and Tadinum from before the war),[1] the Marrucini and the Frentani in the Arnensis, the Paeligni and the Marsi in the Sergia, the Samnites in the Voltinia, some of the Hirpini in the Galeria, a group of south Campanians in the Menenia, and the Lucanians in the Pomptina.[2] The view was put forward in various versions by Beloch and Kubitschek,[3] and defended in a modified form by Salmon,[4] that the states that fought against Rome in the Social War were penalized by being placed in a small number of large tribes, the eight tribes in fact in which Velleius[5] says that the new citizens were placed. The view that every single rebellious town was placed in one of the eight tribes is scarcely tenable,[6] but that does not upset the view that assignment to a large tribal block generally represented a penalty. This quite independent theory has not been disproved by Taylor, for it was wrongly held to be merely part of the theory that there were eight punitive tribes. She also refers to the supposed

[1] For the doubts attaching to some of these cases, see Appendix II.

[2] Cf. the regional lists of tribes, Taylor, *VDRR* 159–64.

[3] Beloch, *It. Bund* 38–43, differently *RG* 578–80; J. W. Kubitschek, *De Romanarum tribuum origine ac propagatione* (Vienna, 1882), 61–76.

[4] *TAPhA* lxxxix (1958), 179–84.

[5] II 20.

[6] For argument against the views of Beloch and Kubitschek see Mommsen, *Hermes*, xxii (1887), 101–6=*GS* v.262–7, with additions by Taylor, *VDRR* 112 nn. 31, 31a. Taylor lists the probable tribes of the rebels as Arn., Clu., Gal., Men., Pom., Ser., Vol. (these seven were allocated to large blocks), Cor., Fab., Fal., Hor., Ouf., Pap., and Qui. Salmon attempted to remove six tribes from this list, namely Clu., Cor., Fal., Hor., Pap., and Qui., in order to reach the eight of Velleius, and his explanations are in some cases convincing, namely that at Ausculum (Pap.), Larinum (Clu.), and Aeclanum (Cor.) there were strong pro-Roman elements as well as ex-rebels. Venusia (Hor.), as the only Latin colony in the revolt, with a tribe already determined before the war, may obviously have been an exception. The Quirina is excluded on the grounds that it was already the tribe of some of the Vestini—special circumstances thus caused the allocation—and indeed the Vestini who revolted seem to have been dissident elements in a pro-Roman area (cf. *VDRR* 112 n. 27). However to reach exactly eight tribes is not important for my purpose. It should be admitted that there is a point of difficulty for the view expounded in the text: namely the effect on the undoubtedly non-rebellious towns enfranchised before the war that found themselves in large tribal blocks, in particular Carsulae, Interamna Nahars, and Tadinum in the Clustumina; however that is a minor discrepancy, and for a way in which these towns may have been helped see below, p. 337 n. 1.

advantages experienced by those who were assigned to large tribal blocks: 'Frentani, Paeligni, and Marsi could make their votes count as units'[1]—but to little purpose, for the Frentani shared a single tribe with the Marrucini (not to mention Italians in at least three other areas), and the Paeligni and Marsi likewise could affect only a relatively minute part of the assembly.[2] The fact that the votes of these peoples were relatively so unimportant naturally had a chain of consequences: it was not a good area in which to bestow *beneficia*—the main reason surely why it was so long before some of the central Italian peoples saw any of their members in high office. If we leave aside suppositions about the attitude of the Marians to the ex-rebels,[3] we must be very much impressed by the fact that most of the rebels were placed in the seven tribes just listed, while of the seven only one received a Latin colony (Latin colonies other than Venusia having kept out of the rebellion).[4] Twenty-five other Latin colonies are known to have been distributed in fifteen other tribes.[5] Apart from Circeii (in the Pomptina), I cannot find any town that was placed in one of these seven tribes although there is definite evidence that it was not rebellious. Further, it is agreed that Italians in general wanted an arrangement whereby they would be distributed among all the rural tribes, which *prima facie* means that they wanted to be members of tribes that were as small as possible. The Clustumina at least I take to have been a 'punitive' tribe in the block of Umbrian territory that was assigned to it after the Social War.[6]

In order to understand the effects of the allocation of towns to a large tribal block or, as in Etruria and part of Umbria, to a

[1] *VDRR* 113.

[2] Mommsen, who disagreed with the 'punitive-tribe' theory of Beloch and Kubitschek, nonetheless recognized that the Marsi and the Paeligni were poorly treated, *Römisches Staatsr.*, iii.180, *Hermes*, xxii (1887), 105=*GS* v.266.

[3] Taylor, *VDRR* 113, argues that Cinna and the Marians would probably not have penalized the new citizens who had been rebels in the Social War; but that does not follow from the fact that they favoured the distribution of the Italians in general in all the tribes. I have questioned above the view that the settlement was the work of the Marians.

[4] The Pomptina received Circeii (Taylor, *VDRR* 114, slips on this).

[5] *VDRR* 110 gives a list.

[6] Taylor's view of the large tribal blocks, that they are to be explained by the 'lack of organised municipal centers' and the 'strength of ethnic ties', which I find at best incomplete, I discuss later, pp. 247–9.

variety of tribes, it is necessary to examine in more detail the effects of such allocations on voting rights. If it was a disadvantage to belong to a large tribe, so that, for example, the Paeligni and the Marsi could between them affect the vote of only one tribe, in how many tribes did the people of Etruria and Umbria carry considerable weight? Explaining at length Murena's degree of success in the consular *comitia*, Cicero mentions that he had held a levy in Umbria: 'dedit ei facultatem res publica liberalitatis, qua usus multas sibi tribus quae municipiis Umbriae conficiuntur adiunxit'.[1] Although we must allow for the possibility that Cicero was exaggerating the effectiveness of various legitimate forms of electoral support for Murena, including this one, he must be at least near the truth. It should incidentally be noticed that there is another case in which we know of the relative electoral strength of a man with connections in Umbria, for a (Minucius) Thermus was thought by Cicero to be likely to profit greatly in the consular elections for 64 from his curatorship of the Via Flaminia.[2]

Yet not surprisingly doubt has been expressed about the number of tribes that were controlled by the Umbrians. The fact that they were in a majority in the Clustumina is obvious enough, and the Lemonia and the Pupinia were probably influenced much more by Umbria than by any other region. The Lemonia was probably very small before the war,[3] and afterwards it received Attidium, Hispellum, and Sentinum in Umbria, and also Ancona and the Latin colony Bononia. The Pupinia was apparently a very small tribe, both before and after the war. Besides Trebula Balliensis near Capua, it contained before the war the unlocated north Umbrian town of Forum Brentanorum and afterwards it received the remote Umbrian Sarsina. Many other tribes were to be found in Umbria, but in every case the tribe was shared with at least one

[1] *Mur.* 42. 'Tribus conficere' is the technical phrase for 'secure the vote of the tribes', cf. Cic. *Planc.* 45, *Fam.* XI 16.3 ('centuriae'), *Comm. Pet.* 18 ('centuriae)', *Lex Malacitana* ii.57 (*FIRA*[2] i (ed. Riccobono), p. 212), *TLL* s.v. *conficere* col. 201.30–34 (Hoppe).

[2] *Att.* I 1.2: 'Nemo est enim ex iis, qui nunc petunt, qui, si in nostrum annum reciderit, firmior candidatus fore videatur, propterea quod curator est viae Flaminiae.' On the identity of the subject cf. Münzer in *RE* s.v. Minucius no. 60 (1932).

[3] Taylor, *VDRR* 99.

substantial community elsewhere in Italy. Thus the Aemilia, for example, which received Mevania and probably Trebiae in Umbria after the Social War, also contained Formiae and Fundi from before the war and three Latin colonies, Suessa Aurunca, Copia Thurii, and Vibo Valentia; the Umbrian voters were clearly in a minority. To take another example: in the Cornelia, which contained the Umbrian towns of Fulginiae (enfranchised before the war), Camerinum, and Matilica, there were in fact more non-Umbrian voters, for it contained Arpinum, Aeclanum, Croton, and several other towns. This in fact applies to *all* the tribes of Umbria except the Clustumina and Lemonia and, perhaps, Pupinia. Cicero's statement that there were many tribes for Murena to gain in Umbria has consequently been interpreted as meaning that there were four or five tribes, including the Clustumina, that it was possible to influence decisively by activity there.[1] In fact if a majority of the substantial citizens in a particular tribe was needed, it was only possible to deal with the Clustumina, the Lemonia, and possibly the Pupinia in Umbria. Yet it is clear that it was possible to *conficere* more than two or three tribes by activity in Umbria, and one can see how it was done. It was surely not at all likely that many voters would come from towns distant from Rome unless their interests were particularly involved,[2] unless, that is, a *patronus* of the town had to be supported, or some particular *beneficium* had to be paid for, or unless local loyalties and the effects of *vicinitas* aroused enthusiasm (obviously this was a factor by which many Italian towns remained unaffected under the Republic). A vision is often conjured up of large numbers of Italians from all over Italy regularly presenting themselves at Rome for the elections,[3] but we should not take too seriously as evidence for this Cicero's rhetorical statement about his own election—'me cuncta Italia, me omnes ordines, me universa civitas non prius tabella quam voce priorem consulem declaravit',[4] for his quite ex-

[1] Brunt, art. cit., 105.

[2] Cf. F. B. Marsh, *CJ* xxviii (1933), 170–1.

[3] Most recently by C. Meier, *Res Publica Amissa* (Wiesbaden, 1966), 193–4; but see below, p. 243 n. 2

[4] Cic. *Pis.* 3. For similar allusions to his election (none, however, so explicit about Italians) see *Agr.* II 4, *Mur.* 17,21, *Vatin.* 6, *Brut.* 323, *Off.* II 59; there are of course numerous references to *cuncta* or *tota Italia* in support of Cicero—see H. Merguet, *Lexikon zu den Reden des Ciceros*, s.vv. *cunctus*, *totus*.

ceptional ties with municipal men, as well as his powers of exaggeration, are well attested. Nor do we find good evidence in Cicero's abuse of Vatinius when the latter failed to win the curule aedileship: 'Sciasne te severissimorum hominum Sabinorum, fortissimorum virorum Marsorum et Paelignorum, tribulium tuorum, iudicio notatum . . .'[1] Rhetoric of this kind is all that there is to persuade us that Italians (of the curial class) regularly turned up *en masse* from all parts of the country. Many Italians did come to Rome at election time, some from far away, when their interest could be stimulated,[2] and probably more regularly from towns that were really close to Rome, but many consular elections, not to mention elections for lesser offices, must have been held in the late Republic that did not engage the interests of many of the voters of, say, Cisalpine Gaul. The purpose of Murena's electioneering in Umbria will not have been so much to persuade voters who were going to attend anyway to vote for him as to persuade favourable voters to come to Rome. Take the case of the Aemilia again, which contained the Umbrian towns of Mevania and Trebiae. Mevania and the other municipalities in the tribe that were nearest to Rome, Fundi, Formiae, and Suessa Aurunca, are all of them more than seventy miles from the city; if it was the case, as seems eminently likely, that few voters came from Fundi, Formiae, Suessa, and so on, except when there was some special involvement, Cicero's statement about Murena becomes much more comprehensible. A man who like Murena had had the opportunity of establishing or strengthening connections with the influential men in Umbria by the holding of the *dilectus*, or a man who like Minucius Thermus had had the opportunity to dispense contracts and other favours, could hope to bring in enough voters to affect many of the tribes of Umbria, not only the Clustumina, Lemonia, and Pupinia, but also the Aemilia, Camilia, Cornelia, Oufentina, Pollia, and Stellatina (these particularly because they each contained more than one Umbrian town). Obviously it was possible for such support to be outweighed by that of other towns in the same tribes for another candidate, yet a particular candidate who had

[1] Cic. *Vatin.* 36.

[2] Cf. Meier, op. cit., 194 (different voters attended, according to who was a candidate).

good connections in Umbria could hope to benefit considerably in elections simply because he would have supporters in a large number of tribes who could be persuaded to turn out in sufficient numbers to carry those tribes. In Umbria after the allocation fourteen of the thirty-one tribes could be found, twelve of them belonging, partly at least, to towns that were enfranchised after the war.

This interpretation can clearly be applied to Etruria as well. Of the tribes that were to be found there after the Social War, two would certainly have been dominated electorally by the Etruscans, if the number of voters from each town who actually voted had been proportionate to the number theoretically available: the Sabatina included Saturnia and probably Visentium and Heba before the war, and received Vulci and Volaterrae afterwards, but no other Italian town before the enfranchisement of the Transpadani. Capena and Graviscae (and possibly Caere) were in the Stellatina before the war, and afterwards Cortona, Ferentium, Horta, Tarquinii, Tuscana, and Nepet were added to it from Etruria, and from elsewhere three small towns in Umbria, and Beneventum. But the full count of tribes in Etruria (in its widest sense) was about fourteen, twelve of them belonging partly at least to towns that were enfranchised after the war.

As another kind of 'political' explanation of the tribal allocations it has been suggested by Taylor that we can detect in them the workings of the interests of certain individual politicians. She concluded from the actual assignments of tribes that the distribution of the new citizens was made 'in the interests of Cinna and his party'[1] and that it showed 'signs of the influence of Marius'.[2] Speaking specifically of Etruria and the part of Umbria outside the Clustumina, she suggested that the tribe-assignments 'are perhaps to be explained as a reward for loyalty',[3] loyalty that is to the cause of Marius and Cinna. Assignment in the interests of Marius and Cinna would not, however, necessarily be a reward for the Etruscans and Umbrians themselves.

[1] *VDRR* 105.

[2] *VDRR* 310; cf. T. F. Carney, *A Biography of C. Marius* (Assen, 1961), 69 n. 293, E. T. Salmon, *Samnium and the Samnites* (Cambridge, 1967), 376.

[3] *VDRR* 312.

In what sort of tribe would a politician prefer to have his *clientes* and those of his friends? A man's own tribe could often be contested or lost, as is obvious from the fact that various tribes were shared by leading senators;[1] but clearly a powerful noble would usually expect to carry the vote of his own tribe, at least when he was standing himself. More important than the whereabouts of a man's own *tribules* or even those of his Roman friends, must have been the tribal allocations of the towns where he could hope to exercise other types of influence. The smallness of the tribe might be an advantage,[2] if control was secure. If a man could call upon extensive support among the Paeligni and Marsi, it would be far less useful than the support of a much smaller number of men in certain Etruscan towns. What then are the signs that, according to Taylor, show that the allocation of the tribes, which she thinks was effectively decided in 87, was made in the interests of Marius and Cinna and Cinna's party? It should be emphasized that we do not know the tribes of a number of crucial figures. Marius was in the Cornelia,[3] Carbo in the Clustumina,[4] Philippus in the Papiria,[5] but what were the tribes of Cinna and Perperna (the censor of 86),[6] or of any of the other consulars who survived under the Cinnan régime? Taylor suggests that certain peoples that had fought against Rome in the Social War 'were made *tribules* of men with whom they had been in alliance in the civil strife of 88–87',[7] but it is most unlikely that such a consideration had any general effect. She has to equivocate about the relationships of the Roman leaders of the period—since it can have been no advantage to the new Umbrian towns in the

[1] Cf. Cic. *Sest.* 114 for Clodius' failure in his own Palatina.

[2] *VDRR* 305.

[3] The evidence for this is that Arpinum was enfranchised in the Cornelia in 188; *VDRR* 232–3.

[4] This is inferred from the tribe of an Augustan Carbo, *RE* no. 36; *VDRR* 241, 310.

[5] Q. Marcius L.f.Pap. in the Pompeian *consilium* of 89 is taken to be a son of the consul of 91; *VDRR* 232, cf. C. Cichorius, *Römische Studien* (Berlin–Leipzig, 1922), 168–9.

[6] The Perpernae may possibly have been in Ser.; cf. *CIL* xi.1812 (C. Perperna C. f. Ser. Geminus—who may, however, be no relation of the senatorial Perpernae). The Sergia is not the tribe of any town in Etruria, and Perpernae other than those in the senatorial family will probably have been enfranchised after the Social War in the regular tribe of an Etruscan town.

[7] *VDRR* 310.

Clustumina to be in that tribe, she suggests that 'there may have been men in them who were opposed to the victors, men whom it was desirable to neutralize by placing them under the patronage of the ruthless Carbo'.[1] What effect the supposed ruthlessness of Carbo was meant to have there, and how this purpose was helped by the Umbrians being members of his tribe, we are not told. She can make nothing of the tribe of Philippus, which became much larger and more scattered as a result of the allocations. In general her assumption seems to be that the most powerful men will have taken the opportunity to acquire new *tribules*;[2] as I have suggested, that was not the most useful thing that they could do for themselves.[3]

It is certainly very striking that Etruria and Umbria received exceptionally advantageous treatment when the allocations were made; they were in a position to exercise a certain amount of direct influence on the *comitia* and they had very definite advantages to offer to the politicians who could deliver their votes. If there were Roman politicians who could deliver these votes, their interests were certainly assisted by the allocations. However it is too simple to say that it was the Marians who therefore benefited. Philippus and Perperna agreed to take a share in the Cinnan régime, but when it collapsed the former came quickly into alliance with Sulla; and as we shall see, in spite of the slaughter and destruction that Sulla undoubtedly caused in Etruria, some powerful local families made their peace with the new régime. The tribal allocations were made, I have suggested, by the *senatus consultum* during the period immediately after the death of Cinna, and they were later accepted by Sulla. This too makes it clear that the allocations in Etruria and Umbria were not intended to give advantages

[1] *VDRR* 310–11.

[2] It does not seem likely that Camerinum would have been much use to Marius in the Cornelia, over which he must already have had a strong hold (we know of no other major contemporary who was in the tribe).

[3] We may have the tribe of one other influential figure of the period of the allocations, a man who 'in senatu consularium auctoritatem adsequebatur' (Cic. *Brut.* 178), P. Cornelius Cethegus (on whom cf. R. Syme, *Historia*, iv (1955), 60). There is some evidence that this most famous manipulator of the tribal arrangements was himself in the compact, if not particularly small, Stellatina, for C. Cornelius M. f. Ste., *RE* no. 17, a *praetorius* in the *consilium* of 129, has been identified, rather optimistically, by Willems (followed by Passerini, Taylor, *VDRR* 207) as a son of M. Cornelius Cethegus, cos. 160.

to a particular group of Roman politicians; the Sullan régime had its local allies among the Etruscans, and of course also retained influence in some towns of Etruria for the simple reason that it had filled them with colonists. What then is the explanation of the variety of the tribes that were allocated to Etruria and Umbria? It is necessary to look back to the Social War. If the large tribal blocks were a disadvantage with which the former rebels were 'punished' (the word is rather strong), then obviously a relative benefit was bestowed on the Etruscans and those Umbrians who were outside the Clustumina. The rebels of the Social War are often thought of as having been near-Romans who only found themselves at war with Rome through a series of political misfortunes, but in Samnium there survived real opposition to the Romans as such,[1] not simply to the anti-Marians, and it can be believed that antagonism continued for a time between Rome and those who had rebelled. The Romans showed no signs of being merciful to those who persisted in fighting—as Brunt points out,[2] with reference to the rebel leaders, all the evidence suggests that the opponents of Rome expected severity if they lost. Part of the explanation of the tribal allocations in Etruria and Umbria is likely to be that the Etruscans and Umbrians had been relatively unwilling to fight against Rome in the Social War, and neither in 84 nor after the Sullan settlement was it thought that opposition to Rome was likely to find effective expression there.

An alternative has been put forward by Taylor to the various theories that the large tribal blocks were in some way punitive. She suggested[3] that 'the explanation for this type of assignment is to be found in the lack of organized municipal centers in the regions and in the strength of ethnic ties'. The lack of organized

[1] The story of Pontius Telesinus' cry that Rome should be completely destroyed, for Italy would never be free until the wolves were rooted out of their lair (Vell. II 27), is in itself rightly suspected by Brunt, art. cit., 96–7; that does not mean that it misrepresented Samnite feelings about Rome or Roman feelings about Samnium. I cannot accept, at least as it stands, Salmon's theory, *Athenaeum*, xlii (1964), 60–79, *Samnium and the Samnites*, 383–4, that Sulla made enemies of the Samnites for internal purposes. For continuing Samnite hostility as shown in their coins see A. Voirol, *Schweizer Münzblätter*, 1953–4, 65–7.

[2] Cf. Brunt, art. cit., 96, referring to the treatment of the Italian rebels in the Hannibalic war, the flight of Poppaedius Silo to the Samnites, the scarcity of rebel Italians whose immediate families were later eminent in Rome, etc.

[3] *VDRR* 113; cf. Salmon, *Samnium and the Samnites*, 376.

municipal centres may *help* us to account for these allocations, but even if we assume that it applies to the central Italian tribes, it certainly does not apply to the Umbrians in the Clustumina,[1] who were organized on the basis of the towns (there is no evidence of any pan-Umbrian organization, but there is on the other hand clear evidence of the independent organization of the towns, including for example Iguvium, among those allocated to the Clustumina). Nor indeed does it apply very well to those Campanians who were put in the Menenia (the people of Herculaneum, Nuceria, Pompeii, Stabiae, Surrentum), nor probably to those Samnites who were put in the Voltinia, nor to the Hirpini in the Galeria.

The expansion of Roman tribes to contiguous areas and by 'orientation'[2] were well-established principles before the Social War, and when it was decided that the Etruscans and Umbrians were to be placed in a number of tribes, these principles came into operation. Of the four tribes that had been created in south Etruria in 387, the Arnensis, Sabatina, Stellatina, and Tromentina, some had been further extended before the war (Heba, Saturnia, and Visentium in the Sabatina, Capena, Graviscae, and Nepet in the Stellatina, possibly Forum Clodi in the Arnensis), and all were extended after the war (Clusium and Blera in the Arnensis, Volaterrae and Vulci in the Sabatina, Cortona, Ferentium, Horta, Tarquinii, and Tuscana in the Stellatina, Perusia in the Tromentina). None of the other tribes that may have been in Etruria proper before the war was extended (no other tribe was in fact certainly there except in so far as the Papiria was already the tribe of Sutrium).[3] Ten allied towns having been put into these four tribes, there are only five or six other towns to consider, Arretium and Volsinii in the Pomptina, Faesulae and Vetulonia (and under Sulla or later Florentia) in the Scaptia, and Saena in the Oufentina; for none of these has it been possible so far to offer any definite explanation. In Umbria, apart from the Latin colonies, the Camilia and Pollia were already established in the *ager Gallicus*, as was the Pupinia, while elsewhere there were the Clustumina, Cornelia, and Oufentina. These last four were all extended

[1] As Taylor in fact recognizes, *VDRR* 114.

[2] On this see Taylor, *VDRR* 83–8.

[3] The Galeria, the tribe of Luna, was extended to Pisae.

after the war, the Pupinia to Sarsina, the Clustumina to the nine towns listed above, the Cornelia to Camerinum and Matilica, the Oufentina to Pitinum Pisaurense and Tuficum. The Umbrian towns placed in the Stellatina, Urvinum Hortense and Mataurense and Mevaniola, may be accounted for by the extension of the Stellatina in and near the Tiber valley in Etruria. There remain seven towns in four tribes, Mevania and Trebiae in the Aemilia, Ocriculum in the Arnensis, Attidium, Hispellum, and Sentinum in the Lemonia, and Asisium in the Sergia. Apart from the possibility that the last case was influenced by orientation, no definite explanation can be offered of why these particular tribes should have been allocated to these particular towns.

One other factor can be seen to have played a part in the allocations. Latin colonies enfranchised after the Social War were probably put into the tribes in which their magistrates had been enfranchised, and a similar principle seems to have affected some formerly federated towns. The cohorts of Camerinum probably entered Marius' tribe, the Cornelia, before the war; afterwards, although in my opinion neither Marius nor his son was capable of enforcing his wishes, the whole community was assigned to the same tribe. There are several other cases in Etruria and Umbria where towns were placed in tribes which already seem to have been those of local people enfranchised before the war. Thus Perusia was placed in the Tromentina, a tribe already known in Etruria. Now there is a good case for supposing that the Vibii Pansae came from Perusia, but C. Vibius C.f. Pansa was a *monetalis* in the 80s and his filiation also argues that he was enfranchised before the war;[1] a Vibius Pansa appears in a clearly republican inscription from Perusia with the tribe Tromentina.[2] Tarquinii was placed in the Stellatina, which was almost certainly the tribe of the family of T. Numisius Tarquiniensis, a legate in 169 and 167, who is quite likely to have been from Tarquinii in spite of the difficulties about topographical *cognomina*.[3] The ancestors of the Saenius who was a senator in 63 and of L. Saenius L.f., suffect consul in 30, were enfranchised before the

[1] See below, pp. 324–5.
[2] *CIL* xi.1994.
[3] On the citizenship and origin of the Numisii, see below, pp. 326–7.

Social War, it is argued below.[1] If this suffect consul was the future consul Balbinus mentioned by Appian,[2] as seems likely,[3] he might be identical with, or related to, the Balbus, son of Lucius and member of the Oufentina tribe, who appears as a witness in the *s.c. de Aphrodisiensibus* of 35 B.C.[4] If so, the family may perhaps already have been in the Oufentina before the Social War. There were a number of other Etruscans and Umbrian individuals who had acquired Roman citizenship before the war, but have left no record of their tribes;[5] it is probable that this factor had a wider influence than we can tell from the existing evidence.[6]

To sum up, the following factors can be seen to have been responsible for the tribal allocations in Etruria and Umbria: (i) punitive treatment of the rebels of the Social War, or those whose loyalty was in some way suspect, and favourable treatment of Etruria and most of Umbria by comparison with the areas of the rebellion; (ii) extension of tribes already belonging to other towns in the area; (iii) extension of tribes already belonging to individual Roman citizens of local origin.

[1] Pp. 323–4.

[2] *BC* IV 50.215.

[3] Syme, *Historia*, iv (1955), 57.

[4] Syme, l.c., cf. Taylor, *VDRR* 251–2, *MRR Suppl.* 9, 55, R. K. Sherk, *Roman Documents from the Greek East* (Baltimore, 1969), 171.

[5] Maecenas, *RE* no. 1, was in the Maecia apparently and seems to be an instance where this principle was not applied.

[6] Syme, *Historia*, xiii (1964), 121, points to the Coponii as an example of a family from a town enfranchised after the Social War (Tibur) that belonged to a different tribe from the one that they had already entered before the war. But the T. Coponius from Tibur who acquired the citizenship by a successful prosecution (Cic. *Balb.* 53) was at best a distant relation of L. Coponius L.f. Col. who was already a senator by *c.* 134. The case of the Munatii Planci is also an interesting one, for as Syme points out, l.c., it appears from *IGRRP* iv.792 that they were in the Camilia; and they acquired a Roman tribe before the general enfranchisement of their home-town Tibur in the Cam., as *ILS* 886 shows—possibly *per magistratum.*

VIII

THE SULLAN SETTLEMENT

1. *Etruria and the Marians*

It is widely believed that Etruria was in the 80s a stronghold, indeed the stronghold, of the *Marianae partes*. In consequence, it can be argued, it was the area that offered the most determined resistance to Sulla, and in consequence of that resistance Sulla singled it out for particularly harsh treatment, including confiscation and colonization.[1] In this view there is much truth, but the actual situation was rather more complicated. As an examination of Marius' following in Etruria and in particular of his actions when he landed at Telamon in 87 has shown, his support in Etruria was of a peculiar kind. Instead of being based, like the Italian *clientelae* of most Roman politicians, on relations with *domi nobiles*, it largely relied on his personal appeal to the mass of the population, including probably the survivors of the old serf class; in Etruria at least, where there was a serious division between social classes, such support from the lower classes was not likely to go with close relations between Marius and the local aristocrats. The support that Cinna and his followers could muster in Etruria was of a decidedly different kind from that of Marius (see below for the prosopographical evidence). Recent writers have emphasized the differences between the interests and policies of Marius and Cinna after their victory,[2] and there certainly seems to have been such a difference in policy towards the Italian enfranchisement. When Marius died and Cinna's policy of compromise, or rather reaction, on the questions of the new citizen's voting rights was put into effect by the censors Philippus and Per-

[1] Badian, *FC* 222–5, 245–6.

[2] Badian, *JRS* lii (1962), 55=*Studies in Greek and Roman History* (Oxford, 1964), 222 (but Marius cannot be given all the responsibility for the proscriptions, cf. J. P. V. D. Balsdon's review in *JRS* lv (1965), 230, and (at length) E. S. Gruen, *Roman Politics and the Criminal Courts, 149–78* B.C. (Cambridge, Mass., 1968), 230–5); C. M. Bulst, *Historia*, xiii (1964), 309–18.

perna, the so-called Marians can certainly not have been regarded as the popular leaders in Etruria. Eventually, when Italian support became more important to the anti-Sullan régime, full effective voting rights were awarded by the *senatus consultum* of 84, and the Italians in general preferred the cause of the government to that of Sulla, whose last action that directly concerned them had been to invalidate the Sulpician law on the tribal allocations. As we have seen, the treatment that the Etruscans and Umbrians received when the tribal allocations were made was preferential; it seems very likely that this advantage was contained in the *senatus consultum*, and that will help to explain the resistance to Sulla in Etruria and Umbria.

That Etruria was particularly favourable to the *Marianae partes* has also been argued on prosopographical grounds. The following magistrates 'under the Cinnan régime' are put forward as 'Etruscan, though . . . not always new citizens':[1] the M. Perpernae, both father and son, the former the censor of 86, the latter a praetor by 82,[2] Burrienus, praetor in 83, C. Carrinas, an anti-Sullan general in 83 and praetor in 82, and C. Verres, quaestor in 84. The Perperna and Carrinas families did indeed derive from Etruria, and although the Perpernae has been in Rome for a long time, they probably retained strong Etruscan connections. The case of Burrienus is much more open: the termination '-ienus' certainly has associations in north central Italy, but in Umbrian, Sabine, and Picene country as well as in Etruria, and there is no epigraphical evidence at all for the name of Burrienus in Italy, though there were once Burii at Caere.[3] To call the praetor of 83 an Etruscan is a guess. Verres is even less likely as an Etruscan, at least of recent origin. The termination of the name is odd, but not exactly paralleled among names of certainly

[1] Badian, *FC* 245 n. 2.

[2] Praetor in 82 according to *MRR* ii.62, but cf. Badian, *Proc. Afr. Class. Assoc.*, i (1958), 9=*Studies*, etc. 86, *FC* 269 n. 3.

[3] On names with endings in '-ienus' cf. R. Syme, *JRS* xxviii (1938), 123 n. 70. Burrienus is 'di origine etrusca o picena' according to E. Gabba, *Athenaeum*, xxix (1951), 207 n. 2, and Badian makes him an Etruscan, *FC* 245 n. 2. The whole of the area described is available, since 'Burr-' cannot really be tied down to Etruria. For Burii at Caere see *CIL* xi.3638–9, and for those in other areas the references in Schulze, *ZGLE* 110 n. 1.

Etruscan origin, and quite apart from his possible connection with the Latin colony of Sora it seems unlikely that, if any connection between Verres and decadent Etruria had been known to contemporaries, it would have gone unrecorded.[1] The political success of the Perperna family was of course no new creation of the Marians or Cinnans; their closest Roman connection was with L. Marcius Philippus, who, it has been argued, had an important *clientela* in Etruria. The Cinnan régime certainly gave way to Philippus and M. Perperna on the subject of enfranchisement policy when they were censors in 86—at least for Marius' true successors it must have been a question of giving way. Philippus and Perperna had their connections with the ruling classes in the Etruscan towns and no doubt looked after their interests during the censorship and afterwards. The same probably applies on a smaller scale to Carrinas. Other Romans whom we know about who had connections in Etruria turn out not to be allies of Marius himself. The case of the Etruscan *hospes*[2] of C. Iulius Caesar Strabo Vopiscus is somewhat obscure: Vopiscus had quarrelled bitterly with Marius and Sulpicius Rufus in 89 or 88 about his candidature for the consulship,[3] and in 87 his Etruscan *hospes*, by name Sextilius, betrayed him to the Marians 'in fundo Tarquiniensi'[4]—but he presumably regarded Sextilius as a faithful *hospes* until it was too late. Q. Ancharius, who was murdered in 87 on the personal instructions of Marius,[5] is another man who may derive from the Etruscan aristocracy.

[1] Schulze, *ZGLE* 287, regarded the Etruscan origin of the name as 'wenigstens nicht unmöglich', with Etruscan **vere, veru*, as the possible original form. For the ending cf. P. Menates (*CIL* i².829=*ILLRP* 463), allegedly derived from Etruscan **menate*. For argument that Verres was in the tribe Romilia and the suggestion that he was connected with Sora, see Taylor, *VDRR* 264. Syme, *Historia*, iv (1955), 71, affirms the Etruscan character of the termination.

[2] So called by Cic. *De Or.* III 10.

[3] Cic. *Brut.* 226, Ascon. 25C, Dio XXXVII 2.12; the conflict probably began in 89, cf. Badian, *Historia*, vi (1957), 336 n. 155=*Studies*, etc. 68 n. 155.

[4] Val. Max. V 3.3. The other sources for this incident are listed by *MRR* ii.51–2. Sextilius had previously been involved in a law-suit at Rome (in which he had been defended by Vopiscus) and it is conceivable that he is P. Sextilius, praetor in 89 or 88, hostile to Marius in 88 (cf. *MRR* ii.41). Some Romans did have property interests in Etruria by this time—cf. the case of Aebutius (below, p. 284). But it is probable that Sextilius was an authentically local personage, for otherwise Cicero would hardly have referred to him as a *hospes Etruscus* (*De Or.* III 10).

[5] App. *BC* I 73.337.

Marius himself was not aligned definitely with, in fact was sometimes opposed to, those who had connections with the ruling classes in Etruria. The Cinnan régime made compromises with such people, with Philippus and Perperna in particular, and in the following of Carbo was to be found C. Carrinas, probably the younger M. Perperna, and perhaps Vibius Pansa, adoptive father of the Caesarian general, a Perusine proscribed in Rome by Sulla.[1]

The care of the Cinnan régime for its connections among the ruling classes of the Italian towns is also illustrated, I suggest, by Appian's account of what happened when Sulla's threat became stronger in 85. He tells us that Cinna and Carbo sent men throughout Italy to collect money, soldiers, and food, they tried to win the support of the powerful by having meetings with them, and they tried to arouse those cities in particular that were newly enfranchised as if it was because of them that they (Cinna and Carbo) were in such great danger.[2] These *δυνατοὶ* are usually taken to be Roman nobles,[3] but it is better to interpret them as the *δυνατοὶ* of the towns: the preceding and succeeding clauses refer to the measures taken in Italy, not Rome, and it would be odd to speak of Carbo and Cinna trying to influence Roman nobles by *συνουσίαι*.

The ruling classes in many Etruscan towns probably looked to those who were involved with the Cinnan régime or with Carbo for the protection of their interests and of the rather favourable arrangements that the *senatus consultum* of 84 had made for them. At the same time the lower classes no doubt remembered the more radical actions of Marius himself in 87 and perhaps hoped for a similar policy from those who were more truly the heirs of Marius. This was part of the following that the anti-Sullans must have hoped to gain when they elected the son of Marius to the consulship of 82.[4]

Most Italians opposed Sulla's seizure of power on his return in 83,[5] expecting that his policy towards them would be like

[1] Dio XLV 17.1.

[2] 76.348: *ὅ τε Κάρβων καὶ ὁ Κίννας ἐς ὅλην τὴν Ἰταλίαν τινὰς περιέπεμπον, χρήματα καὶ στρατιὰν καὶ σῖτον αὐτοῖς ἀθροίζειν, τούς τε δυνατοὺς συνουσίαις ἀνελάμβανον καὶ τῶν πόλεων ἠρέθιζον μάλιστα τὰς νεοπολίτιδας, ὡς δι' αὐτὰς ὄντες ἐν τοσῷδε κινδύνου.*

[3] Cf. Gabba, ad loc.

[4] On the choice of the younger Marius, cf. Badian, *FC* 244.

[5] Cf. App. 82.374–6, 86.388, 393, and Bulst, art. cit., 326. Salmon, *Athenaeum*,

the one that he had followed in 88. In 82, according to a brief notice in the *Periochae* of Livy,[1] he made a treaty with the Italians to the effect that he would not deprive the new citizens of the *ius suffragii*. There were certainly numerous desertions to Sulla,[2] and having arrived at Brundisium with five legions he commanded twenty-three by the end of the war; but the motives for fighting Sulla (and this is true no doubt for some of those who fought against him) must in many cases have been somewhat apolitical. The prospect of booty was raised—as Appian says, Sulla recruited in Italy φιλίᾳ τε καὶ φόβῳ καὶ χρήμασι καὶ ἐλπίσιν;[3] although Sulla had at first restrained his troops,[4] for obvious reasons, they were by this time permitted to plunder and destroy.[5] He made some headway with Italians of various regions: in particular there was support from Picenum and from among the Marsi,[6] and there was probably even some from Etruscans, if Philippus' clients remained loyal to him. However Sulla was fundamentally unpopular with the Italians,[7] and those who, because of their connections with his enemies, could expect to be the victims of land-confiscations had every reason to resist him as long as there was any hope whatsoever of winning. Troops from all over Italy fought against Sulla—there are specifically mentioned Samnites, Lucanians, Praenestines, Campanians, and men from Cisalpine Gaul.[8] Etruscans obviously took part and so almost certainly did Umbrians.[9] But these lists of regions are

xlii (1964), 72, denies this without any real argument (but I agree with his view that the sympathies of the Samnites were more diverse than has usually been recognized).

[1] *Per.* 86: 'Sulla cum Italicis populis, ne timeretur ab his velut erepturus civitatem et suffragii ius nuper datum, foedus percussit.'

[2] See e.g. App. 85.386, 88.401, 90.415, 91.420.

[3] 86.393, cf. 96.447.

[4] Plu. *Sull.* 27, Vell. II 25, Dio fr. 109.

[5] App. 86.389.

[6] Picenum: Plu. *Pomp.* 6, Vell. II 29. Marsi: Plu. *Crass.* 6.

[7] Cf. App. 88.406.

[8] Samnites: App. 87.400, 94.437, etc. Lucanians: App. 91.420—the legion deserted to Metellus. Praenestines: see references to the siege, Greenidge and Clay, *Sources for Roman History, 133–70* B.C.[2] (Oxford, 1960), 205–8; afterwards Romans were spared, Samnites and Praenestines were not, App. 94.437–8. Campanians: Naples resisted, App. 89.411, and Norba, 94.439, and Nola, Gran. Licin. 32F, Liv. *Per.* 89. Cisalpines: App. 86.393.

[9] Cf. the confiscations of Crassus at Tuder, Plu. *Crass.* 6—but they may have been unprovoked, as allegedly in the case of Roscius of Ameria.

incidental—both sides received support, in different proportions, from all over Italy.[1]

When Sertorius was fleeing from Rome to Spain in 82,[2] probably through Etruria, he found it a fruitful recruiting ground and raised forty cohorts there.[3] This, Exuperantius says, was possible because Etruria was 'fidissima partibus Marianis'; his explanation of this is obscure,[4] but there is no reason to doubt that Sertorius did raise such an army there. Subsequently the last serious stand of the anti-Sullan resistance in Italy was, Praeneste apart, in Etruria. However the importance of the Etruscans themselves among Sulla's enemies may seem larger than it really was, simply because in 82 Etruria was almost the only part of Italy not already in Sulla's hands.

It is not necessary to rehearse the whole course of the war.[5] Almost inevitably the resistance to Sulla retreated northwards on either side of the Apennines. In 83 Pompey defeated a force of anti-Sullan cavalry on the river Aesis on the east side of the Apennines.[6] After a winter of rival propaganda another engagement was fought on the Aesis, in which Metellus defeated Carrinas, and 'the whole of the surrounding district passed from the consuls to Metellus'.[7] Carbo then attempted to confront Metellus but was forced to retreat northwards to Ariminum.[8] At an undefined site 'another army of Carbo' was defeated by Metellus, to whom five cohorts deserted in the middle of the battle, and Pompey defeated Marcius (Censorinus, a legate of Carbo) near Sena Gallica on the Umbrian coast, a citizen-colony which he then sacked.[9] At this point in Appian's narrative Sulla entered Rome and having dealt with urgent matters set off for Clusium, where τοῦ πολέμου τὰ λοιπὰ ἤκμαζεν.[10] He won a cavalry battle on the river Glanis

[1] Cf. Badian, *FC* 247.

[2] The date of Sertorius' departure was before the end of 83 according to A. Schulten, *Sertorius* (Leipzig, 1926), 39 n. 210, Gabba on App. 86.392. In Exuperantius he is still in Rome at the end of 83, and that version seems preferable, cf. T. Rice Holmes, *Roman Republic* (Oxford, 1923), i.369; however, he probably did his recruiting before Sulla's *foedus* with the Italians.

[3] Exuperant. 7.

[4] See above, p. 236 n.5.

[5] Cf. Gabba's excellent notes on the campaigns in his Appian commentary.

[6] Plu. *Pomp.* 7.

[7] App. 87.395.

[8] 87.396.

[9] 88.401.

[10] 89.408.

(=Chiani), probably in the valley south of Clusium, and at the same time another part of his army won a victory near Saturnia. Thus he had advanced northwards along the two main roads through central Etruria, the Cassia and the Clodia. Another battle was fought between Sulla and Carbo near Clusium, this indecisive.[1] Pompey and Crassus defeated Carrinas in the plain of Spoletium,[2] Crassus having previously captured the Umbrian town of Tuder[3]—much to his own profit, it was claimed. Carbo still commanded very large forces, for while he was defending Clusium he was able to reinforce Carrinas with another army and to send eight legions to Praeneste. Sulla now concentrated on the siege of Praeneste, and Carbo and Norbanus attacked the Sullan forces under Metellus, who had taken Ariminum and advanced along the Via Aemilia to Faventia. Carbo and Norbanus were disastrously defeated and withdrew to Arretium, thus effectively surrendering the Po valley to the Sullans.[4] Even after the murder of anti-Sullan officers by Albinovanus and the desertion of Norbanus, Carbo still had 30,000 troops at Clusium, two legions under Damasippus, and the other forces under Carrinas and Marcius. After Carbo himself had fled, 'of those who remained those about Clusium were brought to battle with Pompey and lost about 20,000 men. After this immense disaster the remains of the army disbanded and returned to their homes in scattered groups.'[5] Carrinas, Marcius Censorinus, and Damasippus all fought at the Colline Gate and were killed in or after the battle.

In fact Appian's description of the disbanding of the army in Etruria is misleading, for fighting went on which, though forlorn, was in itself serious. The siege of Volaterrae, which was at one time conducted by Sulla himself,[6] was a major military engagement, and probably lasted until the very end

[1] 89.412. Gabba ad loc. equates this battle with the one in Liv. *Per.* 88 which was won by Sulla (cf. the victory of two Servilii 'apud Clusium' in Vell. II 28), but he prefers Appian's account of the result; cf. his references to discussions. Appian's account is fairly carefully constructed and should be accepted.

[2] App. 90.413.

[3] Plu. *Crass.* 6.

[4] App. 91.418–19. Ἀρρήγιον in the MSS. is generally changed to Ἀρρήτιον (see Gabba's references). Ἀρίμινον (Mendelssohn, Viereck, Pareti) makes quite unnecessary difficulties. Arretium was the site of a Sullan colony (see below). For destruction there at this time see below, p. 263.

[5] App. 92.426.

[6] Cic. *Rosc. Am.* 20.

of 80 or into 79.[1] Involved in the siege were not only the Volaterrani themselves, afterwards penalized by Sulla, but other anti-Sullans, for the besieged were, according to Strabo, 'some of the Etruscans and of those proscribed by Sulla'.[2] There was also, again according to Strabo, a devastating siege of Populonium περὶ τοὺς αὐτοὺς καιρούς. The closing of a number of coin-hoards in Etruria in this period is to be associated with the Sullan war: hoards were closed at Capalbio (territory of Cosa) in 81, at San Miniato (in the Arno valley west of Florence) in 80, and at Montiano (near Telamon and Heba) in 79.[3] There is other archaeological evidence that Telamon suffered serious devastation shortly after 85 and Vetulonia in or soon after 81, and these events too can be assigned to the last stage of the Sullan conquest (Lepidus' campaign in 78 is also a possible occasion).[4] Destruction and dislocation at Arretium and Clusium, described in the next section, probably also resulted from this war. There is some evidence of continuing Italian resistance to Sulla in Campania as well—at Nola,[5] no doubt in response to Sulla's decision to establish a colony there. After the siege of Volaterrae the survivors were allowed to go away ὑπόσπονδοι;[6] some no doubt went to Spain, where Sertorius had already gone and where the younger Perperna

[1] The action of the consuls of 79 recorded by Gran. Licin. 32F must have taken place very shortly after its end. For the view that the siege continued into 79 see L. Lange, *Römische Alterthümer*, iii[2] (Berlin, 1876), 161, Gabba on App. 95.440; it is not excluded by Strabo's statement (V 2.6 223C) that the siege lasted for two years.

[2] V 2.6 223 C. They filled four τάγματα (Strabo), probably intended to be four legions (Strabo must have a definite unit in mind, in spite of H. L. Jones' n. in the Loeb edn.; cf. LSJ[9]). The proscribed are also mentioned by Gran. Licin. 32F.

[3] Capalbio: M. H. Crawford, *PBSR* xxxv (1967), 1–3, *Roman Republican Coin Hoards* (London, 1969), no. 258; also closed in 81, a hoard at Carrara, Crawford no. 260; San Miniato: G. F. Gamurrini, *Periodico di Numismatica e Sfragistica*, v (1873), 239–51, Crawford no. 262; Montiano: G. Caputo, *Ann. Ist. Ital. di Numismatica*, vii–viii (1960–1), 326, Crawford no. 266.

[4] For the destruction at Telamon see the evidence cited above, 207 n. 1. For Vetulonia, *NSA* 1895, 295–6 (I. Falchi); the coins are very sketchily reported—the latest dates that can be inferred from the published information are *c.* 87 B.C. for a *denarius* of the Titius family (cf. Sydenham, *Roman Republican Coinage*, 107–8, *MRR* ii.454) and *c.* 81 for a *denarius* of a Marius who must be C. Marius Capito (*MRR* ii.445; Crawford's date is 81). Mr. Crawford kindly tells me that these coins also include the type of Ti. Claudius Ti.f.Ap.n. (Sydenham no. 770) which is slightly later than that of C. Marius Capito.

[5] Liv. *Per.* 89.

[6] Strabo V 2.6 223C.

had probably gone by 81.[1] In spite of what Strabo says, however, many Volaterrani remained, to be punished, as were the Arretines, not only by the loss of much land to Sullan veterans but also by being demoted from the full Roman citizenship to the *ius Ariminensium*.

2. *The Sullan Settlement in Etruria and Umbria*

Sulla's supporters and veterans had to receive their rewards, and the security of the régime was protected in Italy by a number of veteran colonies and other land-distributions. Appian[2] tells us that Sulla distributed much land, and that some of it was land that was still unassigned, by which he must mean that it was *ager publicus* under the terms of the *foedera*, and that some of it was confiscated from the towns as a punishment. Some of the territory assigned in Etruria will certainly have been in the second category, but there may also have been land in the first category in any of the old allied states in Etruria. Unless depopulation had gone further than we have any right to suppose, there was *de facto* confiscation of land on a large scale, for sale as well as for distribution. Appian sets the number of Sullan veterans settled in Italy after the war at twenty-three legions or 120,000 men.[3] Perhaps not all of Sulla's veterans received land, but on the other hand a substantial number received more than the legionary's minimum grant. If we knew the size of such a grant, we should know better how to regard the list of the places where land is known to have been distributed, of which there are only ten or so. It is not likely that veterans received less than the ten *iugera* that seem to have been offered by the proposal of Servilius Rullus in 63.[4] Thirty

[1] *MRR* ii.67 states that Perperna went to Spain after he lost Sicily to Pompey; that is not attested (and he may have gone first to join Ahenobarbus in Africa), but it is likely.

[2] 100.470.

[3] In 100.470 and 104.489 respectively. 'XLVII legiones in agros captos deduxit, et eos his divisit' (Liv. *Per.* 89) is clearly wrong. Carcopino emended to 'XLVII legionarios', referring the notice to Campania alone (*Sylla ou la monarchie manquée*[2] (Paris, 1947), 213 n. 4), which is not plausible; for emendations that make Livy's figure close to Appian's see Viereck's *apparatus*. It is conceivable that only 47,000 men from the twenty-three legions were actually settled on the land.

[4] Cic. *Agr.* II 78: 'Coement praeterea; ista dena iugera continuabunt'; cf. *Att.* II 16.1, where Cicero in 59, learning of the contents of the law on the Campanian land, seems to imply that Rullus' figure is being retained, 'ut dena iugera sint'.

iugera seems to have been the maximum size of a Gracchan allotment,[1] though perhaps more than is likely for the normal allotment at that time,[2] and somewhat later some colonists received 66⅔ *iugera*,[3] so the Sullan one may well have been much more than ten.[4] If 120,000 received only ten *iugera* each, an area of *c.* 1162 square miles was distributed,[5] and since centurions must have received more, it seems unlikely that all the necessary land was found in the places listed below. This is all the more likely because much land was confiscated and settled or sold without the establishment of colonies;[6] we happen to know that there was confiscation at Ameria, Tuder, Beneventum and Larinum, and in Bruttium[7] (and see below on Volaterrae), and there were almost certainly similar proceedings in other places.

Numerous scholars have compiled lists of the Sullan colonies and other settlements,[8] but the cases still need discussion.

[1] Mommsen, *GS* i.103, inferred that the Gracchan allotments were not more than thirty *iugera* from the *Lex Agraria* of 111 (*FIRA*² i (ed. Riccobono), no. 8), line 14 ('agri iugra non amplius XXX possidebit habebitve: is ager privatus esto').

[2] D. C. Earl, *Tiberius Gracchus, A Study in Politics* (Brussels, 1963), 19–20 (but cf. P. Brunt, *Gnomon*, xxxvii (1965), 190).

[3] Hyginus Grom. 199.14–16, 201.3–6L.

[4] Gabba, *Athenaeum*, xxix (1951), 244–5, suggests that the assignments 'non fossero tali da permettere una vita eccessivamente agiata' on the basis of Cic. *Cat.* II 20, but the passage is not really evidence. Nor, I think, is it possible to argue, as Gabba does, art. cit., 231, from the supposed average size of a Pompeian farm (on which cf. E. Lepore, *Pompeiana, Raccolta di studi per il secondo centenario degli scavi di Pompei* (Naples, 1950), 151, K. D. White, *BICS* xiv (1967), 72–3) to the size of the allotments made to the individual Sullan settlers.

[5] 1 *iugerum*=*c.* 0·62 of an acre.

[6] Cf. App. 96.445–6: various charges were made the pretext for taking land from individual Italians.

[7] Ameria: Cic. *Rosc. Am.* 6, etc.; Tuder: Plu. *Crass.* 6; Beneventum: Cic. *II Verr.* I 38; Larinum: *Clu.* 25; Bruttium: Plu. l.c. On Venusia cf. p. 271 n. 2.

[8] The most important is Mommsen's in *Hermes*, xviii (1883), 163–8=*GS* v.205–210 (and notice the summary of his judgements at the end of the article, 211–13=251–3—they are not always stated in the text). Cf. A. W. Zumpt, *Commentationum Epigraphicarum ad antiquitates Romanas pertinentium volumen* I (Berlin, 1850), 250–61, K. J. Beloch, *It. Bund, RG* 511–12, E. Borman in *CIL* xi, s.vv., E. Pais, *Mem. Acc. Linc.*, ser. 6.i (1925), 352–60 (erratic), A. Degrassi, *Mem. Acc. Linc.*, ser. 8.ii (1950), 281–345 (not intended as a full discussion of this question but useful), E. Gabba, art. cit., 270–2. De Ruggiero (*Diz. Ep.* s.v. *colonia*) and Kornemann (*RE* s.v. *coloniae* (1901)) also give lists. For some recent remarks on those in Etruria cf. A. J. Pfiffig, *Studi in onore di Luisa Banti* (Rome, 1965), 275–80, *Die Ausbreitung des römischen Städtewesens in Etrurien und die Frage der Unterwerfung der Etrusker* (Florence, 1966), *passim* (erratic). A. Krawczuk, *Kolonizacja sullańska*, in *Polska Akademia*

Faesulae and Florentia

The cases of Faesulae and Florentia can be discussed together.[1] There was certainly a Sullan colony in the territory of Faesulae, for Cicero refers to the *coloni* 'quos Faesulas L. Sulla deduxit'.[2] At or near Faesulae 'castella veteranorum Sullanorum' were built,[3] that is small fortified places—they could have been on the plain at the site of Florentia.[4] Was Florentia the site of a Sullan colony?[5] According to Florus,[6] various 'municipia Italiae splendidissima sub hasta venierunt', including Florentia, but this is the only direct literary reference to Florentia as existing before the triumviral colony. It has been supposed that Florentia was the name and Roman Florence the site of Sulla's colony and the site of the *castella* of Granius. This suggestion, which is discussed in Appendix III, cannot be entirely excluded, but it is much more likely that there was only one Sullan colony in the area, at Faesulae; its territory may have included the site of Florentia.

Arretium

'Coloni Arretini' are referred to by Cicero as supporters of Catiline in 63.[7] In a letter of 60, describing his own response to Flavius' agrarian bill, Cicero says: 'Volaterranos et Arretinos, quorum agrum Sulla publicarat neque diviserat, in sua possessione retinebam'.[8] The most obvious interpretation of this

Nauk, oddział w Krakowie, Prace Komisji Nauk Historycznych, iv (1960) (91 pp.) is unfortunately known to me only through its French résumé (pp. 89–91).

[1] Faesulae is generally accepted as a Sullan colony (Mommsen, art. cit., 166=207, etc.). For a detailed discussion of the foundation of Faesulae and Florentia see C. Hardie, *JRS* lv (1965), 122–40.

[2] *Cat.* III 14; cf. *Mur.* 49: 'circumfluentem colonorum Arretinorum et Faesulanorum exercitu'.

[3] Gran. Licin. 34F.

[4] 'Certainly the word *castella* cannot refer to Fiesole, but no more can it to Florence. It means fortified villas, more probably not on the plain', Hardie, art. cit., 130. That is too restrictive. For the view that the *castella* were at Florentia, see Beloch, *RG* 511.

[5] Mommsen, discussing the possible triumviral colony at Florentia (art. cit., 176=218), held that it could with at least equally good reason be taken as a Sullan colony, though he rejected the Florus passage as evidence for it. Pais held that land at Florentia was assigned to Sullan veterans, art. cit., 354–5. In Gabba's list it has become a 'certain' colony, art. cit., 271 (as Faesulae also). Hardie rejects all Sullan settlement and accepts the triumviral colony.

[6] II 9.27–8.

[7] *Mur.* 49.

[8] *Att.* I 19.4; the attempt of F. Nicosia, *SE* xxxiv (1966), 277–8, to emend the Arretini out of this text is to be rejected.

is that all or most of the land of Volaterrae and Arretium was confiscated but left undivided, and by 60 much of it was *de facto* in the possession of the non-Sullan locals (if indeed it had ever been out of their possession). Yet the other evidence makes it virtually certain that there was a Sullan colony at Arretium. The town-list in Pliny mentions three sets of Arretini, namely Veteres, Fidentiores (these two categories are epigraphically attested), and Iulienses.[1] The Fidentiores are attested as colonists in an inscription,[2] and they are commonly taken to be Sullan colonists.[3] The division of Arretium under the Sullan arrangements agrees well with what we know about some other Sullan colonies, for example Clusium and Nola.[4] An inscription of the first century B.C. from Arretium refers to two *duoviri*, who are magistrates of a colony and presumably of the Sullan one.[5] But there remains the apparently contradictory evidence in Cicero's letter. This divergence cannot be explained by reference to the Arretines' vindication of their right to the full citizenship,[6] for there were still Arretine colonists in 63, if ever. Possibly we should read 'eos Volaterranos et Arretinos . . .'; and for his settlements Sulla did make use of existing *ager publicus*,[7] that is to say that he may have settled colonists at Arretium without having to make any or much more land into *ager publicus*. The *ager publicus* that he created turned out to be more than was required and no doubt continued in possession of the locals, and this Volaterran land that had been made public by Sulla but not divided was apparently in question in 63.[8]

[1] *NH* III 52.

[2] *CIL* xi.6675: [. . .] (?)P COL(ONORUM) FID(ENTIORUM), perhaps= R(es) P(ublica) COL, etc.; the *Fidentiores* were equated with the Sullan colonists by I. Schmidt, *Bull. Inst.* 1879, 166. The *Arretini veteres* are epigraphically attested in the first or second century A.D., *CIL* xi.1849 (Bormann's date).

[3] Beloch, Pais (but he thinks that the colony perhaps did not last for long, art. cit., 354), Gabba, etc. Mommsen (art. cit., 165=207) was unsure: the contradiction between *Mur.* 49 and Att. I 19.4 means that the assignment must have taken place, but 'in ungültiger oder doch anfechtbarer Weise'; the other evidence inclined him to accept the colony.

[4] For Nola see *CIL* x.1273.

[5] *CIL* i^2.2087=*ILLRP* 548.

[6] As R. G. Nisbet seems to imply in his note on Cic. *Dom.* 79.

[7] App. 100.470.

[8] Cic. *Fam.* XIII 4.2: 'Cum enim tribuni plebis legem iniquissimam de eorum agris promulgavissent, facile senatui populoque Romano persuasi, ut eos cives, quibus fortuna pepercisset, salvos esse vellent.'

In any case the colony must be accepted.[1] Arretium was of course one of the last places where Sulla was resisted, a fact that is confirmed by evidence of a fire and fairly extensive destruction (the walls and other buildings including temples) at about this time.[2]

Clusium

The case for Clusium as a Sullan colony rests substantially on the appearance in Pliny's town-list of 'Clusini veteres, Clusini novi',[3] and on the Clusium inscriptions referring to *duoviri*.[4] The double community of *veteres* and *novi* is appropriate to a Sullan colony, and the case is a fairly certain one. The part played by the town in the Sullan war seems for a time to have been that of Carbo's headquarters and obviously it was liable to punishment. There is much evidence of large-scale dislocation among the inhabitants of Clusium in the early first century, some of it already discussed,[5] and cemeteries used for long periods, but not for long after the beginning of the first century, probably result from the destruction of the local population in the Sullan war.[6]

[1] It is also probable that some Arretine land was confiscated and sold off; Atticus' property there (Nepos, *Att.* 14.3) may have consisted of such land.

[2] See L. Pernier, *NSA* 1920, 183–4, M. Falciai, *SE* i (1927), 102, A. Andrén, *Architectural Terracottas in Etrusco-Italic Temples* (Lund–Leipzig 1940), 267.

[3] *NH* III 52.

[4] *CIL* xi.2116, 2119–21, cf. 2118, 2127–8. The colony is accepted by Beloch, Gabba, etc.; Clusium was the site of *viritim* assignment in Pais's view (art. cit., 355). A. J. Pfiffig has recently argued against the Sullan colony, art. cit., 277, 279–80, *Ausbreitung*, etc. 61–3, making an obscure attack on the general rule that *duoviri* are to be found only in colonies. At Clusium we know of *quattuorviri* as well as of *duoviri* (*quattuorviri*: *CIL* xi.2117, 2122, 7123): Bormann judged the two of these that he knew when he wrote *CIL* xi. p. 372 to be earlier than the *duoviri* inscriptions, and he held that one form of government was superseded by the other (but see below, p. 270 n. 4). The earlier date of 2117 does get some slight support from the form 'Cominia nat(us)', which follows on Etruscan practice. The base of a statue of Sulla found at Clusium (see *CIL* i².723=*ILLRP* 356) is not very substantial evidence for a Sullan colony, *pace* R. A. L. Fell, *Etruria and Rome* (Cambridge, 1924), 165–6 (cf. Pfiffig, art. cit., 280, for good and bad arguments on this point) —though it is difficult to imagine the *Clusini veteres* erecting such a statue.

[5] See above, pp. 210–11.

[6] Cf. the Poggio Gaiella cemetery, in use from the early sixth century onwards and throughout the second century, C. Laviosa, *Fasti Archaeologici*, xvii (1965), 193, and R. Bianchi Bandinelli, *MAAL* xxx (1925), cols. 370–4; and the Colle Lucioli cemetery, Bandinelli, art. cit., col. 280.

Volaterrae

Volaterrae and Arretium were both temporarily reduced to the status of Ariminum.[1] Cicero explicitly stated in 57 that those towns that lost their citizenship (unconstitutionally) under Sulla also lost land (constitutionally), and Volaterrae is the instance specified of such a town.[2] In Sullan eyes if any town deserved to be punished it was Volaterrae after the siege. On the other hand it could be argued that no land, or not much, was actually distributed at Volaterrae, for Cicero did not explicitly say that land was distributed, and in 45 he could write that the Volaterrani 'Sullani temporis acerbitatem deorum immortalium benignitate subterfugerunt'.[3] In 60, in a letter already discussed,[4] he perhaps implied that the land confiscated at Volaterrae had not been distributed. On balance it seems likely that at least some land was distributed, but the case is far from clear. The Caecina family survived, perhaps without any serious losses. C. Curtius, however, a Caesarian senator apparently based at Volaterrae, had suffered an *iniustissima calamitas* under Sulla; although it is not certain that he was of local origin, the *calamitas* probably included material losses at Volaterrae.[5] The land that was proposed for distribution in 63 and 60,[6] that was freed from all danger for ever by Caesar in 59,[7] and that was not only in danger from Caesar but was probably actually distributed by him in 45,[8] was probably land made public by Sulla.

These are the only four specific areas in Etruria where a definite case can be made for Sullan settlement,[9] but land in the

[1] Cic. *Caec.* 102. Assignment of land at Volaterrae under Sulla is generally accepted but thought not to have lasted. According to Gabba, art. cit., 272, it was a not improbable Sullan colony.

[2] Cic. *Dom.* 79: '... ademit eisdem agros. De agris ratum est; fuit enim populi potestas ...'

[3] *Fam.* XIII 4.1, to Q. Valerius Orca, in charge of assignment of land to veterans; perhaps Cicero was referring to an eventual escape.

[4] *Att.* I 19.4.

[5] On this case see *Fam.* XIII 4 and 5.

[6] 63: Cic. *Fam.* XIII 4.1–2; 60: *Att.* I 19.4.

[7] *Fam.* XIII 4.2. Presumably this merely meant that he had decided to omit it from his land law; for Caesar's willingness to give way to particular pressures in this matter see Dio XXXVIII 2.1.

[8] *Fam.* XIII 5.2.

[9] Beloch also gives Cortona as a Sullan colony in Etruria, *It. Bund* 5, 8 (not in *RG*), but Dion. Hal. I 26 is confusing the place with Croton (Mommsen, art. cit., 163 n. 3=205 n. 3).

territory of Populonium, sacked by Sulla, and in the territories of Cosa and Perusia[1] was probably also sold off.

In Umbria, according to Florus,[2] the town of Spoletium came under the hammer, and that may be a confused reference to assignment of land there.[3] When Florus says that 'Interamnium' was auctioned off, however, he is probably not referring to Interamna Nahars in Umbria,[4] but to the Sullan colony of Interamnia Praetuttianorum in Picenum.[5] Another town in Umbria that suffered some losses, including perhaps losses of land, was Tuder, captured by Crassus, who was believed to have taken most of the property for himself and was accused before Sulla.[6] At Ameria Chrysogonus came into the possession of ten sizeable farms, and he probably retained them in spite of the *Pro Roscio Amerino*.

In other parts of Italy Sullan colonists can be detected at Pompeii, Praeneste, Urbana near Capua, probably at Nola, perhaps at Abella (near Nola), and there are a number of still less definite cases.[7]

Some Etruscans lost civil status as well as property. We know

[1] On the estates of the Ahenobarbi at and near Cosa, see below, p. 295. For the murder of a prominent Perusine, Vibius Pansa, see above, p. 254.

[2] II 9.27: 'municipia Italiae splendidissima sub hasta venierunt, Spoletium, Interamnium [*sic*], Praeneste, Florentia.'

[3] Cf. Gabba, art. cit., 272. Spoletium was a Sullan colony according to Beloch *It. Bund* 8, but not in *RG*.

[4] *Pace* Bormann, *CIL* xi. p. 611, Hardie, art. cit., 130; Pais, art. cit., 355, held that land was assigned at Interamna Nahars. On *CIL* i².2510=*ILLRP* 364, which may well refer to Interamna's escape from Sullan confiscation, see C. Cichorius, *Römische Studien* (Berlin–Leipzig, 1922), 185–9, Degrassi in *ILLRP*, cf. L. R. Taylor, *VDRR* 244–5, *MRR Suppl.*, 47. Degrassi now prefers to give the inscription an early imperial date, *Auctarium* (Berlin, 1965), p. 128 (no. 186).

[5] For this colony see *CIL* ix.5074=5075=*ILLRP* 617, Mommsen, art. cit., 166=208, Gabba, art. cit., 235, 271. Florus was evidently not concerned to distinguish colonization from other forms of ill-treatment, since Praeneste was in fact a colony; his statement about Florentia is also probably inaccurate.

[6] Plu. *Crass.* 6. If a particular town is singled out for its participation in the Catilinarian conspiracy, may we not suspect that it had suffered under Sulla? This would add the case of Camerinum to Sulla's victims; that is plausible since it had been specially favoured by Marius.

[7] The first three cases present no problem—see the lists referred to above, p. 260 n. 8. On Nola, see Mommsen, art. cit., 185=226 (although *Lib. Col.* p. 236.3L does not have much independent force). On Abella see Sall. *Hist.* III 97M. Gabba gives Hadria as an 'uncertain' colony, and Forum Cornelii (Cisalpine Gaul), Suessula and Tusculum as 'uncertain' cites of assignment. On the colony at Aleria in Corsica, cf. Gabba, *Athenaeum*, xxix (1951), 20, Badian, *FC* 246. On Venusia see below, p. 271 n. 2.

that Volaterrae and Arretium were deprived of the full Roman citizenship, and it is possible that other towns, for example Clusium and Faesulae, suffered the same. The comment put by Sallust into the mouth of Lepidus—'sociorum et Latii magna vis civitate pro multis et egregiis factis a vobis data per unum prohibentur . . .'[1]—implies that it was a more general measure. More telling is the argument that we know of the cases of Arretium and Volaterrae for particular reasons, because Cicero claimed in the *Pro Caecina* to have established a point of law in the case of the Arretine woman, and because Volaterrae was the town the citizenship of which was in question in the *Pro Caecina* and was in effect established in that case. When he is discussing the impossibility of losing the citizenship in the *De Domo* Cicero mentions only the case of Volaterrae, clearly because it was the one for which he could claim the backing of a legal decision. Thus the fact that we do not hear of the loss of citizenship by other towns does not mean that they did not lose it.

The effects of the Sullan settlement in Etruria were very severe, and they were certainly felt in some Umbrian towns as well. Whatever may have been the possibilities before that Etruria would accept Sulla's government, the settlement necessarily increased and perpetuated local hostility towards Sulla and his system. On the one hand many Etruscans were left with the sole possibility of fighting for the restoration of their property, and that applied to all classes and also to some extent to a number of long-since Romanized Etruscans, such as the younger Perperna and his followers; while on the Roman side it was impossible to dispossess Sulla's veterans, even after Sulla's departure from power, without an immense upheaval. As is often said, Sullan men outlasted the Sullan system, and they retained their property; in the 60s Cicero, and no doubt all but a few other Roman politicians, held that the Sullan veterans should be left in undisturbed possession of their allotments.[2]

There were, however, certainly some who survived the Sullan settlement. The adaptable Philippus was already a Sullan

[1] Sall. *Hist.* I 55.12M.

[2] Cic. *Agr.* III 3 (he says that his opponents have insisted that he wanted to gratify the possessors of Sullan assignments; he replies by pointing out that in fact the Rullan bill does that, not by denying the charge); *Att.* I 19.4.

commander early in 82,[1] and no doubt some of his Etruscan connections benefited from his protection against the Sullan régime. A number of illustrious Etruscan families continued to have a history after Sulla. The Caecinae remained or became again the most influential family at Volaterrae. The Cilnii and Maecenates of Arretium, the Volumnii at Perusia were other families that survived or recovered, no doubt with the help of powerful Roman connections. M. Fulcinius of Tarquinii and presumably other citizens of that town survived apparently unscathed; when Cicero describes the history of that family, clearly going back to a date well before the Sullan war, there is no explicit mention of the Sullan trouble at all. The situation at Ameria was probably repeated at some places in Etruria: some of the Roscii were so definitely on the Sullan side that they were able to safeguard and even to improve their own position. Even after the latest upheaval in Etruria brought about by Octavian, Etruscan names are to be found among the magistrates of Etruscan towns.

3. *The Survival of the Sullan Colonies*

Did the Sullan settlement last? Sulla enacted that land assigned to his veterans should be inalienable,[2] at least for a certain period, but the law was broken.[3] Cicero, speaking against Rullus' proposal in 63, implies that Sullan assignments in general are in the possession of a few men, but such a claim is very much to the advantage of his argument. Ordinary citizens, he says, will get no advantage from the proposed division of the *ager Campanus* because even if they do receive plots and are protected from continuators, *pauci* will take them over, as happened last time there was assignment of land. Conditions at Praeneste, the place specified by Cicero, were not in fact necessarily typical of Sullan colonies,[4] but they were likely to be much

[1] Liv. *Per.* 86.

[2] Inalienability seems to have been a regular feature of agrarian laws, cf. Gabba on App. 9.37.

[3] Cic. *Agr.* II 78: 'ista dena iugera continuabunt. Nam si dicent per legem id non licere, ne per Corneliam quidem licet; at videmus, ut longinqua mittamus, agrum Praenestinum a paucis possideri.'

[4] Although there is rather a lack of specific evidence that Praeneste was villa country for rich Romans before the Empire, cf. H. Dessau, *CIL* xiv. p. 290, G. Radke in *RE* s.v. Praeneste (1954), col. 1550.

better known in Rome than those that prevailed in the others. Cicero also refers to the 'Septimiis, Turraniis ceterisque Sullanorum adsignationum possessoribus', if that is the correct text[1]—in any case there is probably a reference to large-scale holdings of Sullan land. We know of one man in particular who had extensive Sullan possessions south of Rome and perhaps acquired some of them from colonists before 63, namely Valgus, father-in-law of Rullus; he is to be identified with C. Quinctius Valgus, who is attested in many inscriptions.[2] Thus some Sullan settlement failed to last, and this failure is often taken to have been fairly general.[3] A careful analysis of the evidence for the colonies in Etruria shows that that was not the case there. There was an isolated incident at Faesulae in 78 when the colony seems to have given up some of its land to the old inhabitants,[4] but it may have been a temporary concession brought about by the circumstances of Lepidus' revolt. Mazzarino's interpretation of this incident,[5] according to which it shows that the Sullan colonists were 'affascinati dalla tradizione contadina etrusca' and assimilated by the locals—after three years—is sheer fantasy. The other evidence for what happened to the Sullan colonists mostly concerns the Catilinarian rebellion. Some modern writers have stated that the holdings of the Sullan colonists in Etriura had by 63 given way to

[1] *Agr.* III 3. The text given is Madvig's emendation for codd. 'septem tyrannis ceterisque . . .' (*Adversariorum Criticorum* . . . , iii (Copenhagen, 1884), 130). Presumably *tyrannis* was produced by the same word in s. 5. 'Turraniis' is neat (a Turranius was a grazier to whom Varro dedicated *Res Rusticae* ii (praef. 6)); cf. Syme, *Sallust* (Cambridge, 1964), 13 n. 29. But 'Septimiis' has no particular known reference.

[2] He owned much Sullan land (Cic. *Agr.* III 3), including some in the *ager Hirpinus* (II 8) and some at Casinum (III 14). C. Quinctius Valgus, with whom he was first identified by H. Dessau, *Hermes*, xviii (1883), 620–2, was *patronus municipii* at Aeclanum, the chief town of the Hirpini (*CIL* i².1722=*ILLRP* 523) and helped to provide public works at another town (modern Frigento) between Aeclanum and Abellinum (*ILLRP* 598); a freedman of his was buried near Casinum (i².1547=*ILLRP* 565); and Valgus himself was a *duovir*, probably *honoris causa*, at Pompeii (i².1632–3=*ILLRP* 645–6). In face of all this the doubts of H. Gundel in *RE* s.v. Quinctius no. 56 (1963) about the identification are unnecessary.

[3] H. Last, *CAH* ix.302–4, Gabba, *Athenaeum*, xxix (1951), 229–33, cf. P. Brunt, *JRS* lii (1962), 82.

[4] Flemisch reads: 'Hi [complu]ribus occisis agros [e]o[rum] reddiderunt', 'hi' being the Sullan colonists. 'Et compluribus occisis agros suos receperunt' was read in the Bonn edition, p. 45: 'mulieribus occisis' and 'agros captos' were suggested by R. Ellis, *Hermathena*, xiv (1907), 432.

[5] *Historia*, vi (1957), 120.

latifundia.[1] Cicero asserted[2] that the Sullan colonists had been extravagant and therefore were in debt and therefore supported Catiline: he was referring to Etruria among other areas. Similarly Sallust:[3] 'plerique Sullani milites largius suo usi rapinarum et victoriae veteris memores civile bellum exoptabant.' However to be in debt, particularly in the prevailing conditions (Cicero afterwards admitted that the burden of debt had never been greater than in his consulship),[4] was not evidence of particularly incompetent farming; and in any case to be in debt was not to be dispossessed. Sallust indeed does say[5] that some of them had lost their land: 'nonnullos ex Sullanis coloniis, quibus lubido atque luxuria ex magnis rapinis nihil relicui fecerant' (this specifically referring to Etruria). However all these statements about the support given to Catiline by the Sullan colonists have to be treated with great caution; as is argued in detail below, the colonists were of considerable value in anti-Catilinarian invective, and it is not likely in fact that colonists who had lost their farms were the dominant element among Catiline's supporters in Etruria.

In 61 B.C. Octavius as praetor compelled some 'Sullani homines' to give back what they had taken by violence and fear,[6] and in 43 we happen to hear that there was land available for settlement 'ex agris Sullanis'[7]—though in neither case was it necessarily land belonging to colonists that was involved. However, while Sullani continued in uneventful possession of their gains, there was no cause to mention them, and in fact there is other evidence that the colonies survived. *Veteres* and *novi* continue to appear in some of the towns: thus *Clusini veteres* and *novi* in Pliny's town-list, probably referring to the time of Augustus; the *Arretini Fidentiores*, as well as *veteres* and *Iulienses*, also appear on his list, and there is epigraphical evidence for the *Fidentiores* in the first century A.D. Outside

[1] Gabba, art. cit., 232–4. He refers to Cic. *Cat.* II 20, Sall. *Cat.* 16, and to the alleged fact that there was not 'un mutato indirizzo economico' (234).

[2] *Cat.* II 20.

[3] *Cat.* 16.

[4] For the general economic conditions of Italian agriculture at this time see Brunt, art. cit., 73 (not all the difficulties that he mentions applied to Etruria and Umbria). Cic. *Off.* II 84 describes the debt situation in his consulship.

[5] *Cat.* 28.

[6] Cic. *QFr.* I 1.21.

[7] D. Brutus in Cic. *Fam.* XI 20.3.

Etruria there continued to be *veteres* and *novi* also at Nola, for the *veteres* occur in an inscription of the first century A.D.[1] The form of a colony naturally tended to survive, for a colony was privileged by comparison with an ordinary *municipium*[2]—so the mere existence of *duoviri* is no evidence at all that there were any Sullan settlers or descendants of Sullan settlers still in residence; at the time when Cicero tells us that the *ager Praenestinus* was in the hands of a few there was still a colony there.[3] The continuing existence of the distinction *veteres* and *novi* or *veteres* and *Fidentiores* is in fact all the more impressive as evidence for the continuing presence of actual Sullan colonists and their descendants because it outlasted any date at which there can have been two separate communities at Clusium, Arretium, or Nola. There is some evidence that there was a period when *municipium* and *colonia* coexisted at Clusium and at Pompeii;[4] if that had continued to be the case the *Clusini novi* would probably have been local people maintaining the form of a colony. Since the distinction was worth preserving even when a town had a single constitution, it looks as if genuinely differing 'strata' of the population were being distinguished from each other, natives and Sullani. The evidence about the survival of the colonists that comes from Pompeii is fairly clear, and it is reasonable to think that other Sullan colonies developed in a similar way: Sullan settlers were still present in substantial numbers in 62;[5] the name of the dictator continued to appear as a graffito until the last years of the town's existence;[6] so did the names of some Sullan colonists—they tended, it is true, to be absorbed by the local elements (who had a stronger

[1] *CIL* x.1273, 'aetatis ad summum Flaviae', Mommsen, p. 142; offices held at Pompeii are mentioned.

[2] On the preference for the status of a colony cf. Gellius, *Noct. Att.* XVI 13, A. N. Sherwin-White, *Roman Society and Roman Law in the New Testament* (Oxford, 1963), 74–5, etc.

[3] Cic. *Cat.* I 8.

[4] The simultaneous existence of *coloniae* and *municipia* in the same places has been debated. See *CIL* ix.5074=5075=*ILLRP* 617 (Interamnia Praetuttianorum) for an apparent example. It seems likely that the two coexisted for a while at Pompeii, cf. G. O. Onorato, *Rend. Acc. Arch. Nap.*, xxvi (1951), 115–56, against A. Degrassi, *Mem. Acc. Linc.*, ser. 8.ii (1950), 286. It is difficult to think that all the known *quattuorviri* at Clusium (see above, p. 263 n. 4) were earlier than 81.

[5] Cic. *Sull.* 62.

[6] V. Weber, *Historia*, xviii (1969), 376–80.

economic basis than the native population of the Etruscan colonies),[1] but they certainly did not all sell up and depart.[2]

4. *Reaction against the Sullan Settlement*

Three Ciceronian cases were directly concerned with the reaction against the Sullan settlement in Etruria and Umbria, the case of Sex. Roscius of Ameria, the case of the Arretine woman (briefly referred to in the *Pro Caecina*), and the case of A. Caecina. The speeches for Roscius and Caecina both contain much incidental information of interest, but their main importance for this study is their relationship to the Sullan settlement itself.

The case of Sex. Roscius,[3] which was probably tried in 80,[4] concerned a charge of parricide, which according to Cicero was part of a plan made by Chrysogonus and a second faction of Amerian Roscii (T. Roscius Capito and T. Roscius Magnus) to ruin the defendant and deprive him of his property. How strong an attack on the Sullan régime was the *Pro Roscio Amerino*? This familiar question is relevant here because we need to know what measures could be taken against the Sullan settlement, and it is a difficult question, particularly because the published speech evidently differs from the one that was delivered.[5] It should be emphasized—for it is often forgotten—that Sex. Roscius was the defendant and not the plaintiff. The case was begun not on the initiative of Chrysogonus' enemies or of Sulla's, but by Erucius on behalf of Chrysogonus himself. Roscius' purpose was to defend himself on a capital charge, not

[1] Cf. M. L. Gordon, *JRS* xvii (1927), 167.

[2] Note also that sons of probably Sullan centurions were very much in evidence at Venusia during Horace's childhood in the 50s (*Sat.* I 6.71–5, cf. E. Fraenkel, *Horace* (Oxford, 1957), 2–3).

[3] On the facts of the case cf. Drumann–Groebe, *Geschichte Roms*, v (Leipzig, 1919), 249–59.

[4] Gellius, *Noct. Att.* XV 28, gives the date as 80 by the consuls; unfortunately he also gives Cicero's age as twenty-seven, which he did not reach until January 79. The easiest way to resolve the contradiction is to suppose that Gellius' notice derived from a list of consular dates for events in Cicero's life; cf. Badian, *FC* 297. A full bibliography of the question, obscured by Carcopino, is not necessary here; see most recently T. E. Kinsey, *Mnemosyne*, ser. 4.xx (1967), 61–7.

[5] Drumann–Groebe, op. cit., v.258 n. 3, J. Humbert, *Les plaidoyers écrits et les plaidoiries réelles de Cicéron* (Paris [1925]), 100–11, E. Gabba, *Ann. Scuola Norm. Sup. di Pisa*, xxxiii (1964), 10–11, E. Gruen, *Roman Politics and the Criminal Courts, 149–78* B.C. (Cambridge, Mass., 1968), 268, etc.

to make a political point or even to recover his inheritance. Cicero claimed much later that he had shown courage on this occasion by attacking Sulla,[1] but the speech ostensibly exculpates Sulla himself at every opportunity[2]—he did not know what his minions were doing, a failing he shared with Jupiter[3]—and concentrates its attack on Chrysogonus.[4] Thus if the speech was an attack on Sulla it was an indirect one. It is true that the speech portrays the régime in an extremely hostile way—'propter iniquitatem temporum', 'tametsi non modo ignoscendi ratio, verum etiam cognoscendi consuetudo iam de civitate sublata est', 'ea crudelitas quae hoc tempore in re publica versata est', 'cum omnibus horis aliquid atrociter fieri videmus aut audimus'.[5] These passages would, however, if delivered have been both impolitic and unnecessary, for even if Sulla could be dissociated from Chrysogonus he could not be dissociated from the general condition of the state. It is surely likely that they were altered or added at some later date when the speech was being prepared for publication, and such remarks about the Sullan régime were in order;[6] this conclusion can be accepted more easily because many of the passages concerned are concentrated at the beginning and end of the speech. Furthermore Chrysogonus himself was not as important as is sometimes suggested—'adulescens vel potentissimus hoc tempore nostrae civitatis'[7] does not tell us so very much, and except in references obviously derived from Cicero[8] we never hear of him (he is not mentioned in Plutarch's life of Sulla).[9] Even when we reduce the scale of Cicero's attack to something like its actual size (we cannot tell exactly what he did say), the speech

[1] *Off.* II 51: 'Maxime autem et gloria paritur et gratia defensionibus eoque maior, si quando accidit, ut ei subveniatur, qui potentis alicuius opibus circumveniri urgerique videatur, ut nos et saepe alias et adulescentes contra L. Sullae dominantis opes pro Sex Roscio Amerino fecimus . . .' The speech is mentioned without reference to this political aspect in *Brut.* 312, *Or.* 107.

[2] E.g. *Rosc. Am.* 21–2, 25–6, 91, 110, 130–1.

[3] But this sarcasm (*Rosc. Am.* 131) was surely not in the original version, Gabba, art. cit., 10–11.

[4] *Rosc. Am.* 6–7 and *passim*.

[5] *Rosc. Am.* 1, 3, 150, 154—the whole of the final section of the speech is concerned with the cruelty of the times.

[6] Cf. Humbert, op. cit., 101–3, Gabba, art. cit., 10–11.

[7] *Rosc. Am.* 6.

[8] Plu. *Cic.* 3.2, Plin. *NH* XXXV 200, etc.

[9] For this view cf. A. Afzelius, *C & M* v (1942), 213–14.

can hardly have been pleasing to Sulla,[1] but he probably was not making a strong direct attack on Sulla himself.

Much has sometimes been made of the support given to Cicero's client by the *nobilitas*,[2] but their behaviour was ambiguous.[3] Some of its members seem to have sided with Chrysogonus.[4] The other *patroni* of the good Roscius besides Cicero were a woman, Caecilia Metella, daughter of Balearicus and wife of Ap. Claudius Pulcher (consul in 79), and the *adulescens* M. Valerius Messalla.[5] Cicero speaks grandly of the Metelli, Servilii, and Scipiones as having been the friends of the defendant's father,[6] but unfortunately we do not know whether these families were really active in the case. At the beginning of the speech a great number of *nobilissimi homines* are said to be silently present in court on the side of Roscius,[7] but at the end it is admitted that they would have been present in court had it not been for present conditions;[8] they do not dare to speak, Cicero explains, 'propter iniquitatem temporum', 'quia periculum vitant', because if any of them spoke he would be thought to have said much more than he had said.[9] The extent to which the *adulescentes* P. Scipio and Q. Metellus committed themselves to the cause of Roscius is also left unclear.[10] The leaders of the *nobilitas* conspicuously failed to exert themselves on his behalf, presumably to avoid a major conflict with Sulla. No fundamental point of law was made against the Sullan settlement in Roscius' case, as later happened in the *Pro Caecina*; but it was shown that if the Roman connections of a municipal family

[1] Afzelius, art. cit., 216, goes too far in denying this.

[2] See especially Afzelius, art. cit., 214–17, Badian, *FC* 247–50.

[3] Cf. E. Ciaceri, *AIV* lxxix (1919–20), 545–6, Gabba, art. cit., 11–12, Gruen, op. cit., 268–71, who, however, believes that 'the Metellan family's protection of Roscius was demonstrated in conspicuous fashion' (266).

[4] *Rosc. Am.* 140; cf. Gabba, art. cit., 11–12.

[5] Cos. 61 or cos. 53? On Caecilia see above, p. 229 n. 1.

[6] *Rosc. Am.* 15.

[7] *Rosc. Am.* 1.

[8] *Rosc. Am.* 148.

[9] *Rosc. Am.* 1–2. The passages about the support of the *nobilitas* for Roscius may also have been altered in editing, especially as most of them are at the beginning or the end of the speech.

[10] *Rosc. Am.* 77: 'Te nunc appello, P. Scipio, te, ⟨Q.⟩ Metelle; vobis advocatis, vobis agentibus aliquotiens duos servos paternos in quaestionem ab adversariis Sex. Roscius postularit...' (cf. 119, when the social position of those who made the request is emphasized); it looks as if their interest in the case had declined at some point.

were sufficient, and if the particular agent of the Sullan régime who had attacked the municipal family was unimportant enough, the Roman courts could under Sulla's second consulship give protection against certain injustices that resulted from Sulla's own actions. However, as has been said, the case was defensive and it is most unlikely that the younger Roscius recovered his property.[1] It is important to assess the weight of the case correctly: it did not endanger Sulla's position, it did not force him to make any fundamental concession and although it showed that Italians could still be protected by their Roman *patroni* it was protection against a rather vulnerable oppressor—an attack on those noble supporters of Sulla who had profited from the proscriptions would hardly have succeeded.[2] No doubt much of the *nobilitas* was pleased to see humbled a freedman who had pretensions above his rank and had interfered in an Italian town, but there were other profiteers more firmly in possession of their gains.

Cicero said that his defence of the Arretine woman[3] took place 'Sulla vivo'[4] but, he thereby implied, not when Sulla was in office—thus probably in 79 or 78.[5] He also implied later that the speech was another attack on the Sullan settlement[6] and it has been suggested that it in fact took more courage to deliver it than to deliver the *Pro Roscio Amerino*.[7] For our evidence about what took place we are entirely dependent on these two passages of Cicero. In his argument in the *Pro Caecina* about

[1] Cf. T. E. Kinsey, *Mnemosyne*, ser. 4.xix (1966), 270–1.

[2] Gruen, op. cit., 271, seems to me to go too far in saying that the case was a victory over profiteers in general. T. A. Dorey, *Ciceroniana*, ii (1960), 147–8, suggested that the speech was, *inter alia*, an attack on Crassus, who had behaved like Chrysogonus at Tuder and was on bad terms with Metellus Pius (Plu. *Crass.* 6); but to suggest that it was this attack that made Sulla refuse to give Crassus any further public position (ibid.) is to misunderstand the purpose of the speech.

[3] On this see F. Desserteaux in *Mélanges Gérardin* (Paris, 1907), 181–196= *Études sur la formation historique de la capitis deminutio*, i (Dijon, 1909), 195–211, G. Franciosi, *Il processo di libertà in diritto romano* (Naples, 1961), 40–3, and the works on the citizenship issue in the *Pro Caecina* listed below, p. 278 n. 1; cf. Drumann–Groebe, op. cit., v. 259–60.

[4] *Caec.* 97.

[5] Not when Sulla was in office, R. Heinze, *Abh. K. Sächs. Gesell. Wiss., Phil.-hist. Kl.*, xxvii (1909), 966; Desserteaux's suggestion of 81, *Mélanges Gérardin*, 188 n. 1, is much less likely.

[6] *Dom.* 79.

[7] Afzelius, art. cit., 216.

the impossibility of losing the citizenship, Cicero suggests that if citizenship could be taken away, so could *libertas*:

Qui enim potest iure Quiritium liber esse is qui in numero Quiritium non est? Atque ego hanc adulescentulus causam cum agerem contra hominem disertissimum nostrae civitatis, C. Cottam, probavi. Cum Arretinae mulieris libertatem defenderem et Cotta Xviris religionem iniecisset non posse nostrum sacramentum iustum iudicari, quod Arretinis adempta civitas esset, et ego vehementius contendissem civitatem adimi non posse, Xviri prima actione non iudicaverunt; postea re quaesita et deliberata sacramentum nostrum iustum iudicaverunt.

In *De Domo*, again arguing that the citizenship cannot be lost voluntarily, Cicero refers to Sulla's law that took the citizenship away from various *municipia*, and says that the law did not outlast 'illa Sullani temporis arma'. A woman of Arretium had somehow become enslaved,[1] and a *vindicatio in libertatem* was undertaken on her behalf.

What precisely was established in the case of the Arretine woman, and how much difference did it make to the Sullan settlement? It is clear that the Sullan law depriving certain municipalities of the citizenship did in fact outlast both Cicero's defence of the Arretine woman and Sulla's death. They can hardly have been in secure possession of it at the time of Philippus' speech in 77,[2] or indeed at the time of the *Pro Caecina*, although Cicero asserts otherwise.[3] It is not likely that Cicero did demonstrate beyond any doubt in the defence of the Arretine woman that the Lex Cornelia was invalid. It is conceivable that the *decemviri stlitibus iudicandis* decided only that it was possible in fact to lose the citizenship and still retain *libertas* of a sort;[4] more probably they decided that the Arretine woman was *ex iure Quiritium libera*, since the form of the *sacramentum* of an *adsertor libertatis* seems to have been, when it was made before the *decemviri*, 'hunc ego hominem ex iure Quiritium

[1] It is possible to speculate about obscurity in her status resulting from her status in the previous Etruscan system.

[2] Sall. *Hist.* I 77.14M: 'Lepidus . . . placere ait . . . civitatem confirmari, quibus ademptam negat.'

[3] *Caec.* 97, cf. 18.

[4] Suggested by G. Pugliese in *Atti del Congr. internaz. di diritto romano e di storia del diritto* (Verona, 1948, publ. Milan, 1951), ii. 70–1.

liberum esse aio'.[1] However some competent lawyers continued to maintain that Arretium and Volaterrae had really lost the citizenship, for Piso so argued against Cicero in Caecina's case in 69, and Cicero could not deal with the point in a few words, but had to argue it at length. In any case in order to restore the citizenship to the *municipia* that had lost it, something more than the judgement in the case of the Arretine woman was required, a *senatus consultum* or censors who were willing to register the Arretini and Volaterrani, and during the 70s neither was available. Thus the practical results of the defence of the Arretine woman were not very great. From Cicero's point of view, he had undertaken to vindicate the rights of a member of an Etruscan community that had suffered severely from the Sullan settlement, and the case will have helped Cicero along the course that he had taken in the *Pro Quinctio* and *Pro Roscio Amerino* of seeking the support of Italians who had suffered indirectly from Sulla, at a time when few Roman politicians were concerned to offer such help.

The case which was really crucial to the restoration of the citizen rights of Volaterrae and Arretium was Caecina's case in 69; but it was the political circumstances beyond the control of Cicero that determined that it would not be merely a forensic triumph. The facts of the case, as they are given in Cicero's version, were as follows.[2] M. Fulcinius of Tarquinii, who was an *argentarius* at Rome, married Caesennia, also of Tarquinii; with the dowry he bought a farm at Tarquinii, and later when he retired from banking he bought more land there. When he died he left the joint usufruct of all his land to his wife and his son, also M. Fulcinius, who, however, died shortly afterwards. In his will the latter divided his property between the actual *heres* P. Caesennius, his own wife, and his mother, the last of whom received most of it. The estate of the younger Fulcinius was auctioned in Rome, and Caesennia on the advice of her friends and relations decided, it was alleged, to buy the farm near her own Tarquinian property and entrusted the buying to

[1] G. Franciosi, op. cit., 146–7, cf. A. Watson, *The Law of Persons in the Later Republic* (Oxford, 1967), 220–1.

[2] What follows is a summary of *Caec.* 10–23; cf. A. H. J. Greenidge, *Legal Procedure of Cicero's Time* (Oxford, 1901), 556–68, Drumann–Groebe, op. cit., v.358–67, M. Gelzer, *KS* i (Wiesbaden, 1962), 305–11.

Aebutius. Aebutius bought the farm, but in his own name; and it was disputed in the case whether Caesennia had paid Aebutius for it or not. In any case Caesennia, either as a result of the usufruct inherited from her husband or as a result of the purchase possessed the farm and let it out; shortly after the supposed purchase she married her second husband, A. Caecina. Four years after the purchase she died, leaving to her husband 69/72 of her property, to a freedman of her first husband 2/72, and to Aebutius 1/72. Aebutius claimed, as he later did in court, that Caecina could not inherit because he was not a Roman citizen, having lost the Roman citizenship as a citizen of the town of Volaterrae; and he also claimed that the farm was his own in any case, and took legal proceedings to recover it from Caecina, though one of the issues disputed was about which one of them was legally in possession of the farm. Aebutius at some point came into physical possession of the farm; Caecina successfully applied to the praetor P. Dolabella for an interdict, and subsequently challenged Aebutius to a *sponsio*; this was the case before the *recuperatores*. It was one of the grounds put forward by Aebutius in defence that Caecina could never have possessed the farm because having lost the citizenship he could not inherit it.[1]

In order to refute Aebutius' contention that Caecina had been disqualified from inheriting from Caesennia, Cicero put forward two arguments. First, Sulla had added to the law that deprived the Volaterrani of the citizenship the *adscriptio* 'SI QUID IUS NON ESSET ROGARIER, EIUS EA LEGE NIHILUM ROGATUM', and according to the existing *ius* no one could lose the Roman citizenship against his will.[2] His second reply to Aebutius was that Sulla had in fact left the Volaterrani with the *ius Ariminensium* or *ius duodecim coloniarum* and that that was sufficient for Caecina to be able to inherit.

Cicero's argument concerning the impossibility of losing the citizenship, which is here given in its fullest form,[3] was as

[1] There was a particular incentive for Aebutius to use the argument that Caecina could not inherit at all, for if he could prove it he would receive a vastly greater amount for himself under Caesennia's will; cf. Greenidge, op. cit., 560.

[2] *Caec.* 95–102.

[3] Also in *Dom.* 78–9; on which cf. Desserteaux, *Études*, etc., 211–16.

follows.[1] There must be something that the people cannot command or forbid, otherwise the usual *adscriptio* would not be added; for example, it cannot order me, a free man, to be your slave, or vice versa. Cicero claims that his opponent concedes here that the people cannot legally enact whatever it wishes; 'deinde nihil rationis adfers quamobrem, si libertas adimi nullo modo possit, civitas possit.' For the tradition is the same concerning the two things, and if once *civitas* can be taken away, *libertas* cannot be retained. 'Qui enim potest iure Quiritium liber esse is qui in numero Quiritium non est?' There follows his description of the case of the Arretine woman. He also claims that 'in ceteris rebus' everyone who was in the same condition of having lost the citizenship by Sulla's law actually enjoyed the full rights of a citizen without any doubt whatsoever being cast on them. He then discusses the exceptions to the principle that citizenship cannot be lost. Some were cases in which it was given up voluntarily or to avoid a *legis multa* (Latin colonists);[2] in others it was done 'ut religione civitas solvatur' (when a man was handed over to a foreign state by the *pater patratus*—and in such cases if a man was refused by the foreign state he remained a Roman citizen); in another type of case, a man could be sold if it was by the volition of the *paterfamilias* in whose *potestas* he was; in others the people did not take away a man's *libertas* but declared that he had himself repudiated it—if he had evaded military service or the census; again, in the case of those who went into exile, 'non adimitur iis civitas, sed ab iis relinquitur atque deponitur'.[3] Before dealing in full with exiles, who did not lose the citizenship until they took that of a federated state,[4] Cicero puts forward his crowning argument:[5] 'Quod si maxime hisce rebus adimi libertas aut civitas potest, non intellegunt, qui haec commemorant, si per has rationes maiores adimi posse voluerunt, alio modo noluisse.' He claims that there had never been any law or *rogatio* by which *civitas* or *libertas* had been taken away.

[1] On this much has been written. The important works are Mommsen, *Römisches Staatsr.*, iii.43, 146, and in *Juristische Abhandlungen, Festgabe für G. Beseler* (Berlin, 1885), 253–72, Desserteaux, op. cit., Pugliese, art. cit., M. Kaser, *Iura*, iii (1952), 48–89, esp. 74–5.

[2] Cf. *Dom.* 78: Latin colonists gave up the citizenship voluntarily.

[3] *Caec.* 100.

[4] Cf. *Dom.* 78.

[5] *Caec.* 99–100.

As regards the force of the *adscriptio*, it seems that although it was regularly inserted into laws, the actual use of it to invalidate a law was a most unusual proceeding, since Cicero had to argue that the existence of the clause meant that there must be something that the people could not lay down by law. Mommsen[1] objected that Cicero's view of the *adscriptio* meant in effect that any law whatsoever could be invalidated, but without discussing in full the relationship between laws and the *ius civile* one can surely say that if Cicero could show that according to *ius* the citizenship could not be lost involuntarily, the Lex Cornelia was in fact invalid.[2] Evidently it was not universally or even widely believed that it was invalid before the *Pro Caecina*, but Cicero's argument has—thus far—considerable force.

Did *ius* contain the principle that the citizenship could not be lost involuntarily? Cicero argues this partly by saying that it was not within the power of the *populus* to deprive a man of *libertas*, and so citizenship could not be lost either. To this it could be replied that while a man who lost the citizenship did not retain *libertas ex iure Quiritium*, he might have been regarded as retaining another form of *libertas*. There were many non-slaves who did not have *libertas ex iure Quiritium*, Latins and indeed *peregrini* whose states had made *foedera* with Rome. These people did have *libertas* in the sense that they were not slaves, and the *libertas* of *foederati* was guaranteed by their *foedera*.[3] Cicero further argues that there are no cases in which the citizenship is lost in a truly involuntary way, except some that were created by the *ius civile* and not by laws of the people. To show that all these cases were really voluntary, or created by the *ius civile*, required some sophistry.[4] Those who were dis-

[1] *Römisches Staatsr.*, iii.43 n. 2.

[2] To accept this it is not necessary to accept the view of Rotondi, now apparently losing ground among Romanists (cf. S. Di Paola, *Synteleia V. Arangio-Ruiz* (Naples, 1964), ii. 1075), that it was completely forbidden to modify the *ius civile* by a *lex*.

[3] Cf. Cic. *Balb.* 21; cf. Liv. XXVI 34.6–7. According to Kaser, art. cit., 75, those who were free in this sense but not Roman citizens were protected by Roman *fides* against, for example, attempts at enslavement; but provincials could be claimed as free before the *recuperatores* (Cic. *Flacc.* 40).

[4] Cf. E. Levy, *ZSS* lxxviii (1961), 153. These ways of losing the citizenship were discussed by Mommsen in *Römisches Staatsr.*, iii.43–53, who accepted Cicero's view that the citizenship could not be lost involuntarily.

enfranchised by the state for failure to do military service or to register in the census are said to have repudiated the citizenship voluntarily, but the Volaterrani and Arretini who resisted Sulla when he regarded his government as the legally constituted one could easily have been portrayed as having 'voluntarily' repudiated the Roman citizenship. As for the case of the man who was surrendered by the *pater patratus* to a foreign state,[1] he is plainly singled out for involuntary expulsion from the state. He is saving the state from a *religio*, true; when he is accepted, 'est eorum quibus est deditus', true; if he is rejected he retains his Roman citizenship, true; but none of these things alters the fundamental situation. So there was in fact such a thing as involuntary loss of the Roman citizenship.[2] As for the argument that such exceptions were created by the *ius civile*, which created the general principle of the impossibility of involuntarily losing the citizenship, and therefore there could be no other exceptions, that also contains difficulties—was it really the *ius civile* that laid down the rules concerning the loss of citizenship by Latin colonists?

There was a final argument that Cicero used to show that Caecina could inherit, namely that even Sulla did not take away the right of inheritance from the penalized *municipia*—'Sulla ipse ita tulit de civitate ut non sustulerit horum nexa atque hereditates. Iubet enim eodem iure esse quo fuerint Ariminenses, quos quis ignorat duodecim coloniarum fuisse et a civibus Romanis hereditates capere potuisse?' That is all—Cicero then turns to the rhetoric of his peroration. It is not to the point here to identify the twelve colonies—but did they have the right of inheriting from Roman citizens?[3] If it was definitely the case that the Volaterrani had the *ius Ariminensium* (so-called) and that that included the right to inherit from Roman citizens, Cicero's long section on the impossibility of losing the citizenship was completely unnecessary. Yet it was normal enough in forensic oratory to cover oneself by means of such double

[1] Cicero gives the surrender of Mancinus to the Numantines in 137 as an example; it was done *ex s.c.*, *De Or.* I 181.

[2] Cf. Pugliese, art. cit., 70–2, who comments (not always accurately) on the doubtful validity of Cicero's arguments on this point.

[3] The best discussion of the status of these colonies is that of A. N. Sherwin-White, *RC* 96–8; see also A. Bernardi in *Studi giuridici in memoria di P. Ciapessoni* (*Studia Ghisleriana I*) (Pavia, 1948), 237–59.

defences,[1] and Cicero's straightforward statement cannot reasonably be doubted. There may perhaps have been some marginal obscurity, but since this passage is our only direct evidence for this category of Latins, we are not likely to be able to confirm that they had the right of inheriting from Roman citizens. Ordinary holders of the Latin right had the *ius commercii*, which generally meant that they could inherit from Roman citizens, though later there were some obstacles in the way of inheritance by Junian Latins.[2] There is no reason to think that the twelve colonies were less privileged than other Latin colonies,[3] and Cicero's statement about them must be accepted. What this passage does suggest is that the argument about the impossibility of losing the citizenship was given at such length not merely for the purposes of the case in hand but for more political reasons.[4]

The date of the *Pro Caecina* was probably 69. The praetorship of P. Dolabella, who presided at the trial,[5] cannot be dated with certainty. His subsequent governorship of Asia must have succeeded that of Lucullus, which ended in 69,[6] and the case must have been heard before the consulship of C. Piso, Aebutius' counsel, in 67. 69 and 68 are possible years for Dolabella's praetorship,[7] and so is 70, for Lucullus may have been displaced very early in 69, and it is hard to see the Senate leaving Asia without a governor during that year. Caecina's cause is generally assumed to have won, and Cicero's later laudatory reference to the speech makes that probable.[8] It was necessary for the case, but also politically advantageous for Caecina and his fellow-townsmen, that any doubts about the

[1] Cf. Quintil. *Inst.* VII 3.6 for example.

[2] W. Buckland–P. Stein, *A Text-Book of Roman Law from Augustus to Justinian*[3] (Cambridge, 1963), 292.

[3] Pointed out by Sherwin-White, l.c.; cf. F. K. Von Savigny, *Vermischte Schriften* (Berlin, 1850), i.21–5, iii.298, 301.

[4] Cf. Cic. *Caec.* 101.

[5] *Caec.* 23.

[6] Dio XXXVI 2.2: he says that the province of Asia was restored to the praetors in that year.

[7] Greenidge, op. cit., 557, Gelzer in *RE* s.v. Tullius no. 29 (1939), col. 853, *MRR* ii.139, 142 n. 9.

[8] *Or.* 102: 'Tota mihi causa pro Caecina de verbis interdicti fuit: res involutas definiendo explicavimus, ius civile laudavimus, verba ambigua distinximus.' Cf. V. Arangio-Ruiz in *Marco Tullio Cicerone, Scritti di L. Alfonsi*, etc. (Florence, 1961), 203.

validity of Volaterran citizenship should be removed. As one of the leading citizens of the town, as indeed one of the leading men of Etruria,[1] Caecina was able to arouse more interest in his favour than any of the others who had been deprived of the citizenship, and it seems that the Caecina family may have got off fairly lightly from the Sullan war. We happen to know that the younger Servilius Isauricus was *patronus* of Caecina's son in 45;[2] the connection between the two families may well have been formed during or before the Sullan war,[3] and Servilius Vatia's influence (he changed his mind in Pompey's favour at an important moment in 79)[4] was probably helpful in 69. The census of 70–69 had surely not been completed before the case was heard—otherwise there would have been some mention of it in *Pro Caecina*, sections 95–102, for although registration by the censors was not technically complete proof of citizenship, whatever the censors had or had not done would necessarily have had some importance. The censors presumably acted in agreement with the decision of the court in the *Pro Caecina* and accepted the registration of the Volaterrani and probably of the Arretini and any others who had suffered under the Lex Cornelia. There is no evidence that the passing of the Lex Cornelia was ever declared illegal in any other way,[5] or that the situation of its victims was only resolved by the Lex Papia of 65.[6] Pompey must have been willing to assist Italians who could be assisted without altering those features of the Sullan

[1] 'Amplissimo totius Etruriae nomine', *Caec.* 104; their importance is confirmed explicitly by *Fam.* VI 6.9, and by the epigraphical and archaeological evidence, referred to by G. Radke in *RE* s.v. Volaterrae (1961), cols. 736–7; they appear not only at Volaterrae and Tarquinii, but also in office at Volsinii, *CIL* i².2515= *ILLRP* 438; Caecinia at Clusium in this period (i².2027) is no doubt a connection.

[2] Cic. *Fam.* XIII 66.1.

[3] The elder Isauricus was probably one of the two Servilii who were Sullan commanders in 82; cf. *MRR* ii.72 and 74 n. 10. As consul in 79 he was partly responsible for the murder of the proscribed who were forced to leave Volaterrae ('et proscriptos ex oppido dimiserunt, quos equites a consulibus Claudio et Servilio missi conciderunt', Gran. Licin. 32F).

[4] Concerning Pompey's first triumph, Plu. *Pomp.* 14, cf. Frontin. *Strat.* IV 5.1.

[5] I can see no real evidence for the view of G. Tibiletti, *SDHI* xxv (1959), 121 n. 104, and others, that the regulations 'were finally repealed (not declared illegal)'.

[6] Under the law a *quaestio* was probably set up to deal with questions of citizenship, cf. Desserteaux, *Mélanges*, etc., 193 n. 1, E. Weiss in *RE* s.v. *Lex Papia* (1925).

system that were to remain.[1] He realized the political potential of the Italians and assisted the new citizens to become a force at Rome for the first time; for these ends he was prepared to adopt a policy of conciliation (now that it seemed quite safe to do so) even to those who had fought against him and the Sullan settlement in general. The policy was effective, and A. Caecina's son was a loyal Pompeian in the Civil War, together with many other Volaterrans, to judge from the land-distributions there in 45. The limits of the usefulness of such support became painfully clear in the Civil War; one of the reasons for this was surely that while all had been relatively well for those Italians who had been able to protect themselves from the Sullan settlement, there were many in Etruria and elsewhere who never recovered by far the most important of the things that they had lost, namely their property. Pompey's conciliation could never be more than partial.

Cicero's political purpose is made fairly explicit in this section of the *Pro Caecina*: he has spoken at undue length,

> verum id feci, non quo vos hanc in hac causa defensionem desiderare arbitrarer, sed ut omnes intellegerent nec ademptam cuiquam civitatem esse neque adimi posse. Hoc cum eos scire volui quibus Sulla voluit iniuriam facere, tum omnes ceteros novos veteresque civis. Neque enim ratio adferri potest cur, si cuiquam novo civi potuerit adimi civitas, non omnibus patriciis, omnibus antiquissimis civibus possit.[2]

This was surely an appeal to the censors to regularize the standing of all the *municipia* that had lost the citizenship. The cause could be portrayed as the cause of all the new citizens, indeed of all citizens whatsoever; it was a sophistry, but in the first case at least it was a good and eminently topical point. In those towns that were affected by the restoration of the citizen rights Cicero must have become a powerful political influence, as we know that he was by the 60s at Volaterrae.[3] Intelligent

[1] On Pompey's break with his Sullan past before and during 70 see M. Gelzer, *Abh. Preuss. Ak. Wiss.*, 1943 no. 1, 3–10=*KS* ii.146–53, Badian, *FC* 279–84, Taylor, *VDRR* 120.

[2] *Caec.* 101.

[3] *Fam.* XIII 4.1 (45 B.C.): 'Cum municipibus Volaterranis mihi summa necessitudo est. Magno enim meo beneficio adfecti, cumulatissime mihi gratiam rettulerunt; nam nec in honoribus meis nec in laboribus umquam defuerunt', etc.

co-operation with Pompey strengthened his Italian following still further.

There is some incidental information that emerges from Cicero's speech that is of importance, and that is the apparently high degree of Romanization of the Etruscans concerned. They are of course those of the highest class, and the centre of the case is Tarquinii, clearly more exposed to Roman influence than most Etruscan towns were. The families concerned were perhaps more Romanized than most at Tarquinii, the elder Fulcinius having actually carried on business in Rome (apparently in the mid-80s and probably earlier). As far as we can tell the Fulcinii and Caesennii and Caecina were fully at home in the procedures of Roman law, following in full the usual rules concerning wills and the suit itself.[1] The ex-confidant and agent of Caesennia was Aebutius, probably a Roman and not a Tarquinian,[2] and although the *heres* of the younger Fulcinius was one P. Caesennius, a Tarquinian, it was decided to hold the sale of the former's property at Rome rather than at Tarquinii.[3] It would be interesting to know how many of Aebutius' named witnesses[4] were also based at Tarquinii. They were the witnesses of the armed struggle that took place between the two parties at Castellum Axii in the territory of Tarquinii, but they all seem to have straightforwardly Roman names, with the exception of Fidiculanius Falcula.[5]

Many Etruscans went to Spain under the Sullan régime, and many others when the opportunity arose tried to recover their losses by force. In M. Lepidus, the consul of 78, those who had lost land but stayed in Etruria found a champion.[6] The surviving speech attributed to him by Sallust is a rhetorical confection,[7] but it does not seem to misrepresent his position. He

[1] *Caec.* 11–13. On the authentically Tarquinian origin of the Fulcinii cf. M. Cristofani, *Mem. Acc. Linc.*, ser.8.xiv (1969), 253.

[2] Aebutius was a well-established Roman name by the early second century at least.

[3] *Caec.* 15.

[4] *Caec.* 24–8.

[5] The *colonus* of *Caec.* 94 raises a further point of interest, for it is tempting to think that his status developed from that of the old serf class—though *coloni* were beginning to appear in other areas of Italy in this period, cf. P. Brunt, *JRS* lii (1962), 71 n. 31.

[6] Sall. *Hist.* I 67M: 'tunc vero Etrusci cum ceteris eiusdem causae ducem se nactos rati maximo gaudio bellum irritare.'

[7] R. Syme, *Sallust* (Cambridge, 1964), 185–6.

complains that the Italians have been deprived of their votes and the plebs of their land. It was Lepidus' policy to advocate the restoration of land confiscated by Sulla,[1] he advocated the restoration of the citizenship to those Italians who had lost it,[2] and he may also have wanted to rescind all the acts of Sulla.[3] Sallust puts *Etrusci* in general among his supporters, and 'Etruria omnis cum Lepido suspecta in tumultum erat'.[4] Etruria is the only area of Italy specified by Philippus in his speech as being rebellious.[5] How wide Lepidus' support in Etruria must have been we can see from the fact that his main military engagement with the government took place in a very forward position from his point of view, in fact in the outskirts of Rome.[6] The only other geographical indication that we have concerning the rebellion is that the dispossessed at Faesulae extracted concessions from the Sullan colonists[7]—this was surely during the turmoil created by Lepidus. Some Etruscans of all classes probably followed him—Etruscans of all classes had suffered from Sulla, and of the two senators whom we know to have followed him one was the younger M. Perperna, who probably returned from Spain to join him.

The defeat outside Rome was followed by another at Cosa or nearby.[8] The force that Lepidus took with him to Sardinia must have formed the bulk of the large one that Perperna took to Spain after Lepidus' death. There Perperna joined Sertorius with a force that Plutarch puts at fifty-three cohorts,[9] say 25,000 to 30,000 men, usually but unnecessarily dismissed as an exaggeration.[10] It is not to be supposed that this army was

[1] App. 107.501, Gran. Licin. 33F. Cf. Philippus' reference to the loyalty of the 'coloniae veterum militum', Sall. *Hist.* I 77.21.

[2] *Oratio Philippi*, Sall. *Hist.* I 77.14, cf. I 65.

[3] On Lepidus' plans cf. Gabba on App. 107.501, Syme, op. cit., 186–7.

[4] *Hist.* I 67, 69.

[5] 'Etruriam coniurare', *Hist.* I 77.6, 'Etruria atque omnes reliquiae belli arrectae', ibid. 8; cf. Flor. II 11.5.

[6] App. 107.504, Florus II 11.6.

[7] See above, p. 268.

[8] Cf. Sall. *Hist.* I 82, Exuperant. 6, Rutilius Namatianus I 297–8.

[9] *Sert.* 15.

[10] Dismissed by Drumann-Groebe, op. cit., iv.369–70, on the grounds that with such an army P. would have been able to take over Sardinia (on the fighting there see Ascon. 29C)—but there is no need to think that that was or should have been his aim. It was not without a sizeable army that Perperna fought the close battle near Cosa (Exuperant. 6).

an exclusively Etruscan one—it will have contained others of the dispossessed and proscribed—but the Etruscans were strongly attached to Lepidus,[1] and we can infer from the later importance of the Romans of Etruscan origin on Sertorius' staff that there was a massive emigration of Etruscans, following the one that had gone with Sertorius in 82.

The army of Lepidus and Perperna was added to that of Sertorius, whether Perperna was entirely willing or not.[2] Among Sertorius' officers in Spain a number are to be found who are of Etruscan origins,[3] and it is likely that they arrived with Perperna,[4] as neither of the names of Sertorius' known previous officers seems Etruscan and all those who were Etruscan joined later in the conspiracy against him.[5] In Sertorius' company we find besides Perperna himself a Maecenas, C. Tarquitius Priscus, and a Versius.[6] The Etruscan connections of Tarquitius are beyond reasonable doubt,[7] though his exact relationship to the other attested Tarquitii is unknown;[8] the Etruscan origin of Versius[9] is rather specula-

[1] Sall. *Hist.* I 67.

[2] According to Plu. *Sert.* 15, Perperna showed some reluctance and was forced to take the step by his own troops; otherwise App. 113.527. Plutarch's life is extremely hostile to Perperna. He may have claimed to bargain for the command, cf. P. Treves, *Athenaeum*, x (1932), 145.

[3] Syme, *RR* 129 n. 4; cf. Gabba, *Athenaeum*, xxxii (1954), 313.

[4] So Gabba, art. cit., 311.

[5] Sertorius' early commanders: (? Iulius) Salinator, *MRR* ii.78; two Hirtuleii, *MRR* ii.83, 87, *Suppl.* 28–9. On the date of the conspiracy (73 rather than 72) see W. Bennett, *Historia*, x (1961), 459–69.

[6] Maecenas: Sall. *Hist.* III 83; Tarquitius: Sall. *Hist.* III 81, 83, Diod. XXXVII 22 (the full name is from Frontinus, *Strat.* II 5.31); Versius: Sall. *Hist.* III 83.

[7] Cf. Tarquitius Priscus, the expert on *disciplina*, as well as the number of inscriptions from Etruria weighed against the very few from other areas. The most important inscriptions are *CIL* xi.3370 (restored), 7566 (Tarquinii), 2454 (Clusium), 3630, 3634 (cf. 3626–9, 3631–3, and addenda, and 7593–5, with Bormann's note) (Caere), 3801, 3805, 3840, cf. 3802, 3804, 7747 (Veii), 4004 (Capena), 3253 (Sutrium). Cf. Schulze, *ZGLE* 96, 126, J. Heurgon, *Latomus*, xii (1953), 407 n. 5 (arguing for Tarquinian origin).

[8] See Cichorius, *Römische Studien* (Berlin–Leipzig, 1922), 167–8. He may be C. Tarquitius L.f.Fal. (*RE* no. 8), a member of Pompeius Strabo's *consilium* (*ILS* 8888) (it is no obstacle that this man was in a tribe that contained none of the Etruscan towns—some Tarquitii were evidently enfranchised before the Social War), or C. Tarquitius P.f. (*RE* no. 1) who served under the anti-Sertorian governor of Spain C. Annius *c.* 81 (so Heurgon, *Latomus*, xii (1953), 407 n. 5; another of Annius' officers did transfer his loyalties to Sertorius eventually, L. Fabius Hispaniensis, *MRR* ii.77, 120).

[9] Suggested by Gabba, art. cit., 313, referring to Schulze, *ZGLE* 253, who mentions Virsius from *CIL* xi.3505 (Tarquinii, undated).

tive, but may be accepted. Of the conspirators against Sertorius we can name five others,[1] none with real Etruscan possibilities.

Gabba, developing his views about the sympathies of various types of Etruscans in the Social War, explains the presence of men of Etruscan origin in Sertorius' camp as a result of the 'tendenza filomariana delle classi inferiori etrusche'.[2] That is erroneous, for there is no reason at all to think that Perperna, Maecenas, and Tarquitius were representatives of the lower classes. The fact that Maecenas and Versius served Sertorius as *scribae*[3] should not be interpreted in that sense, for *scribae* habitually had equestrian status.[4] I have insisted on the inadequacy of the term 'Marian' as an explanation of the behaviour of Etruscans of the ruling class and their Roman connections. The aim of Perperna and his associates is to be taken as the re-establishment of their rights against the Sullan settlement. There were broadly speaking two ways by which the Etruscans could hope to recover what Sulla had taken from them, by using their remaining Roman political connections and the Roman courts, obviously a method accessible only to a few, or by violence. The first method was eventually successful in regaining the Roman citizenship for those Etruscans who had lost it—but there was little sign of this success in 78. As for confiscated land, the Etruscans who believed that peaceful methods would never recover it were fully justified.

During the 70s the cause of the Etruscans who had suffered from the Sullan settlement continued to win the attention of politicians who attacked the system in general. This we may infer from the work *Pro Tuscis* written by the Marian tribune Licinius Macer,[5] which was probably a speech delivered in his tribunate in 73.[6] 'Quis oportuit amissa restituere, hisce etiam

[1] M. Antonius, Aufidius, L. Fabius Hispaniensis, Manlius (or Mallius), Octavius Graecinus: *MRR* ii.120–1.

[2] Art. cit., 313.

[3] Sall. *Hist.* III 83.

[4] On the status of *scribae* cf. Cic. *Cat.* IV 15, *Dom.* 74, E. Kornemann in *RE* s.v. *scriba* (1923), esp. cols. 850–5. The conspirators seem to have been in Sertorius' inner circle.

[5] Priscian X p. 532H, *HRR* i^2.307, *ORF*^{2} p. 358 (110 fr. 5).

[6] Peter, Malcovati, Münzer in *RE* s.v. Licinius no. 112.

reliquias averrerunt' is the surviving fragment.[1] The occasion cannot be discovered; a particular threat to the rights or property of the Etruscans seems likely.

When Perperna and his followers eventually conspired to assassinate Sertorius it is possible that they hoped to take advantage of a connection between Perperna and Pompey to obtain a tolerable settlement for themselves.[2] Such hopes were illusory, and Perperna complained of Pompey's *saevitia.*[3] In Sicily after the war various fugitives from Spain were put to death by Verres, cruelly and illegally; Cicero contrasted that with the behaviour of Pompey when after the death of Perperna a great multitude of Sertorian soldiers sought refuge with him—'Quem non ille summo cum studio salvum incolumemque servavit?'[4] Some have accepted this at its face value.[5] A contrary tradition rather more convincingly portrayed Pompey as a paragon of cruelty in his actions after Perperna's death,[6] and according to Plutarch none of the conspirators survived, except a certain Aufidius, some of them having been killed by Pompey, others by the Mauretanians.[7] By 70 the armed opposition to the Sullan settlement has been destroyed, and conciliation was the policy of those who wished for Italian support. 'Forum plenum et basilicas istorum hominum [Sertorians, that is] videmus, et animo aequo videmus.'[8] Probably in the same year the Lex Plautia *de reditu Lepidanorum* was passed,[9] a bill that restored the citizenship to them, probably with Pompey's (and Caesar's) support.[10] The policy of conciliation towards those

[1] 'Quos . . .' codd. Either this has to be changed into *quis* or *in* has to be inserted before *amissa*; cf. *ORF*².

[2] This hinges on some claims that Perperna still had to Pompey's gratitude in 72 because of what had happened in Sicily in 82, Plu. *Pomp.* 20. The only event which Plutarch mentions that might have produced such an effect was Perperna's immediate surrender of the island, a charge of which Plutarch absolves him (ibid. 10). For the view that Perperna may have hoped to buy a settlement by murdering Sertorius cf. P. Treves, *Athenaeum*, x (1932), 145–6.

[3] Val. Max. VI 2.8.

[4] *II Verr.* V 153.

[5] E.g. Gabba on App. 115.536.

[6] Val. Max., l.c.

[7] *Sert.* 27.

[8] Cic. *II Verr.* V 152.

[9] On the date see Gabba, *Athenaeum*, xxxii (1954), 294 n. 1 (he cites the important discussions and accepts 70), *MRR* ii.130 n. 4 (70 as a preference). It applied to Sertoriani also, Cic. *II Verr.* V 152, Suet. *DJ* 5, Dio XLIV 47.

[10] So much can be assumed if it was passed in 70, and even if it was a year or two earlier. The sources attribute the success of the bill to Caesar, not yet a quaestor, Suet., Dio, ll.cc.; clearly a later claim, connected in some way with Caesar's later assistance to the sons of the proscribed.

who had hoped to restore their position by fighting shows how completely they had failed.

5. *Catiline*

Those who had lost land cannot have been greatly consoled by the concessions of 70 and 69. The same politician who in youth had helped some Etruscans to regain the citizenship stood firmly by some more essential parts of the Sullan system. 'Ita legibus Sullae cohaerere statum civitatis adfirmat (Cicero), ut iis solutis stare ipsa non possit';[1] this was said in 63 in opposition to a tribunician bill which would have restored the *ius honoris* to the sons of the proscribed,[2] and it was Cicero's line that the beneficiaries of the Sullan confiscations should be allowed to keep their possessions.

It is said that Catiline was supported in Etruria both by disappointed Sullan veterans and by those who had been dispossessed by Sulla.[3] A critical examination of the evidence suggests in fact that it was the dispossessed who were the more important. Manlius was crucial to Catiline's support in Etruria: allegedly he was a Sullan centurion,[4] had been a settler at Faesulae, and was a desperate debtor.[5] Although he could be described as the *satelles atque administer* of Catiline,[6] he was originally an independent force, and he declared war 'suo nomine'.[7] Sallust[8] gives the fullest description of the support that Manlius collected in Etruria: 'plebem ... egestate simul ac dolore iniuriae novarum rerum cupidam, quod Sullae dominatione agros bonaque omnia amiserat, praeterea latrones cuiusque generis, quorum in ea regione magna copia erat,

[1] Quintil. *Inst.* XI 1.85.

[2] For the sources on this proposal see Rice Holmes, *Roman Republic* (Oxford, 1923), i. 253 n. 3. Note the statement of Plutarch (who accepts Cicero's version) that the *proscriptorum filii* were 'neither few nor weak' (*Cic.* 12). Cf. Dio XLIV 47 for their gradual reinstatement, attributed to Caesar. It is not clear that any measures in favour of the *proscriptorum filii* were passed before 49, cf. *MRR* ii.257. See Sall. *Cat.* 58.13 for their support for Catiline.

[3] This is the general modern opinion; however according to Syme, *RR* 89 n. 6, Catiline's supporters were 'largely, but not wholly, disappointed Sullan veterans'.

[4] Cic. *Cat.* II 14, Dio XXXVII 30.

[5] Cic. *Cat.* II 20.

[6] Cic. *Cat.* I 7.

[7] Cic. *Cat.* II 14; cf. Sall. *Cat.* 24.2, Plu. *Cic.* 14.

[8] *Cat.* 28.

nonnullos ex Sullanis coloniis, quibus lubido atque luxuria ex magnis rapinis nihil relicui fecerant.' In this account the dispossessed certainly seem to be more important than the discontented colonists,[1] and this is a description of the support for Catiline that genuinely came from Etruria, not merely a description of those who, favouring Catiline, were to be found in Etruria at a certain time. According to Sallust, Catiline said in addressing his supporters: 'Licuit vobis cum summa turpitudine in exilio aetatem agere, potuistis non nulli Romae, amissis bonis, alienas opes expectare; quia illa foeda atque intoleranda viris videbantur, haec sequi decrevistis'[2]—here Catiline's soldiers are envisaged as being the dispossessed rather than the colonists of 81. The description of some of his supporters as 'multi ex coloniis et municipiis, domi nobiles'[3] is not very clear, but it is likely that long-established local families are meant. Other accounts of Catiline's supporters put more emphasis on the discontented colonists. Thus in the *Pro Murena* Cicero said that before the elections of 63 you could see Catiline 'circumfluentem colonorum Arretinorum et Faesulanorum exercitu; quam turbam dissimillimo ex genere distinguebant homines perculsi Sullani temporis calamitate.'[4] In the *Second Catilinarian* Cicero gives a denigratory list of the supporters of Catiline, including men from the Sullan colonies, 'quas ego universas civium esse optimorum et fortissimorum virorum sentio, sed tamen hi sunt coloni qui se in insperatis ac repentinis pecuniis sumptuosius insolentiusque iactarunt. Hi dum aedificant tamquam beati, dum praediis lectis, familiis magnis, conviviis apparatis delectantur, in tantum aes alienum inciderunt ut, si salvi esse velint, Sulla sit eis ab inferis excitandus.'[5] These people have persuaded some poor *agrestes* to hope for confiscations, 'quos ego utrosque in eodem genere praedatorum direptorumque pono', and both classes Cicero recommends to give up hoping for proscriptions and dictatorships. Four of Cicero's six classes of Catilinarians are people who have got into debt by their own fault (the other two consist of criminals and the morally corrupt), with no mention of the

[1] Other references to the support of the Sullan colonists for Catiline: Sall. *Cat.* 21, 37.

[2] *Cat.* 58.13.

[3] Sall. *Cat.* 17.4.

[4] *Mur.* 49.

[5] *Cat.* II 20.

urban plebs (the speech was *ad populum*)[1] or of those dispossessed by Sulla. Why are the Sullan colonists described as *optimi* and *fortissimi*? Some were in the audience, and although Sulla's confiscations and their beneficiaries were unpopular, it was Cicero's line in 63, as has been said, that they should keep their possessions. The same sort of descriptions reappear in later sources. Thus Sallust, rather inconsistently and without any circumstantial detail: 'plerique Sullani milites, largius suo usi, rapinarum et victoriae veteris memores civile bellum exoptabant...'[2] Plutarch, who naturally derived much information for his life of Cicero from Cicero's own writings,[3] also mentions the influx of discontented Sullan settlers into Rome for the purpose of supporting Catiline in the consular elections: 'these were to be found in all parts of Italy, but the greatest numbers and the most belligerent of them had been scattered in the towns of Etruria and were again dreaming of robbing and plundering the riches that were available. These men, with Manlius as leader, a man who had fought with distinction under Sulla, allied themselves with Catiline.'[4]

The rhetoric in the *Second Catilinarian* should arouse immediate distrust. There are several reasons to suppose that Sullan colonists were not as important a component of Catiline's support as Cicero asserted. It is hardly credible that an army of far more than 20,000 could be raised in Etruria chiefly from Sullan colonists.[5] We may wonder how many colonists could seriously hope that a civil war would justify the risks that it involved. But the most important reason for doubting Cicero's description is simply the rhetorical value of the Sullan colonists that derived from the *invidia* attached to them.[6] This *invidia*, a natural extension of popular hostility to Sulla, is referred to at length by Cicero in the second speech against Rullus' bill,[7] and

[1] On the effects of this cf. Z. Yavetz, *Historia*, xii (1963), 489.

[2] *Cat.* 16, cf. 21, 37. Sallust liked to dwell on the *luxuria* and *lubido* of Sulla's soldiers and colonists, cf. A. La Penna, *SIFC* xxxi (1959), 130, D. C. Earl, *The Political Thought of Sallust* (Cambridge, 1961), 14, 46, 86–8, 105–6.

[3] Cf. D. Magnino's edition of Plutarch's life (Florence, 1963), pp. v–vii.

[4] Plu. *Cic.* 14, cf. Cic. *Mur.* 49.

[5] Cf. Plu. *Cic.* 16. It is admittedly a round and possibly alarmist figure; after desertions Catiline's final army was only 3,000, Dio XXXVII 40.

[6] On which cf. E. G. Hardy, *Some Problems in Roman History* (Oxford, 1924), 86, Gelzer, *Cicero, ein biographischer Versuch* (Wiesbaden, 1969), 73.

[7] *Agr.* II 68–70: 'Quam multos enim, Quirites, existimatis esse qui latitudinem

most of the third speech is devoted to rebutting the charge of favouring the Sullan possessors and imputing it to the authors of the bill. There is no good reason to doubt what Cicero has to say about this *invidia* in the second speech, and so it is hardly surprising that in the highly rhetorical passage in the *Second Catilinarian*—which is fundamental for the view of the Sullan colonists as a main component of Catiline's support—great use is made of them. The *invidia* attaching to *Sullani homines* is attested elsewhere. In 64 Cato attacked those to whom Sulla had given money rewards for killing the proscribed—they were condemned ἡδομένων πάντων.[1] No doubt the attack on the *Sullani homines* of the praetor C. Octavius in 61[2] was a popular action. The passage in *De lege agraria II* is, however, sufficient to establish the point.

It is then reasonable to resolve the inconsistency in the sources about the relative importance among Catiline's supporters of discontented Sullan colonists by discounting as propaganda some of the importance attributed to the Sullan colonists. The accepted account—unsuccessful farming and financial desperation—no doubt did apply to some. Manlius himself was said to have been a Sullan colonist, as was another named Catilinarian, P. Furius;[3] these assertions are not free of doubt, but all manner of *calamitosi* did support Catiline. Among his friends there was also to be found one C. Flaminius, probably *aedilicius*—Catiline stayed 'apud C. Flaminium in agro Arretino' after his departure from Rome[4]—but it is useless to speculate what led him into the party of *novae res*. Catiline's support was variegated, but the bulk of his supporters in Etruria were probably Etruscans who had suffered from the Sullan confiscations.

Some evidence is available on this question from other areas: Cicero's description of affairs at Pompeii in 63 suggests that it was the native Pompeiani rather than the Sullan colonists who

possessionum tueri, qui invidiam Sullanorum agrorum ferre non possint, qui vendere cupiant, emptorem non reperiant, perdere iam denique illos agros ratione aliqua velint? Qui paulo ante diem noctemque tribunicium nomen horrebant, vestram vim metuebant . . . agros partim publicos, partim plenos invidiae plenos periculi', etc.; 98: 'invidiosos agros a Sullanis possessoribus emptos'.

[1] Plu. *Cat. Mi.* 17.5.

[2] Cic. *QFr.* I 1.21.

[3] Cic. *Cat.* III 14.

[4] Sall. *Cat.* 36.1.

favoured Catiline. At least Torquatus charged that P. Sulla, *patronus coloniae*, had encouraged the original Pompeiani to join the *coniuratio*.[1] It is difficult to draw conclusions for the nature of Catiline's support from the list of the other areas which were thought to be particularly susceptible, but some of them are areas where there were Sullan estates but no known colonists.[2]

The close connection of the Etruscan rebellion of 63 with the Sullan colonies is to some extent confirmed by the few geographical references that we have during the course of the revolt: Faesulans were in Rome to support Catiline, Catiline set up a camp in the territory of Faesulae, Faesulae was Manlius' base, P. Furius had been a colonist at Faesulae, and Manlius was sent by Catiline to Faesulae and that part of Etruria.[3] The senator L. Saenius (a significant case of a man of Etruscan origins showing his support for the Ciceronian government)[4] read out a letter in the Senate which he said came from Faesulae, in which it was written that Manlius had taken arms 'cum magna multitudine' on 27 October; the Senate consequently sent Q. Marcius Rex to Faesulae.[5] Eventually Catiline reached Faesulae himself[6] and in the final stage of the rebellion the town was besieged.[7] Arretium is also mentioned several times: it was a source of Catilinarians in Rome,[8] and on his journey northwards Catiline stopped for a few days 'apud C. Flaminium in agro Arretino, dum vicinitatem antea sollicitatam armis exornat'.[9] When Catiline left Rome he travelled

[1] *Sull.* 60: 'Iam vero quod obiecit Pompeianos esse a Sulla impulsos ut ad istam coniurationem atque ad hoc nefarium facinus accederent, id cuius modi sit intellegere non possum. An tibi Pompeiani coniurasse videntur? Quis hoc dixit umquam, aut quae fuit istius rei vel minima suspicio? "Diiunxit", inquit, "eos a colonis ut hoc discidio ac dissensione facta oppidum in sua potestate posset per Pompeianos habere".'

[2] The *ager Gallicus*, Picenum, Apulia (Cic. *Cat.* II 5–6, III 14, cf. Sall. *Cat.* 42—Picenum, Bruttium, and Apulia were the places where actual fighting took place). Cf. Brunt, *JRS* lii (1962), 73.

[3] Faesulans in Rome: Cic. *Mur.* 49; the camp in the territory of Faesulae: Cic. *Cat.* II 14; Manlius' base: Sall. *Cat.* 24.2, cf. Dio XXXVII 30.4; Furius: Cic. *Cat.* III 14; Manlius' mission: Sall. *Cat.* 27.1.

[4] Compare the behaviour of Nigidius Figulus, Cic. *Sull.* 42.

[5] Sall. *Cat.* 30.1, 30.3.

[6] App. *BC* II 3, Dio XXXVII 33.2.

[7] Dio XXXVII 39.2.

[8] Cic. *Mur.* 49.

[9] Sall. *Cat.* 36.1.

along the Via Aurelia[1] to meet armed men who awaited him at Forum Aurelium, so Cicero claimed;[2] this was probably an arrangement of convenience, for a small *forum* in the territory of Vulci was hardly likely to be a centre of rebellion. Although there are some rhetorical implications in contemporary writers that there was wider support in Etruria,[3] it was clearly concentrated in the two colonies of Faesulae and Arretium. Later writers state more specifically that the whole of Etruria revolted.[4] Other neighbouring areas that were involved were Camerinum, Picenum, and the *ager Gallicus*[5] and there were disturbances in several other parts of Italy. A supporter of Catiline from Camerinum is also known, a certain Septimius who was sent by Catiline as an agent to Picenum; it surely cannot be a coincidence that Camerinum was the home of two cohorts enfranchised by Marius before the Social War—that had presumably made it particularly hostile to Sulla in 82, and punishment probably followed.[6]

The followers of Catiline were an amalgam of the discontented, men with widely differing aims. It is not to be doubted that among the debtors of various classes there were those who had done well out of the Sullan proscriptions but in the hard times of 63 again looked to desperate solutions for their financial problems. More important, however, in Etruria, the true home of the rebellion, were those who had been the victims of the previous proscriptions.

6. *62–44*

None of those who fought for Catiline at Pistoriae survived, or virtually none, but naturally that did not altogether remove the sources of discontent in Etruria. The policy of C. Octavius towards the *Sullani homines* in 61 may represent an attempt at

[1] Cic. *Cat.* II 6.

[2] Cic. *Cat.* I 24. Perhaps Cicero was here exaggerating his foreknowledge, cf. Syme, *Sallust*, 74.

[3] Cic. *Cat.* I 5: 'castra sunt . . . contra populum Romanum in Etruriae faucibus conlocata'; cf. II 6, *Sull.* 53, Sall. *Cat.* 28.4: 'Interea Manlius in Etruria plebem sollicitare . . .'

[4] E.g. Plu. *Cic.* 10.

[5] Cic. *Sull.* 53.

[6] On Camerinum see above, p. 265 n. 6. Note also the participation of the Paeligni (Oros. VI 6.7), who had suffered badly from Sulla (Flor. II 9).

conciliation of anti-Sullan Italians. However economic and social dislocation is well attested—brigandage was already a severe problem in Italy,[1] and in 63 it was a particularly serious problem in Etruria;[2] the civil wars were evidently a prime cause. In the 50s the problem continued to exist. Through the abuse poured by Cicero on Clodius, the alleged accomplice of Catiline,[3] we can discern that such things were expected in Etruria; it may be quite untrue that Clodius' armed bands attacked the Etruscans, as asserted in the *Pro Milone*,[4] but it was the sort of thing that happened there.

The wounds inflicted by the Sullan settlement naturally tended to heal, or at least hope of subverting the settlement faded. The old and the new populations became assimilated, the former becoming rapidly more Romanized, and Romanization continued more quickly for other reasons. Roman business and to some extent politics were more open to municipal men. In the 50s and 40s we also begin to have more detailed knowledge of Etruscan and Umbrian land-holdings of wealthy Romans. In part that is an accidental result of the existence of the Ciceronian evidence, but it is likely that the extent of such land-holdings was increasing.

The *praedium Arretinum* of Atticus[5] and the estates of Domitius Ahenobarbus at Cosa and on the nearby island of Igilium, which provided him with troops in 49,[6] may well have been acquisitions of the Sullan period.[7] Besides the *praedium* of Atticus and the property of Flaminius at Arretium, all the evidence for Roman properties concerns either the immediate vicinity of Rome or the coastal area. We have already noted the interests of some Romans at Tarquinii; at Cosa, besides Ahenobarbus, we find P. Sestius in 44;[8] somewhere on the Via

[1] See Cic. *Tull., passim*, and Brunt, l.c.

[2] Sall. *Cat.* 28, quoted above.

[3] Ascon. 50C.

[4] *Mil.* 26, 50, etc.

[5] Nepos, *Att.* 14.

[6] Caes. *BC* I 34.2.

[7] Atticus 'ad hastam publicam numquam accessit', Nepos, *Att.* 6, and since he seems to have avoided having much property in Italy (ibid. 14), it may have been a legacy (cf. 21). Dio (XLI 11.2) says that Ahenobarbus was a Sullan and acquired much land as a result; R. M. Haywood, *AJPh* liv (1933), 150, cast doubt on this, for he was too young, and his father died *c.* 89. The only Domitius Ahenobarbus active in 82–1 (*RE* no. 22) was killed by Pompey in Africa. *AE* 1957, no. 217, provides evidence for the estates of the Domitii in addition to *CIL* i².1995=*ILLRP* 915.

[8] Cic. *Att.* XV 27.1.

Aurelia there had been *possessiones* of P. Clodius,[1] and, according to Cicero, Clodius had forcibly occupied some property of a certain M. Paconius, an *eques Romanus*, on an island in the *lacus Prilius* (in the territory of Rusellae);[2] M. Paconius was probably a member of a long-established family of *negotiatores* of Oscan origin.[3] Property in Umbria that came into Roman hands at the time of Sulla has already been noted, and we can add the *villa Ocriculana* of Milo,[4] and perhaps some property of L. Lucullus at Interamna Nahars, if, as seems likely, he held the quattuorvirate there.[5] We know of these cases from incidental references, and in fact there must have been very many more.

In the Civil War Caesar's cause pretended to be among other things that of the sons of the proscribed,[6] and they recovered their civil rights in 49.[7] It is easy to believe, but impossible to prove, that the dispossessed in Etruria and Umbria were generally favourable to him. The attitude of the substantial classes of Italy towards Caesar is a more complex matter, as is that of the Roman *nobilitas* itself, now known to be fairly equally divided between the two camps.[8] Caesar's Italian support, having been greatly underestimated by Mommsen and Meyer, is since Syme's article on the subject[9] in danger of being exaggerated. While recognizing Caesar's ability as a propagandist he accepted the main claims of the *Bellum Civile* about the welcome that Caesar received, and Etruria and Umbria—about which Caesar did not make any general claim—are thought to have been mainly Caesarian on the strength of Caesar's Marian connection.[10] We can tell little from the course of events: five cohorts, a substantial force by Caesar's standards

[1] Cic. *Phil.* XII 23.

[2] Cic. *Mil.* 74.

[3] On their Oscan origin and Delian activities see Münzer in *RE* s.v. Paconius (1942); note also *CIL* i².948=*ILLRP* 994, from Tarquinii, referring to a slave of a Paconius.

[4] Cic. *Mil.* 64.

[5] *CIL* i².2098=*ILLRP* 616. Taylor, *VDRR* 225, doubts whether this was the L. Licinius L.f. Lucullus; but she is mistaken in giving the inscription an imperial date, and in this case the famous name probably belongs to the famous man.

[6] D. R. Shackleton Bailey, *CQ* n.s.x (1960), 265.

[7] References in *MRR* ii.257; add Dio XLIV 47.

[8] Shackleton Bailey, art. cit., 253–67.

[9] *PBSR* xiv (1938), 1–31.

[10] Art. cit., 19.

at that time, were sent from Ariminum to occupy Arretium,[1] a position of obvious strategic importance. Caesar then learnt that the propraetor Minucius Thermus was holding Iguvium with five cohorts and fortifying it, 'omniumque esse Iguvinorum optimam erga se voluntatem'; he sent three cohorts under the command of Curio. Thermus, 'diffisus municipi voluntati', withdrew, his soldiers deserting him on the way, and Curio occupied Iguvium 'summa omnium voluntate'. 'Quibus rebus cognitis confisus municipiorum voluntatibus Caesar cohortis legionis XIII ex praesidiis deducit . . .'[2] It is possible that events took place exactly thus, but there are several reasons to doubt it: Minucius Thermus, who had some indeterminate family connection with the region of the Via Flaminia[3] and was perhaps not without influence there in 49, may like Domitius have had instructions to withdraw. But the most important reason for scepticism is simply Caesar's exaggerated insistence on the warmth of his Italian reception—during the brief account of the occupation of Iguvium, the key word *voluntas* is used four times, and great emphasis is placed on the rapture of the Italians.[4] The soldiers recruited for Pompey at Camerinum went over to Caesar—how enthusiastically we cannot tell.[5] The whole passage of the *Bellum Civile* reeks of self-justification.[6] Yet Cicero confirms that Caesar was very warmly received—'Municipia vero deum [*s.v.l.*]; nec simulant, ut cum de illo [i.e. Pompey, in 50 B.C.] aegroto vota faciebant.'[7] Pompey had worked to maintain his Italian *clientelae*, and we must suppose that in some places at least the *domi nobiles* preferred his cause; even if the official prayers of the year before were largely a sham, some Italian supporters remained. If Carrinas, son of the anti-Sullan general, Vibius Pansa, adopted son of a man proscribed by Sulla, and Volcacius Tullus were to be found on

[1] Caes. *BC* I 11.4.

[2] Caes. *BC* I 12.

[3] Cic. *Att.* I 1.2.

[4] Cf. *BC* I 15.1: 'libentissimis animis'; 15.2: 'quaeque imperavit se cupidissime facturos pollicentur'; 18.2, 20.4–5, etc.

[5] Caes. *BC* I 15.5, Cic. *Att.* VIII 12B *ad fin.* (Pompey).

[6] See K. Barwick, *Caesars Bellum Civile* (*Tendenz, Abfassungszeit und Stil*) (Berlin, 1951), 41–5, and (better) J. H. Collins, *Propaganda, Ethics and Psychological Assumptions in Caesar's Writings* (Frankfurt-a.-M., 1952), esp. 78; cf. M. Rambaud, *L'Art de la Déformation historique dans les Commentaires de César* (Paris, 1953), 279.

[7] *Att.* VIII 16.1 (4 March 49), cf. IX 5.3.

Caesar's side, Caecina and Nigidius Figulus were for Pompey, as was Ahenobarbus.[1] When land had to be found for veterans in 45, some of it was evidently found at Volaterrae, Caecina's town,[2] Veii, and Capena,[3] and probably at Arretium and Castrum Novum.[4] Even with what little information we have about the attitudes of the Etruscans and Umbrians to the war, we can tell that they were not uniform.

[1] Caecina: Cic. *Fam.* VI 5–9; Nigidius: *Fam.* IV 13.

[2] Cic. *Fam.* XIII 5.

[3] Cic. *Fam.* IX 17.2—but the colony of Lucus Feroniae was probably not Caesarian (see pp. 308–9).

[4] See below, pp. 306–7. On Caesar's provisions for his veterans in general see Gelzer, *Caesar, der Politiker und Staatsmann*[6] (Wiesbaden, 1960), 262 n. 36 (Eng. edn. (Oxford, 1968), 283 n. 1).

IX

THE AUGUSTAN SETTLEMENT

1. *The Perusine War*[1]

LIKE Sulla, the triumvirs and later Augustus on his own sought to reward their veterans by distributing land and founding colonies in Italy. Hence in Etruria, as in Campania, came the last major displacement of the local population by a Roman government and the last real acts of local resistance to Rome. These events, and not the general political history of Augustan Italy, form the subject of this last chapter, for the history of Etruria and Umbria had merged almost completely into the history of Italy.

There may already have been further settlement in Etruria and Umbria between the death of Caesar and the battle of Philippi, for example under the Lex Antonia Cornelia of June 44.[2] The area of Italy that is known to have been affected in this period is the *ager Campanus*,[3] but others may very well have suffered. Of the known Antonian colonies in Italy one at least in another area probably dates from this time, namely Pisaurum,[4] for in 43 the Antonian Insteius was already associated with the place.[5] When they made their agreement at Bononia in October 43 the triumvirs promised their troops that they would give them eighteen cities in Italy as a reward,[6]

[1] For discussions see V. Gardthausen, *Augustus und seine Zeit*, i (Leipzig, 1891), 202–9, T. Rice Holmes, *The Architect of the Roman Empire*, i (Oxford, 1928), 94–100, M. A. Levi, *Ottaviano Capoparte* (Florence, 1933), ii. 20–7, M. Reinhold, *Classical Weekly*, xxvi (1933), 180–2, R. Syme, *RR* 207–13, E. Gabba, *Appiano e la storia delle guerre civili* (Florence, 1956), 189–98, *Appiani Bellorum Civilium Liber Quintus* (Florence, 1970), pp. xvii–lix, H. Buchheim, *Die Orientpolitik des Triumvirn M. Antonius* (Heidelberg, 1960), 29–34.

[2] For the bibliography of the triumviral colonization in Italy see below, p. 303 n. 7.

[3] Cic. *Phil.* VIII 26.

[4] Ἀντωνίου πόλις κληρουχία, Plu. *Ant.* 60.

[5] Cic. *Phil.* XIII 26.

[6] App. *BC* IV 3.10–11; Appian names seven of the eighteen towns that were listed, none of them in Etruria or Umbria.

and it is clear that with two exceptions these towns were actually colonized by Caesarian veterans after Philippi.[1] More legions were probably settled in the event than had been originally intended, thirty-four instead of twenty-eight.[2] There is no certainty that any colonial foundation in Etruria or Umbria belongs to the period after Philippi, nor is there any reason to think that these regions suffered particularly heavily in the proscriptions, but it is likely that some of the Etruscan and Umbrian colonies listed below were triumviral foundations.

How much were the local populations of Etruria and Umbria involved in the Perusine War? The war has sometimes been regarded as the last rising of Italy against Rome,[3] but it was a war of rival factions and their armies,[4] and in most parts of Italy there were partisans of both sides. The reasons why fighting took place in Etruria and Umbria were in a sense accidental: L. Antonius moved northwards from Rome because of the approach from Gaul of Salvidienus, recalled by Octavian, and of the Antonian sympathizers Asinius Pollio and Ventidius;[5] Agrippa and Octavian were led northwards by the necessity of participating in this campaign. Octavian's unsuccessful attacks on Nursia and Sentinum before the siege of Perusia[6] look like attempts to secure places of strategic importance, close to crossings over the Apennines,[7] and we are told that at Nursia he encountered not just the local inhabitants but Titisienus Gallus,[8] a subordinate of Lucius, while at Sentinum he encountered another, C. Furnius.[9] It is hard to make sense of the accounts that Appian and Dio give of the campaign preceding the siege, but it is quite possible to understand how Lucius may have taken up his position at Perusia for reasons

[1] App. *BC* IV 86.362.

[2] App. *BC* V 22.87—an allegation, however, of M. Antonius' agent Manius.

[3] So Syme, *RR* 208 (cf. 287), cf. App. *BC* V 27, Levi, op. cit., ii.25; otherwise E. Gabba, *Athenaeum*, xxix (1951), 242 n. 2.

[4] The armies that fought these wars were themselves largely Italian; cf. G. Forni, *Il reclutamento delle legioni da Augusto a Diocleziano* (Milan, 1953), esp. 159–63, P. A. Brunt, *JRS* lii (1962), 74.

[5] See Dio XLVIII 14.1, App. *BC* V 31.121. Cf. Reinhold, art. cit., 180–1; I accept the main lines of his analysis of the manœuvres preceding the siege.

[6] Dio XLVIII 13.2.

[7] Cf. Reinhold, art. cit., 180 n. 14.

[8] On the name see T. P. Wiseman, *CR* n.s. xv (1965), 19–20.

[9] Dio XLVIII 13.2, 13.6.

unconnected with the views of the inhabitants. He was surely intent on making a junction with Ventidius and Asinius while avoiding the armies of Salvidienus and of Octavian and Agrippa.

Dio and Appian present contrasting views of L. Antonius' opposition to Octavian. According to the former the reasons why Lucius and Fulvia fought against Octavian were in the first place because they did not get the share of land that was due to the Antonian veterans, and because Lucius, *ὡς καὶ ὑπὲρ τοῦ Μάρκου ταῦτα δρῶν*, attempted to gain control of affairs.[1] According to Appian, although Lucius and Fulvia initially tried to obtain some of the credit for the settlement of the veterans for Antony,[2] the real reason for Lucius' opposition was that he was *δημοτικὸς* and opposed to the triumvirate.[3] However, whatever his reasons were, both writers agree that he sought and obtained the support of those who feared or had experienced confiscation at the hands of Octavian.[4] Octavian seems to have made use of this fact in the propaganda that he directed towards the veterans,[5] but it is not to be disbelieved.

The local population of Nursia was opposed to Octavian,[6] and the actions that he took after the surrender of Perusia make it perfectly clear that there too it was not merely the Antonian troops in general who were against Octavian but the native Perusines as well. There are conflicting accounts of what Octavian did to the defeated after the siege:[7] according to Dio most of the Roman senators and knights who surrendered were put to death, and so were the majority of the people of Perusia who were captured; the city itself was completely destroyed by fire, except the temple of Vulcan and the statue of Juno.[8] According to Appian, Octavian pardoned not only the army of

[1] Dio XLVIII 5.2, 6.2; 5.4.

[2] App. *BC* V 14. It is fairly clear that Lucius himself took part in colonization in Italy in this period; Gabba, *PP* xxiii (1953), 101–6.

[3] *BC* V 19.

[4] Dio XLVIII 6.4–5, 10.3, App. *BC* V 19, 27, cf. Vell. II 74.2.

[5] App. *BC* V 39, 43; cf. Gabba, *Appiano e la storia delle guerre civili*, 196–7.

[6] Dio XLVIII 13.6.

[7] On this see K. Scott, *MAAR* xi (1933), 27–8, in addition to the works already cited.

[8] Dio XLVIII 14.3–6. For this version cf. Sen. *de clem.* I 11.1, Suet. *Aug.* 15; the *arae Perusinae* are generally dismissed as a fabrication (cf. Scott, l.c., Syme, *RR* 212).

Lucius but also the Roman senators and knights, although a few of these who were personal enemies of his were killed at the insistence of his soldiers,[1] and the Perusines were pardoned as well, with the exception of the βουλευταί, who were put to death; the town was to have been plundered by Octavian's troops, but before that could happen it was destroyed by a fire started by a deranged Perusine *princeps*, Cestius Macedonicus,[2] the temple of Vulcan alone surviving.[3] The account that is less unfavourable to Octavian has generally been accepted,[4] but that is perhaps an error in view of the improbable effects attributed to Cestius' madness and the evident desire of those who propounded this version to exculpate Octavian. Even if we do take the version that is more favourable to Octavian, it is clear that he behaved savagely towards the Perusines, and more importantly that he behaved more savagely towards them than towards the Roman supporters of Lucius. He must therefore have regarded them as his most implacable enemies.

Opposition to Octavian in Etruria did not disappear after the siege: the coast was sometimes within the range of Sextus Pompey's forces,[5] and when news arrived of the final defeat of Sextus in 36 τὰ τῶν Τυρσηνῶν στασιάσαντα became quiet.[6]

Pisaurum was an Antonian colony and later a *colonia Iulia*; at Perusia the surviving locals were allowed to retain only such land as was within seven and a half stades of the city;[7] at Hispellum the *colonia Iulia* was probably of triumviral date. Apart from these instances, the only triumviral colonies in Etruria or Umbria for which there is any specific evidence are those mentioned in the *Libri Coloniarum*, a source that emerges with little credit when, as in the case of the Augustan colonies, it can be checked against a substantial quantity of other evidence. Falerii, Florentia, Nepet, and Volaterrae in Etruria and Tuder in Umbria are said by the *Libri Coloniarum* to have been

[1] Cf. Vell. II 74.4.

[2] Macedonicus is said to have been a *princeps eius loci* by Vell., l.c.; Cestius is probably an authentically local name, cf. Schulze, *ZGLE* 575, Syme, *Historia*, xiii (1964), 114.

[3] App. *BC* V 48–9.

[4] Rice Holmes, op. cit., 98–9, Syme, *RR* 211–12, Gabba, *Appiano e la storia delle guerre civili*, 198 n. 1.

[5] Cf. Dio XLVIII 30.5—40 B.C.

[6] Dio XLIX 15.1.

[7] Dio XLVIII 14.6.

sites of triumviral colonies, but only in the case of Florentia is there any confirmation; Tuder could also be a real case. *Viritim* assignment of land is also said by the *Libri Coloniarum* to have taken place at Luna and Sena Gallica, and in both cases there is a lack of other evidence for or against the fact. There are in addition several cases of colonies that are well attested as *coloniae Iuliae* and which could quite well be triumviral, namely Castrum Novum, Lucus Feroniae, Pisae, Rusellae, Saena, and Sutrium in Etruria,[1] and Fanum Fortunae in Umbria. The detailed evidence for all these cases is reviewed together with the evidence for the post-Actian colonies and settlement in the next section.

2. *The Augustan Settlement*

A further large quantity of land was bestowed on veterans between Actium and 13 B.C., when such grants were finally replaced by payments of money.[2] The exact amount cannot be calculated, but by 29 some 120,000 colonists had been settled;[3] land was bought in Italy in 14 B.C. as it had been in 30,[4] and altogether more than 300,000 veterans were rewarded with land or money by Augustus.[5] The flourishing of his Italian colonies was evidently a matter of pride for Augustus—'Italia autem XXVIII colonias, quae vivo me celeberrimae et frequentissimae fuerunt, mea auctoritate deductas habet.'[6]

How many of these colonies were in Etruria and Umbria?[7]

[1] Likewise Arretium, although the *Iulienses* are not explicitly attested as colonists.

[2] Dio LIV 25.5.

[3] *RG* 15: 'Et colonis militum meorum consul quintum ex manibiis viritim millia nummum singula dedi; acceperunt id triumphale congiarium in colonis hominum circiter centum et viginti millia.'

[4] *RG* 16: 'Pecuniam pro agris, quos in consulatu meo quarto et postea consulibus M. Crasso et Cn. Lentulo Augure adsignavi militibus, solvi municipis. Ea summa sestertium circiter sexsiens milliens fuit, quam pro Italicis praedis numeravi, et circiter bis milliens et sescentiens, quod pro agris provincialibus solvi . . .'

[5] *RG* 3: '. . . Ex quibus deduxi in colonias aut remisi in municipia sua stipendis emeritis millia aliquanto plura quam trecenta, et iis omnibus agros adsignavi aut pecuniam pro praemis militiae dedi.'

[6] *RG* 28. For the total of twenty-eight cf. Suet. *Aug.* 46.

[7] There have been numerous attempts to list the triumviral and Augustan colonies. The most important discussion is Mommsen's, *Hermes*, xviii (1883), 161–213=*GS* v.203–53; see also the entry for each town in *CIL*, in *CIL* xi by Bormann. Earlier lists that are still of interest are those of A. W. Zumpt, *Commentationum Epigraphicarum ad Antiquitates Romanas Pertinentium volumen* I (Berlin, 1850), 332–9 (triumviral), 347–61 (Augustan), Beloch, *It. Bund.* 1–9; subsequent discussions by E. Pais, *Museo Italiano di Antichità Classica*, i (1885), 37–9 (triumviral), 45–58

The source material that is available for identifying Augustus' colonies in Italy consists mainly of Pliny's lists of colonies in the third book of the *Natural History*, inscriptions, and notices in the *Libri Coloniarum*. The total of twenty-eight colonies given in the *Res Gestae* cannot refer to all the *coloniae Iuliae* and *coloniae Augustae*, for there are too many of them[1]—and Augustus can hardly have given the wrong total; it is probable therefore that some of the *coloniae Iuliae* were foundations of the triumvirate which were not counted among the twenty-eight colonies.[2] Many problems that are not directly relevant to this inquiry arise from the three sources of information mentioned above; the following points are essential. Pliny states in introducing his description of Italy that he is following Augustus' division of the country into eleven regions, but in the order that they occur along the coast; and that in the inland areas he is following the alphabetical order of Augustus' list of towns, indicating the colonies that Augustus gave in that list.[3] He then proceeds to mention some twenty-eight inland colonies and some fifteen coastal ones (not all of them, however, on the coast itself).[4] Of these fifteen, ten had definitely been Roman colonial foundations of earlier periods, but at least four were not,[5] and so

(Augustan), *Storia della colonizzazione di Roma antica*, i (Rome, 1923), *passim*, *Mem. Acc. Linc.*, ser. 6.i (1925), 360–84 (triumviral), 384–403 (Augustan) (these last two works are vitiated by excessive credulity towards the *Lib. Col.*), lists by E. De Ruggiero, *Diz. Ep.* s.v. *colonia*, 445–56, E. Kornemann in *RE* s.v. *coloniae* (1901), cols. 524–6 (triumviral), 535–7 (Augustan). Some pertinent remarks are made by A. Degrassi, *Mem. Acc. Linc.*, ser. 8.ii (1950), 281–345, E. Gabba, *Athenaeum*, xxix (1951), 241–9, *PP* xxiii (1953), 101–10. The cases in Etruria are discussed by A. J. Pfiffig, *Die Ausbreitung des römischen Städtewesens in Etrurien und die Frage der Unterwerfung der Etrusker* (Florence, 1966), *passim*.

[1] Mommsen, art. cit., 187=228, Gabba, *PP* xxiii (1953), 106–10.

[2] Gabba, art. cit., 109.

[3] *NH* III 46: '... praefari necessarium est auctorem nos divum Augustum secuturos, discriptionemque ab eo factam Italiae totius in regiones XI, sed ordine eo quo litorum tractu fiet; urbium quidem vicinitates oratione utique praepropera servari non posse, itaque interiore exin parte digestionem in litteras eiusdem nos secuturos, coloniarum mentione signata quas ille in eo prodidit numero.' On Pliny's method of composition the fullest modern discussion is that of R. Thomsen, *Italic Regions* (Copenhagen, 1947), 17–46.

[4] I omit as specifically non-Augustan Cosa ('a populo Romano deducta', 51) and Ostia ('a Romano rege deducta', 56). It is not necessary to discuss here the difficulties of detail that arise from the list, such as self-contradiction about the status of Venusia.

[5] Fanum Fortunae (113), Concordia (126), Tergeste (127), Pola (129), and also Pisae (50) if Pliny meant to call it a colony (see below).

whatever Pliny's source was for the *periplous* sections of his description, it included some if not all of the triumviral and Augustan foundations. The correspondence between Pliny's lists and the extant inscriptions is, as one would expect, good but not perfect: all the best attested Augustan colonies, the nine known *coloniae Iuliae Augustae* and *Augustae*, appear in his lists as colonies,[1] and of the triumviral-Augustan colonies known from other sources (inscriptions referring to *coloniae Iuliae* and literary evidence) some eighteen or nineteen are registered by him as colonies and between three and seven are not;[2] the cases in which Pliny can be shown to have been wrong turn out, when one makes allowance for the different character of the *periplous* sections, to be very few. When we turn to the *Libri Coloniarum*, however, we are on much less firm ground; Mommsen's attack on their credibility has never really been rebutted, although some writers cite them without a qualm.[3] Of the nine *coloniae Iuliae Augustae* and *Augustae*, four, Capua, Beneventum, Venafrum, and Nola, are within the area that is covered by the notices in the *Libri Coloniarum*. The Augustan colony at Capua is mentioned and the Augustan colony at Beneventum is probably alluded to; but although territorial arrangements at Venafrum by Augustus are mentioned, the colony is mentioned obscurely if at all; and although Nola is explicitly called a *colonia Augusta*, it was supposedly founded by Vespasian.[4] Even if we do not require of the *Libri Coloniarum* comprehensiveness in the areas that they purport to cover, they are not satisfactory. Their list of places where there was triumviral or Augustan settlement simply does not correspond to the list that can be constructed from the other sources. Of the known triumviral and Augustan colonies, some, like Tuder (see below), are listed as such—thus Aquinum is given as 'a

[1] Capua, Nola, Venafrum (63), Beneventum (105), Ariminum, Parma (115), Augusta Taurinorum, Augusta Praetoria Salassorum (123), Brixia (130).

[2] Not listed as colonies by Pliny: Falerio, Nuceria, Parentium, and also Abellinum, Castrum Novum (see below), Cumae, Pisae (see below).

[3] For Mommsen's views see *Die Schriften der römischen Feldmesser* (ed. F. Blume, etc.), ii (Berlin, 1852), 181–8=*GS* v. 173–8, art. cit., 173–84=215–25; Pais's reaction is represented most fully in *Storia della colonizzazione*, etc., *passim*. For a recent reassertion of a Mommsenian view-point see S. Mazzarino, *Il pensiero storico classico* (Bari, 1966), ii.1 226–30.

[4] 213.19–20 (Capua), 232.7–8 (Beneventum), 239.7–10 (Venafrum), 236.3–4 (Nola).

triumviris deducta', Sora, Teanum, and Puteoli are given as Augustan colonies, and Bovianum and Ancona are given as sites of land-assignment in this period;[1] but the entries for Sutrium, Fanum Fortunae, Pisaurum, Hispellum, Suessa, Luceria, Venusia, Hadria, and Asculum fail to show that there was any settlement in the period. Of the places that are said by the *Libri Coloniarum* to have been Augustan colonies and that fall within the area of Pliny's inland lists, Capua, Beneventum, Sora, and Teanum are confirmed by Pliny (and by other evidence), but Acerrae, Arretium (on which see below), Atella, and Veii appear on his *oppida* lists,[2] and 'Divinos' is unidentifiable. Thus as a general rule it is not reasonable to believe in an Augustan colony on the strength of a notice in the *Libri Coloniarum* if there is any evidence against it, Pliny's silence counting as such evidence; the same applies with slightly less force to triumviral colonies. That does not mean that the notices in the *Libri Coloniarum* are completely valueless, but they are of only marginal importance.

The following is a catalogue of the possible cases of triumviral and Augustan colonization and land-distribution in Etruria and Umbria:

ARRETIUM. With the Arretini Veteres and Fidentiores Pliny lists the Arretini Iulienses.[3] The *Libri Coloniarum* refer to an Augustan colony: 'Colonia Arretium, lege Augustea censita, . . .'[4] Since Pliny does not say that it was a colony, there was almost certainly no triumviral or Augustan colony; there was probably either a Caesarian one,[5] or non-colonial settlement by Caesar or by Octavian after Philippi or Actium.

CASTRUM NOVUM. The *colonia Iulia* of Castrum Novum is attested in inscriptions,[6] and must be accepted as authentic

[1] 229.13 (Aquinum), 237.17–18 (Sora), 238.6–7 (Teanum), 236.11 (Puteoli), 231.8–9 (Bovianum), 225.4–5 (Ancona).

[2] In one case, Nuceria, a well-attested triumviral colony (App. *BC* IV 3.11—emended to Luceria by Beloch, *It. Bund* 7, but see Mommsen, art. cit., 171= 212–13) the town is mentioned by Pliny in a *periplous* section (62) without reference to the colony, while in *Lib. Col.* 235.20–1 it is said to have been an Augustan colony.

[3] *NH* III 52.

[4] *Lib. Col.* 215.3.

[5] This solution is generally preferred, Bormann, *CIL* xi. p. 336, etc. Cf. also App. *BC* III 42.174.

[6] *CIL* xi.3576–8 (reign of Gallienus).

in spite of Pliny's silence (in a *periplous* section). His silence suggests that the colony was not triumviral or Augustan, but Caesarian.[1]

FALERII.[2] 'Colonia Iunonia quae appellatur Faliscos a triumviris adsignata et modus iugerationis est datus . . .',[3] and in his description Pliny lists Falisca Etruscorum as a colony in an inland section.[4] The town was designated a colony in inscriptions of the reign of Gallienus—but it was probably only from him that it received the title.[5] Neither a triumviral nor an Augustan colony is in fact possible, for the *municipium* and its *quattuorviri* are well attested;[6] and a colony at Falerii Veteres has been judged from an archaeological point of view to be most unlikely.[7] Mommsen was probably right to find the explanation of Pliny's erroneous entry in a confusion with the Picene town of Falerio.[8]

FLORENTIA. 'Colonia Florentina deducta a triumviris, adsignata lege Iulia, centuriae Caesarianae in iugera CC . . .'[9] The vexed question of the foundation-date of the colony of Florentia is discussed elsewhere,[10] with the conclusion that a Sullan date is unlikely. The greatest difficulty in the view that it was of triumviral or Augustan date is that Pliny lists it among the non-colonies in his description;[11] this may be less of a difficulty if the colony was indeed triumviral and not Augustan, and a triumviral date is the most likely one.

[1] So Bormann, *CIL* xi. p. 530, and most others.

[2] This colony has generally been rejected since Mommsen; see art. cit., 176=217. Beloch, *It. Bund* 11, suggested that the colony may have been at Falerii Veteres=Cività Castellana; but see the text.

[3] *Lib. Col.* 217.5–6.

[4] *NH* III 51.

[5] *CIL* xi.3089, 3091–4. For his connection with Falerii see A. Alföldi, *Num. Chron.*, ser. 5.ix (1929), 269, etc.

[6] *CIL* xi.3083=*ILS* 5373, xi.3116=*ILS* 6585, xi.3125=*ILS* 3111 (the *municipium*); *CIL* xi.3116, 3119=*ILS* 6586, xi.3123=*ILS* 6587 (the *quattuorviri*). The *duoviri* of xi.7501–2 (cf. E. Vetter, *HID* p. 310) do not upset this interpretation.

[7] M. W. Frederiksen–J. B. Ward-Perkins, *PBSR* xxv (1957), 131–2.

[8] On the probable Augustan colony at Falerio see Mommsen in *CIL* ix. p. 517 and art. cit., 173=215. R. Thomsen, op. cit., 44, finds fault with this explanation on the grounds that Falerii was not on the list of inland towns that Pliny used but in one of the *periplous* sections of his description—but that is quite untrue ('Intus coloniae Falisca . . .'). Pliny may very well have got the Argive origin of Falerii from Cato, but (*pace* Bormann, *CIL* xi. p. 465) he hardly took an inland colony from that source.

[9] *Lib. Col.* 213.6–7.

[10] See p. 261 and Appendix III.

[11] *NH* III 52.

GRAVISCAE. 'Colonia Graviscos ab Augusto deduci iussa est';[1] but the town is listed as a non-colony by Pliny, in a *periplous* section,[2] and the entry in the *Libri Coloniarum* is very probably a mistake, referring to the colony of 181 B.C. if to anything.[3]

LUCA. Given as a colony by Pliny in a *periplous* section.[4] An inscription shows that land there was distributed to veterans, definitely before 27 B.C., and probably in the period after Philippi.[5] The colony subsequently appears in two Trajanic inscriptions.[6]

LUCUS FERONIAE. The colony is well attested as 'colonia Iulia Felix Lucoferoniensis' or 'Lucoferoniae'[7] and the town is registered as a colony by Pliny in an inland section.[8] An Augustan or triumviral date is therefore generally assumed,[9] but recently a Caesarian date has been put forward.[10] Distribution of land was carried out in 46 in the territory of Capena,[11] of which Lucus Feroniae must at that time have formed a part, but that does not tell against the fact that Pliny does not generally seem to have registered such few Caesarian colonies as there were in Italy. The title *Felix*, supposed to be contemporary with the only 'securely dated parallel', Sinope (47 B.C.),[12] is in fact well attested as the title of some triumviral or Augustan colonies in Italy, including Pisaurum and Beneventum, neither of which is at all likely to have been a Caesarian colony. Nor is there any reason why *Ludi Victoriae Caesaris*, which seem to have been celebrated at Lucus Feroniae, could not be celebrated in a triumviral or Augustan colony.[13] Since

[1] *Lib. Col.* 220.1.

[2] *NH* III 51.

[3] So Bormann, *CIL* xi. p. 511, cf. Mommsen, art. cit., 179=221.

[4] *NH* III 50.

[5] *CIL* vi.1460=*ILS* 887: 'L. Memmius C.f. Gal. q. tr. pl. frumenti curator ex s.c. praefectus leg. XXVI et VII Lucae ad agros dividundos . . .'. The *cura frumenti* probably belongs before Actium; cf. Gabba, comm. on App. *BC* V, p. lxiii n. 1.

[6] *CIL* xi.1147.vi.60 (the *Veleia Table*), 1525.

[7] *CIL* xi.3938, *NSA* 1953, 14 (G. Foti)=*AE* 1954, no. 162, *RPAA* xxxiii (1960–1961), 173–84 (R. Bartoccini)=*AE* 1962, no. 87.

[8] *NH* III 51.

[9] Cf. Mommsen, art. cit., 183=223.

[10] Taylor, *VDRR* 322 n. 12, made the suggestion. The view is argued at length by G. D. B. Jones, *PBSR* xxx (1962), 192–5.

[11] Cic. *Fam.* IX 17.2.

[12] Jones, art. cit., 194.

[13] *Pace* Jones, art. cit., 194–5.

the town appears in Frontinus as 'Lucus Feroniae Augustinorum',[1] an Augustan date is perhaps preferable to a triumviral one.

LUNA. According to the *Libri Coloniarum* land at Luna was assigned by the triumviral law—'Ager Lunensis ea lege qua et ager Florentinus'.[2] Pliny lists Luna as a non-colony, although only in a *periplous* section,[3] and the epigraphical references to a colony at Luna under the early Empire[4] can be referred to the colony of 177 B.C., so the notice in the *Libri Coloniarum* is unconfirmed.

NEPET. 'Colonia Nepis eadem lege servatur qua et ager Faliscorum',[5] i.e. by the law of the triumvirs. However not only is 'Nepeta' given as an *oppidum* by Pliny but there is also epigraphical evidence for the *municipium*,[6] and a colony of this period must be rejected.[7]

PERUSIA. This town is listed by Pliny as an *oppidum*,[8] and it is not known as a colony in the inscriptions until the time of the Perusine emperor Vibius Trebonianus Gallus. However most of the affluent Perusines were put to death by Octavian after the siege, and those who survived were apparently forbidden to own land more than seven and a half stades from the town.[9] The land beyond that range was available for Octavian to distribute, and the town was reconstituted as 'Augusta Perusia',[10] with *duoviri* instead of the previous *quattuorviri*.[11]

PISAE. The inscriptions from the cenotaphs of C. and L. Caesar at Pisae refer to the colony, the colonists being described as 'colonis Iuliensibus coloniae Opsequenti Iuliae Pisanae'.[12] The known centuriation at Pisae[13] is to be ascribed to this

[1] *De controversiis agrorum*, ii, p. 46.17L.

[2] *Lib. Col.* 223.14.

[3] *NH* III 50.

[4] *CIL* xi.1331=*ILS* 233, etc.

[5] *Lib. Col.* 217.15–16.

[6] Plin. *NH* III 52, *CIL* xi.3214, cf. 3212, x.6440=*ILS* 6277.

[7] Cf. Mommsen, art. cit., 177=218. E. Pais in his later works, *Storia della colonizzazione*, etc., 172–4, *Mem. Acc. Linc.*, ser. 6.i (1925), 375, 380, suggested that the entry in the *Lib. Col.* may have derived from actual *viritim* distribution of land at Nepet; there is no evidence that errors in the *Lib. Col.* arose in this way, but it is possible (cf. below on Volaterrae).

[8] *NH* III 52.

[9] Dio XLVIII 14.6.

[10] *CIL* xi.1924=*ILS* 5503, cf. xi.1929=*ILS* 6612.

[11] *CIL* xi.1924=*ILS* 5503, cf. xi.1941=*ILS* 6615, xi.1945. Cf. Bormann, *CIL* xi. p. 352, etc.

[12] *CIL* xi.1420–1=*ILS* 139–40.

[13] P. Fraccaro, *SE* xiii (1939), 221–29=*Opuscula*, iii (Pavia, 1957), 63–70.

settlement. In the manuscripts of Pliny's description Pisae is not apparently described as a colony;[1] it would be if an emendation of *colonia* to *coloniae* were made, as it perhaps should be. There is no way of deciding whether the colony was set up after Philippi or after Actium.

RUSELLAE. It is listed as a colony by Pliny.[2] He is supported by an inscription in which the abbreviation 'LLCI' probably refers to the *colonia Iulia*;[3] the inscription has been attributed to the early Empire.[4] 'COL RUS' appears in another local inscription,[5] which may be considerably later. Again, there is no way of deciding whether the colony was set up after Philippi or after Actium.

SAENA. Listed as a colony by Pliny, and referred to as a colony by Tacitus.[6] The town is known to have had the title 'Iulia' later, in the *Peutinger Table* (which does not prove that it was a colony). Again, a colony either after Philippi or after Actium.

SUTRIUM. It is listed as a colony by Pliny.[7] The title 'Colonia Coniunc(ta) Iulia Sutrina',[8] although it is reminiscent of the 'coloniae Concordiae' of the triumvirs,[9] is unique, and does not really give us any guide as to whether the colony was founded after Philippi or after Actium. It is usually held to have been an Antonian foundation in the first place because Appian describes it as χωρίον τι χρήσιμον τῷ Λευκίῳ,[10] but the strategic position of the town seems a possible explanation of Appian's remark. Again, the date remains open.

VEII. The town is listed as an *oppidum* by Pliny.[11] It was constituted as a *municipium* by Augustus, witness the title 'muni-

[1] *NH* III 50: 'colonia Luca a mari recedens propiorque Pisae inter amnes Auserem et Arnum ortae a . . .'

[2] *NH* III 51.

[3] A. Mazzolai, *MDAI–R* lxvi (1959), 217–18 (cf. *AE* 1960, no. 329): '. . . L(iberti et) L(ibertae) C(oloniae) I(uliae) . . .'

[4] Mazzolai, art. cit., 218.

[5] *CIL* xi.2618.

[6] Plin. *NH* III 51, Tac. *Hist.* IV 45.

[7] *NH* III 51.

[8] *CIL* xi.3254.

[9] G. Duncan, *PBSR* xxvi (1958), 68.

[10] App. *BC* V 31.122. Cf. Bormann, *CIL* xi. p. 489, etc. *CIL* xi.3322, which has sometimes been used as evidence for an Augustan foundation, is irrelevant, as Duncan, art. cit., 68 n. 9, pointed out.

[11] *NH* III 52.

cipium Augustum Veiens';[1] it was governed by *duoviri*.[2] Land in the *ager Veientanus* was assigned by Caesar in 46 B.C.[3] A very detailed notice in the *Libri Coloniarum* calls Veii a colony,[4] but this has been universally rejected. If the other statements in the notice are correct, Augustus decided to bring to an end the separate government of Veii[5] (which had probably come into existence after the Social War), but later, having increased the population with veterans and others, he reversed the decision.[6] It is probable that the Caesarian settlers were followed by Augustan ones.

VOLATERRAE. 'Colonia Volaterrana lege triumvirale . . . est adsignata. Quam omnem veterani . . . habent . . .'[7] Pliny, however, gives Volaterrae as an *oppidum* in an inland section, and the town continued to be governed by *quattuorviri*.[8] It is possible that the error in the *Libri Coloniarum* arose from the distribution of land that took place at Volaterrae in 45.[9]

There is evidence for triumviral or Augustan colonization or *viritim* settlement in the following areas of Umbria:

AMERIA. The town is listed as an *oppidum* by Pliny.[10] According to the *Libri Coloniarum* 'Ager Amerinus lege imp. Augusti

[1] *CIL* xi.3797=*ILS* 922 (1 A.D.).

[2] *CIL* xi.3805=*ILS* 6579 (26 A.D.).

[3] Cic. *Fam.* IX 17.2.

[4] *Lib. Col.* 220.8–16: 'Colonia Veios, prius quam oppugnaretur, ager eius militibus est adsignatus ex lege Iulia [probably a reference to assignment by Caesar]. Postea deficientibus his ad urbanam civitatem associandos censuerat divus Augustus [presumably before the decision to establish the *municipium Augustum*]. . . . Pars vero camporum et silve . . . a divo Augusto veteranis pro parte data fuit.' (cf. 223.10).

[5] Thus I interpret 'ad urbanam civitatem associandos censuerat', *pace* Pais, *Storia della colonizzazione*, etc., 178, G. D. B. Jones, *Latomus*, xxii (1963), 774–5.

[6] Confirmation of the fact that Veii had been temporarily depopulated is to be found in *CIL* xi.3805, where Augustus' freedman C. Iulius Gelos is honoured by Veii because (among other reasons) 'municip. Veios . . . impensis suis et per filium suum celebrari voluerit'.

[7] *Lib. Col.* 214.10–13.

[8] Plin. *NH* III 52, *CIL* xi.1744, 1746, 1749, 1752. The triumviral colony has been generally rejected, cf. Mommsen, art. cit., 177=219. Pais, *Storia della colonizzazione*, etc., 168, *Mem. Acc. Linc.*, ser. 6.i (1925), 374–5, 380, fails to advance any real reason for doubting this conclusion.

[9] Suggested by Bormann, *CIL* xi. p. 325.

[10] *NH* III 113. All the following references to Umbrian towns in Pliny's list are in the same section.

est assignatus',[1] but there is no other evidence for or against the assertion; it remains merely a possibility.

ASISIUM. The assignment of some of the territory of Asisium that is referred to by Propertius[2] is probably to be connected with the foundation of the colony of Hispellum, which received some neighbouring territory; in any case it is certain that some land that had been in the territory of Asisium was taken away from its proprietors and that that happened in the triumviral period. Asisium is registered as an *oppidum* in Pliny.

FANUM FORTUNAE. The town is given as a colony by Pliny in a *periplous* section. It appears as 'colonia Iulia Fanestris' and 'colonia Iulia Fanum Fortunae' in inscriptions,[3] and as 'colonia Iulia Fanestris' in Vitruvius.[4] It cannot be known whether the colony was triumviral or Augustan.

FULGINIAE. An *oppidum* in Pliny's list, it may like Asisium have lost land to the colony of Hispellum.

HISPELLUM. The town is given as a colony in an inland section by Pliny, and the 'colonia Iulia' appears in an inscription.[5] The *Lex Aelia* under which land in the *ager Spellatinus* was assigned according to the *Libri Coloniarum* may in fact have been a *Lex Iulia*.[6] Since the colony of Hispellum is said by Hyginus[7] to have acquired land from its neighbours, and Asisium undoubtedly lost land to settlers in the period after Philippi, the colony was probably triumviral.[8] Two *duoviri* of Hispellum who appear in an inscription lacked *cognomina*, and therefore as early a date as possible is probably to be preferred;[9] the *quattuorviri* who appear in other inscriptions[10] can be dated earlier than the triumvirate without difficulty.

[1] *Lib. Col.* 224.11.

[2] IV 1.125–30: '... abstulit excultas pertica tristis opes.'

[3] *CIL* xi.6232, 6238=*ILS* 6651.

[4] V 1.6.

[5] *CIL* xi.5278=*ILS* 6624 (cf. xi.5269a).

[6] *Lib. Col.* 224.6. Mommsen, *Die Schriften der römischen Feldmesser*, ii (Berlin, 1852), 178 n. 43.

[7] Hygin. Grom. 179L.

[8] U. Ciotti, *BCAR* lxxi (1943–5), Appendice vol. xiv, pp. 55–6.

[9] The inscription was published by Ciotti, art. cit., 53 (=*AE* 1948, no. 102=*ILLRP* 614), and he pointed out, with appropriate caution, the chronological significance of the lack of *cognomina*.

[10] *CIL* xi.5281, 5288=*ILLRP* 611–12.

PISAURUM. The Antonian colony was transformed into the 'colonia Iulia Felix Pisaurum';[1] it appears as a colony in Pliny, in a *periplous* section.

SENA GALLICA. Land is said in the *Libri Coloniarum* to have been assigned by the triumviral law.[2] There is no other evidence for or against this.

TUDER. 'Colonia Fida Tuder ea lege qua et ager Florentinus'.[3] That there was a triumviral or Augustan colony is certain, for Pliny lists it as a colony (in an inland section), and it is well attested in inscriptions—its full name apparently being 'Colonia Iulia Fida Tuder'.[4] The colony is also referred to by Frontinus.[5] Whether it was founded after Philippi or after Actium cannot be decided with confidence, but since the notice in the *Libri Coloniarum* identifies the colony correctly, it may also have the correct date, i.e. under the triumvirate.[6]

Such an attempt to identify the Augustan colonies can only tell us about part of the settlement that took place. While we can be fairly sure that there were few triumviral colonies that cannot be identified from the existing evidence and that there were very few if any Augustan colonies that are not known at least as colonies of the triumviral or Augustan periods, there were obviously also many places where there was *viritim* assignment of land. Individual opponents and so assignable land were to be found virtually everywhere.

Etruria was with Campania the area that was most affected by the triumviral and Augustan colonization, perhaps because of the desirability of the land in those areas. Of the more important towns in Etruria only Tarquinii, Volsinii, and Clusium may have survived the triumvirs and Augustus fairly untroubled. The displacement of population was not of course limited to the areas that were inhabited mainly by the descendants of real Etruscans—former Roman colonies were just as vulnerable. The settlement must, however, have done a

[1] *CIL* xi.6335=*ILS* 7218, xi.6377.

[2] *Lib. Col.* 226.9–12.

[3] *Lib. Col.* 214.3–4.

[4] *CIL* xi.4646. For veterans of Legion XXXXI who were settled there see xi.4650=*ILS* 2230, xi.4654=*ILS* 2231.

[5] *De controversiis agrorum*, ii.52–3L.

[6] So Mommsen, art. cit., 183=224.

considerable amount to bring the process of Romanization nearer to completion. Since the Lex Iulia and the Sullan colonization it had been inevitable that the process would be completed, but there are still a few signs of Etruscan characteristics in the period of the triumvirate and Augustus. The evidence about the language has already been discussed;[1] the latest known instances of the use of Etruscan are a bilingual funerary inscription from Arretium, another from the tomb of the Volumnii at Perusia and the Etruscan inscriptions from the tomb of the Hepenii at Asciano in the territory of Saena. Even in the most remote parts of Etruria the local language seems no longer to have been used by the literate a few years after the establishment of the Principate.

In spite of the turmoil of the period when the triumviral and Augustan settlements were being made, some local families in the Etruscan towns are specifically known to have survived and to have preserved or even increased their strength. That there were such survivors is quite obvious, but it is worth noting that there is epigraphical evidence to this effect. Local families that rose in station under Augustus while maintaining local connections included the Caecinae of Volaterrae (also powerful in other towns)[2] and the Seii of Volsinii. The Caecina family, having survived the Sullan settlement and the victory of Caesar, not without some difficulties, included a man who acted as an agent for Octavian in 44,[3] and (perhaps the same man) a mutual friend of Antony and Octavian who was used by the latter as a mediator in 41.[4] It may have been as early as this that a certain L. Caecina L.f. rose as high as the praetorship;[5] and under Augustus the family achieved a suffect consulship (A. Caecina, 1 B.C.). Meanwhile at Volaterrae a theatre was constructed, probably in the 30s or in the first years of the Principate,[6] probably by the two A. Caecinae whose names were commemorated in the theatre on a strikingly

[1] Chapter V, Section 3.

[2] On their position see above, p. 282 n. 1.

[3] Cic. *Att.* XVI 8.2—'Caecina quidam Volaterranus'.

[4] App. *BC* V 60.251. That these two references concern the same man was suggested by R. Syme, *CPh* l (1955), 133.

[5] *CIL* i².2515=*ILLRP* 438.

[6] E. Fiumi, *NSA* 1955, 131, gives the theatre a *terminus post quem* of 40–35 B.C.; A. De Agostino, ibid., 178, dates it to the end of the first century.

grand scale.[1] A family tree cannot be worked out, but Caecinae are so few that the fortunes of most of them are likely to have been interconnected.[2] How long the Seii, whose leading Augustan member, the father of Sejanus, rose to be prefect of Egypt, had been at Volsinii we cannot tell, but there is no reason to doubt that they were genuinely local.[3] Among local families that continue to appear in the inscriptions in the two generations after Caesar's death were the Laberii at Arretium and the Hepenii at Asciano, who retained the use of the Etruscan language, and also the Ciartii at Arretium.[4] At Tarquinii two old families, the Spurinnae and Caesennii, survived to erect the famous *elogia*.[5] Even at Perusia there were apparently some survivors of the old local population in the new *municipium* of Augustus, in spite of the fact that all the local senators with the exception of a certain L. Aemilius are said to have been murdered. The last man to be buried in the big family tomb of the Volumnii was 'P. Volumnius A.f. Violens Cafatia natus', whose funerary urn was made of marble and therefore hardly pre-Augustan.[6] P. Volumnius P.f. Violens,[7]

[1] The inscription is described by Fiumi, ibid., 123 (=*AE* 1957, no. 220).

[2] This in spite of the fact that the Caecina of *Att.* XVI 8.2 was not an acquaintance of Cicero's.

[3] The Volsinian origin of Sejanus: Tac. *Ann.* IV 1, VI 8, confirmed by *CIL* xi.2707. The acephalous inscription *CIL* xi.7285=*ILS* 8996 set up at Volsinii by a prefect of Egypt and his family has usually been referred since Cichorius (*Hermes*, xxxix (1904), 461–71) to the father of Sejanus. On this hypothesis Seius married well, Terentia A.f. being the sister of Varro Murena, the consul of 23 B.C. (and so also a relative of Maecenas) (cf. Syme, *RR* 358, etc.). T. P. Wiseman, *Latomus*, xxii (1963), 87–90, suggests that he also married into another senatorial family, namely the Teidii, which is possible. The acephalous inscription from Volsinii has, however, now been referred not to Seius but to C. Caecina Tuscus, prefect of Egypt under Nero and also of Etruscan origin, G. V. Sumner, *Phoenix*, xix (1965), 134–45; on balance this seems more likely.

[4] See *CIL* xi.1856. Evidence of its date: the stone is marble, and Cn. Petronius Cn. f. Asellio in the inscription may well be the Tiberian *tribunus militum* of that name who was in the Pomptina, the tribe of Arretium (*CIL* xiii.6816). The name Ciartia is evidently connected with Etruscan (and especially Arretine) *ciarthisa* (*CIE* 432, cf. *CIE* 428=*TLE* 662 (a bilingual), *TLE* 446).

[5] See above, p. 29.

[6] *CIL* xi.1963=*CIE* 3763=*ILS* 7833. On the dating see J. Thimme, *SE* xxiii (1954), 133. Note the social pretensions indicated by the *cognomen* 'Violens', which was on record as the *cognomen* of the Volumnius who was cos. in 307 and 296 (for a rather visionary discussion of this connection cf. J. Heurgon, *Archeologia Classica*, x (1958), 151–9). The Volumnii of Perusia cannot incidentally be shown to be connected with any of the other known late-republican Volumnii.

[7] *CIL* xi.1944=*ILS* 6618.

who was in all probability his son, was both *quattuorvir* and *duovir*, as was L. Proculeius A.f. Titia gnatus.[1] Given the known facts of Perusia's history, these two probably held the two offices before and after the siege respectively, as Bormann pointed out;[2] both families must have been on Octavian's side during the siege,[3] and when the *municipium* was reconstituted they were rewarded.

Etruria was certainly not under Augustus the 'depleted and unwanted country' that Tenney Frank described.[4] There were new forms of prosperity, manufacture of pottery at Arretium, and the exploitation of the marble quarries near Luna; in the south certain areas of Etruria came to be used much more by the rich from the capital than they had been before.[5] Strabo is a poor guide to the actual state of affairs in Etruria at the time when he wrote—there is no reason to think that he spoke from any first-hand knowledge of the inland area, and even for the coast (he travelled as far north as Populonium by sea) his information is sparse—the only important contemporary reference is to the Luna marble trade and its exports to Rome.[6] The archaeological evidence is more informative, although we should be cautious in inferring general economic conditions from the existence of expensive public buildings.[7] As Rostovtzeff pointed out,[8] the Augustan period was a time when an impressive number of public buildings were erected in Etruria, as in Campania; and he might have added that this was also the case in Umbria. Consider (in the southern part of Etruria) Lucus Feroniae with its Augusteum and Aqua Augusta,[9] the

[1] *CIL* xi.1943=*ILS* 6617.

[2] *CIL* xi. p. 353. Degrassi, *Mem. Acc. Linc.*, ser. 8.ii (1950), 328, was doubtful, and suggested that it was the quattuorvirate *aedilicia potestate* that they held—however it would surely have been stated if that had been the case.

[3] Cf. A. J. Pfiffig, *Studi in onore di L. Banti* (Rome, 1965), 278.

[4] *Economic Survey of Ancient Rome*, v (Baltimore, 1940), 123.

[5] Cf. U. Kahrstedt, *Kulturgeschichte der römischen Kaiserzeit*[2] (Munich, 1944), 91.

[6] V 2.5 222–3C.

[7] We have no way of telling for example how many transactions there were similar to the one at Capua by which, in exchange for land that he made public, Octavian gave to the citizens an aqueduct as well as the territory of Cnossos (Dio XLIX 14.5).

[8] *Social and Economic History of the Roman Empire*[2] (Oxford, 1957), 58, 71. For some substantiation cf. G. D. B. Jones, *PBSR* xxx (1962), 194.

[9] On the Augusteum and Aqua Augusta see Jones, art. cit., 193. He also suggests a date in the first half of the first century A.D. for the small amphitheatre (ibid.),

probably Augustan amphitheatre of Sutrium,[1] the extensive building works of the *duovir* L. Ateius Capito at Castrum Novum,[2] the aqueducts at Caere and Falerii;[3] and (further north) the Augustan baths, the forum and the Augusteum at Ferentium (further work was also done to the theatre),[4] the baths built 'cum omni ornatu' by a prefect of Egypt at Volsinii,[5] the small amphitheatre of triumviral date at Rusellae;[6] and (in northern Etruria) the Augustan theatre at Volaterrae (see above), the baths and theatre at Faesulae,[7] the walls, towers, and theatre at Florentia,[8] the baths and Augusteum at Pisae,[9] the theatre at Luna.[10] This is not an attempt to give an exhaustive catalogue of the public buildings of the region, merely a list of examples of notable buildings that can be fairly well dated. It is sufficient to support the judgement of Rostovtzeff that Augustan Etruria was a prosperous region; and it may be added that this was not a single wave of activity that came to a stop after Augustus' death. In Umbria also there is a similar wealth of public building: for examples we can look to the theatre and amphitheatre at Ocriculum,[11] the theatre at Spoletium,[12] the portico, theatre, and *crypta* at Interamna

but R. Bartoccini, *RPAA* xxxiii (1960–1), 173–84, argued for a later date. These and the subsequent references concerning particular buildings are merely meant to be the most concise possible guide to the evidence.

[1] G. Duncan, *PBSR* xxvi (1958), 70–1.

[2] See *CIL* xi.3583=*ILS* 5515—'curiam tabularium scaenarium subseliarium . . . porticus cenacula . . .' The date of the inscription is, however, open to dispute.

[3] See *CIL* xi.3594 and M. W. Frederiksen–J. B. Ward-Perkins, *PBSR* xxv (1957), 104, respectively.

[4] On the baths see M. E. Blake, *Roman Construction in Italy from Tiberius through the Flavians* (Washington, 1959), 76; on the forum and Augusteum, *CIL* xi.7431; on the Augustan work in the theatre, G. Lugli, *La tecnica edilizia romana* (Rome, 1957), 359.

[5] *CIL* xi.7285=*ILS* 8996.

[6] See C. Laviosa, *SE* xxvii (1959), esp. 14 n. 10.

[7] On the baths, Lugli, op. cit., 639–40, G. Maetzke, *SE* xxvii (1959), 62; on the theatre, Lugli, l.c., Maetzke, art. cit., 45–9.

[8] On the walls and towers see below, p. 343 n. 1; on the theatre, Blake, op. cit., 75.

[9] These are mentioned in the cenotaph inscriptions of C. and L. Caesar, *CIL* xi.1421 (=*ILS* 140), line 23 (baths), ibid. line 1 and xi.1420 (= *ILS* 139), line 1 (the Augusteum).

[10] L. Banti, *Luni* (Florence, 1937), 65.

[11] C. Pietrangeli, *Ocriculum* (*Italia Romana: Municipi e colonie*) (Rome, 1943), 30, 64–6, M. E. Blake, *Ancient Roman Construction in Italy* (Washington, 1947), 236.

[12] Blake, op. cit., 222, Lugli, op. cit., 643.

Nahars (perhaps Tiberian),[1] the theatre at Tuder,[2] the walls of Hispellum, Fanum Fortunae, and other towns,[3] the theatre at Iguvium,[4] the aqueduct at Sestinum.[5]

Those who enjoyed these buildings were Romans, not Etruscans and Umbrians. Roman policies had from the first tended to assist Romanization in some ways; that was the case even in Etruria, though much more so in Umbria and some other parts of Italy. During the period when Rome, in response to the special circumstances of Etruria, left the Etruscans with a high degree of independence, the process continued slowly, gathering momentum only at the end of the second century. The political unification of Italy after the Social War, together with Sulla's settlement, while they left much of the local population undisturbed and of course allowed the local towns to retain some independence, all but completed the history of the Etruscans as a separate nation. The same applied in Umbria, except that the identity of the local population was lost somewhat earlier. After the late Republic it is not possible to regard Etruria or Umbria as separate political entities; Augustus merely hastened the end of the long process of Roman conquest and Romanization, and symbolized it by converting Etruria and Umbria into, respectively, the seventh and sixth regions of Italy.[6]

[1] See *CIL* xi.4206=*ILS* 5645.

[2] Lugli, l.c.

[3] Hispellum: Blake, op. cit., 113, 201–2, following I. A. Richmond, *PBSR* xii (1932), 56–62, *JRS* xxiii (1933), 163–4, 172. Fanum: *CIL* xi.6218=*ILS* 706, xi.6219=*ILS* 104, Blake, op. cit., 113, 204. For Augustan work on the walls at Mevania see Lugli, op. cit., 643 (but cf. C. Pietrangeli, *Mevania* (*Italia Romana: Municipi e colonie*) (Rome, 1953), 60). An Augustan gate at Carsulae: Blake, op. cit., 202.

[4] Blake, op. cit., 220, Lugli, op. cit., 680.

[5] See *CIL* xi.6016=*ILS* 5758.

[6] It is surely incorrect to see the creation of the Italian regions as a homage to local history and traditions, as does G. Tibiletti, *Mélanges d'archéologie, d'épigraphie, et d'histoire offerts à J. Carcopino* (Paris, 1966), 918.

APPENDIX I

Etruscans who acquired Roman Citizenship before the Social War[1]

CARRINAS. Enfranchisement: no Carrinas appears at Rome before C. Carrinas, *RE* no. 1, praetor in 82 (Oros. V 21.10). Did the family have the Roman citizenship before the Social War? E. Gabba, *Athenaeum*, xxxii (1954), 102 n. 1, thinks not. Admittedly it is difficult to say that such a new citizen could not have become a praetor in a year in which one of the consuls was twenty-six. The best-attested case of new citizens obtaining such high office in the 80s is that of the two sons of Minatus Magius of Aeclanum, who, according to their descendant Velleius (II 16.3), who should have known, were both praetors before 81 ('cum seni adhuc crearentur') as a reward for their father's loyalty to Rome in the Social War (cf. also the case of C. Fabius Hadrianus, perhaps from the Latin colony of Hadria,[2] and praetor probably in 84; and the case of Burrienus, pr. 83, above p. 252); Velleius explicitly states that their father was enfranchised for his services in the war, and presumably the sons were too, but two praetorships in this period are difficult to credit. In any case it is surely easier to believe that Carrinas was already a citizen before the war.

Origins: Carrinas was 'presumably Umbrian or Etruscan', Syme *RR* 90 and n. 4 (Münzer, *RE* s.v. Carrinas, who is cited, did not take this view); Etruscan, according to Badian, *FC* 269 n. 3. The evidence referred to is Schulze's view (*ZGLE* 528–31) that names ending in -nas were fundamentally Etruscan,[3] which is sufficient. The name does not occur in inscriptions in Etruria or Umbria, and elsewhere seldom and late (references in Schulze, 530 n. 2; add *CIL* iv.2124b (M. Carr.), *AE* 1927, no. 129, 1940, no. 10); but note Carinia Secundina, wife of the praetorian Vibius Florentinus (*CIL* vi.2516—cf. Schulze, 146). Schulze (l.c.) draws attention to Etr. *carna(ś)*, common at Clusium and Perusia, *CIE* 826, 828, 1957–61, 2506, 2715, 2909, 2964, 4853–4 (*ager Clusinus*), 3815–16, 4229, 4238

[1] See above, pp. 192–201.

[2] Doubt is thrown on his origin by the republican inscription *AE* 1959, no. 272, referred to by Badian, *Historia*, xii (1963), 133.

[3] On this see also G. Devoto, *SE* iii (1929), 261–2, Ernst Fraenkel in *RE* s.v. *Namenwesen* (1935), cols. 1652–3, G. Bonfante, *Mélanges Marouzeau* (Paris, 1948), 57–8, A. Ernout, *Philologica*, iii (Paris, 1965), 33–4.

(Perusia): to which add M. Buffa, *Nuova raccolta di iscrizioni etrusche* (Florence, 1935), no. 445, *SE* xi (1937), 427 (G. Buonamici) (both from Perusia).

There is some evidence for the tribe of Carrinas, cos. suff. 43, son of the praetor of 82 (G. Cousin–G. Deschamps, *BCH* xi (1887), 226–7, R. K. Sherk, *Roman Documents from the Greek East* (Baltimore, 1969), 158, Taylor, *VDRR* 201); he was in the Quirina (or, less probably, the Collina), and therefore probably not in the tribe of an Etruscan or Umbrian town; that increases the likelihood that the family was enfranchised before the war.

MAECENAS. Enfranchisement: C. Maecenas (*RE* no. 3) was a leading (or typical?) *eques Romanus*, one of three who are described as 'illa robora populi Romani' by Cicero because of their resistance to Drusus' *lex iudiciaria* in 91 (*Clu.* 153) together with the rest of the order. It looks as if he was much too prominent to be a recent enfranchisement by Marius (as was suggested by Badian, *FC* 223). Another citizen from before the Social War may occur in *CIL* i^2.2519 (add p. 844) = *ILLRP* 771, which refers to a 'Maecenas D.f.' (*RE* no. 1), *patronus* of a *sunhodos* at Rome. The inscription has been dated by some to the turn of the second century (Münzer in *RE*), but there can be no certainty of that; it has recently been dated to the mid-first century (A. Degrassi, *Auctarium* (Berlin, 1965), p. 210).[1] A further point: the known Maecenates are so few that they are likely to be closely linked,[2] but Maecenas D.f. is in the tribe Maecia[3] whereas the famous Maecenas was in the Pomptina, the tribe of Arretium (*CIL* vi.21771 = *ILS* 7848). If Maecenas D.f. derived directly from Arretium, he was enfranchised before it.

Origins: Maecenas, not Cilnius, was Maecenas' *nomen* (E. Bormann, *Progr. Univ. Marburg*, 1883, pp. iii–v).[4] But whatever is to be made of Augustus' alleged description of him as 'Cilniorum smaragde' (Macrob. *Sat.* II 4.12), Tac. *Ann.* VI 11 makes it very likely that he took the additional name.[5] The Cilnii were believed

[1] Dated to the time of Sulla by R. Paribeni, *Raccolta di scritti in onore di G. Lumbroso* (Milan, 1925), 287–92.

[2] The *praenomen* C. recurs. Note that there is no evidence that Maecenas D.f. had the *praenomen* L., which was that of the father of the famous Maecenas (*CIL* vi.21771, *AE* 1924, no. 5, cf. Nic. Dam. *Vita Caes.*, 133). Degrassi's attempt to extract it from the last letter of the preceding word fails, for the stone is broken in such a way that the whole of the *praenomen* is lost (seen 1962; confirmed by Degrassi's photograph in the *Auctarium*).

[3] 'MAL' is written, presumably for 'MAE'.

[4] Cf. A. Stein in *RE* s.v. Maecenas no. 6 (1930), cols. 207–8. The point is sometimes ignored, e.g. A. J. Pfiffig, *Gymnasium*, lxxi (1964), 27.

[5] Surely Tacitus cannot have been mistaken—yet the name is omitted in inscriptions. Bormann suggested that M. was descended from the Cilnii on his

to have been the dominant family at Arretium (Liv. X 3.2, 5.13), and some probably genuine descendants held office at Rome in the first century A.D. (*PIR*² C 731, 732).[1] It is obvious that Maecenas made some claim to descent from Etruscan kings (Hor. *Od.* III 29.1, 35, I 1.1, *Sat.* I 6.1–4, Propert. III 9.1, and later references); very probably he made claim to a specifically Arretine origin—this we may infer from the phrase 'lasar Arretinum' in Macrobius, the name Cilnius, the known tribe, and perhaps from a reference in Hor. *Od.* I 20.5 (see Nisbet–Hubbard ad loc.). There is no reason to doubt the Etruscan origin of the Roman Maecenates; good confirmation is provided by the suffix of the name (Schulze, *ZGLE* 528–31), and some by the Etruscan name *mehnate*, found in various forms in *CIE* 4180, 4395, 4405 and probably 3888 (all from Perusia); some also by the presence of a Maecenas at the murder of Sertorius (see above, p. 286).

NIGIDIUS. Enfranchisement: a C. Nigidius (*RE* no. 1) was a praetor *c.* 145 (*de vir. ill.* 71) and the name is not known again in the literature until the appearance of the *Pythagoricus et magus* P. Nigidius Figulus (*RE* no. 3), pr. 58. So rare is the name that a connection is likely.

Origins: it was surely possible to be an authority on Etruscan *disciplina* in the first century, like Fonteius Capito perhaps,[2] without being an Etruscan. However the two other best-known experts on Etruscan *disciplina* in the first century, Caecina and Tarquitius Priscus, were of Etruscan origin, and Nigidius too should be accepted as such, especially as he probably understood the Etruscan language.[3] The *nomen* occurs once in *CIL* i² (2640, of the first century according to A. Degrassi, *Auctarium*, p. 220); this is from a Perusine tomb that also contained 2637–9 and 2641–2 (A. Paoletti, *NSA* 1926, 171–6; all six=*ILLRP* 814). 'L. Nigidius L.f. Sors scriba aed(ilium) cur(ulium)' must have been a Roman citizen; but his presumed father 'L. Sortes D.f. Nic(idius)' (2639), a brother of the latter (2638, a first-century inscription according to Degrassi, *Auctarium*, p. 228) and a freedman of the father of these two brothers (2637) have a *nomen* that is common at Perusia in its Etruscan form *surte* (*CIE* 4056, 4227, 4468, 4489, 4491, etc.).[4] It has further been

mother's side (cf. Hor. *Sat.* I 6.3, Schulze, *ZGLE* 149). R. Syme has further suggested, rather fancifully, that Claudius was the source for Tacitus' notion about Maecenas' name, *Tacitus* (Oxford, 1958), 709 n. 3.

[1] Cf. Syme, op. cit., 599 n. 9.

[2] On whom see S. Weinstock, *PBSR* xviii (1950), 44–9. Other Fonteii came from Tusculum (Cic. *Font.* 41).

[3] Cf. above, pp. 6–8.

[4] Fastia, which is presumably to be seen in 'FAS CEAT', i.e. Fas(tia) cnat(us), in i².2638, is also a local name, cf. *CIE* 4491.

suggested that the name Nigidius is based on the translation of Etr. *surte* as Lat. *niger*.[1] The evidence in favour of an Etruscan origin outweighs the concentration of Nigidii at Pompeii pointed out by T. P. Wiseman, *CQ* n.s.xiv (1964), 127 (*CIL* iv.1177, 1179–80, 3785, 4696, x.818, 8071.48), although elsewhere in Italy they are rare (*CIL* ix.4928, 5094 (?), x.3358).

PERPERNA. Enfranchisement: M. Perperna (*RE* no. 3) was sent as a *legatus* to king Gentius of Illyria in 168 (sources: *MRR* i.430), and in 130 his presumed son M. Perperna (*RE* no. 4) achieved the consulship.[2] Valerius Maximus (III 4.5) has a strange story that a certain M. Perperna turned out to have been 'consul ante quam civis', because his father was discovered not to have been a citizen. There are several difficulties in Valerius' story (see Mommsen, *Römisches Staatsr.*, iii.200 n. 1, *Römisches Strafr.*, 858, M. Gelzer, *Die Nobilität der römischen Republik*, 41 n. 5=*KS* i.59 n. 457, Münzer, *Römische Adelsparteien und Adelsfamilien*, 96), but they are not removed by taking the story away from the cos. of 130, to whom Valerius clearly assigns it (*MRR* ii.19 n. 1 associates it with the cos. of 92). It seems unlikely that a member of the Perperna family ever falsely claimed to be a Roman citizen, since they were associated with powerful nobles, in particular with Ap. Claudius Centho (pr. 175) and later with the Claudii Pulchri (see Münzer, op. cit., 95–6). In any case the consulship of 92 suggests that nothing had been found wrong with the family's status (L. Lange, *Römische Alterthümer*, iii[2] (Berlin, 1876), 135), and the father's initial appears in the *Fasti* for 92 (A. Degrassi, *Inscr. It.* xiii.1 129, 164–5, 480–1)—unfortunately we cannot tell whether the grandfather's did as well.[3] The omission of M. Perperna, cos. 92, from the list of the *cuncta nobilitas* in Cicero, *Rab. Perd.* 20, which Gelzer (l.c.) thought could be interpreted as evidence that Cicero regarded as invalid the consulship of the father in 130, can be explained otherwise—even if the consul of 92 was in the Senate in 63 (he died a senator in 49), his presumed son (Münzer, op. cit., 96–7) was the *praetorius* M. Perperna who fought on the side of Sertorius, and a recent *hostis rei publicae* will have disqualified the family from Cicero's list of respected aristocrats. By when was the family given its Roman citizenship? The name Nepos, which the Chronographer of 354 puts in Perperna's place for the cos. of 130, shows (as in similar

[1] E. Vetter, *Glotta*, xv (1927), 226–7, *HID* p. 274, H. Rix, *Das etruskische Cognomen* (Wiesbaden, 1963), 190.

[2] The supposed moneyer Perperna mentioned by Fronto (p. 161 Naber) is to be ignored.

[3] Note also Perpennia, a presumably rather elderly Vestal Virgin in 69; we do not know when she achieved that honour. Cf. *MRR* ii.137 n. 14.

cases) that the man lacked a *cognomen* but claimed a citizen grandfather (A. Degrassi, *Inscr. It.*, xiii.1 126, 346; supported by M. Perperna L.f. in *IG* ix.2 258, line 7), but 168 is the only definite *terminus ante quem.*

Origins: the *nomen* is commonly taken to be Etruscan (cf. Münzer, *RE* s.v., *zweifellos*), and cumulatively the evidence is strong. The termination -erna is a sufficiently well-attested form of the Etruscan-derived -enna, which is very common (Schulze, *ZGLE* 65–107), and the form Perpenna occurs epigraphically (see Schulze, 88) and very frequently in texts; for similar forms cf. Perna (ibid., 85–6), Mastarna (ibid., 85–6), Sepernas (a goddess, *CIL* xi.3868, cf. Schulze, 531, 569).[1] The exact Etruscan form of Perperna is elusive: Schulze (88) suggests that *prpris* (*CIE* 2606, Clusium) was a related name;[2] cf. also *perpran*, *perprathi*, etc., *CIE* 3370–1, 3397, 3399–400, all from Perusia. The name appears in two inscriptions of the republican period from Rome, 1132 (if M. Perpea is M. Perpena, as Lommatzsch thought; the date, p. 580, is the second half of the second century B.C.) and 1356 (=*ILLRP* 773), and in none from Etruria; but cf. *CIE* 2543=xi.2378 ('Perperna Lartha'—Clusium), which shows the Etruscan connection, and also *CIE* 89=xi.7072 (Volaterrae). In *CIL* there are rather more instances in Etruria than anywhere else, although Perpernae are established, e.g., at Velitrae (x.6493: M. M.f., the tribe Sca. indicating Velitrae) and Veii (xi.3805, a *duovir* in the reign of Tiberius). Further, among the connections of the emperor Vibius Trebonianus Gallus, who indulged in Etruscan nomenclature, was the younger son of Decius, to whom the Senate gave the name Perpenna (Aurel. Victor, *Epit.* 30, cf. J. Heurgon, *SE* xxiv (1955–6), 92). Against all this there is the curious mention in Valerius Maximus (l.c.) of the Sabellians who were responsible for the return of the consul's father 'in pristinas sedes' (it is not specified that Perperna was a Sabellian, but it is an obvious inference, cf. 'Sabellus genere' in the epitomator Julius Paris, Val. Max. ed. Kempf, p. 507); that is usually dismissed as merely another mistake by Valerius (cf. Münzer in *RE* s.v. Perperna), which is preferable to denying the other evidence about the origin of the Perpernae.

SAENIUS. Enfranchisement: Saenii were citizens before the Social War if the *monetalis* who appears as C. Sae. in the mid-second

[1] See above on Carrinas; on -erna endings cf. A. Ernout, *Philologica* (Paris, 1946), 29–32.

[2] The text might seem from *CIE* to be 'aeθprpris', without any interpunction; but from the tile itself (seen by me in the Museo Civico at Chiusi in 1969) it is clear that the text should read 'ae·prpris'. E. Vetter's suggested explanation of the inscription, *Jahreshefte des Oest. Arch. Inst.*, xxxvii (1948), *Beiblatt*, cols. 64–5, is a fantasy.

century (Sydenham, *Roman Republican Coinage*, 40 (*c.* 150–133 B.C.); Grueber, *Coins of the Roman Republic in the B.M.*, i.107 (*c.* 172–151)) was a Saenius. This seems very likely, although there are other names beginning with Sae. (cf. Schulze—none of them appears in *MRR*, *PIR* or *CIL* i²). Only one coin of one issue is known to exist, but numismatists seem to accept it as authentic (cf. M. Bahrfeldt, *Num. Zeitschrift*, xxxii (1900), 77, Grueber, op. cit., i.107 n. 3). L. Saenius (*RE* no. 1) was a senator in 63 (Sall. *Cat.* 30) and his probable son (*RE* no. 2) was cos. suff. in 30.

Origins: in 63 L. Saenius 'in senatu litteras recitavit quas Faesulis adlatas sibi dicebat', about Manlius' activities in Etruria (Sallust). Did his family come from Saena? Topographical *nomina* deserve a certain caution when we are looking for origins (cf. E. Badian, *Historia*, vi (1957), 334–5 = *Studies in Greek and Roman History* (Oxford, 1964), 49, on Norbanus' supposed connection with Norba). There is a rare Etruscan name that can be connected with Saenius, saeinal (*CIE* 1777), sainei (*CIE* 589) (both inscriptions are from the *ager Clusinus*; the name also appears in other forms), but that is not in itself very strong evidence. More important, there is good reason to believe that *RE* no. 2 was in the Oufentina, the tribe of Saena (see below, p. 334). And for what such evidence is worth, two areas of Italy have 'concentrations' of Saenii: there are four inscriptions close together at Misenum (*CIL* x.3427, 3625), Puteoli (3029), and Liternum (3715), and probably nine in the area of Asisium (xi.5414) and northern Etruria (2422–3 and probably 2129, Clusium; 1886, Arretium; probably 1742, Volaterrae; and 1613, 1652, and 7041, Florentia); it is plausible to associate the senatorial family, and probably the *monetalis* as well, with the latter area.

VIBIUS PANSA. Enfranchisement: the coins of C. Vibius C.f. Pansa (*RE* no. 15) are dated *c.* 89–88 by Sydenham (105–7), *c.* 87 by Grueber (i.289–96) and by others no earlier than 90 or later than 84 (*MRR* ii.455); he is virtually certain to have been a citizen before the Social War (H. Gundel in *RE* s.v. Vibius (1958), col. 1949, prefers to think that they acquired it during the war). Cf. the filiation of the cos. of 43, who was probably the son of the *monetalis* (cf. Gundel, s.v. no. 15), C.f.C.n.

Origins: Vibius was a common Italic *nomen* and *praenomen*, as well as an Etruscan *nomen*, and by itself establishes nothing. *CIE* 3615 = xi.1994 (Perusia) has 'Vel. Vibius Ar ⟨P⟩ansa Tro' ('Ar' presumably stands for the patronymic as it would in Etruscan; Tro(mentina) was the tribe of Perusia after the Social War). How good an Etruscan name is Pansa? It was already known in the *gens Appuleia* (cos. 300), Cato delivered a speech 'in Pansam' (*ORF*² fr. 205), and the name has a Latin etymology (Schulze, *ZGLE* 365, H. Rix, *Das etruskische Cognomen*, 249; cf. Plaut. *Merc.* 640), but the Etruscan name *panza* is found a number of times (*CIE* 2195, 2913, 2914 (Clusium), 5523 (Tarquinii)).[1] Caetronianus was a *cognomen* of the cos. of 43, and a plausible Etruscan equivalent is available for Caetronius (Schulze, 268, accepted by Syme, *RR* 90, Taylor, *VDRR* 265), but it is not very well established. A L. Vibius also in the Tromentina is cited (*CIL* vi.28774); and there is the Perusine emperor, Vibius Trebonianus Gallus.[2] The early imperial C. Vibius T.f. Clu. Pansa (vi.3542) does not fit in,[3] and the *denarii* issued by Caetronianus *c.* 48 seem to have some reference to Tarracina (which was in the Oufentina) (Taylor, l.c., Gundel, s.v. no. 16); there is also a Vibius Pansa in *CIL* ix.202 (Brundisium—imperial). However the case seems on the whole quite strong for thinking that the Vibii Pansae who were enfranchised before the war were locals of Perusia (so R. Syme, *Historia*, viii (1959), 210). The suggestion of J. Suolahti (*Junior Officers of the Roman Army in the Republican Period* (Helsinki, 1955), 166), that the Vibii Pansae came from Bruttium is without foundation.

VOLCACIUS. Enfranchisement: the family of L. Volcacius Tullus, cos. 66, 'presumably had the franchise before the year 91', R. Syme, *Historia*, xiii (1964), 125. (There is no evidence concerning filiation or the lack of it.) There was also the jurist Volcacius (*RE* no. 10), whose relationship to other Volcacii is unknown, a pupil of Q. Mucius Scaevola (cos. 95).

Origins: the Perusine origin of the Volcacii Tulli is shown by a passage of Propertius (I 22.3), who addressed to Tullus, the nephew of L. Volcacius L.f. Tullus, cos. 33, the line 'si Perusina tibi patriae sunt nota sepulcra'; pointed out by Syme, *RR* 466, *JRS* xxxix (1949), 18, etc. There is confirmation in the inscriptions. C. Volcacius C.f. Labeo was an aedile at Tusculum, *CIL* i^2.1442 = *ILLRP* 689; but i^2 has two inscriptions of Volcacii in Rome, one of which (990 = *ILLRP* 186) refers to 'C. Volcaci(us) C.f. har(uspex) . . .', who is probably Etruscan (cf. above, p. 195 n. 3); in addition the name appears in i^2.2012 = *CIE* 1440 (Clusium) and i^2.2772 (Perusia). Cf. also *CIL* xi.2084 = *CIE* 4361 (Perusia), xi.2336 = *CIE* 1471 (Clusium) (both these have metronymics). For the numerous derivatives from the Etruscan root *velch* see Schulze, *ZGLE* 377–8 (cf. H. Gundel in *RE* s.v. Volcacius (1961)).

[1] Cf. Pansa, *latine*, in *CIE* 3158 (*ager Clusinus*).

[2] Cf. J. Heurgon, *SE* xxiv (1955–6), 92–3.

[3] T. P. Wiseman, *CQ* n.s. xiv (1964), 131, suggests that he may have been a member of the senatorial family, and that Clu., not Tro., may have been its tribe.

There are various cases of families established as Roman by the time of the Social War that have names strongly connected with Etruria or Umbria, but also connected in some way with other parts of Italy. Four cases will be discussed briefly, the Ancharii, Numisii, Petronii, and Sentii.

ANCHARIUS. The Q. Ancharius (*RE* no. 2) killed by Marius' orders in 87 or 86 (App. *BC* I 73.337–8, Plu. *Mar.* 43, Flor. II 9.16) was a former praetor (Plu.).[1] A C. Ancharius Rufus 'e municipio Fulginate' appeared in Cicero's speech *Pro Vareno* (fr. 5 Puccioni) (?80–79 B.C.) (*RE* no. 6), and he too was probably a citizen before the Social War.[2]

The Etruscan name *ancari* is very common at Clusium and Perusia (*CIE* 1689–92, 1696–7, 1699, 1701; 573, 582, 595, 3470, 3539–41, etc ; the form *ancharu* is also found, e.g. in *CIE* 1702).[3] The Latin form appears in *CIE* 1694 ('A. Ancarius A.f. Tolmaca natus', Clusium). There are two Ancharii from Etruria in *CIL* i².2068=*CIE* 3452 ('Ancharia Petroni'—on the latter name see below—from Perusia)[4] and i².2075=*CIE* 4216 ('Thannia Ancharia Lar f', Perusia), which has obvious Etruscan associations (Thannia and Lars being Etruscan names). But there are other inscriptions in *CIL* i².463 (Rome; the text is 'Ancar(i?) Silvi') being the most important, as being 'vetustissima'. Also perhaps relevant to the origins of the family is i².1853=*ILLRP* 487 ('prioris partis saec. I', A. Degrassi, *Auctarium*, p. 154) (Ancharii had vine-groves near Amiternum); also Sabine, but very near Fulginiae, is i².1890 (Nursia), referring to a Q. Ancharius. According to Tertullian (*Apol.* 24.8, *ad nat.* II 8.6), a deity known as Ancharia was worshipped still further east, at Asculum in Picenum.

NUMISIUS. The earliest known citizens are C. Numisius (*RE* no. 2), pr. 177; and T. Numisius Tarquiniensis (*RE* no. 10), a senator by 170 (*s.c. de Thisbensibus* no. 1, *SIG* ii³.646=R. K. Sherk, *Roman Documents from the Greek East* (Baltimore, 1969), no. 2, line 5: *Τίτος Νομίσιος Τίτου υἱός*), a *legatus* in 169 (Polyb. XXIX

[1] He could have held the praetorship well before 88, as the only evidence for his date comes from the career of his probable son, tr. pl. 59, pr. 56; on these grounds 'his praetorship may be dated shortly before 87' in the view of *MRR* ii.44 n. 1. He was in fact an ex-Marian, Badian plausibly argues, *Historia*, vi (1957), 339= *Studies*, etc., 69 n. 177.

[2] There is also in the same period Ancharia, the first wife of Augustus' father, Plu. *Ant.* 31, Suet. *Aug.* 4; and an Ancharius whose *pastores*, according to the prosecution against A. Cluentius, had been harmed by the latter's *vilici* (Cic. *Clu.* 161), presumably near Larinum.

[3] On the form of the name cf. P. Mingazzini, *SE* xxiv (1955–6), 347–8.

[4] This is from a tomb of Petronii, in which one of the four inscriptions is in Etruscan (*CIE* 3450).

25.3–4) (T. Numisius), and on the senatorial commission in Macedon in 167 (Liv. XLV 17.3, adding the name Tarquiniensis). But there is also L. Numisius Circeiensis (*RE* no. 3), praetor of Latium in 340 (Liv. VIII 3.9), explicitly said to have been from a Roman colony, and therefore if Livy was accurate a Roman citizen; in any case not an Etruscan. He has generally been accepted as an historical figure, perhaps wrongly (cf. Syme, *Historia*, xiii (1964), 107).

Even without Numisius of Circeii the early associations of the name Numisius are not exclusively Etruscan, or even primarily so. Numisius was an old name of Mars, and a very similar name appears on an archaic gold fibula from Praeneste.[1] Under the Republic the name occurs in Campania (apparently—Conway, *ID* ii.525, no. 12), at Amiternum (*CIL* i^2.1877), at Ostia (i^2.2379), at Capena (i^2.2436 (add pp. 718, 831) = *ILLRP* 290; the inscription has no clearly Etruscan characteristics, and the reading is disputed), and finally at Asisium (i^2.2114). There is also a bilingual inscription bearing a form of the name in Latin and Umbrian on a bronze strainer of uncertain provenance (M. Lejeune, *REL* xxx (1952), 98–100, *AE* 1953, no. 219 = *ILLRP* 1206).

What is there in favour of Etruria besides 'Tarquiniensis'? C. Numisius C.f. Ste. in Hygin. Gromat. 201L = 164Th has been held to associate the senatorial Numisii with the Stellatina (the tribe of Tarquinii) and with Tarquinii (Taylor, *VDRR* 238). Cf. a Numisius of Tarquinii, who was also in the Stellatina, *CIL* xi.2958. Closely related names are found in Etruscan in various parts of Etruria (*CIE* 423 = *TLE* 670 (Arretium), *CIE* 780, 2501–2 (*ager Clusinus*), 3678, 3679 = *TLE* 591 (Perusia), ? 5191 (Volsinii)), but not at Tarquinii. Taylor suggests that *RE* no. 10 may have earned his *cognomen* for 'special services to Tarquinii', perhaps in connection with the foundation of the colony of Graviscae in 181, which is rather forced. Topographical *cognomina* derived from the names of Italian towns are so rare in the second century that we may suppose that there was some unusual event behind one—such as the rise of an Italian family. The case remains open.

Two other *gentes* are worth mentioning briefly because of the strong connections of their names with Etruria and Umbria; but in both cases there is strong evidence against their having arrived in Rome from Etruria or Umbria in this period.

The first Petronius whom we know at Rome was a *legatus* in 156 (Polyb. XXXII 28.5). The inscriptions bearing the name in *CIL* i^2 that are from outside Latium are from Montepulciano in Etruria

[1] 'Numasioi'—*CIL* i^2.3 = Vetter no. 365 = *ILLRP* 1.

(three) and from Perusia (four); Etruscan forms of the name are very common indeed, especially at Perusia; a *ptrnio* (=Petronius) was a *maro* at Fulginiae (Vetter, *HID* no. 234),[1] and even earlier the name appears in the *Iguvine Tables* (ii. a.21). However it cannot easily be maintained that the senatorial Petronii are likely to have come from these places, in view of *CIL* i².239–40 (and ? 241) and 2471, all from Praeneste and judged by Lommatzsch 'vetustissimae'.

Sentius is a very common name in the inscriptions from Clusium in *CIL* i² and there are well-authenticated Etruscan forms in numerous examples; but as B. Borghesi showed (*Oeuvres numismatiques*, ii (Paris, 1864), 276), with arguments revived and improved by Syme (*Historia*, xiii (1964), 121–2, 156–66), the family of the first Sentii whom we know at Rome came from the *praefectura* Atina in Latium.

A Table of Individuals from Etruria Enfranchised before the Social War

Nomen	Status at first appearance	Its date	Approx. *terminus ante quem* for acquisition of citizenship	Town or area of origin
Carrinas	*legatus*	83	last quarter of second century	?? Clusium or Perusia
	pr.	82		
Maecenas	*eques R.*	91	last quarter of second century	Arretium
Nigidius	pr.	*c.* 145	first quarter of second century	? Perusia
Perperna	*legatus*	168	first quarter of second century	?? Perusia
Saenius	*monetalis*	*c.* 150–133	first quarter of second century	N. Etruria
Vibius Pansa	*monetalis*	*c.* 89–88	last quarter of second century	Perusia
Volcacius	cos.	68	last quarter of second century	Perusia
	privatus (the jurist)	early first century	last quarter of second century	
Ancharius	pr.	before 87 or 86	last quarter of second century	?? Clusium or Perusia
Numisius	pr.	177 (*RE* no. 2)	last quarter of third century	? Tarquinii
	senator	170 (*RE* no. 10)		

[1] The date of this is approximately the second half of the second century B.C., 'doch etwas älter', according to Vetter.

APPENDIX II

A Catalogue of the Tribal Allocations of the Towns of Etruria and Umbria

THE fundamental work on the tribal allocations of the towns of Etruria and Umbria was done by Bormann[1] and Kubitschek,[2] and their results are in most cases still valid. However there are some cases in which detailed discussion is necessary, and some in which new evidence has appeared. Some recent scholars have constructed lists of the tribes which were assigned to the towns, namely L. R. Taylor,[3] who missed only one definite tribe in this area (Sabatina for Heba), but did not cite the evidence in most cases and discussed only some of the difficulties; and A. J. Pfiffig,[4] who attempted to compile a record of the evidence for the tribes of the Etruscan towns, but succeeded in being neither accurate nor complete. In the following list the full body of evidence is discussed in each doubtful case.

Kubitschek made some important distinctions between different types of inscriptional evidence for the tribes, distinguishing, *inter alia*, inscriptions in which the town is actually mentioned in conjunction with the tribe, 'quod testium genus auctoritate praeter cetera insigne est' (category α),[5] inscriptions in which the municipal magistrates appear, and inscriptions in which the tribe is likely to be the result of an emperor's enfranchisement of an individual. Even the fact that a man's *domus* is explicitly said to be a certain town does not of course infallibly establish that his tribe was also that of the town; some cases in which such inscriptions show other tribes are noted below. Nor were local magistrates necessarily in the tribes of their towns. These points obviously make it important to register the number of inscriptions that give a particular tribe for a particular town.

[1] In *CIL*, the Etruscan section being published in 1888 and the Umbrian in 1901.

[2] *De Romanarum tribuum origine et propagatione* (Vienna, 1882), *Imperium Romanum tributim discriptum* (Vienna, 1889) (references to 'Kubitschek' in the catalogue are to the latter work); Kubitschek saw 'schedae' of most of the Etruscan section of *CIL*, but of only a small part of the Umbrian section, and in fact his lists of inscriptions have far more gaps in the Umbrian section.

[3] *VDRR*; a list of communities with their tribes is on 159–64.

[4] *Die Ausbreitung des römischen Städtewesens in Etrurien und die Frage der Unterwerfung der Etrusker* (Florence, 1966).

[5] *Imperium*, etc., p. iii.

Since geographical proximity was one of the things that influenced the tribal allocations after the Social War, I have included in this list all the allocations made in Etruria and Umbria including those from before the war; and for the same reason I have included not only the towns in the regions inhabited by Etruscans and Umbrians, but also the neighbouring towns in the rest of what later became regions VI and VII. For the sake of convenience I have also included two towns whose tribes were in fact determined at later dates, Florentia and Lucus Feroniae. I have of course tried to maintain consistent standards for the verdicts 'certain', 'virtually certain', 'very probable', 'probable', etc.

(A) ETRURIA

ALSIUM. Unknown. *CIL* xi. p. 547, Pfiffig 40. There is no reason to think that the *praefectus Capuam Cumas* and *quaestor* in the Mae. (*CIL* xi.3717) was a local of Alsium, or that the cos. of 123 A.D. (3718) was either. Nor is there any reason to put this town or Castrum Novum, or any other of the towns near Caere, in the same tribe, as Pfiffig does (39–41).

ARRETIUM. Pom. certain. *CIL* xi. p. 336, Kubitschek 81, Pfiffig 66. Inscriptions giving the town as well as the tribe: iii.2678, 6418, vi.2381.b.i.16 and ii.9, 2382.b.10 and 19, 2475, 2478, 2577, 2661, 32519.a.ii.15, x.6123, xi.2594, 5935, xiii.8174. For Maecenates in the Pom. see above, p. 320; for a Cilnius in the Pom. see *CIL* vi.1376 (Tiberian). Two bilingual Etruscan and Latin inscriptions from Arretium, *CIE* 428 = *TLE* 662 and *TLE* 930, have Pom. in the Latin version. On these and other bilingual Etruscan–Latin inscriptions containing Roman tribes, cf. G. Forni in *Studi in onore di E. Betti* (Milan, 1962), iii. 193–207. Some other tribes are found at Arretium, but not in Kubitschek's category α; cf. Kubitschek, l.c., who gives references to other local inscriptions containing Pom.

BLERA. Arn. virtually certain. *CIL* xi. p. 507, Kubitschek 81, Pfiffig 46–7. In category α are vi.221.ii.6, 32519.a.ii.21, and also 2608, which gives Ani., which is commonly confused with Arn. Pfiffig is quite wrong to throw doubts on this. Pal. and Sub. are also found, but the only even nominal possibility other than Arn. is Tro., the tribe of a *quattuorvir* in xi.3338; he perhaps derived from Veii.

CAERE. Uncertain, but Vot. best possibility. *CIL* xi. p. 534, Kubitschek 81–2, R. Syme, *JRS* xxxix (1949), 15, *Historia*, xiii (1964), 106, 110, Taylor, *VDRR* 89 n. 28, E. Badian, *JRS* lii (1962), 208, Pfiffig 38. Vot. is tentatively preferred by Bormann, Taylor; Syme suggested Ste. Gal. is also possible. The evidence for the first is xi.3615, which seems to have derived from Caere (cf. Bormann ad loc., G. De Sanctis in *Scritti in onore di B. Nogara* (Rome, 1937), 154); the subject was a local magistrate. Ste. is argued from xi.3755 = i^{2}.837 = *ILLRP* 443, which was found at Lorium, between Caere and Rome, and is associated with Caere by the fact that the only other epigraphical record of the *nomen* (Sanquinius) is from Caere (xi.7714 = i^{2}.2613). The Sanquinius of xi.3755 was of praetorian rank, and so may not have been of local origin. Galeria is the tribe of a *privatus* in xi.3662, Voltinia apparently that of another in 7613. The Voturia still seems decidedly the strongest possibility.

CAPENA. Ste. certain. *CIL* xi. p. 570, Kubitschek 82, Taylor, *VDRR* 48, Pfiffig 21. Festus 464L ('Stellatin⟨a *tribus dicta non a campo*⟩ eo, qui in Campania est, sed eo qui ⟨*prope abest ab urbe* Ca⟩pena, ex quo Tusci profecti, St⟨*ellatinum illum*⟩ campum appellaverunt') is supported by Liv. VI 4.4, 5.8, and by xi.3958–9 and 4004, all inscriptions of *privati*.[1] A number of other tribes occur, as should be expected near Rome; the only one of possible significance is Fab., belonging to a municipal magistrate, in *NSA* 1953, 22 (G. Mancini) = *AE* 1954, no. 167; the evidence in favour of Ste. is decisive.

CASTRUM NOVUM. Possibly Vol., possibly Ser. *CIL* xi. p. 531, Kubitschek 82, Taylor, *VDRR* 89 n. 29, Pfiffig 39. Taylor tentatively preferred Vol., for which the evidence is vi.951, with an abbreviation 'CCN' filled out to read 'c(oloniae) C(astri) N(ovi)', which is virtually certain. There was of course another Castrum Novum, in region V, its tribe unknown (Pap. is sometimes favoured). Taylor points out that if Vol. belonged to Castrum Novum in Etruria, xi.7613 (Caere) can be referred to it. The other evidence is xi.3584, belonging to a *privatus* in Ser. The case is open, with a slight preference going to the tribe actually known at Castrum, i.e. Ser.

CLUSIUM. Arn. certain. *CIL* xi. p. 372, Kubitschek 83, Pfiffig 63. There are four inscriptions giving the *domus* as well as the tribe Arn. (vi.2500, 2707, xi.2108, *BCAR* liv (1926), 43–8 (A. M. Colini) = *AE* 1930, no. 57, line 21), and many other local inscriptions showing the same tribe (add xi.7122 to those listed by Bormann). Arn. in the Latin version of the Etruscan–Latin bilingual *CIE* 1469 = *TLE* 503 must surely refer to the Roman tribe, in spite of some difficulties; see Forni, art. cit., 199. Qui. in 2106 is irrelevant.

CORTONA. Ste. certain. *CIL* xi. p. 349, Kubitschek 83, Pfiffig 65. There are three relevant inscriptions, vi.3642, xi.1903, 1905, the first two explicitly referring to the *domus*.

[1] xi.4015, however, belongs not to the territory of Capena, but to that of Lucus Feroniae.

COSA. Unknown. Pfiffig's conjecture Sab. (50) is valueless.

FAESULAE. Sca. certain. *CIL* xi. pp. 229, 1266, Kubitschek 83, Pfiffig 72. There are three inscriptions referring to the *domus* as well as the tribe, vi.2484, x.6097, xiii.6957, and other supporting evidence.

FALERII. Hor. certain. *CIL* xi. pp. 466, 1322, Kubitschek 83–4, Pfiffig 27. Although a number of other tribes are found once in the *ager Faliscus*, they all belong to Roman officials; whereas there are at least seven local magistrates in Hor., xi.3099, 3100, 3123, 3125, 3136, 3209, 3930.

FERENTIUM. Ste. certain. *CIL* xi. pp. 454, 1313, Kubitschek 84, Pfiffig 58. Two inscriptions give the *domus* and Ste., vi.2778 and *Bulletin archéologique du Comité des travaux historiques*, March 1927, p. xix = *AE* 1927, no. 34, which is confirmed by at least four local inscriptions.

FLORENTIA. Sca. certain. *CIL* xi. pp. 306, 1267, Kubitschek 84, Pfiffig 72. There are some twenty inscriptions giving the *domus* as well as the tribe; to those in *CIL*, listed by Kubitschek, add *BCAR* li (1923), 70 (P. Mingazzini) = *AE* 1926, no. 46, and *Mainzer Zeitschrift*, xxxiii (1938), 30 (G. Behrens) = *AE* 1940, no. 112.

FORUM CLODI. Arn. or Qui. Kubitschek 85 (Qui.), cf. *CIL* xi. p. 502, Taylor, *VDRR* 48 n. 6, 205 (probably Arn.), Pfiffig 40 (Vot.). Qui. appears in an inscription of Careiae (xi.3770), which may or may not be in the territory of Forum Clodi; the only real evidence is xi.3303, which refers to *duoviri*, one in Arn., the other in Qui. The fact that some Claudii (Marcelli and Nerones in particular) were in Arn. and may have been responsible for the foundation of Forum Clodi favours Arn.; or it can be explained as an extension of one of the old tribes of south Etruria. On the other hand, the emperor Claudius was in Qui., and some of his ancestors may have been (Taylor, however, suggests (205) that Claudius himself transferred the family from Arn. to Qui. 'in order to emphasize the Sabine origin of the house'); and Arn. could be explained as an intrusion from neighbouring Blera.

GRAVISCAE. Ste. virtually certain. *CIL* xi. p. 511, Kubitschek 85, Pfiffig 44. vi.2928 ('L. Coranus L.f. Ste. Valens domo Graviscis . . .') is decisive. In vi.3884.iii.6 ('L. Fullonius L.f. Cl. Magnus Grav(iscis)') (197 A.D.) 'Cl.' must stand for the 'pseudo-tribe' Claudia (on which see G. Forni in *Studi giuridici in memoria di A. Passerini* (Pavia–Milan, 1955), 107–9).

HEBA. Sab. probable. Pfiffig 53. Not mentioned by Taylor, *VDRR*. *NSA* 1955, 40 (G. Maetzke) = *AE* 1957, no. 219, is probably sufficient, although 'Sab.' could be the beginning of a *cognomen* (see

Maetzke's photograph), and the inscription is late, and there is no explicit mention of Heba in the text.

HORTA. Ste. certain. Kubitschek 85, cf. *CIL* xi. p. 463. vi.2380 and viii.4194 both give *domus* and Ste. Arn., mentioned in xi.3071, may be an intrusion from Ocriculum (Pfiffig, 59, ignores the evidence).

LUCA. Fab. certain. *CIL* xi. p. 296, Kubitschek 86, Pfiffig 76. To the eight inscriptions in category α listed by Kubitschek add *Mainzer Zeitschrift*, lix (1964), 64 (W. Von Pfeffer) = *AE* 1965, no. 256.

LUCUS FERONIAE. Vol. virtually certain. *CIL* xi. p. 571, Kubitschek 86, Pfiffig 24. vi.2584, giving *domus* and Vol., is conclusive. Taylor, *VDRR* 322, suggested that Lucus Feroniae, like some other places, may have received the tribe Vol. from Caesar; but the attribution to Vol. is not seriously affected by my rejection of her idea that Lucus Feroniae was a Caesarian colony (for which see above, p. 308).

LUNA. Gal. certain. *CIL* xi. p. 260, Kubitschek, 86, Pfiffig 76. There are four epigraphical references to men with the *domus* Luna and the tribe Gal. (vi.2381.a.i.20 and ii.12, 2382.a.18, 32716b), and local inscriptions showing the same tribe.

NEPET. Ste. probable, Pom. possible. *CIL* xi. p. 481, Kubitschek 86–7 (both giving Ste. with some doubt), Taylor, *VDRR* 163 (Ste.), Pfiffig 30 (Ste.). Only Ste. and Pom. need to be considered. The former is attached to the four names whose tribes survive in xi.3208, which seems to be a municipal document, and it was also the tribe of the *privatus* who is the subject of 3235, which was excavated at Nepet. Pom. occurs only in 3217, belonging to a *quattuorvir*, and in 3205, belonging to a *praefectus fabrum* with no stated connections with Nepet; however, the instances of Ste. may possibly have strayed from neighbouring Capena.

PERUSIA. Tro. certain. *CIL* xi. p. 353, Kubitschek 87, Pfiffig 63. Two inscriptions giving *domus* and Tro. (v.918, vi.2596) are supported by a number of local ones showing Tro.; Lem. is presumably an intrusion from Hispellum.

PISAE. Gal. certain. *CIL* xi. p. 273, Kubitschek 87, Pfiffig 74. At least three inscriptions giving *domus* and Gal. (vi.2530, 2719, x.5912, and apparently xi.1488) are supported by local ones showing Gal. Fab. is an intrusion from Luca and Asculum.

PISTORIAE. Vel. virtually certain. *CIL* xi. p. 298, Kubitschek 87, Pfiffig 73. xiii.6942 has the *domus* as well as the tribe of the subject, and in xi.1541 appears a *quattuorvir i.d.* of Pistoriae belonging to Vel.

POPULONIUM. Unknown.

PYRGI. Pfiffig again conjectures Vot. (41); cf. above on Alsium. The subject of xi.3544, listed in *CIL* under Centum Cellae and Aquae Tauri, was in Lem.; since the inscription was found 'four miles from Tolfa towards Cerveteri' (according to O. Benndorf *apud CIL*), it may well have belonged to the territory of Pyrgi. I suggest that it should be supplemented to read '[...]LIO·L·F· LEM[...] / [...]R·TER·SACER[DO...] / [PYRG]ENSIUM· II[...]'. The priesthood seems to have been at Pyrgi; for the use of the name of the people of Pyrgi rather than of the place, cf. 3367 ('curator Pyrgensium et Ceretanorum'), and for similar usages cf. M. Pallottino, *SE* xxi (1950–1), 153–4. This does not of course establish the tribe of Pyrgi beyond doubt.

RUSELLAE. Unknown.

SAENA. Ouf. virtually certain. *CIL* xi. p. 333, Kubitschek 87–8, Taylor, *VDRR* 251–2, Pfiffig 69. iii.5538 and vii.1345 both give the *domus* of their subjects as well as the tribe; this is supported by xi.1805 and 1815 and by *NSA* 1926, 169 (R. Bianchi Bandinelli) = *AE* 1927, no. 108. Since there are these local inscriptions, it is unnecessary to think that Saena Gallica, whose tribe is unknown, may have been meant in the first two. Kubitschek later came to prefer Saena Gallica for the first two inscriptions (*RE* s.v. *Oufentina tribus* (1942), col. 1904), moved by the wish to find geographical coherence in the tribe (a group of towns in Umbria and the *ager Gallicus*, Forum Flaminii, Pitinum Pisaurense, Plestia, and Tuficum belonged to the tribe); this is unduly schematic. Five other tribes appear in the territory of Saena, of which only Qui. may appear twice (Qui. should perhaps be retained in 1804, in spite of Bormann's conjecture Ouf.). Of these Arn. and Sab. at least can be explained as intrusions from neighbouring towns.[1]

SATURNIA. Sab. certain. *CIL* xi. p. 149, Kubitschek 88, Pfiffig 51. xi.2650 and *Epigraphica*, xxi (1959), 40–3 (L. Gasperini) = *AE* 1962, no. 153, are municipal documents, supported by xi.2661 and 2671.

SUTRIUM. Pap. probable. *CIL* xi. p. 489, Kubitschek 88–9, Pfiffig 30. Pap. is given in two inscriptions in which the *domus* is explicitly mentioned, vi.3884.iii.12 and 32519.a.ii.19; this is supported by xi.3256 and 3258 (local magistrates) and 3267. Sutrium is also given as the *domus* of three men in different tribes, Ani., Pal., and Pol., but these can probably be dismissed with safety.

TARQUINII. Ste. certain. *CIL* xi. p. 510, Kubitschek 89, Pfiffig 44. vi.2381, which gives the *domus*, is supported by a number

[1] Cf. above, p. 245, on the Perperna in Ser. at Saena.

of local magistrates; Arn. (xi.3845) is an intrusion (cf. Bormann ad loc.).

TUSCANA. Ste. probable. *CIL* xi. p. 450, Kubitschek 89 (both these give Ste. with some doubt), Pfiffig 46 (Ste.). xi.2958 and 2970 from Tuscana both give Ste., the former for a *quattuorvir*. Bormann and Kubitschek reasonably suspected that they might refer to Tarquinii.[1]

VEII. Tro. certain. *CIL* xi. pp. 556–7, Kubitschek 89–90, Pfiffig 17. The *municipium* evidently remained in the Tro., into which Veii had been put (cf. Liv. VI 4.4, 5.8). Of the *centumviri* present at the signing of a decree in 26 A.D. only one lacked a *cognomen*, and his tribe was given, Tro. (xi.3805.19); supported by 3801, 3843, cf. vi.221.i.7 (which was referred to Veii by Grotefend, Bormann).

VETULONIA. Sca. certain. Kubitschek 90, cf. *CIL* xi. p. 414, Pfiffig 56. *Domus* and tribe are given in vi.2382.a.16 and perhaps 2472 = 8112.

VISENTIUM. Sab. certain. Kubitschek 90, cf. *CIL* xi. p. 444, Pfiffig 52. *Domus* and tribe are given in vi.2381.b.i.6, supported by inscriptions of local magistrates; to Kubitschek's evidence add *Epigraphica*, xxi (1959), 33–40 (L. Gasperini) = *AE* 1962, nos. 151–2, cf. *ILLRP* 692a (*privati*).

VOLATERRAE. Sab. certain. *CIL* xi. p. 325, Kubitschek 90–1, Pfiffig 69. There are five inscriptions giving *domus* as well as tribe, iii.430, vi.215, 2587, 2683, 2939, and other support.

VOLSINII. Pom. certain. *CIL* xi. p. 424, Kubitschek 91, Pfiffig 57. There are six names in inscriptions with *domus* as well as tribe, vi.2381.b.i.27, 2382.b.14 and b.15, 2513, 2923, 3884.iii.19.

VULCI. Sab. probable. *CIL* xi. p. 447, Kubitschek 91, Pfiffig 49. xi.2930 refers to a *quattuorvir* in Sab., who must be a magistrate of Vulci; otherwise there are three inscriptions of *privati*, two with Sab. (2939a, 2941), one with Qui. (2934).

(B) UMBRIA

AESIS. Pol. certain. *CIL* xi. p. 920, Kubitschek 68. In four inscriptions *domus* and tribe are both given, vi.2380.ii.4, 2381.b.ii.14, 32519.a.ii.4, xi.5643, cf. iii.9742. An instance of Sca. (xi.6206) is of no significance.

[1] Pfiffig attempts to remove this doubt by referring to 'das Bild von der Zuteilung der von den etruskischen *capita* abhängigen Landstädte zu deren Tribus', but it cannot be assumed on the existing evidence that there was such a principle, still less that it applied to Tuscana.

AMERIA. Clu. virtually certain. *CIL* xi. pp. 638, 1368, Kubitschek 69. The inscription that Kubitschek placed in category α was presumably a misreported version of xi.4348, which contains neither *domus* nor tribe. In fact the only inscription in that category is vi.3884.iii.31, giving Pom. Many of the inscriptions from Ameria itself in *CIL* derive from Cosimo Brancatelli, a local cleric at the end of the sixteenth century, who invented and supplemented inscriptions as well as reporting them (cf. *CIL*, ll.cc.). There are in fact no instances of Pom. at Ameria, but there are a number of instances of Clu., including some that do not depend on Brancatelli (or on Pirro Ligorio), xi.4364, 4371, 4382, 4389, 4395 (all these refer to local officials), etc.

ARNA. Clu. probable. *CIL* xi. p. 811, Kubitschek 69. xi.5614 is the only evidence; though it seems to have been found in the neighbouring territory of Asisium, the tribe probably belongs to Arna, for the subject was quaestor of the *alimenta* of Arna.

ASISIUM. Ser. certain. *CIL* xi. p. 784, Kubitschek 69. Two inscriptions give the *domus* and Ser. (vi.3884.iv.31 and xi.5384); another soldier from Asisium was in Ste. (vi.3884.ii.50). The subject of xi.5382, who was in Ouf., evidently regarded Asisium as his *patria* (line 8) and two inscriptions from Asisium refer to *privati* in the same tribe (xi.5339, 5553); however this must result from the influence of Forum Flaminii or Plestia, for there are far more locals in Ser., including officials (5395, 5396) (others: 5387, 5388, 5405, 5543).

ATTIDIUM. Lem. virtually certain. *CIL* xi. p. 825, cf. Kubitschek 69, 78 (Ouf.). The evidence of xi.5675 (a local aedile in Lem.), with 5669 and 5671 (these, however, belonging to a Roman official) and 5678 is sufficient.

CAMERINUM. Cor. probable. *CIL* xi. p. 815, Kubitschek 70. The tribes of three *quattuorviri* are known, two in Cor. (5634 and 5635—but the latter was patron of *complures civitates*), one in Lem. (5633). Cor. was to be found nearby at Matilica (Lem., however, was not much further away). The Camertine cohorts, enfranchised by Marius, probably went into his tribe, Cor., and the whole community probably did so later.

CARSULAE. Clu. certain. *CIL* xi. p. 665, Kubitschek 70. iii.1188 has *domus* as well as tribe, as does an inscription published by H. Bossert—U. B. Alkım, *Karatepe*, etc., ii (Istanbul, 1947), 21 = *AE* 1950, no. 190; there is some local confirmation, including six local magistrates in the tribe. A local magistrate in Pup. with father and brother in Clu. (4575), and two brothers in Pup. with their father in Vol. are strange aberrations, cf. Taylor, *VDRR* 321

n. 10. On Vol. in towns in Clu. see *VDRR* 313, 322; no definite explanation can really be given.[1]

FANUM FORTUNAE. Pol. certain. *CIL* xi. pp. 924–5, Kubitschek 70–1. Seven epigraphical references give *domus* as well as tribe, v.564, 931, vi.478, 3553, 3884.ii.34 and iv.10, xiii.8651; there is local confirmation. An inscription published by L. Gasperini, *Latomus*, xvii (1958), 352–4 = *AE* 1959, no. 174, gives *domus* and the tribe Fab., but that cannot alter the conclusion.

FORUM BRENTANORUM. The existence of this town seems sufficiently attested by Plin. *NH* III 113, *CIL* xi.6055, cf. vi.3884.i.16 (on which see Bormann's n. on xi.6055). Pup. quite probable. Bormann, l.c.; J. Weiss in *RE* s.v. Forum Brentan(i, -orum?) (1912); Taylor, *VDRR* 96 n. 53. Pup. is given in xi.6055—yet the man held no local office and may not have been local; he was also connected with Ancona (ix.5898) in Lem. Not far from where the inscription was first known (Urbino) is Sarsina, in Pup.

FORUM FLAMINII. Ouf. virtually certain. *CIL* xi. p. 1385, quoting an African inscription that gives both tribe and *domus* (*Bulletin archéologique du Comité des travaux historiques*, 1911, p. cliii = *AE* 1911, no. 13), Kubitschek in *RE* s.v. *Oufentina tribus*, col. 1904, Taylor, *VDRR* 92 n. 37.

FORUM SEMPRONII. Pol. virtually certain. *CIL* xi. p. 905, Kubitschek 71. There are four local inscriptions referring to Pol., xi.6117, 6132, 6144, 6155, the second of which gives a *duovir* in this tribe. The two *privati* in Fal. in 6125 must be discounted.

FULGINIAE. Cor. probable. *CIL* xi. p. 755, Kubitschek 71. The subject of xi.5217 was a magistrate of both Fulginiae and Forum Flaminii, and in Cor.; 5246, which belonged to a *privatus* in Cor., was found at Forum Flaminii. (The subject of 5210, a member of the tribe Vol., was not local). Cor. is not otherwise to be found nearer than Camerinum and should be accepted.

HISPELLUM. Lem. virtually certain. *CIL* xi. p. 766, Kubitschek 71–2. xiii.6943 has a soldier 'L. Novellius T.f. Polia Hispelo'; Grotefend and Mommsen took the last word to be a *cognomen* rather than the *domus*, which is not at all convincing. However, at least nine inscriptions give Lem., including the following that refer to local officials, iii.8261, xi.5275, 5278 (twice), 5283, 5286, and 5287,

[1] It is conceivable that the correct explanation may not concern Caesarian settlements, but the fact that some of the towns in question (Carsulae, Interamna Nahars) were already before the Social War in the Clu., a disadvantageous tribe after the war; to protect them from this disadvantage some of the inhabitants may have been assigned to Vol.—admittedly a very irregular proceeding. It is obvious that the suggestion is speculative.

and they are decisive. Other tribes that appear locally are intrusions from neighbouring towns (cf. Bormann).

IGUVIUM. Clu. virtually certain. *CIL* xi. pp. 855, 1395, Kubitschek 72. xi.5802, assigned to Iguvium by Kubitschek, is assigned to Tadinum by Bormann, so there is no evidence of local magistrates in Clu., but it is the tribe of four *privati* (5838, 5857, 5866, 5901); the tribe of a fifth (5898) is shown as C[. . .]. The member of Lem. referred to by Kubitschek (5783) in fact belonged to Sentinum.

INTERAMNA NAHARS. Clu. certain. *CIL* xi. p. 611, Kubitschek 72. vi.221.ii.9, which shows the *domus* as well as the tribe, is supported by numerous local inscriptions and contradicted by virtually none. On Vol. at Interamna, cf. above on Carsulae.

MATILICA. Cor. very probable. *CIL* xi. p. 819, Kubitschek 72. Two inscriptions of local officials (5646, 5650) have Cor.

MEVANIA. Aem. very probable. *CIL* xi. p. 732, Kubitschek 73, *RE* s.v. *Oufentina tribus*, col. 1905, cf. Taylor, *VDRR* 250. Bormann and Taylor assigned the town to Aem., Kubitschek was uncertain; as well he might be at first sight, for at least four genuine tribes (Aem., Fab., Lem., and Ouf.) contained men whose *domus* was said to be Mevania. 'Ael' (vi.3884.iii.27) can be dismissed as a 'pseudo-tribe', and Ouf. (vi.2382.b.4 and b.16) as being from Mediolanum (see Kubitschek, l.c.); the tribe Lem. (xi.5118) is probably an intruder from Hispellum (the subject was 'natus Mevaniae', but *not* a citizen of Mevania—the same applies to another native of Mevania who appears in 4654 at Tuder and was a member of Clu.). There remain the tribes Fab. (vi.3884.ii.42) and Aem. (xi.5029). Fab. is fairly widespread as a result of the activities of the Julian emperors; Aem. on the other hand is supported by a number of local inscriptions, xi.5033, 5051 (twice)—these two inscriptions belong to local officials—5029 ('erga suos municipes'), 5103 (and cf. 5149). Kubitschek seems to have exaggerated the difficulties of the case.

MEVANIOLA. Ste. very probable. *CIL* xi. p. 992, Kubitschek 73. Two local officials (xi.6604, 6605) belonged to Ste.

NARNIA. Pap. almost certain. *CIL* xi. p. 602, Kubitschek 73–4 (who gives Pap. with doubt). Even if in vi.3884.iv.5 the *domus* 'Nar.' could mean Narbo, a local *quattuorvir* was in Pap. (xi.4123—56 A.D.). It was also the tribe of the emperor Nerva who derived from Narnia (4123 is early enough not to have been influenced by that). 4135, evidently very late, has a *privatus* in Pol., which can be discounted.

OCRICULUM. Arn. certain. *CIL* xi. p. 596, Kubitschek 74. The subject of xi.4086 ('patrono civitatis . . . omnibus honoribus /

et oneribus civitatis suae / functo . . .') was in Arn. 4081 belonged to another local official, 4099 to a *privatus*, both in the same tribe.

OSTRA. Pol. virtually certain. *CIL* xi. p. 918, Kubitschek 74. vi.3884.i.9 gives *domus* as well as tribe, and xi.6190 has a local official in Pol. 6195 has a *privatus* in Vel., who must have intruded from Picenum.

PISAURUM. Cam. certain. *CIL* xi. pp. 941, 1399, Kubitschek 74. A variety of tribes are found besides Cam., but the inscription published in *Archivio storico per le Marche e l'Umbria*, i (1884), 381 (later = *CIL* xi.5624), which Kubitschek placed in category α, explicitly refers to a man from Perusia. In view of iii.2014, vi.2381.a.i.14, vii.188, and viii.25741, which all give both *domus* and tribe (cf. xi.6362), and numerous local inscriptions, Cam. is certain.

PITINUM MERGENS. Clu. virtually certain. *CIL* xi. p. 877, Kubitschek 74–5. In xi.5964 one or perhaps two local magistrates are in Clu.; in 5959 a *patronus municipii* is in Clu., but he had a senatorial career and was not necessarily in the local tribe; the subject of 6123, who was in Clu., was a *patronus municipii* and an official of both Pitinum Mergens and Forum Sempronii, and since the latter was in Pol., he is quite likely to have the tribe of Pitinum Mergens (Kubitschek); in 5960 a retired centurion is in Clu. No other tribes are known.

PITINUM PISAURENSE. Ouf. quite probable. *CIL* xi. p. 889 (Clu.), G. Susini, *Epigraphica*, xviii (1956), 15, 21–5 (cf. *AE* 1959, no. 94), Taylor, *VDRR* 114 n. 35. *AE* 1959, no. 94, refers to a local magistrate in Ouf.; Bormann's Clu. was based on xi.6033, which Susini assigns to Sestinum. (The subject was apparently *pontifex Pitini Pisauri patronus municipii*; according to Susini that means that he was *patronus* of some other *civitas*, which for topographical reasons must be Sestinum.)

PLESTIA. Ouf. very probable. *CIL* xi. p. 812, Kubitschek 75. In xi.5621, first recorded in the church at Pistia, a local magistrate, an *octovir*, is in Ouf.; the tribes of all other towns known to have had *octoviri* were different. The reading Ouf. in 5619 (another official) could not be verified by Bormann.

SARSINA. Pup. certain. *CIL* xi. p. 977, Kubitschek 75. vi.2381.b.i.23, 2769 and 2929, and *Rend. Acc. Linc.*, ser. 8. xviii (1963), 264–5 (M. Torelli) = *AE* 1964, no. 23, give both *domus* and tribe; this is confirmed by many local inscriptions. Only Pal. is found otherwise.

SENA GALLICA. Unknown (cf. above on Saena).

SENTINUM. Lem. certain. *CIL* xi. p. 838, Kubitschek 75–6. vi.2379.a.i.57 and 2381.b.i.18 give both *domus* and tribe, and are supported by a number of local inscriptions. xi.5741 apparently refers to a local aedile in Pom., but Lem. must be right.

SESTINUM. Clu. virtually certain. *CIL* xi. p. 884, Kubitschek 76. xi.6010 and 6012 have local officials in Clu. and the tribe is confirmed by 6009, 6011, cf. xi.422 and *NSA* 1942, 61 (A. Minto) = *AE* 1946, no. 216; a third-century magistrate in Pap. can be disregarded.

SPOLETIUM. Hor. certain. *CIL* xi. p. 702, Kubitschek 76. vi.32519.a.ii.27 has both *domus* and the tribe Hor., and at least seventeen local inscriptions have the same tribe (including xi.4793, 4799, 4804, etc., belonging to local officials). For some further confirmation from outside Spoletium see R. Syme, *Historia*, xiii (1964), 113. Single appearances of Qui. and Lem. are insignificant.

SUASA. Cam. certain. *CIL* xi. p. 914, Kubitschek 77. vi.3884.iii.17 has both *domus* and the tribe Cam.; xi.6174 refers to a *VIvir Suasae* and 6173 to a *privatus* in the same tribe. The *patronus municipii* in Lem. (6165) was a Roman senator whose family (the Satrii) are well known in Umbria, especially at neighbouring Sentinum, which was in Lem.

TADINUM. Clu. quite probable. *CIL* xi. pp. 823, 853. This entirely depends on whether xi.5802 belonged to Tadinum or not, and as Bormann argued (853), it is unlikely to have belonged to either Iguvium or Sentinum, because the duovirate held by the man concerned cannot have been in either place, and Sentinum at least was not in Clu. A certain Cn. Disinius is in question; this rare *nomen* is found elsewhere at Sentinum (5786—a woman) and at Perusia (2052), and he may have derived his tribe from one of the other Umbrian towns in the area.

TIFERNUM MATAURENSE. Clu. very probable. *CIL* xi. p. 882, Kubitschek 77. vi.2381.a.i.6 has Clu. and the *domus* abbreviated to 'Tif' can refer to this or the next town. Two local magistrates are known in Clu. (xi.5992 and 5993), the former specifically said to have held offices at Tifernum Mataurense and Ariminum (which was in Ani.).

TIFERNUM TIBERINUM. Clu. virtually certain. *CIL* xi. p. 871, Kubitschek 77. See previous entry. xi.5937 has both *domus* ('Tifernis Tiberinis') and the tribe Clu.; 5949 refers to a *privatus* in Clu., and 5941 to a *patronus municipii* in Clu. (who, however, may have been related to another Petronius Proculus at Ameria (4395), another town in Clu.).

TREBIAE. Aem. more likely than others, but Ser. and Ouf. also possible. *CIL* xi. p. 728, Kubitschek 77 (both non-committal), Taylor, *VDRR* 163 (assigning it very doubtfully to Aem.). Aem., Ser., Ouf., and Qui. all occur once (xi.5005, 5013, 5012, and 5006 respectively). The reason for such confusion in a small town is surely its position on the Via Flaminia. Qui. can be excluded, for the subject of 5006 had the *cognomen* Sabinus and he held office at Nursia (Qui.) as well as at Trebiae and Spoletium. The subject of 5005 (Aem.) is the only known local office-holder in the case, but Aem. is to be found outside Trebiae even nearer than Ouf. and Ser., namely at Mevania. The subject of 5012, a Lafrenius, has a very unusual *nomen*, not known in any of the towns of Ouf.; but the inscription is a dedication by a freedman, and the Lafrenius family probably came from Forum Flaminii or Plestia. 5013 is fragmentary. The case remains open.

TUDER. Clu. certain. *CIL* xi. p. 679, Kubitschek 77–8. Six inscriptions give both *domus* and the tribe Clu., iii. p. 852 ii.33, vi.213, 2382.a.15, 2384.ii.9, 3884.v.14, xi.5176, and many local ones also give Clu. Pol. (xi.6351) is not a serious difficulty, cf. Bormann, p. 679 n. 1. On Vol. in this and other towns in Clu. see above on Carsulae.

TUFICUM. Ouf. certain. *CIL* xi. p. 829, Kubitschek 78. There are no inscriptions in Kubitschek's category α, but many local ones, including inscriptions of magistrates, e.g. xi.5693, 5699, 5713, 5717 ('municip(ibus) suis'), give Ouf.; no other tribes are found.

VETTONA. Clu. virtually certain. *CIL* xi. p. 747, Kubitschek 78. xi.6015 (Sestinum) is dedicated to 'L. Tullio L.f. Clu. Vero Vettonensi' by the plebs of Sestinum; at Bettona there is 5177, a *sevir* in Clu.

URVINUM HORTENSE (for the site, cf. *CIL* xi. p. 747). Ste. certain. *CIL*, l.c., Kubitschek 79. Local magistrates in xi.5175 and 5178 are in Ste., which is not to be found in any of the neighbouring towns. Three inscriptions specify the *domus* Urvinum with the tribe Ste., v.8283, vi.2617, 3884.i.29; cf. next entry.

URVINUM MATAURENSE. Ste. certain. *CIL* xi. p. 894, Kubitschek 78–9. Cf. previous entry. vi.32641.5 (=*Eph. Ep.* iv.888) was thought by Kubitschek to give the *domus* 'Urv. M(at)', but Hülsen could apparently see no 'M'. However there is plentiful local confirmation of Ste., including inscriptions of local magistrates, e.g. xi.6053, 6054, 6056, 6057, 6058, 6060, 6061.

APPENDIX III

The Supposed Sullan Colony of Florentia[1]

THE foundation date of Florentia has been discussed in detail by C. Hardie, *JRS* lv (1965), 122–40, who concluded that there was no colony there before the triumviral one. My conclusion is the same, but since a number of scholars have thought otherwise, I shall indicate which arguments seem to me to carry weight. Some have held that there were Sullan colonies both at Faesulae and Florentia, but it is most unlikely that two colonies were founded simultaneously only three miles apart. Others have suggested that the well-attested colony of Faesulae was only *within the territory of Faesulae* and actually at the site of Florentia.[2] Beloch compared this supposed situation with what happened at Arretium and Clusium, Sullan colonies where the earlier communities continued to exist—but there was no foundation of completely separate new cities in those cases, and at Pompeii, which was also a double community after colonization by Sulla, it is clear that the two communities were different strata within the same city.

'Municipia Italiae splendidissima sub hasta venierunt, Spoletium, Interamnium, Praeneste, Florentia' (Florus II 9.27). The reading 'Florentia' has often been attacked, with insufficient justification in my opinion. Hardie revived the old emendation 'Ferentinum' because in the rest of his list of towns Florus proceeds from north to south; but not all lists in Florus are so systematic, and the emendation 'Ferentinum' is an unsupported guess.[3] However, Florus' statement is questionable in at least one respect, for unless the archaeological evidence is very misleading, Florentia was not already a *splendidissimum municipium*. There is archaeological evidence for habitation at Florentia in the second century B.C., but hardly for a *splendidissimum municipium*.[4] There is then very little positive

[1] See above, pp. 261, 307.

[2] Beloch, *RG* 511–12.

[3] For Hardie's view see art. cit., 130. He argues that it is supported by the reading 'Florentina' in the Ticinensis MS.—but that may be partly explained by the fact that the next sentence begins with the word 'nam'. Nothing else is known of Ferentinum in this period. For another list of Italian towns in Florus that is not geographically straightforward see II 6.11.

[4] For the evidence see G. Maetzke, *Florentia* (*Italia Romana: Municipi e colonie*) (Rome, 1941), 23. It includes coins, for which cf. L. Milani, *MAAL* vi (1895), cols. 52–5.

literary evidence for a Sullan colony at Florentia, and it is hard to believe that if it had existed under that name it would not have been mentioned by some source in connection with the events of 63, when Faesulae is so often mentioned.

The archaeological evidence for early Roman Florence awaits complete publication. Though it has been argued that the brick walls of the city could have been of Sullan date, a triumviral one is, even on strictly archaeological grounds, much more likely.[1] The centuriation of the territory of Florentia is oriented obliquely with respect to the town-plan, which is unusual, but that can be explained without the hypothesis that there were two acts of colonization.[2] It is possible that evidence for a Sullan colony will emerge from the archaeological remains, but the balance of the existing evidence is against one.

Florentia first appears in a literary source other than Florus and the *Lib. Col.* in the context of 15 A.D. (Tac. *Ann.* I 79). Pliny's silence is a difficulty for a triumviral or Augustan colony, but not an insurmountable one.[3] The mediaeval tradition that Julius Caesar was the founder still finds supporters,[4] but it is completely without positive ancient evidence, literary or archaeological, and Caesar founded few colonies in Italy. *Lib. Col.*'s triumviral date is to be preferred.

[1] The walls: Maetzke, op. cit., 26, who argues for a date in the second half of the first century B.C. (a judgement to which he holds, cf. *EAA* s.v. Firenze (1960), 697). Degrassi, art. cit., 293 n. 5, argued for a Sullan date for the walls, comparing those of Verona, Alba Pompeia, and Aquileia (on which cf. G. Brusin, *AIV* xcix (1939–40), 1010 n. 1), but a date in the second half of the first century B.C. or later is surely to be preferred in any case for this type of construction unless strong contrary reasons can be provided.

[2] Cf. Maetzke, op. cit., 30–1, Hardie, art. cit., 134.

[3] Hardie, art. cit., 131, suggests that it may have been 'in strict law a colony of Julius Caesar's reinforced by or actually set in motion by Octavian in 41 B.C.'.

[4] E.g. M. Lopes Pegna, *Firenze dalle origini al medioevo* (Florence, 1962), 32–53. On the formation of the tradition see N. Rubinstein, *JWCI* v (1942), esp. 208–9.

SELECTED BIBLIOGRAPHY

To restrict this list to a reasonable length I have omitted most works that can be considered as standard, and most of the books and articles that are cited on single points.

AFZELIUS, A. *Die römische Eroberung Italiens 340–264 v. Chr.* (Copenhagen, 1942).

—— 'Zwei Episoden aus dem Leben Ciceros', *C & M* v (1942), 209–17.

ALFÖLDI, A. *Early Rome and the Latins* (Ann Arbor, 1965).

ANDRÉN, A. *Architectural Terracottas from Etrusco–Italic Temples* (Lund–Leipzig, 1940).

—— 'Marmora Etruriae', *Antike Plastik*, vii (1967), 7–42.

ANZIANI, D. 'Les voies romaines de l'Etrurie méridionale', *MEFR* xxxiii (1913), 169–244.

ASHBY, T., and FELL, R. A. L. 'The Via Flaminia', *JRS* xi (1921), 125–90.

—— 'La rete stradale romana nell'Etruria meridionale in relazione a quella del periodo etrusco', *SE* iii (1929), 171–85.

BADIAN, E. 'Caepio and Norbanus', *Historia*, vi (1957), 318–46 (reprinted in *Studies*, etc.).

—— 'From the Gracchi to Sulla (1940–59)', *Historia*, xi (1962), 179–245.

—— 'Waiting for Sulla', *JRS* lii (1962), 47–61 (reprinted in *Studies*, etc.).

—— Review of L. R. Taylor, *The Voting Districts of the Roman Republic*, *JRS* lii (1962), 200–10.

—— *Studies in Greek and Roman History* (Oxford, 1964).

BANDINELLI, R. BIANCHI. 'Clusium: Ricerche archeologiche e topografiche su Chiusi e il suo territorio in età etrusca', *MAAL* xxx (1925), cols. 209–552.

BANTI, L. *Luni* (Florence, 1937).

—— *Il mondo degli etruschi* (Rome, 1960).

BARTOCCINI, R. *Vulci, Storia–Rinvenimenti–Scavi* (Rome, 1960).

—— 'Tre anni di scavi a Vulci (1956–8)', *Atti del VII Congr. internaz. di archeologia classica* (1958, publ. Rome, 1961), ii.257–81.

BEAZLEY, J. D. *Etruscan Vase-Painting* (Oxford, 1947).

BISCARDI, A. 'Auctoritas patrum', *BIDR* n.s. xvi–xvii (1953), 213–294.

BLAKE, M. E. *Ancient Roman Construction in Italy* (Washington, 1947).

—— *Roman Construction in Italy from Tiberius through the Flavians* (Washington, 1959).

BOETHIUS, A., and others. *Etruscan Culture, Land and People* (New York, 1962) (Eng. version of *San Giovenale, Etruskerna Landet och Folket*, Malmö, 1962).

BROWN, F. E. 'Cosa I', *MAAR* xx (1951), 5–113.

——, RICHARDSON, E. H., and RICHARDSON, L. 'Cosa II: the Temples of the Arx', *MAAR* xxvi (1960) (whole vol.).

BRUCKMANN, H. *Die römischen Niederlagen im Geschichtswerk des T. Livius* (Münster, 1931).

BRUNT, P. A. 'The Army and the Land in the Roman Revolution', *JRS* lii (1962), 69–86.

—— 'Italian Aims at the Time of the Social War', *JRS* lv (1965), 90–109.

BUCK, C. D. *A Grammar of Oscan and Umbrian*[2] (Boston, 1928).

BUDINSZKY, A. *Die Ausbreitung der lateinischen Sprache über Italien und die Provinzen des Römischen Reichs* (Berlin, 1881).

CAMPOREALE, G. 'La terminologia magistratuale nelle lingue osco-umbre', *Atti e Memorie dell'Accademia Toscana di scienze e lettere "La Colombaria"* xxi (1956), 31–108.

—— 'Sull'organizzazione statuale degli etruschi', *PP* xiii (1958), 5–25.

CAPOZZA, M. *Movimenti servili nel mondo romano in età repubblicana*, i (Rome, 1966).

CASSOLA, F. *I gruppi politici romani nel III sec. a.C.* (Trieste, 1962).

CICHORIUS, C. *Römische Studien* (Berlin–Leipzig, 1922).

COLI, U. 'Formula onomastica romana nelle bilingui etrusco-latine', *SE* xix (1946–7), 277–83.

—— *Il diritto pubblico degli Umbri e le Tavole Eugubine* (Milan, 1958).

—— 'L'organizzazione politica dell'Umbria preromana', *Problemi di storia e archeologia dell'Umbria, Atti del I Convegno di Studi Umbri* (1963, publ. Gubbio–Perugia, 1964).

CORTSEN, S. P. *Die etruskischen Standes- und Beamtentitel, durch die Inschriften beleuchtet, Kgl. Danske Videnskabernes Selskab, Historisk-Filologiske Meddelelser*, xi no. 1 (Copenhagen, 1925).

CRIFÒ, G. *Ricerche sull 'exilium' nel periodo repubblicano*, i (Milan, 1961).

CRISTOFANI, M. *La Tomba delle Iscrizioni a Cerveteri* (Rome, 1965).

—— 'Ricerche sulle pitture della Tomba François di Vulci. I fregi decorativi', *Dialoghi di Archeologia*, i (1967), 186–219.

Dahlheim, W. *Deditio und Societas, Untersuchungen zur Entwicklung der römischen Aussenpolitik in der Blütezeit der Republik* (Munich, 1965).

—— *Struktur und Entwicklung des römischen Völkerrechts im 3. und 2. Jahrhundert v. Chr.* (Munich, 1968).

De Agostino, A. in 'Rivista di epigrafia etrusca', *SE* xxvii (1959), 277–300.

Deecke, W. *Die etruskische Bilinguen* (Stuttgart, 1883), vol. v of Deecke, W., and Pauli, C. (edd.), *Etruskische Forschungen und Studien.*

—— *Die etruskischen Beamten- und Priester-Titel*, vol. vi of the same series.

Degrassi, A. 'Quattuorviri in colonie romane e in municipi retti da duoviri', *Mem. Acc. Linc.*, ser. 8.ii (1950), 281–345.

—— 'Nuovi miliari arcaici', *Hommages à A. Grenier* (Brussels, 1962), i. 499–513.

Della Corte, F. 'Su un elogium Tarquiniense', *SE* xxiv (1955–6), 73–8.

Delplace, C. 'L'intervention étrusque dans les dernières années de la deuxième guerre samnite (312–308)', *Latomus*, xxvi (1967), 454–66.

Dennis, G. *Cities and Cemeteries of Etruria*[2] (London, 1878).

De Rossi, G. B. 'I monumenti antichi Cristiani e loro distribuzione geografica nel territorio dei Capenati', *Bull. Arch. Crist.*, ser. 4.ii (1883), 115–59.

Desserteaux, F. 'Le cas de la femme d'Arretium (Cicéron, *pro Caecina*, 33, 34)', *Mélanges Gerardin* (Paris, 1907), 181–96, repr. in *Etudes sur la formation historique de la capitis deminutio*, i (Dijon, 1909).

Devoto, G. *Gli antichi Italici* (Florence, 1931).

—— *Storia della lingua di Roma* (Rome, 1940).

—— *Le Tavole di Gubbio* (Florence, 1948).

—— *Tabulae Iguvinae*[3] (Rome, 1962).

Duncan, G. C. 'Notes on Southern Etruria, III: Sutri (Sutrium)', *PBSR* xxvi (1958), 63–134.

Earl, D. C. *Tiberius Gracchus, A Study in Politics* (Brussels, 1963).

Finley, M. I. 'Between Slavery and Freedom', *Comparative Studies in Society and History*, vi (1963–4), 233–49.

Forni, G. 'Manio Curio Dentato uomo democratico', *Athenaeum*, xxxi (1953), 170–240.

—— 'Il tramonto di un'istituzione: pseudo-tribù romane derivate da soprannomi imperiali', *Studi giuridici in memoria di A. Passerini* (Pavia–Milan, 1955), 89–124.

FORNI, G. 'Le tribù romane nelle bilingui etrusco-latine e greco-latine', *Studi in onore di E. Betti* (Milan, 1962), iii. 193–207.

FRACCARO, P. 'L'organizzazione politica dell'Italia romana', *Atti del Congr. internaz. di diritto romano* (Rome, 1933), i. 193–208 (repr. in *Opuscula* i).

—— *Opuscula* i–iii (Pavia, 1956–7).

FRANCIOSI, G. *Il processo di libertà in diritto romano* (Naples, 1961).

FRANK, T. 'On Rome's Conquest of Sabinum, Picenum and Etruria', *Klio*, xi (1911), 367–81.

FRANKFORT, T. 'Les classes serviles en Etrurie', *Latomus*, xviii (1959), 3–22.

FREDERIKSEN, M. W., and WARD-PERKINS, J. B. 'The Ancient Road Systems of the Central and Northern Ager Faliscus. Notes on Southern Etruria, II', *PBSR* xxv (1957), 67–208.

—— 'The Republican Municipal Laws: Errors and Drafts', *JRS* lv (1965), 183–98.

FUCHS, H. *Der geistige Widerstand gegen Rom in der antiken Welt* (Basel, 1938).

GABBA, E. 'Ricerche sull'esercito professionale romano da Mario ad Augusto', *Athenaeum* xxix (1951), 171–272.

—— 'Sulle colonie triumvirali di Antonio in Italia', *PP* xxiii (1953), 101–10.

—— 'Politica e cultura in Rome agli inizi del I sec. a.C.', *Athenaeum*, xxxi (1953), 259–72.

—— 'Le origini della Guerra Sociale e la vita politica romana dopo l'89 a.C.', *Athenaeum*, xxxii (1954), 41–114, 293–345.

—— *Appiano e la storia delle guerre civili* (Florence, 1956).

—— Review of E. Badian, *Foreign Clientelae (264–70* B.C.), *RFIC* xxxvii (1959), 189–99.

—— 'M. Livio Druso e le riforme di Silla', *Annali Scuola Norm. Sup. di Pisa*, xxxiii (1964), 1–15.

GAMURRINI, G. F. 'Scavi di Chiusi', *Bull. Inst.*, 1874, 10–17.

GELZER, M. 'Das Römertum als Kulturmacht', *HZ* cxxvi (1923), 189–206 (repr. in *KS* i).

—— *Vom Römischen Staat*, i–ii (Leipzig, 1943).

—— *Kleine Schriften*, i–iii (Wiesbaden, 1962–4).

GERKAN, A. VON, and MESSERSCHMIDT, F. 'Das Grab der Volumnier bei Perugia', *MDAI–R* lvii (1942), 122–235.

GÖHLER, J. *Rom und Italien* (Breslau, 1939).

GRUEN, E. S. *Politics and the Criminal Courts, 149–78* B.C. (Cambridge, Mass., 1968).

HARDIE, C. 'The Origin and Plan of Roman Florence', *JRS* lv (1965), 122–40.

HARDY, E. G. *Some Problems in Roman History* (Oxford, 1924).

HARRIS, W. V. 'Roman *Foedera* in Etruria', *Historia*, xiv (1965), 282–92.

—— 'The Via Cassia and the Via Traiana Nova between Bolsena and Chiusi', *PBSR* xxxiii (1965), 113–33.

HATZFELD, J. *Les trafiquants italiens dans l'orient hellénique* (Paris, 1919).

HAYWOOD, R. M. 'Some Traces of Serfdom in Cicero's Day', *AJPh* liv (1933), 145–53.

HELLMANN, F. *Livius-Interpretationen* (Berlin, 1939).

HERBIG, R. *Die jüngeretruskischen Steinsarkophage* (Berlin, 1952).

HEURGON, J. 'L'elogium d'un magistrat étrusque découvert à Tarquinia', *CRAI* 1950, 212–15.

—— 'L'elogium d'un magistrat étrusque découvert à Tarquinia', *MEFR* lxiii (1951), 119–37.

—— 'La vocation étruscologique de l'empereur Claude', *CRAI* 1953, 92–7.

—— 'Tarquitius Priscus et l'organisation de l'ordre des haruspices sous l'empereur Claude', *Latomus* xii (1953), 402–17.

—— 'Traditions étrusco-italiques dans le monnayage de Trébonien Galle', *SE* xxiv (1955–6), 91–105.

—— 'L'Etat étrusque', *Historia*, vi (1957), 63–97.

—— 'A propos du cognomen Violens et du tombeau des Volumnii', *Archeologia Classica*, x (1958), 151–9.

—— 'Les pénestes étrusques chez Denys d'Halicarnasse (IX, 5, 4)', *Latomus*, xviii (1959), 713–23.

—— 'The Date of Vegoia's Prophecy', *JRS* xlix (1959), 41–5.

—— *La vie quotidienne Chez les étrusques* (Paris, 1961), cited from the Eng. translation *Daily Life of the Etruscans* (London, 1964).

—— 'Posidonios et les étrusques', *Hommages à A. Grenier* (Brussels, 1962), ii. 799–808.

—— 'L'Ombrie à l'époque des Gracques et de Sylla', *Problemi di storia e archeologia dell'Umbria, Atti del I Convegno di Studi Umbri* (1963, publ. Gubbio–Perugia, 1964), 113–31.

HEUSS, A. *Die völkerrechtlichen Grundlagen der römischen Aussenpolitik in republikanischer Zeit, Klio, Beiheft* xxxi (Leipzig, 1933).

HINRICHS, F. T. 'Der römische Strassenbau zur Zeit der Gracchen', *Historia*, xvi (1967), 162–76.

HORN, H. *Foederati* (Frankfurt-a.-M., 1930).

HUMBERT, J. *Les plaidoyers écrits et les plaidoiries réelles de Cicéron* (Paris, [1925]).

JONES, G. D. B. 'Capena and the Ager Capenas', *PBSR* xxx (1962), 116–207, xxxi (1963), 100–58.

Kahrstedt, U. 'Eine etruskische Stimme zur etruskischen Geschichte', *Symbolae Osloenses* xxx (1953), 68–76.

—— 'Ager Publicus und Selbstverwaltung in Lukanien und Bruttium', *Historia*, viii (1959), 174–206.

Kaser, M. 'Zur Geschichte der capitis deminutio', *Iura*, iii (1952), 48–89.

Kiene, A. *Der römische Bundesgenossenkrieg* (Leipzig, 1845).

Klotz, A. 'Ueber die Stellung des Cassius Dio unter den Quellen zur Geschichte des zweiten punischen Krieges', *RhM* lxxxv (1936), 68–116.

—— 'Diodors römische Annalen', *RhM* lxxxvi (1937), 206–24.

Kubitschek, J. W. *De Romanarum tribuum origine ac propagatione* (Vienna, 1882).

—— *Imperium Romanum tributim discriptum* (Vienna, 1889).

Lambrechts, R. *Essai sur les magistratures des républiques étrusques* (Brussels–Rome, 1959).

Leifer, F. *Studien zum antiken Aemterwesen*, *Klio Beiträge*, xxiii (Leipzig, 1931).

Levi, M. A. *Ottaviano Capoparte*, i–ii (Florence, 1933).

Lotze, D. *ΜΕΤΑΞΥ ΕΛΕΥΘΕΡΩΝ ΚΑΙ ΔΟΥΛΩΝ*, *Studien zur Rechtsstellung unfreier Landbevölkerungen in Griechenland bis zum 4. Jahrhundert v. Chr.* (Berlin, 1959).

Lugli, G. *La tecnica edilizia romana* (Rome, 1957).

McDonald, A. H. 'The History of Rome and Italy in the Second Century B.C.', *CHJ* vi (1939), 124–46.

—— 'Rome and the Italian Confederation (200–186 B.C.)', *JRS* xxxiv (1944), 11–33.

Maetzke, G. *Florentia* (*Italia Romana: Municipi e colonie*) (Rome, 1941).

—— 'Presentazione del rilievo di Fiesole antica', *SE* xxvii (1959), 43–63.

Mancini, G. 'Capena, iscrizioni onorarie di età imperiale rinvenute in località Civitùcola', *NSA* 1953, 18–28.

Manni, E. *Per la storia die municipii fino alla guerra sociale* (Rome, 1947).

Martinori, E. *Via Cassia e sue deviazioni* (Rome, 1930).

Matthaei, L. E. 'On the Classification of Roman Allies', *CQ* i (1907), 182–204.

Mazzarino, S. *Dalla monarchia allo stato repubblicano* (Catania, [1945]).

—— 'Sociologia del mondo etrusco e problemi della tarda etruscità', *Historia*, vi (1957), 98–122.

—— 'Le droit des étrusques', *Iura*, xii (1961), 24–39.

MAZZARINO, S. *Il pensiero storico classico* i, ii.1–2 (Bari, 1966).

MEIER, C. *Res Publica Amissa* (Wiesbaden, 1966).

MESSERSCHMIDT, F., and GERKAN, A. VON. *Nekropolen von Vulci* (Berlin, 1930).

MINTO, A. 'Saturnia etrusca e romana', *MAAL* xxx (1925), cols. 585–702.

MOMIGLIANO, A. 'An Interim Report on the Origins of Rome', *JRS* liii (1963), 95–121.

MOMMSEN, T. 'Die italischen Bürgercolonien von Sulla bis Vespasian', *Hermes*, xviii (1883), 161–213 (reprinted in *Gesammelte Schriften*, v (= *Historische Schriften*, ii)).

—— 'Die römische Tribuseintheilung nach dem marsischen Krieg', *Hermes*, xxii (1887), 101–16 (repr. in *GS* v).

MÜLLER, K. O., and DEECKE, W. *Die Etrusker*², i–ii (Stuttgart, 1877).

NICCOLINI, G. 'Le leggi de civitate romana durante la guerra sociale', *Rend. Acc. Linc.*, ser. 8.i (1946), 110–24.

NICOLET, C. *L'ordre équestre à l'époque républicaine (312–43 av. J.-C.)* (Paris, 1966).

NISSEN, H. *Italische Landeskunde*, i–ii (Berlin, 1883–1902).

NOGARA, B. *Gli etruschi e la loro civiltà* (Milan, 1933).

OGILVIE, R. M. *A Commentary on Livy Books 1–5* (Oxford, 1965).

PAIS, E. 'Le colonie militari dedotte in Italia dai triumviri e da Augusto', *Museo Italiano di Antichità Classica*, i (1885), 37–58.

—— *Storia di Roma*, i.2 (Turin, 1899).

—— 'Serie cronologica delle colonie romane e latine dalla età regia fino all'impero', *Mem. Acc. Linc.*, ser. 5.xvii (1924), 311–355, ser. 6.i (1925), 345–412.

PALLOTTINO, M. 'Tarquinia', *MAAL* xxxvi (1937).

—— 'Uno spiraglio di luce sulla storia etrusca. Gli elogia Tarquiniensia', *SE* xxi (1950–1), 147–71.

—— *La peinture étrusque* (Geneva, 1952).

—— *Etruscologia*⁶ (Milan, 1968).

PARETI, L. 'La disunione politica degli etruschi e i suoi riflessi storici ed archeologici', *RPAA* vii (1929–31), 89–100 (repr. in *Studi minori di storia antica*, i).

—— *Studi minori di storia antica*, i–iii (Rome, 1958–65).

PAULI, C. *Etruskische Studien*, i–iii (Göttingen, 1879–80).

PELLEGRINI, G. 'Pitigliano', *NSA* 1898, 429–50.

PFIFFIG, A. J. 'Neues Namenmaterial aus einem etruskischen Familiengrab', *Beiträge zur Namenforschung*, xiii (1962), 28–39.

—— 'Zur historischen Begründung der IIIIviri IIviri in Perugia', *Studi in onore di L. Banti* (Rome, 1965), 275–80.

PFIFFIG, A. J. 'Die Haltung Etruriens im 2. Punischen Krieg', *Historia*, xv (1966), 193–210.

—— *Die Ausbreitung des römischen Städtewesens in Etrurien und die Frage der Unterwerfung der Etrusker* (Florence, 1966).

—— 'Das Verhalten Etruriens im Samnitenkrieg und nachher bis zum l. Punischen Krieg', *Historia*, xvii (1968), 307–50.

PIETRANGELI, C. *Ocriculum* (*Italia Romana: Municipi e colonie*) (Rome, 1943).

—— *Mevania* (*Italia Romana: Municipi e colonie*) (Rome, 1953).

PIGANIOL, A. 'Sur le calendrier brontoscopique de Nigidius Figulus', *Studies in Roman Economic and Social History in Honor of A. C. Johnson* (Princeton, 1951), 79–87.

PIOTROWICZ, L. 'Quelques remarques sur l'attitude de l'Etrurie pendant les troubles civils à la fin de la République romaine', *Klio*, xxiii (1930), 334–8.

PISANI, V. *Le lingue dell'Italia antica oltre il latino* (Turin, 1953).

PLATHNER, H.-G. *Die Schlachtschilderungen bei Livius* (Breslau, 1934).

POULTNEY, J. W. *The Bronze Tables of Iguvium* (Baltimore, 1959).

PUGLIESE, G. 'Intorno al supposto divieto di modificare legislativamente il *ius civile*', *Atti del Congr. internaz. di diritto e di storia del diritto* (Verona, 1948, publ. Milan, 1951), ii. 61–84.

RADKE, G. 'Die Erschliessung Italiens durch die römischen Strassen', *Gymnasium*, lxxi (1964), 204–35.

REINHOLD, M. 'The Perusine War', *Classical Weekly*, xxvi (1933), 180–2.

RICHARDSON, E. H. *The Etruscans* (Chicago, 1964).

RICHARDSON, L. 'Cosa and Rome: Comitium and Curia', *Archaeology*, x (1957), 49–55.

RIIS, P. J. *An Introduction to Etruscan Art* (Copenhagen, 1953).

RIX, H. 'Die Personnamen auf den etruskisch-lateinischen Bilinguen', *Beiträge zur Namenforschung*, vii (1956), 147–72.

—— *Das etruskische Cognomen* (Wiesbaden, 1963).

ROMANELLI, P. 'Tarquinia: Scavi e ricerche nell'area della città', *NSA* 1948, 193–270.

ROSENBERG, A. *Der Staat der alten Italiker* (Berlin, 1913).

RUDOLPH, H. *Stadt und Staat im römischen Italien* (Leipzig, 1935).

SAFAREWICZ, J. 'Rozpowszechnianie się łaciny w Italii w latach 225–81 przed N.E.', *Meander* ix (1954), 157–70.

—— 'Stan językowy Italii za Tyberiusza', *Eos* li (1961), 317–25.

SALMON, E. T. 'Rome's Battles with Etruscans and Gauls in 284–282 B.C.', *CPh* xxx (1935), 25–31.

—— 'Roman Colonization from the Second Punic War to the Gracchi', *JRS* xxvi (1936), 47–67.

SALMON, E. T. 'Roman Expansion and Roman Colonization in Italy', *Phoenix*, ix (1955), 63–75.

—— 'Notes on the Social War', *TAPhA* lxxxix (1958), 159–84.

—— 'The Beginnings of the Latin World', *Report of the Annual Meeting of the Canadian Historical Association*, 1960, 33–43.

—— 'The *Coloniae Maritimae*', *Athenaeum*, xli (1963), 3–38.

—— 'Sulla Redux', *Athenaeum*, xlii (1964), 60–79.

—— *Samnium and the Samnites* (Cambridge, 1967).

—— *Roman Colonization under the Republic* (London, 1969).

SCHMITT, H. H. *Rom und Rhodos* (Munich, 1957).

SCULLARD, H. H. *Roman Politics, 220–150 B.C.* (Oxford, 1951).

SMITH, R. E. 'Latins and the Roman Citizenship in Roman Colonies, Livy XXXIV, 42, 5–6', *JRS* xliv (1954), 18–20.

SORDI, M. *I rapporti romano-ceriti e l'origine della civitas sine suffragio* (Rome, 1960).

STRASBURGER, H. 'Poseidonios on Problems of the Roman Empire', *JRS* lv (1965), 40–53.

SUMNER, G. V. 'The Family Connections of L. Aelius Seianus', *Phoenix*, xix (1965), 134–45.

SYME, R. 'Caesar, the Senate, and Italy', *PBSR* xiv (1938), 1–31.

—— Review of T. R. S. Broughton, *The Magistrates of the Roman Republic*, *CPh* l (1955), 127–38.

—— 'Missing Senators', *Historia*, iv (1955), 52–71.

—— 'Missing Persons II', *Historia*, viii (1959), 207–12.

—— 'Senators, Tribes, and Towns', *Historia*, xiii (1964), 105–25.

—— 'The Stemma of the Sentii Saturnini', *Historia*, xiii (1964), 156—66.

TÄUBLER, E. *Imperium Romanum*, i (Leipzig, 1913).

THIMME, J. 'Chiusinische Aschenkisten und Sarkophage der hellenistischen Zeit', *SE* xxiii (1954), 25–147, xxv (1957), 87–160.

THOMSEN, R. *The Italic Regions* (Copenhagen, 1947).

THULIN, C. O. 'Die etruskische Disciplin', i–iii, *Göteborgs Högskolas Årsskrift*, xi (1905), xii (1906), xv (1909).

TIBILETTI, G. F. 'Il possesso dell'ager publicus e le norme de modo agrorum sino ai Gracchi', *Athenaeum*, xxvi (1948), 173–236.

—— 'Ricerche di storia agraria romana', *Athenaeum*, xxviii (1950), 183–266.

—— 'Le leggi de iudiciis repetundarum fino alla Guerra Sociale', *Athenaeum*, xxxi (1953), 5–100.

—— 'La politica delle colonie e città latine nella Guerra Sociale', *RIL* lxxxvi (1953), 45–63.

TIBILETTI, G. F. 'The comitia during the Decline of the Roman Republic', *SDHI* xxv (1959), 94–127.
TORELLI, M. 'Terza campagna di scavi a Punta della Vipera (S. Marinella)', *SE* xxxv (1967), 331–52.
—— 'Un nuovo attacco fra gli *Elogia Tarquiniensia*', *SE* xxxvi (1968), 467–70.
TOYNBEE, A. J. *Hannibal's Legacy*, i–ii (Oxford, 1965).
TREVES, P. 'Sertorio', *Athenaeum*, x (1932), 127–46.
TRÜDINGER, K. *Studien zur Geschichte der griechisch-römischen Ethnographie* (Basel, 1918).
VAN SON, D. W. L. 'The Disturbances in Etruria during the Second Punic War', *Mnemosyne*, ser. 4.xvi (1963), 267–74.
VETTER, E. 'Die etruskischen Personennamen *leθe*, *leθi*, *leθia*, und die Namen unfreier oder halbfreier Personen bei den Etruskern', *Jahresh. Oest. Arch. Inst.*, xxxvii (1948), *Beiblatt*, cols. 57–112.
—— 'Literaturbericht 1938–1953, Etruskisch, i: Neu veröffentlichte Inschriften', *Glotta*, xxxiv (1955), 47–66.
VEYNE, P. 'Foederati: Tarquinies, Camérinum, Capène', *Latomus*, xix (1960), 429–36.
VITUCCI, G. 'A proposito dei primi contatti politici fra Umbri e Romani', *Problemi di storia e archeologia dell'Umbria, Atti del I Convegno di Studi Umbri* (1963, publ. Gubbio-Perugia, 1964), 291–301.
WALBANK, F. W. *A Historical Commentary on Polybius*, i (Books i–vi) (Oxford, 1957).
WALSH, P. G. *Livy, His Historical Aims and Methods* (Cambridge, 1963).
WARD-PERKINS, J. B. 'Notes on Southern Etruria and the Ager Veientanus', *PBSR* xxiii (1955), 44–72.
—— 'Etruscan and Roman Roads in Southern Etruria', *JRS* xlvii (1957), 139–43.
—— 'Veii: the Historical Topography of the Ancient City', *PBSR* xxix (1961) (whole vol.).
WEINSTOCK, S. 'C. Fonteius Capito and the *Libri Tagetici*', *PBSR* xviii (1950), 44–9.
—— 'Libri Fulgurales', *PBSR* xix (1951), 122–53.
WERNER, R. *Der Beginn der Römischen Republik* (Munich–Vienna, 1963).
WIKÉN, E. *Die Kunde der Hellenen von dem Lande und den Völkern der Apenninenhalbinsel bis 300 v. Chr.* (Lund, 1937).
ZANCAN, L. 'Il frammento di Vegoia e il novissimum saeculum', *A & R* ser. 3.vii (1939), 203–19.
ZUMPT, A. W. *Commentationum Epigraphicarum ad Antiquitates Romanas Pertinentium volumen* I (Berlin, 1850).

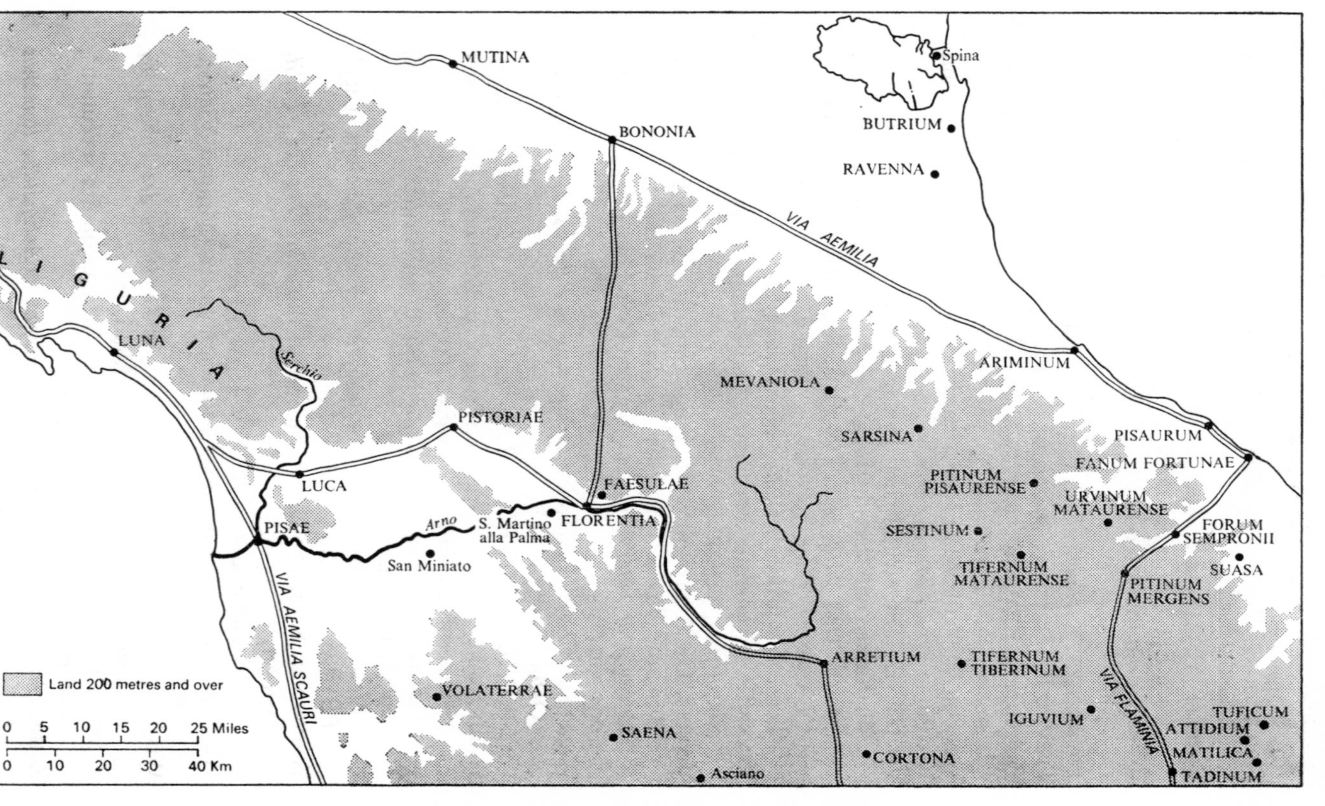

Etruria and Umbria in the Late Republic (North)

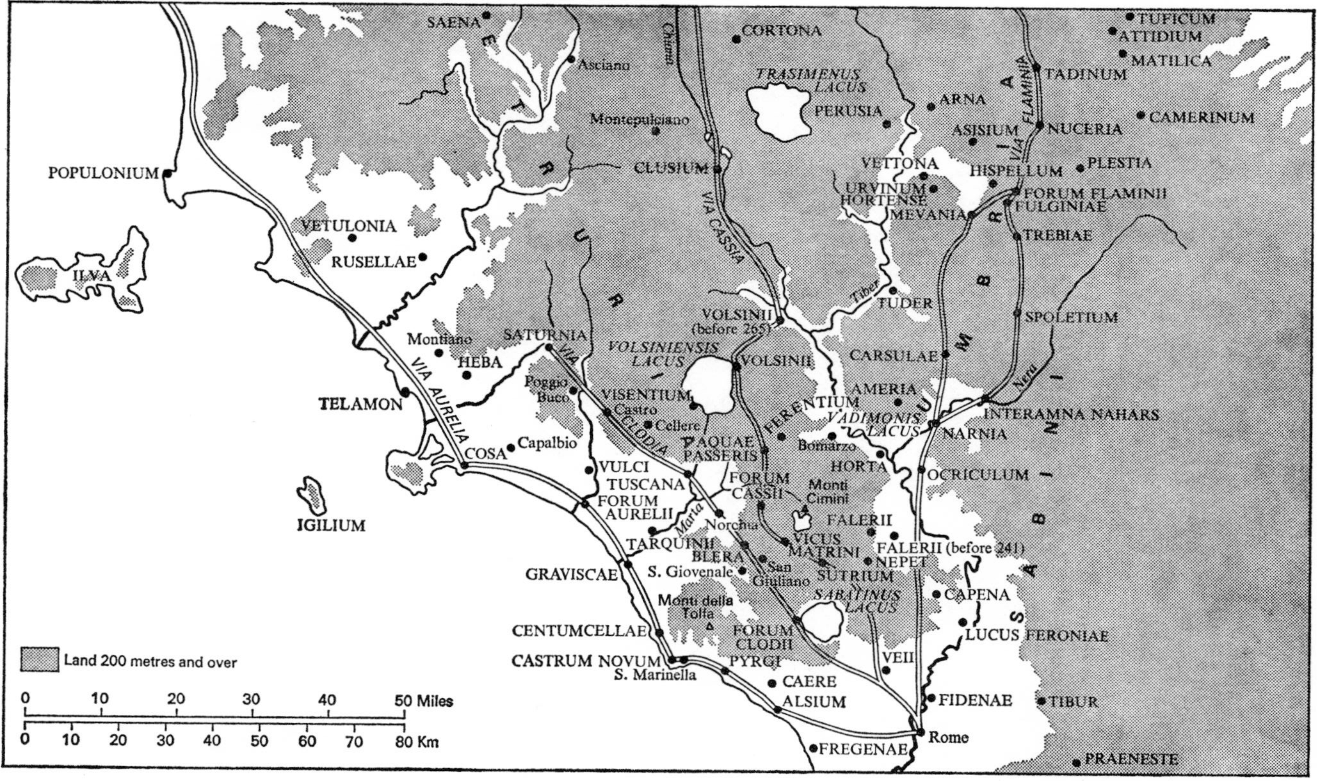

Etruria and Umbria in the Late Republic (South)

INDEX

Note. The appendices have been indexed only in a severely selective way.

coins, Etruscan, 140, 206 n. 8; of some Latin colonies, 159 n. 4